WITHDRAWN
NDSU

SURVEY OF
BRITISH COMMONWEALTH AFFAIRS

SURVEY OF BRITISH COMMONWEALTH AFFAIRS

Problems of Wartime Co-operation
and Post-War Change
1939—1952

BY

NICHOLAS MANSERGH

*Smuts Professor of the History of the
British Commonwealth
and Fellow of St. John's College, Cambridge*

If men could learn from history—what lessons
it might teach us! But . . . the light which
experience gives is a lantern on the stern, which
shines only on the waves behind us.

S. T. COLERIDGE, *Table Talk*

*Originally issued under the auspices of the
Royal Institute of International Affairs*

FRANK CASS & CO. LTD.
1968

Originally issued under the auspices of the
Royal Institute of International Affairs

This new edition is published by
FRANK CASS AND COMPANY LIMITED
67 Great Russell Street, London WC1
by arrangement with Oxford University Press

First edition   1958
New impression   1968

Printed in Great Britain by
Thomas Nelson (Printers) Ltd., London and Edinburgh

TO KEITH

CONTENTS

ACKNOWLEDGEMENTS xi

ABBREVIATIONS xiii

INTRODUCTION xv

PART I
THE COMMONWEALTH AT WAR

CHAPTER I. THE COMMONWEALTH IN 1939: INTERNAL RELATIONS AND EXTERNAL DANGERS 3
   The Status of the Dominions and the Stature of the United Kingdom . 5
   Some Consequences of Equality in the Making of Policy . . . 10
   The Nature of the Nazi Challenge 18
   The Reconstitution of an Imperial War Cabinet? 25

CHAPTER II. COMMONWEALTH CO-OPERATION IN WAR: THE FIRST PHASE, 1939–41 28
   The Mobilization and Employment of Dominion Forces . . . 28
   The Material Foundations of Co-operation 36
   The First Wartime Ministerial Conference 38
   Co-operation in Crisis: Information and Consultation on War Policy, May–September 1940 41
   Britain, Canada, and the United States: (*a*) Destroyers, Bases, and the Defence of the Western Hemisphere; (*b*) Lend-Lease and the Hyde Park Agreement 46
   Irish Neutrality: British Anxieties, United States Diplomacy, and German Plans 58
   South Africa: War and Politics, May–December 1940 . . . 76
   Indian Reactions to the Fall of France and the Establishment of the Eastern Supply Council 79
   Consultation on Defence in the Pacific, June–December 1940 . . 85
   Means and Ends: Canadian and United Kingdom Views on Methods of Co-operation, February–April 1941 90
   Consultation with Dominion Governments on the Decisions to aid Greece and to invade Syria, 1941 95
   The Control and Disposition of Dominion Forces 103
   Dominion Representation in the War Cabinet, 1941 . . . 107
   Australian Proposals for an Imperial War Cabinet and Their Outcome . 110
   The Approach of the Pacific War, July–December 1941 . . . 115

CHAPTER III. COMMONWEALTH CO-OPERATION IN WAR: THE SECOND PHASE, DECEMBER 1941–AUGUST 1945 . . . 124
   A War between Continents 124
   Commonwealth Co-operation: Some Consequences of the Entry of the United States into the War 127

CONTENTS

Australian Reactions to the Pacific War	130
The Pacific War Council	135
The Japanese Onslaught: Australia and South-East Asia	139
India: The Cripps Mission	143
South Africa: The War with Japan, Republicanism, and the Ascendancy of General Smuts	155
United States Belligerency and Irish Neutrality	160
Means and Ends: Debate and Discussion on the Future of the Commonwealth, 1943–4	164
Australian Proposals for a Commonwealth Council or Secretariat	165
General Smuts and the Commonwealth as a Third Force	173
Lord Halifax and a Common Policy	176
The Anzac Agreement, 1944	181
The Prime Ministers' Meeting, 1–17 May 1944	181
The Impact of War upon Commonwealth and Empire	189

PART II
PROBLEMS OF POST-WAR CHANGE

CHAPTER IV. INDIA: PARTITION AND INDEPENDENCE	197
The Wartime Growth of Hindu-Muslim Antagonism	200
The Elections of 1945 and 1946	209
The Cabinet Mission	214
The 'Beloved Pilgrim'	221
The Constituent Assembly	222
A Time-Limit Imposed	225
A Time-Limit Foreshortened	227
The Indian Independence Act	233
The Princes; Pressure and Procrastination	235
15 August 1947: 'A Tryst with Destiny'	237
CHAPTER V. ASIAN MEMBERSHIP OF THE COMMONWEALTH	239
The Secession of Burma	240
Ceylon	246
India: A Republic within the Commonwealth	249
Co-operation Without, Discord Within	256
CHAPTER VI. IRELAND: EXTERNAL ASSOCIATION, THE REPUBLIC AND SECESSION	262
External Association	262
The Republic and the Commonwealth	265
The General Election, 1948	273
The Repeal of the External Relations Act	275
A Republic Proclaimed	289
The Ireland Act, 1949	289
Ireland's Relations with the Commonwealth, 1921–49: A Perspective View	292
The Republic Outside the Commonwealth	298

PART III

PROBLEMS OF INTERNATIONAL AND COMMONWEALTH RELATIONS

CHAPTER VII. THE COMMONWEALTH, THE UNITED NATIONS, IMPERIAL DEFENCE, AND INTERNATIONAL SECURITY, 1945–52   307

    Commonwealth Statesmen and the Post-War International Organization   .   307
    London and San Francisco   .   314
    The Anglo-Egyptian Treaty Negotiations   .   322
    The 1946 Prime Ministers' Meeting   .   324
    The Reorganization of Commonwealth Defence   .   326
    The Commonwealth and Western European Union   .   329
    The North Atlantic Treaty   .   336
    The Commonwealth and the Devaluation of Sterling, September 1949   .   342
    The Colombo Conference, January 1950   .   345
    The Commonwealth and the Korean War   .   350
    The Pacific Security Agreement, 1951   .   352
    India, South Asia, and the Policy of Non-Alignment   .   357
    South Africa, the Western Alliances, and the United Nations   .   361
    The Elaboration of Commonwealth Alliances: A Perspective View   .   363

CHAPTER VIII. THE COMMONWEALTH AT THE ACCESSION OF QUEEN ELIZABETH II   .   367

    The Place of the Crown in the Commonwealth   .   369
    Monarchical and Republican Membership   .   374
    The Representatives of the Crown   .   375
    Nationality and Citizenship   .   382
    The Making of Commonwealth Constitutions   .   387
    The Removal of Surviving Inequalities in Status in New Zealand and Canada   389
    South African Interpretations of Inequality   .   391
    The Incorporation of Newfoundland in the Canadian Confederation   .   397
    Commonwealth Consultation: A Perspective View   .   398
    Prime Ministers and their Meetings   .   410
    Some Problems of Multi-Racial Membership   .   414
    Influence and Power   .   418

APPENDICES

A. GOVERNORS-GENERAL OF THE DOMINIONS, 1931–52   .   422

B. COMMONWEALTH PRIME MINISTERS, MINISTERS OF FINANCE, DEFENCE, AND EXTERNAL AFFAIRS, 1931–52   .   424

C. COMMONWEALTH REPRESENTATION WITHIN THE COMMONWEALTH, 1931–52   431

D. COMMONWEALTH REPRESENTATION IN FOREIGN COUNTRIES, 1931–52   .   437

E. RESULTS OF PARLIAMENTARY ELECTIONS IN THE COMMONWEALTH, 1931–52   440

INDEX   .   445

ACKNOWLEDGEMENTS

SIR CHARLES DIXON of the Commonwealth Relations Office, Mr. George Glazebrook of the Department of External Affairs, Canada, Lord Rugby formerly United Kingdom Representative to Eire, Professor C. H. Philips, Director of the School of Oriental and African Studies in the University of London, Professor F. L. W. Wood of Victoria University College, Wellington, Mr. Gavin Long, Editor in Chief of the Australian War Histories, and the late Major-General Sir Howard Kippenberger, Editor in Chief of the New Zealand War Histories, together with certain of their colleagues have read parts of this book in typescript and I am much indebted to them for their criticisms and suggestions. I would like further to pay a special tribute to General Kippenberger who commented on chapters in this book very shortly before his death and of whose help in conversation at Wellington or in correspondence later I have the most lively recollections. My thanks are also due to many others, some of them directly concerned with events recorded in this book, for their patient answers to inquiries and their discussion of topics in which I was interested. Their anonymity here in no way reflects upon the value of their contributions to my knowledge or understanding. I am also much indebted to former colleagues at Chatham House, chief among them Miss H. G. Oliver of the Editorial Department and Mrs. Cousins and Miss Lindesay Clark, my research assistants in the earlier and later stages of the writing of this book, for their generous assistance, and to Mr. René Hague who prepared the index. My wife has helped me in the reading of the proofs and in listening critically over the years to expositions of various aspects of Commonwealth relations. Finally I should like to record my thanks to the Carnegie Corporation, whose generosity made possible the undertaking of the task in the first instance, and to the Managers of the Smuts Memorial Fund at Cambridge for their help towards its completion. It should be particularly emphasized that no responsibility rests with anyone but the author for the opinions expressed, or the facts included, in the book.

N. M.

St. John's College
Cambridge
November 1957

ABBREVIATIONS

1. OFFICIAL HISTORIES OF THE SECOND WORLD WAR
(a) *Australia in the War of 1939–45.* Canberra, Australian War Memorial, 1952. The following volumes are cited:
Gavin Long, *To Benghazi* and *Greece, Crete and Syria*. Series I (Army).
Paul Hasluck, *The Government and the People, 1939–41* (cited as Hasluck i to distinguish it from the author's forthcoming *The Government and the People, 1942–5*).
S. J. Butlin, *War Economy, 1939–42*. Series 4 (Civil).
(b) New Zealand:
Documents relating to New Zealand's Participation in the Second World War. Wellington, Government Printer, 1949– (cited as *N.Z. Documents*).
F. L. W. Wood, *The New Zealand People at War; Political and External Affairs.* Wellington, Government Printer, 1958 (cited as Wood).
(c) United Kingdom Military Series:
J. R. M. Butler, *Grand Strategy*. Vol. ii: *September 1939–June 1941*. London, HMSO, 1957.
(d) United Kingdom Civil Series, ed. by W. K. Hancock:
W. K. Hancock and M. M. Gowing, *British War Economy*. London, HMSO, 1949 (cited as Hancock & Gowing. Other titles in this series are given in full).

2. CANADA IN WORLD AFFAIRS
The following volumes, with the general title *Canada in World Affairs*, published by the Oxford University Press for the Canadian Institute of International Affairs (cited as *Canada in World Affairs, 1939–41, 1941–4, 1944–6,* and *1949–50*):
Robert MacGregor Dawson, *Two Years of War, 1939–41.*
C. C. Lingard and R. G. Trotter, *September 1941 to May 1944.*
F. H. Soward, *From Normandy to Paris, 1944–6.*
W. E. C. Harrison, *1949 to 1950.*

3. OTHER
Churchill: Winston S. Churchill, *The Second World War*. 6 vols. London, Cassell, 1948–54.
D. Ger. F.P.: *Documents on German Foreign Policy, 1918–45, from the Archives of the German Foreign Ministry*, published jointly by the British Foreign Office and the U.S. Department of State, Series D (1937–45). 10 vols.
Documents on American Foreign Relations: World Peace Foundation, *Documents on American Foreign Relations, 1938–9 to 1951* (later volumes published by the Council on Foreign Relations).
Holborn: Louise W. Holborn, ed., *War and Peace Aims of the United Nations*. 2 vols. Boston, World Peace Foundation, 1943–8.
IMT Nuremberg: *Trial of the Major War Criminals before the International Tribunal, Nuremberg, 1945–6*. Proceedings and Documents in Evidence. 42 vols. Nuremberg, 1947–9.
Langer & Gleason: W. L. Langer and S. E. Gleason, *The World Crisis and American Foreign Policy*, vol. i: *The Challenge to Isolation, 1937–40*; vol. ii: *The Undeclared War, 1940–1*. New York, Harper for Council on Foreign Relations, 1952–3.

ABBREVIATIONS

Mansergh, *Documents*: Nicholas Mansergh, *Documents and Speeches on British Commonwealth Affairs, 1931–52.* 2 vols. London, Oxford University Press for RIIA, 1953.
— *Survey, 1931–9*: Nicholas Mansergh, *Survey of British Commonwealth Affairs; Problems of External Policy, 1931–9.* London, Oxford University Press for RIIA, 1952.

Nicolson: Harold Nicolson, *King George the Fifth.* London, Constable, 1952.

RIIA, *Documents*: Royal Institute of International Affairs, *Documents on International Affairs* (annually).
— *World in March 1939*: Arnold J. Toynbee and F. T. Ashton-Gwatkin, eds., *The World in March 1939.* London, Oxford University Press for RIIA, 1952. (*Survey of International Affairs, 1939–46.*)

Roberts & Trollip: Michael Roberts and A. E. G. Trollip, *South African Opposition, 1939–45.* London, Longmans, 1947.

Sherwood: R. E. Sherwood, ed., *The White House Papers of Harry L. Hopkins.* 2 vols. London, Eyre & Spottiswoode, 1948–9.

Tendulkar, *Mahatma*: D. G. Tendulkar, *Mahatma: Life of Mohandas Karamchand Gandhi.* 8 vols. Bombay, Jhaveri & Tendulkar, 1951–4.

UNCIO: United Nations Conference on International Organization, San Francisco, 1945, *Documents.* 22 vols. London and New York, U.N. Information Organizations and Library of Congress, 1945.

INTRODUCTION

THIS book, like many things, falls into three parts. The first gives some account of the impact of war upon the Commonwealth and upon its individual member nations; the second records the post-war changes in its composition, while the third examines some of the domestic and external problems that confronted the Commonwealth in the bleak mid-years of the century. Each of these topics, if treated exhaustively, would require a volume and what is attempted in this book is no more than the analysis of certain themes which seem to bear most closely on the idea of the Commonwealth and its place in the history of our times.

The theme of the first part is the capacity of the Commonwealth system to sustain unity of purpose and effort among Commonwealth governments and peoples in war; the theme of the second is the adaptability of the Commonwealth to changes which modified its hitherto predominantly British and almost exclusively European membership, and the theme of the third the ability of the Commonwealth to preserve its cohesion and sense of purpose at a time when it was faced with a changing balance of power and interest without and within its frontiers. If these are themes that may usefully be explored in the light of history, they permit of no final treatment at this slight vantage point in time. In examining them an historian of the Commonwealth can hope therefore to do no more—and may do much less—than give to his readers some insight into the ideas, the forces, the hopes, the anxieties, and the conflicts which in these years determined the character of the Commonwealth and the pattern of its development. But he should not for that reason shrink from all attempt to see the Commonwealth experiment and to judge its importance in the longer perspective of history. Coleridge illumined what must be the goal of all such endeavour in saying of our Grecian masters: 'It is the claim of Herodotus that he gives you the spirit of his age—that of Thucydides that he reveals to you his own, which was above the spirit of his age.' But for the Thucydidean 'above' the less presumptuous will prefer for themselves to substitute 'apart from', sensing that for them the summit of aspiration must be at the end to stand aside from events which they have recorded and in some degree experienced in order to try to place them in some larger setting.

The published sources used in this study are indicated in the footnotes— and also the lack of such sources when it seems important that the reader's attention should be specially drawn to it. The evidence available in printed form has been supplemented by personal inquiry and observation. The author had the opportunity of visiting every member nation of the Commonwealth during the years of which he writes and, in the course of his travels throughout this secular community of states, he was at the least not unmindful of the appropriateness to him of the Psalmist's injunction: 'Walk about Sion, and go round about her: and tell the towers thereof—mark well her bulwarks, consider her houses; that ye may tell them that come after.'

This volume is one of a series, the first two of which were written by Professor W. K. Hancock[1] and it follows immediately upon a volume by the present author on *Problems of External Policy, 1931–1939*. Two companion volumes, *Documents and Speeches on British Commonwealth Affairs, 1931–1952*, include the more important source material for the period as a whole.

[1] Professor Hancock's first volume dealt, in the words of its sub-title, with *Problems of Nationality 1918–1936*, and the second, which was published in two parts, with *Problems of Economic Policy 1918–1939*.

PART I

THE COMMONWEALTH AT WAR

Let us therefore brace ourselves to our duty, and so bear ourselves that if the British Commonwealth and Empire lasts for a thousand years men will still say, 'This was their finest hour.'
W. S. CHURCHILL, 18 June 1940

The British Empire is not expected to collapse owing to the peculiar innate force of the political objectives embodied in the conception of the Commonwealth of Nations.
    Report of the Commander-in-Chief, the German Navy, to
        the Führer, 6 September 1940

Our wartime co-operation is not the product of formal institutional unity; it is the result of agreement.
W. L. MACKENZIE KING, 11 May 1944

CHAPTER I

THE COMMONWEALTH IN 1939: INTERNAL RELATIONS AND EXTERNAL DANGERS

IN August 1914 King George V on the advice of the United Kingdom government declared war on Germany on behalf of the whole of the British Empire. In September 1939 King George VI on the advice of the United Kingdom government declared war on behalf of the United Kingdom, India, Burma, and the Colonial Empire, and on the separate advice of the governments of Canada, Australia, New Zealand,[1] and South Africa on behalf of each of these self-governing dominions. The contrast underlines at once the extent of the constitutional changes that had taken place in the intervening quarter of a century and their limitation.

In 1939 as distinct from 1914 the self-governing members of the Commonwealth not only themselves determined whether to remain at peace or go to war but demonstrated to the world their right to make their own decision. In principle this was as true of New Zealand and Australia (whose Prime Minister, Mr. Menzies, stated that it deemed itself to be at war by reason of the King's being at war), both of which with the United Kingdom declared war on Nazi Germany on 3 September, as it was of Canada which, in accordance with its Prime Minister's oft-repeated pledge that Parliament would decide, declared war six days later, on 9 September, and after the Canadian Parliament had in fact so decided, or of South Africa which by a narrow margin of the votes cast at the end of a bitter and prolonged debate in the House of Assembly, decided upon the same course. If further evidence were required of the freedom of choice of the dominions on this issue it was supplied by the Irish government which, with the virtually unanimous support of the members of the Dáil, resolved on neutrality. India's entry into the war, however, was decreed in London and Indian political leaders were not consulted about it.[2]

There was in the dominions both satisfaction and pride in their final responsibility in so great a matter. 'The Parliament of South Africa . . .', said General Smuts[3] in November 1939,[4] 'without any interference from England, decided that it was in the interests of South Africa . . . that we

[1] In the case of New Zealand there is a certain ambiguity in the relevant documentary evidence and it would appear from it that technically the declaration of war was made by the Governor-General, who professed to act under instructions from the King. On this point see Wood, ch. 1.

[2] See Mansergh, *Survey, 1931–9*, ch. x for a full account of how the dominions went to war.

[3] Throughout this book General Smuts, although he was created a Field-Marshal in 1941, is referred to as General Smuts, the title by which he is best known.

[4] In his speech at Bloemfontein on 3 November 1939, reprinted in J. C. Smuts, *Plans for a Better World, Speeches of Field-Marshal Smuts* (London, Hodder & Stoughton, 1942), p. 233.

should take part in this war.' 'Canada's entry into war', said Mr. Mackenzie King, 'was the deliberate decision of a free people, by their own representatives, in a free Parliament. . . . As a nation of the new world we placed ourselves freely at Britain's side because Britain's cause was the cause of freedom.'[1] Moreover the exercise of such sovereign, unfettered choice by the dominions was justly held to be the supreme vindication of the ideals of the British Commonwealth. The choice that was made and the way in which it was made alike showed at the least that autonomy and unity were not incompatible, and suggested that, on the contrary, unity that derived from the free choice of free peoples might rest on foundations more secure than any unity imposed from above. It is true, of course, that that unity was not complete. The final, irrefutable, evidence of dominion autonomy came, as it could only come, from a dominion (for so Eire continued to be regarded by other members of the Commonwealth) which decided not to go to war when the United Kingdom was at war. The Irish right to make this decision was not questioned but inevitably there was a certain ambivalence in the allusions, especially of United Kingdom statesmen, to Irish neutrality. On the one hand, and especially to European and to United States audiences, the fact of Irish neutrality was rightly emphasized as providing conclusive evidence of dominion liberty of action; on the other, and especially to Commonwealth audiences, it was regretted as a 'depressing', 'lamentable', or 'deplorable' breach in the unity of the Commonwealth, according to the outlook and temper of the speaker.

The self-evident independence of the dominions underlined by contrast the continuing dependence of other parts of the Empire, above all India. Never was it more clearly demonstrated that this great country remained outside the circle of the elect. 'In the dominions', wrote Pandit Nehru,[2] 'the decision was taken by popular representatives after full debate and consideration of various points of view. Not so in India, and it hurt.' It stirred resentment. It was felt that there was something 'fundamentally wrong' with a system under which one man, 'and he a foreigner', could plunge 400 million people in Asia into a European war 'without the slightest reference to them'. In Burma, in Ceylon, in the more politically advanced colonial territories throughout the British Empire the way in which the dominions went, or did not go, to war, afforded at least an example that one day their peoples would themselves like to be able to imitate. To that extent the coming of war itself accentuated the demand for full self-government among those who enjoyed it only in part.

The desire for self-government did not detract from the unity of the Empire in 1939; on balance indeed it may well have strengthened it. Even in India, where the Congress felt that India unfree could not participate whole-

[1] *The Times*, 5 September 1941.
[2] Jawaharlal Nehru, *The Discovery of India* (New York, Day, 1946), p. 432.

heartedly in a war for freedom, there was recognition that the ideals of liberty were cherished in Britain even if they were too tardily extended to the government of non-European peoples. At the worst there was the profession of self-government as the goal of British imperial policy, and at the best there were dominion precedents and assurances given in a series of pronouncements carrying, to quote Lord Hailey, 'an authority as complete as any our constitution affords', holding out to all dependent British territories 'the prospect of a progressive development of self-government'. By contrast, the Nazis proclaimed as their goal the rule of a master race which openly declared its mission to be to govern by force the peoples subjected to it, for its own advantage. It was not, indeed, among non-Europeans within the Commonwealth but among extreme conservatives or nationalists, particularly in South Africa, that Nazi doctrines of race and blood elicited some sympathetic response. In the colonial territories and in India popular opinion almost inevitably was antagonistic to the Nazi and Fascist régimes. That the war was a war for freedom from the outset was not in any serious dispute; but for that very reason restrictions upon freedom tended to become more irksome.

The outbreak of war in September 1939 was a landmark in Commonwealth history but neither for the dominions, nor for India, nor for the Colonial Empire did it signify the end of a period. On the contrary, with the coming of war the pressure for change was increased and extended, but the direction of change was not sensibly modified. Self-government and decentralization remained the goal. For Commonwealth statesmen in September 1939, therefore, the all-important questions were the familiar ones—how was autonomy to be reconciled with unity, diversity with strength? But they were posed in the new setting of a war for survival. What were the lessons of peacetime experience? How far were they relevant in wartime? How far was the British Commonwealth, whose capacity for waging modern war was chiefly dependent upon the contribution of a group of states, all of whom with the exception of India were autonomous, fitted politically as well as materially to withstand the challenge of highly organized totalitarian tyrannies?

The Status of the Dominions and the Stature of the United Kingdom

In the period 1919 to 1939 problems of nationality and problems of external policy were of outstanding importance in the history of the British Commonwealth of Nations. The former translated into terms of status were a constant preoccupation of governments and peoples, the latter more nearly of governments alone. Thus while membership, its forms and symbols, received much attention in Parliaments and in newspapers, the foreign policies of the individual dominions were accorded remarkably little, except indeed when they touched on questions of status. This was perhaps to be expected. In these years the dominions, which had long aspired to equality, attained their goal. For Australia and New Zealand, their population overwhelmingly British in extraction, that goal was reached with the recognition by the United Kingdom of the dominion right to participate in the making of foreign policy.

> We were Colonies, we became Dominions. We have been accorded the status of nations.... We, the representatives of the Dominions are met together to formulate a foreign policy for the Empire. What greater advance is conceivable? What remains to us? We are like so many Alexanders. What other worlds have we to conquer?

So said Mr. W. M. Hughes to his colleagues at the Imperial Conference of 1921.[1] But they did not all see things so simply. Ever mindful of the problems of internal unity that derived from the composition of their populations, the representatives of Canada and of South Africa did not speak—indeed could not speak—with the uninhibited accents or in the self-confident tone of the Australian Prime Minister. For them the substance of equality was not enough; they needed the forms as well. For French-Canadian as for Afrikaner nationalists theoretical subordination was still subordination. It was inconsistent with equality. 'A few ancient forms' seemed to them sufficient to wreck the ideal of Commonwealth. They had therefore other worlds to conquer. In 1921 General Smuts was insistent that all surviving inequalities whether legal or conventional should be removed; in 1926 General Hertzog and Mr. McGilligan gave a sharper edge to this demand. The support of the Canadian government of Mr. Mackenzie King ensured its acceptance and the Reports of the Imperial Conferences of 1926 and 1930 represented political agreement which received legal endorsement in the Statute of Westminster. It was the Commonwealth whose relations were thus defined that went to war in 1939.

The defining in convention and in law of the relations between the United Kingdom and the dominions was not, as is sometimes supposed, either unanimously sought or uniformly welcomed by the dominions. It was deemed by many in Australia, New Zealand, and the United Kingdom to be at best superfluous, at worst mischievous and likely to impair imperial unity. To Mr. W. M. Hughes the Balfour Report was 'a wonderful document'.

> It took stock of everything.... It was all things to all men. Every Prime Minister went away perfectly satisfied—Mr. Bruce because it altered nothing that affected Australia, Mr. Mackenzie King because it taught Lord Byng where he got off, and General Hertzog because he was able to assure the burghers that the King of England was no longer King of South Africa, although it was true that the King of South Africa was also King of England.

[1] 20 June 1921. Cmd. 1474, p. 23. In 1942 Mr. Hughes expressly repudiated the notion that the Balfour Report, 1926, was the first authoritative recognition of the new status of the dominions. He described it as an error, for 'the 1926 conference, so far as status is concerned, did no more than reaffirm the very definite and authoritative recognition of the equality of status of the Dominions with Great Britain made in the War Cabinet in 1919 and restated in more precise terms by Mr. Lloyd George at the Imperial Conference in 1921' (7 October 1942, Australia, H. of R. Deb., vol. 172, pp. 1424–30).

INTERNAL RELATIONS AND EXTERNAL DANGERS

But it failed in its intention because, in Mr. Hughes's view, it was an attempt to appease the unappeasable. To Mr. Menzies the Balfour Report was 'in substance a grave disservice', and he believed that 'the whole 1926-31 process' was founded on a misguided attempt to reduce to written terms things that were matters of the spirit and not of the letter.[1] Conservative opinion in New Zealand was no more favourable. 'It's all the fault of that damned Statute of Westminster', complained the New Zealand Attorney-General in a letter to an Australian colleague in comment on a matter for which indeed the Statute could hardly be held accountable. In Britain it was not only right-wing imperialists who contemplated with misgiving all the consequences that might flow from theorizing about imperial relations.

The Times, which under Geoffrey Dawson's editorship[2] devoted much attention to imperial affairs, consistently repudiated the notion that imperial relations needed to be clearly defined. The Report of the Imperial Conference of 1926 was accepted as ' an agreed and authoritative picture of the Empire as it is', but there were recurrent warnings against the attempts of 'legal pedants' to press for further definition, whether of dominion status or of dominion rights, the editor agreeing with Mr. W. M. Hughes that any attempt to crystallize them in a formula would be 'an act of extreme folly'. The Statute of Westminster was dismissed as a piece of mere 'pedantry' for which there was, and could be, no enthusiasm but about which also there would be no great apprehension.[3] At a still more exalted level King George V is said by his biographer to have watched the process of definition and quick decentralization with anxiety. He regretted particularly that the Conference of 1929 on the Operation of Dominion Legislation should have found it necessary to deal with legislation affecting the position of the Crown.[4] 'After following the proceedings of the conference', noted the King, 'and estimating the spirit in which the views of some of the Dominions have been expressed, I cannot look into the future without feelings of no little anxiety as to the continued unity of the Empire.'[5]

[1] Mr. Menzies's comments were made on 25 August 1937 in the debate in the Australian House of Representatives on the Statute of Westminster Adoption Bill (ibid. vol. 154, pp. 85–94). For an account of New Zealand reactions see Wood, ch. ii.

[2] Editor 1912–19 and again 1922–41. His biography has been written by Sir Evelyn Wrench, *Geoffrey Dawson and Our Times* (London, Hutchinson, 1955).

[3] *The History of The Times*, vol. 4: *The 150th Anniversary and Beyond, 1912–1948* (London, The Times, 1952), pp. 879–80.

[4] Cmd. 3479. The terms of reference of the Conference included the following: 'To enquire into, report upon, and make recommendations concerning—(i) Existing statutory provisions requiring reservation of Dominion legislation for the assent of his Majesty or authorising the disallowance of such legislation. . . . (iii) The principles embodied in or underlying the Colonial Laws Validity Act, 1865, and the extent to which any provisions of that Act ought to be repealed, amended, or modified in the light of existing relations between the various members of the British Commonwealth of Nations as described in this Report (i.e. the Report of the Imperial Conference).' The Conference found it necessary to proceed from the discussion of the Colonial Laws Validity Act to a statement of principles concerning laws relating to the succession to the Throne and the Royal Style and Titles.   [5] Nicolson, p. 485.

The Balfour Report was drafted, the Statute of Westminster enacted, because the governments of Canada, South Africa, and the Irish Free State were insistent that conventions and constitutional forms should coincide with political realities and because the United Kingdom, Australia, and New Zealand were prepared to concede so much to the weight of argument and to a realistic appraisal of the balance of opinion within the British Commonwealth. But for them the attainment of equality none the less exacted a price. One part of it, in the words used by Mr. Winston Churchill in the debate on the Statute of Westminster Bill, was the obliteration of 'old, famous landmarks and signposts, which, although archaic, have a historic importance'. More than once he expressed misgivings about their removal to Lord Balfour who

to some extent reassured me, by saying, 'I do not believe in wooden guns'. I thought that a very pregnant remark. He saw no advantage in preserving an assertion of rights and powers on which, in practice, we should not find it possible effectively to base ourselves. I still repose faith in the calm, lambent wisdom of that great man in his later years.[1]

But would Mr. Churchill have reposed such faith in Lord Balfour's wisdom had the guns not been wooden? It seems unlikely. And there were many, perhaps the majority, in Britain who accepted the need for the redefinition of Commonwealth relations in the same spirit of sagacious resignation. For them, as for King George V, there was a feeling that it was a sad destiny that imposed the duty of approving processes of change which might prove to be processes of disintegration.[2] Much has been written about the receding tide of imperial sentiment after 1919; little of the ebbing faith of imperialists in a Commonwealth largely refashioned to meet the claims of dominion nationalists. Yet this also had its impact on the working out of Commonwealth policies and practice between the two world wars.

Conservative imperialists were distressed by the new Commonwealth pattern partly because it was new and partly because it was a pattern. There was in it, so it seemed to them, too little emphasis on the simple virtues of unity and loyalty, too much on theory. Professors and lawyers might find satisfaction in the working out of 'academic constitutional doctrines', but for many men with practical experience of imperial affairs few things were more disturbing than the new intellectual environment. 'The pedantic Statute of Westminster', *The Times* described it; and if the opportunities offered by its text for academic analysis, exposition, and interpretation be regarded as a fair test of pedantry, then the description was warranted. But it was not a description calculated to recommend the Statute, or the transformation in intra-Commonwealth relations which it symbolized, to a public nourished on

[1] 20 November 1931, H. of C. Deb., vol. 259, col. 1190. Doubtless Mr. Churchill placed some emphasis upon 'later'.
[2] Nicolson, p. 474.

British empiricist traditions. While, therefore, the Statute of Westminster Bill had the support of all parties in the House of Commons because it was what dominion governments requested (though in the case of Australia and New Zealand in the interests of conformity and not from conviction), there was little enthusiasm for it in Britain save among left-wing reformers and progressive academics inspired by a Fabian zeal for planning. It was not perhaps altogether chance that the most sanguine interpretation of the transformation from Empire to Commonwealth published in the United Kingdom was by an Oxford professor of European origin.[1]

There was also another factor. 'The Statute of Westminster, as the ensuing India Act of 1935', wrote Sir Harold Nicolson, 'solemnized the renunciation by England of an imperial mission'.[2] Some might question the bleakness of the verdict, some might feel that the new Commonwealth of equal partners would far surpass the old Empire in moral stature and in beneficent achievement, but the great majority welcomed wholeheartedly the rise of the young nations overseas while sensing that with the last surviving traces of inequality in status between the dominions and Britain there would also be taken away something of Britain's standing as a world power. It was not impossible that as the younger nations overseas ascended, Britain herself might decline in power. Some such thought was perhaps in Lord Salisbury's mind some thirty years earlier when in one of his last public speeches he forecast that the colonies, 'our brother nations', 'will go on in their own power, in their own irresistible power, and I have no doubt they will leave combinations behind them which will cast into the shade all the glories that the British Empire has hitherto displayed'.[3] These were prospects about which Canadians and Australians might feel exhilarated, but they had for Englishmen no such warming glow.

It was, therefore, not chance, but the inner logic of British imperial history that stirred enthusiasm among so many overseas for that transformation of Empire into Commonwealth in which the United Kingdom assisted with imaginative understanding[4] but without reforming zeal. They thought of decentralization in terms not of unwelcome necessity but of a policy whose fulfilment was beneficial both for them and for the Empire. 'It is the policy of decentralization', said General Botha in 1911,[5] 'which has made the Empire.' 'Decentralization to the limit' remained the goal of General Smuts, one of the architects of the new Commonwealth, in 1943.[6] Thus while the great majority

[1] Sir Alfred Zimmern, *The Third British Empire*, 3rd ed. (London, Oxford University Press, 1934). [2] Nicolson, p. 473.
[3] Quoted in A. L. Kennedy, *Salisbury, 1830–1903* (London, Murray, 1953), p. 340.
[4] L. S. Amery, *My Political Life* (London, Hutchinson, 1953), vol. 2, ch. xii gives an account of the United Kingdom role in the drafting of the Balfour Report and illustrates the concern of the United Kingdom government to meet and even to anticipate dominion requests for definition and for change. [5] Cd. 5745, p. 70.
[6] Speech to Empire Parliamentary Association, 25 November 1943, reprinted, Mansergh, *Documents*, i. 568.

might acknowledge that decentralization was the condition of continuing unity, it was on the circumference and not at the centre that decentralization itself was thought to be a source of strength. In London, as authority was drained away from what hitherto had been in fact and not merely by courtesy the capital of the whole Empire, this seemed to be the language not of reality but of political paradox. Lord Balfour in 1926 spoke of 'a common interest in loyalty, in freedom, in ideals' as the bond of Empire, adding with surely a hint of sadness—'if that is not enough nothing else is enough'.[1] In the next thirteen years the sufficiency of that seemingly slender bond was tested by the challenge of the dictators in Europe and the menace of Japan in Asia.

Some Consequences of Equality in the Making of Policy

'And, though every Dominion is now, and must always remain, the sole judge of the nature and extent of its co-operation, no common cause will, in our opinion, be thereby imperilled.'[2] This sentence from the Balfour Report is the text to which commentaries on the foreign policies of the independent nations of the Commonwealth before the Second World War must almost of of necessity be related.[3] It was a sentence written at a time when a major war seemed remote to all and unthinkable to many; at a time when the authority of the League, buttressed in the area of greatest danger by the recently negotiated Locarno Treaty, seemed sufficient to discourage any thought of aggression. In such an atmosphere and against such a background, preoccupation with problems of status continued undisturbed by pressing considerations of security. This was fortunate for the future of intra-Commonwealth relations, since it enabled such problems to be examined on their merits, but unfortunate in that it encouraged the dominions to underestimate the urgency of the problems of external policy with which as autonomous nations they were henceforward to be confronted. This underestimate was something which for other reasons they were already predisposed to make. If their anxiety to disentangle their foreign policies from that of the United Kingdom was in principle well advised, their slowness to equip themselves to carry out independent foreign policies was on that very ground the more open to criticism. The distinction made in the Balfour Report between status and function, coupled with the assertion that the principles of equality and similarity appropriate to status did not universally extend to function, inevitably encouraged procrastination and unnecessarily prolonged dependence in practice upon the United Kingdom. There was much to be said for unified control of foreign policy, there was more, in the circumstances of 1926, for individual and separate control, but nothing for the prolongation of a period

---

[1] Blanche E. C. Dugdale, *Arthur James Balfour, First Earl of Balfour, 1906–30* (London, Hutchinson, 1936), p. 382.   [2] Cmd. 2768, p. 14.
[3] It is for this reason much favoured as a topic for discussion by those whose business it is to set examination papers.

of transition in which the United Kingdom continued to discharge functions which were in fact incompatible with equality of status. In the era of Baldwin–Chamberlain administrations the view prevailed in the United Kingdom that this inequality in function was a source of unity, whereas in fact it was more often a source of friction. In the oversea dominions particularly, but also in the United Kingdom, it served to distract attention from what was the greater Commonwealth problem, that of agreement upon major issues of foreign policy after thorough and if possible independent examination of them.

Dominion dissociation from United Kingdom policies and commitments meant that dominion participation in a war in which Britain was engaged could not be presumed. If after the Chanak crisis illusions continued to be entertained on this score there was no justification for them. For this reason after 1922 no United Kingdom government could afford to disregard dominion opinion or fail to take into account likely dominion reactions to any major departure in foreign policy. In the 1930's these were not easy to assess, and partly because two dominion governments, those of Canada and South Africa, preoccupied with problems of internal unity, were wary of comment because they were fearful of commitments, but still more because the strength of that bond of common loyalty of which Lord Balfour spoke had not been fully tested. One consequence, to quote the historian of *The Times*, was that 'Great Britain in 1938 had to face the responsibilities of a world Power in the knowledge that her ability to participate in a world war depended on the support of a number of distant States, bound to her by intangible ties which, however powerful in an emergency, were not strong enough to make a consistent Commonwealth policy easy to formulate.' At this time, moreover, 'the point where Britain was immediately threatened, i.e. in Europe, was of less obvious importance to the Dominions, and Britain's instinct of national self-preservation was constantly checked by the far slower reactions of other members of the Commonwealth'.[1] The historian of *The Times* notes that in these considerations were to be found the principal reasons for the consistent support that newspaper gave to the policy of appeasement in the late 1930's. To its editor imperial, over and above national, unity was a prerequisite of participation in war. When in 1938 the two questions, whether it would be possible for Great Britain and France to resist German plans by force without assured dominion support and whether imperial unity was more important than the integrity of Czechoslovakia, were brutally posed by the German dictator, the Editor of *The Times* had little doubt that the answer to the first was in the negative because the answer to the second was in the affirmative. To most British historians this conclusion has seemed in retrospect at once unworthy and mistaken. But even if so much be allowed, it is to be noted that almost without exception they reached their conclusion the easy way by

[1] *History of The Times*, vol. 4, pt. 2, p. 1021.

ignoring altogether the imperial factor.[1] This was something no government could afford to do. As Geoffrey Dawson wrote in a valedictory letter to Neville Chamberlain,

> I shall always be an impenitent supporter of what is called the 'Munich policy'. No one who sat in this place [Printing House Square], as I did during the autumn of '38, with almost daily visitations from eminent Canadians and Australians, could fail to realize that war with Germany at that time would have been misunderstood and resented from end to end of the Empire.[2]

While making due allowance for the circumstances in which the letter was written, and discounting the use of the over-emphatic 'resented', its substance is not in question. But neither at the time, nor since, has due allowance been made for the new imperial calculation that had entered into the making of British foreign policy. In war a divided Empire would have marked the failure of the Commonwealth experiment, yet the only ultimate assurance of unity could come from dominion assent to, and support for, Britain's foreign policy. European dictators were not disposed to wait upon events. They had indeed in this particular instance every reason to seek to anticipate the consolidation of Commonwealth opinion, though the evidence available suggests that in fact this was a consideration that entered but little into their reckoning.

Agreement upon policy among a group of widely scattered and equal states presents, in any circumstances, a problem of considerable magnitude, and before the Second World War it was greatly accentuated by the isolationist passivity of dominion external policies. The history of the United States indeed suggested that this was likely to be the early fruit of independence, but active dominion participation in the Imperial War Cabinet from 1917–19, dominion pressure for individual representation in the making of the peace treaties in 1919, and the role of General Smuts in the drafting of the Covenant of the League of Nations more than counterbalanced the inexact analogies which history had to offer. In general terms what United Kingdom public opinion expected was that dominion participation in the making of British foreign policy would inject a new spirit at once high-minded and invigorating. Experience in the inter-war years, broadly speaking, substantiated the first but not the second.

A policy which could be defended on grounds of principle alone was apt to be palatable to dominion peoples overseas who for the most part shared the United States revulsion against the power politics, the secret treaties, and the old diplomacy which were widely believed to have been responsible for the outbreak of the First World War. This was doubtless a wholesome

---

[1] This is true of Sir Lewis Namier in *Diplomatic Prelude, 1938–1939* (London, Macmillan, 1948); less true of J. W. Wheeler-Bennett, *Munich: Prologue to Tragedy* (London, Macmillan, 1948); and altogether true, strangely enough, of Churchill, i.

[2] *History of the Times*, vol. 4, pt. 2, p. 1022. The letter was dated 8 November 1940.

INTERNAL RELATIONS AND EXTERNAL DANGERS

and corrective influence; its effect, however, was slight. For this the dominion governments were themselves largely responsible. Their faith in principle was tempered by prudence, which in face of the formidable totalitarian menace of the later 1930's at times led to the nerveless endorsement of Britain's policies. It was not dominion governments but public opinion in some dominions that was outraged by the abrupt announcement of the Hoare–Laval pact in December 1935; it was not dominion governments but some sections of dominion opinion that protested in September 1938 at the sacrifice of Czechoslovakia on the altar of appeasement.[1] But whereas appeasement as a policy—and it was deemed to be neither a dishonourable nor an unprincipled policy—had the full assent of dominion governments other than New Zealand's, their silence, or inaction, in respect of many particular problems of foreign policy in those years was due to a sensible realization of the limitations of their own power and knowledge. It was a realization that had come through experiences that were often painful. They are epitomized in the reaction of the Canadian government to the unwelcome prominence Canada acquired by association with proposals for extended sanctions against Italy in November 1935. It disowned sponsorship and, in the words of Mr. Glazebrook, 'backed from the fame of leadership with rapid steps'.[2]

This was something unexpected by public opinion in Britain. It had been brought up to think of the dominions as young, vigorous states peopled by the hardy descendants of intrepid pioneers who could be trusted to display in peace a resolution that would match the fortitude and courage of their contingents in war. The American desire for detachment was felt to be peculiarly American—and fortunately so. The dominion reputation, first acquired in the South African War, was very different. The quality of their troops and their skill in guerrilla fighting had then elicited a grateful appreciation in the mother country, unkindly pointed by Rudyard Kipling's reflections on her own people who before the outbreak of war in 1899 had 'vaunted' their 'fathomless power' and 'flaunted' their 'iron pride'; who after the early reverses 'fawned on the younger nations for the men who could shoot and ride', and who, when the war was won, again contented their souls

With the flannelled fools at the wicket or the muddied oafs at the goals.[3]

The contrast between the 'old' and, by implication, exhausted mother country and 'younger nations' was much favoured by statesmen. At the Colonial Conference of 1902 Joseph Chamberlain likened England to 'a weary Titan staggering under the too vast orb of his fate' and sought to impress upon

---

[1] The New Zealand government, however, specifically dissociated itself from the Hoare–Laval proposals and was far from approving the Munich Agreement (see Wood, chs. v and vi).
[2] G. P. de T. Glazebrook, *A History of Canadian External Relations* (Toronto, Oxford University Press for CIIA, 1950), p. 411. See also Mansergh, *Survey, 1931–9*, p. 117.
[3] *The Islanders* (1902).

dominion ministers the need for their fresh and youthful peoples to assume a greater share of the burden. In this he was not successful. Dominion ministers thought little of Chamberlain's proposals for a redistribution of imperial responsibilities but seemingly they liked the analogy between age and youth. It coincided well with Sir Wilfrid Laurier's notion that the twentieth would be Canada's century and equally well with the more general idea that the time had come for liberation from Downing Street control. It seemed that the men in the Colonial Office did not understand the urge of young and vigorous nations to be treated on a footing of equality. They were too much preoccupied, they were too tired. Mr. Deakin complained in 1907, with a hint of that thrustfulness which conventional Englishmen were apt to deplore, that Australians found in the Colonial Office

a certain impenetrability; a certain remoteness, perhaps geographically justified; a certain weariness of people much pressed with affairs, and greatly overburdened, whose natural desire is to say, 'Kindly postpone this; do not press that, do not trouble us; what does it matter? we have enough to do already'.[1]

In the Canadian House of Commons five years later Sir Robert Borden spoke of the 'almost impossible burden' thrown upon the British Isles by the growth of naval competition and concluded: 'That burden is so great that the day has come when either the existence of this Empire will be imperilled or the young and mighty dominions must join with the motherland to make secure the common safety and the common heritage of all.'[2] Five years later still General Smuts told the Imperial War Conference of 1917 that 'the young nations are growing into Great Powers'.[3]

In the common experience and the common sacrifices of war all that was asked for was gladly conceded. It was no longer the United Kingdom, it was the dominions who were thereafter apt to express reserve. 'There was a time', so Mr. Lloyd George told the Imperial Conference in 1921, 'when Downing Street controlled the Empire; today the Empire is in charge of Downing Street.'[4] He welcomed the change. 'The hitherto exclusive control of Britain over foreign policy is now vested', he said, 'in the Empire as a whole.' 'The advantage to us', he explained later in the House of Commons,[5] 'is that joint control [of foreign policy] means joint responsibility, and when the burden of Empire has become so vast it is well that we should have the shoulders of these young giants under the burden to help us along.' Once again the analogy was no doubt gratifying to the dominion peoples, but the response of their governments to the notion of joint responsibility was altogether discouraging. But even when that was understood—and because it was so out of line with preconceived ideas some time elapsed before this

[1] Cd. 3523, p. 72.   [2] Canada, H. of C. Deb., session 1912–13, vol. 1, col. 676.
[3] Cd. 8566, p. 48.   [4] Cmd. 1474, p. 14.
[5] 14 December 1921, H. of C. Deb., vol. 149, col. 30.

happened—the expectation remained that the dominions would use their opportunities of influencing the Foreign Office in favour of bold and resolute policies. Lloyd George was voicing it when he forecast that the co-operation of the 'young giants' would introduce 'a broader and a calmer view into foreign policy' which would 'restrain rash Ministers and stimulate timorous ones.'

This expectation was in accord with conventional notions of dominion behaviour, and, as has been remarked already, it was only in part fulfilled. Dominion governments, for reasons which, be it said, seem by no means insufficient in retrospect, unquestionably exercised a restraining influence on successive United Kingdom governments by their firm refusal to enter into major commitments in Europe or Asia. Twice in his career Mr. Mackenzie King believed he had helped to avert major war, and on both occasions by declining to support an adventurous policy. The first was in the Chanak crisis of 1922 when the Canadian government refused to promise military assistance to Britain in support of her Near Eastern policy until the Canadian Parliament had been consulted, and the second in 1935 when the Canadian government disowned the unauthorized initiative of the Canadian delegate to the League of Nations in proposing coal and oil sanctions against Italy. But for the Canadian refusal in 1922 to be stampeded by Mr. Lloyd George, who thus himself provided the classic example of a 'rash minister' restrained by dominion governments, 'a second great European conflict', in Mr. Mackenzie King's opinion, 'might have taken place',[1] while but for the diplomatic retreat of 1935 'the whole of Europe might have been aflame' in 1936. Imperialists were bitterly critical of Mr. Mackenzie King's policy of no commitments; he himself professed to think that 'our country is being drawn into international situations' to an extent that 'is alarming'.[2]

Since not even the most rigorous of critics has suggested that ministers in the Baldwin–Chamberlain era were 'rash', the restraining influence of dominion ministers was not as valuable in the 1930's as it might otherwise have been. It found classic expression when General Hertzog told the Imperial Conference of 1937 that in the attainment of the high object of world appeasement the mission of the Commonwealth stood clearly defined; it encouraged in the Munich crisis the continued pursuit of a policy that was temperamentally congenial to the United Kingdom government and subjected it to no friendly but searching criticism. Late in September 1938 dominion High Commissioners in London sought out Mr. Neville Chamberlain not in order to stiffen his resolution but in anxious perturbation lest a failure to appease the Nazi dictator might bring about a war for which they were unprepared and on an issue to which many of their peoples were in-

[1] 26 March 1928, Canada, H. of C. Deb., 1928, vol. 2, p. 1715. See also ibid. vol. 3, pp. 3479–83 where this statement was discussed acrimoniously.
[2] 11 February 1936, ibid. 1936, vol. 1, p. 98.

different. A dominion stimulus to 'timorous' ministers at that time or earlier might indeed have had beneficial consequences, but it was here that the expectation of Mr. Lloyd George was in the event confounded. Dominion ministers, aware of dangers which no action by middle or small powers would be able to avert, became themselves timorous.[1] The Canadian High Commissioner in London, in conversation with the deputy-editor of *The Times* on 17 September 1938, referred to the 'timid and isolationist Canadian Government' and the 'inert Mackenzie King', though he himself was most strongly opposed to a war on the Sudeten question.[2] The dominions did not favour resolute resistance to aggressors; they favoured appeasement.[3] They did not aspire to fill the role of 'nature's last crusaders'; they eschewed all thought of crusades whether for the League, or for the Empire, or for the rights of small nations.

It is no chance that Mr. Mackenzie King, in so many ways the representative Commonwealth figure of the period, had an avowed dislike of 'crusading'. Canadians, he told the House of Commons in May 1938, while not unmindful of the fate of other democratic governments and the persecution of minorities elsewhere, would be ill advised to join in crusades in other continents. Consideration of geography, of domestic unity, and of economic development alike precluded the pursuit of 'a spectacular headline policy'. Modesty in determining the aims of dominion foreign policy seemed to Mr. Mackenzie King in itself a virtue.[4]

The desire of the dominions was for peace. It was in the light of it that every policy was judged and for it they were prepared to pay a heavy price. General Smuts and Mr. Mackenzie King (who was not temperamentally disposed to lavish encomiums on the United Kingdom government) praised it most highly for the very actions which their own people were later to condemn most bitterly. 'What Britain has done to appease antagonisms in the last few years is something', so Mr. Mackenzie King told the Canadian House of Commons in 1937, 'that the rest of the world hardly begins to appreciate. . . . She has been the great pacifier'.[5] It was a role the Canadian Prime Minister himself sought to emulate.

The major problem of Commonwealth foreign policy before the Second World War was conceived in terms of unity. But the Commonwealth, in fact, was never more firmly united. It was united upon a policy of concession that came perilously close to being the negation of all policy. The self-governing members of the Commonwealth thought alike—which was gratifying, but not enough. What was too much and too easily overlooked in a concern for unity

---

[1] Mr. Baldwin, once asked what he proposed to give Mr. Mackenzie King as a Christmas present, is said to have replied, 'a pair of bedsocks—he always seems to have cold feet'.
[2] *History of The Times*, vol. 4, pt. 2, p. 938.
[3] Other than New Zealand, whose exceptional position is discussed in Mansergh, *Survey, 1931–9*, pp. 202–3 and 437–41.   [4] Canada, H. of C. Deb., 1938, vol. 3, pp. 3175–90.
[5] Ibid. 1937, vol. 1, p. 251 (Mansergh, *Documents*, i. 394).

INTERNAL RELATIONS AND EXTERNAL DANGERS

was the need for judgement and right decision. In the particular circumstances of the later 1930's what was most of all required was not a greater consensus of Commonwealth opinion but the more vigorous expression of independent and conflicting opinion. It was in this respect that the Commonwealth was handicapped by continuing inequality in function. Had the dominion Departments of External Affairs been more strongly staffed, had they been represented by their own ministers or ambassadors in the more important capitals of Europe and Asia, and had they in consequence possessed independent sources of information, it is not likely that there would have been such ready endorsement of the direction of United Kingdom foreign policy. Difference of opinion and judgement would have provoked discussion and discussion could only have been beneficial. Equality of status coupled with inequality in functional responsibility at once encouraged over-much preoccupation with status on the part of the dominions and an exaggerated concern for unity, regardless of its basis and purpose, on the part of the United Kingdom.

Over and above such difficulties, arising from a period of transition within, the Commonwealth was beset with far graver problems and dangers from without. It is a commonplace to observe that democracies are at a disadvantage when confronted by the challenge of dictatorial systems simply because that faith in discussion which is one of the great essentials of their system of government makes for slow appreciation of new dangers in peacetime and often actually precludes prompt measures to meet them. The handicap under which the democracies laboured was increased in the case of the British Commonwealth by the reliance of its self-governing members upon the democratic process not only in the conduct of their domestic affairs but also in the working out of their foreign policies. Agreement could be reached only through consultation between six[1] independent and widely scattered governments, and while improved means of communication had lessened the problems which distance created, most certainly they had not resolved them. For here was no question simply of conveying a decision from the centre to the circumference but one of carrying on a discussion between governments which would go far to determine their individual policies and the measure of agreement that existed among them. If the method seemed to many outsiders, and on occasion to British Foreign Secretaries,[2] slow, illogical, and

---

[1] Seven if one includes the government of India which, though subordinate to London in respect of foreign policy until 1947, was customarily consulted on matters affecting the interests of the subcontinent.

[2] Cf. the observation of Mr. Austen Chamberlain, 18 November 1925, on the impossibility of always waiting upon the expression of dominion views: 'I could not go, as the representative of His Majesty's Government, to meeting after meeting of the League of Nations, to conference after conference with the representatives of foreign countries, and say, "Great Britain is without a policy. We have not yet been able to meet all the Governments of the Empire, and we can do nothing"' (H. of C. Deb., vol. 188, col. 521).

dangerously cumbersome, it was, whatever its defects, congenial to Commonwealth statesmen and derived at root from an inherited belief in the value of conference and discussion as a means of reaching not a quick, but a wise conclusion. It was no accident that Hitler did not share their faith; that he was on the contrary, as he told Lord Halifax, 'a fanatical enemy of conferences',[1] and that in this one revealing phrase he should have exposed the deeper antagonism between the British Commonwealth and the Third Reich.

Under leisurely peacetime conditions the defects of the Commonwealth system were minimized; in time of tension and crisis, as between 1935 and 1939 when in all democracies divided counsels prevailed, its weaknesses were most apparent. It is at such times, too, that the unitary, authoritarian state or Empire enjoys a great advantage. Such a state can pursue policies without waiting on popular consent. It can work out its designs in secret; it can make sudden, disconcerting diplomatic moves[2] which a democratic society finds it difficult to counter. If before the Second World War the countries of the British Commonwealth responded slowly to the dangers that threatened them, that was partly at least because agreement upon policy was dependent upon a double process which in point of time might, and sometimes did, entail a double disadvantage. Both peoples and partners had to be persuaded of the rightness of any given course of action before the Commonwealth could act in unity, and both in those years were often difficult to persuade. Hitler, however, ultimately achieved even this.[3]

The Nature of the Nazi Challenge

During the Munich crisis of September the acting Counsellor at the German Embassy in London warned his government that the destruction of Czechoslovakia would be regarded in Britain as tantamount to a declaration of war.

If our aims [he wrote] were to become other than purely racial, if we digressed from our present policy of wiping out the consequences of the sins of Versailles, and instead advocated imperialist ideas, we must reckon with the fact that the British nation as a whole will be ready to wage war against Germany which, in actual fact, it does not want.[4]

No forecast could have been more exact. Hitler by destroying Czechoslovakia persuaded both the peoples and the governments of the British Commonwealth that there was no alternative to subjection save war. International

---

[1] *D. Ger. F.P.*, i. 63.

[2] It may reasonably be argued that the Hoare–Laval plan and the guarantee to Poland were sudden and disconcerting enough. But a formidable popular reaction compelled the abandonment of the first, while the second, in principle if not in actual form, was the outcome of popular pressure upon the Chamberlain government for a stronger policy.

[3] Cf. Mansergh, *Survey 1931–9*, ch. xi.

[4] *D. Ger. F.P.*, ii. 920; see also a dispatch from the German Ambassador, von Dirksen, dated 18 March 1939, on the same subject (ibid. vi. 36–39).

INTERNAL RELATIONS AND EXTERNAL DANGERS 19

appeasement, accepted by the Imperial Conference of 1937 as the goal of Commonwealth policy, was recognized by all its Commonwealth sponsors, other than General Hertzog, finally to have failed with Hitler's midnight march on Prague on 14 March 1939. For peoples as well as governments that marked the parting of the ways. Thus when Dr. Arnold Toynbee dated the 'true beginning' of the Second World War from March 1939[1] he reflected faithfully the psychological change in the attitude of the British Commonwealth towards Nazi Germany that took place at that time.

Hitler's attitude to the British Empire, like the Kaiser's before him, was ambivalent. At times he thought of an understanding which would guarantee to Britain her imperial possessions, other than the former German colonial territories, and ensure to Germany a dominant position in Europe. The British Empire, as he once remarked to von Rundstedt, was to be looked upon together with the Catholic Church as one of the corner-stones of Western civilization.[2] At other times he was intent upon its destruction and the division of the spoils with Mussolini or Stalin as suited Nazi interests best. But at all times he would seem to have been convinced, as he told the senior commanders of the German forces on 22 August 1939, that 'England's stake in a war is unimaginably great'.[3]

An analogy between the Roman and the British Empires which Hitler had sketched in a few bold strokes for the enlightenment of his Chiefs of Staff at the meeting in the Reich Chancellery in November 1937[4] suggested how he had reached this conclusion. Only the disintegrating effects of Christianity and 'the symptoms of age which appear in every country', he then argued, had caused the fall of Rome, for after the Punic wars the Roman Empire was confronted with no serious political rival from without. But the British Empire had rivals stronger than itself and for that reason could not be compared with the Roman in respect of permanence. Britain might be able to protect herself, but she could protect her colonial possessions only in alliance with other states. 'How, for instance', exclaimed the Führer, with a fine disregard for recent constitutional developments in the Commonwealth, 'could Britain alone defend Canada against attack by America, or her Far Eastern interests against attack by Japan!' Moreover, were there not indications that the Empire could no longer preserve its unity by the exercise of power? Did not events in Ireland, in India, 'where Britain's half-measures had given to the Indians the opportunity of using later on as a weapon against Britain, the nonfulfillment of her promises regarding a constitution',[5] and the emphasis now laid upon the Crown as the symbol of imperial unity all afford convincing evidence of diminishing strength? Externally the position

[1] RIIA, *World in March 1939*, p. vii.
[2] Quoted Alan Bullock, *Hitler* (London, Odhams, 1952), p. 540.
[3] *IMT Nuremberg*, vol. 26, doc. 798–PS.
[4] *D. Ger. F.P.*, i. 29–39. The report of this meeting is generally known as the Hossbach Memorandum.   [5] Ibid. p. 33.

of the British Empire had been weakened in the Far East by Japan, in the Mediterranean by Italy, who 'under the spell of her history, driven by necessity and led by a genius' was challenging Britain's hitherto dominant influence, and even if her imperial position remained 'theoretically sound' it was not 'unshakeable'.

In the light of this analysis, Hitler concluded that in practice the British Empire, this 'hate-inspired' antagonist, presented no insuperable obstacle to Germany's career of planned aggression in Central and Eastern Europe provided that the war came at the right time for Germany. That time could not be later than 1945, when Germany's relative strength would begin to decrease in relation to the rearmament which would by then have been carried out by the rest of the world and when failure to act would mark the 'waning point of the régime'. 'It was while the rest of the world was still preparing its defences that we were obliged to take the offensive. Nobody knew today what the situation would be in the years 1943–45. One thing only was certain, that we could not wait longer.'[1] In 1937, when these words were spoken, Hitler was contemplating the absorption of Austria and Czechoslovakia, but it was his presumption both then and later that if Germany acted with 'lightning speed' the Western democracies might not intervene at all or at least not effectively. Just because the risks of war for Britain were, in his opinion, 'unimaginably great', so he believed she would be correspondingly reluctant to fight. In this he was not altogether mistaken. But at root it was not fear of the destruction of an Empire but an aversion to war and the appalling sacrifices it had entailed between 1914 and 1918 that accounted for that reluctance. That was something Hitler played upon but did not understand, just as British opinion spoke about but did not comprehend the nature of the Nazi ambitions or the foundations of the Nazi state.

Both in his premiss and his conclusion Hitler was expounding commonplaces in Nazi thinking about the British Empire. 'Scarcely any other opinion is given currency by the National Socialists with such diligence as their belief in the doom of the British Empire; they regard its downfall as already an accomplished fact.' So Hermann Rauschning noted before the outbreak of war in 1939.[2] The dominions might think of a mother country wearied with age and worn down with responsibility; the Nazis, seemingly oblivious of the 'vitality' of the younger nations overseas, thought more simply of an exhausted Empire. The 'ageing Empire', explained the geo-politician Haushofer,[3] had grown 'tired', its inclination to pacifism was a special 'symptom of the flagging English will to empire'. 'Subsidence of the British main islands after the fashion of Venice' was the last and almost inevitable stage 'in a curve of dismemberment', for had not England lost 'the flair for rule' in the

---

[1] D. Ger. F.P. i., p. 34.
[2] Hermann Rauschning, *Germany's Revolution of Destruction* (London, Heinemann, 1939), p. 202.　　　　　　　　　　　　　　　[3] Quoted ibid. pp. 202–3.

old, the genuine sense? Did not the Balfour Report afford the most convincing evidence that this was so? 'While apparently at the height of power in territory controlled and in population', the Empire suffered in 1926 'a drastic change of form into a more and more loosely developing association of States'. This constituted, in the opinion of Haushofer, a 'most conspicuous surrender of power' and implied passive renunciation of world dominion. But to some at least in Nazi Germany this renunciation was not necessarily final, and this again accounted for the ambivalence in Nazi attitudes towards the British Empire. Many elements in England were believed to remain 'undemoralized by the democratic poison', the country itself had always been 'ready for metamorphosis at the right moment', and hope was not to be abandoned that it could be brought on terms into membership of the front of renovating powers.[1] National-Socialism might indeed recommend itself to a nation of rulers 'so old and experienced, but temporarily weary and slackening as the British especially by the effective political element of a new doctrine of rulership'. Nazi doctrines of race, the doctrine of the inequality of men and races 'sweeps away all the sentiment acquired under the burden of centuries by so reflective and sensitive a race of rulers, rather feminine in their sensibility, as the Anglo-Saxons'. Such doctrines expressed a clear will to rule 'in contrast with the doctrine of equality, with all its corollaries of self-determination, material dismemberment, and concern for all shades of material and religious thought, a doctrine that weakens every Empire'. If, therefore, the Anglo-Saxons 'still like to consider it their special mission to bear "the white man's burden" nothing is better calculated to facilitate their task than the new racial doctrine, the new rulership of the dynamic nations'. Indeed the greater part of the burden might be taken from 'her tired shoulders' by a partnership with the Third Reich. But the condition of any such partnership was the renunciation of liberalism. It was 'the liberalism of the English mind' that constituted 'the essential and almost insuperable obstacle to an alliance between England and Germany'. It might well prove ineradicable but fortunately it was in itself evidence of 'the extinction of the will to live, the surrender of the will to power'.

The reliance of Commonwealth statesmen and peoples upon improvisation, their inherited faith in ultimate individual responsibility, coupled with their distaste for abstract political thought, led them, for their part, to explain Nazi actions by contrast in seemingly superficial terms. Hitler was another Tamburlaine threatening the world in 'high astounding terms', and his principal associates were criminals who in bringing ruin and destruction upon the world had misled most of all their own people. Explicitly or by implication a distinction was thus commonly drawn between the 'tyrannical régime'[2]

---

[1] Ibid. p. 216. The argument that follows is based upon Rauschning's summary of Nazi thinking about the redistribution of world power. See especially pp. 201–19.
[2] Cf. Mr. Mackenzie King, Canada, H. of C. Deb., 1939, 2nd session, p. 19.

and the German people, pacific at heart, compelled to obey its behests. In turn, this encouraged the presumption, so very acceptable to those schooled in the liberal tradition which had shaped the Commonwealth, that the aggression of Nazi Germany—which in its military aspect was not underestimated—was politically a terrible but transient phenomenon. The conceptions on which it rested, its roots in the past and its challenge to the liberal tradition, were less widely understood though not altogether overlooked. In November 1939 Mr. Peter Fraser, the Deputy Prime Minister of New Zealand, showed an anxious awareness of their existence. Speaking as an observer from 12,000 miles away, who had watched the European situation deteriorate so that all feeling of humanity seemed to have been suppressed, all sense of fair dealing discarded and 'the word of the Nazi dictators, brittle as glass . . . given only to be broken', Mr. Fraser wondered what had happened—what had 'gone wrong with the great German nation'.[1] Few could have answered his questions better, had they cared to, than the German professors who expounded the political ideas of Hegel and von Treitschke.

The Hegelian dialectic, whose impact on modern German history has been so great, has been used to interpret the evolution of the British Empire. Some have seen in its recent development the thesis of nationalism confronted with the antithesis of imperialism, producing the synthesis of Commonwealth. But such analysis, conforming to a fixed pattern, invites questions more searching than those to which it suggests an answer. The essence of Hegel's interpretation of history was to be found in a conception alien to the main tradition of English thought, namely that the dynamic motive force in history provided by the constantly renewed interaction of thesis, antithesis, and synthesis is one of struggle, of tension and reconciliation followed by a renewal of the struggle at a higher level. It is because of this underlying idea of recurring tension that the existence of the Hegelian state was bound up with war and exalted it in a way not easily comprehended by those brought up in the individualistic, liberal traditions of the English-speaking world.

The state, Hegel maintained, was to be thought of 'as above and beyond what is made, as self-begotten and self-centred, as divine and perpetual',[2] from which it followed that it was a law unto itself and that its actions were not to be judged by the traditionally accepted standards of morality. Among his successors von Treitschke[3] was less absolute in relation to the moral law, for he allowed that the authority of the state should be subject to Christian teaching, but he identified its aim more closely with the pursuit of power. It is because 'the state is power' that 'it is normal and reasonable that a great

---

[1] Broadcast from London, 8 November 1939. Reprinted in Peter Fraser, *In Time of War* (Wellington, Govt. Printer, 1946), p. 8.

[2] Quoted in Rohan D'O. Butler, *The Roots of National Socialism, 1783–1933* (London, Faber, 1941), p. 76.

[3] H. W. C. Davis, *The Political Thought of Heinrich von Treitschke* (London, Constable, 1914), remains the standard critique in English.

nation should, by its physical force, embody and perfect this power in a well organized army'. By fighting for the state the individual was most completely engulfed in it, and that was as it should be. It was von Treitschke's view that 'the individual must forget the claims of his own ego, and feel himself a member of the whole'; he must recognize 'how trifling is his life compared with the welfare of the state. In that consists the grandeur of war, that trivial things are entirely lost sight of in the great idea of the state.' Von Treitschke recognized that 'it is not necessary for an army to be always fighting; the silent work of preparation is continued in time of peace'. But he maintained that 'over and over again it has been proved that it is only in war that a people becomes in very deed a people'. He wrote of 'the moral sublimity of war', which indeed was to be conceived as 'an institution ordained of God'.[1]

The abasement of the individual, which was the essential part of Hegel's political thought, deeply impregnated the German mind and provided the theoretical foundation for the exaltation of the state under the First and the Third Reich. This emergence of the all-powerful state, with its glorification of war and its identification of might with right, was not the work only of Bismarck, of the Kaiser, or of Adolf Hitler. The political outlook of generations had been conditioned by thinkers at least as much as by their rulers to believe in the final authority of the state as a positive good and to regard its actions as above the moral law. The freedom of action this gave to the rulers of such a state in diplomacy and in war is written large on the pages of history. Moreover, were not diplomacy and war the same thing? To that Clausewitz gave a confident answer. War is merely diplomacy by other means. All war in his view 'supposes human weaknesses', and it is these weaknesses which must be exploited. 'Often', he observed, 'wars are not much more than an armed neutrality, or a threatening position in support of negotiations, or a moderate attempt to put ourself in a slightly advantageous position and then to await events'.[2] But the moderation was in method, not in aim. 'The political instability of the world situation', declared Field-Marshal von Blomberg in a directive on the Wehrmacht to the Commanders-in-Chief in June 1937,[3] '. . . demands constant preparedness for war on the part of the German armed forces in order (a) to meet attacks at any time and (b) to be able to exploit militarily any favourable political opportunity that may offer itself.'

It is not suggested that the association of the state with the pursuit of power and with war was Germany's only contribution to political thought in the last hundred years, but it was the conception that lay behind the Nazi régime and that ultimately brought the German people into conflict with the greater part of the world. For the British Commonwealth the challenge was therefore a challenge to their liberal political tradition over and above a

[1] Quoted Butler, *Roots of National Socialism*, p. 148.
[2] Ibid. p. 97.
[3] RIIA, *Documents, 1939–46*, i. 8.

challenge to existence. Of the two principal protagonists of the early years of the war the one underlined the ultimate authority of the state, the other the final responsibility of the individual; the one that war is the natural state of nations, the other that peace is a supreme good. If to say so much is to generalize about and over-simplify a contrast in political outlook at a given moment in history, it is not to enter into the treacherous field of comparative national morality. Faith in peace and discussion were in some measure at least the product of easy circumstances and satiated appetite; reliance upon war the outcome of defeat and physical as well as psychological repression. 'I see the world as it actually is': said Mussolini in his first speech on foreign policy in the Italian Chamber of Deputies; 'that is, a world of unchained egoisms'.[1] This was a way in which Commonwealth statesmen[2] neither saw it nor for the most part had reason to see it.

Faced with a struggle against states conceived of as existing for war and organized for the winning of it, could the members of the British Commonwealth continue to rely upon methods of internal government and external co-operation well fitted, if not first fashioned, for spacious days of peace and material progress? The Australian Prime Minister, Mr. Menzies, in his first wartime speech to the House of Representatives, maintained that in internal government at least they could and should.

> I do not seek [he said] a muzzled Opposition. Our institutions of parliament, and of liberal thought, free speech, and free criticism, must go on. It would be a tragedy if we found that we had fought for freedom and fair play and the value of the individual human soul, and won the war only to lose the things we were fighting for.[3]

That commanded general assent in respect of domestic policy. But posed in its external setting the answer seemed less certain. Could the partner nations of the British Commonwealth hope to wage war successfully against such antagonists without some radical modification of their individualistic decentralized peacetime relationship, involving as it did separate control of foreign and defence policies? Was not, indeed, a more centralized Commonwealth, more consciously organized for the conduct of war, with wide powers vested in the hands of some single authority, the only way to overcome the disadvantages of geographical dispersal and divided counsel? Was there not perhaps, even apart from the immediate claims of war, some truth which the Commonwealth would do well to heed in Mussolini's assertion that all the political experiences of the contemporary world were anti-liberal, and in his forecast that the twentieth century would be that 'of authority, a century of the "Right" '?[4] Such were the questions which, though customarily phrased

---

[1] RIIA, *World in March 1939*, p. 521, n. 1.
[2] Among them General Smuts perhaps would have understood best what Mussolini meant, for he had thought most deeply on the often unpleasant problems of power in the modern world.   [3] 6 September 1939, Australia, H. of R. Deb., vol. 161, p. 36.
[4] Quoted in RIIA, *World in March 1939*, p. 521, n. 3.

INTERNAL RELATIONS AND EXTERNAL DANGERS 25

in a less theoretical form, underlay discussion on methods of Commonwealth co-operation from the outbreak of the Second World War to the meeting of Commonwealth Prime Ministers in the spring of 1944. They were questions commonly debated in the context not of political principle, but of Commonwealth history, and in particular of Commonwealth history in the years before the outbreak of war. Lord Halifax observed in his speech at Toronto on 24 January 1944 that 'the magnificent response of the Dominions in 1939 was not, thank God, too late to save the cause for which the Commonwealth and Empire stood and stands; but there is a real sense in which it was too late to save the peace.'[1] Those who felt at the outbreak of the war that, in part at least, this was so, concluded that only a Commonwealth institutionally more tightly knit could overcome the tardiness which had had such well-nigh fatal consequences.

The Reconstitution of an Imperial War Cabinet?

The history of the First World War seemingly furnished an appropriate precedent in an Imperial War Cabinet. Yet no such Cabinet was reconstituted on the outbreak of the Second World War. This was something Mr. Amery, who had first proposed the creation of such a body, much regretted. In so doing he expressed a view widely entertained by statesmen of an older generation. For them at least the Imperial War Cabinet of 1917–18 grew in reputation as the years went by. It came to be regarded as the symbol of the great days of imperial co-operation, and all that had happened since was interpreted by many of them as a falling away from the ideal it had come to symbolize. Nor indeed is it to be disputed that it was the waning of imperial sentiment after the First World War that was in a large measure responsible for the refusal of dominion governments to contemplate the continued existence of that Cabinet in peacetime. But it was not wholly responsible. The Imperial War Cabinet suffered from defects which told alike against its survival in time of peace and its revival in time of war. It was not a Cabinet in the strict sense of the term at all. Its members were not collectively responsible to any legislature but were individually responsible, as the Canadian Prime Minister, Sir Robert Borden, had been careful to emphasize, to their own individual parliaments and people. He spoke of it as 'a cabinet of governments', a convenient description which defied definition. Mr. Amery argued that 'in so far as it worked as a single body of colleagues all concerned with the same end and each contributing the best of his individual judgement, it deserved the title of Cabinet as fully as any Cabinet that I have ever attended'.[2] But even if constitutional realities be put on one side, the common sense of responsibility for a common cause which bound the members of the Imperial War Cabinet together could not, for any long period,

[1] Mansergh, *Documents*, i. 575–9.
[2] Amery, *Thoughts on the Constitution* (London, Oxford University Press, 1947), p. 120.

provide a sufficient substitute for collective responsibility to a single parliament. Moreover, there was a price to be paid in the absence of members of the Imperial War Cabinet from their own countries, from contact with their Cabinet colleagues and with their own parliaments and peoples. In 1917–18 that price had not been negligible. Over a long period any such divorce of political leaders from those to whom they were primarily responsible was something not to be contemplated without the most careful consideration of possible consequences. This was the more necessary in view of the extension of dominion responsibilities in the intervening twenty years. By September 1939 dominion governments were themselves individually responsible for foreign policy and defence. In their hands lay the conduct of day-to-day affairs and the making of great decisions of policy. They had their own defence departments, their own departments of external affairs, they were all represented in London by High Commissioners, some of them had representatives in foreign capitals.[1] None the less, despite these differences, some of them in some instances admittedly still of theoretical rather than of practical importance, the record and achievements of the Imperial War Cabinet deeply influenced thinking about methods of Commonwealth co-operation at the outbreak of the Second World War, and for that reason the critics of prevailing practice were to be found, not among those who felt that new circumstances demanded new devices, but among those who believed that it was possible to go back on history.

In all debate about methods of co-operation in wartime, something more was usually in mind than the effectiveness of machinery. Discussion might be focused on practical measures, but even with the coming of war it was rarely free from undercurrents of emotion, familiar to students of Commonwealth history. On the one hand imperialists felt that in wartime at least the need for central direction demanded some degree of centralized machinery which, once established, might well survive when the dangers that had called it into existence had passed. On the other hand, and for that very reason, the more nationalist dominions with their 'anti-Downing Street complex'[2] approached all such proposals with wariness lest indeed they might pave the way for some such revival of centralized institutions. This is a field in which the psychology of Commonwealth relations has its own special importance and for this, if for no other reason, the historian is well advised to beware of generalizations about Commonwealth co-operation in wartime. It is something that cannot be understood by a meticulous study of constitutional or conventional arrangements but only by the unravelling of a relationship as it worked and as it developed during the war years. The theory of the Commonwealth in this context especially needs to be closely related to its practice, and

[1] See Appendix D, below pp. 437–9.
[2] The phrase is used by Amery, *Thoughts on the Constitution*, p. 146. Mr. Mackenzie King was thought to suffer notably from it.

INTERNAL RELATIONS AND EXTERNAL DANGERS

if the account of Commonwealth co-operation during the war which is attempted in the following pages often seems haphazard and illogical, in that at least it is true to one of the most deeply cherished of Commonwealth traditions. What has to be considered after all is not the working out of some carefully devised machinery but the elaboration of old and the improvisation of new methods of co-operation in time of mortal danger.

CHAPTER II

COMMONWEALTH CO-OPERATION IN WAR: THE FIRST PHASE, 1939–41

> *This is the midnight—let no star*
> *Delude us—dawn is very far.*
> *This is the tempest long foretold—*
> *Slow to make head but sure to hold.*
> RUDYARD KIPLING

The Mobilization and Employment of Dominion Forces

THE difficulties that arose and the delays that took place in mobilizing the Commonwealth for war sprang at root not from any insufficiency of discussion or inadequate expression of opinion after the outbreak of war but from lack of preparation on the part of all Commonwealth governments before it began. No machinery of consultation, however excellent, could have restored the lost opportunities of the years that the locust had eaten. Remoteness from Europe, coupled with contemporary emphasis, in Britain as well as in the dominions, upon the importance of the economic weapon in modern war, encouraged dominion governments and peoples to regard their countries as sources of supply and reinforcement to the Western democracies, but not as constituting a first line of defence. It is true that in a report to the 1937 Imperial Conference the Chiefs of Staff had pointed out that the first phase of a war against Germany could be the most dangerous for Britain and therefore for the Empire as a whole, and that in this early phase help from the dominions could be of the highest value. 'However willing any Member of the British Commonwealth . . . may be to throw its weight into the war', the report continued, 'her contribution during this earlier phase will be dependent upon the preparatory measures . . . taken in time of peace'.[1] But in no instance was this opinion acted upon to the extent that any dominion was in a position to offer equipped and trained contingents to serve in the main theatre of operations on the outbreak of war. In 1939, notes the official Australian war history,

the now-adult nation possessed an army little different in essentials from that of the young Australia of 1914. It was fundamentally a defensive force intended if war broke out to go to its stations or man the coastal forts and await the arrival of an invader. History had proved and was to prove again the futility of such a military policy. The measures that had been taken in the few years of 'rearmament' were insignificant in the face of the threat offered by two aggressive Powers, one of which desired to master Europe, the other East Asia.[2]

---

[1] Long, *To Benghazi*, p. 21. [2] Ibid. p. 32.

The eastward direction of the first German onslaught encouraged the notion that, despite the spectacular success of German arms, the war might be one of limited liability for the dominions. On 8 September 1939 Mr. Mackenzie King quoted with approval a statement of Sir Henry Gullett, Australian Minister for External Affairs, to the effect that the Australian government had not seriously considered dispatching an expeditionary force overseas. He avowed his own belief that conscription for overseas service would not be necessary and repeated his pledge that no such measure would be introduced in Canada by his administration.[1] In Canberra Mr. Menzies was equally categoric, stating on 20 October 1939: 'It must be made clear that there is no obligation for service abroad, except in the case of a volunteer for such service.'[2] In Cape Town General Smuts, while pledging South African assistance, if need arose, to British colonies in Southern Africa, 'the northern outposts of the Union', restricted service outside the Union to volunteers, and it was not till March 1940 that a voluntary oath was taken by the great majority of the members of the Union Defence Force to serve 'anywhere in Africa'. The New Zealand documents contain evidence that New Zealand, also, lacked a sufficient sense of urgency. The government of the dominion which alone had doubted the wisdom of appeasement, which had most clearly foreseen its probable outcome, and whose policy was for ever epitomized in Mr. Savage's ringing declaration 'where she [Britain] goes, we go, where she stands, we stand',[3] had no detailed plans worked out with the United Kingdom government about the use of its troops outside New Zealand and its area of local security on the outbreak of war. In part this was due to the fact that the aggressor, as always, enjoyed the initiative and could choose where and when he would strike, but even more was it to be attributed to the reluctance, more pronounced in other dominions, to contemplate realistically the demands that total war would make.

The disposition of dominion forces and the mobilization of dominion resources were planned in collaboration with the government of the United Kingdom. Thus the Canadian government, in announcing its early war programme on 19 September 1939, specifically stated that it was the outcome of close consultation with the government of the United Kingdom so as to ensure 'the maximum effective' Canadian contribution to the successful prosecution of the war. It had been agreed by the two governments, so the statement continued, that Canada could be of most assistance at that time by facilitating the purchase by the United Kingdom of essential supplies in the dominion, by stepping up her production of war material and munitions of all kinds, and by providing naval craft, naval and air personnel, and technically trained men for the forces. Canada was also to recruit one army division to

---

[1] Canada, H. of C. Deb., 1939, 2nd session, pp. 35–36 (Mansergh, *Documents*, i. 472).
[2] *Sydney Morning Herald*, 21 October 1939.
[3] Broadcast 5 September 1939 (Mansergh, *Documents*, i. 489–91).

be available for overseas service, if and when required, with a second division to be recruited 'as a further measure of preparedness'.[1] There was to be a sufficient force for home defence, though in Canada home defence was not an overriding preoccupation in the making of war plans as it was in the Pacific dominions.

On 4 September 1939 the New Zealand government invited the United Kingdom government to suggest ways in which its forces might usefully be employed in the war effort. The New Zealand government would, so the Governor-General assured the Secretary of State for Dominion Affairs,[2] 'give the fullest consideration to any suggestion of the British Government as to the method, or methods, by which this Dominion can best assist in the common cause'. On 8 September 1939 the Secretary of State for Dominion Affairs, in a telegram[3] to the United Kingdom High Commissioner in Wellington, indicated in the light of alternative hypotheses how and where the New Zealand army might best be used. The hypotheses were (a) that Japan was neutral and adopted a friendly attitude towards the democracies, and (b) that Japan was neutral but adopted an attitude of reserve towards them. Should the first hypothesis prove justified, the United Kingdom government hoped that New Zealand would be able to 'exert her full national effort, including the preparation of her forces with a view to the despatch of an expeditionary force', but should the second prove correct, then the United Kingdom government felt it would be unwise for New Zealand to dispatch an expeditionary force overseas, and that she could best assist the common cause by holding formations ready at short notice for the reinforcement of Singapore and Fiji or of British and French islands in the south-west Pacific. There was warning that there must be preparation for a long war.

In a parallel telegram to Australia drafted on the same assumptions the hope was likewise expressed that Australia would 'exert her full national effort including preparation of her forces with a view to the dispatch of an expeditionary force', but it was not yet felt to be possible to make any suggestion about the destination and composition of any such force which Australia might provide. It was, however, thought that the Commonwealth government, while awaiting some further disclosure of Japanese intentions, might consider whether it would prefer, in the event of there being sufficiently reassuring information about them, to relieve United Kingdom units and formations in, say, Singapore, Burma, or India as brigades became available, or to delay the dispatch of any troops until complete divisions could be sent to a main theatre. As in the case of New Zealand, the dispatch of any large-scale expeditionary force was thought to be largely conditional upon evidence

---

[1] Statement issued by Defence Department, September 1939, reprinted in *Canada in World Affairs, 1939–41*, pp. 286–9.
[2] *N.Z. Documents*, vol. 1, no. 9, p. 6. For reply see no. 10, p. 7.
[3] Ibid. no. 24, pp. 17–19.

of a friendly attitude on the part of Japan, and if that were not forthcoming, then it was suggested that Australia could best assist by holding formations ready at short notice for the reinforcement of Singapore, New Zealand, or the British and French islands in the Pacific.[1]

The New Zealand government in its reply, dated 13 September 1939,[2] said that were the first hypothesis made in the United Kingdom telegram of 8 September to prove correct, a fully trained division, given adequate equipment, could leave for France or any more appropriate theatre within eight months, while troops sufficiently trained for garrison duty could be ready within a period of two to four months according to the number required. The appointment of a Commander for what was to be the 2nd New Zealand Expeditionary Force was perhaps inevitably a matter of time and opportunity, but it was not till 15 November 1939, 'after full consideration of his record and brilliant service',[3] that the appointment was given to General Freyberg, who had offered his services and stated his desire to serve once again with his compatriots on 16 September 1939.[4]

The Australian government and Chiefs of Staff were less disposed than their colleagues in New Zealand to make tentative plans on the assumption that the attitude of Japan would not be hostile. On 25 October 1939 the Australian War Cabinet decided to inform the Dominions Office that the period needed to train the Second Australian Imperial Force up to the stage at which it might be possible to send units abroad for garrison duty and further training would 'afford a further opportunity for the international position to clarify itself as to the possibility of the dispatch of an expeditionary force from Australia'.[5] But the period it had in mind was shortened by the public announcement, made without the foreknowledge of the Australian government, that the First New Zealand Echelon was proceeding overseas. The story of how this happened is a curious one.

An incident which occurred at the time of the Munich crisis had impressed the New Zealand Prime Minister, Mr. Savage, with the inadequacy of the liaison between the New Zealand and Australian governments. It appears that at that time an Australian paper on the *Defence of Australian Ports* was submitted to the Committee of Imperial Defence and, after some discussion of its contents in London, was sent to New Zealand as a United Kingdom paper, while at the same time a parallel New Zealand paper on the *Defence of New Zealand Ports* was following the same process in reverse.[6] To avoid the recurrence of such incidents Mr. Savage suggested the direct exchange of information between the two governments. The Australian Prime Minister, Mr. Lyons, responded sympathetically, agreeing in principle that the exchange of information between dominions in the same geographical region

---

[1] Long, *To Benghazi*, pp. 35–36.
[2] *N.Z. Documents*, vol. 1, no. 25, pp. 20–22.
[3] Ibid. no. 33, p. 27.
[4] Ibid. no. 27, p. 23; see generally Wood, ch. viii.
[5] Long, *To Benghazi*, p. 43.
[6] *N.Z. Documents*, vol. 1, app. iii, pp. 338–9.

could not but be beneficial, though adding some cautionary remarks about the inadvisability of laying down hard and fast rules about the classes of documents that should be exchanged.[1] In accordance with this arrangement and because of common interests and anxieties, and more immediately because of a domestic political situation in which his own course would be easier if Australia and New Zealand acted together, Mr. Lyons's successor, Mr. Menzies, on 21 November 1939 placed some of his problems about the dispatch of Australian forces overseas before his New Zealand colleagues. Australia, like New Zealand, had at the time a division enlisted for service at home or abroad and, despite a reassuring survey of the situation in the Far East which he had just received from the Foreign Office, Mr. Menzies felt that there was still real uncertainty about the attitude of Japan, especially should Germany overrun Holland and the East Indies be cut off from the mother country. Moreover, while Australian public opinion would warmly support the sending of troops to Europe if land warfare there assumed a critical character, their dispatch did not yet seem to be very urgent. 'With only five British divisions in France and as yet no casualties' the situation did not suggest that dominion reinforcements were greatly needed, and, while not wishing to get out of step with New Zealand, the Australian government would have preferred to watch events for some weeks longer before taking a decision.[2] On the day before Mr. Menzies's telegram was received the New Zealand government had, however, decided, on the advice of the United Kingdom and on the assumption that the matter was 'one of common arrangement with our Ministers in London',[3] to announce its decision to send the First Echelon of its Special Force overseas. Mr. Menzies, pained at this precipitate action, alluded austerely to the principles of co-operation which the New Zealand government had itself proposed in September 1938 and had now neglected to put into practice.[4]

The New Zealand announcement, as Mr. Menzies had surmised, precipitated sharper controversy in Australia between that section of the public which was still psychologically unprepared for all-out participation in war and the growing and already perhaps larger section which was increasingly impatient of half measures. On 28 November the Australian Cabinet, feeling that further procrastination was now undesirable, decided that the 6th Division should go overseas when it had reached a suitable stage in its training early in 1940.[5]

This incident, which might serve as a further illustration of dominion unpreparedness psychologically as well as militarily for war, reflects more surely the doubts and perplexities of Commonwealth governments and peoples

---

[1] *N.Z. Documents*, vol. 1, app. iii, pp. 339–40.
[2] Ibid. no. 52, pp. 42–43. See also Long, *To Benghazi*, pp. 64–65.
[3] *N.Z. Documents*, vol. 1, no. 54, pp. 44–45. Mr. Fraser and Mr. Casey were attending a Commonwealth conference (see below, p. 38). [4] Ibid. no. 56, pp. 46–47.
[5] Long, *To Benghazi*, p. 65. The first convoy sailed for the Middle East in January 1940.

at this time about how the war was likely to develop. As Mr. Hasluck remarks in a volume of the Australian war history, 'It may be true to say that wars can only be won by fighting but during this "twilight war", as Churchill has called it, Australia could not see where to fight'.[1]

In the Union of South Africa there were, added to such external uncertainties, internal divisions. Parliament had decided that the Union should go to war side by side with Britain and with her sister dominions, but the majority in Parliament was small and at least one informed and experienced observer doubted whether an election held after the Nazi victories in Poland would have returned General Smuts to power.[2] Certainly the two sections of Afrikaner Nationalists, the followers of General Hertzog and those of Dr. Malan, unable to agree in principle about the nature of a South African republic or the way in which it was to come into existence, were firmly united in a desire, not for the successful prosecution of the war with Nazi Germany, but for peace. In January 1940 General Hertzog, for a brief moment and as a result of a verbal compromise on the republican issue, leader of a reunited Nationalist party,[3] moved in the House of Assembly that 'the time has arrived that the war with Germany should be ended and that peace be restored'. The debate that followed underlined some of the problems that preoccupied the government of the Union in determining the character of South Africa's contribution to the war effort of the British Commonwealth.

General Hertzog submitted his motion, the ambiguous phrasing of which left it open to question whether he was advocating a general or a separate peace, because he remained altogether unconvinced that there had been any sufficient reason for the South African declaration of war in September 1939. If, he argued, one looked for the true origin of the war, disregarding the 'discoloured splashes along the wagon's trail', was it not clear that it was to be found in the German desire for the restoration of the authority and the territorial unity of their country 'so scandalously dislocated and broken up by the Treaty of Versailles?' Such 'oppression and humiliation' could not be carried on without necessitating a reply on the part of Germany itself. And did not responsibility for the continuation of the war also rest with the Allies who refused to discuss peace terms with Hitler? The only explanation of their uncompromising attitude, so it seemed to General Hertzog, was that they were out to destroy Germany or at least to compel the enemy to acquiesce in otherwise wholly unacceptable conditions 'with the knee on his chest and the sword at his throat, as had happened at Versailles'. If so, that made continuation of the war 'a crime by which international murder and robbery are

---

[1] Hasluck, i. 157.
[2] For an account of South Africa's entry into the war see Mansergh, *Survey, 1931–9*, pp. 381–400, and the contemporary opinion on the possible outcome of a later election see *Round Table*, December 1939, p. 211.
[3] See Roberts & Trollip, pp. 20–37, for a detailed account of the negotiations between the Hertzogite and the Gesuiwerde (Purified) Nationalists about Hereniging (Reunion).

elevated and legalized to a national virtue'. South Africa should at once dissociate herself from participation in action which was not in her interests but in those of the British Empire.[1]

General Hertzog's conviction that the Treaty of Versailles was the source of almost all contemporary evil was indeed familiar,[2] but the conclusions to which it led him in January 1940 accorded so ill with the known facts of the European situation at that time as to weaken his own case. His overstatements in particular caused embarrassment to some of his supporters, and Dr. Malan was careful to explain that support for the motion did not necessarily imply pro-Nazi sympathies.[3] The Prime Minister, in answer to what he described as 'the most amazing speech which has ever yet been delivered in this Parliament',[4] had little difficulty in disposing of General Hertzog's principal argument, for the Nazis themselves had rendered it otiose by their seizure in March 1939 of Czechoslovakia, a country that was German neither in population nor by history. It is, indeed, sad to recall that so honourable and distinguished an Afrikaner patriot in his old age should have lent his voice to so tainted a cause.[5]

General Hertzog's motion commended itself to Afrikaner Nationalists. They were for the most part indifferent to the rights or wrongs of European nations. They believed that the war was the Empire's war. It was not South Africa's war and it was not a war fought in the interests of South Africa. General Smuts had done wrong, complained Dr. van der Merwe, not to distinguish the position of South Africa from that of Australia and New Zealand with their overwhelmingly British populations. It was their war in a sense in which it was not South Africa's. But with the Prime Minister 'it is a matter of Empire first, and it is also a matter of being the first in the Empire'; and for that he had committed 'a crime against the people'.[6] Mr. Louw compared the position of South Africa with that of Ireland, 'which also was a British dominion; but which has broken the fetters', and he believed that it was because of South Africa's continuing dominion status alone that she, too, had been unable to stay out of the war.[7] The imperialist press within South Africa and without desired to turn 'every Afrikaner into a lackey of the Empire with the soul of a national scout', alleged Mr. Pirow, and he charged

---

[1] 23 January 1940, South Africa, H. of A. Deb., vol. 37, coll. 38–44.

[2] See Mansergh, *Survey, 1931–9*, pp. 418–21. On this occasion he alluded also to 'the scandalous torture' Germany had to endure as a consequence of Versailles.

[3] 24 January 1940, South Africa, H. of A. Deb., vol. 37, col. 93. For his speech see coll. 91–102.   [4] 23 January 1940, ibid. col. 45.

[5] It is possible that a German agent, Herr Denk, was right in supposing that Hertzog was 'favourably influenced' towards Germany as a result of communications which may have been passed on verbally to him shortly before he introduced his motion in the House of Assembly; but there is no conclusive evidence that this was so (*D. Ger. F.P.*, viii. 711). It may equally be that his expression of extreme views on international issues was deliberately calculated as a means of strengthening his position as leader of the reunited Nationalist party at home.

[6] South Africa, H. of A. Deb., vol. 37, col. 379.   [7] Ibid. col. 79.

the Prime Minister with abetting it.[1] 'There today sits C. J. Rhodes redivivus', exclaimed Dr. Malan[2] pointing to General Smuts, who, like Rhodes, had used his great opportunity not to unite but to divide the people of South Africa. Since the declaration of war, added Dr. Malan, he himself despaired of peace between the two sections of the European population.

While the condemnation of the government's war policy was thus uninhibited, it was not altogether unreserved. There was South-West Africa which seemingly no one wished to see restored to Germany, there was the protection afforded by the Royal Navy with its base at Simonstown which was more often than not tacitly accepted, and, more important still, there was the defence of 'white civilization' in Africa. If that were in danger then, as Mr. Pirow allowed,[3] help would be forthcoming from Nationalists in large numbers. But where were the frontiers of white, or European, civilization? In the opinion of Mr. Pirow the European colonists to the north of the Union were within them, North Africa without so far as the Union was concerned. Some weeks after the defeat of General Hertzog's peace motion by 81 votes to 54, General Smuts, in introducing a War Measures Bill, made much of the defence of white civilization as the criterion by which the defence limits of the Union, deliberately left undefined in the Defence Act of 1912,[4] should be determined. Thus he spoke of Tanganyika and Kenya, the strategic 'outposts of the Union', as being 'to a large extent the frontiers of our European civilization', and he argued that South Africa, 'the leading European community in this sub-continent'—and here he was quoting a phrase used by Mr. Pirow as Minister of Defence in 1936—of necessity had imposed upon it wide responsibilities in time of war.[5] It is true that General Smuts favoured a liberal while the Nationalists preferred a restricted interpretation of such responsibilities. Yet the difference between them was not great. General Smuts quoted from a memorandum drafted by Mr. Pirow in 1933 in which the possibility of co-ordinating the defence of the Union with that of Kenya, Tanganyika, Uganda, and Nyasaland was contemplated to show that his own interpretation of the defence of South Africa, announced to the House of Assembly on 11 April 1940, was at the least not inconsistent with these earlier ideas.[6] Moreover, partly as a gesture of conciliation, he gave emphatic assurances that no member of the Defence Forces would be compelled to give any service in areas not included in a limited interpretation of the Defence

---

[1] Ibid. col. 63.   [2] Ibid. col. 98.   [3] Ibid. col. 61.

[4] South African citizens were 'liable to render in time of war personal service in defence of the Union in any part of Africa whether within or outside the Union' (South Africa Defence Act, 1912, c. i, s. 1).

[5] 7 February 1940, South Africa, H. of A. Deb., vol. 37, coll. 981–2. An interesting sidelight on this preoccupation with white civilization was the pained observation of one Nationalist that he expected 'white righteousness even from his enemies' but he failed to find it in General Smuts (26–27 January, ibid. col. 382).

[6] Ibid. vol. 38, coll. 4786 ff.

Act, and that forces which, in case of need, would go northwards would be composed entirely of volunteers. No troops would serve outside Africa.

At the outbreak of the war the ability of the Union to defend her own frontiers was limited by grave deficiencies in her preparations for war. Both numbers and equipment fell far short of what had been planned and voted by the House of Assembly. For whatever reason, Mr. Pirow's five-year plan announced in 1937 for the reorganization of the Union's defences had been left largely unfulfilled. General Smuts charged in the House of Assembly on 14 March 1940[1] 'that all his grandiose, all his great plans, have remained in the air, and that after the six years that he has been Minister of Defence they have still remained plans, and they have not got beyond that'. He then proceeded to quote figures; the 56,000 trained men provided for in the plan were 37,000 short, the artillery had not enough ammunition for a single day's fighting, and of the money voted by Parliament for defence reorganization only £186,000 out of £1 million had been spent in 1938–9; of the £3 million voted for 1939–40 only £100,000 had been drawn up to August 1939. Not all the blame rested with Mr. Pirow, for arms were not easily acquired on the eve of the war. But whatever might be his share of the responsibility—and it was on any reckoning no small one—the fact remained that of all members of the Commonwealth the Union was the least prepared for battle. It was General Smuts's greatest task and his supreme responsibility to remedy this grave deficiency in the short time that remained before the war came to Africa. In so doing he could not afford, even had he wished, to antagonize still further Nationalist sentiment; on the contrary an effective war effort was dependent upon a growing measure of Afrikaner support, avowed or tacit, for South Africa's participation in the war. One consequence was that, while there was close collaboration and consultation with the government of the United Kingdom, it was not unduly publicized.

The Material Foundations of Co-operation

The assertion that the members of the British Commonwealth were unprepared for war needs to be counterbalanced by the statement that the members of the British Commonwealth were well prepared for co-operation in war. This is something the importance of which tends to be undervalued. Yet the British Commonwealth could hardly have survived the year when it stood alone had not the foundations of wartime co-operation been well and securely laid long before the outbreak of war. For some thirty years the Chiefs of Staff in the United Kingdom and in the dominions, in accordance with principles outlined by the Committee of Imperial Defence,[2] had aimed

---

[1] H. of A. Deb., vol. 38, col. 3435; see also *Round Table*, June 1940, pp. 712–16.

[2] The minutes of the Committee of Imperial Defence are not open to inspection by students. Though command was not a function of the Committee, as Lord Haldane had emphasized, its advice on particular and on general problems of Imperial defence necessarily carried weight with dominion governments.

at the fullest co-ordination in the training of their forces and in the use by all of them of standardized weapons and equipment. This was something which enabled the great Imperial army which fought in North Africa from 1940 to 1943 and which comprised Australian, New Zealand, South African, and Indian, as well as United Kingdom, divisions to operate as a single, effective, fighting unit. Nor was the long standing policy of co-ordination and standardization any less important in respect of war supplies. The United Kingdom, despite the development of some war industry in Canada and Australia,[1] was the arsenal of the Empire in the early and most critical period of the war. In the first fifteen months the United Kingdom provided 90·7 per cent. (in terms of value) of the supplies of munitions from all sources to British Commonwealth countries and for the entire period of the war the proportion contributed by the United Kingdom remained as high as 69·5 per cent.[2] Moreover the United Kingdom, by placing orders overseas and especially in Canada, gave a much needed stimulus to munitions production both before and after the outbreak of war. The aim from the beginning, writes Mr. Duncan Hall,[1] was the development of dominion war potential by creating new munitions capacity. Despite early disappointments this policy achieved outstanding success.

The presumption of wartime co-operation was likewise implicit in the proposals under consideration at the outbreak of war for an Empire Air Training Scheme. They originated with the United Kingdom government and had as their principal purpose air training in Canada on a Commonwealth basis. Late in 1939 a Conference at Ottawa at which the governments of the United Kingdom, Canada, Australia, and New Zealand were represented, and over which the Canadian Prime Minister presided, approved the proposal in principle and as a result the Empire Air Training Scheme came into existence. In conception and in execution this scheme constituted one of the most telling of Commonwealth contributions to ultimate victory.

In sum, therefore, there was within the Commonwealth not only a will to co-operate but also the necessary provision for effective co-operation. It had been assumed throughout the inter-war years that the members of the Commonwealth would once again be fighting side by side in the event of a Second World War and it had been tacitly accepted that all preparations for war should proceed on this assumption. What this meant in practice when war came is recorded in the military and civil histories of the United Kingdom and the dominions. The political relations between Commonwealth governments,

---

[1] The development of munitions industries in Canada and Australia from 1936 onwards is described in H. Duncan Hall and C. C. Wrigley, *Studies of Overseas Supply* (London HMSO and Longmans, 1956) (*History of the Second World War*, United Kingdom Civil Series), pp. 46–65 and 425–42.

[2] See H. Duncan Hall, *North American Supply* (London, HMSO and Longmans, 1955) (*History of the Second World War*, United Kingdom Civil Series), p. 3.

[3] Ibid. p. 23.

which are our principal concern, were conducted in the belief that the foundations for their common war effort were securely laid.

The First Wartime Ministerial Conference

On the outbreak of war suggestions were made in London for the constitution in some form of an Imperial War Council. They received a tepid response from the United Kingdom government. Thus the Prime Minister, Mr. Chamberlain, asked in the House of Commons on 21 September 1939 to consider such a possibility, replied that there was already close contact with the dominion governments and that the constitution of an Empire Council with a representative in the War Cabinet was not immediately practicable.[1] The United Kingdom government did, however, invite dominion governments to send ministers to confer with British ministers in London. This invitation, as Mr. Eden, then Secretary of State for Dominion Affairs, explained on 4 October, was intended to 'supplement the existing arrangements for collaboration between the Governments of the British Commonwealth . . . [and] to co-ordinate to the best advantage the contribution which each of us can make to our common task.'[2] Mr. Mackenzie King, in Ottawa, firmly repudiated the suggestion that this was to be an Empire War Cabinet or Conference.[3] It was to be a conference of ministers concerned not with war policy but with practical co-operation in many fields, and it constituted, therefore, an elaboration of existing methods and not in any sense a supersession of them or a departure from them. Constitutionally indeed this was the important feature of this first wartime ministerial conference.

The ministerial conference to which Mr. Chamberlain, Mr. Eden, and Mr. Mackenzie King referred took place in London in October and November 1939. Its membership underlined the functional nature of its responsibilities. Mr. Crerar, Minister of Mines and Natural Resources, represented Canada, Mr. R. G. Casey, Minister for Supply and Development, Australia, Mr. Peter Fraser, Deputy Prime Minister, New Zealand, Colonel Deneys Reitz, Minister of Native Affairs, South Africa, and in answer to an Indian request Sir Muhammad Zafrullah Khan, a member of the Governor-General's Executive Council, was nominated to watch over Indian interests. The conference concerned itself principally with problems of finance, of production and supply, of transport and the general co-ordination of the war efforts of the countries represented at it. In the House of Commons on 16 November 1939 the Chancellor of the Exchequer, Sir John Simon, reported favourably on the usefulness of the meeting and told the House of Commons that the discussions had shown once again the great value of direct and personal contact.[4]

---

[1] 21 September 1939, H. of C. Deb., vol. 351, col. 1061. It was in this rather curious form that dominion representation in the War Cabinet was suggested by Mr. Ellis Smith, Labour Member for Stoke-on-Trent.   [2] Ibid. col. 1962
[3] *Canada in World Affairs, 1939–41*, p. 19.   [4] H. of C. Deb., vol. 353, col. 874.

During their visit to London dominion ministers engaged in discussions on questions of some magnitude, including the possible attitudes of Japan and the United States towards the war and a possible declaration of war aims,[1] outside the immediate scope of the conference itself, and their conclusions or impressions influenced the making of dominion policies. Thus the New Zealand government, on learning from Mr. Peter Fraser that it was the general opinion in London that the situation in the Far East was sufficiently clear to justify sending the First New Zealand Echelon[2] overseas, agreed to its dispatch to Egypt.[3] The further opportunity taken by dominion ministers to visit France, to confer there with the French Prime Minister, M. Daladier, and with General Gamelin, and to meet the British and French General Staffs, enabled them to make their own individual assessments of the war situation which in due course were communicated to their cabinet colleagues. Mr. Crerar on his return to Canada spoke of the grim determination and harmony of effort which he had found on the Western Front.[4] But Mr. Casey and Colonel Reitz were much disturbed and insisted on seeing Mr. Chamberlain. Colonel Reitz, after inspecting the British positions, and mindful of his experience in the same area in the First World War, warned the Prime Minister, 'Sir, if you will pardon my saying so, the Germans will go through there like a knife through cheese.'[5] Mr. Casey endorsed his opinion and told Mr. Chamberlain bluntly that with the defensive positions as they were he was bound to advise the Australian Cabinet against allowing any Australian troops to be placed in so hopeless a situation.[6] Mr. Chamberlain took refuge in the opinion of his military advisers and left Colonel Reitz with an impression of being 'somewhat vague and aloof'. But action followed. Mr. Casey, who complained orally to his colleagues in Canberra of the 'self-satisfaction' of the Secretary of State for War, stated in a memorandum for their information that, as a result of the interview with the Prime Minister, General Ironside went to France to investigate, and while there was 'considerable bother', work on the defences was speeded up.[7] More generally it is clear that Mr. Casey's impressions and general appreciation of the war situation were of first importance to his Cabinet colleagues in Canberra.

From the outset of the war the Prime Ministers of Canada, Australia, New

[1] On this see especially Wood, ch. ix. Mr. Fraser pressed strongly for a more explicit definition of war aims.

[2] This term, instead of contingent, which for a time replaced it in the Middle East, was first officially used by New Zealand Army Headquarters on 29 August 1939 (*N.Z. Documents*, i. 21).

[3] Ibid. nos. 46 and 47, pp. 38–39. The agreed conclusions of discussions between officials at the War Office on 2 November 1939, reprinted as Appendix 1, p. 333, are also relevant both to the dispatch of the First New Zealand Echelon and for the light they throw on the matters brought forward for discussion by visiting Commonwealth ministers. See also above, p. 32.

[4] *Canada in World Affairs, 1939–41*, p. 19. It is to be noted that this was an opinion expressed in public.

[5] Deneys Reitz, *No Outspan* (London, Faber, 1943), pp. 255–6.

[6] Hasluck, i. 170–2. [7] Ibid. p. 171.

Zealand, and South Africa were sent a daily telegram from London recording the progress of operations for their most secret and personal information, and after the German invasion of the Low Countries in May 1940 these telegrams were sent twice daily. They were also sent copies of the Chiefs of Staff *Weekly Résumé* but only by ocean mail for security reasons.[1] The Secretary of State for Dominion Affairs met the dominion High Commissioners daily for a general discussion of the war situation and of problems of mutual interest. If such elaboration of existing methods did not altogether satisfy dominion desire for information about the actual and probable course of military developments, there was at least no suggestion in the early months of the war that dominion governments lacked adequate opportunity for the expression of their views, whether by written or telegraphic communication or personally at the official or ministerial level. On 21 March 1940 Mr. Chamberlain spoke with confidence of the complete effectiveness of the organization of Commonwealth consultation. 'The closest contact', he said, 'is maintained both directly between Governments, through High Commissioners in London and in the Dominion capitals, and through an immense variety of technical and subordinate liaison arrangements covering every field of our relations.'[2] This opinion was endorsed by the Australian Minister for External Affairs, Mr. McEwen, in the House of Representatives on 19 April 1940. He stated[3] that the Australian government was making full use of the system of consultation which had grown up in the preceding years and assured the House that the views of the Australian government were not only sought by the United Kingdom government but also 'acted upon'. In a very real sense the voice which the dominions had in the common policy of the British Commonwealth since the outbreak of the war, he continued, was one that accorded fully with their status and with their individual responsibilities. The communications which passed between the United Kingdom and the New Zealand governments, and which have since been published by the New Zealand government in two volumes,[4] substantially confirm this view. Neither Mr. Mackenzie King nor General Smuts favoured the meeting of an Imperial Conference, as was proposed by the United Kingdom government in April 1940, partly because of their own stated inability to attend but still more because of their satisfaction with existing methods of co-operation. If the governments of Australia and New Zealand acquiesced in, but did not welcome, this negative conclusion[5] they, too, were at the least satisfied in the early phases of the war that they were in a position to make their views known in London and

---

[1] Butler, *Grand Strategy*, ii. 262–3.
[2] H. of C. Deb., vol. 358, col. 2147.
[3] Australia, H. of R. Deb., vol. 163, p. 203.
[4] Their issue marked a departure from a convention which had hitherto precluded the publication, save on specific issues, of communications between His Majesty's governments until the normal period of fifty years had elapsed.
[5] Cf. Butler, *Grand Strategy*, ii. 558.

that there such views were assured of careful and usually of prompt consideration. It was only later that the Australian government concluded that while comment might lead to modification of policy it was not tantamount to a voice in the formulation of policy.

Co-operation in Crisis: Information and Consultation on War Policy, May–September 1940

In the period 1939–41, that is to say until the entry of the United States into the war, the outward flow of information and opinion from London was of decisive importance in the determination of dominion war policies. So far as it is possible to judge from the evidence so far published, dominion governments were not seriously misled by the advice they received from London at the most critical times on the probable course of events in Europe. On the contrary, they would seem to have been well served. The cool and careful appreciation of the military situation prepared by the Chiefs of Staff and sent out on 4 May 1940[1] was a model of its kind. Its assessment of Italian strength, of Spanish intentions, of Balkan possibilities, and of Russian reluctance to embark on further adventures proved in the sequel realistic, as was the analysis of the balance of forces in Italy at 'a stage of dangerous equilibrium between peace and war' sent to dominion governments on 26 May 1940.[2] The United Kingdom government, however, tended to take a more sanguine but not unrealistic view of the situation in the Far East. In a dispatch dated 4 May 1940 the Foreign Office considered that while Japan's ultimate policy would be determined by the outcome of the war in the West, her early intervention was unlikely, not only because of her heavy commitments in China but also because she 'is fearful of American policy'. The Chiefs of Staff considered 'as very remote' the possibility of direct attack upon Australia or New Zealand.[3]

The German offensive of the spring and early summer of 1940 left the United Kingdom with little to transmit to dominion governments but a catalogue of military disaster and a courage that never wavered. In order to keep the dominion governments as fully informed as possible throughout those critical days without extending the risk to security, the Cabinet agreed on 5 June that the Dominions Office should, with the approval of the Service Departments in important cases, communicate to dominion Prime Ministers for their secret and personal information the substance of Cabinet papers of special interest relating to the military aspects of the war.[4] Mr. Churchill personally 'kept in the closest contact with my old friends now at the head of

---

[1] There had been a particular request for such an appreciation from the Australian government on 1 May (Hasluck, i. 217). It is reprinted in full in *N.Z. Documents*, vol. 1, no. 135, pp. 100–3, and it may be presumed that the substance of the telegram was sent to other dominion governments as well. There were several occasions on which the Australian Cabinet requested either fuller information or a strategic appreciation from London.

[2] *N.Z. Documents*, vol. 1, no. 12, pp. 9–10.

[3] Ibid. no. 135, p. 102.

[4] Butler, *Grand Strategy*, ii. 262–3.

the Governments of Canada and South Africa'. On 5 June he expressed doubts, in a telegram to Mr. Mackenzie King, about the possibility of keeping France in the war but solid confidence 'in British ability to continue the war, defend the Island and the Empire, and maintain the blockade'. He differed from General Smuts, who 'far off in South Africa and without the latest information upon the specialised problems of Insular Air Defence' viewed 'the tragedy of France according to orthodox principles' of concentration of force at the decisive point, and made his critical decision to retain in Britain the fighter squadrons essential for the defence of the island contrary to Smuts's advice. But none the less, urged Mr. Churchill, 'always give me your counsel, my old and valiant friend'.[1] With the full assent of the Canadian government the first Canadian division embarked for France in early June.[2] But the situation was past repair. On 16 June 1940, to lessen the shock of the impending French capitulation, Mr. Churchill composed a message to all the dominion Prime Ministers in the Cabinet Room at No. 10 Downing Street. In it he explained that Britain's resolve to continue the struggle alone was 'not based upon mere obstinacy or desperation' but upon an assessment of 'the real strength of our position', which he then proceeded to examine in some detail. He showed the draft to Air Marshal Newall, the Chief of Air Staff, in the garden of No. 10. He was 'evidently moved' and, records Mr. Churchill, 'when I read the message over the final time before sending it off I felt a glow of sober confidence. This was certainly justified by what happened. All came true.'[3]

At this time Britain's leadership was decisive for the Commonwealth and for the world. But the resolve of the United Kingdom government to fight on against any odds after the fall of France, and if need be alone, was proudly approved by the governments of the oversea dominions. On 18 June 1940 Mr. Churchill told the House of Commons that he had

fully informed and consulted all the self-governing Dominions, and I have received from their Prime Ministers, Mr. Mackenzie King, Mr. Menzies, Mr. Fraser and General Smuts, messages couched in the most moving terms in which they endorse our decision and declare themselves ready to share our fortunes and to persevere to the end.[4]

Throughout the anxious days that followed the dominion governments, to quote Mr. Fraser, were 'kept closely, indeed daily, in touch with the position by His Majesty's Government in the United Kingdom'.[5] In a telegram dated 27 June 1940[6] to General Smuts Mr. Churchill with a remarkable foresight wrote: 'If Hitler fails to beat us here he will probably recoil eastwards. Indeed, he may do this even without trying invasion.'

[1] Churchill, ii. 128–30.   [2] Ibid. p. 130.
[3] Ibid. pp. 172–4, where the message is printed in full.
[4] H. of C. Deb., vol. 362, col. 58.
[5] 20 June 1940, New Zealand, H. of R. Deb., vol. 257, p. 301.   [6] Churchill, ii. 200.

On 10 July 1940 Italy tempted, as Count Ciano later and apologetically explained, by the thought of easy spoil and of 'a chance which comes only once in five thousand years', declared war on Britain and France. The sense of outrage throughout the English-speaking world was voiced by President Roosevelt who on that same day declared that 'the hand that held the dagger has struck it into the back of its neighbor'.[1] Mr. Mackenzie King declared that the new peril would serve only to increase Canada's determination to fight to the end by the side of Britain and France, and with due regard to the doctrine that 'Parliament will decide', a resolution was submitted by the government to both Houses, also on 10 June, inviting their approval of 'the entry of Canada into a state of war with Italy'. It was unanimously adopted.[2] Australia, New Zealand, and South Africa declared war on Italy on 11 June, in each case by Royal Proclamation and without prior parliamentary consultation.[3] The Prime Minister of New Zealand stated that his government had sent a message to the United Kingdom government asking it that Italy be informed that New Zealand had that day declared war. He expressed New Zealand's strongest indignation at Italy's 'cynical and cold-blooded attack at a moment plainly chosen in the belief that it will afford the maximum embarrassment to the Allied arms' and renewed assurances of all possible assistance.[4] The South African Proclamation specifically stated that Parliament would not be consulted, in conformity with the statement of the Prime Minister in March 1940, that the emergency powers vested in the government gave it full authority to act. Later this view was to be sharply challenged by the Opposition. But in general perhaps no single event in the summer of 1940 served more to harden the resolve of the peoples of the Commonwealth to fight to the last than the circumstances of Italy's entry into the war. In the month that followed it 41,000 men enlisted in the Australian Imperial Forces, a number larger than any recorded for a single month in the First World War.

In these critical months action often preceded consultation or even information. In particular, dominion governments were not consulted about Mr. Churchill's offer of union to France in June 1940 (which for them might have had far-reaching implications), but the desperate situation in which the proposed declaration was drafted precluded discussion.[5] None of the dominions was consulted about the ultimatum delivered to the French naval forces in July 1940, even though for Canada at least the decision was one of moment.

[1] Langer & Gleason, i. 516. See Churchill, ii. 116 for the satisfaction with which the President's outspoken condemnation was greeted in Britain.

[2] Canada, H. of C. Deb., 1940, vol. 1, pp. 651–5.

[3] Cf. the procedure adopted in Australia in 1941 (Australia, H. of R. Deb., 1941, vol. 169, pp. 1088–9) where the Australian Parliament was asked to approve a declaration of war on Japan, Finland, Hungary, and Rumania already made by the Governor-General on the advice of the Australian Prime Minister.

[4] *The Times*, 12 June 1940; see also Mr. Fraser's speech, New Zealand, H. of R. Deb., 19 June 1940, pp. 204–7.

[5] Churchill, ii. 182–4.

After the bombardment at Oran there were indeed some misgivings in Ottawa lest Quebec should view unfavourably the action which the United Kingdom government had felt compelled to take in order to prevent the French naval forces from falling into German hands. These fears, however, were not realized. While French Canadians could not echo the confident prediction of General Smuts that on the day of liberation 'the entire French people will recognize in gratitude that the hand that smote them was the hand that saved them',[1] none the less for the most part they acknowledged, however sadly, that Britain had no alternative. *Le Canada*, the leading Liberal newspaper in Quebec, entitled a leading article 'La Grande Bretagne a fait ce qu'il fallait faire'.[2]

> I am sure [said Mr. Mackenzie King] that it is the prayer of the people of Canada who owe so much to the memory of France, that the French people will recognize that if the Bordeaux government acted under the compulsion of the conqueror, the British Navy acted equally under the compulsion of its great responsibility for the preservation of the liberties of the world.[3]

The painful episode at Oran was mercifully brief, the engagement at Dakar, a 'good example of bad luck' as Mr. Churchill later described it,[4] unhappily protracted. The decision to attempt to wrest Dakar from Vichy France was taken by the War Cabinet in London but the initiative was Mr. Churchill's. He himself records that he undertook in 'an exceptional degree' first the advocacy and then the initiation of the expedition in the firm conviction that despite the military and political hazards so obviously involved the gamble was worth-while. 'Dakar was a prize; rallying the French colonial empire a greater', and both warranted the taking of risks.[5] 'I kept General Smuts fully informed', Mr. Churchill records in his *History of the Second World War*, but by implication other dominions were merely warned of Britain's intentions in more general terms.[6] Canada, as well as South Africa, was deeply concerned with the outcome. Quite apart from the ties of kinship between Quebec and France, Canada had no wish to see German submarine and aircraft bases established in West Africa. But the interest of South Africa was certainly the more immediate. General Smuts had earlier impressed upon Mr. Churchill the importance of not neglecting Africa or allowing the French and Belgian colonies to fall into hostile hands, and he needed no reminder from him that

---

[1] *The Times*, 6 July 1940.
[2] 5 July 1940.
[3] 4 July 1940, Canada, H. of C. Deb., 1940, vol. 2, p. 1359. For a general account of Quebec's reactions to the fall of France see Mason Wade, *The French Canadians, 1760–1845* (London, Macmillan, 1955), pp. 832–40.
[4] Churchill, ii. 432.
[5] Ibid. p. 423.
[6] So much would seem to be implied in the opening sentence of Mr. Churchill's telegram to General Smuts dated 22 September 1940 and reprinted ibid. pp. 431–2. It reads: 'You will have seen my message about Dakar'.

Dakar under German control and used as a U-boat base would have consequences to the Cape route that 'would be deadly'.[1] But it would not seem that General Smuts was brought actively into the discussions about the dispatch of the expedition, for in his telegram of 22 September Mr. Churchill, after summarizing the arguments for it, commented 'anyhow, the die is cast'.

The enterprise proved a failure. 'To the world at large', Mr. Churchill recalled later, 'it seemed a glaring example of miscalculation, confusion, timidity, and muddle.'[2] Paradoxically enough the sharpest criticism within the Commonwealth came not from Canada or from South Africa but from Australia, whose immediate interests were somewhat remote, though the cruiser *Australia* had taken part in the operations. On 29 September 1940 Mr. Menzies expressed his concern to Mr. Churchill in terms of some asperity. 'We are very disturbed', he cabled,[3] 'in regard to Dakar incident, which has had unfortunate effect in Australia.' On the point of substance the Australian government could not understand why the attempt was made unless chances of success were overwhelming and on the point of procedure 'it is absolutely wrong that Australian Government should know practically nothing of details of engagement and nothing at all of decision to abandon it until after newspaper publication'. Mr. Menzies refrained from public criticism but privately he told Mr. Churchill that the 'absence of real official information from Great Britain has frequently proved humiliating'. On receiving Mr. Churchill's aggrieved rejoinder Mr. Menzies allowed that his telegram had been 'somewhat crudely expressed',[4] but he re-emphasized the point that 'we, at this distance, will learn the lessons of events the more rapidly if information about those events can come to us as promptly and as fully as possible'. Mr. Churchill agreed. The delay in the case of Dakar was evidently due in part to the lack of information from the commanders of the expedition early enough to forestall news published in Berlin and Vichy, but it seems doubtful in any case if Mr. Churchill fully realized the importance to an Australian government far removed from the scene of operations, with a precarious majority and confronted by a highly critical Opposition, of being able to comment on events with authority.

In a broader context the rapid dissemination of information about operations which were in progress was, however, not necessarily always wise. It was as important not to send too much as to send enough information. In December 1940 Mr. Churchill recommended to the Secretary of State for Dominion Affairs that, while specially full information should be given in respect of theatres where dominion troops were serving, this should not necessarily be circulated to other dominions whose forces were not engaged.

---

[1] Ibid. p. 431. On 11 July 1940 Admiral Raeder had drawn Hitler's attention to the importance of Dakar 'for warfare in the Atlantic' (*Brassey's Naval Annual, 1948*, p. 115. This volume reprints the *Führer Conferences on Naval Affairs, 1939–45*).

[2] Churchill, ii. 437.   [3] Ibid. app. D, p. 645.   [4] Ibid. p. 647.

There should be an effort 'not to scatter so much deadly and secret information over this very large circle. . . . There is a danger that the Dominions Office staff get into the habit of running a kind of newspaper full of deadly secrets, which are circularised to the four principal Governments with whom they deal.'[1] One important lesson to be drawn from the Dakar incident was that the dissemination of information to dominion governments demanded more judgement and discrimination than outside critics normally allowed.

Britain, Canada, and the United States: (a) Destroyers, Bases, and the Defence of the Western Hemisphere

'In these summer days of 1940 after the fall of France we were all alone. None of the British Dominions or India or the Colonies could send decisive aid, or send what they had in time.' So writes Mr. Churchill;[2] and it is not to be doubted that it was 'upon the resolution and the example of this small island' that 'our own British life and the long continuity of our institutions and our Empire'[3] at that time depended. And not of the Empire only but of 'the whole world, including the United States'. The United States government and people were, however, by no means so convinced that this was so. It was only gradually and under the compulsion of events that they were persuaded to accept the Churchillian view that there was an underlying community of interest in the defence of the Western hemisphere between a belligerent United Kingdom, a belligerent Canada, and a neutral or non-belligerent United States, and to act upon that assumption.

Mr. Churchill told President Roosevelt of the perils that confronted Britain within five days of his appointment as Prime Minister.

If necessary, [he wrote on 15 May 1940] we shall continue the war alone, and we are not afraid of that. But I trust you realise, Mr. President, that the voice and force of the United States may count for nothing if they are withheld too long. You may have a completely subjugated, Nazified Europe, established with astonishing swiftness, and the weight may be more than we can bear.

What Britain needed, he continued, in her desperate struggle was above all 'the loan of forty or fifty of your older destroyers' to bridge the gap until new British construction put in hand at the beginning of the war became available.[4] The reply from the President was sympathetic but discouraging. The moment was inopportune; any such transfer of destroyers would require the authorization of Congress and that was unlikely to be forthcoming.[5] Moreover there were doubts in Washington, which became more marked with the complete

---

[1] Churchill, ii, app. A, p. 631.   [2] Ibid. p. 225.
[3] Extracts from Mr. Churchill's famous speech of 18 June 1940 to the House of Commons (H. of C. Deb., vol. 362, col. 60).
[4] Churchill, ii. 22–23.
[5] For an account of the position as seen from Washington see Cordell Hull, *The Memoirs of Cordell Hull* (New York, Macmillan, 1948), i. 831–43.

collapse of the French armies in June, about whether Britain could hold out alone. The United States Ambassador in London, Mr. Joseph P. Kennedy, shared them.¹ The conviction of Nazi invincibility, Mr. Mackenzie King reminded the Canadian House of Commons later in the year, was held 'to a surprising degree' in the United States at this time. 'Public attention there', he recalled, 'became concentrated on the extent of American preparedness to meet the threat to this hemisphere which would follow the defeat of Britain. The myth of isolation was dissolved in an almost frenzied preoccupation with self-preservation.'² The retention of equipment and munitions desperately needed by Britain was urged upon the administration and 'ominous rumours' spread and gained ground that Britain could not hold out. It was in this atmosphere that the ultimate destiny of the British fleet became a matter of growing concern to the United States administration.

With the state of American opinion much in mind, Mr. Churchill impressed upon the Canadian Prime Minister and the British Ambassador to Washington alike the need for realism in discussions with the United States government. 'We must be careful', he cabled Mr. Mackenzie King on 5 June 1940, 'not to let Americans view too complacently [the] prospect of a British collapse, out of which they would get the British Fleet and the guardianship of the British Empire, minus Great Britain.'³ On 9 June he told Lord Lothian that he should 'discourage any complacent assumption on United States' part that they will pick up the *débris* of the British Empire by their present policy'.⁴ He further recommended to him on 28 June a 'bland and phlegmatic' mood, being firmly convinced that 'what really matters is whether Hitler is master of Britain in three months or not'.⁵ But by late June opinion in Washington at least was changing. The fear lest any aid afforded might be too little and too late and be lost to no lasting purpose in the apparently unfinished catalogue of Western European disasters was more and more counterbalanced by the hope that Britain's resolution to fight on, given the means to do so, might halt the Nazi advance and save the Americas from immediate peril. There followed the British action against the French fleet on 3 July which would seem to have had a possibly decisive effect on United States opinion.⁶ More important still, Britain, to quote Mr. Mackenzie King once more,⁷

did hold out, and held out magnificently. The world's vision cleared, Great Britain stood forth as she has through the centuries, an impregnable fortress of freedom. On this side of the ocean despair vanished. The English Channel came to be viewed as the first line of defence of the United States and of the new world.

The unwavering confidence of the United Kingdom government chiefs in ultimate victory contributed significantly to the growing conviction in

¹ Langer & Gleason, i. 481 ff. and 712.
² 12 November 1940, Canada, H. of C. Deb., 1941 session, vol. 1, p. 53.
³ Churchill, ii. 128.   ⁴ Ibid. p. 355.   ⁵ Ibid. p. 201.
⁶ Langer & Gleason, i. 710.   ⁷ Canada, H. of C. Deb., 1941 session, vol. 1, p. 54.

Washington that Britain would survive. The government of the United States was furnished with two British memoranda dated 27 June and 3 July 1940, analysing Britain's position and setting forth her most urgent needs. The first of them has been described by two American historians as 'a remarkable expression of moral courage'[1] in that it dealt less with the requirements for defence than with the conditions of victory. But for the United States at that time the essential thing was that Britain should continue to be successfully defended. As President Roosevelt is reported to have remarked to Mr. Morgenthau, the Secretary of the Treasury, 'If we want to keep out of this war, the longer we keep them [the British] going, that much longer we stay out of this war.'[2]

It was against this background of calculation well grounded in a sense of community of interest and of outlook that the Anglo-American bases for destroyers deal was negotiated in the late summer of 1940. Mr. Churchill on 31 July 1940 cabled President Roosevelt about Britain's now imperative need for destroyer reinforcement.

> We could not [he said] sustain the present rate of casualties for long, and if we cannot get a substantial reinforcement the whole fate of the war may be decided by this minor and easily-remediable factor. . . . Mr. President, with great respect I must tell you that in the long history of the world this is a thing to do *now*.[3]

But while greater reassurance in the United States about the future of the Royal Navy made negotiation easier, there were continuing difficulties. Any such transfer of naval craft might well be regarded by Germany as an act of war, and even were the President prepared to discount that risk, he could act only within the terms of the Naval Appropriation Bill Amendment of 28 June 1940, which laid down that no item of military equipment could be turned over to a foreign government without a certificate from the Chief of Naval Staff stating that it was not essential for the defence of the United States. It was this last obstacle that was so fully circumvented by a proposal, originating in the United States[4] and commended to Mr. Churchill by the British Ambassador, that the United States should be leased bases in the Caribbean in return for the transfer of some fifty over-age destroyers. There was, as Mr. Churchill has noted, 'no comparison between the intrinsic value of these antiquated and inefficient craft and the immense permanent strategic security afforded to the United States by the enjoyment of the island bases'.[5] Mr. Churchill moreover disliked the notion of a bargain and he would have preferred the granting of the facilities without stipulation of a return, confident that the United States would give the aid Britain most desperately needed. From the United States point of view, however, this seemed impracticable,

---
[1] Langer & Gleason, i. 709. [2] Ibid. p. 713. [3] Churchill, ii. 356.
[4] Langer & Gleason, i. 749–50. Their account is based largely on State Dept. papers. See also Hull, *Memoirs*, i. 831–43 and Sherwood, i. 175–7.
[5] Churchill, ii. 357.

COMMONWEALTH CO-OPERATION IN WAR

the President sensing 'that he could put the deal over to Congress and the people only if it represented a really good bargain'.[1] Since British needs were great and there were unquestionably considerable political and strategic advantages to Britain in the transfer, the United States view was not further disputed. The deal was concluded on 2 September 1940. It was coupled with assurances about the future of the British Fleet which the President felt he must have to strengthen his position with Congress and which Mr. Churchill gave, though he deemed them to be superfluous and more relevant if required of the German Navy.

Mr. Churchill regarded the leasing of bases and the transfer of fifty American destroyers as parallel transactions; the President presented them to Congress as a connected whole.[2] The transaction as set out in the documents exchanged had, itself, a twofold character. The bases in the Caribbean were part of a formal exchange, those in Newfoundland and in Bermuda were, on Mr. Churchill's insistence, a gift from the United Kingdom government. The British Ambassador, Lord Lothian, in his communication[3] of 2 September 1940 to the Secretary of State, Mr. Cordell Hull, made clear the distinction. First,

> In view of the friendly and sympathetic interest of His Majesty's Government in the United Kingdom in the national security of the United States and their desire to strengthen the ability of the United States to cooperate effectively with the other nations of the Americas in the defense of the Western Hemisphere, His Majesty's Government will secure the grant to the Government of the United States, freely and without consideration, of the lease for immediate establishment and use of naval and air bases and facilities for entrance thereto and the operation and protection thereof, on the Avalon Peninsula and on the southern coast of Newfoundland, and on the east coast and on the Great Bay of Bermuda.

Then in addition His Majesty's government agreed to make available to the United States, on a ninety-nine year lease and for immediate use, air bases and facilities on the eastern side of the Bahamas, the southern coast of Jamaica, the western coast of St. Lucia, the west coast of Trinidad in the Gulf of Paria, in the island of Antigua and in British Guiana within fifty miles of Georgetown 'in exchange for naval and military equipment and material which the United States Government will transfer to His Majesty's Government'. The transaction was confirmed in a letter from the Secretary of State to the British Ambassador, also on 2 September 1940,[4] which stated that 'in consideration of the declarations above quoted, the Government of the United States will immediately transfer to His Majesty's Government fifty United States Navy destroyers generally referred to as the twelve hundred-ton type'.

The distinction was in effect a compromise between the conflicting wishes

---

[1] Langer & Gleason, i. 765.
[2] Churchill, ii. 368.
[3] *Documents on American Foreign Relations*, iii. 203–5.
[4] Ibid. p. 205.

of President and Prime Minister. In itself of little importance it none the less illumined something of the spirit that inspired what was at once and on both sides a transaction and an act of faith. The President spoke of 'an epochal and far-reaching act of preparation for continental defense in the face of grave danger';[1] Mr. Churchill of 'memorable transactions' completed 'to the general satisfaction of the British and American peoples and to the encouragement of our friends all over the world'.[2] Nor was Hitler left in doubt about its implications. On the afternoon of 6 September 1940 the Commander-in-Chief of the German Navy reported to the Führer that the agreement would in his view 'necessarily lead to closer co-operation between Britain and the U.S.A.'[3] That indeed was its principal and abiding significance for the British Commonwealth of Nations.

No country was more concerned with measures to protect the Western hemisphere in 1940 than Canada, the only self-governing state in the Americas at war with the Axis Powers. While the United Kingdom government was generally responsible for the lease of bases in the Caribbean, in Bermuda, and in Newfoundland, whose dominion status had lapsed in 1934, this responsibility was exercised so far as possible in agreement with the local governments, or, in the somewhat anomalous case of Newfoundland, with the Commission of Government. There was also in the case of Newfoundland due acknowledgement of Canada's existing and reversionary interest, for Newfoundland was recognized to be at once the key to Canada's Atlantic defences and the tenth province which Canadians hoped one day to be able to welcome into the Canadian Confederation. Throughout the summer of 1940 there was much consultation between London and Ottawa about the possible lease of bases in this island. On 20 August Mr. Churchill told the House of Commons that the President 'has recently made it clear that he would like to discuss with us, and with the Dominion of Canada and with Newfoundland, the development of American naval and air facilities in Newfoundland and in the West Indies'. Mr. Churchill spoke of the very close harmony in 'all this line of thought'[4] between the governments of the United Kingdom and of Canada. Nor is the contribution of the Canadian government to the successful outcome of the negotiations to be dismissed as being of secondary importance. Mr. Brooke Claxton, in the Canadian House of Commons, on the contrary, spoke of 'a leading part' played by Mr. Mackenzie King 'in bringing about . . . the greatest act of co-operation among English speaking peoples since the war of independence'.[5]

Mr. Mackenzie King's understanding of the United States and personal

[1] *Documents on American Foreign Relations*, iii. 206.
[2] Churchill, ii. 367.
[3] *Brassey's Naval Annual, 1948*, p. 134.
[4] H. of C. Deb., vol. 364, col. 1170. Mr. Mackenzie King drew the attention of the Canadian House of Commons to this comment (Canada, H. of C. Deb., 1941 session, vol. 1, p. 54).
[5] 8 November 1940, Canada, H. of C. Deb., 1941 session, vol. 1, p. 6.

friendship[1] with its President were indeed never of greater advantage to his country than at this time, when parallel to the destroyer-bases deal an agreement was negotiated between Canada and the United States for the setting up of a Joint Board on Defence. Though there was a Canadian Army Corps in Britain, whose 'bayonets were sharp' and whose 'hearts were high' and who would have been proud 'to strike the decisive blow for Britain and Freedom',[2] posted 'most conveniently', as Mr. Churchill later recalled, 'between London and Dover' during July and August 1940, Canada herself had felt little of the impact of war. But with the fall of France her immunity from all risk of attack was ended. Though Mr. Churchill, as has been seen, discountenanced discussion of the possible evacuation of the United Kingdom government and the transfer of the Royal Navy to the senior dominion of the Crown, it was not a possibility that could be altogether ignored. The Canadian government in these circumstances sought and was freely granted emergency powers 'to mobilize all our human and material resources for the defence of Canada'. National registration followed, though not national service, and the pledges already given about conscription for overseas service were reaffirmed.[3] But even the otherwise 'violent acceleration' of Canada's war effort, it seemed, might not suffice to meet immediate dangers. There was accordingly an appeal to the United States government for its co-operation. It was embarrassing in its timing because of the United States government's greater preoccupation with national defence and with the defence of Latin America (which seemed a more likely target of attack than Canada), but not unwelcome in principle. President Roosevelt decided that at the least common problems of North American defence should be discussed, and he invited the Canadian government to send military representatives to Washington for this purpose in July 1940.[4] Mr. Mackenzie King, however, while himself prepared to wait, felt bound to express to the United States Minister in Ottawa a growing feeling in all parties that a joint defence agreement between the two countries was desirable. The outcome was an invitation from the President to the Prime Minister to meet him at Ogdensburg on 17 August 1940. There the President, 'in an exhilarated and expansive frame of mind', confident now of Britain's capacity to endure, himself proposed a joint United States–Canadian Defence Board with civilian as well as military membership. Mr. Mackenzie King was 'perfectly delighted' and 'almost with tears in his eyes' told the President that his courage and initiative would tremendously encourage the people of Canada and of Britain in their struggle.[5] On 23 August the Canada–United States

[1] The phrase would seem to be justified, though from the published records the friendship evidently meant more to Mr. King than to the President, whose accomplishment in the art of winning friends is not to be overlooked.   [2] Churchill, ii. 264.
[3] See *Canada in World Affairs, 1939–41*, pp. 40–49, for an account of the measures taken.
[4] Langer & Gleason, i. 703.
[5] Ibid. pp. 703–5. Their account is based principally on State Dept. papers and the Roosevelt papers. For a Canadian account see *Canada in World Affairs, 1939–41*, pp. 240–1 and Mr. Mackenzie King's speech to the Canadian House of Commons on 12 November 1940.

Permanent Joint Board on Defence was duly constituted.[1] One of its earliest decisions was the immediate strengthening of the defences of Newfoundland through the reinforcement of the Canadian garrisons on the island and the establishment of adequate air patrols. Later, in November 1940, a report of the Board recommending the building of air and sea ports by the Canadian government for use by United States planes and ships in the event of an attack on Canada was approved by the President and by the Canadian government. So, also, was the Board's proposal for the immediate preparation of a detailed plan for the defence of North America which was in fact drawn up and agreed some months before the Japanese attack on Pearl Harbour.[2]

The most important thing in 1940 about the Ogdensburg Agreement was that it associated the United States with a belligerent Commonwealth; the most important thing about it on the longer view was that the Joint Board it established was permanent. Both President and Prime Minister were careful to emphasize that each was moved by considerations of national advantage, but Mr. Mackenzie King further underlined[3] in the Canadian House of Commons that the agreement was the outcome of a policy of friendship and association with the United States pursued by his government over many years. In particular was it to be regarded as a logical development of the principles enunciated by the President and the Prime Minister at Kingston on 20 August 1938, the eve of the Munich crisis. 'The Dominion of Canada', the President had then observed,[4] 'is part of the sisterhood of the British Empire. I give to you an assurance that the people of the United States will not stand idly by if domination of Canadian soil is threatened by any other Empire.' And the Prime Minister had then replied that Canada, too, had her 'obligations as a good, friendly, neighbor, and one of them is to see that, at our own instance, our country is made as immune from attack or possible invasion as we can reasonably be expected to make it'. Formal endorsement of these assertions came with the Ogdensburg Agreement two years later.

In the United States and in Canada the news of the agreement was widely acclaimed. This was partly due to time and circumstance. It was a gesture of assurance in a summer of doubt. For the United States it had the particular attraction of completing the chain of defence agreements covering the Western hemisphere from the Antarctic to the Arctic. Mr. Stimson thought it 'one of the most momentous talks' in which he had ever participated; Mr. Mackenzie King doubted whether 'any conference between representatives of neighboring countries could possibly have been more complete in its accord from beginning to end, or more significant in its relation to world affairs'.[5] It was,

---

[1] The text of the agreement is reprinted in Mansergh, *Documents*, i. 547.
[2] Langer & Gleason, ii. 169.
[3] 12 November 1940, Canada, H. of C. Deb., 1941 session, vol. 1, pp. 53–60.
[4] See Mansergh, *Survey, 1938–9*, pp. 128–9.
[5] Langer & Gleason, i. 705, quoting a letter from Mr. Mackenzie King to President Roosevelt.

so he told the Canadian House of Commons later,[1] 'part of the enduring foundation of a new world order' in the furtherance of which 'Canada, in liaison between the British Commonwealth and the United States, is fulfilling a manifest destiny'. One resonant voice did not, however, join in this general acclaim. Mr. Churchill was not altogether well disposed to 'new world orders', nor was 'manifest destiny' a phrase in the vocabulary of the *British* Empire.

The Ogdensburg Agreement and the destroyer-bases deal were interrelated in time and in significance. Both provided for closer defence co-operation between the Atlantic members of the British Commonwealth and the United States in the war and for more intimate political co-operation in war and in peace. That had been the avowed aim of Canadian policy in both negotiations and of United Kingdom policy in the destroyer-bases deal. When late in August Mr. Churchill, still wedded to the idea of granting the bases 'in friendship and good will', discussed the possibility of announcing to the British people that they were being given as a free gift and that the transaction had acquired the appearance of a deal only to meet United States constitutional political difficulties, he was dissuaded by Lord Halifax's plea that the matter should be handled as the President desired, 'because the idea of the English–United States tie-up on anything is of more value than either bases or destroyers'.[2] This was unquestionably true; it was also true that the lease of the bases coupled with the Ogdensburg Agreement did mark a shift in the Western balance of power favourable to the United States. Extravagant Axis propaganda could be largely discounted, but the comment of the Commander-in-Chief of the German Navy in his report, already quoted, of 6 September to the Führer was not without insight. 'The leased islands', he noted, 'are of great significance to the U.S.A. They represent a considerable gain in prestige and a decisive step forward in the pursuit of the Pan-American objective'. On the longer term he foresaw in consequence not the collapse of the British Empire, because of 'the peculiar innate force of the political objectives embodied in the conception of the Commonwealth of Nations', but the most drastic changes leading 'very likely' to its re-emergence as an Anglo-Saxon Empire. Canada's role was evidently to be a passive one for he noted that 'understanding between the U.S.A. and Britain concerning Canada' was a prerequisite of any such transformation.[3] Here, alas for the correctness of this Teutonic diagnosis, Canada showed no predisposition to so self-effacing a role.

During negotiations early in 1941 between the United Kingdom and United States governments about a formal agreement on the Newfoundland bases the interest, earlier recognized, of the Canadian government would seem to have been overlooked. A protest from Ottawa followed, too late to affect the

[1] 12 November 1940, Canada, H. of C. Deb., 1941 session, vol. 1, p. 57.
[2] Langer & Gleason, i. 768.
[3] *Brassey's Naval Annual, 1948*, p. 134.

form of the agreement itself but in time to ensure the addition to it of a protocol of which the first two provisions read as follows.[1]

(i) It is recognized that the defence of Newfoundland is an integral feature of the Canadian scheme of defence, and as such is a matter of special concern to the Canadian Government. . . .

(ii) It is agreed therefore that, in all powers which may be exercised and in such actions as may be taken under the Agreement for the use and operation of United States bases dated the 27th of March, 1941, in respect of Newfoundland, Canadian interests in regard to defence will be fully respected.

Here was a forceful reminder that in relations between governments also there was a North Atlantic triangle.

(b) *Lend-Lease and the Hyde Park Agreement*

The Commonwealth with its exiled European allies fighting on alone after the fall of France was furnished by the United States with many of the weapons and the supplies essential to the waging of the war. More than half a million machine guns, 25,000 automatic rifles, 21,000 revolvers, some mortars, with supplies of ammunition for all these weapons, were sold to Britain and transported thither in British ships in midsummer 1940.[2] But continuing supplies and larger aid were conditional upon two things: first, and once again, the conviction of the government and people of the United States that helping Britain was the best means of defending North America, and second the continuing capacity of the British to pay cash for ever-increasing supplies and to transport them in their own ships, constantly depleted by the attacks of U-boats, to United Kingdom or Middle Eastern or other ports where they might be most effectively used. Britain's resolution in the summer months of 1940 convinced the people of the United States, as has already been noted, that support for Britain, to put it no higher, would help to keep them out of the war, but the second, a more technical, was also a more intractable problem.

In the summer crisis of 1940 there was for Britain only one problem—survival. The cautious earlier policy of conserving dollars so as to pay for vital purchases in the United States as they became necessary was for this reason cast aside in favour of a simpler plan, more suited to the desperate needs of the hour. It was, in the words of Mr. Churchill, 'to order everything we possibly could and leave future financial problems on the lap of the Eternal Gods',[3] and in the expressive phrase of the head of the British Purchasing Mission in Washington, Mr. Arthur Purvis, 'to shoot the wad'. The decision to take over the French arms contracts after the fall of France at a cost of $600 million was the most dramatic illustration of the new policy. Though some Americans affected to believe that Britain's dollar resources

---

[1] See *Canada in World Affairs, 1939–41*, pp. 215–17, where the text of the protocol is printed in full.   [2] Hancock & Gowing, pp. 227–8.   [3] Churchill, ii. 492.

were far from exhausted, it was the case that by the end of 1940 she was, if not in the contemporary phrase 'stripped to the bone', at the least without the dollar resources to carry her over more than a few months if the policy of purchase, unlimited by immediate financial consideration, were to be continued.[1]

The exhaustion of Britain's dollar reserves was viewed with concern by the United States administration. The arms embargo of the first phase of the war had been replaced, in accordance with the policy of friendly neutrality, by 'cash' and 'carry', and by late 1940 'cash' and 'carry' was, clearly, a programme with a limited life before it. On 8 December 1940 Mr. Churchill, in what he described as one of the most important letters of his life, put the position before the President of the United States. To ease the burden of 'carrying' by the merchant navy he proposed to the President the reassertion by the United States of the doctrine of the freedom of the seas so that United States ships should be free to trade with countries against which there was not an effective legal blockade and that they should where necessary be provided with armed escort. As for 'cash', he left the initiative to the President and confined himself to a statement of the position as seen from London:

> The more rapid and abundant the flow of munitions and ships which you are able to send us, the sooner will our dollar credits be exhausted. They are already, as you know, very heavily drawn upon by the payments we have made to date. Indeed, as you know, the orders already placed or under negotiation . . . many times exceed the total exchange resources remaining at the disposal of Great Britain. The moment approaches when we shall no longer be able to pay cash. . . . I believe you will agree that it would be wrong in principle and mutually disadvantageous in effect if at the height of this struggle Great Britain were to be divested of all saleable assets, so that after the victory was won with our blood, civilisation saved, and the time gained for the United States to be fully armed against all eventualities, we should stand stripped to the bone.[2]

In respect of 'cash' the President's response was Lend-Lease—'the most unsordid act', Mr. Churchill termed it, 'in the history of any nation'[3]—made possible constitutionally by an act of 1892 which allowed that the Secretary of War 'when in his discretion it will be for the public good' could lease army property, if not required for public use, for a period of not longer than five years, and politically by the far-sighted generosity of President and people. Nor was it an act to give Britain alone the sinews of war but, as the President himself acknowledged, aside from United States current and historic interest in the survival of democracy in the world as a whole, it was equally important from the point of view of American defence that the United States should do everything possible to help the British Empire to defend itself. 'There are . . . millions in Britain and elsewhere bravely shielding the great flame of

---

[1] This was understood by members of the United States administration. See Langer & Gleason, vol. 2, ch. viii, 'The Origins of Lend-Lease'.   [2] Churchill, ii. 494–501.
[3] Ibid. p. 503. See also for United States' accounts of this arrangement Sherwood, i. 220–8 and Hull, *Memoirs*, ii. 922–6.

democracy from the blackout of barbarism. . . . Our country is going to be what our people have proclaimed it must be—the arsenal of democracy.'[1] It was, however, some time before the United States production lived up to this description.[2]

As the Commonwealth had its vital role to play in ensuring that democracy should survive, so too its members collectively had a vital interest in these transactions between the United Kingdom and the United States. While the immediate results of Lend-Lease were somewhat disappointing,[3] the all-important fact remained that this financial arrangement made possible long-term British plans of vast extent worked out in agreement with the United States, which ensured that in time the supply position of the British Commonwealth as a whole would be transformed because, apart from direct United States aid to other members,[4] a Britain more liberally supplied could in turn afford to allocate supplies more generously to the oversea dominions. For the remainder of the war the 'barrier of the exchanges' no longer impeded the war production of the Western democracies.

The Lend-Lease Act received Congressional approval in March 1941, and what Mr. Morgenthau called the 'cash on the barrelhead era'[5] of American aid came to an end. In April that year the Prime Minister of Canada and the President of the United States, meeting at Hyde Park, concluded an agreement making a parallel though by no means identical arrangement to ease Canada's problems of finance and supply. In the first nine months of the war Britain made but limited use of Canada's (as of the United States') industrial capacity. Up to 30 June 1940 total contracts and commitments on behalf of the British Supply Board were about $100 million. In the succeeding three months, that is until 30 September 1940, they totalled $216 million, while by 30 September 1941 the total was little short of $1,000 million.[6] In the case of Canada, as of the other dominions, there were no reservations about cash and carry. All were engaged upon a common struggle in which victory was to be won by a common effort on the battlefield, on the seas, on the farm, and in the factory. But in the case of Canada, lying, unlike the other ·dominions, outside the sterling area and bordering upon the United States, there were particular currency difficulties. By the end of 1940 it became apparent that the deficiency in United Kingdom's payments to Canada could be met only in part by British exports, by repatriation of Canadian dollar securities, and by the transfer of gold. Accordingly early in 1941 the United Kingdom received an

---

[1] U.S. Dept. of State, *Peace and War; United States Foreign Policy, 1931–41* (Washington, 1943), pp. 634 and 637. See also Langer & Gleason, ii. 247–50.
[2] Hancock & Gowing, pp. 384–6.
[3] Ibid. pp. 235–47. See especially diagram on p. 237.
[4] Reciprocal Lend-Lease Agreements between the governments of the United States and Australia and New Zealand were concluded in 1942. That with Australia is reprinted in Mansergh, *Documents*, i. 555–7.   [5] Langer & Gleason, ii. 421.
[6] *Canada in World Affairs, 1939–41*, pp. 217–18.

assurance from the Canadian government that British requirements would continue to be met, even though it meant the accumulation on the part of Canada of large sterling balances.[1] Early in 1942 Canada made a gift of $1,000 million to the United Kingdom to make easier further purchases of munitions, war materials, and foodstuffs.

In the meantime, and despite the re-export of gold received from the United Kingdom, Canada's deficit with the United States continued to grow with her demands for materials for war production to meet her own needs and those of the United Kingdom. The principal purpose of the Hyde Park Agreement was to meet this difficulty and to ensure that it did not restrict the scale of North American war production. Canadians, Mr. Mackenzie King told the House of Commons in Ottawa,[2] could not possibly have embarked upon their existing programme of war production 'if we had not lived side by side with the greatest industrial nation in the world'. But the purchase of essential tools, machines, and materials in the United States, required 'both for our own Canadian war effort, and in the production of war supplies for Britain', had brought into existence 'the most urgent problem we faced in our economic relations with the United States'. Coupled with it, though distinct from it, was the growing danger of waste and duplication in Canadian and United States war production. The Hyde Park Agreement, resting upon the principle that 'in mobilizing the resources of this continent' each country should provide the other with the articles it was best able to produce, contemplated the co-ordination of their production programmes. Canada was to supply the United States with materials needed for its defence programme which would help Canada in paying for her essential purchases in the United States, and further Canadian purchases of materials or components to be used in war supplies for Britain were to be made available under the terms of the Lend-Lease Act.

The Hyde Park Agreement[3] was described by the Canadian Prime Minister 'as the economic corollary of Ogdensburg'. It resulted in the setting up of machinery, in the form of a Materials Co-ordinating Committee in May 1941, and of two Joint Economic Committees[4] in June 1941. If it did not wholly solve Canada's exchange problem it marked a new stage in United States–Canadian co-operation, a stage the more important in that it contemplated close co-ordination of United States–Canadian production not only for its own sake but also for the explicit purpose of aiding Britain. In this respect it went further than Ogdensburg.

While the problem of 'cash' was being thus resolved, the problem of 'carry' assumed new and ever more formidable dimensions as the Germans sought to

[1] Cf. ibid. pp. 217–29.
[2] 28 April 1941, Canada, H. of C. Deb., 1941, vol. 3, pp. 2286–7.
[3] Canada, Treaty Series, 1941, no. 14 (Mansergh, *Documents*, i. 548–9).
[4] Cf. *Canada in World Affairs, 1939–41*, pp. 254–9, and Langer & Gleason, ii. 431–2.

bring Britain to her knees by cutting the Atlantic lifeline. The sustained Nazi attacks on British shipping and the extended area of German U-boat operations brought the Atlantic battle nearer to the United States. In January 1941 Mr. Churchill alluded to the use that could be made in the spring of another thirty over-age American destroyers; in March he sent to the President an Admiralty report showing the grave extent of British naval losses. The President responded with such limited aid and expedients as the administration felt free and able to adopt.[1] A larger step was, however, taken on 10 April when the President decided on an extension of the United States patrol area—a fitting retort to Germany's extension of the combat area—as the essential part of a programme for saving the situation in the Atlantic.[2] On the same day, and with the same purpose in view, it was announced that the Danish government had placed Greenland under the temporary protection of the United States and authorized the American government to construct bases there, and that the Red Sea region was removed from the list of combat areas forbidden to United States shipping since June 1940. In a message to Mr. Churchill on 11 April the President summarized the total effect of these measures and the assistance they would give to Britain. The extension of the security and patrol zones was designed to make possible a greater degree of assistance to British convoys in the Atlantic, while, with the reopening of the Red Sea area, the United States proposed to send all types of goods in unarmed American flag-ships to Egypt or any other non-belligerent port via the Red Sea or Persian Gulf. This, as the President pointed out, would free a large amount of British shipping 'for direct haul to England'.[3] Short, therefore, of providing convoy escort, as some members of his administration advised, the President had done as much as seemed possible to ease, if no more than temporarily, Britain's position in the Atlantic battle.

On one point, to which Mr. Churchill attached the utmost importance, the President proved unable to help him. This was not from any lack of trying. Ambassador Winant, Colonel Donovan, and the warm-hearted Mr. Wendell Willkie all sought to persuade Mr. de Valera 'to provide the hard-pressed British' with 'desperately needed bases in Eire's ports'. All confessed 'total failure'.[4] To understand why, it is necessary to examine the problem of the Irish ports not in isolation but in relation to the broader question of Irish neutrality which was—politically as well as strategically—of much significance to the Commonwealth.

Irish Neutrality: British Anxieties, United States Diplomacy, and German Plans

The governments of the United Kingdom and of the oversea dominions continued to regard Eire as a member of the British Commonwealth even after the enactment of the External Relations Act in 1936 and of the new

[1] Langer & Gleason, ii. 423; see generally ch. xiv.
[2] Ibid. pp. 426–7.   [3] Quoted ibid. p. 435.   [4] Ibid. p. 447.

Constitution in 1937. Despite Irish repudiation of allegiance to the Crown, one of the conventional characteristics of dominion status as defined in the Balfour Report and restated in the preamble to the Statute of Westminster, they agreed to regard the Constitution as not effecting a 'fundamental alteration' in the relationship of the Irish Free State (henceforward to be described in accordance with the relevant provision of the new Constitution as Eire or Ireland) to the British Commonwealth of Nations.[1] If there was an element of unreality, even absurdity, in thus maintaining that a state which expressly repudiated allegiance to the Crown continued in fact to pay it, the importance of the consequences that flowed from this interpretation of what had taken place is not open to question. Since, in the British view, Eire remained a dominion, then it was in that view also a dominion which remained neutral in September 1939. Irish neutrality thus became a test of dominion neutrality, and if under other circumstances Britain would have respected Eire's right to determine her own wartime policy, this interpretation of Eire's status assuredly strengthened the arguments for so doing. Any questioning or invasion of Irish rights was thereby made tantamount to a questioning or invasion of dominion rights. Paradoxically, therefore, Eire, which did not regard herself, and did not wish to be regarded, as a dominion benefited from British insistence that she should be so regarded; while Britain's own freedom of action throughout the war was restricted by this very insistence which made Eire against her own will the symbol and supreme example of unfettered dominion sovereignty. It was the dominion that did not deem itself to be a dominion that demonstrated to all the world the sovereignty which the dominions enjoyed under the Statute of Westminster. Alternately gratified at the demonstration and dismayed by its consequences, the United Kingdom could do nothing to impair its effect. 'Previous bad experience, ... as well as regard for America and the Dominions', noted the German Minister in Eire in a dispatch to Berlin dated 8 October, 1939, 'may impede the consideration of possible [British] steps against Ireland'.[2] This was understatement. And it was no less ironic that Mr. de Valera, who had fomented civil war in 1922 because he believed that dominion status could never lead to national independence, was now the principal beneficiary of a status which he had so vigorously repudiated and which he believed he had finally discarded in 1937.

'Mr. de Valera's attitude will not be challenged or resented by any Englishman who knows and has pondered the past. He will observe, rather, that this is the first occasion on which the great majority of Irish nationalists have not acted up to their historic maxim: "England's difficulty is Ireland's opportunity".' These sentences from the leading article in the *Round Table* after the outbreak of war,[3] even if easier to write in the autumn of 1939 than in the summer of 1940, reflect an approach admirable alike in its understanding and

---
[1] See Mansergh, *Survey, 1931–9*, pp. 304–7, and for texts Mansergh, *Documents*, i. 321–67.
[2] D. Ger. F.P., viii. 241–2.   [3] *Round Table*, December 1939, p. 13.

its restraint. But while Britain acquiesced with good grace in Irish neutrality, Germany considered whether it might not be of positive advantage to her. In the dispatch of 8 October 1939 already referred to, the German Minister in Eire, after noting that the declaration of neutrality and the government's subsequent careful, consistent adherence to it had the support of the great majority of the Irish population, observed that it had 'visibly strengthened Irish national self-consciousness'. In this he was unquestionably right, and he thought the correct policy for Germany was to continue 'to support consolidation of Irish neutrality and independence on a broad national basis, which is also important in its effect on the Dominions, India, and America as a symptom of the loosening of the ties of Empire'.[1]

In the early years of the war Mr. de Valera was much preoccupied with the activities of the minority of Irish nationalists who had not discarded the ancient maxim to which the *Round Table* alluded, and who believed that the coming of war afforded them opportunity for the intensification of the violent protest against the continuance of partition. In Ireland the first nine months of the war witnessed a determined attempt by the members of the new Irish Republican Army to put their ideas into practice and in so doing to challenge the authority of the lawfully elected government of their country. The most spectacular of their exploits was a raid on 23 December 1939 on the Magazine Fort in Phoenix Park, Dublin, from which over a million and a half rounds of .303 rifle and Thompson sub-machine gun ammunition were taken.[2] It was this daring exploit which finally prompted Mr. de Valera, always reluctant to act strongly against republicans still faithful to the physical force tradition which in different circumstances he had himself once cherished, to act with some decision and effect. But more than ever was he mindful thereafter of the divisions within the country which, he believed, in themselves predicated a policy of neutrality. It was possible, he had told the Dáil on 29 September,[3] to divide the people of the country into two large classes, namely the great bulk of the population, who, whatever might be their particular sympathies, desired above all that Eire should remain neutral, and a minority composed of those who felt so strongly about the issues at stake that they wished to involve their country in the war on one side or the other. Mr. de Valera was resolved that neither the pro-German nor the pro-British section in this second category should succeed. One of his principal weapons, rigorously employed, was a press censorship designed to keep the political temperature low.

Mr. de Valera's concern with unity was realistic. In so far, however, as he suggested by linking them together that the extremes in political allegiance might be regarded as cancelling each other out, he was misleading, for there was in fact no balance between them. The history of the preceding two

---

[1] *D. Ger. F.P.*, viii. 241, 242.
[2] For a dramatic first-hand account of the raid see S. O'Callaghan, *The Easter Lily* (London, Wingate, 1956), ch. xvii.   [3] *Round Table*, December 1939, p. 140.

decades had demonstrated with a finality rare in politics that the pro-British element was politically impotent. Its support for a particular cause was not an asset but a liability. With the extreme nationalists the position was quite different. They were in the main stream of the nationalist tradition, they could and did claim that they alone were the uncorrupted and incorruptible heirs of the national-republican revolution, and their appeal to nationalist sentiment, uncompromising but authentic, might in conditions favourable to them influence decisively public opinion or the course of events.[1] With Ireland partitioned and with the ending of partition by force as their goal, they were for the most part pro-German by compulsion of circumstance rather than by choice. If Germany was to exploit the opportunities afforded to her by Irish neutrality, here were her natural allies. Of this the German government was well aware. But while it was in German interests to establish contact with the leaders of the new Irish Republican Army, so as to be prepared to take advantage of any favourable turn in events, it was equally important in the meantime to support and strengthen Mr. de Valera as the principal and consistent advocate of neutrality. It was, therefore, as important from the German point of view to be ready to act should circumstances prove favourable, as it was not to act too soon and thereby invite British intervention, and risk losing the advantages that accrued to Germany through the existence of a neutral state on Britain's western seaboard.

The German government was judiciously advised to this effect by Herr Eduard Hempel, German Minister in Eire from 1937 to 1945. He noted in his dispatch of 8 October 1939 that 'the personal attitude of the Government toward me is definitely friendly', that Irish opinion after the Nazi pact with Soviet Russia and the conquest of Poland was 'to a large extent anti-German but at the same time strongly anti-British', and that the I.R.A. recognized the danger of premature activity. He advised that Germany should continue to 'support consolidation of Irish neutrality', should avoid interference in domestic disputes, should give 'the greatest possible consideration' to Ireland in the blockade, and that German submarines should avoid Irish territorial waters if possible and, if impossible, should exercise the greatest caution.[2] On 14 November 1939[3] the German Minister reiterated his plea for 'complete restraint' in view of the fact that 'the I.R.A. is hardly strong enough for action with promise of success or involving appreciable damage to England and is probably also lacking in a leader of any stature'. 'Sensible adherents of the radical nationalist movement' were, so he reported, opposed to coming out in the open, especially in view of the determination shown by Mr. de Valera's government to maintain neutrality. German interference 'would, even in their opinion, prematurely endanger the whole nationalist movement', because moderate nationalist opinion would accuse the I.R.A. of making

[1] Cf. O'Callaghan, *Easter Lily*, ch. xviii on the I.R.A. hunger strikes of 1939–40 and their impact on the public. [2] *D. Ger. F.P.*, viii. 241–2. [3] Ibid. pp. 405–6.

national interests dependent on Germany. This, in view of 'the widespread aversion to present-day Germany, especially for religious reasons, could rob the I.R.A. of all chances of future success.' Moreover, it would give Britain an excuse to intervene. The situation, the German Minister allowed, 'would presumably change if Irish neutrality were definitely violated' and 'perhaps also if a considerable weakening of England were to make the prospects of regaining Northern Ireland appear more favorable'. In such circumstances 'the friendship of all Irishmen' might be assured by a German declaration stating that at the end of the war Ireland would have German support for the return of Northern Ireland. Such at least was the hope he had heard expressed and which he believed to be entertained in some government circles, 'although hardly by De Valera so far'. But even for such a declaration of aims—the Minister believed—'the proper moment' had not yet arrived.

On 30 November the Minister renewed his plea for special treatment for Ireland should the German blockade of Britain be intensified and advised that if Irish neutrality were to be violated Britain, if at all possible, should be allowed to take the first step. Should Britain in fact do so action against the German Legation was to be expected and the Minister had been informed by the I.R.A. that in such circumstances they would defend its staff and take them to a place of safety. He mentioned, doubtless with satisfaction, that 'the provisional British representative here is considered in greater danger at present than we [are] and is constantly under the strictest surveillance'.[1] In January and February 1940 the German government was considering the possibility of returning Seán Russell, a prominent I.R.A. leader, to Ireland by submarine but while it was considered practicable it was not thought timely.[2]

On the assumption that the German Minister's advice was heeded in Berlin, Mr. de Valera was faced not with an immediate but only with a contingent Nazi threat to Irish neutrality in 1939 and early 1940. Nothing, however, is more apparent from the Minister's own dispatches than that his advice carried no weight outside the German Foreign Office. In November 1939 he could only allude to 'rumours' of 'alleged German support of the Irish Republican Army';[3] in December he complained of German propaganda distributed 'to radical Irish-nationalist personalities' and 'allegedly very strong'[4] in content about which he had himself evidently not been consulted, despite, or perhaps because of, warnings he had already given against the distribution of such material.

Mr. de Valera referred not infrequently in the early phase of the war to

[1] D. Ger. F.P., viii. 466–7.
[2] Ibid. pp. 693 and 760. Seán Russell in fact never reached Ireland; on 22 November 1950 Mr. Seán MacBride informed a questioner in the Dáil that 'it appeared reasonably certain that Russell died as a result of illness while a passenger in a German submarine in 1940' (*The Times*, 23 November 1950). For a further comment see O'Callaghan, *Easter Lily*, pp. 158–9.   [3] D. Ger. F.P., viii. 405.
[4] Ibid. p. 545; see also O'Callaghan, *Easter Lily*, pp. 158–9.

COMMONWEALTH CO-OPERATION IN WAR

dangers threatening Eire from both sides. In this he was in part but not wholly employing the accepted vocabulary of neutrality. The violation of Irish neutrality by British forces was something which Mr. de Valera thought could not in all circumstances be excluded. In particular he feared that Britain at some critical moment might attempt to seize the ports restored to Irish sovereignty under the Anglo-Irish Agreement of 1938. They were fears to be understood only in the light of history.[1]

Under Article 7 of the Anglo-Irish Treaty of 1921 the government of the Irish Free State agreed to afford to His Majesty's Imperial Forces in time of war or strained relations 'such harbour and other facilities as the British Government may require' for the purpose of coastal defence and more particularly the ports at Berehaven and Cobh in the south-west and Lough Swilly in the north which were to be made available to them at all times. This arrangement was terminated and the ports were restored to Irish sovereignty in 1938. There was then no attempt by the Irish government to disguise the fact that, apart from national sentiment, it desired the restoration of the ports because their retention by Britain seemed likely to prejudice the practical possibility of maintaining neutrality in a war in which Britain was engaged. No suggestion that Mr. Chamberlain's government for its part entered into the 1938 agreement unaware of the likelihood of Irish neutrality survives examination. Nor indeed has it been advanced by the apologists of Mr. Chamberlain's policy. The betterment of Anglo-Irish relations was Mr. Chamberlain's aim and he was prepared to sacrifice much to achieve it, but he did not enter into the 1938 agreement without first having a careful examination made of the strategic considerations involved. Lord Chatfield has placed on record the advice tendered to him by the Chiefs of Staff.[2] It was their view, all attempts to obtain Irish agreement to a defensive alliance in any form having proved fruitless, that the practical alternatives in the event of war were a neutral Ireland or a hostile Ireland. In either case the possibility that the ports would have to be defended against Irish forces could not be discounted, and for the adequate defence of each of the ports and its hinterland a brigade would be required. 'Such a position', notes Lord Chatfield, then Chief of Naval Staff, 'with a series of Gibraltars' scattered round the coast, was 'in view of our meagre military position at that time divorced from realities'. The General Staff, especially in view of Britain's Continental commitments, were 'not only strongly averse to accepting such a responsibility' but were also anxious to relieve the army of its peacetime responsibilities for guarding the ports. The Admiralty moreover believed that even if the

---

[1] For a discussion of the 1938 agreement see Mansergh, *Survey, 1931–9*, pp. 312–17. For the sake of continuity of argument and narration some aspects of the agreement are here recalled.

[2] Lord Chatfield, *The Navy and Defence*, vol. 2: *It Might Happen Again* (London, Heinemann, 1947), ch. xviii. See also his letter to *The Times*, 4 February 1942 (extract in Mansergh, *Survey, 1931–9*, p. 316).

Irish port facilities were lost to them they could hold the position with France as an ally and Norway as a friendly neutral. In the circumstances envisaged in 1938 their judgement, Lord Chatfield insisted, proved correct. But with Nazi seizure first of the Norwegian and then of the French Atlantic ports the situation was transformed. It is true that the cession of the Irish ports had obtained the assurance of a non-hostile Ireland, but was this sufficient compensation for the loss of Irish bases from which to fight the battle of the Atlantic? Mr. Churchill, who had denounced their transfer in 1938 in one of the most formidable of his philippics,[1] most emphatically thought not. At the Admiralty as First Lord during the first eight months of the war he complained constantly and bitterly of the unfair burden that in consequence had been placed upon the Royal Navy.

On 5 September 1939 Mr. Churchill called for a special Admiralty report[2] upon the questions arising 'from the so-called neutrality of the so-called Eire', among them being the restriction of the radius of British destroyers which resulted from their not having the use of Berehaven and other South Irish anti-submarine bases, and the refuelling, with the connivance of 'Irish malcontents', of German U-boats in lonely west-coast inlets. On 24 September Mr. Churchill summarized his views of the Irish situation.[3] Three-quarters of the Irish people 'are with us, but the implacable, malignant minority can make so much trouble that De Valera dare not do anything to offend them'. There seemed to be 'a good deal of evidence' that U-boats were being succoured

from West of Ireland ports by the malignant section with whom De Valera dare not interfere. And we are debarred from using Berehaven, &c. If the U-boat campaign became more dangerous we should coerce Southern Ireland both about coast watching and the use of Berehaven, &c. However, if it slackens off under our counter-attacks and protective measures, the Cabinet will not be inclined to face the serious issues which forcible measures would entail. It looks, therefore, as if the present bad situation will continue for the present. But the Admiralty should never cease to formulate through every channel its complaints about it, and I will from time to time bring our grievances before the Cabinet. On no account must we appear to acquiesce in, still less be contented with, the odious treatment we are receiving.

A minute giving direction to a department, it needs in this instance to be underlined, is something very different from a Cabinet minute recording governmental agreement on policy. Mr. Churchill's comments and the course which he would appear from this minute to have been prepared to sponsor in certain eventualities had no prospect of acceptance so long as Mr. Chamberlain remained in office. His language indeed represented as much continuing resentful protest against Mr. Chamberlain's earlier policy as against Irish neutrality and more particularly Irish refusal to make Berehaven or some

---

[1] Mansergh, *Documents*, i. 384–90.   [2] Churchill, i. 335.
[3] Ibid. pp. 582–3. See also p. 577.

other port available for British use. It is not to be doubted that the Royal Navy's ability to extend protection to ocean convoys was reduced by some 200 miles owing to the lack of an advanced destroyer fuelling base on the west coast of Ireland. Yet no one in fact had posed more cogently than Mr. Churchill in 1938 the arguments against forcible seizure of the Irish ports once they were restored to Irish sovereignty.

> You had the rights. You have ceded them. You hope in their place to have good will, strong enough to endure tribulation for your sake. Suppose you have it not. It will be no use saying 'Then we will retake the ports'. You will have no right to do so. To violate Irish neutrality should it be declared at the moment of a great war may put you out of court in the opinion of the world, and may vitiate the cause by which you may be involved in war.[1]

It was largely for these very reasons that the German Minister in Eire thought any forceful British action to regain the ports improbable despite Irish fears that it might be taken.[2] Mr. Churchill's bitterness, coupled with his idiosyncratic assessment of political forces in Ireland, led him to embark upon a course of recrimination which, if anything, hardened Irish resolve to withhold the ports and lost to Britain some of the advantages that might otherwise have accrued from unqualified recognition, in time of extreme peril, of an agreement freely negotiated some few years earlier.

When the German armies launched their spring offensives in 1940 the practicability of Irish neutrality in a war in which Britain was not merely engaged but fighting for survival against a power which was soon to control the Western European seaboard from northern Norway to the Pyrenees was put to its crucial test. On this point the Irish government entertained few illusions. Mr. de Valera, addressing a Fianna Fáil convention at Galway on 12 May, said of Holland and Belgium so ruthlessly invaded by the Nazi forces: 'Today these two small nations are fighting for their lives, and it would be unworthy of this small nation if, on an occasion like this, I did not utter a protest against the cruel wrong that has been done them.' The majority of the Irish people shared his sentiments and, as the German Minister in Dublin himself testified, feeling in Eire towards the Third Reich 'noticeably deteriorated'.[3] The German Minister protested at de Valera's unfriendly comments but, contrary to German records, no apologies were tendered by 'the deputy of the Irish Foreign Minister' in Dublin.[4] Meanwhile there was evidence of undiplomatic German activity in Eire. Some few parachutists were dropped and some agents landed by submarine. One among them, and presumably others, was instructed to make use of personal connexions with the Irish for action against Britain but activity against the

---
[1] 5 March 1938, H. of C. Deb., vol. 335, col. 1104.
[2] D. Ger. F. P., viii. 241–2, 405–6, 466–7.
[3] Ibid. ix. 422–4. This dispatch from the German Minister is an interesting assessment of Irish attitudes towards the principal belligerents at this time.
[4] Ibid. pp. 401–2 and personal information.

Irish government was expressly forbidden.[1] The arrest and trial of two of them was a matter of embarrassment to the Irish government and of some concern to the German lest this evidence of Nazi espionage should further alienate feeling from the Third Reich.[2] The Irish government was advised through the German Minister of the attitude it was expected to adopt in these circumstances.

> The Irish Government [read the German démarche] must be clearly aware that the struggle between the German Reich and England was now entering upon its decisive stage. We were conscious of the fact that the measures we had to take for carrying out this struggle against England... might also affect Irish interests.... We believed that Ireland, whose enemy through history was known to be England, was fully aware that the outcome of the struggle would also be of decisive importance for the Irish nation and the final realization of its national demands.

In such circumstances the German government believed it could count on the 'greatest possible understanding' from the Irish government despite its neutrality.[3] The representatives of the Irish government responded with due 'understanding' to this approach in respect of lack of publicity for the trial of captured Nazi agents but not otherwise.[4]

Mr. de Valera, meanwhile, aware of misgivings within and dangers without, resolved to do what could be done to preserve the independence and the neutrality of a small country, without modern arms or equipment, with no navy and a negligible air force. On 28 May 1940 a National Defence Council was formed in agreement with the opposition and its first meeting was held on 30 May. On 1 June Mr. de Valera spoke of the immediate and imminent danger with which the country was faced and expressed his conviction that the only chance of safety lay in the mobilization of the resources the country possessed so as to make invasion too costly an enterprise for an aggressor to undertake.[5] None but the wilfully blind, he said in the Dáil on 6 June,[6] could fail to see that Ireland was well within the war zone and that it might suit any one of the belligerents to 'interfere with the liberties which we claim to be ours'.[7] Attack, he insisted, might be expected from any quarter. On

---

[1] *D. Ger. F.P.*, viii. 490–1. For some light on their objectives and association with the I.R.A. see ibid. x. 110–11.

[2] See especially the details given in the German Minister's dispatch of 24 May about the capture of a man named Held about whom the Minister had previously given warnings of an unknown character to Berlin (ibid. pp. 431–2). See *Round Table*, September 1940, pp. 864–7, for a contemporary Irish account.   [3] *D. Ger. F.P.*, ix. 573–4.

[4] Ibid. pp. 601–3 and vol. x, pp. 36 and 110–11.

[5] *Round Table*, September 1940, p. 870.   [6] Dáil Deb., vol. 80, col. 1666.

[7] On 17 June Mr. Walshe, Secretary of the Department of External Affairs, repeated to the German Minister his earlier assertions that fears of an English attack on Ireland still occupied first place. This was doubtfully true. The report of the interview with its expressions of 'great admiration' for the German achievements and hopes that Hitler's reported absence of intention to destroy the British Empire did not mean the abandonment of Ireland suggests strongly a desire to appease a probable aggressor (*D. Ger. F.P.*, ix. 602–3).

16 June, the day on which France fell, a national recruiting campaign culminated in a great meeting in College Green, Dublin, at which for the first time since the civil war the leaders of all the principal parties appeared on the same platform. Unity was Mr. de Valera's theme and in an allusion to the I.R.A. he appealed to 'any Achilles in his tent' to come out and 'fall in behind the rest of us'.[1] This was certainly not the language that would have moved Achilles long ago, and it made no perceptible impression upon the members of the new I.R.A. None the less it was never more apparent that Mr. de Valera, with the great weight of Irish opinion behind him, desired at all costs to preserve unity. His statement to the German Minister on 19 June was impressive in its exposition and unqualified assertion of such intention. If Germany invaded Eire, said Mr. de Valera, the Irish government would resist with English support just as likewise, and presumably with German support, they would resist an English invasion. But, Mr. de Valera observed, without excluding the possibility of change, Irish neutrality had been so far respected by Britain.[2] Whether Mr. de Valera succeeded or failed in his endeavours to preserve neutrality in fact depended less on Irish policy than on the intentions of the principal belligerents and of the United States.

In 1940 the President of the United States and the State Department gave evidence of growing concern about the possible fate of this small neutral state in the eastern Atlantic. In March of that year Mr. David Gray, a kinsman of Mrs. Roosevelt, was appointed United States Minister to Eire, and in April he discussed the Irish question with members of the British Government, including Mr. Churchill, in London before taking up his appointment in Dublin. Mr. Gray was much interested in the possibility of a bargain by which Mr. de Valera would abandon neutrality in return for unity and would thereby make possible co-ordinated defence of the island.[3] At a distance this seemed a simple and attractive notion; it had already occurred to others without first-hand knowledge of recent Irish history. Members of the British government assured him that they were willing to see a negotiated settlement of the Irish question but stipulated that it should involve no coercion of Ulster. On arrival in Dublin, however, Mr. Gray discovered that Mr. de Valera would hear nothing of 'bargaining with Ireland's neutrality'.[4] The Irish Prime Minister suggested that Mr. Gray should see Lord Craigavon in Belfast. The United Kingdom representative in Dublin assured Mr. Gray that London had 'prepared the way' for such a visit. Lord Craigavon appeared, however, to the disappointment of the United States Minister, to be 'quite unmoved by any instructions he may have had from London', flatly declined to take the initiative, and eschewed all thought of compromise. Mr. Gray, commendably anxious 'to get at the root of the difficulty', had now

---

[1] *Round Table*, September 1940, p. 871.   [2] *D. Ger. F.P.*, ix. 637–40.
[3] Langer & Gleason, i. 484. Their commentary is based on telegrams and letters from Mr. David Gray to the President.   [4] Ibid.

completed the circle, and his one conclusion was that on the score of obstinacy there was little to choose between the Prime Ministers of Northern Ireland and Eire.[1]

On 23 May Mr. de Valera assured the British Government that Eire would fight if attacked by Germany and would call in British help the moment it became necessary but he also insisted that there could be no question of inviting in British troops before an actual German invasion had begun. The Chiefs of Staff, while recommending that military support should be provided on these terms, believed that the Irish forces would be unable to offer serious resistance to a German invasion, and considered it essential that strong British forces should be stationed in the south of Ireland before an invasion took place. A further approach was thereupon made to Mr. de Valera to find out what were the smallest political concessions required to induce him to admit British troops and ships forthwith.[2] But then, as always, he was not prepared to bargain.

Mr. Churchill in the meantime was exploring other possibilities with Mr. Roosevelt. In his first message as Prime Minister to the President, Mr. Churchill drew Mr. Roosevelt's attention to the risk of German parachute or airborne landings in Eire and suggested that the visit of a United States naval squadron to Irish ports would be invaluable.[3] On 5 June, in a telegram to Mr. Mackenzie King, Mr. Churchill again among other and even more important matters said that any pressure the Canadian Prime Minister could apply to encourage the visit of an American squadron to Irish ports would be invaluable.[4] On 11 June, with the French armies in collapse, Mr. Churchill cabled President Roosevelt once more: 'We are also worried about Ireland. An American squadron at Berehaven would do no end of good, I am sure.'[5] The President, however, was not to be persuaded. In a cable dated 13 June he said he could not send a squadron to Berehaven because of other United States naval commitments which he listed and all of which he professed to consider more important.[6] But it is hardly to be doubted that it was not strategic but political considerations that determined the President's negative response. In an election year the President had no desire to pull English chestnuts out of the Irish fire. Indeed, in Washington as in Dublin, fears were entertained lest the government of the United Kingdom in those desperate days of late June and early July might be tempted in self-defence to seize control of the Irish ports. They were heightened by the British action against the French fleet at Oran. The United States government, however sympathetic to Britain in her hour of trial, was convinced that any such step would be a grave political error. Accordingly, on 8 July Mr. Cordell Hull warned Lord Lothian that any such action would cause serious offence to Irish American

---

[1] Langer & Gleason, i. 523–4.
[2] This account is given by Butler in *Grand Strategy*, ii. 276.   [3] Churchill, ii. 23.
[4] Ibid. pp. 128–9.   [5] Ibid. p. 136.   [6] Quoted in Langer & Gleason, i. 523.

opinion. The British Ambassador reassured him. The British government had no plan to move in unless the Germans moved in first.[1] There was other, and more concrete, evidence that this was so.

The Irish government had made no sustained attempt to equip its forces with modern weapons before the outbreak of war and thus found itself in the crisis of 1940 virtually unarmed by contemporary standards. There were desperate appeals to Washington. On 4 June the Irish government asked urgently for 25 fully equipped fighter planes, 17 armoured cars, and 1,000 rifles as well as ammunition and other items. Its pleas were supported by the British government, providing only that the supply of arms did not impede or delay the consignments to Britain.[2] Had there been any intention at that time of coercing Eire to obtain possession of the ports, such support would not have been forthcoming. It is rather to be regarded as evidence of the seriousness with which the British Chiefs of Staff regarded the prospect of a German assault, perhaps of a diversionary character, upon Ireland. Several attempts indeed were made to reach a prior understanding with the government of Eire about the precise steps to be taken in the event of any such invasion, but they elicited a negative response, on the understandable ground that, if known, any agreement on them would in fact invite aggression. All that was agreed, therefore, was that in the event of actual invasion British aid would be sought at once in a common effort to repel the invader. The United States government, like that of the United Kingdom, believed that no such last-minute appeal would suffice to avert disaster.

The Irish appeals to Washington for arms were backed by the United States Minister in Dublin—other than an additional request for one or more American destroyers, of which Mr. Gray remarked 'the Irish Government has no more use for one destroyer than I have for a white elephant'[3]—but first they got lost in 'the mazes of Washington bureaucracy' and then the United States government evaded them.[4] Any arms supplied to Eire should come, so it was decided in Washington, out of the allocation made to Britain and at the discretion of the United Kingdom government. 'Those dear people you are with', wrote the President to Mr. Gray on 15 August 1940, 'must realize that in the end they will have to fish or cut bait—while, of course, they know that Irish independence is very close to the American heart, nevertheless, there can be no question as between invasion by Germany and protection by England.' When the United States Munitions Board referred to the President Canadian and Irish requests for 80,000 surplus rifles, the President noted on the memorandum 'O.K. for Canada'.[5] Irish requirements, so the Irish Minister in Washington was told, should be met out of the British allocation and that, in fact, was what happened. The purpose of the President and the State Department was to impress upon the

[1] Ibid. p. 718. [2] Ibid. p. 524.
[3] Ibid. p. 717. [4] Ibid. p. 524. [5] Ibid. p. 718.

Irish government that the United States had an important stake in Britain's survival and that it desired the Irish government to co-operate with the British in safeguarding the security of their country against Nazi assault.[1] It was a new experience for the Irish government to find a United States administration so much concerned with the safety of Britain, and a new experience for a United States government to find that Irish independence meant not merely independence of Britain but independence without qualification.

To what extent and in what ways did Ireland figure in German war strategy? What in fact were the chances of a German invasion of Ireland in the summer or early autumn of 1940? To these questions the answer, or at least a substantial part of it, is on record. Germany was anxious not to drive Eire into association with Britain before any possible German invasion had been launched. A memorandum prepared by the Economic Policy Department of the German Foreign Ministry dated 1 June 1940 weighed the advantages and disadvantages of including Eire within the German blockade and concluded on both economic and political grounds that it would be wiser to exclude Ireland from it; the most telling argument for doing so was that any such blockade, being a violation of Irish neutrality, 'might give rise to the idea in Ireland that in an emergency Ireland was to some extent still linked to England for better or worse'.[2] Hitler accepted this conclusion and in his order for the intensification of the blockade in the waters round England and off the French coast to the extent of the original United States combat zone expressed his wish that an exception be made in the case of Ireland 'as otherwise Ireland, instead of being separated from England, will be forced into her arms'.[3] A decision in respect of invasion, which was in any event conditional and contingent in character, was longer delayed.

The German campaign in the Low Countries and France, planned with masterly thoroughness, had been conceived by Hitler as an end in itself— the German knock-out blow in the West—and not as a prelude to the invasion of Britain. The first reference to such a possibility in the minutes of the German Naval Conferences was on 21 May 1940, when Hitler and Raeder discussed in private 'details concerning the invasion of England';[4] it was not again mentioned till 20 June and it was not until six weeks in all had gone by that on 7 July Hitler directed that preparations were to begin. On 11 July he spoke of invasion 'as a last resort',[5] and it was only on 15 July that, changing his mind, he fixed a date, 15 August, by which all preparations were to be completed.[6] This, however, did not mean that Admiral Raeder or the German Naval staff conceived of the invasion as an easy or even a possible undertaking or that they had any enthusiasm for it. On the contrary Admiral Raeder,

---

[1] For an account of United States policy towards Ireland throughout the war see Hull, *Memoirs*, ii. 1351–60.   [2] *D. Ger. F.P.*, ix. 500–1.   [3] Ibid. p. 525.
[4] Report of C-in-C Navy to the Führer, 21 May 1940 (*Brassey's Naval Annual, 1948*, pp. 105–6).   [5] Ibid. p. 115.   [6] Ibid.

especially after he had been informed of the demands of the German General Staff first for the transport of 25–40 divisions, and then more modestly of 13, for the first wave of the landing, was filled with misgivings. On 31 July he recommended postponement till the spring of 1941.[1] Hitler then and later was reluctant to agree, and preparations proceeded for an invasion of south-eastern England to be completed by the date which Raeder considered the earliest possible, namely 15 September 1940. In these plans Ireland had no place. Transport was assembled but 'the operational state which the Naval War Staff . . . gave as the most important pre-requisite for the operation', namely 'clear air superiority in the Channel area and the extinction of all possibilities of enemy Air Force action in the assembly areas', was not achieved. The famous few had postponed, for ever as it proved, Hitler's invasion of Britain. He was extremely loath to admit it[2] and when weather conditions clearly made an attempt impossible in the winter of 1940–1 his mind turned to other means of bringing Britain to her knees which might not involve hazards so great as those of crossing the Channel in the teeth of British naval and air forces. It was at this point that he thought of a German invasion of Ireland. The Naval Staff were instructed to investigate the possibilities, and on 3 December 1940 their report, tendentiously entitled 'The Question of Supporting Ireland against Britain',[3] was tabled.

The memorandum of the German Naval Staff was a well-reasoned case against the invasion of Ireland so long as Britain remained supreme at sea. The first condition for the transfer of troops, it said, was naval supremacy along the routes to be used, and that supremacy could never be attained by Germany in view of the vastly superior British Home Fleet even for the duration of one transport operation. Britain had naval superiority in the ratio of at least 2 to 1 in battleships, 20 to 3 in cruisers, and 70 to 6 or 8 at most in destroyers. There was no possibility of surprise or of establishing a supply line which could be defended. Moreover, 'although the Irish might willingly open their ports to us, they would also be open to the enemy pursuing us'. If a force were successfully landed the topography of the country would afford it little protection, and without supplies or reinforcements it would soon be subject to increasing pressure from a British force landed under the protection of a British Navy enjoying supremacy at sea. Air support would be conditional on the weather and, as the memorandum truly noted, 'Ireland, the westernmost island of any size in the northern Atlantic, is known to have a heavy rainfall and consequently low clouds and very frequent damp and foggy weather.' In addition the airfields were inadequate and 'every attempt at transporting troops by Ju 52's would be in great danger from British

[1] Ibid. pp. 122–5.
[2] Ibid. pp. 136–7. See also F. H. Hinsley, *Hitler's Strategy* (Cambridge University Press, 1951), chs. iv and v.
[3] Reprinted in full, *Brassey's Naval Annual, 1948*, pp. 157–8.

fighters'. It was concluded, therefore, that it would not be possible 'to follow up an Irish request for help by sending an expeditionary force and occupying the island'. The decisive factor was British naval supremacy. All that was held out to Hitler by his naval advisers was the bringing of occasional blockade runners into Irish harbours with weapons and ammunition 'as long as there is still no state of war between Britain and Ireland, and as long as the Irish co-operate'.

Hitler showed some reluctance in accepting this negative conclusion. He allowed that a landing in Ireland could be attempted only if the Irish requested help. The German Minister should, therefore, ascertain whether de Valera desired German support and also whether he might like to have his military equipment supplemented with captured British guns and ammunition which could be sent to him on single steamers. Ireland, too, was important for the Luftwaffe as a base for attack on north-western British ports, though weather conditions still needed investigation. But above all the project was attractive because, as Hitler said, 'the occupation of Ireland might lead to the end of the war'.[1] Accordingly he sought further information, and it is evident from German plans captured in October 1944 that some preliminary preparations were put in hand.[2] But, while weighing the possibilities, Hitler was contemplating a more dramatic move which, while more likely to bring resounding successes to German arms, was less likely to finish the war. The invasion of Ireland and the invasion of Russia were in the first instance at least not part of one plan but alternative courses of action. Hitler decided on the latter.[3]

The invasion of Ireland on a large scale was considered by Hitler and his military advisers only because their plans for the invasion of Britain had been frustrated. The same considerations, notably the superiority of the British naval and air forces, told against it. But even after German abandonment of plans for an invasion of England the superficial attractions of an Irish operation which might end the war remained. Yet if it were seriously to be considered in the face of British air strength and naval superiority, the German forces had to be assured at least of the acquiescence and preferably of the co-operation of the Irish government. Hitler's principal inquiry after the discussion of 3 December was, therefore, on this point. The answer to it had in fact already been given by Mr. de Valera to the German Minister in Dublin some few months before and transmitted by him to Berlin.[4] It was an answer free from ambiguity and must have convinced all who read the record of it that the political consideration which would have encouraged German plans

---

[1] *Brassey's Naval Annual, 1948*, p. 157.

[2] A set of maps prepared for an invasion of Great Britain and Ireland was discovered in Brussels in 1944 after its evacuation by the Germans; it included such items as street plans of every town and village in Great Britain and Ireland and maps of their coasts, with comments on conditions to be expected. The dates of printing were 1940 and 1941; the latest revisions were made in 1943 (*Manchester Guardian*, 18 October 1944).

[3] See Hinsley, *Hitler's Strategy*, chs. v and vi.   [4] See above, p. 67.

for the invasion of Ireland was lacking. In this respect Mr. de Valera had served his country well by unequivocal reassertion of its resolve to defend neutrality against all who threatened it.[1]

The threat of Nazi invasion overhanging both Britain and Ireland in the second half of 1940 helped, by underlining their common danger, to bring their governments into closer accord. The United States government, which was kept informed of the progress of discussions for common defence between London and Dublin, was much reassured to note an improvement in their relations in the autumn of 1940. Mr. Gray, who described the policy of Eire in the summer of 1940 as one of 'nervous neutrality' and who reported in August the conviction of some Irish leaders that Nazi Germany was bound to win, noted by late September, when the threatened invasion of Britain had not been launched and evidence accumulated that London and the principal cities in the United Kingdom could 'take' the savage bombing to which they were subjected, a greater willingness on the part of the Irish government to concert measures to meet a German invasion of Ireland with the government of the United Kingdom. Discussions to this end began in October 1940. It has been claimed with some reason that United States diplomacy had played some part in easing a highly critical situation.[2]

In the winter of 1940–1 and the spring of 1941 as the battle of the Atlantic moved towards its climax a severe strain was once more imposed on Anglo-Irish relations. There were frequent and sometimes provocative references to the burden imposed upon the Royal Navy by its inability to use the Irish ports in the Parliaments both of the United Kingdom and of the oversea dominions.[3] While there was evident concern in London that nothing should be said which would seriously impair relations between the two countries,[4] it was a matter about which strong opinions were entertained. Mr. Churchill continued constant in public and private protest. On 22 November the Prime Minister, stirred by some complaints from Dublin about a critical article in *The Economist*, minuted the Secretary of State for Dominion Affairs that 'the claim now put forward on behalf of de Valera is that we are not only to be strangled by them, but to suffer our fate without making any complaint'; and he asked that the United Kingdom representative in Eire, Sir John Maffey, 'should be made aware of the rising anger in England and Scotland, and especially among the merchant seamen, and he should not be encouraged to think that his only task is to mollify de Valera and make everything, including

---

[1] In writing this section the author, thanks to the assistance of Mr. F. H. Hinsley and of Captain B. H. Liddell Hart, had the opportunity of putting certain points which seemed to require clarification to Field-Marshals von Kesselring and von Manstein and to Generals Blumentritt and Warlimont and of taking their comments upon them into consideration.
[2] Langer & Gleason, i. 719.
[3] Cf. H. of C. Deb., vol. 365, coll. 1261–89 and vol. 371, coll. 743–6; Canada, H. of C. Deb., 1941, vol. 1, pp. 26–27.
[4] e.g. Mr. Duff Cooper, Minister of Information, H. of C. Deb., vol. 365, col. 1047.

our ruin, pass off pleasantly'.[1] On 8 December 1940, in a letter to President Roosevelt recording shipping losses 'on a scale almost comparable to those of the worst year of the last war', Mr. Churchill said that 'denied the use of the ports or territory of Eire in which to organise our coastal patrols by air and sea . . . we have now only one effective route of entry to the British Isles, namely, the Northern Approaches, against which the enemy is increasingly concentrating'. He hoped for

> the good offices of the United States and the whole influence of its Government, continually exerted, to procure for Great Britain the necessary facilities upon the southern and western shores of Eire for our flotillas, and, still more important, for our aircraft, working to the westward into the Atlantic. If it were proclaimed an American interest that the resistance of Great Britain should be prolonged and the Atlantic route kept open . . . the Irish in the United States might be willing to point out to the Government of Eire the dangers which its present policy is creating for the United States itself.[2]

Mr. Churchill, anxious to retain the understanding of the United States in an Irish policy, in which resentment sometimes seemed to outweigh judgement, cabled President Roosevelt once again on 13 December. North Atlantic transport, he wrote, remained the prime anxiety. Britain was so hard pressed that she could no longer carry the 400,000 tons of feeding stuffs and fertilizers hitherto brought by convoy to Eire, and Mr. de Valera was to be so informed. Nor were the subsidies on Irish agricultural produce to be continued. Mr. Churchill hoped these restrictions would make Mr. de Valera more ready to consider common interests.

> You will realise also [he concluded] that our merchant seamen, as well as public opinion generally, take it much amiss that we should have to carry Irish supplies through air and U-boat attacks and subsidise them handsomely when de Valera is quite content to sit happy and see us strangled.[3]

The President was sympathetic, but United States representations to the Irish government to modify its policy of neutrality to the extent of permitting access by British shipping to the Irish ports if anything hardened the Irish resolve to assert and maintain its chosen policy. In his 1941 St. Patrick's Day broadcast to the United States Mr. de Valera complained that Eire was being blockaded by both sides. In Washington this observation made 'a painful impression'.[4] The administration felt that it had no alternative to continued refusal of supplies of arms and of wheat to Eire because it could not be maintained that Eire was contributing to the national security of the United States

---

[1] Churchill, ii. 614.   [2] Ibid. pp. 495–6, 498.
[3] Ibid. pp. 535–6. There was no reference by Mr. Churchill to food supplies from Eire to Britain or to the extent to which, with the adoption of a more constructive policy, they might be increased in time by mutual agreement between the two governments and to the mutual advantage of both countries.   [4] Langer & Gleason, ii. 447–8.

and in Washington at this time the extreme gravity of the British shipping situation and its implication for the United States was the overriding preoccupation. On 27 May 1941 President Roosevelt revealed that the current rate of Nazi sinkings of merchant ships 'was "more than three times the capacity of British shipyards to replace" and "more than twice" the current combined British and American output'.[1] If two American historians speak, not of June 1940, but of May and June 1941 as being Hitler's golden opportunity[2] and as the time when he was closer to victory than ever in the war, the course of the Atlantic battle is their principal and substantial justification. 'Everything was going hellward',[3] exclaimed the depressed, almost defeatist, Mr. Hull. But in Dublin other considerations were uppermost.

There was some resentment in Ireland at United States pressure on a small and virtually defenceless country to take action which might well call for sudden and terrible Nazi retaliation on its people, while the United States, a great and powerful nation seemingly secure on the western side of the Atlantic, remote from all immediate danger, remained conspicuously aloof from the war. There was also some continuing misgiving about Britain's intentions. The Irish government, with the support of the people, had indeed one all-absorbing preoccupation, the preservation of neutrality. It was a policy endorsed by the Dáil, approved by the country, and within the full competence of the Irish Parliament and people, whether the status of Eire at that time be regarded as that of a dominion or a state externally associated with the British Commonwealth of Nations. The ports themselves had been returned by the United Kingdom government at a time when war was evidently imminent and after consideration of the political and strategic factors involved. There was, therefore, no constitutional or political claim which the United Kingdom could advance for their return. Neither Mr. de Valera nor his colleagues desired to see Great Britain 'strangled', a term employed twice by Mr. Churchill, and suggesting positive, malignant feelings on the Irish side. It was possible to explore the treacherous field of moral obligation and some ventured to do so, though they were rarely resolved upon a cool examination of the issues involved. In any event Irish opinion took the view that there was no greater obligation resting upon them to resist Nazi aggression than that resting upon any small country in Western Europe, and none had entered the war except when invaded. There was in fact a dangerous and intractable conflict of immediate interest between a belligerent Britain fighting on alone against the might of Nazi Germany and a neutral Eire preoccupied with the maintenance of a neutrality that had come to be regarded as the final vindication of independence. It is much to the credit of the governments both of the United Kingdom and of Eire that on the whole at this time they persevered in statesmanlike forbearance the one towards the other.

[1] Ibid. p. 460.   [2] Ibid. p. 494.   [3] Ibid. p. 457.

South Africa: War and Politics, May–December 1940

Italian participation brought the war to Africa. Paradoxically this eased the problems facing General Smuts at home. The Union became thereafter no longer a spectator of events taking place in another continent, their interpretation a source of interminable disputation, but an active belligerent on the soil of her own continent. Psychologically this was important; important in the factories which now produced almost all the equipment required by the Union forces—it was no mean achievement—and to the thousands wearing the orange flash on their shoulder straps who had volunteered for service anywhere in Africa. Now they pushed forward through East Africa to take part in the campaign that was destined to overthrow Mussolini's short-lived empire in Abyssinia and thence on to join their comrades from almost all parts of the Commonwealth in the desert war.

It is not, however, to be supposed that the Nationalist Opposition, temporarily reunited in Parliament under the leadership of General Hertzog, were prepared to let pass the hour of Nazi triumphs in the West without seeking once again to challenge the government's policy of participation in the war. Was not the long-expected hour of crisis at hand when the defeat of Britain and the disintegration of the Commonwealth would open the way at last for an Afrikaner republic? The administration was tense and watchful, while ardent republicans prepared for the day of destiny. On 14 July General Hertzog addressed a public letter to the Prime Minister; two days later, with Dr. Malan as a co-signatory, he published a manifesto. In it they protested against continued participation in the war and called on all true Afrikaners to hold demonstrations in favour of peace. Late in August, still seemingly convinced of the inevitability of an early Axis victory, the Herenigde (reunited) Nationalist party sponsored a motion in the House of Assembly, deploring the action of the government in persisting in its war policy and advocating a separate South African peace with Germany and Italy. It was introduced by General Hertzog.[1] His argument was twofold. On the one hand there was the virtual certainty of Britain's defeat: 'England today stands within her own borders a fugitive from the continent of Europe, defeated and threatened, with nearly all her original armaments, munitions and other war material in the hands of the enemy', pursuing the war 'in a spirit strongly permeated by despair', her population of some 50 million facing 80 to a 100 million victorious Germans and an Italy 'well equipped at sea as well as on land and in the air and with its 5,000,000 to 7,000,000 well trained soldiers already in possession of war achievements; nowhere, so far as we are aware, in this conflict, so far surpassed by British acts of bravery....' On the other there was the plight of 'poor South Africa', too weak to be able to contribute anything either to the benefit of Europe or to her own defence against either of 'the two giants

[1] South Africa, H. of A. Deb., vol. 40, coll. 79–89; cf. Roberts & Trollip, p. 38.

against whom it has so irresponsibly declared war', and 'now doomed like a second Sancho Panzo to serve as Europe's imperial satellite'. With the war already 'hopelessly' lost it would be 'fatal folly' for South Africa to continue to participate in it. Favourable consideration from the victors was dependent upon peace now. 'If Germany wins this war', argued Dr. Malan in a more clearly-reasoned utterance supporting the same policy of a separate peace, 'we are in the position . . . that the war aims of Germany and our desire to have a republic in South Africa clash with each other, unless we make it clear to Germany that the people of South Africa repudiate the Prime Minister and his declaration of war and his continuance of the war.'[1] But were the republic to be declared, then, argued Dr. Malan, Germany might possibly be satisfied because 'she will say that the separation of a dominion from the British Empire, weakens that empire and that is her object'. The choice before them, he concluded, was therefore 'a republic or annexation by Germany, a Hitler republic'. Dr. Malan's chief concern was to avoid the second alternative, and so while the opportunity remained he wished to place South Africa in a favourable position to negotiate with Germany in the event of a Nazi victory.

The deep-rooted conviction of Afrikaner Nationalists that dominion status was not synonymous with sovereignty, but was rather a shackle by which South Africa had been dragged into the war by imperialists in South Africa and in Britain, reinforced strongly their desire to extricate themselves from the war and to declare a republic. Eire, it was argued, enjoyed greater freedom because she had renounced dominion status, and Dr. Malan discerned in the Ogdensburg Agreement a move by Canada 'to get free from England'.[2] 'There is only one way of getting rid of this terrible condition of affairs', declared Mr. Strijdom, 'and that is by doing away with the British connection and getting a free South African Republic. Then we could not be dragged into such a war as we have now been dragged into.'[3]

It seems, therefore, that the prospect of a Nazi victory, the desire to make favourable terms with the victor, a continuing sense of the subordination of South Africa to Britain despite the free vote in the House of Assembly early in September 1939, and more positively hopes of an Afrikaner republic and of Afrikaner unity all played their part in strengthening the Nationalist demand for peace with Italy and Germany. The motion they sponsored was defeated in the House of Assembly on 31 August 1940 by 83 votes to 65, but none the less it marked the high tide of Nationalist strength in critical wartime divisions.[4] For the government this was the crucial challenge. Thereafter the actual voting strength of the Opposition in important divisions declined, owing more to internal divisions than to an early appreciation of the changing fortunes of war.

[1] 30 August 1940, South Africa, H. of A. Deb., vol. 40, col. 273.
[2] Ibid. col. 267.   [3] Ibid. col. 324.
[4] The government majority (ibid. coll. 415–19) was smaller than in the two previous motions of neutrality.

Some considerable time elapsed before Nationalist expectation of a Nazi victory, which by no means all the members of the reunited party desired, was seriously undermined, but on the long term it was at the least imprudent, as Dr. Malan would seem to have sensed, for General Hertzog to relate his motion for separate peace in August 1940 so closely to his belief that the Axis would win the war. Ultimately few things redounded more greatly to the advantage of General Smuts. He at least had been sufficiently clear sighted to back the right horse. Moreover it served also to associate the Nationalist party, which was a 'constitutional' party in the public mind, with Opposition groups, unconstitutional in their methods and in their aims.

The Ossewa Brandwag, founded at Bloemfontein in October 1938, the centenary of the Great Trek, was chief among them, its first formal constitution dating from May and its first congress from July 1940. Originally intended to perpetuate the idealism which the 1938 convention had inspired, its commando organization with a Kommandant-Generaal at its head, coupled with the military discipline imposed on its members, acquired a fresh significance in the summer of 1940. More openly totalitarian in aim and method was the New Order group of which the egregious Mr. Pirow became the acknowledged leader. Both were a source of genuine concern to Dr. Malan, who disliked their methods, resented their implicit challenge to the authority of the Nationalist party, and adjured the faithful to follow experienced and well-tried leaders lest they be led to disaster.[1] The great majority of Afrikaner Nationalists were, in fact, averse to violence and sincerely desirous that their republican ideals should be achieved by constitutional means on the broad basis of the people's will. For this reason the tolerant attitude of the Union government to the Ossewa Brandwag and the New Order group was well founded in calculation. If under the impact of Nazi victories the Nationalist movement as a whole inclined perceptibly towards Nazi doctrines of 'Blut und Boden', it remained predominantly a constitutional movement.[2] Faithful Hertzogites could never embrace totalitarian doctrines which so evidently conflicted with all that their venerable leader had taught about the ultimate mingling of the two streams of European culture in one South African republican nation, whilst the more numerous Malanites, though resolved upon a republic that was predominantly Afrikaner in culture and in race, none the less firmly repudiated the notion of a republic imposed by force and authoritarian in character. The growing strength of the Ossewa Brandwag in late 1940 was therefore a threat to the parliamentary Nationalist party and its leadership which they could not afford to ignore.

The parliamentary Nationalist party was not itself united. General Hertzog's neutrality motion at the outbreak of the war had seemingly paved the way for the reunion of Afrikanerdom and 4 September 1939 was spoken of by

[1] Cf. Roberts & Trollip, ch. iv. [2] Ibid.

Nationalists as the date of the rebirth of Afrikanerdom.[1] Though Hertzog was too obstinate and too proud to disavow his past, and too principled to abandon his ultimate aim of equality between the two European races, a compromise formula led, as has been seen, in January 1940 to his election to the leadership of a reunited parliamentary Nationalist party. But at heart there was no reconciliation, above all on the supreme issue of how and in what circumstances a republic was to come into being—whether, as Hertzog insisted, with English acquiescence won and with full equality for English-speaking South Africans, or, as Malan contemplated, at the will of Afrikaners and essentially for Afrikaners with English-speaking South Africans either being assimilated or occupying some ill-defined but inferior status. And because there was no reconciliation on fundamental questions, intrigues nourished on unforgiving resentments plagued the reunited party. General Hertzog was fully aware of the bitterness of many of the purified Nationalists against him and, always intolerant of opposition, he was not prepared to be a leader on sufferance. When, therefore, his views were challenged on 6 November 1940 in his own Orange Free State in the very heart of Afrikanerdom, he resigned dramatically from the leadership and from the party with his faithful lieutenant, Mr. Havenga, as ever beside him.[2] But even with his resignation party unity lay in the future. And so, while domestic divisions preoccupied his opponents, General Smuts, with his clear, consistent advocacy in good and evil days of war till victory was won, slowly but surely strengthened a position that in September 1939 and again in the summer of 1940 had been precarious.

INDIAN REACTIONS TO THE FALL OF FRANCE AND THE ESTABLISHMENT OF THE EASTERN SUPPLY COUNCIL

The Viceroy declared war on behalf of India in September 1939 under authority vested in him by the Government of India Act, 1919, which remained in force in respect of the central government because the federation contemplated in the Government of India Act, 1935 had not come into existence, owing to princely non-co-operation. Within India all the principal parties, the Congress, the Muslim League, and the princes were united in the condemnation of Nazi aggression but in little else. The Congress was affronted by the manner in which war was declared, and the Viceroy's 'imposed decision', as the Working Committee described it, was 'necessarily' opposed by it. 'If cooperation is desired in a worthy cause', so the Congress claimed, 'this cannot be obtained by compulsion and imposition.'[3] But the Congress had never doubted that resistance to Nazi or Fascist aggression was 'a worthy

[1] Cf. Rev. S. W. Naudé, South Africa, H. of A. Deb., vol. 40, col. 235.
[2] See Roberts & Trollip, pp. 46–54, and C. M. van den Heever, *General J. B. M. Hertzog* (Johannesburg, A.P.B. Bookstore, 1946), pp. 278–91.
[3] *Indian Annual Register, 1939*, ii. 226–7.

cause' and indeed for many years had been foremost in its denunciations of the new European tyrannies. Its co-operation in the war effort was, therefore, withheld because of India's continuing subjection to British rule. The Muslim League, less critical of the declaration of war by an external authority, was fearful lest the British government, in its endeavours to enlist Congress support by conceding if only in part its constitutional demands, should prejudice Muslim interests and so it became the more vehement in its assertion of them. If the resignation of the Congress ministries in the provinces was celebrated as a day of deliverance from Congress oppression, in December 1939, if federation was rejected and Pakistan declared to be the goal of Muslim India at Lahore in March 1940,[1] these were primarily intended as formal and final repudiation of all thought of Muslim acquiescence in Congress rule, but they served also as warnings to the British government of the risks of concessions to Congress claims. As such they were well heeded in London where there was little, and in Delhi where there was less, disposition on the part of the British rulers to hasten the transfer of power. Dominion status, it is true, was the goal of British rule, but was it part of Britain's responsibility or, indeed, of the course of wisdom to continue to try to bring nearer the day of its realization? If during the early months of the war the Secretary of State for India, Lord Zetland, had some passing doubts, they were not shared by the Viceroy.

After all [wrote Lord Linlithgow in response to an expression of them] we framed the Constitution as it stands in the Act of 1935, because we thought that way the best way—given the political position in both countries—of maintaining British influence in India. It is no part of our policy, I take it, to expedite in India constitutional changes for their own sake, or gratuitously to hurry the handing over of controls to Indian hands at any pace faster than we regard as best calculated on a long view, to hold India to the Empire.[2]

The most the Viceroy was prepared to concede was that with the progress of the war it might become necessary to consider a new approach to the Indian problem, but he did not think the time for so doing had arrived in the winter of 1939–40. Indeed it seemed likely that Lord Linlithgow would not easily be persuaded that the right time had ever come.

By May 1940 the Indian political situation had hardened in the mould set on the outbreak of the war.[3] The British raj was engaged in the war without qualification, the Indian princes with some few reservations lent their support, the attitude of the Muslim League was acquiescent but not unco-

---

[1] See Mansergh, *Survey, 1931–9*, pp. 354–7 and below pp. 205–6.
[2] Marquess of Zetland, *'Essayez'; the Memoirs of Lawrence, Second Marquess of Zetland* (London, Murray, 1956), pp. 276–7.
[3] For a fuller account of events following the outbreak of war see Mansergh, *Survey, 1931–9*, pp. 407–14.

operative, that of the Indian National Congress non-cooperative. Congress non-cooperation was, however, not absolute but conditional. India unfree, so the Congress maintained, could not fight for freedom, or, to restate the condition of co-operation in its familiar constitutional context, Congress support for the war effort was dependent upon acceptance by the British government of its demand that the Government of India Act of 1935 should be set aside and that, in the words of the all-Indian Congress Committee's resolution of October 1939, India 'be declared an independent nation and present application . . . given to this status to the largest possible extent'.[1] This was a concession the British government was not prepared to make and a demand which the Muslim League was not prepared to support, for while the League agreed with the Congress that the Act of 1935 should be scrapped, its continuing co-operation in the war effort was conditional upon assurances that no new constitution should be framed without the consent and approval of the League, 'the only organization that can speak on behalf of Muslim India'. Confronted with conflicting claims the government of India favoured the not uncongenial policy of waiting upon domestic developments.

The deadlock was not broken by the events of 1940 but the relationship of the three principal parties was modified. This was due principally to the weakening of the power and prestige of the British raj as a result of the German victories in the West. The position hitherto enjoyed by the government of India was destined never to be regained. Slowly but inevitably the realization that this was so introduced the final and most bitter phase in the struggle for power within India. In such circumstances the British government could not continue to rule India on what at times was perilously close to a negation of all policy. Inaction was the privilege of unquestioned authority.

The attitude of all sections of Indian opinion to Britain in her hour of peril was in itself, and by contrast with predominant Afrikaner Nationalist sentiment, markedly sympathetic. 'We do not seek our independence out of Britain's ruin', said Gandhi. 'England's difficulty is not India's opportunity', said Pandit Nehru, but it was no use asking India 'to come to the rescue of a tottering imperialism'.[2] There was, he recorded later, a powerful current of sympathy for England and France after Dunkirk and during the air blitz. There were some people 'who thought that England's difficulty and peril were India's opportunity, but the leaders of the Congress were definitely opposed to any such advantage being taken of a situation full of disastrous foreboding for England'.[3] A civil disobedience campaign which was about to begin was accordingly called off.

---

[1] *Indian Annual Register, 1939*, ii. 226–8. See also Sir Reginald Coupland, *India, a Re-Statement* (London, Oxford University Press, 1945), pp. 196–8.
[2] Quoted Coupland, *India*, p. 199.
[3] Nehru, *Discovery of India*; see pp. 442–6, for his reflections on this period.

In the summer of 1940 Gandhi favoured both for Britain and for India 'a nobler way' than fighting. It was the way of non-resistance. For Congressmen to aid the war effort or to set their hand to the war machine, he warned, would be 'a disaster of the first magnitude'. The Congress, none the less, was not prepared to commit itself as an organization to a policy of out-and-out pacifism. While publicly absolving Gandhi of all responsibility for it, the Congress adopted a programme which envisaged the organization of defence and of public security by Congressmen, though not in co-operation with the government. On 7 July it went further; it showed itself prepared, for co-operation with the government on terms less absolute than those advanced hitherto. Its principal condition was the formation of a provisional national government at the centre so constituted as to command the confidence of all sections of the Legislative Assembly. Statutory and constitutional changes were left dependent upon future discussion and, in Mr. Nehru's words, until 'a more favorable opportunity', provided only that 'India's claim to complete freedom was recognized'. This represented a toning down of the earlier and oft-repeated Congress demands and Pandit Nehru records that 'it was no easy matter for the Congress to put forward this proposal after all its past declarations and experiences'. 'I agreed chiefly because of larger international considerations', he writes, 'and my desire that, if it was at all honorably possible, we should identify ourselves completely with the struggle against fascism and nazism.'

The concessions the Congress was prepared to make were threefold. First there was the professed readiness to enter into a composite government so as to meet the claims of the minorities and especially of the Muslim League; secondly there was agreement that the Viceroy should remain as Head of State until otherwise decided; and thirdly that continuing control over war administration should be exercised by the Commander-in-Chief. In sum these concessions were by no means insubstantial. Gandhi publicly dissented from them on the ground that in no circumstances should the Congress agree to undertake responsibility 'for a violent war effort', and this time he broke with his colleagues and the Congress. The Viceroy, however, was little stirred. 'Heavy of body and slow of mind', writes Pandit Nehru bitterly, 'solid as a rock and with almost a rock's lack of awareness, possessing the qualities and failings of an old-fashioned British aristocrat', Lord Linlithgow sought 'with integrity and honesty of purpose to find a way out of the tangle. But his limitations were too many; his mind worked in the old groove and shrank back from any innovations . . . ; he distrusted . . . fundamental political and social changes.' Behind the Viceroy Pandit Nehru discerned the formidable figure of Mr. Churchill, an uncompromising opponent of the Government of India Act and remembered by Indian nationalists as the man who had said in 1930 'sooner or later you will have to crush Gandhi and the Indian Congress and all they stand for'. But even though 'the gulf between Mr.

Churchill and us was vast', Pandit Nehru acknowledged that 'he was a big man who could take a big step'.

The British government did take a step. It was not, however, a big step. Nor did it carry it in the direction the Indian National Congress wished it to move. The government's so called 'August offer' agreed that there should be a new constitution, its drafting to be 'primarily the responsibility of Indians themselves'; but first British obligations in respect notably of defence, of minority rights, and of treaties with the Indian princes would have to be fulfilled, and secondly minority opinion should not be overridden. 'It goes without saying', continued the United Kingdom government's statement, 'that they could not contemplate the transfer of their present responsibilities for the peace and welfare of India to any system of government whose authority is directly denied by large and powerful elements in Indian national life.' Nor could constitutional issues be discussed at a moment when 'the Commonwealth is engaged in a battle for existence'. After the war an Indian constitution-making body would be set up and in the meantime there would be some enlargement of the Central Executive Council and the establishment of an Advisory Council.[1]

The 'August offer' concluded with the hope that all parties would co-operate in the war effort and so pave the way for India's attainment of free and equal status in the British Commonwealth of Nations. That hope was not fulfilled. The League, it is true, welcomed the statement as evidence that minority interests would be respected. It meant, as interpreted in the resolution of the League's Working Committee, that 'no future constitution interim or final' would be created 'without the League's assent', and that in effect meant that the partition of India, on which the League had taken its stand, was henceforward 'the only solution'.[2] For the Congress the 'August offer' was an open rebuff. The President of the Congress, Maulana Azad, declined to discuss it with the Viceroy. Pandit Nehru regarded it as 'an insolent repulse' which failed to camouflage 'Britain's determination to hold on to India at all costs'.[3] Thereafter the whole conception of dominion status for India was 'dead as a doornail'. The treatment of minorities, complained the Congress Working Committee, 'has been made into an insuperable barrier to India's progress'.[4] Yet it may be that the Congress, by its flat rejection of an admittedly unpalatable offer—excluding even discussion of it—missed an opportunity. 'In wartime', V. P. Menon has noted, 'there was no question of converting the Executive Council into a national government. Lord Linlithgow was firm on this issue and so was His Majesty's Government.' Had the Congress frankly recognized that this was so, and had it consequently temporarily

---

[1] Cmd. 6219. [2] *Indian Annual Register, 1940*, ii. 243–5.
[3] Nehru, *Discovery of India*, p. 447.
[4] *Indian Annual Register, 1940*, ii. 196–8. See also Coupland, *India*, pp. 202–3, where this and other extracts are quoted.

withdrawn its demand for a national government and agreed to join the Viceroy's Executive Council, then the way would have been open for the Congress ministries to come back into power in the provinces and, concludes V. P. Menon, 'the political situation would have changed immensely to the advantage of the Congress'.[1] As it was, however, the events of the summer of 1940, which at first had seemed to narrow the gulf between British and Indian opinion, ended in bringing about a new and greater estrangement between the government of India and the Indian National Congress and between the Indian National Congress and the Muslim League. Variously though responsibility may be allocated, the outcome could not on any reckoning be regarded as reflecting credit on the skill or insight of British statesmanship.

In the Indian Ocean as in the Atlantic Ocean the fall of France, the entry of Italy into the war, and the overhanging threat of Nazi invasion of Britain encouraged the Commonwealth countries in the area to assume new regional responsibilities. The virtual severance of the traditional lifeline of the Empire through the Mediterranean and the Suez Canal brought together representatives of the Commonwealth countries east and south of Suez in the autumn of 1940 in an attempt to plan the better use and distribution of the resources collectively at their disposal. They met in Delhi in October, and Lord Linlithgow at the opening meeting suggested that the Eastern Group Conference, as it was described, fell into a category 'almost unique' in the political experience of the British Commonwealth.[2] The novelty, in so far as it existed, lay in the assumption of responsibilities by a group of Commonwealth countries in the interests of the whole. Those responsibilities were, first to attempt to make the Commonwealth countries in the area self-supporting in respect of their war needs, and secondly to help in increasing measure in supplying the war needs of the United Kingdom. The pooling of resources and the planning of production over a wide field were the means employed.

Australia, New Zealand, South Africa, India, and Burma were represented at the Delhi Conference, as well as Southern Rhodesia, Ceylon, Hong Kong, Malaya, and Palestine, among colonial and mandated territories, and the United Kingdom, which sent a Ministry of Supply mission. When its deliberations ended a standing conference was established known as the Eastern Group Supply Council, but its machinery was not completed until the Central Provisions Office was set up in March 1941, with the responsibility of provisioning the troops in the Middle and Far East and of co-ordinating the military demands of countries within the region which could not be satisfied from their indigenous production. The Council itself undertook the collection of information about the resources and production capacities of the

---

[1] V. P. Menon, *The Transfer of Power in India* (London, Longmans, 1957), p. 97.
[2] Marquess of Linlithgow, *Speeches and Statements, 1936–43* (New Delhi, Bureau of Public Information, 1945), pp. 256–60 (Mansergh, *Documents*, i. 542–4).

Eastern Group countries, the handling of their requests for assistance in procuring stores which were in short supply, and the investigation of the possibilities of their supplying materials required by the Indian army. In the course of its work the Council assembled much information, some of lasting as well as of immediate value, about the productive capacities of the area.

The usefulness of the Eastern Group Supply Council was related to the amount of food and war materials produced by its member countries. In some instances this was notably increased under stress of war. On the other hand one of its members, Australia, co-operated only with important reservations,[1] and more generally the effective discharge of the Council's responsibilities was dependent upon the availability of shipping[2] and other means of transport. Its period of useful existence was shortlived. Within six months of the outbreak of war in the Far East the Council became dependent for the bulk of its supplies on the resources of two countries, India and South Africa. In 1943 its functions were transferred to the Ministry of Supply Mission.

The Eastern Group Supply Council had relieved Britain of some share of her overseas military supply responsibilities, especially in the Middle East, at the most critical phase in the European war, and in so doing afforded some further evidence of the extent to which decentralization of responsibilities might contribute to the effectiveness of the war effort. The pattern set in Delhi in 1940 was followed in July 1941 with the creation of the Middle East Supply Centre in Cairo. Its far greater importance was reflected in the appointment of Mr. Oliver Lyttelton, a member of the War Cabinet, as its Chairman. None of the dominions were, however, directly represented. The contributions of the Eastern Group Supply Council and the Middle East Supply Centre, while valuable, were possibly over-valued, and encouraged later a somewhat undiscriminating predisposition to create Commonwealth regional organizations and groupings for political or economic purposes.

Consultation on Defence in the Pacific, June–December 1940

Mr. Menzies's expostulations about lack of information on Dakar were symptomatic of, and prompted by, concern about what appeared to the Australian government to be inadequacies in the system of Commonwealth consultation and co-operation. Mounting Australian anxieties about the Pacific further underlined the deep misgivings already entertained on this

[1] For an account of the Australian reservations see Hasluck, i. 302. The prior claims of home defence were restated and any policy of Australian dependence on India was rejected, firstly because of the Imperial Conference principles of responsibility for local defence and self-sufficiency in munitions, secondly because of the wartime risks of sea transport, and thirdly because of such political factors as the possible attitude of India after the attainment of self-government. There is further discussion of the Australian position in Butlin, *War Economy, 1939–42*, pp. 335–41.

[2] Cf. C. B. A. Behrens, *Merchant Shipping and the Demands of War* (London, HMSO and Longmans, 1955), pp. 202–6.

score. The dramatic victories of the Reichswehr in the west in the early summer of 1940 could not but encourage Japanese militarists to feel that their hour too had come at last. On 28 June 1940 the United Kingdom government, hitherto reassuring in its communications, expressed the belief, in a telegram to the governments of Australia and New Zealand, that 'in spite of the possible hostility of the United States of America and Russia, the deterrent of the Japanese commitments in China, and our military and economic strength', Japan must be contemplating how best to take advantage of this favourable moment to improve her position. While the Chiefs of Staff did not regard war with Japan as necessarily imminent, they recognized how great for her must be the temptation to strike a sudden blow. The security of imperial interests in the Far East depended upon Britain's ability to control sea communications in the south-west Pacific, and that was conditional upon the presence of an adequate fleet based on Singapore. But with the French collapse this became impossible. As the Chiefs of Staff stated, 'we must retain in European waters sufficient naval forces to match both the German and Italian fleets, and we cannot do this and send a fleet to the Far East'.[1] Even the possibility of a Japanese invasion of Australia and New Zealand, which for so long had haunted the minds of many Australians, could no longer be discounted. Mr. Churchill, in what he described as a brief foreword (it was in fact of some considerable length), to this strategic appreciation offered the Prime Ministers of the two dominions such reassurance as lay in his power. 'If . . . contrary to prudence and self-interest', he wrote on 11 August 1940, 'Japan set about invading Australia or New Zealand on a large scale, I have the explicit authority of the Cabinet to assure you that we should then cut our losses in the Mediterranean and sacrifice every interest, except only the defence and feeding of this Island.' Such were the bleak realities with which the government of the United Kingdom confronted the Pacific dominions. Its first preoccupation was to gain time.

> We are trying our best to avoid war with Japan [wrote Mr. Churchill] both by conceding on points where the Japanese military clique can perhaps force a rupture, and by standing up where the ground is less dangerous. . . . In adopting against the grain a yielding policy towards Japanese threats we have always in mind your interests and safety.[2]

There were doubts, most marked in New Zealand and frankly expressed by its government, about the wisdom of such a policy, but they were not pushed to the point of disagreement.[3]

On 27 June 1940 Mr. R. G. Casey, appointed first Australian Minister to Washington in January 1940, and Mr. Cordell Hull took part in discussions on the situation in the Far East with Lord Lothian. Australia supported

---

[1] *N.Z. Documents*, vol. 1, no. 214, pp. 158–9. [2] Churchill, ii. 385–6.
[3] See Wood, ch. xviii for New Zealand reactions.

United Kingdom proposals for overtures designed to end the 'China incident', and Mr. Casey expressed Australia's willingness to resume exports of iron ore to Japan, if Japan, China, and Britain were prepared to make concessions in the Far East to restore peace there.¹ Britain and Australia,² negotiating from a position of extreme weakness, were in fact tempted to buy time in the Far East by conciliatory gestures, whereas the United States from a position of strength had no need to be accommodating. But it is to be noted that Mr. Churchill at any rate had no greater faith in a policy of appeasement in the East than he had had earlier in the West, and on 20 July 1940 he minuted the Foreign Secretary suggesting 'we might go very slow on all this general and equitable, fair and honourable peace business between China and Japan', if only because 'I am sure that it is not in our interest that the Japanese should be relieved of their preoccupation.'³ None the less Britain acceded to the pointed Japanese request for the closing of the Burma Road, because of fear of a Japanese onslaught on South-East Asia should she refuse, while the Australian appointment of Sir John Latham as first Australian Minister to Japan in August 1940 indicated Australia's desire at once to improve her relations with Japan and to acquire independent information about Japanese policies and intentions.⁴ There was, however, no fundamental difference in United Kingdom and Australian attitudes towards Japan in the summer and autumn of 1940, though there is some evidence to suggest that the Australian government had more constantly in mind at this time the desirability of the closest co-ordination of British and United States policies.

The Australian government was somewhat concerned lest its belated appointment of Ministers to Washington and Tokyo should be taken to imply a dissociation of Australian from United Kingdom policy. The appointment of an Australian Minister to Japan would, so Mr. McEwen told the House of Representatives on 20 August 1940,⁵ 'in no sense alter the very close collaboration between the Governments of Australia and the other dominions and the Government of the United Kingdom in reference to all matters affecting foreign policy and especially Far Eastern policy'. 'I wish to remove that misapprehension', said his successor, Sir Frederick Stewart, some six months later on the same point,⁶ 'by stating clearly and emphatically that there is no such differentiation in policy and that Australia's desire is to share in the responsibilities of the British Commonwealth and to preserve its unity.' Consultations between Britain, Australia, and the other dominions on Far Eastern policy at this time would seem fully to substantiate these assertions.

On 18 July 1940 Lord Halifax's announcement of Britain's decision not to extend the Anglo-Japanese Agreement beyond the end of 1940 provoked

---
¹ Hull, *Memoirs*, i. 896–9. See also Langer & Gleason, vol. 1, ch. xvii and vol. 2, *passim* for a detailed account of United States policy in the Far East.   ² Cf. Hasluck, i. 524–7.
³ Churchill, ii. 571.   ⁴ Australia, H. of R. Deb., vol. 164, p. 420.
⁵ Ibid.   ⁶ Ibid. 3 April 1941, vol. 166, p. 687.

inquiries, prompted largely by knowledge of United States interest in this aspect of British policy, as to whether the Canadian Prime Minister had been consulted before a decision had been reached. Lord Halifax replied that Canada had been kept fully informed of what the government had in mind.[1] The next day Mr. Mackenzie King, however, explained that 'no advice was tendered by the government of Canada to the government of the United Kingdom'. 'If the government of Canada', he added, 'had felt at the time that it was advisable to comment, it would have been done, but no comment was made.'[2] On the other hand the Australian Minister for External Affairs, Mr. McEwen, assured the House of Representatives on 6 August 1940 that the Australian government in common with the government of New Zealand had been taken fully into consultation by the United Kingdom government and that Australian views had been a real factor in all discussions with the United Kingdom and the Japanese governments in respect of the Burma Road and other outstanding issues.[3] This was elaborated on 28 November 1940 when the new Minister for External Affairs, Sir Frederick Stewart, confirmed that on 17 July the British government, after consultation with the Australian and other dominion governments, undertook to close the Burma Road for a 'period of three months', and later declared its intention not to renew this agreement on its expiration on 18 October. This step, he said, had been taken with the full concurrence of the Australian government.[4]

The lack, as it seemed to the Australian government and its military advisers, of any sufficient sense of urgency in London about remedying defence deficiencies at Singapore prompted more critical observations. A proposal made in August by the United Kingdom Chiefs of Staff for a Far Eastern Defence Conference engaged the attention of the Australian and New Zealand governments in the autumn of 1940. An Australian suggestion that the Conference should be held in Melbourne gave way to a decision to hold it in Singapore. The Conference accordingly took place there from 22 to 31 October 1940, and reviewed the defence position and requirements of the South-East Asian and Pacific areas in the event of a Japanese attack. The United Kingdom view was that Singapore was the key to the British Commonwealth's defensive position, and that Australia and New Zealand and the British possessions in the Far East would best be defended by an adequate concentration of forces in Malaya. The possibility of a major expedition against Australia and New Zealand initially was ruled out, but home defences against raids and forces for convoy and other duties had necessarily to be maintained. In the light of information received from the Australian delegation to the Conference, Mr. Menzies informed the Advisory War Council on 25 November of 'the alarming position in regard to the defence of Singapore'.[5]

[1] H. of L. Deb., vol. 116, col. 1043. [2] Canada, H. of C. Deb., 1940, vol. 2, p. 1765.
[3] Australia, H. of R. Deb., vol. 164, p. 188. [4] Ibid. vol. 165, p. 251.
[5] Hasluck, i. 296; see also pp. 294–8 from which this account is drawn.

There was general agreement that Mr. Menzies should go to London to talk about this and other matters with Mr. Churchill. On 1 December the Australian government cabled the Dominions Office[1] urging that immediate steps be taken to remedy the deficiencies in the army and air forces at Singapore in view of the inadequacy of the naval forces available. There was an 'unenthusiastic' offer of Australian troops for Malaya. On 2 December the Australian War Cabinet agreed that Mr. Menzies should communicate with London about the possibility 'of basing three or four capital ships at Singapore as a deterrent to Japanese action in this region'. But, as Mr. Hasluck observes, 'the pathetic extremities in which the British Commonwealth found itself are revealed most pointedly in the plain facts' that the weapons and above all the naval strength on which Far Eastern security was based were not available.

It was this lack of all adequate defence and seemingly of a sufficient sense of urgency about it in Britain that prompted successive Australian governments to send special personal missions to London in an attempt to bring about a greater awareness of Australian anxieties, more effective representation of Australian views, and a larger Australian share in the making of critical decisions involving the disposition of forces in the Far East and the ultimate security of Australia herself. It could be regarded as axiomatic, said Mr. John Curtin, the leader of the Labour party, that people and Parliament in Australia hoped for the closest collaboration between governments of the British Commonwealth, in respect both of the conduct of the war and also of the conduct of international relations which was inseparable from it, but collaboration meant something very much more than being informed about developments and

being in the position of having to accept whatever may be the situation without any attempt to deal with it. I submit that collaboration means not only receipt by the Commonwealth Government of the views of the Imperial Government, but also the consideration of those views and rejoinder and even a negativing of these views.[2]

Mr. W. J. McKell, then leader of the New South Wales Labour Opposition, went one step further, saying that Australia should insist on representation in London where war policy was decided.

It is our duty [he said] to see that Imperial War Policy should be decided and carried out in a manner which will ensure that our men shall not be used in half-hearted ventures. . . . Australia must have its say in the conduct of the war. It cannot do so by telephone or cable. The nation demands representation in an Empire War Cabinet.[3]

This was an overstatement. No less a personality than the redoubtable Mr. W. M. Hughes, a survivor of the Imperial War Cabinet of 1917–18, dissented,

---

[1] This cable was repeated to the New Zealand government.
[2] Australia, H. of R. Deb., vol. 164, p. 189.
[3] Sydney *Daily Telegraph*, 27 September 1940.

maintaining on behalf of the government that an Imperial War Cabinet would not achieve more than the existing methods of consultation. But the Australian people, politically divided, oppressed by new responsibilities and new anxieties, aware that the Royal Navy no longer shielded the long Australian coastline from invasion, for the most part concluded that direct Australian representation in the War Cabinet in London would be in their interests, if only because it would ensure that the United Kingdom government, in its pressing preoccupation with the air assault at home and the growing German and Italian strength in North Africa, would not neglect Pacific needs or overlook Pacific anxieties. Labour support for the government on this issue, significant in itself, notably strengthened the hand of the Australian government, and more particularly of Mr. Menzies on his visit to London in the early spring of 1941.[1]

Means and Ends: Canadian and United Kingdom Views on Methods of Co-operation, February–April 1941

The United Kingdom government at no time expressed strong views about the desirability or otherwise of the reconstitution of an Imperial War Cabinet. Its role was that of an honest broker and if, on occasion, in ministerial speeches, some trace of impatience obtruded at reiterated criticisms evidently based on imperfect acquaintance with the existing methods of co-operation, that did not qualify repeated assurances that in this respect the United Kingdom government was willing to do as the dominions wished. For its part, however, it was not prepared to take the initiative, and on 3 December 1940 the Deputy Prime Minister, Mr. Attlee, stated categorically that the Prime Minister did not contemplate the addition of representatives of the dominions to the United Kingdom War Cabinet.[2] But it was from a dominion statesman, appropriately perhaps, that the question received its first authoritative examination. In a speech on 17 February 1941 in the Canadian House of Commons[3] Mr. Mackenzie King analysed the reasons for and against any substantial modification of the existing machinery for Commonwealth consultation and wartime co-operation. He recognized that the imposing title Imperial War Cabinet had for many a certain appeal, and he allowed that an Imperial War Council composed of the Prime Ministers of the dominions and of the British Secretary of State for Foreign Affairs and presided over by the Prime Minister of Great Britain would in fact be an imposing body. It would also suggest opportunities for direct and intimate conference in the shaping of common war policy such as did not at that time exist. Yet, Mr. Mackenzie King argued, imposing externals mattered little, and what needed to be examined was whether the creation of any such body would or would not be

[1] See below p. 95.
[2] H. of C. Deb., vol. 367, col. 435.
[3] Canada, H. of C. Deb., 1941, vol. 1, pp. 811–13 (Mansergh, *Documents*, i. 528–32).

the most effective means of achieving the desired end. He maintained that it would not. Already, he argued, such a Council existed in reality although it had no physical form. Those matters of high policy which came before the Imperial War Cabinet at the close of the First World War were today discussed between the several governments of the Commonwealth by direct communication. Since 1918 the cable had been supplemented by the wireless and the transatlantic telephone. Each dominion had its Department of External Affairs efficiently organized and in a position to supply the information essential for the proper discussion of any problem.[1] Moreover dominion governments were all represented in London, and the United Kingdom in all the dominions, by High Commissioners who were at all times available for consultation with the government to which they were accredited.

There were, Mr. Mackenzie King explained, three sending and three receiving sources through each of which special classes of communication were sent and received. The first, relating to matters of high policy, was from Prime Minister to Prime Minister direct, the second was from the Secretary of State for Dominion Affairs to the Secretaries of State for External Affairs, and the third special communications, supplementing those from the two sources already mentioned, between High Commissioners and Prime Ministers or Secretaries of State. Not a day passed, said the Canadian Prime Minister, but that communications in considerable number came backwards and forwards between London and Ottawa, and in general the means of communication and consultation in all matters seemed to him to be so effective and comprehensive that he doubted if a more efficient arrangement could be devised. It was a real, if invisible, Imperial Council that was made possible by these means of constant and instantaneous conference, and it had one all-important advantage which would be denied to an Imperial War Cabinet sitting in London. It afforded to the Prime Minister of each of the dominions an opportunity of discussing immediately with his colleagues in his own Cabinet every question raised. Here indeed was the crux of the whole question. A minister, even a Prime Minister, in London or away from his own country, could speak only on his own authority. Great though that might be by reason of his office or of his personal eminence, it could not carry the same weight as the opinion of a whole Cabinet. Under the system that existed the view that was expressed was a Cabinet view because the Cabinet could be assembled by the Prime Minister at short notice to formulate it. Members of an Imperial War Cabinet in London confronted with the need for a prompt decision on a difficult question would be faced with the alternatives either of acting on their own exclusive responsibility without reference to their colleagues, or of delaying decisions while they communicated with them, whereas,

---

[1] Except New Zealand, where the establishment of a separate Department of External Affairs may be dated to 1943. For further particulars see Mansergh, *Survey, 1931–9*, p. 71, n. 1.

argued Mr. Mackenzie King, a Prime Minister in his own country and in his own capital could consult with his colleagues and reach a decision promptly in the sure knowledge that it represented authoritatively and finally the view of the government as a whole.

Mr. Mackenzie King, in repudiating the suggestion that an Imperial War Cabinet would have merits greater than those of the conference of governments made possible by modern means of communication, did not dispute the desirability of periodic personal discussions by ministers or Prime Ministers with the United Kingdom government. On the contrary, he emphasized the very great value of the numerous visits by Canadian ministers to Britain since the beginning of the war.[1] But periodic visits for specific or general purposes and for a comparatively short time were a very different thing from the prolonged absence of a Prime Minister from his own country. Would not any Parliament prefer in a moment of crisis, such as arose in Canada on the sudden collapse of France, to have its Prime Minister at home at the head of the country which had elected him to office rather than overseas? As to the suggestion that there might be a representative in London who was not the Prime Minister, Mr. Mackenzie King saw very little advantage in it. Such a minister, a Minister for Overseas Affairs was a title proposed, would in fact tend to duplicate the functions and the responsibilities of the Canadian High Commissioner, Mr. Vincent Massey, who had long experience and was himself a member of the Canadian Privy Council. Was it likely that a minister newly appointed and also resident in London could add anything to the authority with which Mr. Massey could already express the views of the Canadian government? Membership of the Canadian Cabinet would add little to his status. Moreover, apart from personalities, if a Canadian minister were seconded for service in London, would he not be placed in the dilemma that if he made a practice of consulting his colleagues in Ottawa he would seem to have little authority himself, while if he failed to consult them the result would be uncertainty of jurisdiction? For all these reasons it seemed to Mr. Mackenzie King that the reconstitution of an Imperial War Cabinet or the creation of an Imperial War Council would add nothing to the united war effort of the Commonwealth and might well hamper it.

The Canadian Prime Minister's argument was couched in general terms and applied with equal force to all members of the Commonwealth. But there was one consideration which would seem to have weighed more with him than he allowed to appear in his speech. Only in passing did he allude to the advantages of immediate personal contact between the Prime Minister of Canada and the President of the United States at critical moments in the war and the importance to Canada and to the Commonwealth of such relations. Personal contact between President and Prime Minister would be

[1] Five members of the Canadian government visited London between September 1939 and February 1941.

precluded at any given moment were the Prime Minister to be absent in London.

The Canadian Prime Minister's conviction that the existing machinery for consultation and co-operation was to be preferred to any suggested alternative was not disputed in London. In April 1941 Lord Elibank asked the government whether in consultation with the governments of the dominions they would consider the desirability of forming an Imperial War Council to co-ordinate action upon major questions of imperial policy arising out of the war and in the making of peace.[1] Lord Elibank would seem to have had in mind some modification of the existing machinery as well as its strengthening at the highest level. He drew attention to one remediable weakness when he pointed out that the Secretary of State for Dominion Affairs, Lord Cranborne, was not a member of the War Cabinet. The value of the daily meetings between the Secretary of State and the dominion High Commissioners that took place during the war would obviously be greatly reduced if the opinions they expressed should not be voiced, when occasion justified, in the War Cabinet itself. Was it not, therefore, of cardinal importance that the Secretary of State should be a member of the War Cabinet? Lord Cranborne thought it was not essential. He explained that while he was not a member of the War Cabinet he attended its meetings (though apparently not all of them), so as to enable him to keep the dominions in the closest possible touch with events. While this was to the good so far as it went it hardly went far enough, for in wartime especially a great many matters might come up in discussion when the Secretary of State was not present which did not relate directly to the Commonwealth but might have considerable bearing upon Commonwealth policies or interests. Moreover the role of a minister who is not a member of the Cabinet but is in attendance at Cabinet meetings must necessarily be somewhat restricted and passive. He is, for example, hardly in a position to champion vigorously an unpalatable dominion point of view. Lord Elibank's criticism, therefore, was fully met only by the appointment in 1942 of Mr. Attlee, the Deputy Prime Minister, as Lord Cranborne's successor at the Dominions Office. On the broader issue, Lord Elibank added little of importance or of immediate relevance. Lord Chatfield, however, following him and speaking with the authority of a distinguished senior member of the Committee of Imperial Defence, like Mr. Mackenzie King though for different reasons felt that the creation of an Imperial War Council would not really contribute to speedy action or speedy decision, or bring victory sooner.[2] Since the war of 1914–18 there had been set up the Chiefs of Staff Committee, which had under it a vast organization able to advise the Minister of Defence, who was also the Prime Minister, about strategy. The Committee consisted of the Prime Minister and the three Chiefs of Staff; it met daily and in Lord

[1] H. of L. Deb., vol. 118, coll. 952–8 (Mansergh, *Documents*, i. 532–7).
[2] H. of L. Deb., vol. 118, coll. 961–2.

Chatfield's opinion seemed to be far the best organization to advise the War Cabinet as a whole on how strategy should be carried out. Its creation had rendered otiose many specious proposals for closer imperial defence co-operation.

Lord Cranborne,[1] in recording the satisfaction of the United Kingdom government with the existing machinery for Commonwealth co-operation, traversed much the same ground as the Canadian Prime Minister had covered earlier in the year. He, too, attached much importance to the presence of High Commissioners in all Commonwealth capitals, and he supplemented what Mr. Mackenzie King had said in dwelling upon the value of the daily conferences which he held with dominion High Commissioners in London. These conferences were in his opinion an essential point of liaison between the United Kingdom and the dominions. 'I see the High Commissioners every day of the week', he remarked, 'and I should be seeing them at this moment if it were not for this debate.' At these meetings the Secretary of State gave the High Commissioners all the latest official confidential information on the international situation and kept them in touch with the decisions and deliberations of the United Kingdom government in matters affecting the dominions. Nor was it only a one-way traffic in information or ideas. Often, Lord Cranborne said, he received personal suggestions from the High Commissioners which he passed on to the Cabinet or the departments concerned. He also emphasized the value of visits by dominion ministers to London in supplementing written communications, and referred to the fact that since his arrival in London at the end of February Mr. Menzies had taken a full part in the deliberations of the United Kingdom War Cabinet. He also alluded to the 'immensely valuable' discussions which Mr. Eden had had with General Smuts in the Middle East.

Behind this discussion lay one simple fact. In wartime it was not easy for Commonwealth Prime Ministers to meet in conference. Official and ministerial visits for particular purposes could normally be arranged as occasion required, but a meeting of dominion Prime Ministers in London was dependent upon the war situation as it affected their individual countries and upon the political conditions prevailing in them. Both combined to discourage General Smuts from coming to London in the first three years of the war, and to the second must be attributed the otherwise strange silence of this famous survivor of the historic Imperial War Cabinet of 1917–18 in all debate at this time about its reconstitution. It was not a topic, one may be certain, on which he had no views to express but rather one on which, in view of political tensions in the Union, he thought it might be dangerous to embark. If in the other dominions there was no such cleavage of opinion as continued to exist in South Africa on the question of participation in the war, none the less internal political conditions played an important part in deter-

[1] H. of L. Deb., vol. 118, coll. 967–73.

mining the timing and frequency of visits of their Prime Ministers to London. Moreover, quite apart from such domestic considerations, it was almost impossible in the changes and chances of war to foresee what decisions would have to be made at what particular time, and for that reason not easy to foretell when the presence of dominion Prime Ministers in London would be of greatest value to their own countries and to the Commonwealth war effort. But difficulties in timing were much reduced in the case of individual Prime Ministerial visits.

Consultation with Dominion Governments on the Decisions to aid Greece and to invade Syria, 1941

In 1941 both Mr. Menzies and Mr. Fraser, who succeeded Mr. Savage as Prime Minister of New Zealand on 4 April 1940, were in London for considerable periods, Mr. Menzies from 21 February to 20 May and Mr. Fraser from 21 June to 26 August. Both attended meetings of the War Cabinet for the period of their stay, and for that reason their presence in London afforded some opportunity of judging how far such representation in the Cabinet simplified and accelerated the process of consultation, assisted in the making of hard and difficult decisions involving, as it happened, the use of dominion forces, and more particularly lessened Australian anxieties about the defence of the Pacific which in the first place had brought Mr. Menzies to London.

Mr. Menzies, leaving Australia on 24 January 1941, visited the Australian forces in the Middle East on his way to London. At the time of his departure the principal preoccupation of the Australian War Cabinet was, as has already been seen, the situation not in the Middle East but in the Far East. This had one consequence of some importance. Neither Mr. Menzies nor his colleagues had devoted serious attention to the unfolding drama in the Balkans, where bravely won Greek victories over Italian forces made German assistance to her discredited ally almost inevitable in the spring of 1941. Could Britain, in such an eventuality and whatever the risks, abandon at once her opportunity of creating a Balkan front and her one remaining and most gallant ally on the continent of Europe? Yet if she were not to do so, Australian and New Zealand divisions in the Middle East would almost certainly have to make up an important and perhaps a major part of any relieving force. This in itself added a further and a complicating element in the making of a painful and difficult decision, for the governments of Australia and New Zealand, less influenced it may be than that of the United Kingdom by the political and psychological factors involved, did not find it easy to conceive a situation in which Britain would abandon a successful campaign in Africa to try to establish a Balkan front, and the Australian Cabinet at least was slow to envisage or to discuss such a possibility. The chief responsibility for this tardiness lay with the United Kingdom government, which did not at any early date 'pose' the major question of policy. It did, however, telegraph background information to the Australian government, which in November 1940 was, moreover, specifically asked to agree to the dispatch of an Australian brigade to Crete. None the less, Mr. Hasluck states categorically, no question regarding policy in the Balkans was brought before the Australian Cabinet or raised by any minister until telegrams were received from the United Kingdom government late in February 1941.[1] Yet if the Australian government collectively by reason of its failure to make timely inquiries, must take a share of the responsibility, the fact remains that the United Kingdom government was guilty of a serious oversight in neglecting to consult its dominion partners from the outset about a dangerous enterprise in which dominion forces were bound to play a major part. Nothing is more revealing on this point than the Instructions drafted for the Foreign Secretary, Mr. Eden, and formally approved by the Cabinet before his departure on a mission to the Middle East, the principal object of which was stated to be 'the sending of speedy succour to Greece'.[2] In them Mr. Eden was fully empowered 'to formulate with the Greek Government the best arrangements possible in the circumstances' and while asked to keep His Majesty's government informed, he was authorized in an emergency to act as he thought best. Dominion approval was not sought for these Instructions, though dominion troops might well be committed as a result of the authority vested in the Foreign Secretary by them. The result was that major decisions in both the military and the political fields which ought to have been made after, were being made before, consultation between the Commonwealth governments concerned.

In all this, chance, as always, played its part. It so happened that Mr. Menzies failed to meet either Mr. Eden or Sir John Dill while in the Middle East. He had, however, some conversations with General Wavell, who had been considering the possibility of sending aid to Greece for some time, and apparently found Mr. Menzies very ready to give him certain latitude in the use of Australian forces for the execution of any such plan.[3] But this conversation would seem to have been on the general outlines of a provisional plan and Mr. Menzies 'apparently first gave close attention to its details after he reached London on 20th February'.[4] Only then did he become fully acquainted with the risks involved and thereafter he participated in the discussions of the War Cabinet on them.

'As regards the general prospects of a Greek campaign', Mr. Eden telegraphed on 21 February from Cairo, 'it is, of course, a gamble to send forces to the mainland of Europe to fight Germans at this time.' But the stakes were high and opinion in the Middle East felt the risk should be taken. On 24

---

[1] Hasluck, i. 335; see generally pp. 333–41. It is clear from Wood, ch. xiv, that the New Zealand government, and presumably other dominion governments, were fully informed about the situation in January.
[2] See Churchill, iii. 60–62 for text of these instructions.
[3] Ibid. p. 59.   [4] Hasluck, i. 336.

February Mr. Churchill telegraphed back to Mr. Eden to say that the Chiefs of Staff had endorsed the plans made for the dispatch of Imperial forces from North Africa to take part in the defence of Greece and that the members of the War Cabinet, who had considered the question that day, had agreed unanimously. The Australian Prime Minister, he said, was present and was in full agreement; but, added Mr. Churchill, 'of course Mr. Menzies must telegraph home'.[1] Mr. Menzies did so, concluding: 'with some anxiety, my own recommendation to my colleagues is that we should concur'.[2] It was in the light of this personal message that the Australian War Cabinet considered on 26 February a telegram from the Dominions Office setting out the proposals for aid to Greece and asking for Australian concurrence. It will be noticed that in London Mr. Menzies entered actively into the discussions not in their preliminary stage but near the moment of decision.

Mr. Churchill presumed[3] that Mr. Eden had settled with the New Zealand government 'about their troops' and anyway felt there was no need 'to anticipate difficulties' either from the New Zealand or the Australian governments. But in fact Mr. Eden would not seem to have discussed the matter with the New Zealand government at all, and he did not meet General Freyberg. On 25 February the Secretary of State for Dominion Affairs sent two telegrams to Wellington, the first on the same lines as the Dominions Office telegram to Canberra summarizing in balanced terms the arguments for sending an expeditionary force to Greece, and the second stating that the immediate dispatch of the 2nd New Zealand Division was an essential part of the plan for the reinforcement of Greece.[4] In the second telegram the New Zealand government was informed that the whole plan had been discussed with Mr. Menzies at the Cabinet meeting on 24 February and that the Australian Prime Minister was asking his colleagues in Canberra to endorse his own conditional agreement to the dispatch of two of the Australian divisions to Greece from North Africa. The New Zealand government, influenced in particular by a cable from General Freyberg which was taken as implying that he had no objection to the expedition[5] and by Mr. Menzies's approval as represented in the cable from the United Kingdom government, in reply expressed its agreement on the understanding that the New Zealand division would be fully equipped before leaving and accompanied by an armoured brigade. It showed itself very much aware that the task confronting an expedition of the size contemplated would be most formidable and hazardous. It asked particularly for assurances that the risks had been taken fully into account and that full consideration had been given to the question

---

[1] Churchill, iii. 69. [2] Hasluck, i. 336.
[3] He has not recorded why he did so. Mr. Eden was authorized by his instructions to communicate direct with Iraq, Palestine, and Arabia and with the government of India, as well as with Greece, Yugoslavia, and Turkey (see Churchill, iii. 60–62).
[4] *N.Z. Documents*, vol. i, nos. 335–6, pp. 239–41. [5] Ibid. no. 274.

of whether the force was in fact adequate to meet the probable scale of attack.[1] These assurances were duly given.[2]

The response of the Australian government, which was also favourable, reflected similar anxieties. In a message dated 28 February Mr. Fadden, the acting Prime Minister, cabled Mr. Menzies that the Australian War Cabinet had decided to concur in the proposed use of two Australian divisions in Greece on the understanding that its consent to their participation was to be regarded as 'conditional on plans having been completed beforehand to ensure that evacuation, if necessitated, will be successfully undertaken and that shipping and other essential services will be available for this purpose if required'. In the British Cabinet Mr. Menzies 'received assurances on all points'.[3]

In the planning of earlier campaigns in East and North Africa the opinion of General Smuts was greatly valued, Mr. Churchill having expressed his gratitude 'above all for your surefooted judgment, which marches with our laboriously reached conclusions'.[4] On this occasion his counsel was invited at an earlier stage than that of his dominion colleagues, but then he had himself taken the initiative, which they had not, in expressing his opinion on strategy and policy in the Middle East and in the Balkans.[5] He went to Cairo at Mr. Eden's 'earnest request' in February 1941 and took part in discussions there. Mr. Churchill sought his opinion on the 'grave and hazardous decision' that had been taken to sustain the Greeks and to try to make a Balkan front.[6]

Mr. Churchill more than once alluded to the 'grave Imperial issues'[7] raised by committing New Zealand and Australian troops to an enterprise which with the passage of time seemed not less but more hazardous. At a meeting of the United Kingdom Cabinet on 6 March Mr. Menzies pointed out that the governments of Australia and New Zealand could not feel bound by an agreement signed by a British general in Athens without their approval and on instructions which had never received the sanction of their governments. Their approval, he argued, should be sought not on a commitment to which they had not been a party but on the ground that militarily there was a fair chance.[8] On 7 March 1941 Mr. Churchill impressed upon Mr. Eden the necessity of being able to tell the

New Zealand and Australian Governments faithfully that this hazard, from which they will not shrink, is undertaken, not because of any commitment entered into by a British Cabinet Minister at Athens . . . but because Dill, Wavell, and other Commanders-in-Chief are convinced that there is a reasonable fighting chance.[9]

---

[1] N.Z. Documents, vol. 1, nos. 337 and 339, pp. 242–3. Two replies were sent because the first of the two telegrams from the Secretary of State was apparently delayed and not at first available for consideration.
[2] Ibid. no. 343, pp. 245–6.   [3] Hasluck, i. 337.   [4] Churchill, iii. 19.
[5] See his telegram of 8 January 1941 to Mr. Churchill in ibid. pp. 14–16.
[6] Ibid. p. 85.   [7] Ibid. p. 90.
[8] Butler, Grand Strategy, ii. 447–8.   [9] Churchill, iii. 92.

Mr. Eden replied on the same day that the whole position had been reviewed with the Commanders-in-Chief and with General Smuts, and 'while we are all conscious of the gravity of the decision, we can find no reason to vary our previous judgment'.[1] When the issue was brought before the War Cabinet Mr. Churchill, believing, incorrectly as it would seem in the case of the Australian and New Zealand commanders, that the men on the spot had been 'searchingly tested',[2] and reassured by the fact that 'Smuts with all his wisdom, and from his separate angle of thought and fresh eye, had concurred', sensed that the time had come for a final and affirmative decision. In making it, however, notes the editor of the British Military History of the Second World War, 'the military arguments had to be taken at second hand—or indeed at third hand, since Dill and Wavell had not reconnoitred the terrain'. And he adds that it was 'remarkable that no "precise military appreciation" such as Mr. Churchill had asked for, was ever received from Cairo', nor was account seemingly taken in London of 'the drain on our resources in Egypt which a prolonged campaign in Greece would imply; in fact, no considered estimate was made of how much we were prepared to lose'.[3] Mr. Menzies 'on whom', as Mr. Churchill allowed, 'a special burden rested, was full of courage'; but it remains open to question till further documentary evidence is available whether he was in all important respects as 'fully informed' as circumstances permitted.[4]

The New Zealand government, which had always regarded the operation 'as highly dangerous and speculative' and which recognized that it had now become 'obviously much more hazardous',[5] none the less agreed that the decision to proceed was the right one in a most difficult situation and 'with a full knowledge of the hazards to be run' aligned itself with the views of the United Kingdom government, confident that the New Zealand troops in the area would be the first to approve of its action. Mr. Churchill paid warm tribute to this reply, which 'whatever the fortunes of war may be, will shine in the history of New Zealand and be admired by future generations of free men in every quarter of the globe'.[6] It is, however, to be noted that before this second New Zealand assent was given half of the New Zealand division was in Greece.

In April Mr. Fraser arrived in Cairo,[7] and unquestionably it was much to the advantage of the Commonwealth that Mr. Menzies should be in London

---

[1] Ibid. p. 93.
[2] Ibid. p. 94. Later Mr. Menzies came to the conclusion that, far from his being 'searchingly tested', 'some pains had been taken to suppress the critical views of General Blamey' (Hasluck, l. 336).
[3] Butler, *Grand Strategy*, ii. 447. See generally Wood, ch. xiv.
[4] See on this point Long, *Greece, Crete and Syria*, ch. i.
[5] N.Z. Documents, vol. 1, no. 353, p. 257.
[6] Churchill, iii. 95 and *N.Z. Documents*, vol. 1, no. 354, p. 257.
[7] Ibid. nos. 370 and 371, pp. 272–3, record how his views were sought by the Australian government as well as his own government.

and Mr. Fraser in the Middle East during the gallant but unavailing effort of the Imperial forces committed to an unequal struggle to save Greece and Crete from Nazi conquest. The fact that the expeditionary force was so largely manned by Australian and New Zealand troops did raise, as Mr. Churchill had foreseen, grave imperial issues. In Australia the Labour party complained that the Australian Advisory War Council had not been consulted beforehand about the employment of the Australian Imperial forces in Greece.[1] Mr. Menzies defended his failure to do so on the ground that the Greek expedition represented a major decision in war strategy of the highest possible order of secrecy, and that for this reason it would have been inappropriate to have had it discussed in the War Council. In retrospect it seems doubtful if his decision on this point was a wise one. The fact that the Labour party was in no way associated with the decision to send the Australian divisions to Greece gave to the subsequent controversy a touch of party acrimony which it might not otherwise have acquired. Moreover, in New Zealand Mr. Fraser had submitted the question not only, as has been seen, to his Cabinet colleagues but also to the leader of the Opposition, who approved the decision taken.[2] Yet on the principal point at issue Mr. Menzies and Mr. Fraser were in complete agreement. Both stated in the most emphatic terms that their governments had been fully consulted before the decision had been made and that they were fully aware beforehand of the risks involved. The difficulties of the Greek campaign, said Mr. Menzies in a broadcast from London to Australia on 23 April 1941,[3] were always understood by the British, the Australian, and the New Zealand governments. As a matter of principle the Australian government was always consulted before Australian forces were moved to any new theatre of operations, and in this particular case the question of their employment in Greece came before him at the first War Cabinet meeting that he attended in London. It was also, he recalled, the subject of extensive communications between the governments of the United Kingdom and of the Pacific dominions, and between himself and his Cabinet colleagues in Canberra. Every question, he observed with reference presumably to the period after his arrival in London, that could properly be raised was raised, examined, and debated, and it was as a result of these investigations that they had come to the conclusion that while the sending of land forces to Greece was a hazardous undertaking it was one which had some real prospects of military success.

In Australia the Deputy Prime Minister, Mr. Fadden, amply confirmed what his Prime Minister had said from London. Any suggestion, he said in Brisbane on 20 April 1941,[4] that the Australian government was not in the closest contact with the British government and the officers commanding troops in the Middle East must be silenced immediately. The Australian

---

[1] Hasluck, i. 338; see also *The Times*, 22 April 1941. [2] Ibid. 26 April 1941.
[3] Ibid. 24 April 1941. [4] *Argus* (Melbourne), 21 April 1941.

government had been consulted before every troop movement affecting Australian forces had commenced and the only reason why the facts could not always be made known immediately was the overriding demands of wartime security. If criticism was not in fact altogether silenced by these assurances, it was at the least deflected from the question of prior consultation to that of the adequacy of the military and political appreciation on which the decision to reinforce Greece was made. In New Zealand, where there was no outburst of criticism comparable to that which took place in Australia, the War Council passed a formal resolution on 29 April 1941 retrospectively expressing full support for the government's action in agreeing to the dispatch of New Zealand troops to Greece.[1] Mr. Fraser went out of his way to assert[2] that the decision had been reached after the most able and accurate appreciation of the situation, and two months later in London he maintained[3] that there never was a problem discussed more fully and in more detail between the New Zealand and the British governments than the question of 'our forces assisting the Greeks'. Yet it is the case, despite these assertions made at the time, and in part influenced by a desire to still criticism at home and to counter propaganda abroad, that the Australian and New Zealand governments did not have a say in the formulation of policy to which their military contribution to the expedition would have entitled them. Their subsequent restraint in comment is therefore evidence of the cohesion of the Commonwealth rather than of their satisfaction with the way in which decisions had been reached.

The controversy over the Greek campaign had its importance. It helped public opinion throughout the Commonwealth to understand that any appearance of division even on the technical question of how decisions should be and had been reached would be exploited by their enemies in a way that they had never intended. German broadcasts emphasizing supposed dissension between the British and Australian governments, and the Japanese press happily deducing from the controversy that the British Empire was 'crumbling to pieces' prompted sobering reflections about the desirability of voicing criticisms of any given course of action in such a way as to make it unmistakably clear that unity of purpose in the waging of the war was unshaken and unshakeable.[4] 'There is no political disunity in Australia', declared Mr. Curtin,[5] 'in the prosecution of the war'. He was right, but the Australian press was unhappily not uniformly mindful of the impression its language might create outside the Commonwealth.[6] But when all is said, what remains is that the Australian and New Zealand governments, to their honour and

[1] *The Times*, 30 April 1941. [2] Ibid.
[3] *Manchester Guardian*, 23 June 1941.
[4] Cf. New Zealand, H. of R. Deb., vol. 259, p. 297.
[5] *Sydney Morning Herald*, 28 April 1941.
[6] See Hasluck, i. 340 on the need felt by members of the Australian Cabinet to counteract this impression.

lasting credit, having made a difficult decision, indulged in no recrimination when the enterprise which they had approved failed of its immediate purpose. Any other decision, said Mr. Fraser,[1] would have involved 'eternal dishonour'. Mr. Menzies, who felt that a very particular responsibility rested on him through his presence in London at the time when the decision was reached, told the House of Representatives on his return that the decision made was the right one in the circumstances and that he had 'no regrets that the people of Australia were associated with one of the most gallant actions in the history of modern war'.[2] In London on 6 May Mr. Eden told the House of Commons that General Smuts, with whom he had consulted in Cairo, was in complete agreement with the decision arrived at. Thus none of those who had participated at whatever stage and in whatever way in the making of a fateful choice later shrank from the responsibility of having done so. But neither the Australian nor the New Zealand governments were prepared to have it taken in the same way in the future.

The campaigns in Greece and Crete were soon followed by a campaign in Syria where Australian forces played the leading, and this time a victorious, role but where political consultation seemed to Australian critics once more belated and inadequate. In brief the sequence of events was as follows. In June 1940 the Australian government was consulted about and concurred in a United Kingdom declaration to the effect that Syria and the Lebanon would not be allowed to fall into the hands of any hostile power or to become a danger to Middle Eastern countries which Britain was pledged to defend. Subsequently it was kept informed by the Dominions Office of developments in the area. In May 1941 there was ground for fearing that Syria would pass from Vichy to German control and the Free French pressed for intervention. On 24 May, the day on which Mr. Menzies returned to Australia, Mr. Stanley Bruce, the Australian High Commissioner in London, cabled Canberra to express his 'grave concern' at the situation in the Middle East and his opinion that 'the paramount requirement' there was 'to prevent the Germans from establishing themselves in Syria'. He urged a review of the whole situation in the Middle East, observing that 'in this review, Australia should be fully and—having so many of her troops in the Middle East—specially consulted'. On 28 May General Wavell was instructed to occupy Syria, on 29 May the Australian High Commissioner informed Mr. Menzies of this decision, and on 30 May General Blamey informed the Australian government that with other Allied forces the 7th Australian Division were to move against Syria. Australian concurrence was not in question at any time—indeed throughout the campaign the Australian government favoured the most vigorous action—but, as in the case of Greece, the decision to invade Syria had been taken 'without effective Australian participation'.

[1] *The Times*, 26 April 1941.   [2] Australia, H. of R. Deb., vol. 167, p. 23.

COMMONWEALTH CO-OPERATION IN WAR

From these experiences [writes Mr. Hasluck] one conclusion was clear. Consultation through an exchange of telegrams was not enough. To have an effective voice in decisions on the higher conduct of the war which directly affected Australia, the Dominions must be represented in the place where the decisions were made—in the War Cabinet itself.[1]

Of this more was to be heard.

The Control and Disposition of Dominion Forces

It would seem appropriate at this point to say something of the relationship between United Kingdom and dominion forces in the field, for the Greek campaign especially confronted the commanders of the Australian and New Zealand Expeditionary Forces with some difficult questions. Dominion governments, advised on the strategic situation by their own commanders, retained throughout the war control over the disposition and use of their forces in the field. This control was exercised in that spirit of free co-operation which was the life-blood of the Commonwealth in war as in peace.

The relationship of Canadian forces serving overseas with United Kingdom forces was determined in law by a statute enacted in 1933 which provided *inter alia* that forces outside Canada operating with British forces might alternatively be designated as 'serving together' with British forces, in which case each remained under its own commanding officer, or 'in combination', in which case they were subject to a single commanding officer. Under a Canadian Order in Council dated 3 April 1940 Canadian forces in the United Kingdom were generally designated as 'serving together' with British forces, but when dispatched to the Continent they passed into the second category. The Order, however, also vested discretionary authority in the hands of Canadian commanders to enable them to detail Canadian army and air formations in the United Kingdom for service 'in combination' as they saw fit, and in fact this discretionary authority was used for this purpose in the early years of the war.[2] The ultimate authority of the Canadian government in respect of the disposition of Canadian forces was at all times preserved. Colonel Ralston, the Minister of National Defence, explained in the Canadian House of Commons on 1 April 1941 that in the event of operations in the United Kingdom the British commander would consult with General McNaughton, then Commander of the Canadian Corps, who in turn would consult with the Chief of the Imperial General Staff about any operation to which the Canadian Corps might be committed. That, said Colonel Ralston, was not only what should happen but what had been happening in practice since the Corps had landed in Britain. With regard to the use of Canadian troops outside the

---

[1] Hasluck, i. 341–5.
[2] Canada, Order in Council of 3 April 1940, P.C. 1066 (see *Canada in World Affairs, 1939–41*, pp. 229–31).

United Kingdom the decision, he said, rested entirely with the Canadian government. It was in accordance with that principle that the approval of the Canadian government was expressly sought and given in the spring of 1940 for the use of Canadian troops in Norway and France.[1] In the intervening year no suggestion of any kind had been made to Canadian military authorities or to the Canadian government that its forces should serve beyond the United Kingdom, except in one instance when the British government requested and the Canadian government approved the dispatch of a small detachment of Canadian troops to carry out special work at Gibraltar. This procedure was followed throughout the war, and the Canadian government, to give one notable illustration, was consulted and was in full agreement with the use of Canadian troops for the raid on Dieppe in August 1942. Such agreement was not invariably forthcoming. On one occasion at least the Canadian government declined to consent to the use of Canadian forces in an enterprise which it deemed imprudent. As Colonel Ralston observed, the final word rested with the Minister of National Defence, if for no other reason than that Canadian Service authorities were not in a position to authorize the embarkation of Canadian forces from the United Kingdom without his consent.

Other dominion governments would seem to have enjoyed equally effective control over the disposition and movement of their forces. 'The Commonwealth Government', said Mr. Fadden in April 1941,[2] 'has been consulted before every troop movement affecting Australian units has commenced', and never did it 'relinquish control or direction of those armed forces which it has raised and for which it is wholly responsible to the people of Australia.' Negatively at least, therefore, dominion governments possessed in theory a partial veto in the sense that operations largely or wholly dependent upon the use of dominion forces could not be undertaken without the approval of their respective governments advised by their respective commanders.

The instructions given to dominion commanders overseas were in these circumstances important. Those given to General Freyberg, the Commander of the Second New Zealand Expeditionary Force, were admirably clear. Dated 5 January 1940, they were addressed by the Prime Minister to the General Officer for the time being commanding the Second New Zealand Expeditionary Force overseas and their principal provisions read as follows:

> The General Officer Commanding will act in accordance with the instructions he receives from the Commander-in-Chief under whose command he is serving, subject only to the requirements of His Majesty's Government in New Zealand. He will, in

---

[1] Canada, H. of C. Deb., 1941, vol. 2, pp. 2047–9 (reprinted in *Canada in World Affairs, 1939–41*, pp. 297–301).

[2] *Argus*, 21 April 1941. But see above, p. 102, where the timing of events would seem to make it clear that the government could not have been 'consulted' about the movement of the 7th Australian Division to Syria at the end of May 1941. On the other hand in this instance the views of the Australian government were known.

addition to powers appearing in any relevant Statute or Regulations, be vested with the following powers:

(a) In the case of sufficiently grave emergency or in special circumstances, of which he must be the sole judge, to make decisions as to the employment of the 2nd New Zealand Expeditionary Force, and to communicate such decisions directly to the New Zealand Government, notwithstanding that in the absence of that extraordinary cause such communication would not be in accordance with the normal channels of communication. . . .

(b) To communicate directly with the New Zealand Government and with the Army Department concerning any matter connected with the training and administration of the 2nd New Zealand Expeditionary Force.

(c) To communicate directly either with the New Zealand Government or with the Commander-in-Chief under whose command he is serving, in respect of all details leading up to and arising from policy decisions.[1] . . .

The relevant provisions of the Charter issued to General Blamey as General Officer Commanding the Second Australian Imperial Force, drafted on similar lines, were equally explicit. They read as follows:

(a) The Force to be recognised as an Australian force under its own Commander, who will have a direct responsibility to the Commonwealth Government. . . . No part of the Force to be detached or employed apart from the Force without his consent.
Questions of policy regarding the employment of the Force to be decided by the United Kingdom and Commonwealth Governments, in consultation; except that, in an emergency, the Commander of the Force may, at his discretion, take a decision on such a question, informing the Commonwealth Government that he is so doing.

(b) The Force to be under the operational control of the Commander-in-Chief of the theatre in which it is serving.[2]

These instructions in full were dispatched to the Dominions Office on 9 March 1940 and approved by the United Kingdom government on 26 March.[3]

The relationship between the commander of a dominion force and his Commander-in-Chief could not, however, be settled merely by paper definitions of responsibility. It was something to be worked out by a process of trial and error, especially where dominion forces, as in North Africa, combined with United Kingdom and Indian troops to form one imperial army. Some of the practical problems likely to arise in such circumstances came to light early in 1941.

Neither General Blamey's nor General Freyberg's opinions about the decision to aid Greece would seem to have been adequately stated in communications to their governments. It is true that on 15 November 1940

[1] *N.Z. Documents*, vol. 1, no. 39, pp. 31–32.
[2] Reprinted in Long, *To Benghazi*, p. 101. See also above, p. 32.
[3] Hasluck, i. 217, n. 1.

General Blamey drew the attention of Mr. Menzies to the risks of piecemeal land warfare[1] in the Balkans and proposed as an alternative policy the prepared defence of Crete and Rhodes. On 10 March he cabled to Mr. P. C. Spender, the Minister for the Army, an appreciation of the situation in Greece where 'we must be prepared to meet overwhelming forces completely equipped and trained'. On 27 March 1941, however, Mr. Fadden cabled Mr. Menzies about the resentment felt by the Australian Cabinet at the insufficiently full and frank opinions it had received from the Australian commander, and also at discussions taking place about the proposed expedition to Greece at which 'Blamey's views as G.O.C. of the force which apparently is to take the major part in the operations should not have been sought'.[2] Had he been fully consulted and had he felt at liberty to do so, Blamey would apparently have expressed grave misgivings. As it was he was faced with the choice of criticizing the policy or even the decision of his military superiors or 'remaining silent despite his fears'. When Mr. Fraser reached the Middle East in April 1941 he learned likewise and with surprise that General Freyberg had at no time believed that the dispatch of the Expeditionary Force to Greece could achieve a successful result. When he pointed out that General Freyberg's communications to the New Zealand government had not adequately expressed his misgivings, General Freyberg agreed, explaining that it was difficult for him to transmit advice which ran counter to that of his superior officers. Mr. Fraser replied that it was the duty of the New Zealand commander in the field to transmit his own views to the New Zealand Cabinet even when they ran counter to those of the Commander-in-Chief. On 7 June he cabled from Cairo to the acting Prime Minister in Wellington,

I ... am surprised to learn now from Freyberg that he never considered the operation a feasible one, though, as I pointed out to him, his telegrams to us conveyed a contrary impression. In this connection he has drawn my attention to the difficulty of a subordinate commander criticising the plans of superior officers, but I have made it plain to him that in any future case where he doubts the propriety of a proposal he is to give the War Cabinet in Wellington full opportunity of considering the proposal, with his views on it.[3] ...

Mr. Fraser's interpretation was endorsed by the New Zealand government. Thereafter the two dominions would seem to have been fully and frankly advised of the opinions entertained by their respective Commanders-in-Chief.

By contrast, dominion commanders from time to time had positive opportunities of influencing even high-level strategic planning. In the summer of 1940 General Freyberg was among those who maintained that defence must

---

[1] John Hetherington, *Blamey, the Biography of Field Marshal Sir Thomas Blamey* (Melbourne, F. W. Cheshire, 1954), pp. 92–93.
[2] Long, *Greece, Crete and Syria*, p. 19.
[3] *N.Z. Documents*, vol. 1, no. 447, p. 323.

be thought of and planned from the point of view of the Empire as a whole, and that accordingly all available equipment should not be concentrated in the United Kingdom to guard against the risk of invasion but should be distributed so as to defend the critical communications of the countries of the Empire. He was invited by Mr. Churchill to put his views in writing, and they were printed and circulated to the War Cabinet.[1] Mr. Mackenzie King in 1943 went so far as to say that General McNaughton knew the mind 'of the staff in Great Britain as well as any member of the staff knows his own mind. And they know General McNaughton's mind.'[2] On the influence of General Smuts, who exceptionally among dominion leaders combined the role of Prime Minister and strategist, in the making of war policy it is superfluous to write, though it is relevant to recall here the weight attached to his opinion by the United Kingdom in early 1941 even though there was no question of the dispatch of South African troops to Greece.

General Blamey complained in November 1941 that the United Kingdom commanders in the field 'had difficulty in recognising the independent status of the Dominions and their responsibility for the control of their own forces'.[3] This was probably true enough. But the relationship between the forces of the independent nations of the Commonwealth in any circumstances would have presented problems that were at once novel and exceptional in character. In the Middle East there was a United Kingdom Command with reservation to subordinate dominion commanders of administrative control, of direct contact with their own governments, and of the right of appeal. It was, as an Australian war historian has remarked, a 'peculiar system'.[4] No theorist would have devised it. It posed difficult problems to which a solution had to be found. But it worked. It was a system under which an army composed of units from all over the Commonwealth was welded into a famous fighting force. For the system had one outstanding merit. It recognized political realities and, in conformity with the practice and, above all, the spirit of the Commonwealth, it sought to reconcile autonomy with unity.

Dominion Representation in the War Cabinet, 1941

Mr. Churchill failed to persuade General Smuts to come to London and 'do a month's work in the War Cabinet as of old',[5] but after Mr. Menzies left in May 1941 Mr. Fraser arrived on 21 June, for a two months' visit. He was, therefore, in London when Germany invaded Russia. Dominion governments were not consulted about the terms of Mr. Churchill's famous broadcast on 22 June, the evening of the Nazi invasion, declaring that 'any man or state who fights on against Nazidom will have our aid'.[6]

For quite palpable reasons [said Mr. Menzies in Canberra] it was not possible for

[1] Ibid. no. 195, p. 145. [2] 1 February 1943, Canada, H. of C. Deb., 1943, vol. 1, p. 44.
[3] Long, *Greece, Crete and Syria*, p. 553. [4] Ibid. p. 552. [5] Churchill, iii. 95.
[6] Churchill, *The Unrelenting Struggle*, compiled by Charles Eade (London, Cassell, 1942), p. 179.

him [Mr. Churchill] to consult effectively all of the governments of the dominions before making the statement, and I take no exception to that. This was a matter upon which the views of the British Government should at once be announced.[1]

And the statement was 'completely accepted' by the government of Australia. It was warmly endorsed in New Zealand, and coolly approved in South Africa and Canada. 'Everyone who engages our enemy', said Mr. Mackenzie King, 'advances our cause'.[2]

In London Mr. Fraser took part in the deliberations of the War Cabinet about mutual assistance between the British Commonwealth and the Soviet Union. He subscribed to the opinion that a declaration proposed by Russia, guaranteeing mutual help without 'any precision as to quantity or quality' and providing that neither country should conclude a separate peace, should be signed as soon as the dominions of Canada, Australia, and South Africa had been consulted and their approval had been obtained.[3] This in fact was done by 15 July 1941, when Mr. Churchill publicly announced the terms of the Anglo-Russian Agreement which, in his words, carried with it 'the full assent of the British and Russian people and all the great Dominions of the Crown, for united action against the common foe'.[4] It is to be noted that in his communication to the United Kingdom Ambassador in Moscow Mr. Churchill would seem to have presumed that the presence of the New Zealand Prime Minister in the War Cabinet rendered formal consultation between the United Kingdom and New Zealand governments superfluous. Though Mr. Fraser himself was in fact in communication with his own government, this was a presumption that would almost certainly not have won unanimous dominion approbation.

Mr. Churchill has recorded that Mr. Menzies's prolonged visit to London was 'most valuable',[5] but Mr. Menzies was not satisfied either with his share in the making of policy or with a system which allowed Australia a voice in the United Kingdom War Cabinet only while the Prime Minister was in London. On the first count he had legitimate cause for complaint. Secret Anglo-American staff talks held in Washington from January to March 1941 resulted in an agreement for Anglo-American co-operation short of war and for full co-operation if Axis aggression forced the United States into war. Fundamental to the agreement was the conclusion that should the United States be involved in war with both Germany and Japan, a decision would have to be sought first in the vital theatre—Europe. 'I believe', wrote President Roosevelt to Mr. Churchill in May, 'that the outcome of this struggle is going to be decided in the Atlantic and unless Hitler can win there he cannot win anywhere else in the world in the end.'[6] This implied a holding

---

[1] Australia, H. of R. Deb., vol. 167, p. 284.
[2] *Canada in World Affairs, 1939–41*, p. 268.
[3] Churchill, iii. 341–2.
[4] H. of C. Deb., vol. 373, col. 463.
[5] Churchill, iii. 365.
[6] Langer & Gleason, ii. 450.

war in the Far East. But while conceding so much in principle, the United Kingdom representatives at the staff talks insisted upon the vital importance to Britain of her position in the Far East with Singapore the key to its security. The American delegates did not dissent, but for their part insisted that Britain must continue to bear the responsibility for the defence of Singapore and resisted all British pleas for a diversion of sufficient American naval forces from Pearl Harbour to ensure its impregnability. The American view prevailed, and the upshot was an understanding that in the event of the United States being involved in war, Britain would send six capital ships to defend Singapore and the United States Navy would assist the Royal Navy in the Atlantic.[1] The Australian government was informed that staff talks were taking place, but the decision of the United States government, consequent upon the provisional agreement reached at them, to transfer the Pacific Fleet to the Atlantic in May 1941, was wholly unexpected. The presence of a United States fleet in the Pacific hitherto had been considered to be 'the main deterrent to any further Japanese aggression'. The Australian War Cabinet allowed that the move involved a 'nice judgment on very uncertain factors', but 'the concern, almost the consternation', of Australia was chiefly due to the fact that, 'at a time when her armed strength was being expended overseas on the expectation—or even a gamble—of security in the Pacific, the main conditions could be changed in consultation with Britain but with only tardy reference to Australia'. Circumstances made the neglect the more irritating to Mr. Menzies. For two months he had been in London, attending the meetings of the British War Cabinet, in constant touch with the Chiefs of Staff, and specially concerned to represent the needs of the Pacific. Yet 'no rumour or whisper reached him of the contemplated change'. He learnt of it only when supplied with a copy of a routine telegram by the Dominions Office which had been sent out to Australia the previous day. Later he 'told the British War Cabinet pretty plainly that this was not good enough'.[2] As a result of his protest final decision was delayed until dominion governments had expressed their views.[3]

Mr. Menzies left London with the impression that Mr. Churchill exercised too much power in the conduct of the war.[4] While acknowledging his outstanding qualities, Mr. Menzies felt, and told his colleagues in the Australian War Cabinet and War Council, that Mr. Churchill had no conception of the dominions as 'separate entities' and that 'the more distant the problem from

---

[1] For a full account see Sherwood, i. 271–4. See also, for an account of their implications for Australia, Hasluck, i. 353, and especially Langer & Gleason, ii. 285–9.

[2] Hasluck, i. 345–6; see also Butler, *Grand Strategy*, ii. 500–3.

[3] Butler, *Grand Strategy*, ii. 502.

[4] Cf. the impression of Harry Hopkins as communicated to President Roosevelt on 14 January 1941: '*Churchill* is the gov't. in every sense of the word—he controls the grand strategy and often the details—labour trusts him—the army, navy, air force are behind him to a man' (Sherwood, i. 244).

the heart of the Empire the less he thought of it'. Mr. Churchill was 'a great European', but on questions in which dominion interests were involved the attitude of his mind was 'unsatisfactory'.[1]

Australian Proposals for an Imperial War Cabinet and Their Outcome

The conclusions Mr. Menzies reached after his stay in London were at the least not lacking in clarity. He felt that a radical change in the higher direction of the war effort was essential and that it could best be effected by the formation of an Imperial War Cabinet containing representatives of each of the four self-governing dominions.[2] He submitted his proposals formally to Mr. Mackenzie King, General Smuts, and Mr. Fraser. None of them favoured such a change. Mr. Mackenzie King, still the decisive figure in the shaping of Commonwealth relations, 'deployed', in the words of Mr. Churchill, 'formidable constitutional arguments against Canada's being committed by her representative to the decisions of a council in London'.[3] Mr. Churchill, sensible of the weighty objections to the course the Australian Prime Minister advocated, himself took the opportunity, in expressing a hope that Mr. Menzies would soon be able to visit London once again, to point out that it would not be possible for a dominion minister other than a Prime Minister to sit in the War Cabinet because representatives of all four dominions would then be involved and that would result in too large a permanent addition to its numbers. Mr. Menzies's counter-suggestion that a single dominion minister should represent all the dominions had no chance of acceptance in the other dominions and was indeed remote from political reality.

Mr. Menzies's criticisms of the central conduct of the war are important in themselves and also because they represented a recurrent element in Australian thinking about imperial relations whether in war or in peace. On both counts the arguments he advanced merit some detailed consideration. It was Mr. Menzies's principal contention that in a war characterized by extraordinarily sudden changes and developments it was not enough for the opinion of the Australian government to be known and understood. Australia's voice must also be 'directly heard in the place in which the major decisions are inevitably made'.[4] This implied no criticism of the United Kingdom War Cabinet, the members of which had been 'in the highest degree co-operative' during Mr. Menzies's visit to London, but the fact remained that, in the Australian view, the best results for the British Empire as a whole would be achieved by having matters of high war policy which concerned any particular dominion discussed freely and frankly at the right place by authoritative spokesmen of that dominion. Where was the right place? That was the crux of the whole question. For successive Australian governments the right place

---

[1] Hasluck, i. 347. [2] Churchill, iii. 365. [3] Ibid.
[4] Australia, H. of R. Deb., vol. 168, pp. 10–11. (Extracts from this debate are reprinted in Mansergh, *Documents*, i. 537–8.)

was in London and later in London and Washington. Mr. Menzies fully realized the impracticability of a Prime Minister of Australia being indefinitely, or for a long period, away from his own country, but that limitation in point of time left the force of the general proposition 'quite unimpaired'. It did, however, detract from the prospects of its practical application. The Canadian and South African Prime Ministers evidently felt that the right place for them was in Ottawa and Pretoria respectively, where they were in touch with their own Cabinets, Parliaments, and public opinion. Mr. Mackenzie King in February had already stated his position on this point in unmistakable terms; and there were compelling reasons why General Smuts should remain in Pretoria. It was he more than any single man who had brought the Union into the war on the side of the Allies in September 1939; it was his leadership which was winning a growing measure of support for the war effort despite many allied setbacks and disappointments, and it was his experience of war as well as of politics that made his personal decisions about the disposition and use of South Africa's forces seemingly indispensable. This feeling was intensified after the German invasion of Russia in June 1941, when the war politically as well as militarily was thought in the Union to have entered upon a new and unpredictable phase. 'Widespread agreement of opinion exists . . .',[1] noted the South African correspondent of the *Round Table* in September 1941, 'that Field-Marshal Smuts's place is in the Union, whence he can be in momentary touch with the British Cabinet and at the same time keep his sensitive and firm hand upon the reins of South African military affairs.' For exactly the same reasons there was not, reported the same correspondent, 'much support in the Union for the suggestion that there should be an Imperial War Cabinet or even an Imperial War Conference in London'. Moreover in the case of South Africa one of the strongest personal arguments was lacking. No one doubted that General Smuts was consulted by Mr. Churchill on matters affecting South Africa and indeed many other places and things.

Mr. Churchill's suggestion that Mr. Menzies might shortly revisit London showed a proper indifference to the astringencies and mounting uncertainties of Australian domestic politics. On 9 August 1941 the Australian Prime Minister started on a tour of the Australian capitals; on 11 August he abandoned it ostensibly on receipt of critical information about the situation in the Far East. Members of the Opposition were sceptical and openly described the cancellation as a political stunt. This is a point on which it is not necessary here to pronounce judgement. It is, however, relevant to note that on 9 August two cables were received from London, one about a forthcoming meeting of Mr. Churchill and President Roosevelt in the Atlantic, and another about the possibility of an agreed Anglo-American warning to Japan, the terms of which were to constitute a principal topic for discussion at the

[1] *Round Table*, September 1941, p. 810.

Atlantic meeting. The second cable was well calculated by reason of its contents to revive Australian anxieties lest decisions on a matter of vital concern to Australia might be taken without her views being sufficiently weighed.[1]

On Mr. Menzies's return to Canberra the Australian War Cabinet concluded, with these communications from London before it, that Mr. Menzies should proceed thither once again in order to represent Australian interests in the British War Cabinet. When its conclusion was communicated to the Advisory War Council on 14 August it provoked Labour members to anger and indignation. Some, with Dr. Evatt, believed that Mr. Menzies was trying to go away 'on the condition that he should not be deposed';[2] others that the gravity of the war made it essential for Australia to have her Prime Minister at home to direct the organization of a total war effort. All were united in opposition to the suggestion that Mr. Menzies should proceed to London as Prime Minister. On the other hand, irrespective of party, there was agreement that arrangements should be made with the United Kingdom government for Australian representation in London so as to ensure that Australian views on war policy would be constantly before the War Cabinet.[3]

Representation in the United Kingdom War Cabinet would seem, moreover, to have been regarded as a matter of right by the Labour party. Thus Mr. Curtin maintained in the House of Representatives:

> The Parliament, the Government, and the people of Australia are warranted, in view of all that Australia has done, is doing, and proposes to do, in saying to the Government of the United Kingdom: 'We desire to have our view of war policy placed before the Cabinet in Great Britain by such a representative as we deem most suitable for the purpose. . . . Whilst in the past it has been a matter of general practice that the Prime Minister of Australia should, as a gesture of courtesy, be admitted to the discussions of the British War Cabinet, . . . the exigencies of the war now make it necessary that that gentleman shall remain in Australia to lead his Administration. Therefore, as it is important that our view should be put before you, we ask you to accept, not the representative of Australia that you would choose, but the representative of Australia which the Australian Government may choose.'[4]

This was a request verging upon a demand which implicitly discounted Mr. Churchill's known reluctance to enlarge his Cabinet (for if one dominion received representation all were entitled to it), and which explicitly challenged the United Kingdom Prime Minister's final voice on the membership of his Cabinet. It was not one in which Mr. Churchill was prepared to acquiesce.

On 29 August Mr. Menzies fell from office. To his successor, Mr. Fadden, who like Mr. Menzies enjoyed a majority of one in the House of Representatives, Mr. Churchill summarized his views on the question of dominion

---

[1] Hasluck, i. 495–6. See below, pp. 118–19.
[2] Ibid. p. 498.
[3] Australia, H. of R. Deb., vol. 168, pp. 77–78.
[4] Ibid. p. 79.

representation in the War Cabinet in a telegram[1] that takes its place beside Mr. Mackenzie King's speech of February 1941 as an exposition of the principles at stake in all discussions on the constitution of an Imperial War Cabinet or Council. The tenor of Mr. Churchill's argument was that the Cabinet which he had the honour to lead was responsible to Parliament and held office because its members collectively enjoyed the support of a majority in the House of Commons. The presence of an Australian minister who was responsible to the legislature of the Commonwealth of Australia as a member of that Cabinet would involve organic changes. While in practice a dominion Prime Minister was always invited to sit with the United Kingdom government and to take full part in government deliberations during the period of his visit, that was because he was the head of the government of a sister dominion and might be presumed to be in a position to speak not only on instructions from home but with the authority of the dominion of whose government he was the head. But a dominion minister other than the Prime Minister would not be a principal at all but only an envoy. That deprived him of authority and made his possible contribution to the discussions of the War Cabinet unequal to the disadvantage of greater numbers which his presence implied. The Prime Ministers of Canada, South Africa, and New Zealand, noted Mr. Churchill, had said that they did not desire such representation, and some of them had taken a very strongly adverse view on the ground that no one but the Prime Minister could speak for their government except on instructions. What might happen otherwise was that the liberty of action of dominion governments might be prejudiced by any decisions to which their minister in London became a party. From the point of view of the United Kingdom the proposal was equally objectionable. The addition of four dominion representatives would involve the retirement from the War Cabinet of an equal number of British ministers. That would destroy the basis of the coalition government, since Mr. Churchill was not prepared to increase the War Cabinet's numbers so that they became too large for the efficient conduct of business.

Mr. Churchill suggested to Mr. Fadden the possibility of the appointment of a special envoy to discuss any particular aspect of the common war effort, but he pointed out that such an envoy would not and could not be a responsible partner in the daily work of government, and if he remained in London as a regular institution there would be the risk of duplication of function between such an envoy and the Australian High Commissioner in London. If such a risk could not be obviated, none the less its existence had to be frankly faced, especially in view of the fact that the whole system of the High Commissioners in daily contact with the Secretary of State for Dominion Affairs was working well.

The Australian government, with Mr. Churchill's suggestion of a special

[1] Churchill, iii. 758–60 (Mansergh, *Documents*, i. 540–2).

envoy before it, decided to proceed with the appointment of a ministerial representative to the British War Cabinet. Mr. Fadden's tenuous majority added to the difficulties of selection. The choice fell on an elder statesman and former Prime Minister, Sir Earle Page, at the time of his appointment Minister of Commerce. Before he reached London, however, the Fadden government fell. Mr. Curtin's Labour government which replaced it invited Sir Earle Page to continue as Australia's Envoy Extraordinary to the War Cabinet, but the authority which he could reasonably hope to command was undermined by the fact that he was now a member not of a government but of an Opposition party. On his arrival in London Sir Earle Page defined the nature of his mission in terms which suggested that it was partly representative and partly exploratory. His function, he was reported to have said, was

to establish personal Cabinet liaison between the United Kingdom and Commonwealth Governments. The primary purposes of his mission would be the presentation of Australia's point of view on certain immediate problems of war strategy and the arrangement of the best mechanics for maintaining a system of direct Cabinet representation in London.[1]

It is apparent from the earlier discussions in the Australian War Council that what the Labour leaders desired was the exercise of a strong personal influence on the making of Pacific war policy, and, as Mr. Curtin in effect allowed, membership of the War Cabinet was not an end in itself but a means to that end.[2] Whether Sir Earle Page was in a position to exercise such an influence was now very open to question, but there was at least much to be said for learning from experience whether Australian representation in the War Cabinet could be secured without bringing about substantial and undesirable changes in its composition and without leading to duplication of function with the Australian High Commissioner.

While Australia, passing through a succession of political crises at home, was expressing through Mr. Menzies, Mr. Fadden, and Mr. Curtin (her three Prime Ministers in two months) in turn a sense either of uneasiness or of open dissatisfaction with the system of Commonwealth co-operation at the highest level, Mr. Mackenzie King, who arrived in London in August 1941, went out of his way to pay the warmest tributes to its efficiency. He could not, he said, conceive of a more effective means of communication than those which existed at present. What they had in actual practice was the most perfect, continuing conference of Cabinets that any group of nations could possibly have. An Imperial War Cabinet in London might seem more effective in reaching the necessary decisions, but speaking from long experience he asserted that the existing method was infinitely better. In times of emergency it was particularly important that decisions should not be those of one man but of a united government, and because decisions had been reached on that

[1] *The Times*, 8 September 1941.   [2] Hasluck, i. 535–6.

basis the system of Commonwealth co-operation had worked admirably since the outbreak of war and, continued Mr. Mackenzie King,

> So far as relations between the two Governments are concerned, there never has been a time when they were closer. No single point of difference has arisen since the beginning of the war between us in matters which are essential. In the last War differences did arise continually. The reason for the present position is that before an important step is taken we have been consulted; we have had the opportunity of expressing our views, freely and frankly, and we have considered all aspects of the matter under review. Then a general consensus of opinion is reached.[1]

Neither General Smuts nor Mr. Fraser was so forward in his praises but they, too, were satisfied. They did not wish for radical change and above all—and this was of cardinal importance—they did not desire representation in the United Kingdom War Cabinet. In practice, therefore, Mr. Churchill was confronted not with the question of over-weighting his Cabinet with four dominion representatives, but with the much simpler question of including a single Australian envoy.

The contrast between the views of the Canadian and the Australian governments on methods of imperial co-operation was further underlined. Where Mr. Menzies returned from London dissatisfied with the working of the system of dominion representation on the War Cabinet, Mr. Mackenzie King came back to Canada wholly content and, as he remarked in Montreal, 'more firmly than ever opposed to the formation of an Imperial War Cabinet'.[2] These differences derived in part at least from the different situations of the two countries. By contrast with Australia's isolation and exposure to attack from the Pacific, Canada lay in the heart of the Western world, well placed not only for rapid consultation with London but, equally important, for rapid consultation with Washington. Canada in fact throughout the war was close to the points at which decisions were made, Australia was far removed from them. And the two powers principally concerned in the making of those decisions, the United Kingdom and the United States, were agreed in any eventuality upon a strategy of 'Hitler first' which well accorded with Canada's traditional eastward outlook, whereas Australia, isolated in the Pacific, could derive no comparable satisfaction from an order of priorities which, if correct in strategic terms, none the less gravely accentuated the dangers to which she was exposed.

The Approach of the Pacific War, July–December 1941

Mr. Churchill was saddened by the news of Mr. Menzies's downfall on 29 August 1941, and, while scrupulously refraining 'from all interference in Australian politics', he could not but feel that it was a great pity that all the knowledge Mr. Menzies had acquired, especially during the two months in

---

[1] *The Times*, 22 August 1941. [2] Ibid. 9 September 1941.

which he had sat in the United Kingdom War Cabinet, should be wasted.¹ But so in large measure it was, for Mr. Menzies's offer to serve in a national government was rejected. It may be that there was much to be said for a coalition Cabinet in Australia so long as the balance of the parties was so even, though it is to be noted that in this respect none of the dominions followed the example of the United Kingdom. Mr. Churchill's regrets, however, were doubtless accentuated by the less easy relations he enjoyed with Mr. Menzies's successor governments.² At the very outset of Mr. Fadden's short-lived administration there began an acrimonious dispute about the relief of the Australian division in Tobruk which continued after Mr. Fadden's fall from office. For a variety of reasons, none of which were to be lightly disregarded, Mr. Fadden's government demanded the immediate relief of these Australian troops by other forces. Primarily and as seen from Canberra this was not a political but a military matter, in which the Australian War Cabinet acted upon the advice given to it by the commander of the Australian forces in the Middle East, General Blamey, and the United Kingdom government upon the advice of the Commander-in-Chief, General Auchinleck. General Auchinleck in fact repudiated vigorously the suggestion that these troops should be withdrawn; Mr. Churchill sought to dissuade Mr. Fadden, finally sending him, on 11 September, with a covering and persuasively worded dispatch, General Auchinleck's private telegram to London about the relief of the Australians in Tobruk. But Mr. Fadden was not to be persuaded, and on 15 September Mr. Churchill yielded. 'Orders', he cabled Mr. Fadden, 'will at once be given in accordance with your decision'.³ To General Auchinleck Mr. Churchill expressed his grief at the Australian attitude, but added: 'I have long feared the dangerous reactions on Australian and world opinion of our seeming to fight all our battles in the Middle East only with Dominion troops.' He urged especially reconsideration of General Auchinleck's decision, 'painful to us', to place the 50th British Division in Cyprus, since Cyprus, thought to be a position of special danger when the movement was made, had ceased to be so with the outbreak of the war in Russia.⁴ General Auchinleck, however, was so deeply affronted by the insistence of Mr. Fadden on the withdrawal of Australian forces from Tobruk against his advice that he wished to tender his resignation on the ground that he no longer possessed the confidence of the Australian government. Mr. Churchill, thereupon, enlisted the good offices of the Minister of State in Cairo, Mr.

¹ Churchill, iii. 365–6. Mr. Menzies did, however, continue as a member of the Advisory War Council, which was to retain its influence for some time yet.   ² Ibid. p. 367.
³ Ibid. p. 368. See also Hasluck, i. 544 and, for a full account of the situation based upon a study of the Australian Cabinet records, app. 10, pp. 616–24. There are some important differences in emphasis between this account and that given by Mr. Churchill. Here we are concerned not with the substance of the dispute but with its bearing on relations between the two countries and the means by which they were conducted.
⁴ Churchill, iii. 368–9.

Oliver Lyttelton, sending him a complete copy of the exchanges between the Australian and United Kingdom governments, with the comment that while he was himself 'astounded' at the decision of the Australian government, it was imperative that no public dispute should arise between the United Kingdom and Australia. Once again, added Mr. Churchill, the trouble had arisen largely 'through our not having any British infantry divisions in the various actions, thus leading the world and Australia to suppose that we are fighting our battles with Dominion troops only'.[1] General Auchinleck was appeased. Mr. Fadden fell from office. Though Mr. Churchill in his own words hastened to put himself 'in friendly touch' with Mr. Fadden's successor, Mr. Curtin, any hope he may have entertained that the new government might prove more malleable than its predecessors about the relief of the Australians in Tobruk was destined to be promptly and sharply dispelled.[2] The troops were withdrawn. The insistence of successive Australian governments on this being done in itself suggests that the reasons for it were more substantial than either General Auchinleck or Mr. Churchill was prepared to allow.

Mr. Churchill concludes his account of the Tobruk incident with the remark that 'the Australian Governments had little reason to feel confidence at this time in British direction of the war'.[3] This lack of confidence is to be attributed principally to the course of events in the Middle East and especially to the outcome of the Greek campaign. But, quite apart from the actual conduct of the war in the Middle East, there was a deeper difference of opinion about strategic priorities which somewhat impaired good relations between them. It would be a grave over-simplification to say that the United Kingdom accorded to the Middle East as well as to the Atlantic area priority over the Far East, for in fact the Chief of the Imperial General Staff, Field-Marshal Sir John Dill, positively reasserted in May 1941 as an accepted principle of imperial strategy that 'in the last resort the security of Singapore comes before that of Egypt'.[4] This was a view which the United States military advisers also entertained.[5] But Mr. Churchill strongly dissented.

This [he wrote later] was indeed a tragic issue, like having to choose whether your son or your daughter should be killed. For my part I did not believe that anything that might happen in Malaya could amount to a fifth part of the loss of Egypt, the Suez Canal, and the Middle East. I would not tolerate the idea of abandoning the struggle for Egypt, and was resigned to pay whatever forfeits were exacted in Malaya.[6]

And in such matters Mr. Churchill's view was apt to prevail. Of this the Australian government was only too well aware, and the knowledge brought it

---

[1] Ibid. p. 369.   [2] Ibid. pp. 370–1.   [3] Ibid. p. 372.
[4] Ibid. p. 375.   [5] Sherwood, i. 313–14.
[6] Churchill, iii. 379. Admiral Raeder agreed with him; see Bullock, *Hitler*, pp. 586–8 for Raeder's attempts to persuade Hitler of the possibilities in the Middle East in the summer of 1941.

no reassurance. The Japanese were in effective occupation of Indo-China by late July 1941, and action taken by the United States, the United Kingdom, and the Netherlands governments to freeze all Japanese assets, thus bringing trade to a standstill and depriving Japan of her overseas oil supplies, might provoke her at any moment to launch an attack from Indo-China upon an exposed and well-nigh defenceless Malaya and a Singapore which the Australians at least at no time deemed impregnable.

The United Kingdom government by no means discounted the impending danger in the East, recognizing that with the higher priority given to home defence and to the Middle East there could be little confidence about the Empire's capacity to withstand a Japanese assault. There was a somewhat belated recognition of the need for a firmer direction of United Kingdom policies in the threatened area, Mr. Churchill in late July appointing Mr. Duff Cooper Chancellor of the Duchy of Lancaster (to enable him to retain his seat in the Cabinet) and Minister of State in the Far East with prospective headquarters in Singapore. This appointment was welcomed by the Australian government. Mr. Duff Cooper was, however, invested with no overriding authority in military matters, his responsibility being to ensure the greater co-ordination of the civilian administrative services and dominion and allied policies in the area.[1] At this late hour these were no longer matters of the greatest moment.

Early in August 1941 Mr. Churchill advised the Prime Ministers of the dominions of his impending meeting with President Roosevelt in Newfoundland waters, Mr. Menzies, as has already been noted, receiving the telegram at the outset of his tour of the Australian states. This was accompanied by the inquiry from the Dominions Office to all dominion governments about a possible warning to Japan,[2] and Mr. Menzies also received a supplementary personal message from Mr. Bruce, Australia's High Commissioner in London, in which he outlined possible courses of action with regard to the Japanese threat to Thailand. After discussion in the Australian Cabinet, a message was addressed direct to Mr. Churchill, and repeated to all dominion Prime Ministers, stating that the Australian government favoured the course advocated by its High Commissioner, namely a declaration to Japan made on behalf of the British Empire as a whole, or preferably the British Empire and the United States, making any Japanese invasion of Thailand a *casus belli*.

We are of the opinion [cabled Mr. Menzies] as the Government of one of the two British Dominions which are most directly affected that the first question should be answered 'yes' [i.e. about a British Empire declaration] and that while every pressure should be maintained upon the United States, it would be an error to condition our action upon American action, though actual objection by the United States of America would of course be fatal.[3]

[1] Churchill, iii. 379; and for a fuller account Duff Cooper, *Old Men Forget* (London, Hart-Davis, 1953), ch. xviii.
[2] See above, pp. 111–12.
[3] Hasluck, i. 530–1.

In the *White House Papers of Harry L. Hopkins* it is said that Mr. Churchill consulted the dominions in advance about policy towards Japan as a matter not merely of courtesy but also of prudence, because he hoped 'some momentous agreement' might come from the Atlantic meeting which would require ratification by dominion governments. 'The agreement that Churchill hoped for', proceeds Mr. Sherwood, 'was definitely not the Atlantic Charter: it was the establishment of a common policy of resistance to further Japanese aggression.'[1] Though Mr. Churchill does not himself concede that this was so, it is the case that he brought with him drafts of 'Parallel communications to the Japanese Government' which might be sent by the United States and the United Kingdom governments, but only on arrival and at the President's suggestion prepared one for an agreed statement of war aims such as was embodied in the Atlantic Charter.

In respect of the Far East, Mr. Churchill impressed upon the President, and especially upon Mr. Sumner Welles,

that some declaration of the kind he had drafted with respect to Japan was in his opinion in the highest degree important, and that he did not think there was much hope left unless the United States made such a clear-cut declaration of preventing Japan from expanding further to the south, in which event the prevention of war between Great Britain and Japan appeared to be hopeless.[2]

Mr. Churchill further expressed his conviction that if such a declaration were made by the United States, by Britain and the Dominions, the Netherlands, and possibly the Soviet Union, it 'would definitely restrain Japan'. The President agreed emphatically ' "that every effort should be made to prevent the outbreak of war with Japan". But—the question eternally was: Would a tough line, a medium line, or a soft line best suit that purpose?'[3] The answer on the part of the United States was once again a medium line. A warning was conveyed by the President on his return to Washington to the Japanese Ambassador. There were no joint or parallel British and United States declarations. Both the Australian and the United Kingdom governments were disappointed at this non-fulfilment of expectations about which Mr. Churchill had felt sufficiently sanguine to cable Mr. Menzies on 15 August in explicit terms,[4] but they reacted differently. Mr. Churchill, thereafter, believed that Britain should wait upon a United States lead; the Australian government continued in its view that if the United States was not prepared to align herself with Britain in issuing a warning to Japan, the British Commonwealth should issue such a warning and underwrite the consequences without United States backing. Both, and perhaps especially the Australian government, would have been somewhat reassured had they seen the text of

---

[1] Sherwood, i. 351. The 'parallel communications' are reprinted pp. 354–5. See also Churchill, iii. ch. xxiv; Sumner Welles, *Where Are we Heading?* (New York, Harper, 1946), pp. 2–15, and Langer & Gleason, ii. ch. xxi.
[2] Sherwood, i. 355.   [3] Ibid.   [4] Churchill, iii. 399.

a memorandum dated 11 September 1941, submitted by the United States Chiefs of Staff, General Marshall and Admiral Stark, to the President. In it were listed 'major national objectives', and second only to the preservation of the territorial, economic, and ideological integrity of the United States was rated 'prevention of the disruption of the British Empire'.[1]

The concrete results of the meeting between President and Prime Minister in Newfoundland waters served primarily to strengthen Britain's position in the West. The terms of the Atlantic Charter, which received the prior approval of the United Kingdom Cabinet reinforced by the presence of the New Zealand Prime Minister, but not of dominion governments (which were however kept fully informed), were calculated, despite the language of universality employed, to appeal most directly to the oppressed and suffering peoples of Europe. The inclusion in the sixth section of a reference to the 'final destruction of Nazi tyranny' was tantamount to a challenge on the part of the non-belligerent United States to Nazi Germany, which, as Mr. Churchill remarks, 'in ordinary times would have implied warlike action'.[2]

The members of the Labour government which took office in Australia in mid-October 1941, with their long-standing preoccupation with home defence, were even less disposed than the Menzies–Fadden administrations to acquiesce in the prevailing Anglo-American view, implicitly reaffirmed at the Atlantic meeting, of the secondary place of the Pacific in the strategy of the war. Throughout earlier discussions about Australian representation in London the Labour leaders had shown anxiety as pronounced as that of their political and traditionally more imperialist opponents that the Australian voice should be heard effectively in the making of political and strategic decisions in London. There was nothing paradoxical in their attitude; on the contrary, it was the logical outcome of their desire to substitute their own conception of strategy in the Pacific for traditional and, as they believed, outdated ideas which rested on an overestimate of the importance of naval as against air power, and more particularly of the power of the Royal Navy to determine the course of a Pacific war. While confirming their predecessors' decisions about Australian troops in the Middle East they underlined more heavily the importance of co-operation with the United States (which was not in itself indeed disputed), and in so doing were tempted to overestimate first the deterrent influence and secondly the naval power of the United States available at the time for the waging of war in the Pacific. The unhappy upshot was that, while only too well justified in their misgivings about the adequacy of traditional sources of Australian security, they were misled by

---

[1] Sherwood, i. 414.
[2] Churchill, iii. 394. According to the account in the *White House Papers* the Americans were astonished 'at the speed of communication and of action thereon' between Mr. Churchill on the *Prince of Wales* and Whitehall (Sherwood, i. 362).

their over-confidence in the influence and power which the United States could exert in the Pacific. In conjunction the two contributed to the shrillness of the Australian official reaction to the grave events of December 1941.

There was the proverbial lull before the storm. The Labour government took office at a time of rising hopes in the possibility of averting war with Japan. A *Review of the Situation in the Far East*,[1] prepared in General Headquarters Far East at Singapore and dated 26 September 1941, expressed the view that since May 1941 the situation had changed from being very much in favour of Japan to being very much against her. The 'more positive' attitude of the United States, the violent reaction in the Commonwealth and elsewhere to the Japanese occupation of Indo-China, the military alliance between Britain and Russia, and 'the virtual certainty of a military undertaking between the British and Dutch in the Far East' were considered the main factors in bringing about this change. It was also thought that the German attack on Russia, coming so soon after Hitler had encouraged the Japanese to sign the Soviet-Japanese non-aggression pact, had 'confused the minds' of the Japanese —though not so much as to obscure the fact that for them it would be 'madness' to embark on a war in the south while strong Russian forces remained in the maritime provinces, and more 'attractive' to attack the Soviet Union. This assessment proceeded to sanguine speculation as to whether the Japanese might be moved to withdraw from Indo-China by strong 'diplomatic pressure'.

Two ministerial travellers, the one eastward and the other westward bound on impossible missions, sensed this strange illusion of security. Mr. Duff Cooper on his way to Singapore found opinion in the United States 'curiously optimistic', and being assured on excellent authority in Washington that it would be suicidal for the Japanese to enter the war, reminded his audience that the Japanese, as a people, were addicted to suicide. At Pearl Harbour there seemed to be less consciousness of the threat of war than on the east coast of America, whilst in doomed Singapore 'the same optimistic atmosphere' prevailed.[2] Sir Earle Page on his way to London discussed the memorandum on the Far Eastern situation referred to above at a meeting at which the Commanders-in-Chief, Far East, and Mr. Duff Cooper were present on 29 September. In general outline it was accepted, but, with a note of realism that deserves to be placed on record, those present concluded with the 'emphatic opinion' that the only real deterrent to further Japanese aggression would be a British fleet based on Singapore, and in the absence of such a fleet Japan would be able to strike at her selected moment.[3] Sir Earle Page proceeding on his journey saw General MacArthur, Commander of the United States Army Forces in the Far East, at Manila on 6 October; from him he heard the reassuring opinion that Japan was facing a

---
[1] Hasluck, i. 541–2. For an account of the situation as seen from Washington, see Sherwood, i. ch. xix and Hull, *Memoirs*, ii. ch. lxxiv.
[2] Cooper, *Old Men Forget*, pp. 291, 293.
[3] Hasluck, i. 542.

critical situation, that she was overextended, and that after the five years of war in China she would need a long period of recuperation before she could undertake another major war.[1] On 26 October a telegram from Mr. Churchill to Mr. Curtin expressed the view that Japan would not run into war unless or until Russia was decisively broken. On 1 November Mr. Duff Cooper sent a report to London concerned alike, it would seem, with sound if spacious speculation about the future of Asia, minor reorganization of United Kingdom departmental representation, and a recommendation that a Commissioner General for the Far East be appointed to preside over a Far Eastern War Council. Mr. Menzies was his choice for the post. But while Mr. Duff Cooper's report was printed as a Cabinet paper, its author had no subsequent evidence of any interest in it, possibly because it was not circulated until early December.[2]

On 5 November in London the Australian High Commissioner and the Australian Envoy Extraordinary to the British Cabinet—to give Sir Earle Page his appropriate designation—now arrived at his destination, submitted a 'strongly prepared' case for the strengthening of the Singapore defences on the assumption that a policy of deterrents had a reasonable chance of success. It was discussed by the War Cabinet a week later on 12 November. At this meeting Mr. Churchill expounded the view that the correct strategy was to move armed strength from theatre to theatre as the situation changed, and that consequently it would be an error to move forces to the Far East, as Australia desired, because they might 'remain inactive for a year'.[3] Dr. Evatt, the Minister for External Affairs, fully aware of the risk of a Japanese attack before the British position could be reinforced and anxious at all costs to gain time, was seemingly convinced even late in November that 'the Japanese are clearly anxious to avoid war'.[4] There followed a protracted correspondence between the Australian and United Kingdom governments seeking to define precisely the circumstances in which the countries of the Commonwealth would go to war. Again there was some divergence of view, Mr. Churchill stating on 1 December 1941 when Sir Earle Page and Mr. Bruce called upon him that the British policy was 'to march in line with the United States of America', not to anticipate the American reaction to further Japanese aggression in South-East Asia but to support it. On 6 December his point of view was reported in a telegram from Mr. Averell Harriman to Mr. Harry Hopkins.

The President should be informed [wrote Mr. Harriman] of Churchill's belief that in the event of aggression by the Japanese it would be the policy of the British to postpone taking any action—even though this delay might involve some military sacrifice—until the President has taken such action as, under the circumstances, he considers best. Then Churchill will act 'not within the hour, but within the minute'.[5]

[1] Hasluck, i. 543.   [2] Cooper, *Old Men Forget*, pp. 297-9.
[3] Hasluck, i. 548.   [4] Ibid. p. 549.   [5] Sherwood, i. 428.

COMMONWEALTH CO-OPERATION IN WAR

The Australian view, however, remained that the British nations should act with or without American assistance.[1] On the evening of 6 December Mr. Casey, who would not seem to have been cognizant of all the information intercepted by the United States Government,[2] cabled Canberra from Washington to say that the President had decided to send a message to the Emperor, and to issue a warning on 9 December; and that a warning to be issued on behalf of the governments of the British Commonwealth would follow on 10 December. The text of the latter was delivered to the President on 7 December. It concluded,

If Japan attempts to establish her influence in Thailand by force or threat of force she will do so at her own peril and His Majesty's Governments will at once take all appropriate measures. Should hostilities unfortunately result the responsibility will rest with Japan.[3]

Whether the President ever read the text of this proposed British warning, the product of such protracted consultation, is uncertain. By the night of 7 December he had other preoccupations. The Japanese by then had placed themselves beyond the reach of warnings and added to the history of our times 'a date that will live in infamy'.

[1] Hasluck, i. 554. For an account of the more cautious New Zealand views see Wood, ch. xv.   [2] Cf. Langer & Gleason, ii. 902–37.   [3] Sherwood, i. 429–3.

CHAPTER III

COMMONWEALTH CO-OPERATION IN WAR: THE SECOND PHASE, DECEMBER 1941–AUGUST 1945

A War Between Continents

DECEMBER 1941 was for Japan a favourable but not the most favourable moment to enter the war. If the resources of the Commonwealth alone were at all times unequal to the waging of a major war in the East and in the West simultaneously, the most desperate period of Britain's struggle for survival in the West reached its climax in the spring of 1941. It was then, with the Atlantic lifeline most dangerously threatened by German U-boats and with the German army still uncommitted in Eastern Europe, that Japanese intervention might have had its most devastating effect. Hitler himself sensed the moment and the greatness of the opportunity that lay open before the members of the Tripartite Pact. On 5 March 1941 he issued his *Basic Order No. 24*, 'regarding collaboration with Japan'.[1] Its contents and the reports of the discussions between Hitler and Ribbentrop on the one hand and the Japanese Ambassador and Foreign Minister, Matsuoka, on his visit to Berlin on the other, afford conclusive evidence that Hitler at that time wanted the Japanese to enter the war at the earliest possible moment.[2]

In March 1941 Hitler sought to persuade Japan to strike a deadly blow at the British Commonwealth by an assault on Singapore. Britain was the principal enemy of Nazi Germany, and the capture of Singapore, so Hitler felt, might convince her that her cause was lost, and without actual invasion compel her to sue for peace. It was a course which seemingly might also yield great advantages to Japan by enabling her to realize her dreams of domination in Eastern and South-Eastern Asia. 'Few situations', Hitler told Matsuoka on 27 March 1941, 'could be envisaged which offered greater facilities for the realization of Japanese aims and larger possibility of success.' England was 'tied down in Europe'; America could either arm herself or assist England or wage war on another front. If she helped England she could not arm herself; if she abandoned England, England would be destroyed and 'America would find herself confronting the powers of the Three-Power Pact alone. In no case ... could America wage war on another front.' So Hitler reasoned, and in contemplating this seemingly favourable opportunity for the destruction of the British world Empire he became almost lyrical about the prospects before

---

[1] *IMT Nuremberg*, vol. 34, doc. 075–C; cf. also Bullock, *Hitler*, pp. 577–8.
[2] *Nazi-Soviet Relations*, pp. 280–324.

Germany and Japan. 'There could never in human imagination', he told Matsuoka in 1941, 'be a better condition for a joint effort of the Three-Power Pact countries than the one which had now been produced. . . . Such a moment would never return. It was unique in history.' He allowed there was a certain element of risk, but it was extraordinarily slight at a moment in which Russia and England were eliminated and America was not yet ready. The Japanese, German, and Italian peoples 'would achieve great successes if they drew the necessary conclusions from the present unique situation'. Matsuoka, though alluding pointedly to the risks liable to be incurred by any agressive action, agreed. But 'a people found such a Führer once in a thousand years. The Japanese people had not yet found their Führer.' There were accordingly doubts and uncertainties in the making of Japanese policy.[1] Hitler and Ribbentrop tried hard to dispel them. There was particular emphasis on Singapore. 'Japan', insisted Ribbentrop on 29 March 1941, 'would best help the common cause if she did not allow herself to be diverted by anything from the attack on Singapore' at the earliest possible date. He asked Matsuoka for maps, 'so that the Führer, who certainly must be considered the greatest expert of modern times on military matters, could advise Japan as to the best method for the attack.'[2] But, while the Japanese Foreign Minister was seemingly willing to believe that the German nation in Europe and the Japanese in the Far East were associated by a divine command to bring about the break-up of the British Empire and establish a new order, he remained non-committal about the role Japan would play. Hitler concealed from the Japanese his intention to invade Russia, and the Japanese Foreign Minister, the emissary of a deeply divided government, also kept his own counsel.

Hitler's attempts to focus the attention of the Japanese upon Singapore indicated at once his own confidence in the ability of Germany unaided to erase 'the Russia of Stalin' from the map and his desire to see the forces of his Eastern ally concentrated on an attack upon a British imperial base whose fall would wreck British defence arrangements for the Pacific–Indian Ocean area, without necessarily giving cause to the Americans to intervene. In March 1941 he professed indeed to believe that a Japanese capture of Singapore would strengthen the hands of non-interventionists in the United States. By July, however, Hitler had changed his mind. Despite the initial success of German arms in Russia he now wanted Japan to attack Vladivostok as well as, or in preference to, Singapore.

. . . the present Japanese Government [cabled the egregious Ribbentrop to the German Ambassador in Tokyo on 10 July] would really act inexcusably toward the future of their nation if they would not take this unique opportunity to solve the Russian problem. . . . It is simply impossible that Japan should not settle the matter of Vladivostok and the Siberian area as soon as her military preparations are

[1] Ibid. pp. 292–3.   [2] Ibid. p. 298.

completed. ... I ask you to employ all available means in further insisting upon Japan's entry into the war against Russia at the earliest possible date.[1]

But the Japanese were not amenable. They entertained ambitions they were not prepared to abandon for the sake of an ally whose reliability they had so much reason to doubt.

The Japanese attack on Pearl Harbour in December 1941 was, therefore, not only later in time than Hitler had urged but in direction also disregarded altogether the advice he had tendered to them in March and in July 1941. Far from strengthening the non-interventionists in the United States, as Ribbentrop hoped, the Japanese by their attack on the American Fleet had done the one thing necessary to unite popular sentiment behind an interventionist President.

Hitler had been neither consulted nor forewarned, save in general terms, by the Japanese about their intentions. Japanese allusions to the possibility of their provoking war with the United States, according to Count Ciano, filled the Germans with misgivings. But once the attack was made Hitler professed to be delighted with it. Disregarding the possible advantages of holding his hand, he declared war on the United States on 11 December.

> I can only be grateful to Providence [he said] that it entrusted me with the leadership in this historic struggle which, for the next five hundred or a thousand years, will be described as decisive, not only for the history of Germany but for the whole of Europe and indeed the whole world. ... A historical revision on a unique scale has been imposed upon us by the Creator.[2]

Mussolini, who soon liked to describe himself as 'the foremost pro-Japanese in the world'[3] as some small antidote to his growing subservience to his overbearing German ally, remarked on learning of the impending Japanese attack on the United States: 'Thus we arrive at the war between continents, which I have foreseen since September 1939.'[4] The language was grandiose but so also were the circumstances.

The extension of the war brought into alliance with the British Commonwealth not merely in Western Europe, as in the First World War, but in almost every part of the world the state which had seceded from the British Empire more than a century and a half earlier. If this association in war carried with it reassurance of an ultimate victory and, especially for the United Kingdom and the dominions, the prospect of a welcome partnership of the Anglo-Saxon peoples in a common cause and a supreme crisis, Japanese intervention opened up for the British Colonial Empire in Asia a period of trial to which politically as well as militarily it proved unequal. Hitler was not

---

[1] *IMT Nuremberg*, iii. 384 (doc. 2896–PS).
[2] Quoted in Bullock, *Hitler*, pp. 608–9.
[3] Galeazzo Ciano, *Ciano's Diary, 1939–43*, ed. by M. Muggeridge (London, Heinemann, 1947), p. 456.
[4] Ibid. p. 405.

mistaken about the vulnerability of the British colonial possessions in Asia. Nor was he seemingly at fault in advising the Japanese that the spring of 1941 was for them a most favourable moment to strike. As it was they achieved spectacular victories but no major ends. That was largely because, to quote Mr. Hinsley, 'The attack on Pearl Harbour was a striking example of the disunity of the Axis Powers'.[1] The major effort of Germany and Italy in the West was spent before the Japanese ally irrupted in the East. Within six months of Pearl Harbour the United States Navy had recovered its strength, had a success in the Coral Sea, and won a victory at Midway Island. But if the Japanese onslaught was checked within that brief period of time (except in New Guinea where they retained the initiative till early 1943) the consequences of their overpowering the Western colonial empires in Asia were lasting. Japan failed to establish a colonial empire of her own; she inflicted upon the Western colonial empires in Asia a mortal wound.

Commonwealth Co-operation. Some Consequences of the Entry of the United States into the War

The first and the critical phase of Commonwealth co-operation in the Second World War came to an end with the Japanese attack upon the United States in December 1941. The years 1939–41 had been for the peoples of the British Commonwealth a period of improvisation, of great danger, of fortitude unexampled in their history and of leadership of those European peoples who preferred to perish rather than submit to Nazi tyranny. If until June 1940 the higher direction of the war in the West was exercised by the French and British governments, and after December 1941 by the governments of the United States and the United Kingdom—or more precisely by the President of the United States and the Prime Minister of the United Kingdom advised by the Joint Chiefs of Staff Committees in Washington and in London and with such degree of co-operation with the Soviet Union as proved possible—in the intervening period, and especially for the year when the Commonwealth stood alone, the dominions exercised their greatest influence on war policy and on the making of strategy. That influence, considerable though it was, should not, however, be overestimated. Mr. Menzies was correct in stating, after his experience in the United Kingdom War Cabinet in 1941, that power was concentrated to a remarkable degree in Mr. Churchill's hands. But it is not only or even chiefly by their part in the making of policy that the contribution of the dominions is to be measured. It was the presence of Canadian forces in the United Kingdom, of Australian, New Zealand, South African, and Indian forces in the Middle East, comprising as they did so large a proportion of the trained forces at the disposal of the British Commonwealth after the evacuation from Dunkirk, that ensured survival. It was their presence and their prowess on the battlefield that gave to the dominions individually and

[1] Hinsley, *Hitler's Strategy*, p. 189. See generally pp. 176–91.

collectively a place in the Commonwealth and in the world such as they had not hitherto enjoyed.[1]

With the entry of the United States into the war the importance of exclusively Commonwealth organizations declined. This was inevitable. The higher direction of the war in all its aspects was henceforward concentrated in Washington and London, and on the supply side final responsibility was vested in the Anglo-American Combined Boards. Three of these Boards were established as a result of the Prime Minister's first Washington visit in December 1941—January 1942. They were the Munitions Assignments Board, which consisted of two committees under the Combined Chiefs of Staff in London and in Washington, the Combined Shipping Adjustment Boards, which were established in both capitals, and the Combined Raw Materials Board, which had headquarters in Washington and its counterpart in London.[2] To these were added notably the Combined Production and Resources Board and the Combined Food Board, both in June 1942. Dominion governments were not represented on them, all the Combined Boards being at first wholly Anglo-American in membership. Liaison with other members of the Commonwealth was, however, maintained through their missions in Washington and the offices of the High Commissioners in London. In particular various Commonwealth committees were established in London which were supplementary to the Combined Boards and worked through them.[3] Of particular importance was the Empire Clearing House, whose first meeting was held in March 1942, and which was concerned with the purchase and allocation of raw materials. Its duties were merged with those of the Commonwealth Supply Council in October 1942, and the new body was charged with responsibility for the co-ordination of arrangements for supply throughout the Empire. Canada was not a member either of the Empire Clearing House or of the Supply Council because of her already established relationship with the supply organization in Washington.

Canada alone of the dominions had special arrangements with the United States in respect both of defence and of supply before the American entry into the war in December 1941, and she continued to enjoy comparatively favourable treatment thereafter. In November 1942 Canada, in view of her increasing importance in the war effort and more particularly of the contribution she could make to the supplies necessary for the winning of the war, was included in the top-level membership of the Combined Production and Resources Board, and in October 1943 of the Combined Food Board.[4] The way

---

[1] The part played by dominion forces (other than those of South Africa) in the Second World War is being fully recorded in their own official war histories.

[2] Cmd. 6332.   [3] Hancock & Gowing, pp. 394–5.

[4] For an account of Canada's position in relation to the Boards see H. G. Skilling, *Canadian Representation Abroad* (Toronto, Ryerson Press for CIIA 1945), pp. 316–23. The Canadian government, in seeking membership of some of these Boards, seems to have felt that Canada's contribution to various phases of the Allied war effort, and not her vital interest in the policies

in which Canada became a member of the Combined Food Board throws some light on the attitudes of the United States and United Kingdom governments to the separate representation of Commonwealth countries.

In August 1943 Mr. Hull, at the instance of the War Food Administrator, suggested to the President that Canada, Australia, and New Zealand, which were making large contributions to Allied food supplies, should be represented on the Board. Mr. Roosevelt accordingly proposed this to the British government, which agreed to Canada's membership but preferred that Australia and New Zealand should be represented only on the London Food Council—a matter on which 'the United States took the position that the status of the London Food Council was a matter of Empire concern and hence did not require its approval'.[1] The President approved a draft message of invitation to Canada and sent it to Mr. Churchill, who redrafted it in a form which, said Mr. A. A. Berle, 'cuts down recognition of Canada's right to be consulted. We do not agree; but it is not worth a fuss'.[2] Thereupon the invitation was sent and accepted. It is clear that the United States government recognized the dominion governments as in no way subordinate to the United Kingdom; nevertheless, it still held the view that the United Kingdom could speak for the Commonwealth as a whole, and, as earlier,

> set its face steadily against separate approaches to it on supply matters. . . . The Administration insisted . . . that the Commonwealth countries should first co-ordinate their needs with the British Government and should use a common channel for their approach to the American Government. . . . This was an independent and unchanging American policy, although it happened to coincide with the policy preferred by London. . . .[3]

In general the setting up of the Anglo-American Combined Boards meant that the control of the resources of the united nations, other than Russia, passed under the authority of the two great Western powers with a completeness that was demanded by the needs of the war situation but was not altogether agreeable to the smaller Allied powers. Even Mr. Mackenzie King was moved to observe[4] that at some stage a more representative character should be imparted to the bodies invested with the supreme direction of the war, while New Zealand and Australian leaders were outspoken in their complaints. Australia,

---

adopted, was its qualification. 'Where Canada has a special contribution to make, a special "function" to perform, Canadian representation has been sought, in accordance with what has been described as a "functional" theory of international organization. "It is a tribute to Canada's importance, and also a recognition of the functional principle", Mr. Pearson, Canadian Minister to Washington, has said, "that she alone has been included in the top-level membership of two of these boards . . . along with the United States and the United Kingdom" ' (ibid. pp. 319–20). See also below, pp. 312–13.

[1] S. McKee Rosen, *The Combined Boards of the Second World War* (New York, Columbia University Press, 1951), p. 232.   [2] Quoted ibid. p. 233.
[3] Hall, *North American Supply*, p. 100; the author adds 'and its fellow members of the Commonwealth'. This is questionably true of Australia apart from Canada.
[4] Canada, H. of C. Deb., 1943, vol. 5, p. 4558.

said Dr Evatt in 1943, was not a member of the Munitions Assignments Board, which took its general directive on strategic requirements from the Joint Anglo-American Chiefs of Staff Committee, on which Australia also was unrepresented. While she could submit her point of view through her representatives in London and Washington, 'nonetheless, any claims made by Australia in relation to aircraft, shipping, army or naval strength are dealt with by such bodies in a way that places us in the role of a petitioner'.[1]

Dominion participation at the highest level in the work of the Combined Boards, however, continued to be exceptional, partly because in the general interests of efficiency the United States government preferred so far as possible to deal with the Commonwealth as a unit. The greater, therefore, the degree of preliminary agreement that could be reached about the requirements and supplies of the Commonwealth countries before submission to the Combined Boards, the better the system worked in practice. In turn this underlined the importance of the Commonwealth machinery for co-operation, especially in the Middle East, in Asia, and in the Pacific. But what was supremely important for the future of the Commonwealth was that the setting up of the Combined Boards, taken in conjunction with the Lend-Lease agreements and above all with the direction of the higher strategy of the war by the Joint Chiefs of Staff, heralded a new age of Anglo-American co-operation which developed, despite passing setbacks and differences, in such a way as to transform thinking about future relations between the Commonwealth and the United States.

Australian Reactions to the Pacific War

In the winter of 1941–2 such widening prospects everywhere seemed remote and nowhere more so than in Australia and New Zealand. On 7 December 1941[2] their worst fears had been realized. In one night, with one deadly, treacherous blow, Japan had secured command of the Pacific. Australia's trained divisions were overseas, she was denuded of aircraft,[3] and her long coastlines were indefensible. If on the longer view the attack on Pearl Harbour made it certain that the Axis powers would lose the war, on the shorter, with which the Australian Cabinet was properly concerned, it meant that unless forces were diverted to the Pacific, Australia in the meantime might 'go'.

[1] Australia, H. of R. Deb., vol. 176, p. 569. Australian demands for separate representation were not unrelated to General MacArthur's views on how a greater share of war supplies might best be secured for the Pacific War. At times the voice of the Australian government and the voice of MacArthur were not easily distinguishable.

[2] In Australia the date was in fact 8 December, owing to her position on the other side of the international date line from Pearl Harbour.

[3] Mr. Curtin recalled in 1944 that when Singapore fell 'our small naval forces were divided in several areas. Our militia forces were only partly trained and were very short of modern equipment. We lacked air support, possessing no fighters whatever, and our bomber and reconnaissance aeroplanes had been reduced to about 50 machines' (*The Times*, 5 May 1944).

For the Australian government, therefore, the higher strategy of the Allied powers now acquired supreme and critical importance. Its anxieties on this count were not fully shared by its New Zealand colleagues, some of whom at least, while equally aware of the dangers in the Pacific and by no means sure of Britain's ability to defend Commonwealth interests there, remained none the less more ready than their Australian colleagues to recognize that the security of their country depended upon the survival of Britain and on the defence of the Middle East. Yet New Zealand needed to be reassured.

I sense your [reproach at our] having been misled by a too complacent expression of military opinion in the past [cabled Mr. Churchill to Mr. Fraser on 17 January 1942] on probable dangers in the Pacific area in general and to New Zealand in particular. If you have thought us unmindful of your necessities in the past, although indeed we have never been so, I can assure you that the vast distance in miles which separates London from Wellington will not cause us to be unmindful of you or leave you comfortless in your hour of peril.[1]

The Australian government lacked full confidence not only in Britain's appreciation of Pacific perils, but also in her readiness to help within her range of active comprehension, because of the strategic preconceptions her government entertained. So it was that in the face of military and naval disasters which seemed daily to bring nearer the prospect of Japanese invasion,[2] many Australians concluded that Britain had deliberately neglected the Pacific in an understandable if mistaken concentration on the European and Middle Eastern theatres of war, and, more seriously, that her strategy was determined by an incorrect and complacent underestimate of Japanese power.

The Australian government was outspoken in complaint. Its members, believing that Australia's exposure to the full violence of a Japanese assault was in part at least to be attributed to the fact that they had been seriously misled by the United Kingdom military advisers over the years, did not hesitate to say so. In 1933, recalled Mr. Curtin in the course of an astringent correspondence with Mr. Churchill, the Australian High Commissioner in London had pointed out to the Committee of Imperial Defence the grave consequences that would flow from the loss of Singapore, or from the denial of its use to the main British fleet in the Pacific, and had stated that the whole internal defensive system of Australia was based on the integrity of Singapore and the presence of a capital fleet there. In 1937 the Australian government had received assurances that 'it was the aim of the United Kingdom Government to make Singapore impregnable'. It was upon this assumption that Australian defence plans had been made before the war and which after its outbreak had influenced the Australian decision to dispatch forces overseas from the relatively small resources 'we possess in relation to our commitments in a Pacific

[1] Churchill, iv. 11–12.
[2] The Japanese had no plans to invade Australia but then neither had Hitler to invade Britain when he attacked on the Western front.

war'.[1] Fundamental to Mr. Curtin's complaint was the feeling that the dangers of the Pacific situation had been more clearly foreseen in Australia than in Britain. 'Just as you foresaw events in Europe', he observed in a later telegram to Mr. Churchill, 'so we feel that we saw the trend of the Pacific situation more clearly than was realised in London.'[2] This claim was not without foundation.[3] It has been elaborated by Australian war historians, notably by Mr. Gavin Long, who is highly critical of undue Australian dependence in defence planning on advice from London, of the inadequacies of British defence appreciations of the Pacific in the inter-war years, and of the 'somewhat parochial' outlook of the Committee of Imperial Defence, which 'carried out continuously the study of Imperial war problems, but without an influential contribution from the Dominions'.[4] There was, therefore, on the Australian side criticism on technical as distinct from political grounds. Neither lacked foundation, but a lively sense of grievance is not usually an aid to balanced judgement.

At this moment of tension and of increasing peril Mr. Curtin turned to the United States for aid. On 26 December 1941, he appealed directly to the President of the United States for immediate American assistance for Malaya.[5]

> Reinforcements earmarked by the United Kingdom for dispatch to Malaya [he wrote] seem to us utterly inadequate, especially in relation to aircraft. . . . It is in your power to meet the situation. Should the Government of the United States desire, we would gladly accept an American commander in the Pacific area.

Mr. Roosevelt had said that Australia would be a base of increasing importance, but, argued Mr. Curtin, 'in order that it shall remain a base, Singapore must be reinforced'. The following day, 28 December, there appeared in the Melbourne *Herald* a signed article by Mr. Curtin[6] which, in the words of Mr. Churchill, 'was flaunted round the world by our enemies'. In the company of many others who, unlike him, did not know the facts Mr. Churchill may well have exaggerated its importance. Mr. Curtin's views were reasonable, even if his expression of them was undiplomatic and his way of publicizing them unorthodox. The article was in essence a challenge to the Anglo-American strategic policy which gave priority to the European theatre. 'We refuse', said Mr. Curtin, 'to accept the dictum that the Pacific struggle must

---

[1] Telegram from the Prime Minister of Australia to the Prime Minister of the United Kingdom, 18 January 1942 (Churchill, iv. 12–13).

[2] 22 January 1942 (ibid. p. 15).

[3] See, for example, views expressed by the Chiefs of Staff on the defence of Malaya, 28 June 1940 (*N.Z. Documents*, vol. 1, no. 214, pp. 158–9) and the reports of the Australian Commissioner in Singapore, Mr. Bowden, which are reprinted in Churchill, iv. 6–7.

[4] Long, *To Benghazi*, pp. 17–18.

[5] Reprinted in Churchill, iv. 5–6. The telegram was addressed to both Prime Minister and President, Mr. Churchill being in Washington at that time.

[6] Quoted in part in Mansergh, *Documents*, i. 549–50.

be treated as a subordinate segment of the general conflict.' On the contrary Australia, without claiming that other theatres should be subordinated to the Pacific, asked for 'a concerted plan evoking the greatest strength at the Democracies' disposal, determined upon hurling Japan back'. The Australian Prime Minister stated that his government regarded the Pacific struggle as one in which the United States and Australia 'must have the fullest say in the direction of the Democracies' fighting plan'. He made it

quite clear that Australia looks to America, free of any pangs as to our traditional links with the United Kingdom. We know the problems that the United Kingdom faces. We know the constant threat of invasion. We know the dangers of dispersal of strength. But we know too that Australia can go, and Britain can still hold on. We are therefore determined that Australia shall not go, and we shall exert all our energies towards the shaping of a plan, with the United States as its keystone, which will give to our country some confidence of being able to hold out until the tide of battle swings against the enemy.

The impact of the article upon the public in Australia and in the United Kingdom was the greater because the earlier debates between the two governments upon the strategy and conduct of the war were unknown to them. Mr. Curtin in effect was continuing in public an argument that had begun and was to conclude in private.

Mr. Curtin's emphasis upon the supreme importance of United States aid in the Pacific, in itself altogether realistic, did not lessen the insistence of the Australian government on the need for representation in London such as would enable Australia to participate in the making of major decisions there. The influence of tradition was still great upon one professedly prepared to break with it.

Sir Earle Page, it will be recalled, was in London as special Australian envoy to the War Cabinet when the Japanese entered the war. His mission was exploratory in the sense that it was one of his responsibilities to make recommendations for Australian representation in the War Cabinet on a more lasting basis. In a broadcast to Australia on 13 January[1] he concerned himself, however, mostly with proposals for improved consultation on the administrative plane. The political machinery of consultation, to which he thought over-much attention had been paid, needed in his opinion a firmer administrative foundation with dominion representation in the Cabinet secretariat to influence and to assist in the process of working out the ideas from which policies derived. Since 1924 Australia had had in fact a liaison officer within the Cabinet Offices, but one concerned only with foreign policy. What was now needed, in Sir Earle Page's judgement, was an extension of this system to provide correspondingly close liaison between the fighting and supply services in the two countries. If here he foreshadowed some of Mr. Curtin's later

[1] *The Times*, 14 January 1942.

proposals, such administrative improvements as he recommended seemed in Australia at the time woefully inadequate to the needs of the hour. The unstated premiss from which Sir Earle Page's conclusions derived was that the need for Australian representation in the War Cabinet was met by his own appointment as Envoy Extraordinary. The Labour government, however, unduly influenced perhaps by its tenuous majority in Parliament, would seem to have displayed questionable judgement in its decision to continue as its country's special representative in London a man who was not a member of the Australian Cabinet and who was therefore unlikely in any circumstances to be authorized to make decisions on its behalf. It was this simple political fact that deprived Sir Earle Page's mission of all chance of major achievement. In London he was given every facility. On 27 January 1942 Mr. Churchill explained that Sir Earle Page had attended meetings of the War Cabinet and also of the Defence Committee when matters of war policy and matters of Australian interest were under discussion, adding 'as a matter of fact this has always been interpreted in the most broad and elastic fashion'.[1]

On 1 January 1942 Mr. Curtin asked for the agreement of the United Kingdom government to the appointment of a representative of the Australian government who should have 'the right to be heard in the War Cabinet and in the formulation of and direction of policy'. Mr. Churchill acceded to the request, noting that while South Africa and Canada would probably continue to feel that there was no need for their separate representation, New Zealand, in view of the perils threatening her, also felt bound to ask for similar representation.[2] But what precisely was he agreeing to? By referring once again to the problems created by the presence at meetings of the War Cabinet of representatives who had no power to take decisions and could only report to their governments, Mr. Churchill implied that he at least expected that the new Australian representative to the War Cabinet would in fact possess no greater authority than that hitherto enjoyed by Sir Earle Page. The important distinction seemed one of status, not function. The new representative, it appeared, would be entitled to attend meetings of·the Cabinet as of right. Mr. Menzies, commenting on the proposals in the light of his visit to London in the preceding year, strengthened this impression by observing that while such an appointment could not produce that perfect result at which Australians were aiming, none the less it would at least be an advantage to have someone in the Cabinet when arguments were shaped and tentative decisions made. Mr. Menzies emphasized particularly how important it was that any such representative should be present all the time, because of the uncertainty that necessarily existed about the topics that would come forward for discussion at any particular meeting. Only later did it emerge that the new Australian representative did not enjoy this right, or the status that would confer it.

[1] H. of C. Deb., vol. 377, coll. 613–14 (Mansergh, *Documents*, i. 550–2).
[2] Mansergh, *Documents*, i. 551.

Dr. Evatt told the House of Representatives on 25 February 1942[1] that the presumption that he was to do so was ill founded, for Mr. Churchill had subsequently explained that his granting of 'our special request gave us no more rights than Sir Earle Page had already been receiving'. Confusion was now complete. Even the Australian government acquiesced and decided to continue Sir Earle Page's representation on 'the present footing'.

Sir Earle Page continued for a short time in the new capacity of Australian representative, but with his old status of Envoy Extraordinary, in the War Cabinet, but during his indisposition in the early spring of 1942 Dr. Evatt, Minister for External Affairs, sat in his place at Cabinet meetings, and in June that year Mr. Bruce, Australia's High Commissioner in London, was appointed as a permanent successor. He thus became, and remained till the end of the war, at once High Commissioner for the Commonwealth of Australia and representative for the Commonwealth government in the United Kingdom War Cabinet. Had this simple arrangement been adopted in the first instance it might have saved some rather heated correspondence and more confusion of purpose.

The Pacific War Council

In Dr. H. V. Evatt the Commonwealth of Australia acquired a Minister for External Affairs of outstanding forcefulness who was by temperament disposed, and by conviction resolved, to secure for his country what he conceived to be her due share in the making of policy. Not for him the half-light in which Mr. Mackenzie King delighted to move, but the full glare of public attention and popular acclaim. Nor was the range of his interest or activity narrowly regional. Not long after his accession to office he drew the attention of Whitehall to a 'strange feature of the present struggle'. The countries of the British Commonwealth, he pointed out, remained at peace with Finland, Hungary, and Rumania, despite a Russian request for a declaration of war against these satellite states. A continued refusal on the part of Commonwealth governments to accede to the Russian request, in Dr. Evatt's opinion, 'might well be disastrous to Russian morale and dangerous to our own'. Accordingly the Australian government proposed that Stalin should be consulted and his wishes carried out. Action followed. 'Our suggestion', Dr. Evatt told the House of Representatives,[2] 'was adopted by the Government of the United Kingdom', and 'finally, ultimatums were addressed by the United Kingdom Government to the three governments concerned'. Whether so full a share of the credit is correctly to be attributed to Australian initiative is open to question, but at least there was no doubt about the impact of

[1] Australia, H. of R. Deb., vol. 170, p. 53.
[2] Ibid. vol. 169, p. 1088. Dr. Evatt's action would seem in part at least to have been prompted by his interest, already expressed in the constitutional procedure adopted for the separate Australian declaration of war on Japan, in the forms of Australia's action in such circumstances (see Mansergh, *Survey, 1931–9*, pp. 380–1).

Australian views on a matter of much closer concern to her government and people.

After the outbreak of the Pacific War, one of the first considerations of the Australian War Cabinet, mindful of the short-lived Council established in Singapore, was the constitution of a supreme authority for the higher direction and control of allied strategy in the Pacific. As early as 11 December representations were made to the United Kingdom government for the creation of an inter-Allied Council, but there was no immediate response.[1] As a result, however, of the visit of Mr. Churchill to Washington in December 1941–January 1942, the text of an agreement for a unified command in the south-west Pacific under General Wavell was submitted to the governments concerned. The Commonwealth government gave its immediate assent, only to learn from a later communication that the smaller powers, including Canada and Australia, would not participate in the higher direction of the Pacific War. The Australian government protested sharply. The states endangered by the Japanese advances, they maintained, should have a direct part in the making of strategy, and they advocated the immediate formation of a Pacific War Council. It was their idea that the Council should itself be responsible for the higher direction of the war in the Pacific and that its headquarters should be in Washington. What they desired above all, to quote Dr. Evatt, was that the Council should give to Australia 'the opportunity of conferring as an ally with the United States of America and China at the same council table and on a common footing'.[2]

Australian anxiety to have the headquarters of a Pacific War Council in Washington provoked 'strong differences'[3] of opinion within the British Commonwealth. New Zealand supported the Australian view, but Mr. Churchill was insistent upon the claims of London. For a brief period his will prevailed. On 27 January 1942 he told the House of Commons[4] that a Pacific Council on a ministerial plane was to be set up in London, composed of representatives of Great Britain, Australia, New Zealand, and the Netherlands. Assisted by the Chiefs of Staff and the organizations which served them, the Council was to have as its primary purpose 'to try to form and focus a united view' which would enable the British Commonwealth to act as a whole, and facilitate collaboration at the appropriate levels in the spheres of defence, foreign affairs, and supply. If, according to Mr. Churchill, the members of the Council reached an agreed view, it would be transmitted at first on the Chiefs-of-Staff level to the joint Chiefs of Staff Committee sitting in Washington, while in the event of differences of view, it would be the responsibility of the President of the United States and the Prime Minister to

---

[1] Australia, H. of R. Deb., vol. 170, p. 51 (Mansergh, *Documents*, i. 552–3).
[2] Ibid. pp. 51–52.
[3] Walter Nash, *New Zealand: a Working Democracy* (London, Dent, 1944), p. 80.
[4] H. of C. Deb., vol. 377, coll. 611–12.

reach an agreement. The Prime Minister's language then and later[1] suggested no enthusiasm for the Pacific Council, and the account of its functions which he gave to the House of Commons suggested an impossible compromise between conflicting views.

On 9 February it was formally announced in London that the Pacific Council had been set up. Mr. Churchill presided, and, of Commonwealth countries, Australia, New Zealand, and later India[2] were represented. No provision was made at this stage for Canadian representation (or indeed for that of the United States), and this evoked some inquiries in Ottawa. Mr. Mackenzie King, who entertained less exalted notions of the possible functions of such a Council than did Dr. Evatt, alluded to the lack of Canadian representation in philosophic terms. Sometimes, he observed in a deprecating allusion to Australian methods, an individual achieved most not by asserting but by effacing himself, and by taking into account difficulties which others had to meet. He defined the duties of the Council as being directly related to questions of regional defence of the areas in the south-west Pacific and South-East Asia against which Japanese offensive action was aimed, explaining that since Canada's sector of the Pacific front fell outside that region, her immediate membership of the Pacific Council was not necessitated by strategic developments, while her expectations about future membership were known in London and Washington.[3] Moreover Mr. Mackenzie King felt that the Canadian government was in sufficiently close touch with Washington, which in his view also was of cardinal importance, to be confident of being able to ensure that Canada's interests should not be overlooked. The Australian government entertained no such confidence in respect of Australia.

On 25 February 1942 Dr. Evatt alluded to the unfortunate consequences of the United States not having representatives on the Pacific Council. The two predominant partners in the Pacific War were separated from each other and from the war zone by immense distances. The smaller states whose survival was endangered by the war had acquired in the Pacific Council a means of meeting together and with one of the predominant partners, so that for the first time there could be discussion about problems of policy, of strategy, and of supply. Yet the Pacific Council was not 'a true inter-allied' body. The second predominant partner in the war, the United States, was not represented at its meetings, and 'at no point whatever does any representative of this country [Australia] meet any representative of the United States of America in any council, committee, or strategic body directly concerned in the controlling of the Allied war against Japan.'[4] That was the gap the Australian, and also the New Zealand, government desired to close. The

[1] Churchill, iv. 16–17.
[2] See H. of C. Deb., vol. 377, col. 1569, for Mr. Amery's statement on Indian representation. The Netherlands and later China were also represented.
[3] Canada, H. of C. Deb., 1942, vol. 2, pp. 1632–3.
[4] Australia, H. of R. Deb., vol. 170, pp. 52–53.

insistence of both on Washington as the meeting place of the Pacific Council was, therefore, in no way modified after the setting up of a Council in London. In January Mr. Churchill had transmitted their views on this point to the President, but in Washington opinion was divided. 'The Army and Navy', records Harry Hopkins, 'never had much enthusiasm for it [the Pacific Council], because they were afraid it would require too much of the time of the military people'.[1] Hopkins, however, was himself impressed by the Australian arguments and felt that it was 'essential' that there should be a common meeting ground for the Pacific countries. On his recommendation the President decided to set up in Washington a counterpart to the Pacific Council in London.

The first meeting of the Washington Council was held on 1 April 1942 while the tale of defeat from the Eastern theatres of war still continued. Under Australian pressure President Roosevelt presided, with Hopkins as deputy Chairman. There were now not one but two Pacific Councils.[2]

Technically the Council in Washington was coequal with the Council in London, and, in the words of President Roosevelt at its opening meeting, would be 'in intimate contact'[3] with it. But in fact in the eyes of its members it quickly assumed a greater importance. This was reflected in its membership. At the first meeting of the Washington Council Australia was represented by Dr. Evatt and New Zealand by Mr. Walter Nash, the Deputy Prime Minister, who was also Minister to the United States from 1942 to 1944. 'In effect', noted Mr. Nash later, the Washington Council 'took precedence over the London body'.[4] In respect of location, therefore, the arguments of the Pacific dominions were justified. The swift Japanese onrush through South-East Asia, the fall of Singapore, the loss of the East Indies, the retreat from Burma all told catastrophically against Britain's position in the East. If she could not spare sufficient reinforcements to save Singapore, how could she detail forces to protect Australia? It was on 17 March 1942 that it was announced that General MacArthur was to take over the supreme command of the United Nations forces in the Pacific area, including the Philippine Islands, in accordance, as the official announcement from Washington stated,[5] with the request of the Australian government. A phase in history had ended. The Australian government realized that the balance in the East had changed and that where the Royal Navy had once reigned supreme, the hopes of the white man on the lonely island continent in the far south now rested upon the strength and resources of the New World.

In other respects, however, the Washington Pacific Council failed to fulfil the hopes of its sponsors. At no time did it play any important part in the

---

[1] Sherwood, ii. 520.
[2] To be exact a Pacific Council in London and a Pacific War Council in Washington.
[3] *Documents on American Foreign Relations*, iv. 244.
[4] Nash, *New Zealand*, p. 80.   [5] *Documents on American Foreign Relations*, iv. 245.

making of decisions, whether strategic or political. As Mr. Mackenzie King had shrewdly surmised, from the outset it proved in fact to be a purely consultative body. At its first meeting, recorded Harry Hopkins, 'not much happened. The President outlined the problems in the whole Pacific Area, but kept away from the tough tactics which are now in progress. It is perfectly clear, however, that this body wants to talk about military strategy and the distribution of munitions.'[1] This was an understatement. What some members wanted was for the Council not merely to talk but to take decisions. That it never did. The most that could be said of it was said by Mr. Nash, who noted that it did good work and served a useful purpose by enabling the smaller countries represented on it to be kept fully informed about developments in the Pacific War and by giving them an opportunity of stating their case in the presence of those in whose hands major decisions continued to rest.[2] Such an opportunity was a psychological necessity for the Pacific dominions, abruptly confronted with the actual danger of invasion and sensitive, especially in the case of Australia, lest their peril be overlooked in the making of global strategy. 'The war', wrote Mr. Churchill, in a disparaging allusion, 'continued to be run by the old machinery, but meetings of the Pacific War Councils enabled those countries which were not represented in this permanent machinery to be consulted about what was going on.'[3] He never fully realized how important that was to those close to the point of danger but far from the place of decision. But equally Dr. Evatt did not appear to understand that the role of secondary powers in a major war must remain a secondary one and that no elaboration of machinery could sensibly modify a relationship determined by relative power.

The Japanese Onslaught: Australia and South-East Asia

Early in 1942 the Japanese had command of the seas and they could, therefore, move almost at will upon Australia and New Zealand to the south-east or upon the British and Dutch possessions in South Asia and the Indian Ocean to the south-west. Mr. Churchill seemingly never doubted that the Japanese would use their freedom of manœuvre first to seize the long-coveted wealth of the South-East Asian archipelago,[4] and he was prepared to act upon that assumption. The Australian government was not. Here was occasion for further differences.

Australia's fear of invasion from Eastern Asia was not something that dated from Pearl Harbour; it was a fear long and deeply implanted in the Australian mind. In December 1941 it began to assume a hideous reality. Even if the main Japanese advance was south-westward along the coast of Asia, the forces available to Japan were not precisely known and her movements, as Pearl Harbour had demonstrated, were sudden, violent, and unpredictable. In

---

[1] Sherwood, ii. 520. [2] Nash, *New Zealand*, p. 80.
[3] Churchill, iv. 17. [4] Ibid. p. 138.

such circumstances it would have required rare courage and foresight on the part of any Australian Prime Minister to assent to the continued absence overseas of Australia's own contingents in the seemingly forlorn hope of saving something from the wreckage of South-East Asia. Nor indeed is it by any means clear that any such decision would have been warranted. Australia was threatened, for Japan was pushing southward by Rabaul and elsewhere in New Guinea even while the main weight of Japanese forces was engaged in Asia, and the first responsibility of the government of a country is to protect its own people. The Japanese air raid on Port Darwin on 19 February 1942 was carried out by a strong force of bombers and dive bombers.[1] There was much damage and many casualties and the raid was above all a reminder of the inability of Australia to defend her long coastline without the return of her own forces or their equivalent and additional assistance as well. The obstinacy of the Australian government, therefore, in insisting on the return to Australia as soon as opportunity allowed of all the trained Australian divisions overseas, and the unforgettable welcome accorded to the first United States forces to land at Melbourne at the end of February 1942 alike stemmed from this realization. Australians needed reassurance that their island continent was not in fact destined to be left 'the orphan of the Pacific' at the mercy of a Japanese invader possessing so many of the dreadful attributes of a legendary Yellow Peril.

Mr. Churchill, proceeding on the twin assumptions that a Japanese invasion of Australia was probably not imminent and that in any event her defences were being sufficiently strengthened by the United States, asked Mr. Curtin on 20 February 1942, the day after the Japanese raid on Darwin, for permission to divert the leading Australian division returning home from the Middle East to Rangoon.[2] Without such reinforcement Burma could not be saved; with it there was, in his opinion, some prospect that the Japanese advance might be halted there. Mr. Churchill enlisted President Roosevelt's support for his appeal, and the President cabled Mr. Curtin asking him, 'in the interests of our whole war effort in the Far East', to reconsider the decision to return the 7th Australian Division to Australia. He pointed out that the United States was better able to reinforce, and was already reinforcing the Allied right flank, comprising Australia and New Caledonia, while the left flank in Burma and India properly remained a British responsibility. It sorely needed the reinforcement that the veteran Australian division alone could give.[3]

The immediate position was, however, not such as to encourage any easy affirmative Australian reply to the Prime Minister's forceful and the President's persuasive appeal. Hong Kong, among the defenders of which was a

---

[1] See C. L. A. Abbott, *Australia's Frontier Province* (Sydney, Angus & Robertson, 1950), chs. xi and xii for a first-hand account of the raid and its impact. Mr. Abbott was Administrator of the Northern Territory, 1937–46.

[2] Churchill, iv. 138–9.   [3] Sherwood, ii. 512–13.

Canadian brigade, had fallen, isolated and unaided, on Christmas Day 1941; the defences of Malaya were quickly penetrated; Singapore was invested and finally captured on 15 February with the 8th Australian Division under Major-General Gordon Bennett among the defenders, and the main strength of the British and Dutch fleets in the Far East was destroyed in the Java Sea in the last days of that same disastrous month.

Already, on 21 February, the Supreme Commander, General Wavell, conceded that the defence of the vast area of the A.B.D.A. command, staffed, as Mr. Churchill noted, after the most elaborate consultation in strict proportion to the claims of the different powers, and 'all in triplicate for the Army, Navy, and Air', had collapsed.[1] On 23 February orders were sent to Wavell by the Combined Chiefs of Staff to dissolve the command, one day after President Roosevelt had taken the painful decision to order General MacArthur to leave the heroic defenders of Corregidor so that he might in due course take up command of the south-west Pacific area with his headquarters in Australia. No move he could make, it seemed to the President, 'would be so well calculated to bolster the morale of the people of Australia and New Zealand'. But the news was not announced until General MacArthur arrived in Australia three weeks later, and in that interval 'a sense of panic was developing throughout the entire South-West Pacific area, for it seemed that all the ambitious attempts to establish unified command, or any command at all, had collapsed'.[2]

No one was more conscious of the calamitous course of events in South-East Asia and in the Pacific than Mr. Curtin, and partly for that reason his reply to Mr. Churchill's request for the temporary diversion of the Australian division to Rangoon on 22 February 1942 was a blank negative. 'The movement of our forces to this theatre', he wrote, '... is not considered a reasonable hazard of war, having regard to what has gone before, and its adverse results would have the gravest consequences on the morale of the Australian people.'[3] In alluding to 'what has gone before' Mr. Curtin was thinking chiefly but not only of what had happened and was happening in South-East Asia; he thought also of what had happened in Greece. In the light of all past experience he did not believe that a limited commitment was practicable; on the contrary he feared that if one Australian division was committed in Burma, further Australian reinforcement would almost certainly be required.

Mr. Churchill, already apparently informed of the views of the Australian government by Sir Earle Page, none the less assumed 'a favourable response' from Mr. Curtin and diverted the Australian division to Rangoon without awaiting his reply. The Australian Prime Minister was indignant that Australian approval in a matter of such moment should be taken as a matter of form. 'We feel', he rejoined, 'a primary obligation to save Australia not only for itself, but to preserve it as a base for the development of the war against Japan', and 'in the circumstances it is quite impossible to reverse a decision

[1] Churchill, iv. 118. [2] Sherwood, ii. 513–14. [3] Churchill, iv. 141–3.

which we made with the utmost care, and which we have affirmed and reaffirmed'.[1] The Australian division was returned via Colombo. Burma fell. It seems improbable in any event that it could have been saved by the reinforcement of one division. But if so much is necessarily speculative, one thing at least this prime ministerial controversy painfully illumined. The presence of an Australian Envoy Extraordinary in London did not necessarily ensure regard for Australian views.

The possible diversion of an Australian division to Burma was not to be the only source of Anglo-Australian governmental discord at this time. There was also the strange case of Mr. Casey. On 12 March 1942 Mr. Churchill cabled Mr. Curtin that he was thinking of appointing Mr. R. G. Casey, Australian Minister to Washington, as Mr. Oliver Lyttelton's successor as Minister of State in Cairo, and he inquired if Mr. Curtin could spare him.[2] On 13 March Mr. Curtin replied that he was sensible of the compliment being paid to Mr. Casey and that he believed that Australian opinion would be gratified. But, he proceeded, Mr. Casey's presence in Washington was most valuable to Australia and his replacement would be difficult. 'All things considered', concluded Mr. Curtin, 'probably it would be in [the] interests of us all if [the] approach [is] not made at this juncture.' Mr. Churchill replied on the same day to say that he had consulted his ministerial colleagues and the Chiefs of Staff and both were agreed in wanting Mr. Casey 'for this most important post'. Mr. Churchill moreover had learned from Mr. Casey when in the United States that he was 'very anxious for a change'; he ventured to suggest that Mr. Menzies might replace him in Washington and explained that he was himself much attracted by the idea of an appointment which 'strikes the note of bringing statesmen from all over the Empire to the highest direction of affairs'. Mr. Curtin replied on 14 March that the Australian government would not stand in the way of Mr. Churchill's desire but hoped that Mr. Casey would stay in Washington to meet Dr. Evatt on his impending visit. 'That', said Mr. Curtin, 'is [the] full extent of our demurrer.' Mr. Churchill thereupon cabled to Mr. Casey, who accepted the Middle East appointment. Mr. Churchill announced the acceptance, the news was broadcast, and Mr. Curtin learned of it in this way before he received official intimation of Mr. Casey's acceptance either from Mr. Casey or from London. He complained about the procedure while specifically excluding Mr. Churchill from all reproach. The telegrams which passed between the two Prime Ministers were thereupon published. It was thought strange by some in Australia that at that most critical moment in its history Mr. Churchill should have urged his views so strongly upon the Australian government and deprived

---

[1] Churchill, iv. 144. There is a serious discrepancy in the account given of the conclusion to this incident in Sherwood, ii. 513, where it is stated that Mr. Curtin agreed to send the division to Burma, but that Rangoon had fallen before the troops could get there.

[2] The correspondence was issued from 10 Downing Street on 21 March 1942, and printed in *The Times*, 23 March 1942.

it of the services of a Minister in Washington which it evidently esteemed so highly, while venturing to suggest that a former Prime Minister and leader of an Opposition party should replace him.[1]

In itself the Casey incident, as it may most fittingly be described, acquired significance only from its association with other and more important events. President Roosevelt, who felt that the decision to send Mr. Casey to the Middle East was a wise one, expressed himself to Mr. Churchill as greatly disturbed about 'the publicity from the Casey business' because of the encouragement it afforded to the enemy,[2] and because it seemed to be symptomatic of 'a rather strained relationship at this critical time between the United Kingdom and Australia' at which he sensed in the United States 'a growing feeling of impatience'.[3] It is not to be doubted that here again there lay at root differing if not conflicting appreciations of the war in the East. Dr. Evatt spoke—and some American leaders were prepared to think—of a situation that was 'practically desperate',[4] while Mr. Churchill, with the experience of equally grave or still graver events in Europe behind him, thought in more sanguine terms and acted with undiplomatic disregard of anxieties that oppressed others. Because of this the possible advantages of the appointment of an Australian, even though in a personal capacity, as a member of the United Kingdom War Cabinet, were perhaps insufficiently weighed in Canberra.

India: The Cripps Mission

'A Japanese invasion of India', wrote Pandit Nehru in 1939, 'could become a practical proposition only if China has been completely crushed, and if the United States, the Soviet Union and England have all been effectively humbled. That is a large undertaking.'[5] It was indeed; but in March 1942 it was well nigh accomplished. The Japanese navy commanded the Bay of Bengal, Rangoon went the way of Hong Kong and Singapore on 7 March, and the remnant of British forces in South-East Asia under the intrepid leadership of General Alexander retreated painfully towards the Indian frontier. Nor was this the sum total of the Empire's loss. Mr. Churchill spoke of the fall of Singapore as 'the greatest disaster to British arms which our history records'.[6] If the verdict seemed and perhaps was too emphatic militarily, it is not to be doubted that politically, whatever the outcome of the war, the inglorious surrender of this island base set a term to the British Empire in Asia. The Japanese had achieved something more than a military, they had won a psychological victory, all the more momentous in its consequences

[1] Cf. *Sydney Morning Herald*, 21 March 1942; *The Age* (Melbourne), 22 March 1942. See also article by Sir Keith Murdoch in *Manchester Guardian*, 23 March 1942.
[2] For German comment see *Völkischer Beobachter*, 23 March 1942, *Frankfurter Zeitung*, 23–24 March 1942; and for Italian *Giornale d'Italia*, 22 March 1942.
[3] Sherwood, ii. 513.
[4] Ibid. p. 511.
[5] Nehru, *The Unity of India* (London, Drummond, 1948), p. 25. [6] Sherwood, ii. 506.

because it undermined the faith of English people themselves in the colonial system. Hardened as they were by 1942 to retreat, destruction, and loss in Europe, these things in Asia would not in themselves have achieved so much. Indeed it was not, save to the few, the magnitude but the manner of the collapse there that caused so strong an emotional reaction. Indolence and ineptitude, complacency and procrastination were held indiscriminately to be characteristic of colonial rulers,[1] and in revulsion against a system of government which the British people for the most part had supposed to be founded firmly upon the loyalty of the indigenous inhabitants, there was implanted in the minds of a widening circle hitherto little influenced by radical or socialist criticisms, a pronounced anti-colonial bias. In Australia the reaction was sharper still.

At such a time and in such an atmosphere India became the focus of much anxious attention. Within British India the political deadlock remained unbroken. The rejection of the 1940 'August offer' was followed by a campaign of civil disobedience on a modest scale designed, so Gandhi explained, to voice a moral protest and not seriously to inconvenience the war effort of the government of India. In consequence, it was in prison that Pandit Nehru learned of the four freedoms of the Atlantic Charter and of Mr. Churchill's categorical assertion that the Charter did not apply to India.[2] No single event did more to aggravate Indian suspicions of Britain's intentions. 'It is difficult', wrote Sir Reginald Coupland in 1942 in the light of his near contemporary experience in India,[3] 'to exaggerate the disquieting effect of one particular incident—Mr. Churchill's statement in September, 1941, that the Atlantic Charter was primarily intended to apply to Europe.' It was, he noticed, the cause 'of a new and uncomfortable suspicion' which began to spread beyond nationalist circles. President Roosevelt early in 1942 stated that the Charter 'applies not only to the parts of the world that border the Atlantic, but to the whole world'.[4] But in this he spoke for the United States alone, and the geographical limitation in the British interpretation of the Atlantic Charter confirmed in the minds of the Congress leaders the correctness of their conclusion that India unfree neither could nor should fight for freedom. So it was that as Calcutta prepared to resist, or to share, the fate of Moulmein, Singapore, and Rangoon, Indian suspicions of British intentions were deepest and the prestige of the British raj at its lowest ebb. In these circumstances it is not surprising that some Indian leaders were unmindful of the longer-term factors which presaged an Allied and a British victory.

Heightened suspicion between ruler and ruled as danger approached the Indian border was not accompanied by any lessening of tension between the

[1] The impressions of Mr. Duff Cooper as recorded in *Old Men Forget* give little ground for questioning such conclusions.
[2] Nehru, *Discovery of India*, p. 449.
[3] Coupland, *The Cripps Mission* (London, Oxford University Press, 1942), p. 22.
[4] Sherwood, ii. 512.

two great communities which comprised so great a proportion of the population of British India. On the contrary there continued to be an overriding anxiety on the part of each lest the rival community or party should turn a situation fraught with so much danger to its own advantage. On 8 February 1942, the day on which the Japanese landed on the island of Singapore, *Dawn*, the official newspaper of the Muslim League, inscribed across its front page a student manifesto proclaiming, 'Pakistan is our deliverance, defence, destiny. . . . Pakistan is our only demand . . . and by God we will have it.'[1] Many Congressmen were only too ready to take up the heady challenge, though the wiser leaders recognized, however reluctantly, that in the last resort unity could not be imposed by force. Rajagopalachari, in particular, who had initiated the Congress proposals for a settlement in 1940, was now speaking in terms which allowed that some sort of compromise between Congress and League claims would be necessary, and that the Congress could not maintain, as it had done, that it represented the majority of Muslims as well as Hindus.[2] In principle, however, the attitude of the Congress as of the League to the war remained unchanged. 'The only strategy that will outwit Japan', declared Rajagopalachari on the eve of the fall of Singapore, 'is the acknowledgement of India's indefeasible right to freedom'.[3] Mr. Churchill's confidence, however, continued to rest in strong government and the proven valour of India's martial peoples. He discounted the possibility of breaking the political deadlock even in acknowledging, albeit reluctantly, the desirability of making public endeavour to do so.

Mr. Churchill to all outward appearance was wholly resolved to pursue the Indian policies thought best by his Cabinet colleagues and by himself regardless of any pressure from the United States or other Allied powers. President Roosevelt, who spoke to him in Washington about India 'on the usual American lines' in December 1941, provoked so strong and so lengthy a rejoinder that he never raised the matter with Mr. Churchill verbally again;[4] while in February 1942 Generalissimo Chiang Kai-shek, seeking to stimulate Indian resistance to the Japanese, was firmly discouraged from embarking upon intended conversations with Gandhi at Wardha.[5] That same month Mr. Churchill formed a sub-committee of the Cabinet under the chairmanship of Mr. Attlee to advise the War Cabinet on Indian affairs. The Secretary of State for India, Mr. Amery, Sir John Simon, Sir John Anderson, Sir James Grigg, Mr. R. A. Butler, and Sir Stafford Cripps were the other members of it. A proposal, submitted by Sir Stafford Cripps and contemplating a representative Indian constituent assembly to enable Indians to decide on their own future, was accepted by the Committee and approved by the Cabinet.[6] On 4 March Mr. Churchill cabled President Roosevelt to say that the Cabinet

---
[1] Quoted Coupland, *Cripps Mission*, p. 32. [2] Ibid. p. 33.
[3] *The Hindu*, 14 February 1942, quoted ibid. p. 34. [4] Churchill, iv. 185.
[5] Ibid. p. 183. [6] C. R. Attlee, *As It Happened* (London, Heinemann, 1954), p. 180.

was earnestly considering whether a declaration of dominion status after the war, carrying with it the right to secede, should be made to India, adding, by way of admonition against hasty or ill-conceived Presidential conclusions, that the Muslims must not be antagonized, the princes and the Untouchables must not be abandoned, and India must not be thrown 'into chaos on the eve of invasion'.[1] On 11 March the President replied at some length trying to approach 'the problem from the point of view of history', and suggesting that the experience acquired in the inception of the government of the United States between 1775 and 1789 might by analogy give a new slant on the Indian question.[2] Mr. Churchill, however, did not think so. 'It is probable', writes Mr. Sherwood,[3] 'that the only part of that cable with which Churchill agreed was Roosevelt's admission that it is "none of my business"'. Mr. Churchill by implication confirms that this was so. Yet United States and indeed Allied interest in India at this time, however misconceived it seemed to Mr. Churchill, was a factor of greater importance than British historians have customarily allowed. The inspiration of the Cripps Mission is to be traced back to pre-war conversations between Sir Stafford Cripps, Mr. Attlee, and Pandit Nehru;[4] the agreement of Mr. Churchill and his Conservative colleagues derived from immediate circumstances, but not least among them was the need to work in reasonable harmony with the United States, on whose broad shoulders had fallen responsibility for the defence of the Pacific and the higher direction of the war in the East. On this point it would seem that Indian interpretation of events was nearer to the truth than that of the British constitutional adviser, Sir Reginald Coupland.[5]

On 11 March 1942 the Prime Minister, in a statement to the House of Commons, foreshadowed a new departure in British policy. 'The crisis', he said, 'in the affairs of India arising out of the Japanese advance has made us wish to rally all the forces of Indian life to guard their land from the menace of the invader.'[6] The 'August offer' of 1940 had promised that as soon as possible after the war, and subject to agreement among the various communities and classes in India and to existing treaty obligations to the Indian states, the subcontinent should attain dominion status under a constitution to be framed by Indians themselves. The intention now was 'to clothe these general declarations with precision'; and in order to 'convince all classes, races and creeds in India of our sincere resolve' to do so, the War Cabinet proposed not to set forth immediately the terms of their new 'constructive British contribution, to aid India in the realization of full self-government', but to send a member of the War Cabinet to India 'to satisfy himself upon the spot,

---

[1] Churchill, iv. 185–6.   [2] Ibid. pp. 188–90; Sherwood, ii. 515–16.
[3] Sherwood, ii. 516.   [4] Attlee, *As It Happened*, p. 181.
[5] Coupland, *Cripps Mission*, p. 44. See also Hull, *Memoirs*, ii. 1482–7 for a statement of United States aims and policies in respect of India at this time.
[6] For an account of the exchange of views between the Prime Minister and the Viceroy which preceded this announcement see Menon, *Transfer of Power*, pp. 115–22.

COMMONWEALTH CO-OPERATION IN WAR

by personal consultation, that the conclusions upon which we are agreed, and which we believe represent a just and final solution, will achieve their purpose'.[1] Their chosen emissary was Sir Stafford Cripps, recently returned from Moscow, endowed with all the prestige of an Ambassador whose mission ended with the forging of a famous wartime alliance, with the reputation of an intellectual whose visions had in part come true and of a wayward political rebel who in the hour of his country's peril was proving himself an administrator of passionate, dedicated purpose. Had Mr. Churchill's administration fallen following upon the disasters in the East, it might well have been Sir Stafford Cripps who, under pressure of public opinion, would have been called upon to succeed him as Prime Minister. In such circumstances it is understandable that Mr. Churchill should not have been dismayed at the thought of Sir Stafford's departure for distant climes on a mission in whose success he reposed no confidence. For Sir Stafford himself it was an opportunity at once to serve his country and, as he believed, to clear its reputation of the charge of procrastinating imperialist policies in India by ensuring agreement upon the earliest possible transfer of power. If the choice of a friend of Nehru and the Congress caused some uneasiness among the Muslim leaders, it was slight by comparison with that occasioned by the selection of a former advocate of a Popular Front, of an intellectual socialist anti-imperialist recently returned from Moscow, among the Viceroy[2] and his immediate entourage. The War Cabinet had momentarily at least recaptured the political initiative in India; that was something the League, the Congress, and the Viceroy from their very different viewpoints were all prepared to allow.

Sir Stafford Cripps arrived in New Delhi on 23 March, and on 29 March, after some discussions with the party leaders, he published the War Cabinet's draft Declaration.[3] The aim was defined as

the creation of a new Indian Union which shall constitute a Dominion, associated with the United Kingdom and the other Dominions by common allegiance to the Crown, but equal to them in every respect, in no way subordinate in any aspect of its domestic or external affairs.

The means by which it was proposed to achieve this end was the setting up of an elected constituent assembly charged with the task of framing a new constitution for India 'immediately upon the cessation of hostilities'. Unless the Indian leaders agreed otherwise before the ending of hostilities, this con-

---

[1] H. of C. Deb., vol. 378, coll. 1069–70 (Mansergh, *Documents*, ii. 614–15).
[2] The Viceroy had had occasion in December 1939 to consider earlier proposals for an Indian settlement which Sir Stafford Cripps had formulated while in opposition, and the principal one among them concerning the setting up of a constituent assembly 'did not carry the faintest shadow of conviction to his mind' (Zetland, *Essayez*, p. 275). Cf. also Churchill's reassuring cable quoted in Churchill, iv. 190, and comments of a later date by W. L. Philips, *Ventures in Diplomacy* (London, Murray, 1955), ch. xxii.
[3] Reprinted in Mansergh, *Documents*, ii. 616–17.

stituent assembly was to be elected by the entire membership of the Lower Houses of the provincial legislatures acting as one electoral body and voting according to the principles of proportional representation. They were to elect about one-tenth of their number to the constituent assembly, and the Princely States were to be invited to appoint representatives to it in the same proportion to their total population as in the case of the representatives of British India as a whole. His Majesty's Government undertook 'to accept and implement forthwith the Constitution so framed' subject only to:—(i) 'the right of any Province of British India that is not prepared to accept the new Constitution to retain its present constitutional position', or, should such non-acceding provinces so desire, 'His Majesty's Government will be prepared to agree upon a new Constitution, giving them the same full status as Indian Union', and arrived at by an analogous procedure, and (ii) the negotiation of a treaty between the United Kingdom government and the constitution-making body covering matters arising out of the transfer of power. No restriction was to be imposed 'on the power of the Indian Union to decide in the future its relationship to the other Member States of the British Commonwealth'. Finally the Declaration stated that during the 'critical period which now faces India and until the new Constitution can be framed His Majesty's Government must inevitably bear the responsibility for and retain control and direction of the defence of India as part of their world war effort', but it invited the immediate and effective participation of the leaders of the principal sections of the Indian people 'in the counsels of their country, of the Commonwealth and of the United Nations'.

The draft Declaration was an attempt to bring about present co-operation upon the basis of assurances of future constitutional advances. If it was not too little, it seemed to many in the early spring of 1942 too late. Gandhi was not alone in thinking of it as a post-dated cheque upon a bankrupt Empire. For this reason Sir Stafford Cripps was negotiating from a position not of strength but of weakness, in which, be it said, even the undoubted sincerity of his own conviction was at something of a discount. If it be conceded that the draft Declaration was sound in principle and statesmanlike in approach, it has still to be noted that it was produced at a desperate hour to ease a well-nigh desperate situation. It was in the 1930's, or at latest in 1940, not in 1942, that opportunity offered.

The Cripps Mission failed. The precise allocation of responsibility for the rejection of the conditional offer of the United Kingdom has been variously attributed and some of the evidence essential for a final judgement is not yet available. It is not, however, to be doubted that it rested principally with the Indian National Congress. The princes, whose position was amply safeguarded, had no reason to do other than say they were, as always, in the interest of the motherland prepared to make their contribution; provided also, as always, that the contribution asked of them was 'compatible with the sovereignty and integrity of the States'.[1] The Working Committee of the Muslim League, which, as was its prudent custom, delayed the issue of its formal statement on the draft Declaration until the views of the Congress had been made known, expressed 'their gratification that the possibility of Pakistan is recognized by implication by providing for the establishment of two or more independent Unions in India', but went on to regret that the creation of more than one union was 'relegated only to the realm of remote possibility'. In so far as the main object of the United Kingdom was to constitute one Indian Union composed of the two principal nations, Hindus and Muslims, it seemed to the All-India Muslim League Working Committee 'neither just nor possible' in the light of past failure and the bitter experience of Musulmans.[2]

While the Muslim League thus complained that the idea of a separate Muslim state was relegated to the realm of remote possibility, the Indian National Congress complained with equal vehemence[3] of 'the acceptance beforehand of the novel principle of non-accession for a Province', which was at once likely to cause discord and 'a severe blow to the conception of Indian unity'. 'Congress has been wedded to Indian freedom and unity and any break of that unity . . . would be . . . exceedingly painful to contemplate.' None the less the Congress did not think in terms of compulsion against the declared and established will of the people of any territorial unit, though equally and on the same principle it held that compulsion should not be exercised on other substantial groups within that area. In general the Working Committee felt that the terms of the Declaration would encourage separatist tendencies instead of efforts to reconcile the fullest possible autonomy for Muslim majority provinces with the ideal of a strong national state, and Sir Stafford Cripps subsequently allowed that this objection was 'a most substantial one'. He himself remained, however, convinced that it was not in the circumstances possible to find a fairer solution than the one in the Declaration, which aimed and provided for a single, united India but which also provided that, if in the last resort the principal communities could not agree upon a form of constitution which would enable them to work together, then the Muslims should be allowed to opt out of the Union in those provinces where they commanded a majority of votes of the whole electorate.[4] However, though the difference in approach of the United Kingdom government and of the Congress to the possible creation of a separate Muslim state was important, it was not in itself

[1] Resolution of the Indian States Delegation contained in a letter to Sir Stafford Cripps from His Highness the Chancellor of the Chamber of Princes, dated 10 April 1942 (Mansergh, *Documents*, ii. 617–18). A full account of the reactions of the States to the British offer is to be found in V. P. Menon, *The Story of the Integration of the Indian States* (Calcutta, Orient Longmans, 1956), ch. iii.

[2] Resolution of All-India Muslim League Working Committee, 11 April 1942, Cmd. 6350 (Mansergh, *Documents*, ii. 621–3).

[3] Resolution of the Congress Working Committee, 11 April 1942, Cmd. 6350 (ibid. pp. 618–21).

[4] 28 April 1942, H. of C. Deb., vol. 379, coll. 826–43 (ibid., pp. 625–32).

responsible for the failure of the Mission. Nor were acrimonious Congress comments on the treatment in the Declaration of the 90 million people in the states, as 'commodities at the disposal of their Rulers' who would nominate their representatives to the constitution-making body and thereby negate the principles of democracy and self-determination alike. Indeed, to balance such complaints was the recognition that future independence 'may be implicit in the proposals' and the realization, as a result largely of Sir Stafford Cripps's personal explanations, that the future Indian Union would be free to secede from the Commonwealth and in this important respect therefore conformed to Congress ideas of what independence for India should mean. The share of Gandhi's responsibility for the rejection of the War Cabinet's proposals has been variously estimated. Pandit Nehru points out[1] that he took no part in the negotiations; he was for much of their duration absent from Delhi. Nevertheless, the Congress must have been aware of his opposition to the settlement offered, as it was certainly aware of his disapproval of any idea of any Indian co-operation in the war, and it is hard to believe that his influence, whether or not deliberately exerted, played no part in the final decision to reject proposals which he thought 'ridiculous'.[2] Gandhi discounted future possibilities and it is a chief criticism of the Congress that, lacking in foresight, it too weighed them insufficiently as against the immediate issues on which in fact the breach came.

The draft Declaration stated that the United Kingdom government must retain ultimate responsibility for the conduct of the war, but that co-operation of Indian leaders should be sought to ensure a broader measure of popular support for it. This was something easier to state than to interpret. Both Sir Stafford Cripps and the Viceroy agreed that it would be difficult for the representative Indians on the Viceroy's Executive Council and responsible for civil administration to rouse the people to the defence of India unless they could say with justice that at least some part of that defence was the responsibility of a representative Indian, and so of the Indian people. Yet if Indian leaders were to be more fully associated with the war effort, what responsibilities were they to discharge? Control and direction of the defence of India as part of Britain's world war effort was something the government of the United Kingdom was not prepared to relax, and it was at least agreed that the technical conduct should continue to be the responsibility of the British Commander-in-Chief. But if so much were excluded from Indian control how much in reality remained?[3] Nothing, it seemed, was calculated to stir the enthusiasm of Indian leaders, for it was contemplated that this remainder

---

[1] Nehru, *Discovery of India*, p. 472.
[2] Tendulkar, *Mahatma*, vi. 90–91. For a fuller analysis of Gandhi's views made public after the failure of the mission see below, p. 207. See also Menon, *Transfer of Power*, pp. 136–8.
[3] See Sir Stafford Cripps's speech to the House of Commons (H. of C. Deb., vol. 379, coll. 832–41).

would consist largely of responsibility for public relations, petroleum, canteens, stationery and printing, social arrangements for foreign missions and amenities for troops. 'This list', commented Pandit Nehru later, 'was remarkable and made the position of an Indian defense member ludicrous.'[1] Yet the problem was more difficult than this intemperate language allows. Sir Stafford Cripps made many efforts to resolve it and, after much discussion, redefined and somewhat enlarged the admittedly limited scope of such responsibilities by devising a new formula allocating to the Commander-in-Chief as War Member of the Viceroy's Executive all the administrative functions vital to the efficient prosecution of the war, leaving what remained as the responsibility of a representative Indian defence member of the Council.[2] Sir Stafford Cripps, and the War Cabinet behind him, were satisfied they could concede no more; the Indian National Congress that it was not enough. But yet again, while contributing to the breakdown, this was not the occasion of it. It came, in Cripps's words, on 'the form of the temporary government that should be in power until the end of the war and the coming into operation of the new constitution'. To the Congress Working Committee 'the essential fundamental prerequisite for the assumption of responsibility by the Indian people in the present is their realization as a fact that they are free and are in charge of maintaining and defending their freedom'.[3] What they demanded was tantamount to an immediate transfer of power before a constitution could be drafted, leaving the reconciliation of violently conflicting viewpoints to be worked out within an India threatened with invasion. It was in effect a restatement of the demand made by the Congress on 10 October 1939, when the Working Committee passed the resolution stating that 'India must be declared an independent nation and present application should be given to this status to the largest possible extent'.[4] There were risks involved that the British Government was not prepared to take in 1939 and still less in 1942.

In assessing responsibility for the failure of the Cripps Mission too much importance may easily be attributed to the occasion and too little to the cause of the breakdown. The offer contained in the Declaration was made conditional upon the outcome of Sir Stafford Cripps's discussions with the Indian leaders and in any event was not to take effect until the end of the war. The condition was not fulfilled because first the Congress and then the League rejected the proposals. Congress rejection was due at root to the fact that it seemed to Congress leaders that 'in today's grave crisis it is the present that counts' and in the British War Cabinet's proposals 'there would appear to be no vital changes in the present structure contemplated'. This was essentially true. The Congress demand that the Executive Council should henceforward

[1] Nehru, *Discovery of India*, p. 469.
[2] See H. of C. Deb., vol. 379, coll. 837–8.
[3] Resolution of Congress Working Committee, 11 April 1942 (Mansergh, *Documents*, ii. 620).
[4] Indian National Congress, *The Background of India's Foreign Policy* (Delhi, 1952), p. 70.

operate as a Cabinet and as a 'free government' with the Viceroy acting as constitutional head of the state was rejected, because in Sir Stafford Cripps's opinion, such a reform would mean a transformation of the existing system of government and would for that reason require major legislative changes the enactment of which could not be contemplated in wartime.[1] Defence was thus a part of the large question as to whether final responsibility for government should continue to rest with the Viceroy and ultimately with Parliament and the Secretary of State for India, or whether it should be transferred.

At any time [noted the Resolution of the Working Committee] Defence is a vital subject; during war-time it is all-important and covers almost every sphere of life and administration. To take away Defence from the sphere of responsibility at this stage is to reduce that responsibility to a farce and nullity, and to make it perfectly clear that India is not going to be free in any way and her Government is not going to function as a free and independent Government during the pendency of the war.[2]

About the conclusion there was no room for dispute. The War Cabinet did not deem it feasible to bring such a free and independent government into existence during the war. In the light of its constantly reiterated assertion that India unfree could not fight for freedom, the Congress could have demanded no less than it did; in view of its responsibilities for the conduct of the war at this time of crisis in the East the British War Cabinet could concede no more.

Too late though the Cripps Mission must be adjudged, it was not wholly barren of achievement. Not since Edwin Montagu in 1917 had a Cabinet Minister come to India and been prepared to debate and to discuss in public over a period of seventeen days proposals of the British Government with every important group in Indian political life, with liberals, Scheduled Castes, Sikhs, and orthodox Hindus of the Mahasabha, as well as with the princes, the Congress, and the League. By every account Sir Stafford Cripps's press conferences in particular created a marked impression upon their Indian audiences and made possible a better understanding of British intentions. Especially illuminating were Sir Stafford's explicit replies to questions about membership of the Commonwealth and secession from it.[3]

Will the Indian Union be entitled to disown its allegiance to the Crown?

Yes. In order that there should be no possibility of doubt, we have inserted in the last sentence of paragraph (c) (ii) the statement: 'but will not impose any restriction on the power of the Indian Union to decide in the future its relation to the other Member States of the British Commonwealth'. The Dominion will be completely free either to remain within or to go without the Commonwealth of Nations.

Will the Indian Union have the right to enter into a treaty with any other nation in the world?

Yes.

---

[1] Cf. Nehru's own account, *Discovery of India*, pp. 468–70.
[2] Mansergh, *Documents*, ii. 620.   [3] Quoted in Coupland, *Cripps Mission*, pp. 47–49.

Can the Union join any contiguous foreign countries?
There is nothing to prevent it. Canada can join the U.S.A. tomorrow if it wants to.
Can it?
Of course it can. . . .
Can you tell us clearly what you are going to give us? What is required is one simple word, 'freedom'.
We used what we thought simple, 'full self government'. We followed it by a definition which we believed would convey the right meaning. There is no conceivable doubt that this allows complete and absolute self-determination and self-government for India.

Lord Mountbatten was later to profit from Sir Stafford's example and with equal or even greater success to use press conferences as a means of spreading knowledge and understanding of British policies.

In London Mr. Churchill found himself able to bear the news of the failure of the mission which he had thought probable from the beginning with fortitude. President Roosevelt's plea for a reopening of the negotiations which Mr. Churchill characterized as being in the circumstances 'an act of madness' was fortunately precluded by Sir Stafford's prompt departure from New Delhi.[1] Harry Hopkins, who was in London and 'who loved to use the phrase "meeting of minds", was by now convinced that the subcontinent of India was one area where the minds of Roosevelt and Churchill would never meet', and accordingly took the position that 'there was not much sense in burning up the transatlantic cables with more messages on this subject'.[2] The Viceroy, whose attitude to the Cripps Mission was correct, was also able to contemplate its failure with equanimity.

On the breakdown of negotiations the government of India took action to reaffirm its political authority while the Congress, inspired by Gandhi, and faced, as its leaders believed, with a choice of evils, decided on a policy of non-violent non-resistance. If a free India could not fight as an equal among the United Nations which were its natural allies then, so it was argued, it must choose some way of asserting its own claim to freedom. The outcome was the 'Quit India' resolution approved by the All-India Congress Committee in August 1942. Freedom, it read, would 'enable India to resist aggression effectively with the people's united will and strength behind it', but 'inaction and submission to a foreign administration is not only degrading and reducing her capacity to defend herself and resist aggression but is no answer to that growing peril [from Japan] and is no service to the United Nations'. Once again there was an appeal to Britain and the United Nations to give India her freedom 'in the interest of world freedom', but having made it the Congress Working Committee felt it was no longer justified 'in holding the nation

---

[1] For an adverse criticism of the abrupt ending of negotiations see Menon, *Transfer of Power*, pp. 135–6. See also ibid. p. 121 for the insufficiently precise definition of responsibilities which contributed to it. [2] Sherwood, ii. 536.

back from endeavouring to assert its will against an imperialist and authoritarian Government which dominates over it'. Accordingly the Committee sanctioned, 'for the vindication of India's inalienable right to freedom and independence, the starting of a mass struggle on non-violent lines under the inevitable leadership of Gandhiji'.[1] The resolution was passed on 8 August 1942; the government reacted strongly. On 9 August the Congress leaders were arrested. There was extensive damage to communications, especially in the United Provinces and Bihar, and the supply lines of the armies facing the Japanese were threatened. But while disturbances were on a considerable scale, order was largely restored by the end of the year. Some 36,000 were imprisoned by the middle of 1943, and the principal Congress leaders, including Gandhi and Nehru, spent most of the remaining years of the war in jail.

The 'open rebellion' thus launched by the Congress was formally condemned by the Muslim League as a means by which the Congress sought to secure control of the government of the country. Though some Congress men listened to the appeals of Subhas Chandra Bose from Berlin, and were tempted to think that India should take advantage of a Japanese invasion, and with the aid of a Japanese-recruited Indian National Army secure Indian independence, the great majority were profoundly antagonistic to the aims and ideas of the militarist aggressor powers and were resolved that they should win and preserve their own freedom by their own means. Gandhi thought in terms of non-violent non-resistance to Japanese and British alike; Nehru was at all times insistent that the Japanese should be resisted by force. What united them was the belief that all Indian resistance to the invader should be inspired and directed by the Indian people and their own leaders.

What happened in India in August 1942 [wrote Pandit Nehru two years later, imprisoned in Ahmadnagar Fort] was no sudden development but a culmination of all that had gone before. . . . Behind it all lay an intense feeling that it was no longer possible to endure and live under foreign autocratic rule. All other questions became secondary. . . . Only the overwhelming desire to be rid of it remained. . . .[2]

'Quit India' was largely the expression of a mood crystallized by the Cripps Mission, the hopes it aroused, and its subsequent failure. The question, therefore, remained—was it statesmanlike to give to the Indian people in 1942 the glimpse of a promised land which they might at best see from afar but which they could not reach until a war of continents had ended?[3] The doubt is strengthened by recollection of the disadvantages of negotiating in an hour of defeat and peril. In 1940 the British government reacted to the fall of France with the 'August offer'; in 1942 to the surrender of Singapore with the Cripps Mission. In the long months between the outbreak of war and the

---
[1] Nehru, *Discovery of India*, p. 487.   [2] Ibid. pp. 489–90.
[3] A former Secretary of State for India, Lord Zetland, described the failure of the Mission as 'inevitable' (*Essayez*, p. 296). If this view is accepted the question surely merits a negative answer.

invasion of the Low Countries it took no important initiative. If its action, in 1942, was ill timed not least because it had the appearance of being prompted not by conviction but by calamity, that was because earlier inaction had made some move almost imperative.

South Africa: The War with Japan, Republicanism, and the Ascendancy of General Smuts

The South African declarations of war on Japan and the Axis satellites in Europe prompted the first Nationalist motion in the House of Assembly for the declaration of a South African republic. This was not so paradoxical as at first sight it might seem. War and the Constitution were deemed, and not by Nationalists alone, to be inextricably associated. As Indian Congressmen believed that the subcontinent was threatened by Japan only because it was a part of the British Empire, so Afrikaner Nationalists believed that only the Union's association with the British Commonwealth had brought about its participation in the war and that, as Mr. Strijdom had asserted in August 1940, there was only one way of getting rid of 'this terrible condition of affairs', and that was by doing away with this British connexion and getting a free South African Republic.[1]

In the successive phases of the war the themes republicanism, independence, peace, were restated, but with perceptible changes in emphasis as the prospects of Nazi victory first waxed and then waned. By 1941 the precedent of Ireland, the dominion which had thrown off the shackles of dominion status and was now neutral, attracted the particular attention of the Malanites, who desired to establish the republic by constitutional means. Thus at Stellenbosch, on 24 March that year, Dr. Malan reminded those who had thought of establishing a republic by force following upon a German victory that the 'path opened to us before the war is still possible; that is to follow in the footsteps of Ireland'.[2] And a month later the Federal Council of the Herenigde Nasionale party noted that 'If . . . this road [i.e. a republic brought into being as the result of an Axis victory] remains closed, the republic would have to be reached along the only other possible road—namely that which Ireland took', for 'Afrikanerdom is now unanimous on the breaking of the British connection and the establishment of a republic'.[3]

In the House of Assembly on 13 January 1942 Dr. Malan, maintaining that 'a great constitutional change must be brought about in the country, and South Africa from being a Dominion under the British Crown must be converted into a free independent republic', introduced a formal motion on behalf of the Nationalist party for the establishment of a republic.[4] 'Our highest national interests', he asserted, 'can only be served by the conversion of South

---
[1] South Africa, H. of A. Deb., vol. 40, coll. 324–5. See above, p. 77.
[2] *Cape Times*, 25 March 1941.   [3] *The Friend*, 11 April 1941.
[4] South Africa, H. of A. Deb., vol. 43, col. 34.

Africa into a republic dissociated from the British Crown and Empire and free and independent of any other foreign power.' But such a republic, he argued, with an eye on his pro-Nazi critics, 'should not be cast on any foreign model, but shall be built up in accordance with our own national character and traditions, based upon the principles of national government as embodied in the two former South African Republics', and eschewing 'anything false and dangerous to the nation contained in the British liberalistic democracy as existing in this country'. Such a republic should be Christian and national in character, it should be based upon the true observance of equal language and cultural rights of both sections of the European population; it should be made safe for the European race and its civilization and 'protected effectively against the capitalistic and parasitical exploitation of its population as well as against the undermining influences of hostile and unnational elements'. He condemned the existing dualism in South Africa under the British connexion and represented republicanism as the way to final national unity.

So long as the British connection prevails [he contended] the ideal of a united South African nation based on the sound and friendly relationship of the two white races is hopeless.... The question what will become of the British connection crops up every time as a disturbing element on every occasion we touch any of South Africa's vital problems. In that way it is impossible for us to render South Africa secure to ourselves and the white races. We must achieve another basis. The other basis is a South African basis, the basis of our being able to enjoy our own nationhood.[1]

In all this Dr. Malan had the support of Mr. Pirow. It was a dubious asset. Mr. Pirow extended the full support of the New Order to the motion in spite of the fact that 'it asks for much less than we should like to get and notwithstanding the primitive party political wording in which it is framed'.[2]

The United party, delighted with the bitter taunts that betokened continuing division within the Nationalist ranks, were psychologically in a much stronger position in January 1942 than in the summer of 1940. There was no disposition, however, on their part to discount the appeal of republicanism to Afrikaner sentiment. On the contrary supporters of the Government were at some pains to bring home the grave constitutional and political consequences which they believed would follow upon the achievement of the Nationalists' goal. Thus Mr. Marwick emphasized that a republican constitution, involving of necessity the elimination of 'His Majesty from the Act of Union and as a constituent element of the legislative power of the Union', would be 'contrary to law and entirely unconstitutional';[3] while Mr. Blackwell gave warning that such a republic, 'the apotheosis of Little South Africa', would jeopardize all hopes of a greater South Africa. 'By this motion . . .', he said, Dr. Malan is

---

[1] South Africa, H. of A. Deb., vol. 43, coll. 45–46.
[2] Ibid. col. 130.
[3] Ibid. coll. 180–1.

'for ever . . . slamming the door against the rest of Southern Africa. Gone for ever, should his republic come into being . . . is any chance of . . . amalgamation with either of the two Rhodesias . . . Gone for ever is any idea of a greater South Africa.'[1] This was well-founded criticism, and yet it missed its mark. Renewed Nationalist emphasis on a republic in fact reflected a desire, partly subconscious, for withdrawal from a world in which Nationalists found so many things uncongenial to them. The ascendant power of the United States made them increasingly fearful of North American cultural and economic penetration, evidence of the might of the Soviet Union appalled them, while resurgent nationalism in Asia filled them with misgivings for the future of white civilization. Isolationalism was implicit in their republicanism, which seemed to offer if not protection at least escape from an unfriendly or critical world. All this had its importance for the future, and because of that the debate of January 1942 on the republic remains a significant landmark in South African political history.

General Smuts on 13 January submitted an alternative motion in comprehensive terms:

That in view of the fact that the Union is at war with Germany and Italy, and that Japan, Bulgaria, Hungary, Rumania and Finland are taking an active part in the war on the side of those powers, this House approves the Union's declaration of war also against these countries. This House also affirms the continuance of South Africa's membership of the British Commonwealth of Nations and expresses its strongest disapproval of the raising at a time like the present when the country is at war, of issues involving a fundamental change in its constitution.

The motion, which was carried on 17 January by 81 votes to 55,[2] was at once a statement of war aims and a declaration of faith. On constitutional questions the United party were the champions of the *status quo*. 'I stand firm for our rights as set out in our Status Act and the Statute of Westminster', said General Smuts later, and 'nothing that I do will ever be to the detriment of that position, and any course, whether Right or Left, that touches the present position will meet my strongest opposition.'[3] Immobility, however, was not without its dangers in a changing Commonwealth, as the United party was later to learn.

Shortly after the debate in the House of Assembly there appeared in the Afrikaans press a draft republican constitution which was understood to have provided a basis for discussion about the nature of a future republic. Though Dr. Malan later, in 1948,[4] repudiated any connexion with this draft constitution and charged that it was a creation of the Ossewa Brandwag, *Die Burger*, in publishing it in 1942, stated that the Nationalist party had accepted the scheme in principle and in broad outline.[5] The draft constitution contemplated

---

[1] Ibid. col. 83.   [2] Ibid. col. 536.   [3] *Manchester Guardian*, 18 March 1944.
[4] South Africa, Senate Deb., 1948, col. 1089; see generally coll. 1084-1102.
[5] Quoted in *Review of the Dominions Press*, series E, no. 129, 10 April 1942.

a Republic of South Africa on Christian-national principles with the abdication of British kingship over, and hence the status of British subjects within, the republic. It proposed to confer 'burger' citizenship discriminately on European subjects who could be relied upon to 'behave in a manner helpful to the upbuilding of the volk'. Article 4 created a State President 'directly and solely answerable before God and towards the volk for his acts in the execution of his duties', under whom would be appointed a Head Minister and a Council of Ministers, all dismissable by the President. The content of the draft was well calculated to deepen United party suspicions of Nationalist intentions, and in so far as it contemplated not the fusion of English and Afrikaans-speaking South Africans in a future republic, but the creation of an exclusivist Afrikaner republic, it marked also a repudiation of Hertzogite and the triumph of Krugerist principles. Politically the publication of this fundamentalist document at this juncture was a liability for the Nationalists, who cast doubt upon its origins and authenticity, and an asset to the United party because it brought home to moderate opinion what the consequences of Nationalist rule might be.[1]

There was in Afrikaner eyes a clear distinction between Germany and Japan. Germany was a European, Japan was an Asian power. Moreover, past German sympathy with the Boer republics, a lively sense of German humiliation at Versailles, the appeal of Nazi doctrines of blood and race, all combined to instil in the minds of Afrikaner Nationalists a predisposition towards friendship rather than enmity with the Third Reich. But it was far otherwise with Japan. She was a non-European power which was inflicting defeat and humiliation upon Europeans. When General Smuts declared on 2 February 1942 that 'the passage is open from the Pacific into the Indian ocean',[2] his statement had implications unwelcome and alarming to all white South Africans irrespective of party. Defeat of Britain by Germany might have had its considerable compensations for many Nationalists; defeat of Britain by Japan had none. It is likely, therefore, that Nationalist assertions that Japanese advances did not threaten the Union, and their consequent denunciation of the use of South African troops for the precautionary occupation of Madagascar (for which General Smuts sought the retrospective sanction of Parliament), further weakened their position in the country.[3]

The principal trend in South African politics at this time, though in part obscured by the continuing asperity of party warfare, was the progressive consolidation of South African resources and opinion behind the Union's war effort. On 27 January 1943 General Smuts felt his position sufficiently secure to recommend the use of South African forces 'beyond the continent'

[1] Cf. Dr. A. Keppel-Jones, *When Smuts Goes* (London, Gollancz, 1947) for a considered forecast full of foreboding about its implications for the future of English-speaking South Africans in the Union. [2] South Africa, Senate Deb., 1942, col. 246.
[3] South Africa, H. of A. Deb., vol. 44, col. 3567. For Nationalist opposition to any active participation in war against Japan see ibid. *passim.*

on the basis of voluntary recruitment, in view of 'the prospect of the early expulsion of the enemy from the continent of Africa'.[1] Later in the same year popular backing for his war policy was impressively demonstrated by the results of the general election. The United party increased their strength in the House of Assembly from 72 to 84, and the total number of members supporting South Africa's participation in the war advanced from 87 to 110. This was more than a triumph for a party; it was the triumph of a cause and of the man who symbolized it. In 1939 General Smuts had changed the course of South African history; in 1943 his courage and his insight received from the electorate its due reward. Secure at home he was now free to expound before a wider audience ideas which were to influence the shaping of the post-war Commonwealth and of the post-war world.

The election of 1943 had one other notable consequence. It left the Nationalist party in sole possession of nationalist representation in the House of Assembly.[2] Mr. Pirow's New Order group, which had commanded 16 seats in the old House, was eliminated, and the same fate befell the faithful remnant of General Hertzog's followers who lost all their 8 seats. But while the total strength of the Opposition groups fell from 68 to 43, the strength of the Nationalist party increased from 41 to 43. Within the ranks of Nationalist Afrikanerdom this was regarded as a notable victory for the advocates of constitutionalism. It was also interpreted as a triumph for a policy of no compromise on the republican question. 'The H.N.P. has written republic on its banner', declared Dr. Malan after the election. 'Perhaps we had to give up political gain as a result; but where the National Afrikaners were not republican, they are so now.'[3] Mr. C. R. Swart, at the opening of the Herenigde Nasionale party Congress in November 1943, defined the most important immediate aim of the party as 'the severance of the British connection and the establishment of a republic'. Mr. Strijdom on the same occasion was inspired by a transcendental interpretation of South African politics at once to cast scorn on the defeated Ossewa Brandwag, New Order, and Greyshirt rivals and to hold out the prospect of a promised land to his Nationalist party colleagues.

Unfortunately [he said] there are some who saw a possibility of our liberation only in a German victory and now that this victory seems uncertain, they say that we will never again come to power. We will win and rule because the Lord placed us here with a certain intention. And his intention is not based on a Russian, German, or British victory.[4]

Forecasts of England's weakened position in the post-war world afforded new grounds for hope.

In this war [Dr. Malan affirmed in October] England has been put in the shade in

[1] Ibid. vol. 45, coll. 405 ff.
[2] See Roberts & Trollip, chs. v and vi for an analysis of the significance of the election from the point of view of the Nationalist Opposition.
[3] *Die Transvaler*, 13 November 1943.   [4] *Die Volksblad*, 17 November 1943.

the military field by other nations. Financially they are irrevocably mortgaged to America.... Through all this the breaking up power in the Empire has been strengthened as opposed to the building together power. The time is ripe for South Africa to gain freedom.¹

But whatever the future might hold by way of possible consolation, 1943 was for the Nationalists a year of signal defeat.

United States Belligerency and Irish Neutrality

On the evening of Sunday 7 December Mr. Churchill first learned from the B.B.C. nine o'clock news of the Japanese attack on the United States. He telephoned the President of the United States for confirmation, and on receiving it instructed the Foreign Office to prepare at once a declaration of war upon Japan. Then his thoughts turned to what had always lain near to his heart, and in the early hours of 8 December 1941 he sent this cryptic message to Mr. de Valera: 'Now is your chance. Now or never! A nation once again! I will meet you wherever you wish.'² Mr. de Valera, aroused in the early hours of the morning, was unresponsive. He was not then or at any time prepared to bargain neutrality for unity. Ireland's position after the entry of the United States into the war he described as that 'of a friendly neutral', but, he added,

from the moment that the war began there was for this state only one policy possible—neutrality. Our circumstances, our history, the incompleteness of our national freedom through the partition of our country made any other policy impracticable. Any other policy would have divided our people, and for a divided nation to fling itself into this war would be to commit suicide.³

On 11 January 1942 he discounted explicitly all suggestion of a bargain:

We have laid down our policy clearly from the beginning, and that is that we do not intend to enter into this war if we can possibly avoid it, and we will avoid it, please God, unless we are attacked. If we are attacked we have to take it as God's will and sell our lives as dearly as we can.... There are no bargains. When this war started I said that there was no inch of our national territory for sale. Our policy has been this—we will defend ourselves against attack from any quarter.⁴

Here was an occasion when a dispassionate Irishman was not to be moved by the pleas of an impassioned Englishman or, and this is the more remarkable fact, by the pressures of a hitherto non-belligerent and now very belligerent United States.

As early as October 1941 Mr. Churchill suggested to President Roosevelt that, in view of the contemplated dispersal of Britain's military strength in

---

¹ *Die Transvaler*, 11 October 1943.   ² Churchill, iii. 539.
³ *Irish Times*, 15 December 1941. Mr. de Valera was speaking at Cork on 14 December 1941.   ⁴ Ibid. 12 January 1942.

aggressive action against the enemy in 1942, 'it would be a very great reassurance and a military advantage of the highest order' if a United States Army Corps and Armoured Division with air support were to be stationed in Northern Ireland at the invitation of the governments both of the United Kingdom and of Northern Ireland itself.[1] This suggestion was once more submitted to the President, now the head of an Allied power, by Mr. Churchill on his visit to Washington in December 1941.[2] The President responded sympathetically[3] and so, later, did Mr. Stimson, the Secretary for War, and the United States' Chiefs of Staff. In the broad strategy of the war the move had much to recommend it. It was an earnest of the intention of the United States to intervene directly in the European war; it might serve to detain German troops in the West during the critical years of the war in Russia; it would release trained British troops from garrison duties at home and it would serve as an additional deterrent against German thoughts of an invasion of the British Isles. Over and above these substantial strategic reasons there was the thought in Mr. Churchill's mind that, as he expressed it in the first instance to President Roosevelt in October 1941, 'the arrival of American troops in Northern Ireland would exercise a powerful effect upon the whole of Eire, with favourable consequences that cannot be measured'.[4] In fact the arrival of the United States forces in late January 1942 in Northern Ireland had consequences that were easily measured. It made no significantly favourable impact upon opinion in Eire and it elicited a sharp protest from Mr. de Valera.

> The people of Ireland [he said] have no feeling of hostility towards, and no desire to be brought in any way into conflict with, the United States ... but it is our duty to make it clearly understood that, no matter what troops occupy the six counties, the Irish people's claim for the union of the whole of the national territory, and for supreme jurisdiction over it, will remain unabated. Four years ago the British Government and Parliament recognized fully the sovereignty of the Irish nation[5] over that part of the national territory included in the 26 counties, and the bond has been honourably kept in that regard. But the maintenance of the partition of Ireland is as indefensible as aggression against small nations elsewhere, which it is the avowed purpose of Britain and the U.S. in this war to bring to an end.[6]

The bond was honourably kept and Irish neutrality respected to the end. The Irish government had, however, no explicit assurance that this would be so, and in the later phases of the European war it was subjected to considerable psychological pressure from London and more especially from Washington.[7] One instance deserves recall. On the eve of the Allied invasion of

---

[1] Churchill, iii. 482–3.   [2] Ibid. p. 576.   [3] Ibid. p. 590.   [4] Ibid. p. 483.
[5] An allusion to the restoration of the Treaty Ports to Irish sovereignty in 1938.
[6] *Irish Times*, 28 January 1942.
[7] Cf. a letter from Mr. David Gray, at that time United States Minister to Ireland, published in ibid. 31 May 1950.

Europe the continued presence of Axis legations in Dublin prompted a formal United States *démarche* to the Irish government. While the initiative came from Washington, there was encouragement from London. On 2 February 1944 Mr. Churchill minuted the Secretary of State for Dominion Affairs that he was preparing a telegram to be sent to President Roosevelt concerning the information about Anglo-American troop convoys and, more especially, about altered preparations for the invasion of Europe, which 'will certainly be passing in a stream' to the enemy unless measures were taken to prevent it.[1] On 21 February a United States Note[2] requesting as 'an absolute minimum' the recall of the Axis diplomats in Dublin was presented to the Irish government. The text was not made public for some three weeks, and during this interval between presentation and publication Mr. de Valera uttered one of his more sombre warnings about the dangers that threatened Eire as 'the efforts of the belligerents against each other reach their climax'. 'At any moment', he went on, 'this war may come upon us and we may be called upon to defend our rights and our freedom with our lives.'[3] Nothing came, however, more formidable than the American Note itself. This was an essay in transatlantic 'tough' diplomacy which was not well calculated to achieve the ends in view.

The American Note alleged in general terms that the neutrality of the Irish government

has in fact operated and continues to operate in favor of the Axis powers and against the United Nations on whom your security and the maintenance of your national economy depend.

Associated with this broad allegation was the particular charge that

one of the gravest and most inequitable results of this situation is the opportunity for highly organized espionage which the geographical position of Ireland affords the Axis and denies the United Nations.

The ejection of the Axis representatives was accordingly requested by the United States government. Mr. Churchill stated in the House of Commons that, while the initiative in the making of those representations was taken by the United States, its government was in consultation with the government of the United Kingdom throughout, and its action had the full concurrence of the United Kingdom government and of the governments of the oversea dominions.[4] Mr. de Valera's attempts to enlist the support first of the Canadian and then of the Australian Prime Minister for the withdrawal of the American Note in the interests of Eire's relations with the United Nations were notably unsuccessful.

The Irish rejoinder,[5] a classic example of Mr. de Valera's dialectical skill,

---

[1] Churchill, v. 606–7. [2] *Documents on American Foreign Relations*, vi. 675–6.
[3] *Round Table*, June 1944, p. 265.
[4] H. of C. Deb., vol. 396, coll. 1252–3. It would not seem, however, that the dominions were consulted. [5] *Documents on American Foreign Relations*, vi. 676–8.

gave the most emphatic assurances that every means had been taken to prevent the leakage of information and declared that not a single instance of neglect on the part of the Irish government was alleged in the Note. More generally his reply expressed surprise at the terms used by the United States government, which seemed to be out of harmony with the traditional friendship between the two countries, and suggested that it was 'perhaps not known to the American Government that the feelings of the Irish people toward Britain have, during the war, undergone a considerable change, precisely because Britain has not attempted to violate our neutrality'.[1]

The United States request for the removal of the Axis representatives was firmly rejected. Mr. de Valera's decision to do so had the support of all parties in Eire. It was the almost universal conviction there that while the German and Japanese diplomatic missions endeavoured to exploit any possibilities of espionage to the best of their ability, their opportunities for so doing, because of their geographical isolation reinforced by governmental precautions, were so restricted as to be virtually non-existent. The American Note itself allowed that the good faith of the Irish government in its efforts to suppress espionage was not in question, but on the eve of the Allied landings in Normandy their effectiveness was what mattered to the Allied governments. The Irish rejection of the Note, which did not exclude further stringent measures to restrict German espionage, stemmed from the belief that neutrality was the final vindication of sovereign status. What had begun as a policy had ended by becoming a symbol. For that reason—it is a paradoxical fact—representations from the traditionally friendly United States for the removal of two unpopular Axis legations were regarded as an attempted infringement of national sovereignty. If the request was further intended to weaken Mr. de Valera's position at home it was singularly ill advised. No man was happier than he when championing the sovereignty of his country against all who threatened to impair it. Following the rejection of the American Note he dissolved the Dáil and at the polls won what was destined to be his greatest political triumph.

Two things may be noted in concluding this account of a controversy highly charged with emotion but of no great importance. The first is that the British and the United States governments alike consistently overestimated the potential influence of the United States upon Irish opinion. Sentimental appeal is one thing, practical politics another, and nowhere is the distinction better understood than in Ireland. The second is that while Irish neutrality was a liability to the Allied cause there were, to quote a statement by the Under-Secretary of State for Dominion Affairs, at the end of the war in Europe 'no grounds for suggesting that the Eire Government committed un-

---

[1] Mr. Churchill complained in his Victory Broadcast that Mr. de Valera 'frolicked' with the German and Japanese representatives in the hour of Britain's peril. Had Mr. de Valera foreseen this he might have worded his reply rather differently. He rarely frolicked with anyone.

neutral acts to the disadvantage of this country'.[1] On the contrary the unimpeded, and in Ireland unpublicized,[2] flow of Irish volunteers to the British forces was to the advantage of the Allied cause. Their number, variously but uncertainly estimated, was probably not far short of 40,000, and their quality was high, perhaps because they were all volunteers. A semi-official list of their distinctions published by the United Kingdom government was a well-deserved tribute to men who fought and died in a cause which their country had not, for reasons which to many of them seemed sufficient, made its own. If their enlistment did not infringe the letter of Irish neutrality, it materially strengthened the forces at the disposal of the British Commonwealth.

Means and Ends: Debate and Discussion on the Future of the Commonwealth, 1943–4

The changes in the balance of world power made evident as the tide of battle turned became a recurrent theme in the speeches of Commonwealth leaders in 1943–4. The changes themselves were on the greatest scale and confronted Commonwealth statesmen with the question of what would, and what should, be the role of the Commonwealth in the new constellation of world powers that would emerge when Germany and Japan were defeated. It was no accident that the first considered reflections upon these questions were voiced by Commonwealth statesmen overseas, by Mr. Curtin, by General Smuts, by Lord Halifax from his vantage point in the Embassy at Washington, and by Mr. Mackenzie King. The decline of Europe, the ascending power of the United States and of the Soviet Union, was something that Western Europeans, engulfed in the most deadly war in history, had little time or disposition to contemplate, whilst across the oceans there was at once acute awareness of them coupled with a conviction that, in accordance with the shift in world power, means should be found whereby the wisdom and the vigour of new societies should be enabled to make a full contribution to world peace and progress when victory was won. The relationship between the dominions and the United Kingdom, so recently restated in terms of equality, was an important part of this larger whole, and seemed to deserve reconsideration in this wider world context. For if the

[1] Cf. H. of C. Deb., vol. 407, col. 132, when in reply to criticism the Under-Secretary of State for Dominion Affairs said, 'There is no conspiracy of silence [about the number of volunteers in H.M. Forces from Eire] . . . it is just the fact that it has not been possible to decide what numbers of His Majesty's Forces come from Eire and which do not. We have made great efforts to find out, but it has not been possible.' Some incomplete figures were given later (ibid. vol. 421, col. 58). The figure tentatively suggested in the text does not include Irishmen domiciled in Britain.

[2] In pursuance of its resolve to keep the political temperature low, the Irish censorship prohibited the publication of all information about Irish volunteers serving in H.M. Forces. Its edicts were, however, on occasion circumvented. An *Irish Times* report that a former member of its staff was fully restored to health after a recent serious 'boating accident' was an allusion to his being one of the survivors of the sinking of the *Prince of Wales* in Malayan waters.

power of the United Kingdom relative to that of the greatest powers had declined, that of the dominions, and especially of Canada and Australia, relative to the large grouping of middle powers had ascended. But none the less they still remained, in the language of the day, middle powers. They need not follow but they could not lead. Their old reliance on the United Kingdom had gone, but what was to replace it? Was there not here at once a need and a case for a realistic reappraisal of dominion relations with the United Kingdom? For if within the Commonwealth equality of status was still unmatched by equality in stature, the margin in power between the United Kingdom and the dominions had sensibly declined, while, without, the Commonwealth was confronted by a world for long likely to be dominated by powers whose resources the members of the Commonwealth collectively could not match.

Changes in the balance of world power subtly modified the attitudes of the older dominions to the United Kingdom. Fear of entanglement in the policies of a great power began to give way to anxiety to sustain its authority in the face of a greater. When, therefore, it seemed timely to re-examine the foundations of Commonwealth co-operation in a new pattern of world power, dominion governments showed themselves, not indeed unconcerned, but assuredly much less concerned with questions of status than in the past, and much more preoccupied with the broad aims of Commonwealth policies and with the means by which these aims might best be realized. Different views about ends and means were formulated in different parts of the Commonwealth and particular experiences in the war and pre-war years played the decisive part in influencing them. Yet partly because so much that was of fundamental importance in that experience was shared, the discussion that followed was focused on the means to achieve rather than on the ends to be achieved.

Australian Proposals for a Commonwealth Council or Secretariat

When the crisis of the Pacific War broke upon the island continent of Australia its people reinterpreted their past experience of Commonwealth relations in the light of their present dangers. They found it not altogether reassuring. It seemed to many of them that the means for conserving effective unity of purpose and action among the self-governing members of the British Commonwealth had proved defective, and that progressive decentralization of responsibility from Britain to the dominions was likely to render them altogether inadequate unless new machinery were introduced to close the gap caused by the progressive disappearance of the old. In particular the Imperial Conference, conceived of as the cornerstone of the Commonwealth had, in the prevailing Australian view, perceptibly and regrettably declined in prestige and importance. Should not its status be restored in such a way that it might serve as a body through which a foreign policy for the British Commonwealth might be worked out with due regard to the views and the regional interests of the self-governing members of the Commonwealth and to the changes in the world scene?

Before and during the war Australian misgivings about lack of dominion participation in the making of policy were sharpened by experience. It was the convention, agreed in 1926 and again in 1930, that each dominion government should inform its partners of all treaty negotiations in which it was engaged so as to give them the earliest possible opportunity for the expression of their views. It was the understanding that if there were no comment within a reasonable period the negotiating government was entitled to assume that there was no objection to the policy it proposed to follow. This understanding worked well so long as time and circumstance permitted. Thus Australia was consulted at all stages in the negotiation of the Anglo-Egyptian Treaty of 1936.[1] Again in 1938 the Munich Agreement, though in no sense a formal treaty, was reached after dominion governments had had every opportunity of influencing United Kingdom policy. Very different in this respect, however, were the circumstances surrounding the guarantees to Poland, Greece, and Rumania in March–April 1939. In each instance the dominions were kept informed but in no case were they consulted. The decision to extend the guarantees was that of the United Kingdom Cabinet alone, which believed Nazi aggression against these Eastern European states to be imminent. As a result the dominions had no opportunity of expressing in advance their opinions in particular about the guarantee to Poland, which in the sequel committed them not formally but none the less certainly to war. This gave rise to considerable uneasiness in Australia. It was accentuated, as has been seen, during the war years by the 'humiliation' of Dakar, by experience in the Middle East, and by the widespread feeling that United Kingdom opinion, more interested in Europe than in Asia, had been complacent about developments on the Pacific seaboard and had dangerously underestimated the power of Japan. Australia's minor role in the making of Pacific strategy and her absence from the Cairo Conference further account for the continuing resolve of Australian governments to secure for themselves a place in the inner sanctuaries where Britain's policies were made.

Mr. Curtin was a member of the Australian War Council from the time of its formation but the first Cabinet offices which he held were those of Prime Minister and Minister for Defence. It was this which perhaps accounted for his tendency to speak on topics on which his official advisers, not to mention his ministerial colleagues, might have had useful observations to make without consulting them beforehand and also for his seeming unawareness of the impression which his public pronouncements were likely to produce.[2] If he was unpleasantly surprised by the interpretation placed upon the words

[1] See Mansergh, *Survey, 1931–9*, p. 159.
[2] *Round Table*, March 1944, p. 170. See generally pp. 168–73 for an interesting contemporary commentary on Mr. Curtin's proposals.

of his famous (or notorious) article in the Melbourne *Herald* in December 1941, he was agreeably impressed by the interest shown in the suggestions which he made for an Imperial Secretariat and Council in August–September 1943. But if the presentation of the ideas was personal[1] and if in both instances Mr. Curtin underestimated the impact of his observations, especially outside Australia, that was a matter of formal rather than fundamental importance. Nothing could be more misleading than to suggest that Mr. Curtin was going ahead of party opinion on imperial policy; still less was he deviating from it. He was, at the time he advanced these proposals, engaged in the election campaign of 1943, which resulted in the return of his party with the largest majority in its history. Australian Labour was then, as at other times, a strictly disciplined party, and Mr. Curtin was fully alive to the fate of his predecessors who had strayed from the party line. If he did not consult he certainly did not fail to take into account the known opinion of the Labour caucus in putting forward his proposals for new imperial machinery. Nor did he misjudge it; for in December 1943 when he outlined them to the party conference there was no dissent from the opinions he expressed.[2]

The acceptance by Australian Labour of the conception of more precisely formulated imperial policies and the establishment of machinery for their elaboration marks an important stage in the evolution of its external policy. Mr. Menzies noted with appreciation that in fact the Labour Prime Minister had now learned from experience the wisdom of his opponents' policies and was accordingly adopting them. This explanation has about it a pleasing simplicity; unquestionably, too, it contained some truth. In the War Council and still more in office the Labour leaders, confronted with the greatest crisis in the history of the Federation, gained a new understanding of the nature and importance of Australia's ties with Britain and the British Commonwealth. Australia, as the German radio never tired of repeating, was the orphan of the Pacific, and her perilous isolation in 1941–2 played the most important part in shaping proposals whose origins could be traced back over many decades.

What did Mr. Curtin in fact propose? In Adelaide on 14 August 1943 he suggested that some more formal machinery for imperial consultation had become necessary in the light of wartime experience.

I do not believe [he said] that Britain can manage the Empire on the basis purely of a government sitting in London. I believe some Imperial authority must be evolved so that the British Commonwealth of Nations will have, if not an executive

[1] In the second case it seems likely that he was indebted to the Defence Department, and perhaps particularly to the Secretary for Defence, Sir Frederick Shedden, for ideas on closer collaboration on defence between Britain and Australia which had been developed at the time of the 1937 Imperial Conference.

[2] See L. F. Crisp, *The Australian Federal Labour Party, 1901–1951* (London, Longmans, 1955), p. 105, where the Labour party's 'notable warming to British Commonwealth links' over the years is contrasted with its refusal of other international affiliations.

body, at least a standing consultative body. With all the scientific facilities for communication, these meetings must be frequent in the years to come. . . .[1]

In a statement a few weeks later[2] the Australian Prime Minister indicated more precisely but still not very precisely what he had in mind. He spoke of an Imperial Council similar in constitution to the Pacific Council, at which dominion governments might ordinarily be represented by their respective High Commissioners and occasionally at short appropriate intervals by ministers. The Council he conceived of as a permanent body, holding regular meetings; and because of 'everything that is inherent in Dominion status' these meetings should be held in dominion capitals as well as in London. The creation of such a Council, he thought, would make possible prompt consideration by a central Commonwealth body of any issue of importance whenever it should happen to arise. Even though the Council, like its prototype, the Pacific Council, would be a deliberative body, it would offer some assurance that dominion, and especially Australian, views would be taken into account from the outset in the making of imperial policy. While under existing arrangements the dominion High Commissioners met frequently with the Secretary of State for Dominion Affairs and at times exercised their right of access to the United Kingdom Prime Minister, there was no formal body in existence, as Mr. Curtin explained, expressly designed to elicit and ensure consideration of dominion views before decisions were made. It was this gap that the Imperial Council was intended to fill. In order to do so effectively, however, it would require, in Mr. Curtin's view, the services of a permanent secretariat 'as expert in the problems of peace' as those who were at that time advising the governments of the Empire and of the United Nations were expert in the problems of war. Neither Council nor Secretariat was to be invested with, or apparently intended to discharge, any executive responsibilities, though the Australian Prime Minister's language was, perhaps deliberately, ambiguous on this second point, and he himself did not exclude the possibility of their doing so.

It is not certain to what extent Mr. Curtin intended that the Imperial Council and Secretariat should ultimately supersede the existing machinery of Commonwealth consultation, and it seems likely that this was an important question to which he had given little consideration. On the shorter view it is clear that he thought to supplement rather than replace it. To that extent, therefore, he was concerned with methods rather than with principles. But that was not the way in which his proposals were interpreted outside Australia, and the controversy which they provoked is to be attributed to the simplification which overtook such boldly sketched ideas once they crossed the Pacific.

In Cape Town, in London, and most of all in Ottawa Mr. Curtin was commonly judged to have suggested reforms that would change the direction in

[1] Mansergh, *Documents*, i. 562.
[2] Press statement of 4 September 1943 (ibid. p. 563).

which the Commonwealth had been travelling since 1919. This was only partly true. Decentralization may not have had for Mr. Curtin the cherished associations it had for General Smuts, but neither was he a champion of centralization in any traditional sense. At root his proposals derived from an awareness of a change in the balance of power within the British Commonwealth itself. Britain might remain the predominant partner, but in the course of the war the dominions had acquired an increased stature in the eyes of friend and foe alike. Did this not imply that the greater responsibility thrust upon the oversea dominions in time of war should be matched by their greater participation in the making of policy when it was ended? The place which Australia would occupy in the Pacific after the war, said Mr. Curtin, 'can never be the same as it was up to 1939'.[1] For that very reason Australia should hav the advantage of a concerted Empire policy so that she could stand effectively for democracy in the South Pacific, while in turn 'Britain's power as a force for peace in the future will be strengthened in the world if a firm voice against aggression comes from the Empire and not merely from London'. In sum this was an argument for co-ordination of policies coupled with a great and growing measure of devolution of regional responsibility. In so far as it presupposed British Commonwealth policies it pointed to centralization, but it was not centralization in the accepted sense of a concentration of power in the hands of Britain, for the ultimate purpose was that not only Britain but also the dominions, each in respect of its own area, should have a greater share in the making and execution of policies.

In October 1943[2] Dr. Evatt spoke in balanced terms of the deficiencies in the system of imperial consultation which had prompted Mr. Curtin's proposals. He allowed that information was always readily forthcoming from the United Kingdom government on all important issues and that also 'as a general rule' there was an opportunity for the Australian government to express its views in advance of decisions taken.

> We have [he said], for example, been fully informed of the discussions and negotiations relating to the surrender of Italy, the Badoglio Government's becoming a co-belligerent, the formation of a Mediterranean commission, and also as to the arrangements and proposals to be discussed at the Three-Power meeting in Moscow.

But it was necessary to take the question rather further. What happened in the ordinary way was that the United Kingdom government placed a proposal before all the dominion governments. Each dominion, after examining it, expressed its opinion and sent it through the Dominions Office to the appropriate department in London, or if necessary to the Cabinet. Since from time to time the dominions were bound to express different views, the final decision had often to be taken by the United Kingdom government on its exclusive responsibility. Dominion governments tended to acquiesce in any decision

---

[1] *The Times*, 7 September 1943. [2] Australia, H. of R. Deb., vol. 176, p. 576.

reached in the United Kingdom, partly because consultation among them on a political level was usually out of the question in time of crisis and still more in time of war. What therefore was needed, urged Dr. Evatt in support of his Prime Minister—possibly qualified by reflections on Mr. Curtin's failure to consult his Cabinet colleagues at all times before the public enunciation of his ideas—was some additional machinery by which this gap in the system of consultation could be closed, and dominion governments assured that at all times there existed a means by which their views individually and collectively could be brought to the attention of the United Kingdom government before decisions were made.

The arguments of politicians were more fully developed in the press. One extract from an article published in *The Age* in December 1943 reflects the widespread uneasiness that existed at that time in Australia about the making of imperial policies. The writer, after noting that decisions on policy involving issues of peace and war had on occasion reached the stage of definite commitment before each responsible government in the Commonwealth had been given an opportunity of expressing its views, proceeded:

Important foreign policy engagements of this order ultimately involve the whole Empire in their practical consequences. In the fevered days before the war momentous and crucial attitudes toward other countries were shaped at Westminster. If the Dominions were 'kept informed', that seemed to be as far as their participation in decisions went. The Munich crisis was succeeded by guarantees to Poland, to Roumania, to Greece. Right or wrong, these pledges were not the result of any integrated foreign policy by the British Empire. The Dominions were interested spectators, later to become—certainly by their spontaneous action in support of Britain—participants in redemption of pledges which were a precipitating factor in bringing a state of war. When the die had been cast, it mattered little whether or not Australia and the other Dominions would have accepted the pledges as equally binding on themselves. Much wider issues than the merits of specific engagements to this or that country threatened by aggression were involved. A main purpose in Mr. Curtin's plan is to ensure that each self-governing nation of the Empire should have an effective voice in the formation of foreign policies which involve questions of war or peace, and for this reason are of direct concern to the Empire in each part.[1]

There was here some overstatement. Australia, for example, had not only been consulted but had been among the foremost in urging that the Czech crisis of 1938 should be peacefully disposed of without too precise an inquiry into the sacrifices demanded of Czechoslovakia.[2] But if the detail was

[1] *The Age*, 16 December 1943, quoted in J. G. Allen, *Editorial Opinion in the Contemporary British Commonwealth and Empire* (Boulder, University of Colorado Studies, 1946), pp. 399–400. Mr. Allen's book has made it possible to survey in a convenient, though by its nature not complete, form the editorial comment called forth by this and other proposals throughout the Commonwealth, and incidentally makes clear how much public interest there was in all the dominions in these rather abstract questions about the organization of the Commonwealth.

[2] Mansergh, *Survey, 1931–9*, pp. 168–71.

exaggerated the problem remained. Was it, however, of a kind that could conceivably be resolved by the creation of an Imperial Council and secretariat with duties that were purely consultative? It was to this question that Mr. Curtin's critics devoted most of their attention. They maintained that if the proposed new imperial bodies failed to take decisions urgently demanded in moments of crisis, they would not fulfil the principal purpose for which they had been created, while if they did it would mean that decisions would be taken without the concurrence of dominion governments.

It was apparent from the initial reaction to Mr. Curtin's proposals that neither Canada nor South Africa would be prepared to contemplate any delegation of executive authority to any central Commonwealth body, while the New Zealand response, warmly phrased but ambiguously worded,[1] suggested at the least no uncritical welcome. Even if specially appointed ministers were to be members of such an Imperial Council, even if the Prime Ministers of each dominion were to attend its sessions personally, there remained great, and in some instances extreme, reluctance on the part of dominion parliaments and peoples to invest them with an authority which would allow them to commit their countries to explicit actions or policies without consultation with their Cabinet colleagues or their Parliaments. Such reluctance would have been transformed into open opposition at the slightest suggestion that a central secretariat might take decisions without reference to governments. This point was underlined in a South African comment published in the *Cape Times*:

> Surely consultation nowadays is as close as it could possibly be? The creation of a special secretariat may improve the filing of Dominion Prime Ministers' decisions, but it cannot hasten or improve those decisions. No secretariat can make decisions unless it has been given plenipotentiary powers; and we doubt whether any Dominion—even Australia—would be willing to give the right of decision to someone in a distant part of the world, when its own Prime Minister, with the privilege of being able to consult his Cabinet at any time, can receive information and give his judgment at the lifting of a telephone.[2]

That doubt was sufficiently well founded to prove fatal to Mr. Curtin's proposals.

The association of Mr. Curtin's ideas with earlier suggestions for an Imperial

---

[1] Cf. Mr. Fraser's comment of 10 September 1943 on Mr. Curtin's proposals: 'I am strongly in favour of any scheme which will bring the Dominions into closer consultation and co-operation with the United Kingdom and with each other'. That co-operation, he said, was Mr. Curtin's clear intention and the proposal would receive the New Zealand Government's careful and friendly examination. There were, however, daily consultations with Britain on all matters of importance, and co-operation between the countries of the British Commonwealth had been very close, effective, and beneficial during the war. If a scheme for providing a workable basis for a permanent British Commonwealth organization were put forward it would be welcomed by New Zealand (*The Times*, 11 September 1943).

[2] *Cape Times*, 5 May 1944, quoted in Allen, *Editorial Opinion*, p. 413.

Consultative Council or Imperial Federation prejudiced their reception. So far as Mr. Curtin himself was concerned, the analogy was mistaken and superficial. He was not a second Ward coming to champion the lost cause of imperial federation; he was an Australian nationalist with no desire to see the identity of his country submerged in a wider imperial unity, a dominion leader with a steady resolve to secure for the Commonwealth of Australia a greater share in the making of British policy. His aim was to safeguard Australia. It was not academic reasoning; it was the bombs that had been dropped on Darwin, the midget submarines that had pierced the harbour defences of Sydney and the large submarines that had bombarded it, which persuaded him that the days of easy security and complacent acceptance of British policies were ended. For this reason Mr. Curtin coupled his proposals for new imperial machinery with an implicit and at first sight contradictory demand for a greater devolution of regional responsibilities within the British Commonwealth. Australia desired for the future an assurance not merely that her views would be heard in the making of Pacific and Far Eastern policies at the earliest possible moment, but, further, that in association with New Zealand she should take the initiative in their formulation and perhaps in their application, that the policies so decided upon should have the support of all the Commonwealth countries interested in that area, and that Australia should be the spokesman for them. It was a recurrent theme in the speeches of Australian leaders that after the war Australia would play a new role in the Pacific, but if that role were to be played effectively, Australia would need to be assured of the support of other members of the Commonwealth, and above all of the United Kingdom.

But how could this support be assured unless methods of co-operation were tightened? If, therefore, the search was not for common policies, at least it was for policies made in common, and the first step was to establish a means whereby that might be done. The principal aim was to compensate for lack of power by enlisting the support of the United Kingdom and other members of the British Commonwealth for Australia's Pacific policies. This larger purpose behind Australian proposals, frequently alluded to in Dr. Evatt's speeches, was little considered, at least in public, by comparison with the means intended to achieve it. Yet it invites the question whether Australia, even after her formal association with New Zealand in the Anzac Agreement of 1944,[1] was as yet of sufficient international stature to assume such responsibilities for the British Commonwealth as a whole in the Pacific area as her government apparently desired. There was little to be gained by Australia acting as the spokesman of British interests there if the great powers bordering on the Pacific were not prepared to pay heed to what she said. In terms of power the real question was whether any member of the Commonwealth, whatever the backing it received from its fellow members, would be in a

[1] See below, p. 181.

position to exercise a major influence in the determination of Pacific policies after the war, and the risk was lest over-ambitious notions of leadership there might be translated into policies insufficiently related to the realities of power.

General Smuts and the Commonwealth as a Third Force

Canada and South Africa had themselves no wartime experiences of the kind that had prompted Australia's continuing anxiety to secure for herself a share in the making of policy, for New Zealand alone was comparably endangered. Yet the distinction must not be pressed too far, for in some important respects their problems were not dissimilar. They, too, were middle powers, and in so far as the Australian initiative voiced the protest of 'middle nations' against exclusive great-power control of war strategy, it was something which they could understand and with which they could sympathize even if they decided that circumstances called for acquiescence in it. There were also general, if less tangible, sources of irritation with the great, the chief among them being their seeming indifference to the aspirations and exertions of those less powerful than themselves. 'The natural concentration of Americans upon their own war effort', noted two Canadian historians,[1] 'left them with little opportunity to notice the activities of their associates aside from criticizing their shortcomings.' This, among other things, made the probable decline in Britain's power after the war a matter for some anxious consideration by the dominions, for the special claims they had on Britain's attention could not be advanced with equal force elsewhere. It was not surprising, therefore, that Mr. Curtin's proposals opened a far-ranging discussion on the role the Commonwealth should play in a post-war world in which the one thing that seemed certain was that great powers would become still greater, and that Britain for the first time for centuries would not be numbered with the greatest.

Mr. Curtin was preoccupied with the problem of power and security in the Pacific. General Smuts, in a provocative address delivered to the Empire Parliamentary Association in London in November 1943,[2] was thinking of the same problem in a wider context. 'This war has taught us', he said, '. . . that we cannot get away from the problem of power.' All high aspirations for a better and more peaceful world stood 'no ghost of a chance' of realization unless governments resolved this fundamental question. 'Peace unbacked by power', he argued, 'remains a dream'. Freedom, like patriotism, was not enough. There must be leadership, and leadership in international society could come only from the powerful.

Such was General Smuts's premiss. In terms of practical politics it led inescapably to the conclusion that due place must be given to leadership and to power in the international organization to be created after the war. He did

[1] C. C. Lingard and R. G. Trotter in *Canada in World Affairs, 1941–4*, p. 149.
[2] *The Times*, 3 December 1943 (extracts in Mansergh, *Documents*, i. 568–75).

not shrink from that conclusion; he seemed even to welcome it. He was, but he did not speak as, the representative of a middle power and he had little sympathy with the resentments of such powers against the predominance of the great.[1] As Great Britain, the United States, and Russia formed the trinity at the head of the United Nations in war, so too in peace, he urged, 'we shall have to see to it that in the new international organization the leadership remains in the hands of this great trinity of Powers'. Mutual respect, mutual fear, not mutual affection—though General Smuts did not say so openly— would afford the one assurance of peace among the triumvirs themselves. But would not the whole edifice, resting upon an uneasy balance, collapse were one of the three to be outdistanced in the race for power and two left to face each other, after the imagery of Hobbes, in the state and posture of gladiators? That was the half-expressed anxiety that troubled General Smuts most profoundly, for he feared that it would be Britain that would be outdistanced.

General Smuts understood that in post-war Europe there would be a great vacuum in power to the west of Russia, where three of the traditional great powers had suffered defeat and two of them, France and Italy, might never regain their former stature. Germany, too, would be weakened for generations. Russia, therefore, would be left as a colossus bestriding the continent, and with the ultimate defeat of Japan there would also be no counterpoise to her power in Asia. On the other side of the ocean there would be the United States of America, with enormous assets, with wealth and resources and 'potentialities of power beyond measure'. Between them lay the British Commonwealth. Britain herself might emerge from the conflict 'with a glory and an honour and a prestige such as perhaps no nation has ever enjoyed in history', but from a material, an economic point of view she would be a poor country. The political consequences of impoverishment would be accentuated through the dispersal of her power by contrast with its concentration in the Soviet Union and in the United States. Britain, in short, would be vulnerable. Should her position, therefore, be strengthened by closer union with the United States? General Smuts thought not—as a political axis it would not do. 'If you were to pit the British Commonwealth plus the United States against the rest of the world, it would be a very lopsided world.' Opposition and enmity would follow. The course of wisdom would be rather for Britain to strengthen her position in Europe by working closely together with those smaller countries of Western Europe 'which are of our way of thinking, which are entirely with us in their outlook and their way of life, and in all their ideals'. In the Commonwealth there was a group of nations working together while retaining all the attributes of sovereignty, and neighbouring nations, living the same way of life and with the same outlook, could with perfect safety say 'That is our group; why are we not there?'

[1] See below, p. 319, on the drafting of the United Nations Charter.

General Smuts thought that any such association with Western European states was not in itself sufficient to ensure equality among the trinity of great powers. There must also be a strengthening of the Commonwealth system. There should be a reorganization of the Commonwealth and Empire as a whole. 'We must look to our own inner strength, our inner coherence, our system, our set-up and pattern, to see that it is on safe lines for the future.' As it was there was a dual system in Commonwealth and Empire. That dual system might prove a source of weakness, for in it two conflicting principles were to be found. 'In the Commonwealth we follow to the limit the principle of decentralization', and 'this group of ours had become wholly decentralized as sovereign States. The members of the group maintain the unbreakable spiritual bonds which are stronger than steel, but in all matters of government and their internal and external concerns they are sovereign states.' In the Colonial Empire, on the other hand, the opposite principle of centralization was followed. It was from London that colonial policy was controlled.

The question that arises in my own mind, looking at the situation objectively, is whether such a situation can endure. To have the Empire centralized and the Commonwealth decentralized, to have the two groups developed on two different lines, raises grave questions for the future.

General Smuts's analysis of the twofold character of the Commonwealth posed a question of profound importance. His own answer to it, however, carried little conviction. In colonial policy he advocated decentralization of power not to individual colonies but to regional colonial groupings, and the closer association of such groupings with neighbouring dominions. Since General Smuts was a South African, it was to Africa that his answers might first be thought to apply. But from the outset it was evident that devolution of power on the lines he suggested would elicit strong, probably violent, opposition in the African colonies. In the past even the white settlers north of the Limpopo had displayed little enthusiasm for South Africa in the role of an elder brother, and while an association with the Union might be imposed on non-Europeans, it would not be willingly accepted. Elsewhere, though less controversial, the idea of colonial development in close association with the self-governing dominions met with a tepid response. Canadians were more than ready to welcome Newfoundland, which was not a colony but a dominion in suspense, as the tenth province in the Canadian Confederation, but were reluctant to assume any formal share of responsibility for West Indian development. Only in the Pacific did General Smuts's words find a sympathetic echo, and some provisions of the Australia–New Zealand Agreement of 1944[1] and the later establishment of the South Pacific Commission[2] represented a partial realization of his line of thought.

[1] See below, p. 181.
[2] For the text of the agreement to set up such a Commission see Cmd. 7104 (Mansergh, *Documents*, ii. 1050–2).

General Smuts, like General Botha before him, never doubted that decentralization had been and must remain the guiding principle in Commonwealth development. In relations between its self-governing members that principle had been followed, and in his view rightly followed, to the limit. Yet to place in antithesis General Smuts's plea for the extension of this same principle of decentralization to the Colonial Empire and Mr. Curtin's plea for more centralized control of Commonwealth policies could be misleading. In fact they proceeded from much the same premisses to conclusions which were more sharply contrasted in form than implication. Fundamental to the thought of both was the conviction that new measures would be needed to sustain the Commonwealth in the post-war world, that regional groupings within the Commonwealth would increase its strength, and that the discharge of regional responsibilities by the dominions on a scale not contemplated before 1939 presupposed a more active and a more influential part in the making of policy and its execution. More generally both felt that that period of functional inequality, to which the Balfour Report alluded, was drawing to its close, but they differed on the question of where dominion influence in the shaping of Commonwealth policies might most usefully be exerted. Mr. Curtin believed it to be at the centre, General Smuts at the circumference.

Lord Halifax and a Common Policy

To predominant opinion in Canada, Mr. Curtin's proposals for a Commonwealth Council or Secretariat and the peacetime leadership of a triumvirate of great powers, which was the principal theme of General Smuts's address, were alike distasteful. Canadian opposition to any form of Commonwealth centralization was so firmly established as to have become part of the national tradition; while reliance upon the peacetime leadership of the great powers, and the preservation of peace through the creation of a balance between them, seemed to most Canadians a counsel of despair,[1] for would not the coming into existence of any such balance prove to be the precursor of a third world war?

In January 1944, while politically-conscious Canadian opinion was still analysing the explosive ideas of Mr. Curtin and General Smuts—and in the Canadian view the former were the more highly charged—Lord Halifax, the British Ambassador in Washington and a member of the War Cabinet, a statesman widely respected throughout Canada and especially in the Province of Quebec, took the opportunity of a visit to Toronto to discourse upon the place of the Commonwealth in the post-war world. The topic was important, the theme he developed austere, and the speech, which had not been approved

---

[1] Cf. the intemperate leading article in the *Winnipeg Free Press*, 6 December 1943, and its temperate but critical successor of 30 December 1943, quoted in Allen, *Editorial Opinion*, pp. 305–7 and 312–14.

by the War Cabinet, echoed with startling reverberations across the wide extent of the dominion. This was not altogether surprising. United Kingdom statesmen in office, with a possibly exaggerated notion of the sensitivity of dominion governments and peoples, were not at this period much given to speculation about the future development of the Commonwealth, while the choice of the imperialist city of Toronto for the enunciation of Lord Halifax's views was well calculated to heighten their impact upon Canadian opinion. So much, if theoretically understood, would yet seem to have been insufficiently appreciated by Lord Halifax's advisers, for it is hardly to be supposed that he deliberately intended to rekindle the dying embers of a debate charged with emotions that could prove disruptive of Commonwealth unity.[1] If, therefore, the British Ambassador's excursion into the field of Commonwealth politics can scarcely be regarded as an object lesson in the art of diplomacy, assuredly it contributed to the crystallization of Commonwealth opinion on some of the more important questions that Commonwealth statesmen had to resolve as the war moved towards its victorious close.

Lord Halifax[2] was as much concerned with the problem of policy-making which had prompted Mr. Curtin's proposals as with the problems of power which had inspired General Smuts's address. As a former Foreign Secretary he recalled understandingly the circumstances in which the dominions had gone to war. They had themselves been in no direct danger of attack. They had not been parties to the treaty of guarantee to Poland which was the immediate cause of Britain's ultimatum to Germany. They had influenced, but they had not been responsible for, Britain's foreign policy. They had, it is true, received regular information and been in constant consultation with the United Kingdom government, but the control of policy had been in the hands of a minister 'whom they had not appointed, and who was responsible to a Parliament in which they were not represented'. In fact and in theory they were uncommitted, but because of the sense of community upon which the British Commonwealth rested, they recognized that Britain's danger and Britain's interests were their own. Yet was that position altogether satisfactory? Clearly equality of status had not by 1939 been matched by equality of function. The dominions had not had an adequate, still less an equal, voice in the making of policies in the consequences of which they were involved. Their response in 1939 was not too late to save the cause of freedom but there was, in Lord Halifax's telling but misleading phrase, already quoted, which epitomizes his whole argument, a real sense in which it was too late to save the peace.[3] On 3 September 1939 the dominions were faced with this

[1] It is not without significance that Lord Halifax does not even refer to this speech in his autobiography, *Fulness of Days* (London, Collins, 1957). It was not a major pronouncement by intention but by reason of place and timing.
[2] His speech was published in British Information Services, New York, *British Speeches of the Day*, vol. 3, no. 6, pp. 12–17 (Mansergh, *Documents*, i. 575–9).
[3] See above p. 25. In so far as Lord Halifax implied that the dominions as distinct from

dilemma—either they must confirm the policy which they had had only a partial share in framing, or they must stand aside and see the unity of the Commonwealth broken perhaps for ever. Every time there was a crisis in international affairs, proceeded Lord Halifax in a generalization which a closer examination of the facts does not wholly sustain, the dominions were faced with the same inexorable dilemma. How could such a situation be avoided? Lord Halifax saw two possibilities. The dominions might relapse into isolation and so adopt the course they had rejected in 1939. The alternative was to bring the peoples of the Commonwealth into closer unity of thought and action in all fields of common interest, which Lord Halifax defined as embracing foreign policy, defence, economic affairs, colonial questions and communications.

The Statute of Westminster [he said] was in a sense a Declaration of Independence. But it was more than that. It was also a Declaration of Interdependence . . . it left the greatest latitude for development, in the conviction that, in working out our fate together, we should discover that independence and interdependence . . . were not only complementary but necessary to each other.

Thus far in his line of argument Lord Halifax followed closely in the footsteps of Mr. Curtin. Both were concerned with the interdependence of the members of the Commonwealth, both seemingly anxious that the dominions should effectively influence the making of policy. But in inspiration Lord Halifax was closer to General Smuts than to Mr. Curtin. In the conclusion to his speech he reverted to the theme of great-power predominance in the post-war world. In the company of the Titans Britain, apart from the rest of the Commonwealth and Empire, could hardly claim equal partnership with the United States and the Soviet Union. Not only was her population smaller but she would emerge from the war impoverished. If, therefore, in the future Britain was to play her part without assuming burdens greater than she could sustain, she must have the same support from the Commonwealth in peace that she had had in war. 'Not Great Britain only', concluded Lord Halifax, 'but the British Commonwealth and Empire must be the fourth power[1] in that group upon which, under Providence, the peace of the world will henceforth depend.'

In Canada majority opinion was highly critical of Lord Halifax's analysis and conclusions. Canadians of almost all shades of political opinion viewed with dismay the prospect of a post-war world in which power politics would prevail, and in which the British Commonwealth would need to measure its strength against that of the colossi of East and West. Running through the speeches both of Lord Halifax and of General Smuts the *Winnipeg Free*

the United Kingdom had it within their power to 'save the peace' he was almost certainly wrong. There is no evidence, least of all in the published German documents, that would lend countenance to any such suggestion (see Mansergh, *Survey, 1931–9*, pp. 444–7).

[1] Lord Halifax added China to General Smuts's list of post-war Great Powers.

Press[1] detected the 'clear note of fear'. These statesmen were obsessed by the thought of power; hence their fear lest the United Kingdom would not qualify as the fourth master nation without the assured support of the dominions. But that meant centralization, however disguised, and a return to a centralized Empire which would be 'a step along the road to yesterday'. The emergence of four colossal power blocs would 'doom the human family', to quote the words of Mr. Coldwell, the leader of the Commonwealth Co-operative Federation, 'to a third world war', while any serious attempt 'to rigidify and centralize the British Commonwealth of Nations would destroy it'.[2]

The Progressive Conservative party neither joined in this denunciation of Lord Halifax's ideas nor welcomed them. Their implications indeed were nicely calculated to sow division within a party whose frequent changes in leadership and in name alike[3] betokened desperate attempts to recapture electoral support after long, debilitating years in the political wilderness. Its leaders accordingly were restrained in comment, recommending that the whole question of intra-imperial relations should be examined without undue heat and without prejudice when the conference of Dominion Prime Ministers met in the spring of 1944 in London. But it was instructive that they, too, should place emphasis on the need to preserve intact full dominion autonomy. It never could be considered, said Mr. John Bracken, the leader of the Progressive Conservative party, in a statement[4] made some three months after Lord Halifax's speech, 'that there should be such rigidity to any plan as would subtract from our sovereign rights'. But Mr. Mackenzie King had no reason to favour such Fabian tactics. He knew his own mind, and the mind of the party he led. He took the exceptional course of defining his position in the House of Commons, where he strongly repudiated both the idea of a common foreign policy for the nations of the Commonwealth, and the concept of a post-war world controlled by the great-power blocs. It was a major pronouncement, not only on Canadian but also on Commonwealth affairs.

Mr. Mackenzie King[5] referred to the concrete issue of external policy that had been raised in the speeches of Lord Halifax and of General Smuts, in which both expressed the view that the future peace of the world depended on the attainment of an equal partnership in strength and influence between the great powers among the United Nations, and then went on to say:

Both took the position that the resources and manpower of the British isles were

[1] 26 January 1944, quoted in Allen, *Editorial Opinion*, p. 317.
[2] *Winnipeg Free Press*, 26 January 1944, quoted in ibid. p. 339.
[3] Between 1920 and 1955 the party had five different names and also five leaders. For an account of its depressing fortunes at this time see John R. Williams, *The Conservative Party of Canada* (North Carolina, Duke University Press, 1956).
[4] The enunciation of his view in a press statement rather than in the House of Commons was a matter not of tactics but of necessity. He had failed to secure election. The statement is summarized in *Canada in World Affairs, 1941–4*, p. 297.
[5] Canada, H. of C. Deb., 1944, vol. 1, p. 41 (Mansergh, *Documents*, i. 579–85).

too small to enable the United Kingdom to compete with the United States and the Soviet Union in power and authority after the war. Both, therefore, argued that it was necessary that the United Kingdom should have the constant support of other countries, in order to preserve a proper balance. Field Marshal Smuts thought that this might be achieved by a close association between the United Kingdom and 'the smaller democracies in western Europe'; he had little to say of the place of the British commonwealth as such. Lord Halifax on the other hand declared: 'Not Great Britain only, but the British commonwealth and empire, must be the fourth power in that group upon which, under Providence, the peace of the world will henceforth depend.'

Mr. Mackenzie King disagreed both with the diagnosis and with the proposed remedies. He allowed that the peace of the world would depend on preserving on the side of peace a large superiority of power, but he questioned whether the best way of attaining it was to seek to create a balance between three or four great powers. 'Should we not, indeed must we not, aim at attaining the necessary superiority of power by creating an effective international system inside which the cooperation of all peace-loving countries is freely sought and given?' And in the building up of such an international system co-operation, not rivalry, between the great powers was essential. A competition in strength would be disastrous. Therefore from this point of view alone the idea that the prime Canadian commitment should be to pursue, as Lord Halifax had suggested, in 'foreign policy, defence, economic affairs, colonial questions, and communications', a common policy to be framed and executed by all the governments of the Commonwealth, was ill conceived. Apart from practical questions about the working out of such a common policy, it was a conception that ran counter to the establishment of effective world security, and therefore was 'opposed to the true interests of the commonwealth itself'. Collaboration inside the British Commonwealth would rightly continue to have a special degree of intimacy but it should not, in aim or method, be exclusive. 'In meeting world issues of security, employment and social standards we must join not only with the commonwealth countries but with all likeminded states, if our purposes and ideals are to prevail.'

Mr. Mackenzie King's language suggests that he underestimated altogether the underlying tension between the Soviet Union and the Western powers at that time and did not make due allowance for the intolerable strain which it would place upon the working of any international organization. But in other respects he was supremely realistic. In Canada his pronouncement was welcomed, for it reflected faithfully the dominant trends in Canadian thinking, both in its psychological mistrust of centralized machinery within the Commonwealth and in its dislike of the broader concept of a Commonwealth organized to play a part in a world dominated by power. In other Commonwealth countries his speech served to harden opinion against any thought of a retracing of steps 'along the road to yesterday'.

The Anzac Agreement, 1944

On 21 January 1944 an agreement (known as the Anzac Agreement) was signed in Canberra between His Majesty's government in the Commonwealth of Australia and His Majesty's government in the dominion of New Zealand. 'The purpose of the Agreement was to provide on a more formal basis than hitherto for the fuller exchange of information regarding both the views of each Government and the facts in the possession of either bearing on matters of common interest'; to give mutual assurances 'that, on matters which appear to be of common concern, each Government will, so far as possible, be made acquainted with the mind of the other before views are expressed elsewhere by either', and to seek 'the maximum degree of unity in the presentation, elsewhere, of the views of the two countries'. More specifically there was agreement to act together in matters of common concern in the south-west and south Pacific areas. In order to achieve these common purposes the two governments agreed 'to adopt an expeditious and continuous means of consultation' and detailed provisions for the establishment of a 'Permanent Secretariat' to be known as the 'Australian–New Zealand Affairs Secretariat' were set out in the penultimate section of the agreement.[1]

The Anzac Agreement was concerned with future security, with the welfare of native peoples in the Pacific, with civil aviation and, on the shorter term, with the prosecution of the war. It was founded in the new sense of regional responsibility; it was thought of as bringing into existence a regional zone of defence based on Australia and New Zealand but forming part of a wider whole, for the agreement was in no way intended to be, in the words of Mr. Curtin, either 'exclusive' or 'monopolistic'.[2] On the contrary it was intended to be part of, and a contribution to, the general post-war system of world security.

Mr. Fraser claimed that the agreement marked a new and important step in the political development of the Pacific dominions.[3] In this he was justified not so much because of what the agreement contained but because of what it foreshadowed. 'What we have done', said Dr. Evatt, 'is to take the initiative.'[4] The fact that they had done so was of significance for the Commonwealth as a whole, and the way in which it was done made possible the realization within a limited Pacific context of many of the ideas which Mr. Curtin would like to have seen extended to the whole field of British Commonwealth relations.

The Prime Ministers' Meeting, 1–17 May 1944

It was evident some time before the Commonwealth Prime Ministers assembled in London in May 1944 that differences of opinion about the

[1] Cmd. 6513. The text of the agreement and of speeches on it by Mr. Peter Fraser and Dr. H. V. Evatt is reprinted in Mansergh, *Documents*, ii. 1157–68. See also below, p. 312.
[2] Quoted by Dr. Evatt, ibid. p. 1167.
[3] Ibid. p. 1164.
[4] Ibid. p. 1167.

future organization of the Commonwealth would not necessarily be the subject of formal debate. The Prime Ministers were indeed not committed in advance to any such discussion, and the lack of any formal agenda for their meetings left the way open for a more personal approach to the subject. More important, as the discussion on the ideas and the assumptions implicit in Mr. Curtin's, in Lord Halifax's, in General Smuts's, and in Mr. Mackenzie King's speeches proceeded, there emerged a remarkable consensus of view about the main lines of future Commonwealth development. In a debate on imperial affairs in the House of Commons in April 1944 Mr. Emmanuel Shinwell[1] supported Lord Halifax to give a strangely assorted sponsorship to 'centralist policies' which otherwise received no backing from party leaders. Mr. Churchill[2] took up a middle position, at one moment giving encouragement to those who would like to see new machinery for the closer co-ordination of Commonwealth policies and at another suggesting that any such machinery would be superfluous. It was, however, to the latter view that he himself somewhat cautiously inclined. 'We have not', he said, 'got to consider how to bind ourselves more closely. It would pass the wit of man to do so.' The question therefore that the Prime Ministers had to consider was for him narrowed to the point of deciding whether the Commonwealth could gain greater results from its already close ties, and in this context he alluded to the possibility of some continuing peacetime machinery undertaking responsibilities comparable to those discharged by the Committee of Imperial Defence in wartime. The second outstanding war leader in the Commonwealth, General Smuts, though in some respects even more reserved than Mr. Churchill about what he would like to see done in respect of relations between the self-governing members of the Commonwealth, was outspoken in his comments on what he did not want done. Thus on the one hand when he was asked about the proposals which Lord Halifax had made in Toronto for the strengthening of the British Commonwealth in order to enable it to play a part in maintaining a world balance after the war, he remarked that Lord Halifax had suggested something which he himself had not discussed, and again that the subsequent difference of opinion between Lord Halifax and the Canadian Prime Minister was something that 'is out of my sphere'.[3] But on the other hand he had no hesitation in saying that he was wholly opposed to any idea of a super state, or a federal state in the British Empire. To him the ideas of closer union and of 'union now' were mere illusions belonging to 'a past which is dead'. 'The road we have followed', he said, 'has been away from Federation and not in the direction of a closer bond inside the Empire.'[4] It was the better road to tread, for along it the dominions were able, while retaining their full sovereignty, to remain within that circle of friends, and by consultation and co-operation to make their way in the world and to safeguard themselves against

---

[1] H. of C. Deb., vol. 399, coll. 390–401. [2] Ibid. coll. 577–86.
[3] 17 March 1944, South Africa, H. of A. Deb., vol. 48, col. 3357. [4] Ibid. col. 3360.

danger from without. The General, it was clear, was to be numbered with those opposed to all thought of Secretariat or Council.

The weight of opinion in favour of the development of existing, rather than the creation of new, machinery for Commonwealth co-operation would seem to have discouraged Mr. Curtin in any notion he may have entertained about the desirability of submitting formal proposals for its reform or renovation to his Commonwealth colleagues. In the speeches he made after his arrival in London he struck a tentative and exploratory note, and it was evident once again that his principal anxiety was to ensure that Australia would have the backing of the British Commonwealth in its Pacific policies. Yet equally he was not prepared to see his ideas of new machinery for the closer co-ordination of Commonwealth policies rejected out of hand, and he remarked in evident allusion to Canadian opposition, that it was better to go forward with three brethren than with none.[1] It was an observation which made it only too apparent how greatly he had misjudged political realities and the minds of his Commonwealth partners.

The Prime Ministers' Meeting in London in May 1944 was an event of some importance in the history of the Commonwealth. That was partly because it assembled, in Mr. Churchill's words, at the 'most deadly climax' of the war and partly because of its character and composition. If the Prime Ministers met at a time of much stress, on the eve of the Allied invasion of Europe, they also met at a time of great encouragement. The victory of Allied arms was then assured, the reputation of the Commonwealth had not been higher in its history. One important task before the Meeting was to state and discuss the provisional views of Commonwealth governments on the proposed United Nations organization and to clarify opinions about the part which the Commonwealth itself might play within that wider whole.

Yet the Meeting is more likely to have a place in history not by reason of anything that was debated or decided in the course of its deliberations, but because it was the first of its kind to be held. In the past discussions at the highest level between Commonwealth leaders had taken place at Imperial Conferences which in the inter-war years had met in London in 1921, 1923, 1926, 1930, and 1937. The Meeting of 1944 was not an Imperial Conference. On that point General Smuts was categorical.[2] It was a Meeting of Commonwealth Prime Ministers, a smaller and altogether less formal gathering. The Prime Ministers met for an 'exchange of views'—a non-committal phrase which featured prominently in Mr. Mackenzie King's vocabulary of Commonwealth relations—and at the conclusion of their discussions no report of the proceedings such as had been usual in the case of Imperial Conferences was published. There were other differences. At Imperial Conferences Prime Ministers had customarily been accompanied by one or more Cabinet colleagues and by numerous official advisers. But an exchange of views among

[1] *The Times*, 5 May 1944.   [2] Ibid. 18 May 1944.

Prime Ministers demanded the attendance of neither and the visiting Prime Ministers were accompanied for the most part by the official heads of their own departments and of their respective Departments of External Affairs. The lack of a large-scale official entourage was partly to be explained by wartime conditions, but equally it gave to the Prime Ministers' Meeting an air of intimacy and informality which the Imperial Conferences had not possessed, and which Mr. Mackenzie King regarded as being in itself an asset. The Prime Ministers could speak more frankly when they were secluded in the Cabinet room at No. 10 Downing Street and without the constraint which the presence of senior civil servants imposes upon all but the most self-assured. Likewise the decision not to tie down Prime Ministerial deliberations by adherence to a fixed agenda broadened the scope of discussion.

The value of the 1944 Meeting is not to be judged by the generalities contained in its final communiqué. Its informal character in itself, quite apart from considerations of wartime security, precluded the publication of any detailed report of its proceedings. The Prime Ministers themselves deemed the Meeting an outstanding success. Most impressive was the verdict of General Smuts, who had unequalled knowledge of the Imperial Conferences of the past, and who remarked at the conclusion of this 'new model' gathering that in his experience it had achieved a success that under war conditions was 'amazing' and that there had been at it a spirit and atmosphere unlike any that he had known in the past.[1] This tribute was the more striking because General Smuts remarked at the same time that he could not recall discussion of such a range of far-reaching, fundamental problems at any Imperial Conference. By its very success the 1944 Meeting helped to dispel some at least of the doubts and misgivings of those who felt that the existing machinery of Commonwealth consultation was no longer altogether adequate. It was perhaps with this in mind that Mr. Churchill spoke of the 1944 Meeting as one of the 'important milestones in the history of our united association'.[2]

From evidence that later became available[3] it would seem that there was a general discussion among the Commonwealth Prime Ministers about the desirability of strengthening the machinery for consultation. It was initiated by Mr. Curtin, who argued that the aim of all machinery must be to provide for full and continuous consultation, but that such consultation had to be consistent with sovereign control of policy by each individual government. No machinery, he said, could be more satisfactory than periodical conferences of Prime Ministers provided they were held frequently, but they should in any case be supplemented or reinforced by meetings of other ministers. In the interval between them there should be, he urged, monthly

---

[1] *The Times*, 18 May 1944.   [2] Ibid. closing speech at the Meeting.
[3] One important source of information is Mr. Curtin's speech to the Australian House of Representatives, 17 July 1944 (Australia, H. of R. Deb., vol. 179, pp. 38–44; Mansergh, *Documents*, i. 589–93. See also ibid. pp. 585–6).

meetings of the United Kingdom Prime Minister with all the dominion High Commissioners, and in addition machinery should be created or procedures adopted appropriate to the very different needs and interests of each dominion to facilitate its co-operation with the United Kingdom in defence and foreign policy. More specifically he suggested that an examination should be made of the desirability of some centralization of Commonwealth effort in financial, economic, and social questions.

In the discussion that followed the United Kingdom ministers contented themselves with putting forward 'certain lines of thought' about imperial defence co-operation. General Smuts maintained his attitude of reserve, and at no time expressed an opinion on Mr. Curtin's proposals. The position of Canada had been unmistakably defined and in any event Mr. Curtin argued that Canada and South Africa were both so far removed from the main theatres of war and so comparatively free from any risk of direct aggression against their frontiers that they were psychologically precluded from understanding or entering fully into the anxieties which had prompted the Australian proposals. If, therefore, they did not share Australia's dissatisfaction with the working of the machinery of Commonwealth co-operation, that was not necessarily because the existing machinery was effective but rather because their fate had at no time depended upon its effectiveness. Such arguments, however cogent, did not apply to New Zealand. It is true that New Zealand did not lie in the immediate line of the Japanese advance in 1942, but on the other hand when Japan struck at Pearl Harbour New Zealand, like Australia, was denuded of ships and aircraft, her land forces were overseas, and she was exposed to possible invasion, since it was by no means essential for the Japanese to gain a foothold in Australia in order to launch an attack upon the sister dominion.[1] Traditionally, too, New Zealand, the most loyal of the dominions, was well disposed towards any suggestion for a tightening of the bonds of Empire. After the First World War indeed it had been New Zealand's constant complaint that those bonds were being unwisely loosened. Yet the New Zealand Prime Minister's response to Mr. Curtin's proposals, as we have seen, had been ambiguous from the outset. At the Prime Ministers' Meeting it would seem that, while sympathetic understanding was once more forthcoming, support was not; Mr. Fraser apparently contenting himself with the observation that there was little in the Australian proposals with which he disagreed. This was helpful so far as it went, but from Mr. Curtin's point of view it did not go very far. Only the strongest backing from New Zealand

[1] The Japanese would hardly have ventured upon a major assault, however, without first capturing Fiji and then lengthy preparation would have been required for a full-scale invasion though raids and bombing attacks by carrier planes could have done great damage. Moreover with the passage of time New Zealand's capacity to resist increased. Major-General Sir Howard Kippenberger (Editor in Chief, New Zealand War Histories) suggested to the author that raids on New Zealand by small land forces would have met strong resistance from mid-1941 and by mid-1942 serious invasion, by say two divisions, would have been no walkover.

could have influenced the course of the discussions in a way favourable to his ideas, and that was not to be had. It is apparent indeed that the New Zealand government was in no way convinced of the desirability of structural reform in the Commonwealth.[1] When Mr. Fraser visited Ottawa after the Meeting in London he went out of his way to express views that in essentials coincided not with those of Mr. Curtin but with those of Mr. Mackenzie King. He spoke of the United Kingdom and not of the British Commonwealth as the permanent member of the suggested Security Council, and observed that there was no question

about any of our prime ministers or countries delegating to the United Kingdom or any other dominion the right to speak for our respective countries. That is fundamental. . . . Cooperation, solidarity, help in peace and war, yes, but not subordinating any opinions that our respective governments arrive at.[2]

Mr. Mackenzie King, who was present, observed with understandable gratification 'that sounds all right to my ears'.[3] When he returned to his own country Mr. Fraser explained that his own attitude in respect of Mr. Curtin's or any other proposals was that if he could be shown any scheme that would be an improvement on what already existed he would be in favour of it. But the implication was unmistakable—he had not been shown any such scheme, and in the light of his own prudent and practical criterion no case for change had been established.

The United Kingdom government agreed to Mr. Curtin's suggestion that over and above the daily meetings with the Secretary of State for Dominion Affairs the High Commissioners should have a monthly meeting with the Prime Minister, and both Mr. Fraser and Mr. Curtin alluded with appreciation to its adoption on their return. In fact, however, its importance was transient. Some few such meetings were held but the great pressure of duties that lay upon a wartime Prime Minister who was also a Minister of Defence precluded their ever taking place as a matter of routine and soon they lapsed altogether. Yet if this positive proposal did not produce any lasting result it would be a mistake to measure the contribution of the 1944 Prime Ministers' Meeting to the strengthening of the unity of the Commonwealth by this alone. The communiqué[4] published at the conclusion of the Meeting made it clear, as much by what it omitted to say as by what it said, that this was to be done not by the creation of new but by the development of existing methods of co-operation. By its very occurrence, by the evidence it afforded that the chief aim of some and a dominant concern of all Commonwealth statesmen, however they might differ in their opinions about the best way of attaining it, was the unity and strength of the Commonwealth, the 1944 Prime

[1] See Wood, ch. 22.
[2] Text quoted by Mr. Mackenzie King in Canada, H. of C. Deb., 1944, vol. 6, p. 5910.
[3] *Canada in World Affairs, 1944–6*, p. 221.
[4] *The Times*, 18 May 1944 (Mansergh, *Documents*, i. 585–6).

Ministers' Meeting bore striking testimony to the vitality of this group of nations, all of whom for five years had manfully shouldered the burdens thrust upon them by the changes and chances of modern war and one of whom, the United Kingdom, had felt its full impact.

On 11 May the Canadian Prime Minister addressed both Houses of Parliament at Westminster.[1] The theme of his speech was the intimacy of the association between Commonwealth governments. It was true, said Mr. Mackenzie King, that there was not sitting in London a visible Imperial War Cabinet or Council. But there was something which was more important, though invisible—a 'continuing conference of the Cabinets of the Commonwealth'. It was a Conference of Cabinets which dealt from day to day, and not infrequently from hour to hour, with policies of common concern. The decisions taken were not the decisions of Prime Ministers, or other individual ministers; they were decisions reached after mature consideration and with a full consciousness of responsibility to the respective Parliaments. Let us, he said, by all means seek to improve where we can, but let us also beware lest in changing the form the substance be lost, and reality be sacrificed to appearance. The wartime co-operation of the Commonwealth was not the product of formal institutional unity; it was the result of agreement upon policies of benefit to all. After the war the strength and unity of the Commonwealth could be maintained not by exclusive policies but only by policies which could be shared with other nations. It was Mr. Mackenzie King's conviction that the future of all peace-loving nations would depend in large measure on the capacity of the Commonwealth to give leadership in the pursuit of policies which in character were not exclusive.

The arguments which Mr. Mackenzie King employed, the conclusions which he advanced were not seriously challenged in principle at the time or later. In a real sense his speech summed up and in so doing marked the end of a transitional phase in Commonwealth relations. Henceforward, even in Australia, interest shifted from how things should be done to what should be done. But if a consensus of views about the future of intra-Commonwealth relations had emerged, the deeper cause of the debate of 1943–4 remained. Behind the problem of organization, and giving to it its renewed importance, lay the problem of power. Dominion statesmen in their search for a pattern of post-war Commonwealth relations consistent with their varied needs and aspirations were moved above all by their awareness of the great changes in world power taking place before their eyes—changes which were, as will be seen later, the principal factor determining their attitudes towards the United Nations and problems of international security.

As many men are remembered not for what they did but for what they did not do, so, too, the study of certain political societies is usually approached by

[1] Mansergh, *Documents*, i. 587–9.

an account not of what they were but of what they were not. Such an approach has at times much to commend it. Foreigners seeking to understand the British Commonwealth find it enlightening to be told what it is not. It is not a federation, a confederation, or an alliance; nor is it an organic union. Having learned so much they will at the least be better prepared for the assertion that the Commonwealth comprises a community of peoples who mistrust overmuch definition of the nature of that community in constitutional terms, preferring to think that it falls within no known category of political society, and who have greater confidence in improvisation than in formal organization. It is largely because of the consequent lack of a constitution or of formalized machinery for the conduct of Commonwealth affairs that within the Commonwealth as well as outside it the Statute of Westminster on the one hand and proposals to formalize, to institutionalize the Commonwealth system on the other, customarily receive more attention than is their due. The notion of an Imperial Council or Secretariat suggests something concrete and comprehensible while a flexible, if working, system of co-operation is less easy to explain and for that reason may attract comparatively little notice. Yet the one hitherto has proved a transitory illusion, the other has shown a continuing capacity for development. If, negatively, there is a lesson to be learned from the protracted discussions of 1943–4 on the desirability of common policies and of central institutions to shape them, it is one about what the Commonwealth is not and about the things it cannot do. And if, positively, there is something always to be kept in mind, and especially in reading the record of wartime differences, it is that these differences found their expression within a context of agreement not only upon wartime co-operation but also upon the essential nature and purposes of the British Commonwealth. The settlement of major constitutional questions between 1926 and 1939 combined with force of circumstances to create a relationship in which dominion governments were less disposed to concern themselves with matters of status and commitments, partly because such matters were for the most part resolved to the satisfaction of dominion governments, and still more because they were also preoccupied with the practical problems of waging war together. Viewed in this light problems, especially perhaps of Anglo-Australian co-operation, may be regarded as posing some of the larger questions involved in wartime relations between great powers and small, and as having by no means exclusively Commonwealth implications. In its more general aspect the outcome of practical co-operation in wartime was to be seen in less inhibited and friendlier relations between Commonwealth governments and administrators than had hitherto been known. In this context the rejection of proposals for more formal machinery for the co-ordination of Commonwealth policies may reasonably be regarded as evidence of a degree of unity in aims and outlook which made additional machinery superfluous at that time.

The Impact of War upon Commonwealth and Empire

The war in Europe which began on 3 September 1939 ended on 8 May 1945, and the war in Asia which began on 7 December 1941 ended on 15 August 1945. At its outset the countries of the British Commonwealth were ill prepared for a 'war for survival'; at its close their resources were devoted to the waging of war on a scale which few had contemplated when Hitler's armies crossed the Polish frontiers. Statistics can tell but a part of the story of their achievement and of their losses, yet it is a part that should not go unrecorded here.[1]

Manpower of Commonwealth Forces in 1945

	Navy	Army	Air Force
United Kingdom	880,987	933,000	133,000
Canada	92,209	491,942	181,080
Australia	39,851	383,383	173,622
New Zealand	10,557	55,217	36,313
South Africa	9,455	132,194	44,569
India	37,863	2,049,000	207,632*

* The figures for the Indian Army and Air Force are not comparable in all respects with those of the United Kingdom and the dominions.

Casualties: Killed and Missing

United Kingdom	397,762
Canada	39,319
Australia	29,437
New Zealand	11,671
South Africa	8,681
India	36,092

(*Official sources*)

Mobilization on so great a scale over so long a period imposed strains not only on the manpower and resources of the sparsely populated oversea dominions but also, especially where there was cultural variety in the composition of their population, upon their unity as well. The continuing rancour of party politics in the Union of South Africa, the Canadian reinforcement crisis of the winter of 1944–5, resolved by adroit political manœuvre rather than by conscientious devotion to principle on the part of Mr. Mackenzie King,[2] were reminders that in these countries unity was something not to be lightly assumed but at all times to be carefully nurtured. Yet the waging of war on so grand a scale against so hateful a tyranny contributed perhaps even more to the forging of national unity. The breaking down of cultural and

---
[1] A much more detailed record is of course to be found in the official war history of each country.

[2] For a near contemporary account see *Canada in World Affairs, 1944–6*, pp. 31–39. Some details of the crisis and the means by which it was resolved remain matters of dispute on which the forthcoming official biography of Mr. Mackenzie King is expected to throw fresh light. For a detailed account of French-Canadian reactions to the crisis see Wade, *French Canadians*, pp. 994–1088.

provincial barriers, the widening of experience, participation in a sustained common effort, the sharing in common disasters, the rejoicing in final victory —all these are things that contributed to the making of nations. They fostered national sentiment and pride in membership of a Commonwealth, which had endured from first to last, and which, as Mr. St Laurent was later to observe, had proved itself 'stronger than any alliance in history'. Yet even if so much be allowed there were other and less reassuring entries to be made in the balance sheet.

At the outset of the war the dominions had conceived their military role as one of reinforcement of the Franco-British armies on the Continent. The collapse of France, brutally dispelling such preconceptions, seemed to them not only catastrophic but incredible.[1] That 'awful moment in history', that 'most deadly catastrophe of all',[2] as General Smuts described it, when France fell, left its mark upon Britain and upon the Commonwealth overseas, whose peoples had become accustomed to thinking, too complacently as events proved, of France as the great and friendly land power on the Continent. And while Britain's decision to fight on alone was grimly applauded and wholeheartedly supported by the Commonwealth overseas, the break-through of the panzer divisions in the Ardennes, their later triumphant sweep across northern France in those lovely summer days of 1940, destroyed many things which even victory could never restore. Foremost among them was the unquestioning confidence of the English-speaking world in the invincibility of the Western European Allies. Even where Britain's decision to fight alone was most admired, people asked with growing insistence as the tide of war turned what Britain's position would be when victory left her with resources attenuated by the very magnitude of her sacrifices in a common struggle. France had fought one war too many. Might not that be true of other Western powers as well? Nazi propagandists persistently proclaimed that whatever the outcome of the war, Britain and her Commonwealth would emerge as satellites of the United States. Extreme Nationalists in South Africa echoed that whatever might have been said for association with Britain in the days of her greatness—and they had not themselves found it particularly convincing —there was nothing whatever to be said for 'hitching our waggon to a waning star'. Hitler had described Britain's stake in a world war as 'unimaginably great'. In this it seemed he was not mistaken.

However much the wishful thinking of hostile or unfriendly countries might be discounted it was apparent by the close of 1942 that whatever the future might hold for Britain in Europe and for the dominions overseas, the decline of Western power and prestige in Asia was indisputable and perma-

[1] Even General Smuts, so his son records, found it difficult to believe in May 1940 that France was collapsing; and to reassure himself kept muttering 'Now France will throw in her reserves. The Frenchman was a wonderful fighter in the last war'. But there were no reserves. (J. C. Smuts, *Jan Christian Smuts* (London, Cassell, 1952), p. 412.)

[2] *The Times*, 22 October 1942.

nent, and Britain's position as a world power could not but be affected by it. In October 1942 General Smuts rightly emphasized that the almost total loss of the entire Allied possessions in the Far East and in South-East Asia was due to the fall of France. It was the Vichy government that in Indo-China had opened the door to Singapore, and it was through that unexpected opening that the flood had poured into Siam, Malaya, and Burma. No one could have conceived that that door would be opened 'by our ally against us', and Singapore was therefore attacked from a direction from which the planners had conceived no attack would ever come.[1] Yet though so much was true it was not the whole truth. It was also the fact that once possessions not merely of Britain but of the Western powers in Asia were exposed to direct assault, the superficial air of endurance which they had possessed vanished overnight. Even by the autumn of 1942 it was apparent that never again would Western colonialism re-establish itself in its traditional form in Asia. It had perished in Saigon, in Singapore, and in the running battle of the Java Sea in those dark months of early 1942. If Gandhi was wrong in that same year in dismissing the Cripps offer of dominion status for India as a post-dated cheque upon a bankrupt Empire, he was right in sensing that the day of European rule in Asia was drawing to its close. This was something, in itself momentous, which could not fail to have repercussions in Africa, in the Caribbean, in the Pacific, and in every part of the world where colonies continued to exist.

While it was the Japanese who with brutal violence overthrew the colonial governments and administrations of South-East Asia, they were anti-Western rather than anti-colonial in outlook and in principle. If in Asia at that time the two were virtually synonymous, the distinction between them on a wider view was by no means without importance. It was, in fact, not Britain's enemies but her two great allies in the war who were anti-colonial in principle, the one by reason of doctrine, the other by reason of history. To Stalin, as to Lenin, imperialism was the final manifestation of capitalist society engaged upon its own self-destroying struggle for markets and for power, while to President Roosevelt the rule of one people over another was incompatible with the dignity, the happiness, and above all the equality of man for, as he observed on 15 March 1941, 'There has never been, there isn't now, and there never will be, any race of people on earth fit to serve as masters over their fellow men'.[2] Each alike placed his own interpretation upon words susceptible of many variations in meaning and charged with emotional overtones.[3] Yet

[1] This was not, however, true of those serving in Singapore. See A. E. Percival, *The War in Malaya* (London, Eyre & Spottiswoode, 1949), for an account of his views from 1937 to 1941, chs. i–iii.
[2] Quoted in F. R. Dulles and G. E. Ridinger, 'The Anti-Colonial Policies of Franklin D. Roosevelt', *Political Science Quarterly*, March 1955. See also generally Coral Bell, 'The United Nations and the West', *International Affairs*, October 1953.
[3] See R. Koebner, 'The Emergence of the Concept of Imperialism', *Economic History Review*, 2nd series, no. 1, pp. 1–29, for an analysis of the meanings attached to the word 'imperialism' at different times by different peoples.

while Soviet criticism, deriving from an economic interpretation of history, was focused primarily on imperialist economic exploitation, and the American, stemming from eighteenth-century notions of the rights of man, directed chiefly against the element of political and social subordination implied in imperial rule, there was at the least a shared conviction that the ending of colonialism was something to be desired and to be hastened.

We had definite ideas with respect to the future of the British colonial empire [noted Mr. Cordell Hull] on which we differed with the British. It might be said that the future of that Empire was no business of ours; but we felt that unless dependent peoples were assisted toward ultimate self-government and were given it when, as we said, they were 'worthy of it and ready for it', they would provide kernels of conflict.[1]

Mr. Churchill was not slow in sensing the existence of such ideas or backward in the defence of the future integrity of the British Empire. It was not his Axis foes but his Russian and especially his American allies whom he had in mind when he uttered what Mr. Wendell Willkie[2] illuminatingly termed his 'world-disturbing remark': 'We mean to hold our own. I have not become the King's First Minister in order to preside over the liquidation of the British Empire.'[3] Indeed the future of colonialism in the traditional meaning of the term was a deep-seated, though at times almost wantonly exaggerated, difference in the approach of President and Prime Minister to the major problems of war and the post-war settlement. When Mr. Churchill was first confronted with United States trusteeship proposals at Yalta he 'exploded', and before the proposals were explained, warned his American allies that under no circumstances would he ever consent 'to the fumbling fingers of forty or fifty nations prying into the life and existence of the British Empire'. On this occasion, however, the proposals related to enemy territories and to Indo-China which, partly as a result of British protests, was restored to French sovereignty—with lamentable consequences. Yet if in this particular instance Mr. Churchill's indignation was misplaced, it was not ill founded. United States hostility to colonialism, as seen in the perspectives of American history, was no distinguisher of Empires.[4]

The 'war between continents' ushered in by the Japanese attack on Pearl Harbour had thus at one and the same time exposed the British Colonial Empire to direct assault by a major power which it was ill equipped to withstand, and associated Britain with the principal anti-colonial powers in a war with states who were certainly envious of the vast extent of the British Empire, but who, in so far as they wished to disrupt it, desired to replace it not by a multitude of independent national states or by international trustee-

[1] *Memoirs*, ii. 1477–8.
[2] Wendell Willkie, 'One World', in *Prefaces to Peace, a Symposium* (New York, Simon & Schuster, 1943), p. 127.
[3] *The Times*, 11 November 1942.
[4] Edward R. Stettinius, *Roosevelt and the Russians* (London, Jonathan Cape, 1950), pp. 207, 210–13, 218–19.

ship territories but by the imposition of their own imperial rule. Before the war Hitler had constantly complained that Germany, having won late a place in the sun, had been wrongfully deprived of it after the First World War, but what he meant then by a settlement of the colonial question was the restoration of Germany's colonies, not the ending of colonialism.[1] During the war he outlined in spacious terms, first, in November 1940, to an unappreciative Molotov[2] who, sheltering in the basement of the Reich Chancellery from British bombs, was not easily to be persuaded that the war was in fact already won, and later to a more receptive Matsuoka, his plans for the redistribution of the British Empire among the presumed victors in the war.[3] What was at issue between the Axis and Great Britain in this respect was, therefore, the possession of colonies—what was at issue between Britain and her greater allies was colonialism as a system of government.

In theoretical distinctions of this kind there is inevitably much oversimplification. The aim of Britain's colonial policy was, for example, self-government by a gradual process of evolution, and in practice, therefore, it was closer to the United States' democratic ideas than to the Nazi notion of domination by force. But the distinctions none the less were historically of importance, first, by their influence on Anglo-Russian and again more especially on Anglo-American relations, and secondly, by their focusing of world opinion on the future of colonies. Mr. Churchill was emphatic that the provisions of the Atlantic Charter in no way qualified 'the various statements of policy which have been made from time to time about the development of constitutional government in India, Burma, or other parts of the British Empire'. Such statements would be found, he said, 'to be entirely in harmony with the high conception of freedom and justice which inspired the Joint Declaration', but they were in origin and inspiration distinct from it.[4] The progressive evolution of self-governing institutions in territories owing allegiance to the Crown, he argued, was a problem quite separate from the restoration of the liberties of European nations under the Nazi yoke which 'we had in mind primarily' at the Atlantic meeting. But neither in Asia nor in the United States, nor indeed in many parts of the Commonwealth, was this restricted interpretation of the Atlantic Charter accepted or welcomed. In principle, it was difficult to insist on a geographical limitation for the application of principles enunciated as though they possessed a universal validity; in practice Mr. Churchill's assertions paid too little regard to the experience of the war and the climate of world opinion. 'The British', noted Mr. Wendell Willkie,[5] 'have no doubt—and, so far as I can see, little regret—that the old

[1] Cf. Mansergh, *Survey, 1931–9*, pp. 240–52.
[2] *Nazi-Soviet Relations*, pp. 234–47.
[3] For a more detailed examination of German economic needs and colonial demands related to them see *D. Ger. F.P.* ix. 476, 479, and 500.
[4] 9 September 1941, H. of C. Deb., vol. 374, coll. 68–69.
[5] Willkie, 'One World', p. 127.

imperialism must pass and that the principles of the British Free Commonwealth of Nations must be extended at a rapidly accelerating pace to all corners of the British Empire.' Mr. Churchill, it seemed, entertained both. Yet Mr. Willkie had seized upon one point of essential importance for the future. As the reputation of all colonial governments had been severely shaken, not by the inability of those in South-East Asia to withstand the onslaught of a great Asian power, but by their apparent acceptance of outdated notions of Western superiority, their seeming inefficiency, and by the evident indifference of the great body of their subjects to their sudden collapse, so the prestige of the self-governing dominions had been significantly enhanced by their capacity to stand as free and equal nations with Britain, for a year alone, and from first to last against the Axis powers. If the days of colonialism were seemingly numbered, the idea of Commonwealth had acquired new significance and renewed vitality. No one perceived this earlier or more clearly than General Smuts.

On his first wartime visit to London in the autumn of 1942 he sought to interpret the meaning of events in broad and balanced perspective in an address to members of the two Houses of Parliament[1] which, broadcast that evening, made a deep impression upon the British people. He took the occasion in a year of disappointments in North Africa and of humiliating surrender in Singapore to acknowledge in strangely moving terms the debt the free world owed to the people of Britain and to reaffirm his faith in the idea of Commonwealth. 'The people of this island', he said, 'are the real heroes of this epic drama, and I pay my small tribute to their unbending, unbreakable spirit.' And he spoke of the Commonwealth, holding out more successfully than ever under the most searching test as the 'greatest human experiment in political organization, this proudest political structure of time, this precedent and anticipation of what one hopes may be in store for human society in the years to come'. Yet the Commonwealth with its enhanced, and the Colonial Empire with its diminished, reputation were parts of a larger whole. One of the more important consequences of the war was to bring about a lessening of the division between them by encouraging a transformation of Empire into Commonwealth on a scale not hitherto contemplated.

[1] *The Times*, 22 October 1942.

PART II

PROBLEMS OF POST-WAR CHANGE

... and he that will not apply new remedies must expect new evils; for time is the greatest innovator: and if time, of course, alter things to the worse, and wisdom, and counsel shall not alter them to the better, what shall be the end?

FRANCIS BACON, *Of Innovations*

CHAPTER IV

INDIA: PARTITION AND INDEPENDENCE

I was quite determined that India should not be another Ireland.
STANLEY BALDWIN

I dream a dream, not of some far distant future . . . when you make bravely, spontaneously, that beau geste of abdication, for that is what lies at the root of our demand. When you have abdicated nobly your claim and title, when you have by your own abnegation of many imperialistic material interests risen to the height of your own spiritual greatness, stretch your hand in fellowship and we shall not be lacking in the response that bids you 'Hail but not farewell'.

MRS. SAROJINI NAIDU at the Indian Round Table Conference, 1931

'THE proudest day in English history.' So, in a famous speech, Thomas Babington Macaulay, Secretary of the Board of Control for India, foresaw the possibility that 'by good government we may educate our subjects into a capacity for better government' so that 'having become instructed in European knowledge, they may, in some future age, demand European institutions'. He thought of this, not as something to be averted or retarded but as something that would constitute a crowning tribute to the excellence of English laws and English institutions.[1] His thought—often indeed with but small variation the phrase 'the proudest', 'the finest', or 'the noblest' day in English history—was expressed by those well-nigh legendary figures, Malcolm, Munro, Mountstuart Elphinstone, the Lawrences, who laid or strengthened the foundations of British rule in India. But with the Mutiny and with the passing of the years this clarity of vision was dimmed, the present overshadowed the future, that strange phenomenon of history[2] in which a small European island people ruled over an Asian subcontinent of fabled wealth came to be thought of no longer as something either remarkable or transient, but as something that

---

[1] 10 July 1833, H. of C. Deb., 3rd ser., vol. 19, col. 536.

[2] Macaulay described it in measured periods in the speech from which a quotation has already been made. 'That a handful of adventurers from an island in the Atlantic should have subjugated a vast country divided from the place of their birth by half the globe—a country which at no very distant period was merely the subject of fable to the nations of Europe—a country never before violated by the most renowned of Western Conquerors—a country which Trajan never entered—a country lying beyond the point where the phalanx of Alexander refused to proceed;—that we should govern a territory 10,000 miles from us—a territory larger and more populous than France, Spain, Italy, and Germany put together—a territory the present clear revenue of which exceeds the present clear revenue of any state in the world, France excepted—a territory, inhabited by men, differing from us in race, colour, language, manners, morals, religion;—these are prodigies to which the world has seen nothing similar. Reason is confounded. We interrogate the past in vain. General rules are almost useless where the whole is one vast exception' (ibid. coll. 515–16).

would, and should, endure. Not all Englishmen, indeed, lost that earlier sense of wonder or even of misgiving as the anxious consideration given by the Regius Professor of History at Cambridge in 1882 to the possible consequence of England's association with the traditions of Oriental despotism in India[1] bears witness. But for the most part administrators in India and statesmen in London looked forward less and less to 'the proudest day' and concentrated more and more upon the indefinite extension of British rule in India. At the Grand Durbar in 1902, Lord Curzon, never relaxing in the pursuit of his high purposes, had the hymn 'Onward Christian Soldiers' removed from the Order of Service in Delhi's Red Fort because of its undesirable allusion[2] to the passing of earthly empires. New Delhi, with the Secretariat and Viceroy's Palace which crown its splendid vista, was designed and built after the First World War, when the clamant demand of Indian political leaders for British political institutions might have suggested that the day of abdication—Macaulay's 'proudest day', though the words have now an ironic flavour—was fast approaching, and their building at this time elicited from an old and embittered French traveller,[3] as he looked down from the hills upon a city which boasted the memorials of so many empires, the savage comment—'They will make the finest ruins of them all'.

It was not only time and a hardening of the arteries,[4] though both indeed played an important part, that made so many Englishmen in the twentieth century so unwilling to contemplate the act of renunciation so hopefully foreseen by their early Victorian forebears. There was also a change of circumstances. Where formerly England had held the balance of European, and therefore of world, power, now she was insecurely poised between powers greater than herself. India, which to Napoleon and Lenin alike seemed to be the gateway to world domination, she retained; and so long as she did so, she commanded, if not as in Curzon's day the greatest, still a formidable and perhaps the most efficient land force in Asia. Renunciation of political control, therefore, meant renunciation of military power at a time when new forces and new weapons exposed Britain herself and the traditional life-line of her Empire to dangers greater than any experienced since the heyday of Napoleon's power. It was not merely instinct and dislike of change, therefore, that made the Conservative party in England reluctant to contemplate an early transfer of power to Indian hands; it was also their concern with the strength and safety of Britain

---

[1] J. A. R. Seeley, *The Expansion of England* (London, 1883).
[2] 'Crowns and thrones may perish
Kingdoms rise and wane'
The troops deprived of their favourite hymn, were thought to sing less lustily than was their wont. For an account of the incident see Philip Woodruff, *The Men Who Ruled India* (London, Cape, 1953–4), vol. 2: *The Guardians*, pp. 198–200.
[3] Georges Clemenceau.
[4] The phrase in this context is Philip Woodruff's. James Bryce noted the symptoms as early as 1888 on a visit to India (see H. A. L. Fisher, *James Bryce* (London, Macmillan 1933), i. 259–60).

and of the British Empire. It was no chance that the most relentless opponent, even of the partial transfer contemplated in the 1935 Government of India Act, should have been Mr. Winston Churchill, the man most preoccupied with imperial strategy and imperial defence against the ascendant power of new European dictatorships. Nor was it altogether chance that the Labour party —most of whose leaders at that time found problems of Empire, and more especially of imperial defence, irksome and uncongenial and preferred either to discount the risks of war or to repose their faith in the League of Nations— should have disregarded such unwelcome considerations in inscribing and retaining independence for India in their party programme. Yet if in so doing they may be charged on one count with lack of foresight, on another they rendered none the less signal service to their country. One of the great English parties was irrevocably committed to independence for India after 1919. That was something Indians never forgot.

In 1939 a Conservative government was in office which had made substantial concessions to its right-wing critics in the Government of India Act, 1935 but had not been deflected from its principal purpose, which was to reaffirm in statutory form its conviction that a federal India in due course should become a self-governing member of the Commonwealth. It was a conviction based on experience, not founded in hope. There was on the part of the Conservative government no haste to reach the goal. On the contrary there was the belief that the journey thither should and would be protracted. This was illustrated in some exchanges of view between the Secretary of State for India Lord Zetland, and the Viceroy, Lord Linlithgow, in 1939.

In January 1939 Lord Zetland—mindful, not of Macaulay's but of Munro's opinion expressed in December 1824 that India should be looked upon as a possession to be maintained until the natives in some future age should have become sufficiently enlightened 'to frame a regular Government for themselves and to conduct and to preserve it' and that then it would probably be best for both countries that British control over India should be gradually withdrawn—wondered whether such a time had perhaps already come.[1] He penned his thoughts to the Viceroy, restating the aim of British policy as set out in the Preamble to the Government of India Act of 1919, and reaffirmed by Lord Irwin in 1929, but noting the uncertainty about the means by which 'the gradual development of self-governing institutions with a view to the progressive realization of responsible self-government in British India as a part of the British Empire' was to be brought about. This had been made no clearer, he recalled, in the discussions on the Act of 1935 partly because of concentration on its highly complex detail and partly because 'the general feeling of most of us who were concerned with the fashioning of the Act of 1935 was—"Sufficient unto the day is the evil thereof".' They had indeed little expectation of rapid progress because of India's domestic divisions, her

[1] *Essayez*, pp. 265–8.

inability to defend herself effectively for a long time to come and, above all, because of the inertia of the East. 'With such comforting assurances in mind', continued Lord Zetland, 'the rate of advance seemed much more likely to be that of a stage-coach rather than an express train.' But, alas, the disturbing thought intruded that suppositions based on previous experience of 'the conservatism and inertia of the immemorial East' were 'being surprisingly falsified'. If in these circumstances the princes were to capitulate before the Congress, that 'might well result in the final stages of the journey to Dominion Status being made at even greater speed than is the present stage'. Defence and the cleavage between Hindu and Muslim remained, but the tentative conclusion of the Secretary of State was 'that the really effective drag on the wheels of the coach is the unreadiness of Congress, or of any other political party, to guarantee the country against either external aggression, or internal upheaval'.[1] The outbreak of war evidently increased the prospect of change. 'I do not believe', noted Lord Zetland to the Prime Minister on 1 December 1939, 'that the picture of India moving towards the goal which we have set before her, by smooth, measured and leisurely stages—which is what we have hitherto had in mind—is likely to be realized.'[2]

The Viceroy was seemingly not unduly moved by the Secretary of State's misgivings or his forebodings of change. While any comments which Lord Linlithgow may have made on Lord Zetland's letter of January 1939 have not been made public, rumours of impending change circulating in Bengal later in the year elicited a forceful expression of viceregal opinion.

No one [wrote Lord Linlithgow with reference to them] can, of course, say what, in some remote period of time, or in the event of international convulsions of a particular character, may be the ultimate relations of India and Great Britain... but, that there should be any general impression (if in fact it exists) that public opinion at home, or His Majesty's Government, seriously contemplate evacuation in any measurable period of time, seems to me astonishing.[3]

Yet if the Viceroy was destined to be astonished there were others who understood better the signs of the times. Among them was Sir Harry Haig, Governor of the United Provinces, who favoured Britain's 'going a very long way' to meeting the Congress partly on political calculation and still more because of the principles in defence of which Britain had taken up arms in the Second World War. He much impressed the Secretary of State with his unexpected views.[4]

The Wartime Growth of Hindu-Muslim Antagonism

If British rule foreclosed with a suddenness that surprised many of the rulers, the reasons for its extension until after the end of the Second World War are more likely to preoccupy historians. They are not, indeed,

[1] *Essayez*, pp. 266–8.   [2] Ibid. p. 263.   [3] Ibid. p. 265.   [4] Ibid. p. 280.

at first sight difficult to determine. The continuance of British rule in India beyond what might seem to have been its natural term was chiefly due to divisions within India. But for such divisions, Jinnah told the Constituent Assembly of Pakistan in August 1947,[1] 'we would have been free peoples long ago. No power can hold another nation, and specially a nation of 400 million souls, in subjection ... but for this.' Gandhi agreed with him. 'Let no one imagine', he said in 1940, 'that the Hindus constitute the majority community and that they can win swaraj for India or even for themselves ... without the backing or support of the other communities ... I must be impatient for Hindu-Muslim unity, because I am impatient for swaraj.'[2] Yet, while at one in their diagnosis of communal divisions as the reason for the prolonged deferment of India's hopes of independence, Jinnah and Gandhi were not at one in their interpretation of its cause. Where Gandhi believed it was the outcome of a deliberate British policy of divide and rule, Jinnah maintained that its principal manifestation derived from the existence within India of two nations, even two civilizations, members of which neither intermarried nor interdined.[3] In both instances their beliefs went far to determine the policies of their respective communities or parties, for while Gandhi, especially during the war years, with his belief in out-and-out non-violence, was often at variance with the Congress High Command on particular issues, no one had a surer instinct or a better judgement than he of what the Indian masses were thinking.[4] Jinnah, for his part, was more than the spokesman of the Muslim League; he was, despite his own denials, its leader, the maker of its policies, the decider of its tactics, with a voice in its councils as dominant as that of Parnell in the days when he commanded the votes of a solid, oath-bound phalanx of Irish members at Westminster. Traditionally parties, like snakes, are moved by the tail, but if this was questionably true of the Congress, it was manifestly untrue of the League.

The conflicting opinions of Jinnah and Gandhi, of the Muslim League and of the Indian National Congress, as to the root cause of those communal divisions which were deemed by both to have been chiefly responsible for the delay in *swaraj*, had at once an historical and a political importance. Congress critics maintained that the British rulers of India had deliberately fomented communal antagonisms, and more especially the antagonism between Hindu and Muslim, in order to extend the period of their rule in India, and the entrenchment of the principal minority communities by means of separate electorates and of weightage of seats in their favour is adduced as evidence of such intention. 'It has been the traditional policy of Britain to prevent

[1] *Address of Quaid-i-Azam to the Constituent Assembly of Pakistan* (Karachi, Pakistan Govt. Press, 1948). [2] Tendulkar, *Mahatma*, v. 184.
[3] Presidential Address to the All-India Muslim League at Lahore, March 1940 (Mansergh, *Documents*, ii. 609–12).
[4] The letters that came to the Mahatma's *Ashram* from simple people all over India provided him with a source of information denied to more conventional leaders.

parties from uniting', complained Gandhi with unusual bitterness in 1940 after the rejection of the 'August offer' of that year by the Congress. '"Divide and Rule" has been Britain's proud motto. It is the British statesmen who are responsible for the divisions in India's ranks and the divisions will continue so long as the British sword holds India under bondage.'[1] The existence of such a policy is as vigorously disputed by British writers,[2] who maintain that this is to confuse consequence with cause and that separate electorates were adopted because the Muslims, sensing themselves to be a separate community, demanded them. Until fuller documentary evidence is available, it would be prudent to suspend judgement, though it is indeed unlikely that conclusive support for either view will in fact be found in hitherto unpublished state papers. The pursuit of a settled imperial policy by successive British governments of differing political complexions is something inherently improbable, and while there is already evidence enough to show that Indian allegations of a policy of 'divide and rule' at particular times by particular persons are well founded,[3] evidence of a consistent official policy of this kind is wholly lacking. Moreover, evidence of intention such as documents might supply is by no means enough to determine the issue. For what has first to be determined is whether there were in India two nations or one. History records examples of a political nation supreme over the nationalities comprising it, but such states were formed in an age when the principle of national self-determination had not been formulated. Thereafter the task was rendered more difficult especially, as John Stuart Mill so clearly understood, when the system of government was to be democratic. 'Free institutions', he wrote,[4] 'are next to impossible in a country made up of different nationalities.' If, therefore, as Jinnah claimed, there were two nations in India, then its ultimate partition may be thought to derive from this, and the British responsibility for it on such reckoning to be secondary; if, however, there were in India different communities, essentially part of one nation, then the allegation that the British rulers of India provoked and fostered antagonism between them is far graver in its implications. Fundamental, therefore, to the dispute is the question 'what is a nation?' A great Asian, Sun Yat Sen, offered an answer appropriate to the circumstances of India. 'A nation', he said, 'is a community that feels itself to be a nation.' But this in turn poses the question why and at

[1] Tendulkar, *Mahatma*, vi. 11.
[2] Cf. Sir Ivor Jennings, *The Commonwealth in Asia* (Oxford, Clarendon Press, 1957), pp. 28–29.
[3] Mary, Countess of Minto, *India, Minto and Morley, 1905–10* (London, Macmillan, 1934), provides much quoted evidence to this effect, e.g. pp. 45–47, and see also the Marquess of Zetland's comment in a letter to the Viceroy in April 1940: 'The diehards over here are secretly delighted at the widening of the gulf between the Muslims and the Hindus; but, taking a long view, I should myself doubt very much if a cleavage . . . as fundamental as that contemplated by the present leaders of the All-India Muslim League would prove to be to our advantage' (*Essayez*, p. 292).
[4] *Considerations on Representative Government* (London, 1861), p. 289.

what times did the Muslims of India feel themselves to be a nation? And that can be answered only by a careful historical study of Muslim separatism analysing especially the reasons for the ebb and flow of separatist sentiment.

Whatever the verdicts of history—and it seems a matter on which historians are unlikely to agree—the Congress conviction that Britain had in fact pursued and was still pursuing a policy of 'divide and rule' in the last phase of British rule had its own historical importance, because the Congress interpreted almost every action of the British government in the light of this presupposition. Thus, at the very outset of the war in October 1939, Gandhi complained that the Viceroy's declaration of aims 'simply shows that the old policy of "divide and rule" is to continue'.[1] 'The Viceregal statement', echoed the Working Committee of the Congress, 'is unequivocal reiteration of the same old imperialistic policy', and it regarded 'the mention of the differences among several parties as a screen to hide the true intention of Britain'.[2] But neither the Congress, nor, still less, Gandhi, credited Britain with responsibility for the existence of the communal problem. It existed; it was of the heritage of earlier conquest, but in its view it was essentially a communal and domestic problem to be resolved by Indians when they were free. So long as the British regarded it as an imperial problem which the imperial power had a duty to resolve before withdrawing, then the British would 'continue to feel the necessity of holding India as a dependency'.[3] Gandhi, indeed, would seem to have doubted at times whether it was a problem that could ever be solved so long as 'the third party', the British, remained. If after 1940, and certainly after 1942, they stayed, pending a solution of the communal problem, then he feared they might find reason to stay for ever. In sum, therefore, while to the British a solution of the communal problem was a condition of their departure, to Gandhi their departure was a condition of its solution. For this reason expressions of profound concern for the depressed classes on the part of unrepentant imperialists, including Mr. Churchill, aroused only suspicion. If this concern was authentic, was it not somewhat belated? And was it not explicitly coupled with the assertion that Britain could not lay down her heavy burden or responsibility until assured of fair play for such minorities? 'We in this House', said Lord Birkenhead in the House of Lords in 1927, '... have the responsibility not for a loudly articulate India but for the real India as a whole—that India which consists ... of 300,000,000 people.'[4] The implication that Congress with its great and growing membership could speak only for an 'unreal' India was not one its leaders relished and if seriously intended was dangerous nonsense. Yet in one form or another it was frequently asserted in the House of Commons and the surprise[5] which Congress successes in the 1937 provincial elections occasioned is largely to be attributed to it.

[1] Tendulkar, *Mahatma*, v. 227. [2] Cmd. 6121. [3] Ibid. p. 249.
[4] H. of L. Deb., vol. 69, col. 239. [5] Zetland, *Essayez*, p. 267.

The Congress, or Gandhian, interpretation for its part carried implications unacceptable to the British and the Muslim League alike. It led, as has been noted, directly to the conclusion that the problem of the minorities was, in Gandhi's words, 'purely a domestic one', which Indians were bound to solve if they were to live at peace with one another, but which no one else could solve. So long as the imperial power remained, minorities would advance claims designed as much to strengthen their bargaining position when the imperial power was withdrawn as to ensure reasonable protection for themselves. Britain had hitherto held power by the playing of the minorities against the majority, not necessarily, Gandhi conceded, as a matter of deliberate policy, but because such was an inevitable consequence of imperial rule. This made agreement between the communities 'wellnigh impossible' by encouraging conflicting claims, by inflaming mutual antagonisms, and by seemingly providing cause for indefinite delay in the transfer of power at a time when, so Gandhi wrote, 'patriots impatient for deliverance will fight, non-violently if I can guide them, and violently if I fail and perish in the attempt'. Yet were power to be wholly transferred in one bold, generous gesture, then the solution to this formidable problem would be reached. 'Once', to quote Gandhi again, 'a declaration to free India from bondage, not in stages but at once, is made, an interim solution will be found to be easy'. Protection of the rights of minorities would become simple, for 'the game of seesaw' would cease.[1]

A story is told, the authenticity of which matters little, that in 1939 the Viceroy, Lord Linlithgow, inquired of Gandhi whether he had ever read the text of the Government of India Act, 1935. Gandhi replied that he had not so much as glanced at it, whereupon the Viceroy commented that this was the saddest thing he had ever heard in his life. It was no doubt very regrettable, but it was also understandable. Apart from the fact that the Mahatma was little interested in constitutions which he professed not to comprehend and the consideration of which he left to Pandit Nehru, there remained a wide gulf of principle. It had been the consistent demand of the Congress that a constitution for India should be devised in India, drafted by Indians, and implemented by an Indian government. This is what happened in Canada, in Australia, in South Africa, and in the Irish Free State. Why should India in this be an exception to conventional Commonwealth practice? Not only was it unjust, it was also unwise. For an Indian constituent assembly alone could work out by agreement the protection to which the minorities were entitled. Gandhi, morally as well as politically preoccupied by the question they presented, was 'compelled' by Pandit Nehru to study 'the implications of a constituent assembly' and became an enthusiastic convert to it.[2] Such an assembly, elected on an 'unadulterated adult franchise both for men and

---

[1] Tendulkar, *Mahatma*, v. 249.
[2] Ibid. p. 251.

women' would, so it seemed to him, provide the surest index to popular feeling. Its members would have the responsibility of drafting a constitution which would give protection to the rights of minorities 'to the fullest extent and in one single step', for in Gandhi's view 'no charter of freedom will be worth looking at, which does not ensure the same measure of freedom for the minorities as for the majority'.[1]

The essential demand of the Congress was embodied, therefore, in the demand for the creation of an all-Indian constituent assembly to draft a constitution for a United India wholly free to determine its own future, whether in respect of domestic or of external affairs. By implication it struck at the very root of the Muslim demand for Pakistan, as formulated at Lahore in March 1940, for it assumed that there were in India not two nations but one. It was not intended as a challenge, for the Congress insistence upon a constitution drafted in India had long preceded the Muslim demand for a separate state. But it was in effect a challenge, for obviously one constituent assembly would not be an appropriate body to draft constitutions for two separate states. It presumed indeed that the question of the minorities was, as Gandhi asserted, a domestic question and that the 80 million Muslims in India constituted admittedly a large minority, but still a minority. But this was precisely what the Muslim League denied. The Muslims, in its view, were not a minority; they were a separate people, and therefore proposals for the protection of minorities were irrelevant, whatever views might be entertained of their adequacy—and since the days of Sayyed Ahmed the majority of the Muslims had been convinced that under a democratic franchise ultimate power, however diluted on paper, would rest in practice with the majority community. For the Muslims, in the view of the Muslim League as enunciated at Lahore in 1940, did not constitute a minority but a nation. The complaint against the British was not that they had sown division, but rather that they had created an 'artificial' unity dating from their coming and maintained, in Jinnah's words 'by British bayonets'. It was only a dream of the British that 'Hindus and Muslims can ever evolve a common nationality' and that democracy, which presumed the existence of such a common nationality, could ever work in India. 'Muslims', he declared, 'are a nation, according to any definition of the term, and they must have their homelands, their territory and their state.'[2] As such their demand was no longer for special electorates, or for weightage, or for provincial power strongly entrenched against a weak federal centre, but for the equal treatment given to separate nations. Jinnah was logical therefore, if indeed there were two nations in India, in demanding of the Viceroy not specially favourable representation for Muslims, whether on the Viceroy's Executive Council or in determining the future government of India, but

[1] Ibid. p. 249.
[2] Presidential Address to the All-India Muslim League at Lahore, March 1940 (Mansergh, *Documents*, ii. 609–12).

equal representation with the Hindus. The Muslim League and the Congress alike, in this view, were representatives of separate peoples and separate nations, the Congress the recognized voice of Hindustan, the Muslim League of Pakistan. This claim involved repudiation of the Congress pretension to speak for the whole of India, relegated Muslim members of the Congress, including Maulana Azad, its sometime President, to the role of quislings, and implicitly asserted the authority of the Muslim League to speak for all the Indian Muslims. Even more important, it identified party with community and community with state. The demand for Pakistan was the demand of the Muslims for a separate state for the Muslim community, and the demand of the Congress, to be equated with it, was therefore a demand for a separate Hindu state. The first proposition might be true; the second, despite the great preponderance of Hindu membership in the Congress, was manifestly false.

The Congress did not, as it claimed, speak for all India, but equally it spoke for more than the Hindus, and even under pressure of Muslim League assertions and Muslim League demands, it refused to narrow its pretensions or to restrict its goal. The ideal of the Congress remained a secular state in which loyalty to the state transcended the separate loyalties of the many communities which comprised it, whereas the goal of the Muslim League was a Muslim state, communal both in its origin and so far as possible in its composition, and to be brought into existence, should need arise, by the waging of a *jehad*, a holy war, to safeguard the way of life of the faithful.

The Congress and the British alike were slow to credit the nature of the Muslim demands and to understand their full significance. The vivisection of India was something too painful for cool consideration by most of the Congress leaders,[1] while the British, believing that the unity of India was the chief monument of their rule, contemplated the possibility of India's ultimate partition with extreme reluctance. Yet each wartime attempt to resolve the constitutional deadlock served at once to drive deeper the barriers between the Congress and the League and to deprive the Viceroy of freedom of manœuvre. Thus, as has been noted,[2] the 'August offer' of 1940, contemplating a new constitution 'primarily the work of Indians themselves', subject to the fulfilment of Britain's obligations as to the safeguarding of minorities and to the general assertions that the British government would not contemplate the transfer of responsibility to any system of government 'whose authority is directly denied by large and powerful elements in India's national life', was

---

[1] Cf. Gandhi's observation on the Lahore resolutions (Tendulkar, *Mahatma*, v. 333-8) where he describes the 'two nations' theory as 'an untruth', with particular reference to the common racial origins of Hindus and Muslims in Bengal; and see also vi. 343-9, where in discussions with Jinnah he advanced similar arguments. They served to convince Jinnah that Gandhi was the spokesman only of the Hindus and that one of the chief difficulties of disoussion with him was that he did not recognize this.

[2] See above, pp. 83-84.

rejected outright on behalf of Congress by its President Maulana Azad, angered Nehru and Rajagopalachari, deeply distressed the Mahatma who organized the civil disobedience campaign that followed as a moral protest against it, but was interpreted by the Muslim League as an assurance that no new constitution would be enforced without the consent of the minorities, and seized upon by Jinnah as an opportunity to assert the Muslim League claim to parity of representation with the Congress as a condition of participation in an enlarged Executive Council and to repudiate all suggestion that any solution of the Indian problem was practicable other than partition. As a result of statement and restatement, it was not the British Government or the Congress, but the League which had perceptibly moved nearer to its goal. The outcome of the Cripps Mission[1] at the least confirmed this advance. The Congress Working Committee regarded 'the novel principle of non-accession' as a severe blow to 'the conception of Indian unity', but conceded that it could not think in terms of compelling people of any territorial unit 'to remain in an Indian Union against their declared and established will'. The Muslim League, gratified that the principle of non-accession had been accepted, none the less rejected the Cripps proposals, chiefly on the ground that the creation of more than one Union was 'relegated only to the realm of remote possibility'. Yet Gandhi, who considered that the British government had advanced proposals for resolving the deadlock 'too ridiculous to find acceptance anywhere', now concluded that attainment of independence was impossible until 'we have solved the communal tangle', and 'we may not blind ourselves to the naked fact.... If the vast majority of Muslims regard themselves as a separate nation having nothing in common with the Hindus and others, no power on earth can compel them to think otherwise.' He believed that there were only two ways of solving 'what has almost become insoluble', one by violence, the other by 'the royal way of non-violence'.[2] But deep as his faith continued in the second way, he allowed that it was by no means universally shared by his Hindu and Sikh compatriots.

The Muslim League took no part in the 'Quit India' campaign which followed the rejection of the Cripps proposals and once again the sequence of events favoured it rather than the Congress, for while the principal Congress leaders were imprisoned for their participation in it, the Muslim League leaders, without in any way compromising their demand for independence, strengthened their organization in order to bring into being that separate state without which independence in their view could prove a snare and a delusion. The talks between Jinnah and Gandhi in September 1944, intended to open the way to compromise and reconciliation between the Congress and the League, served chiefly to underline the points in dispute between them.[3] The result

---

[1] See above, pp. 143–53.   [2] Tendulkar, *Mahatma*, vi. 89–92.
[3] All-India Muslim League, Central Office, *Jinnah-Gandhi Talks* (1944); see also Bolitho, *Jinnah, Creator of Pakistan* (London, Murray, 1954), pp. 148 ff. For an account of Gandhi's

was that, as the war in Europe drew to its close, the British government was confronted by the older demand of the Congress that it should 'quit' and the newer demand of the League that it should 'divide and quit'.

In June 1945 the Governor-General, Lord Wavell, following the release of the Congress leaders, summoned a conference[1] to meet at the summer capital at Simla, whence an Anglo-Irish Viceroy looking across the mountains towards China some eighty years before had thought of the Manchu Emperor as the only other man on earth bearing responsibility for the welfare of so many people. The responsibility remained, but the power to exercise it was fast draining away. The Simla Conference failed in its major purposes, but it was by no means without importance. It made plain that the British raj was resolved on the final abdication of its awful responsibility; it brought the imprisoned Congress leaders at once into personal relations with their British rulers and their League opponents; it opened the way for elections to ascertain not so much any modifications in the attitudes of the principal political parties, since they were already too firmly fixed for change, but their relative strength, and in particular the extent to which the League was, or was not, entitled to speak for the Muslims of India.

Before the Conference at Simla was convened, the Congress had agreed, as a gesture of conciliation, that there should be parity of Congress and League representation at it. But it remained altogether unyielding to the further suggestion that the League alone had a right to nominate Muslims as representatives, for to do so would have been to abandon its pretensions to be a national party. Dr. Azad's presence at Simla, as a Congress representative, was in itself an assertion of its claim and duly regarded by the principal League newspaper, *Dawn*, as a more than 'symbolic affront'.[2] At the Conference itself bitter dissensions arose about representation in the more influential and all-Indian Executive Council contemplated by the British government, the League maintaining that in it there should be not only parity as between Muslims and Caste Hindus but, further, that all Muslim members of any such Council should be chosen from the League, the Congress challenging and the Viceroy disputing this second claim.[3] Jinnah was unyielding. Parity of representation was in itself a considerable concession for the Hindus, for it meant, as the Hindu Mahasabha underlined, that they would have minority representation in an Executive Council selected on this principle, despite their overwhelming majority in the country. Yet it must also be allowed that in essentials the position of the Hindus was secure, for they could reasonably count on the support of the Sikhs, the scheduled castes, and the Christians, and so secure a majority.

position see Tendulkar, *Mahatma*, vi. 332–56; for Jinnah's see *Times of India*, 7 September 1944 and *Speeches and Writings*. See also Menon, *Transfer of Power*, pp. 163–6.

[1] Cmd. 6652.
[2] Quoted in E. W. R. Lumby, *The Transfer of Power in India, 1945–7* (London, Allen & Unwin, 1954), pp. 49–50.
[3] For a detailed account see Menon, *Transfer of Power*, pp. 200–2.

The Muslims, by contrast, could not, and accordingly the League feared lest any concession in respect of their demands for parity of representation and exclusive nomination of Muslim representatives should prejudice the attainment of their goal.

Behind the disputes about representation lay the bigger question of 'whether we are to have a constitution or constitutions', and that, said Jinnah on 30 June, must 'be settled first'.[1] His insistence on this being done, if anything had become sharper, for, in his own words, 'the combination consisting of Gandhi and Hindu Congress, who stand for India's Hindu national independence as one India' had been reinforced at Simla by 'the latest exponent of geographical unity, Lord Wavell'.[2] If Congress designs thus ominously backed by the imperial power were to be frustrated there could be no question, in Jinnah's view, of the secession of a Muslim state from an independent India; from the outset there must be two independent states. 'Pakistan', Gandhi had written as long ago as 1940,[3] 'cannot be worse than the foreign domination.' But Hindustan, in Jinnah's eyes, could and would be worse. He was, therefore, prepared to let independence wait upon division, while the Congress was not prepared to let independence wait upon unity.

The Elections of 1945 and 1946

There was one point on which the Congress and the League were agreed at the Simla Conference. It was that there should be new elections for the Central and the Provincial Legislatures, the last election to the former having taken place in 1934 and to the latter in 1937. But their reasons were not the same. The Congress desired elections in order to rally the many disparate elements within the Congress fold behind a renewed demand for immediate independence, the League chiefly in order to substantiate Jinnah's claim that it could speak for 90 per cent. of India's Muslims. So it was that while the Congress looked to the elections to unite the Indian people in support of a single demand, the League looked to them as an opportunity for the elimination of Muslim parties, notably the Punjab Unionist party, independent of the League, which might, and hitherto had, sensibly impaired its claim to speak for Muslim India.

The elections planned to take place in India in 1946 were, however, less important for the future of the subcontinent than the British general election already held in the summer of 1945. It was perhaps significant that twice as many Labour as Conservative candidates alluded to India in their election addresses though, in each instance, the proportion of the total was small.[4] Among those who made such particular allusion on the Labour side were

---

[1] Lumby, *Transfer of Power*, pp. 54 ff. and see also for the background to this, Bolitho, *Jinnah*, pp. 150–1.   [2] Quoted in Tendulkar, *Mahatma*, vii. 13.   [3] Ibid. v. 338.
[4] R. B. McCallum and Alison Readman, *The British General Election of 1945* (London, Oxford University Press, 1947), pp. 98–99.

Mr. Pethick-Lawrence, who was to serve as Secretary of State in Mr. Attlee's administration and who declared that India must attain full self-government in friendly association with Britain and the dominions at the earliest possible date, and Sir Stafford Cripps, who informed the electors of Bristol East that in 1942 he had gone to India with their good wishes as the representative of the British people.[1] The Labour party's landslide victory meant for India very much what the Liberal victory forty years earlier had meant for the Boer republics. Henceforward India's leaders could rely not only on an assurance that self-government was the goal of British rule, but also upon sympathetic understanding of their desire for its early attainment. The Labour party, long since pledged to India's independence, was now triumphantly returned to office for the first time with a clear majority over all other parties, and its resolve to give effect to this point in its programme was beyond question. Where the predominant Conservative approach to Indian self-government in the last phase of British rule was one of reluctant acquiescence, the predominant Labour attitude was one of tempered optimism.

In India, however, the pall of suspicion that surrounded British intentions was not wholly dispelled by Labour's victory. Maulana Azad, the Congress President, it is true, conveyed through Mr. Attlee warmest congratulations to the people of Great Britain on behalf of the people of India on election results which demonstrated 'their abandonment of the old ideas and acceptance of a new world'.[2] But there was an expectation of dramatic and revolutionary change, in part deriving from a failure to understand the influence exerted by Labour ministers upon the policy of Mr. Churchill's wartime coalition, which was not, and, perhaps, could not be fulfilled. Disappointment led early to disillusion. Imperialist designs, it seemed, remained in essence unchanged. Sir Stafford Cripps, in retrospect, might cherish the notion that he had gone to India as the representative of the British people, and the electors of Bristol might welcome the thought, for there was much goodwill in Britain toward India. But in India Sir Stafford had not been so regarded, even by those most sympathetic to him and to his party. Sir Stafford, in their view, and constitutionally it was the correct view, had come to India not as the representative of the British people but of the British government. 'I have no doubt about his goodwill', Gandhi had commented from Sevagram in April 1942, but he deemed it a misfortune that the bearer of a 'ridiculous' proposal should have been one who was 'acclaimed as a radical among the radicals and a friend of India', for 'the fact is that Sir Stafford Cripps, having become part of the imperial machinery, unconsciously partook of its quality'.[3] Indian leaders were not altogether unwise in thus emphasizing the continuing element in imperial government, since at the least it should have precluded impossible hopes of a spectacular transformation in policy. Yet at the last

---

[1] McCallum and Readman, *British General Election*, pp. 112-13.
[2] Tendulkar, *Mahatma*, vii. 13-14.
[3] Ibid. vi. 90-91.

their suspicions clouded their judgement. The advent of Labour to office in Britain in fact portended change in the temper of imperial policy none the less real because often embalmed in understatements which were the especial gift of the principal artificer of Labour's Indian policy, Mr. Attlee.[1]

The accession of the Labour party to office in Britain had another consequence. Its political bias, its belief in centralization and planning, its concept of a socialist state, all predisposed its leaders in favour of the aspirations of the left wing of the Congress, and made them if not antipathetic, at least allergic to Muslim League demands for partition and a separate Muslim state. The traditionalist outlook of so many members of the Muslim League High Command did nothing to qualify a reaction founded in instinct and reinforced in many instances by personal friendships between British Labour and Indian Congress leaders. Where Conservative governments and the English ruling classes, distrusting the more volatile intellectual Hindu, understood better the outlook and way of life of the Muslims, and thought of them as the principal of India's martial races and, in Lord Cranborne's words, as 'our best friends in that country',[2] the Labour party leadership at the least felt a closer affinity to the more intellectual and more progressive elements in the Congress. The importance of this, subsequently much exaggerated in Pakistan, was none the less real. In the last phase of British rule the concern of the rulers was to hand over responsibility for a united India to an Indian government. The whole bias of their minds was against partition on economic and social as much as on political grounds; they were notably less sympathetic to princely pretensions than their Conservative opponents; and, far from wishing to 'divide and rule', they wished to unite and abdicate. In turn this meant on the one hand that the Muslim League demand for Pakistan had to be impressed upon those unwilling to be convinced, and on the other that the cause of Indian unity at the least would not go by default. By 1947 some Congressmen had begun to think and to speak not of the British but of the Muslims as the 'third party' in India without whom settlement would be easy. A 'third party' numbering some 80 million souls was not, however, easily wished out of existence.

Labour's electoral triumph was followed in August by consultations between members of the new administration and the Viceroy, and in September by the announcement[3] that a constituent assembly would be summoned in India as soon as possible after the elections there. Despite the definite terms of the announcement on this all-important point and accompanying evidence that preparations were being made for an early transfer of power, it received no very cordial welcome in India. The All-India Congress Committee meeting in Bombay in September described Labour's programme as 'vague and

[1] Many delightful examples of it are to be found in Mr. Attlee's *As It Happened*.
[2] H. of L. Deb., vol. 145, col. 1051.
[3] *The Times*, 20 September 1946.

inadequate and unsatisfactory' and reaffirmed the quit-India resolution of August 1942.[1] Jinnah was little less critical. Both Congress and League indeed assumed that what was now important was not the first step but the second; not the summoning of a constituent assembly, but the decision to be taken when the principal parties in that assembly failed to agree. Yet the Labour government was not prepared to take the second without assaying the first. The Indians, like the Irish later, underestimated Mr. Attlee's composure and resolution in a tense and difficult situation.

In the autumn and winter of 1946 India moved a step nearer to civil war. For this all the principal parties shared some measure of responsibility. 'Swaraj seems to be near.' So Gandhi wrote[2] early in 1946, and the sense of its imminence was the root cause of mounting and dangerous passions. Britain was abdicating her position; there was a struggle among the principal claimants to the succession in the conference room, on the hustings, and in the streets. Jinnah was prepared to fight a holy war for Pakistan; many Hindus, disregarding the precepts of the Mahatma, were only too willing to take up the challenge rather than see India partitioned, while the Sikhs, their homeland in the Punjab threatened with possible partition and they themselves moved toward violence, were ready to cause or to take advantage of trouble. 'I believe in chaos', said Master Tara Singh some years later, and his bearded followers, wearing their long *kirpans*, moved round the cities of central India, angry portents of the chaos that was to come.

But if such were the general causes of mounting tension, there were also some that were more particular. The All-India Congress Committee in its resolution of September 1946 on 'the Struggle of 1942 and after' was understanding in its condemnation of those who had been 'goaded' by the 'provocative action of the government' into departing from the Congress method of peaceful and non-violent action, and in its resolution on the Indian National Army formed by Subhas Chandra Bose under Japanese auspices from among Indian prisoners of war in Malaya and Burma, pointed out that it would be a 'tragedy if these officers were punished for having laboured, however mistakenly, for the freedom of India'.[3] Both resolutions suggested a Laodicean faith in non-violence, and the latter association of the principal Congress leaders[4] with the defence of the Indian National Army prisoners when placed on trial in the Red Fort in Delhi heightened that impression among Muslim and British observers.[5] Yet the Congress leaders were seemingly moved less

---

[1] Tendulkar, *Mahatma*, vii. 16.   [2] Ibid. p. 59.

[3] Ibid. pp. 15–16. Subhas Chandra Bose enjoyed a great and lasting reputation, especially in Bengal, where many refused, even after a government inquiry, to believe that he had been killed in an air accident in 1945, and where twelve years later candidates of every party in the General Election of 1957 sought to establish connexion with him, and make use of his name. On the second point, see *New York Times*, 16 February 1957.

[4] Nehru was present in barrister's robes which he had not worn for thirty years (Tendulkar, *Mahatma*, vii. 17; see also Menon, *Transfer of Power*, pp. 222–4).

[5] Cf. Lumby, *Transfer of Power*, pp. 66–68.

by any change in their convictions—and far from all of them subscribed in their hearts at any time to Gandhian principles of 'out-and-out non-violence' —than by electoral considerations. Criticism of the British government on the one hand, even if it were a Labour government whose accession to office had so recently been hailed with such warming words, and understanding that verged on open approbation of the actions of all who had striven for liberation on the other, seemed best to serve the cause of unity, and to that all else was subordinated. The Congress election manifesto[1] issued in October proclaimed that the Congress stood for the unity of all communities and for a federal constitution allowing a large measure of autonomy to the constituent units. The majority of the Congress leaders, despite Jinnah's constant and vehement reiteration of the League's demand for the concession of the principle of Pakistan before the meeting of a constituent assembly, at this time hardly credited the reality of his aim. And in so far as they believed that the demand was indeed an end and not a means to an end, the majority were evidently not unprepared to contemplate violent resistance to a violent and unwelcome assertion.

The elections were a triumph for the Congress and the League at the centre and in the provinces alike. The Congress party won all the 'general' constituencies in the elections to the Central Assembly, thus eliminating the Mahasabha and the Nationalist party, while similarly the Muslim League won every reserved Muslim seat.[2] In the provincial assemblies, where the results were not known till the spring of 1946, the Congress increased its strength from 704 to 930 seats; it gained an absolute majority in 8 provinces and constituted the second largest party in the remaining 3. The advance of the Muslim League in the provinces was no less striking. It won 428 of the 492 Muslim seats, as compared with 109 in 1936, the Unionist party in the Punjab being a significant casualty. Where ten years earlier the Congress and the League had stood side by side, now they stood face to face in mounting anger and frustration.

The elections in simplifying the political scene made the more apparent the complexities inherent in the demand for Pakistan. Here was no claim for a unified state comprising the Muslims of India, but the demand for the creation of a state consisting of two component and widely separated parts, which ran counter to almost every consideration of economics or strategy, and comprising, of geographical necessity, only a substantial proportion of the widely-scattered Indian Muslim community. Jinnah claimed for Pakistan: Sind, Baluchistan, the North-West Frontier Province, and the Punjab in the west; Assam and Bengal in the east. Yet after the elections it was not the League but the Congress which was in a position to form a government in Assam and in the North-West Frontier Province, where Abdul Ghaffar

[1] *Indian Annual Register*, *1946*, i. 225–8.   [2] Ibid. p. 229.

Khan, 'the frontier Gandhi', maintained the Congress loyalty of an overwhelmingly Muslim population. In the Punjab a coalition government composed of the Congress, the remnant of the Unionist party, and the Akali Sikhs took office, with the Muslim League the largest individual party in opposition, while in Bengal and Sind the League took office without, however, enjoying an absolute majority over all other parties. So it was that apart from British Baluchistan, which was not a ministerial province, the League was able to form a government in only two of the five remaining provinces claimed for Pakistan, and in none of these did it in fact, despite its success at the polls, command an absolute majority. If, however, this was a fair indication of the complexities inherent in partition, it was not a fair representation of Muslim strength in the areas claimed for Pakistan. The Congress victory in the North-West Frontier was built up on the assurances of Ghaffar Khan that the province should be free to choose its own government and constitution, while in the Punjab and in Bengal the League suffered from the weightage given under the communal award to the smaller communities. The upshot was admittedly to reduce the strength of the Congress, but even more markedly in Bengal and the Punjab of the League, depriving them of the opportunity of securing the clear majority in both provinces which the Muslim majority might have yielded them.[1] After 1947 many Muslims felt that earlier acceptance of the idea of 'weightage', which told in their favour in the provinces in which they were a minority, proved at the last to be the fatal tactical error of their leaders.

The Cabinet Mission

On 25 January 1946 the Viceroy announced the determination of the British government to establish a new Executive Council composed of India's political leaders[2] and to bring into existence an Indian constituent assembly. On 19 February the Prime Minister told the House of Commons[3] that 'in view of the paramount importance not only to India and to the British Commonwealth but to the peace of the world of a successful outcome of the discussions with the leaders of Indian opinion' the government had decided to send out to India a special mission of Cabinet Ministers to seek an agreement on constitutional issues in association with the Viceroy and in agreement with India's leaders. The members of the Mission were to be Lord Pethick-Lawrence, Secretary of State for India, Sir Stafford Cripps, President of the Board of Trade, and Mr. A. V. Alexander, First Lord of the Admiralty. 'My colleagues are going to India', said Mr. Attlee, 'with the intention of using their utmost endeavours to help her to attain that freedom as speedily

---
[1] In Bengal Muslims comprised 55 per cent. of the population, but the seats reserved for them in the Bengal Legislative Assembly amounted only to 48 per cent. of the total. These figures are taken from the Cabinet Mission Report (Mansergh, *Documents*, ii. 545 ff.).
[2] *The Times*, 26 January 1946.
[3] H. of C. Deb., vol. 419, coll. 964–5.

and fully as possible.' India's future form of government was for her own people to decide and it was the purpose of the Cabinet Mission to help in setting up machinery to enable her to do so. It was no part of its task to keep India within the Commonwealth. The Prime Minister hoped that the Indian people might elect to remain within and believed that India would find great advantage in so doing, but 'if she does so elect, it must be of her own free will'. The British Commonwealth and Empire was not 'bound together by chains of external compulsion'; it was an association of free peoples, and if India elected for independence, 'in our view she has a right to do so' and 'it will be for us to help to make the transition as smooth and as easy as possible'.[1] The Cripps offer had contemplated the secession of an Indian dominion from the Commonwealth, but not Indian election for independence without a period as a dominion. The distinction was not without psychological importance. India's freedom of choice was now to be altogether unrestricted; what remained was for Indian leaders to agree on how it should be exercised.

The members of the Cabinet Mission and the Viceroy discussed India's future with the Provincial Governors and with leaders of political opinion throughout the country. They had private talks among others with Nehru, Jinnah, Rajagopalachari, and with Gandhi, Lord Pethick-Lawrence later recording that Gandhi was not an easy person with whom to conduct negotiations, principally because of 'the subtlety of his mind which made it impossible to assess at their true value the precise meaning of his words'.[2] They were confronted with familiar difficulties—the pressure of the Congress for an independent, united India with constitutional safeguards where necessary for minorities, but if possible a common franchise; the demand of the League for partition before a British abdication of authority; the growing anxiety of the Sikhs lest their homeland in the Punjab should be partitioned in the greater partition of a subcontinent; the desire of the scheduled castes for a separate electorate; and the concern of the princes to retain in a self-governing India their own personal rule in their own states.[3] Yet amid this conflict of interest and aspirations one thing was clear. The voluminous evidence submitted to the Mission showed, as stated in their report,[4] 'an almost universal desire, outside the supporters of the Muslim League, for the unity of India'. Because of it, and because of the difficulties inherent in partition, the Mission concluded in principle in favour of a Union of India. On that, the central issue, the Mission in essence endorsed the Congress view. It was not, however, the view that was destined to prevail.

The Cabinet Mission's negative conclusion did not deter them from examining the possibility of partition; indeed the conclusion was in part the result

[1] 15 March 1946, ibid. vol. 420, col. 1421.
[2] 'Indian Constitutional Government; the Last Stage Before Self-Government', *Asian Review*, 19 January 1954.
[3] Cf. ibid. See also and generally Menon, *Transfer of Power*, chs. x and xi.
[4] Cmd. 6821 (Mansergh, *Documents*, ii. 644–52).

of such examination. They were 'greatly impressed by the very genuine and acute anxiety of Muslims lest they find themselves subjected to a perpetual Hindu-majority rule' and they recognized that it had become so strong and widespread 'that it cannot be allayed by mere paper safeguards'. Yet they noted also that the concession of the full Muslim League demand for a fully independent state of Pakistan, comprising two areas, one in the north-west consisting of the Punjab, Sind, North-West Frontier, and British Baluchistan, the other in the north-east consisting of Bengal and Assam, would result in the inclusion of a large non-Muslim majority within its frontiers. The figures were as follows:

North-Western Area	*Muslim*	*Non-Muslim*
Punjab	16,217,242	12,201,577
North-West Frontier Province	2,788,797	249,270
Sind	3,208,325	1,326,683
British Baluchistan	438,930	62,701
	62·07 per cent.	37·93 per cent.
North-Eastern Area		
Bengal	33,005,434	27,310,091
Assam	3,442,479	6,762,254
	51·60 per cent.	48·31 per cent.

These figures showed that the creation of Pakistan, with the frontiers claimed by the Muslim League in order to make of it a viable state, would not solve the communal minority problem, while the Cabinet Mission for their part believed that there was no justification for including within a sovereign Pakistan those districts of the Punjab and of Bengal and Assam in which the population was predominantly non-Muslim. 'Every argument', they concluded, 'that can be used in favour of Pakistan can equally, in our view, be used in favour of the exclusion of the non-Muslim areas from Pakistan.' The Mission turned their attention, therefore, to the possibility of a smaller state of Pakistan, confined to Muslim majority areas alone. Jinnah was contemptuous of such 'a mutilated, a moth-eaten and truncated Pakistan', and at that time the possibility was not considered practicable by the Muslim League. The Cabinet Mission accepted its view, partly on that ground, but also because it would involve the partition of Bengal and the Punjab against the wishes of a very large proportion of their inhabitants and, furthermore, in the Punjab it would divide the Sikhs, leaving substantial bodies of them on either side of the frontier.

More general considerations reinforced the particular arguments against any partition of India. Administrative services, defence, and communications had been built up to serve India as a whole, and their disintegration, all the greater in its impact because of the separation of the two parts of Pakistan by some 700 miles of Indian territory, could not but injure and perhaps even endanger both parts of a divided India. Nor were the problems likely to arise in the association of the Indian states with a divided British India overlooked.

On all those counts, therefore, the Cabinet Mission felt unable to advise that 'the power which at present resides in British hands should be handed over to two entirely separate sovereign states'. Nor did they regard compromise Congress proposals, largely inspired by Maulana Azad, for a flexible, federal constitution adequate to the needs of the situation, or indeed wholly practicable on technical grounds. Accordingly the Cabinet Mission propounded recommendations of their own for consideration by the Indian parties and the princes.

The Cabinet Mission prior to the publication of their Report outlined their own recommendations in a letter from Lord Pethick-Lawrence to the party leaders suggesting one further attempt to reach agreement between them.[1] In this letter the Mission put forward a proposal for a three-tier constitutional structure for British India. At the apex there would be a Union government, dealing with foreign affairs, communications, and defence; then in an intermediate position three groups of provinces, the one comprised of predominantly Hindu, the remaining two of predominantly Muslim, provinces, dealing with all such subjects as the provinces comprising each group might desire to have dealt with in common; and at the base the provinces themselves dealing with all other subjects and possessing all the residuary sovereign rights.

The Indian leaders were invited to discuss these 'purposely vague'[2] recommendations at a further conference at Simla where the British believed, despite much past discouragement, that the cool air of the hills and remoteness from the fevered capital enhanced the prospects of agreement. But while there was consideration and discussion of the proposals, once again there was no agreement. Accordingly the Cabinet Mission decided to issue their Report and to make public their recommendations in detail on 16 May. The three-tier constitutional structure remained, and there were elaborated particular safeguards for Muslims, first in the form of a proviso stating that any question raising a major communal issue in the Union legislature should require for its decision a majority of the representatives present and voting of each of the two major communities, as well as a majority of all the members present and voting, and secondly in the further proviso that any province might by majority vote of its legislative assembly call for a reconsideration of the terms of the constitution at the end of each period of ten years.

The Mission's constitutional proposals were intended not to provide the draft of a constitution but to bring together the two communities so that they might themselves draft a constitution. The Mission's principal interest, therefore, was not in the form of a constitution but in setting up the machinery for drafting it. Here they suggested that the constitution-making body should

[1] Cmd. 6829. See also H. of C. Deb., vol. 425, coll. 1397–8 for Sir Stafford Cripps's explanation of them.
[2] The description is that of Sir Stafford Cripps, ibid. col. 1397.

be indirectly elected by the provincial legislative assemblies so that each member should represent 1 million of the population, that the seats so allocated to each province should be divided between three main communities— 'General', Muslim, and Sikh (the first including all who were neither Muslims nor Sikhs)—and that the representatives allocated to each community should be elected by members of that community in the legislative assembly. It was contemplated that the States should be represented on the same basis, i.e. in relation to population, but that the method of selection in their case should be determined later by consultation with their rulers. In due course this procedure was adopted, but the end in view was not attained, for while the members of the constituent assembly were duly chosen, they never met in a single body.

The election of a constituent assembly and the fulfilment of its allotted task on any reckoning were bound to take time. Meanwhile, the government of India had to be carried on, and the Cabinet Mission attached the 'greatest importance' to the immediate formation of an interim government with popular support to do so. Not only would such a government with full British backing best discharge the day-to-day responsibilities, but also it might reasonably be expected to bring about as rapid and as smooth a transition as possible. This, in essentials, was a task already attempted at Simla in 1945, and it was to prove no easier as the shadow of violence fell dark across the land some twelve months later. Violence, chaos, and civil war were the alternatives, as the Cabinet Mission saw them, to acceptance of a plan which, if not satisfying to all parties, none the less seemed to them to offer an opportunity of a peaceful settlement at a supreme moment in Indian history.

The Cabinet Mission's proposals have a threefold importance. They demonstrated once again the British conviction that continued unity alone was practicable, they offered a considered and in some respects ingenious attempt to reconcile that unity with the entrenchment of minority-community rights; and, finally, they afforded conclusive evidence of the British desire to withdraw from India at the earliest possible moment. The response of the Indian parties and leaders at the outset was not unfavourable. Gandhi, in his prayer discourse on 19 May, told his audience that the Mission had brought forth something of which they had every reason to be proud, which showed that the English were not incapable, as some maintained, of doing the right thing, and that the plan contained the seed to convert 'this land of sorrow into one without sorrow or suffering'.[1] On 20 May Gandhi wrote in *Harijan* that after four days of searching examination

my conviction abides that it is the best document the British Government could have produced in the circumstances. It reflects our weakness, if we would be good enough to see it. The Congress and the League did not, could not agree. We would grievously err, if, at this time, we foolishly satisfy ourselves that the differences are

[1] Tendulkar, *Mahatma*, vii. 142–3.

a British creation. The mission have not come all the way from England to exploit them. They have come to devise the easiest and the quickest method of ending British rule.[1]

But he appended an interpretation to this welcome which seemed to Lord Pethick-Lawrence later to illustrate the difficulties of negotiating with one whose language was so full of subtlety and refinement. 'My compliment', said Gandhi, 'however, does not mean that what is best from the British standpoint is also best, or is even good, from the Indian. Their best may possibly be harmful.'[2] There followed qualified Congress acceptance of the principle of grouping and searching Congress inquiries into the procedure to be adopted in the making of the constitution and in the formation of the interim government. A final Congress decision on the proposals as a whole was delayed. 'I know you think that we are difficult people to pin down to an answer', observed Pandit Nehru to Lord Pethick-Lawrence,[3] 'but you must realize that if you and we do come to an agreement, you are laying down a burden and we are picking it up.'

Protracted Congress consideration of the Cabinet Mission's proposals resulted in the League's view being first made known. On balance it was favourable, and in principle the League accepted the plan. One reason for this was the Viceroy's acceptance of the principle of parity.[4] Jinnah, who had personally criticized the Cabinet Mission's proposals in May on the ground that they rejected the demand for Pakistan even while acknowledging the strength of feeling behind it 'in order to appease and placate Congress', said on 6 June, at a meeting of the Muslim League Council—'the Parliament of the Muslim Nation', as he now described it—that the attainment of the goal of a 'full sovereign Pakistan' remained 'the unalterable objective of the Muslims in India, for the achievement of which they will . . . employ every means in their power, and consider no sacrifice or suffering too great'. But in so far as the League Council considered that 'the basis and the foundation of Pakistan' were inherent in the Mission's proposals and prompted by 'its earnest desire for a peaceful solution', it was prepared to co-operate in the constitution-making machinery 'in the hope that it would ultimately result in the establishment of a complete sovereign Pakistan, and in the consummation of the goal of independence for the major nations, Muslims and Hindus, and all the other people inhabiting the vast subcontinent'.[5]

On 26 June the Congress also announced its conditional acceptance of the plan, agreeing to participate in the work of the constituent assembly but declining to enter the interim government. Even this partial acceptance was qualified by insistence on its own interpretation of matters raised with the

---

[1] Quoted in ibid. p. 142.   [2] Ibid. p. 143.
[3] 'Indian Constitutional Government', *Asian Review*, 19 January 1954.
[4] Bolitho, *Jinnah*, p. 160.   [5] Cmd. 6861, p. 8.

Cabinet Mission inevitably in a sense contrary to that placed upon them by the League and in many instances contrary to that of the Cabinet Mission themselves.[1] The Viceroy, faced with League agreement and Congress refusal to enter an interim government, did not proceed, as Jinnah deduced from the text of the statement made on 16 June,[2] with the formation of an interim government from among those who had declared their willingness to enter it, and which would necessarily therefore have been a predominantly Muslim government, but to the appointment of a caretaker government of civil servants until the elections for the constituent assembly had taken place. In the opinion of the Viceroy and of the Cabinet Mission, the statement of 16 June made membership of the interim government conditional upon acceptance of the plan, and both the Congress and the League had done so. 'When Congress ultimately came to their final decision . . . to accept the statement of May 16, while unfortunately rejecting the Interim Government', said Lord Pethick-Lawrence, 'they quite clearly became equally eligible with the Moslem League for inclusion in the representative Government.'[3] The Viceroy's duty, therefore, was to work for a basis of agreement between them. Jinnah, however, wrote to the Viceroy, 'You have chosen to go back on your pledged word'.[4] Thereafter, the area of misunderstanding between the Viceroy and the British government on the one hand and the League on the other widened still farther. On 18 July Lord Pethick-Lawrence in the House of Lords[5] and Sir Stafford Cripps in the House of Commons,[6] while allowing that the Muslim League was to be regarded as the major representative of Muslim interests, stated that the British government could not accept Jinnah's claim that the League should have 'a monopoly of Muslim appointments'. On 22 July the Viceroy, seeking to bring both parties into the interim government, sought agreement on the vexed question of representation by offering 6 seats to the Congress, 5 to the League, and 3 for other minorities, as against an earlier 5 : 5 : 2 formula. Jinnah replied in bitter terms, concluding with the complaint, 'Your present proposal clearly destroys the principle of parity . . . and gives a clear majority to the Congress as against the League'. On 28 July Jinnah told the Council of the League in Bombay that he felt 'we have exhausted all reason', and since Muslims could look for help from no other source, the only tribunal to which they could go was 'the Muslim Nation'. On 29 July he alluded to the League's desire 'not to allow the situa-

---

[1] Cmd. 6861, pp. 7–8. For the exchange of correspondence see also Cmd. 6835.
[2] The relevant paragraph read: 'In the event of two major parties or either of them proving unwilling to join in the setting up of a Coalition Government . . . it is the intention of the Viceroy to proceed with the formation of an Interim Government which will be as representative as possible of those willing to accept it' (Statement of 16 June, Cmd. 6861, p. 16). See also the account in Menon, *Transfer of Power*, pp. 276–9.
[3] H. of L. Deb., vol. 142, col. 587.
[4] Cmd. 6861, p. 34.
[5] H. of L. Deb., vol. 142, col. 586. See generally coll. 579–91.
[6] H. of C. Deb., vol. 425, col. 1406. See generally coll. 1394–1418.

tion to develop into bloodshed and civil war'. But Muslim India had learnt its bitterest lesson and now there was 'no room left for compromise'.[1] Acceptance of the Cabinet Mission's plan was withdrawn, and 'direct action' to secure Pakistan approved,[2] 16 August being chosen as 'Direct Action Day' when the change in Muslim policy was to be explained to the Muslim people. On that day communal rioting on a terrible scale broke out in Calcutta and through the autumn months massacres in Bengal and Bihar wrote out in blood and suffering the tale of one more disputed succession to power.

Meanwhile, as distrust between the Viceroy and the League was intensified, co-operation between the Viceroy and the Congress increased. On 24 August, as a result of the discussions between the Viceroy and Pandit Nehru, the names of 12 of the 14 members of the interim government were announced. Pandit Nehru himself, Sardar Vallabhbhai Patel, and C. Rajagopalachari were among the 5 caste Hindus and there were in addition 1 Congress member of the scheduled castes, 1 Sikh, 1 Christian, 1 Parsee, and 3 non-League Muslims one of them a member of Congress, included in the government. Even though the announcement of their appointment was coupled with assurances that the way was open for the Muslim League to propose the names of five members and a consequent reconstruction of the government, the League leadership was outraged.[3] On 2 September when the interim government took office, Jinnah asked all members of the Muslim League to fly black flags from their housetops 'in silent contempt for the Hindu government'. Early in October, however, by which time the risks of continued abstention had become apparent, the League accepted the offer of five seats in the interim government, and, while Jinnah remained without, Liaqat Ali Khan, his principal lieutenant, entered the government as the principal League member, assuming the Finance Minister's portfolio. No government in British history, it may safely be assumed, held office with less sense of collective responsibility. It was the destiny of Lord Wavell, the least loquacious of soldiers, to preside over its deliberations. It was an assignment for which taciturnity was not the supreme attribute; in which silence was not golden.

The 'Beloved Pilgrim'

'If India is destined to go through a blood bath', said Gandhi in July 1946, 'it will do so.'[4] On 16 August 1946, the day named by the Muslim League as

[1] Bolitho, *Jinnah*, pp. 163, 165.
[2] The declaration read: 'The Council of the All-India Muslim League is convinced that now the time has come for the Muslim nation to resort to direct action to achieve Pakistan, and get rid of the present slavery under the British, and contemplated future caste Hindu domination' (quoted by Sir Stafford Cripps, H. of C. Deb., vol. 431, col. 1348). See also Menon, *Transfer of Power*, ch. xii.
[3] For an account of the formation of the government and further negotiations between the Viceroy and Jinnah see Sir Stafford Cripps's speech, ibid. coll. 1348–50.
[4] Tendulkar, *Mahatma*, vii. 195.

'Direct Action Day', there began the 'Great Calcutta Killing'.[1] Four thousand people were killed, 10,000 injured, a tale of casualties in communal rioting greater than in any year since British rule began. In early September rioting broke out in Bombay; in October destruction and disorders in East Bengal led to panic-stricken Hindu evacuations; in October and November there followed a holocaust of Muslims in Bihar.[2] There were bitter accusations as terror provoked counter-terror and concerted and courageous appeals by political leaders were slow to still the fears and passions which in part they themselves had inflamed. The Viceroy and members of the interim government, Nehru, Patel, Liaqat Ali Khan, and Abdur Rab Nishtar, visited Calcutta and some among them went on to Bihar in the autumn of 1946, seeking to check the fearful slaughter there. But there was one man in India to whom in this moral crisis of a people all eyes were turned. Gandhi, now in his seventy-seventh year, did not fail them. Entering upon the last and the noblest period of his life, he journeyed to Bengal on his venture in faith, staying in villages desolated by rioting and arson till Hindus and Muslims had learned to live together as brothers again. In the early months of 1947 he decided to travel from place to place, from village to village where death and destruction were greatest by slow day's marches on foot. 'Beloved pilgrim', wrote Mrs. Sarojini Naidu, 'setting out on your pilgrimage of love and hope, "Go out with God". I have no fear for you—only faith in your mission.'[3] If the peace brought to the villages through which he passed and in which he prayed did not always endure, Gandhi by force of example and his teaching of non-violence brought solace to the suffering and imposed some restraint upon the fanatical and the violent. As has happened so often in history, terrible suffering and inhuman passions called forth the highest in man. An Australian Governor of Bengal[4] wrote of the Mahatma as a saint among politicians and a politician among saints. No one who had dealings with him could afford to forget the astute politician; few who followed him on his pilgrimage or heard him at his prayer meetings in a sweepers' colony at Delhi in those dark days of communal strife could doubt that here was one whom men of other faiths could number with those whom their own had sanctified.

The Constituent Assembly

The Constituent Assembly, its membership diminished by the absence of the Muslim League representatives, its proceedings overshadowed by violence without, met none the less in an atmosphere not of dejection but of hope. The Constituent Assembly was a sovereign body, Pandit Nehru disposing

[1] For a soldier's account see Sir Francis Tuker, *While Memory Serves* (London, Cassell, 1950), ch. xii: 'The Great Calcutta Killing', ch. xiv: 'Disturbance in East Bengal', ch. xv: 'The Butchery of Muslims in Bihar'. Both text and illustrations bring home the horror of what took place.
[2] For figures killed see Sir Stafford Cripps, H. of C. Deb., vol. 431, col. 1351.
[3] Tendulkar, *Mahatma*, vii. 346. For a detailed account with many illustrations, see ibid. *passim*. [4] R. G. Casey, *An Australian in India* (London, Hollis & Carter, 1947), p. 3.

cavalierly of such limitations on its freedom of action as the Cabinet Mission had deemed it wise to impose, and at long last it had come into being to draw up the constitution of a new India, which, partition or no, would surely reemerge as one of the great independent nations of Asia and indeed of the world.

We are at the end of an era ... [said Pandit Nehru, moving the Objectives Resolution[1] on 13 December 1946] and my mind goes back to the great past of India, to the 5,000 years of India's history, from the very dawn of that history ... till today. All that past crowds upon me and exhilarates me and, at the same time, somewhat oppresses me. Am I worthy of that past? When I think also of the future, the greater future I hope, standing on this sword's edge of the present between the mighty past and the mightier future, I tremble a little and feel overwhelmed by this mighty task. We have come here at a strange moment in India's history. I do not know, but I do feel that there is some magic in this moment of transition from the old to the new, something of that magic which one sees when the night turns into day and even though the day may be a cloudy one, it is day after all, for when the clouds move away we can see the sun again.[2]

Though night by night even in the capital itself, the assassin fulfilled his deadly mission, there was in Delhi in the winter of 1946–7 a sense of magic side by side with fear. For Indian nationalists it was a time of high romantic exaltation when the old order and the new worked side by side, the one in hope, the other with a sense of duty to be honourably discharged whatever might be the heaviness of the heart within, and together they invested the time with something of the grandeur demanded of so great a moment in history.

The Constituent Assembly resolved that India should be 'an independent sovereign republic', comprising a Union of the provinces of British India and such Princely States and other territories as 'are willing to be constituted into the independent sovereign India'. Residuary power was to rest with the constituent units of the Union, the powers of the central government to be specifically assigned to it. But it was also resolved that all power and authority both at the centre and in the units would derive from the people. Equality of status and opportunity, freedom of faith and worship, adequate safeguards for minorities and for backward areas were to be provided. In sum, therefore, what was contemplated was a federal constitution, conceding the principle of non-accession, with protection for minorities promised, but with no pronounced bias towards the constituent units and indeed some indication that the outcome would be a federation less on the Australian (despite the retention by the units of residuary powers) than on the Canadian model. Indeed the use of the term 'union' itself suggested a unitary state with many of the characteristic features of federalism rather than a federal state in which the

[1] It was passed unanimously on 22 January 1949.
[2] India, Constituent Assembly Deb., vol. 1, no. 5, pp. 57–61 (Mansergh, Documents, ii. 652–8).

power of the centre and of the units were co-ordinate. Such, indeed, had been the consistent aim of Congress and, since the Muslim League decided not to participate in the proceedings of the Assembly, it was likely to prevail.

Pandit Nehru in moving the Objectives Resolution noted regretfully that 'there are many absentees here and many members who have a right to come here who have not come',[1] and reminded those who attended that there 'is a duty cast upon us and that is to bear the absentees in mind, to remember always that we are not here to work for one party or one group, but always to think . . . of the welfare of the four hundred millions that comprise India'. That was well said. Jinnah, however, was not a man to be satisfied with the passing thoughts of others. The policy of abstention had but one meaning, and in the closing months of 1946 the Congress leaders, for the most part for the first time, realized what it was. There was little point in drafting a constitution to reconcile the irreconcilable.

The decision that India should be an independent, sovereign republic was a matter of concern to other members of the Commonwealth. The Irish Constitution of 1937 had stated[2] that Ireland was a sovereign, independent democratic state. Members of the Indian Constituent Assembly criticized the omission of the word 'democratic' from the Objectives Resolution. Pandit Nehru explained that it was not used, partly because the Resolution as a whole made it clear that the aim was the fullest democracy, including 'economic democracy', and partly because 'we thought it obvious that the word republic contains the meaning of that word and we did not wish to use unnecessary or redundant words'. This, however, according to legal opinion was precisely what had been done by the inclusion of both 'sovereign' and 'independent', and in the preamble to the later Constitution of the Republic of India 'independent' was deleted and 'democratic' inserted so that the sentence of the Preamble read, '*We, the People of India*, having solemnly resolved to constitute India into a Sovereign Democratic Republic . . .'.[3] In 1926 the word 'independent', which appeared in a draft formula defining dominion status submitted to the Imperial Conference of 1926 by General Hertzog, was deleted, partly because Mr. Mackenzie King disliked its American overtones, and 'autonomous' substituted. But the Irish precedent and Congress demands for full independence had accustomed Commonwealth statesmen to such terminology. Sir Stafford Cripps in 1942 indeed had emphasized the independence India would enjoy if and when his proposals were given effect.

The implication of the word 'independent' for most Congressmen was independence outside the Commonwealth, but it was not necessarily so elsewhere in the Commonwealth. There it was not India's future independent sovereign status but her contemplated adoption of a republican constitution

---

[1] Ibid. Negotiations were proceeding with the rulers of the states and their representatives did not attend unless and until these were concluded.
[2] Art. 5.
[3] Mansergh, *Documents*, ii. 838.

that gave cause for thought. In the Balfour Report and in the Preamble to the Statute of Westminster common allegiance to the Crown was listed as one of the conventional and indispensable conditions of dominion status. British policy towards the Irish Free State since 1931, and indeed since 1921, rested on the twin assumptions that common allegiance was a condition of dominion status and that a repudiation of that allegiance was tantamount to secession. The Irish accepted this premiss and Eire was not named a republic in the Constitution of 1937, partly in order to avoid forcing the question of secession at that time. Outside India the Objectives Resolution was, therefore, only to be interpreted as a declaration of India's intention to secede from the Commonwealth. Yet it is to be noted that in Delhi Pandit Nehru alluded specifically to Irish precedents, remarking that the House would recall 'that even in the British Commonwealth of Nations today, Eire is a Republic and yet in many ways it is a member . . . so it is a conceivable thing. What will happen, I do not know, because that is partly for this House and partly for others to decide.' But in any event there was no doubt about a republican constitution for India. 'It is our firm and solemn resolve to have an Independent Sovereign Republic. India is bound to be sovereign, it is bound to be independent, it is bound to be a Republic.' It was not worth-while going into the arguments about a monarchy, for 'we are not going to have an external monarchy and we cannot begin a search for a legal heir from among local monarchies. It must inevitably be a Republic.' The fact that this was likely to be somewhat displeasing to the rulers of the Indian states disturbed neither the Assembly nor, least of all, Pandit Nehru, who, as he had often said before, did 'not believe in the monarchical system anywhere'.[1] In his argument, and indeed in that of other speakers, republicanism was associated with full independence, whereas apart from other considerations the monarchical constitutions for the older dominions were held to confer something less. 'One King, one flag, one cause . . . Britain is at war, therefore Australia is at war', were phrases used by Mr. Menzies on 3 September 1939.[2] If they were to be precisely interpreted, did not that mean that dominion monarchical constitutions and common allegiance allowed of something less than full independence in foreign policy? If only a doubt, it was a doubt the Indian Constituent Assembly wished to remove. Secondly, there was also the thought that the rulers of India before the British came were the Grand Moguls. In the Hindu-dominated Assembly there was even less disposition to consider a return to that more distant past.

A Time-Limit Imposed

In December 1946–January 1947 there were negotiations, on the now familiar triangular pattern, seeking to end the Muslim League boycott of the

[1] Speech moving the Objectives Resolution, quoted above, p. 223.
[2] See Mansergh, *Survey, 1931–9*, p. 378.

Constituent Assembly. They proved unavailing not, as many close to the event supposed, because of differences about the detailed interpretation of the Cabinet Mission's plan, but because of a difference in aim.[1] If the Cabinet Mission's proposals had modified momentarily the League's insistence on the concession of Pakistan before any transfer of power, the events of the late autumn and perhaps also Jinnah's conversations in London in December 1946 (where he went at Mr. Attlee's invitation in company with the Viceroy and the Congress leaders), had once more hardened them in their earlier resolve. There was not, therefore, a failure on the part of the three principal parties to negotiate a reasonable settlement on the basis of League participation in the work of the Constituent Assembly; there was a conflict in aim which precluded it and which made further attempts at negotiation otiose. Accordingly Mr. Attlee's administration decided to put a limit to discussion and dissension. It was 'their definite intention', said an official statement of 20 February,[2] '... to effect the transference of power into responsible Indian hands by a date not later than June 1948'. It was their desire to hand over responsibility to authorities established by a constitution approved by all parties in India in accordance with the Cabinet Mission plan, but if it should appear that such a constitution would not have been worked out by a fully representative assembly, then

His Majesty's Government will have to consider to whom the powers of the Central Government in British India should be handed over, on the due date, whether as a whole to some form of central Government for British India or in some areas to the existing Provincial Governments, or in such other way as may seem most reasonable and in the best interests of the Indian people.

The statement marked a departure from the tradition of British imperial policy hitherto at all times supremely mistrustful of the explicit and the predetermined. But there are times when it is wise to depart from tradition. This was assuredly one of them. The Indian political scene had been too long overshadowed by many contingencies, and the announcement of 20 February introduced at least one element of certainty. The Conservative Opposition alleged that the statement at once extinguished the last hope of Indian unity and, further, allowed of a period too short for the working out of constitutional arrangements whether for a united or a divided India. Mr. Churchill, because of the narrow franchise on which the Constituent Assembly was elected, maintained in one of the more memorable miscalculations of great men that 'in handing over the Government of India to these so-called political classes we are handing over to men of straw, of whom, in a few years, no trace will remain'.[3] But in the House of Lords for the first, but not for the last time,

---

[1] For a fuller account see Lumby, *Transfer of Power*, pp. 122–36.

[2] Cmd. 7047 (Mansergh, *Documents*, ii. 659–61).

[3] H. of C. Deb., vol. 434, col. 674. See generally coll. 663–78 and especially speeches of Mr. R. A. Butler (coll. 759–63) and Mr. Attlee (coll. 763–72).

a Conservative ex-Viceroy, Lord Halifax, felt unable to condemn the judgement of the Labour government.[1]

Great decisions are often the outcome of many lesser ones, and so it was in this instance. In 1944 the British members of the Indian Civil Service numbered only some 500 because of progress in Indianization of the Service and the cessation of recruitment since the outbreak of the war in 1939, while with demobilization there was also a rapid decline in the proportion of British to Indian officers in the armed services. The government, before making its statement of 20 February, was advised that British rule could not be maintained on its existing basis with adequate efficiency after 1948.[2] This was not in itself decisive. It would have been possible to reinforce both the administrative and the military services, a course which Mr. Churchill favoured. But it would have meant, and would have been interpreted in India as representing, a fundamental change in British policy indicating, if necessary, a willingness to use force. It is possible that by such an implied reversal of policy the prospect of unity in India would have been increased. The Congress and the League might well have united against the British.

In India the imposition of a time-limit had a salutary effect. Though Indian political leaders by long habit scrutinized British state documents with suspicion and care, on this occasion there appeared to them no subtlety or possibility of equivocation. Both the Congress and the League welcomed the announcement. The Congress, noting that at long last its demand for a transfer of power without waiting upon agreement among the communities or the drafting of the constitution was in effect conceded, prepared to assume responsibility for the government of India; the League understood that resolution could now achieve the goal of Pakistan, for the partition of India was implicit in the phrasing of the announcement.

A Time-Limit Foreshortened

In March 1947 Lord Mountbatten succeeded Lord Wavell as Viceroy. It was his unenviable lot to end British rule in India. He came to Delhi as the last of a long line of representatives of the British Crown; he was welcomed with curiosity by political leaders, with indifference by the inhabitants of the capital, and, while his task was difficult because of the complexities of Indian politics, it was seemingly one that offered little scope for personal initiative or imaginative statesmanship. Yet within a few brief months the last British Viceroy had become one of the outstanding personalities in India, a political

---

[1] H. of L. Deb., vol. 145, coll. 1013–21. Earl Attlee, as he later became, recalled in 1957 that Lord Halifax's speech prevented a division in the House of Lords at a time when 'the acceptance of the Indian proposals of the Labour Government hung in the balance' (*Listener*, 23 May 1957, p. 837).

[2] Lord Pethick-Lawrence, H. of L. Deb., vol. 145, coll. 940–81. For an illuminating and critical appreciation of the outlook and importance of the Indian Civil Service see H. V. Hodson, *Twentieth Century Empire* (London, Faber, 1948), ch. vii.

force in his own right, known from end to end of the subcontinent, invited by the first independent government of India to serve as its first Governor-General, hailed in triumphal procession by surging crowds on Independence Day, when among the cries of '*Jai Hind*' were to be heard cries of 'Mountbatten *Ki Jai*', and leaving India within little more than a year of his arrival surrounded by every sign of popular esteem and personal affection. If Lord Mountbatten made no such happy impact upon the people of Pakistan, that detracts but little from a personal triumph which lent lustre to the last days of British rule in India and invested its passing with a sense of achievement shared alike by British, Indians, and Pakistanis together. The 'Philistine on Mount Parnassus' would surely have acclaimed the manner of Britain's withdrawal, recapturing as it did something of that sense of 'the proudest day in British history', and have recorded it in prose which Lytton Strachey would as surely have deplored. Perhaps Pandit Nehru was right; perhaps there was some magic in the air at the moment of transition from the old to the new.

Lord Mountbatten's viceroyalty opened with a re-examination of the points of agreement and of disagreement among the Indian leaders. This was no formal inquiry in the traditional manner, inviting a restatement of community or party views, but an attempt on the part of the Viceroy to enter into the fears and hopes that filled the minds of India's leaders. In this he was notably successful in respect of the Congress, less so in respect of the League. 'I will enter into discussion on one condition only' was Jinnah's opening to his first conversation with the Viceroy, an opening interrupted by Lord Mountbatten's saying, 'Mr. Jinnah, I am not prepared to discuss conditions or, indeed, the present situation until I have had the chance of making your acquaintance and knowing more about you yourself.'[1] But according to Mountbatten's recorded comment, it took most of the interview 'to unfreeze him'. The leader of the weaker party can little afford to display cordiality in hard negotiation. Yet it is open to question whether Jinnah, making every allowance for the difficulties of his position, most advanced the cause he had at heart by his lack of compromise in manner as in matter.

The Viceroy concluded within a fortnight of his arrival that the need for a solution was much more pressing than it had appeared to be in London, and that the time-limit of June 1948, far from not allowing enough time, was too remote.[2] Communal rioting, even if spasmodic in most areas, threatened to develop into civil war, and indeed in March-April 1947 many were concerned less with that possibility than with the question who would win it. The morale of the civil service, the continuing immunity of the armed forces to communal division, the functioning of government in the provinces even more than at the centre, could hardly survive the stress of a protracted period of

[1] Alan Campbell-Johnson, *Mission with Mountbatten* (London, Hale, 1957), p. 57. It should be noted that there is no published record of Jinnah's impressions known to the author.
[2] Ibid. p. 55; see also Menon, *Transfer of Power*, ch. xx.

uncertainty. Nor could it any longer be seriously supposed that such a period would serve to bring the parties closer together; on the contrary, it was likely to heighten the claims of communities, to encourage the pretensions of princes, and to bring the subcontinent to the verge of chaos.[1] Yet a quick solution demanded not only the bringing of issues to the sharp point of decision, but also a readiness on the part of the British government and of its successors alike to let constitution-making wait upon independence.

Partition was implicit in the statement of 20 February 1946, provided—it was an unlikely contingency—that the League did not weaken in its demand for Pakistan. This it did not do. Gandhi, in a desperate attempt to arrest a final split, suggested to the Viceroy that the Congress should withdraw from the interim government and that the Muslim League should be invited to form a government on its own with Congress support so as to lessen their fears of Congress rule. But while the Viceroy did not dismiss this ingenious idea, closer examination of it suggested that it offered no adequate long-term solution and that in any event the Congress was not prepared for such self-sacrifice.[2] On 21 April Pandit Nehru conceded publicly that the League would have Pakistan if it wished, but on the understanding that it did not include areas where the majority had no wish to be included. On 28 April Dr. Rajendra Prasad told the members of the Constituent Assembly that India must be prepared for the division both of the subcontinent and of some of its provinces.[3] The Viceroy, confronted by the League threat that any attempt to impose unity would cause the bloodiest civil war in the history of Asia, was convinced that there was no alternative to partition. Gandhi was the last among Congress leaders to acquiesce, and with extreme reluctance, in the impending vivisection of India.

Partition accepted in principle, the chief obstacle to an early transfer of power was removed, and indeed the prospect of partition was made less unpalatable to the Congress leaders by the realization that this was so. There was now no purpose to be served by procrastination, and what remained was to determine the manner in which power was to be transferred and the time required to arrange for the partition and all that it implied, administratively, economically, as well as politically. On 3 June 1947 Mr. Attlee outlined in the House of Commons the government's plan for an early transfer of power.[4] It was favourably received by the Congress, the League, and the Sikhs. The plan,[5] recognizing that all attempts to preserve the future unity of India by agreement had failed, proposed the creation of a new and separate Constituent

[1] For some contemporary impressions, see the author's *The Commonwealth and the Nations* (London, RIIA, 1948), ch. v.
[2] *Mission with Mountbatten*, pp. 52 and 61.
[3] *Annual Register, 1947*, p. 150. The article on India is by H. V. Hodson, Reforms Commissioner to the Government of India, 1941–2.
[4] H. of C. Deb., vol. 438, coll. 35–40.
[5] Cmd. 7136 (Mansergh, *Documents*, ii. 661–9).

Assembly consisting of the representatives of those areas which decided not to participate in the existing Assembly. 'When the Muslim League demanded the partition of India', said the Viceroy in his broadcast to the people of India on the evening of 3 June,[1] 'Congress used the same arguments for demanding in that event the partition of certain Provinces. To my mind that argument is unassailable.' Accordingly the all-important detail of the plan was concerned with the way in which the provinces should be divided. It was not uniform. In Bengal, the Punjab, and Sind, the decision was left to the recently-elected provincial legislative assemblies, and in Bengal and the Punjab the assemblies were to meet in two parts, one representing the Muslim majority districts which were listed in an appendix to the statement, and the other the rest of the province. The members of the two parts of each legislative assembly, sitting separately, were to be empowered to vote whether or not the province should be partitioned. If a simple majority of either part decided in favour of partition, it would take place, and in that event a decision would be made by the same process to determine which constituent assembly the areas it represented should join. If either or both provinces elected in favour of partition, they would be divided provisionally on the basis of Muslim and non-Muslim majority districts with a Boundary Commission appointed in consultation with those concerned to make a later and final demarcation on the basis of contiguous majority areas of Muslims and non-Muslims, but being also instructed to take into account other factors. If Bengal opted for partition, the district of Sylhet in the predominantly non-Muslim province of Assam, being contiguous to Bengal and predominantly Muslim, was to be allowed to determine its own future by referendum, and the same device was to be employed to determine the future of the North-West Frontier Province. Means were also to be taken to ascertain the wishes of British Baluchistan. In every instance the determination of the future was thus to rest in Indian hands.

The British government's plan of 3 June was not a British award imposed from above; it was a plan to make possible a settlement in accordance with the wishes of the inhabitants of the areas in dispute between the Indian parties. As such it was recognized by the principal Indian leaders (including the Sikhs likely to lose so much by the partition of the Punjab) with greater or lesser degree of reluctance, for none had attained in full what they had demanded. The time had come when there seemed no practicable and acceptable alternative to partition. 'There can be no question', said Lord Mountbatten, 'of coercing any large areas in which one community has a majority to live against their will under a Government in which another community has a majority. And the only alternative to coercion is partition.'[2] In 1947 it was a conclusion Gandhi questioned, but which even he did not

---

[1] Earl Mountbatten of Burma, *Time Only to Look Forward* (London, Kaye, 1949), pp. 10–13 (ibid. pp. 667–8).   [2] Ibid. p. 11.

dispute at the last. That is not, however, to say that the Congress or most Hindus were finally reconciled to partition. That was something time alone could bring about and for which even time might not suffice.

The statement of 3 June opened the way not only for a second partition in British Commonwealth history but also for the addition of two new dominions to the self-governing membership of the Commonwealth. 'The most expeditious, and indeed the only practicable way' by which Indian desire for the earliest possible transfer of power could be met was, so it seemed to the British government, by a transfer of power on a dominion status basis to one, or two, successor authorities, as the case might be. The British government proposed accordingly to introduce legislation for this purpose during the current session of Parliament, being careful at the same time to emphasize that the grant of dominion status as a matter of temporary convenience in no way prejudiced the right of the Indian constituent assemblies to decide whether or not to remain within the British Commonwealth. None the less, Indian acceptance of a transfer of power on a dominion-status basis was rightly regarded in other parts of the Commonwealth as a hopeful portent for the future. On 4 June Mr. Mackenzie King[1] assured the peoples of India of the sympathetic understanding and goodwill of the government and people of Canada and thought that the outcome might be to enlarge the number of states within the British Commonwealth. Dr. Evatt considered that the peoples of India could pursue all their national aspirations while maintaining the Commonwealth link,[2] while General Smuts thought that it might well be that India—whether as one or two dominions—would find 'that the advantages of Commonwealth association outweigh all other considerations or inducements to chart her future course alone'.[3] But it was Mr. Fraser who spoke most directly to Indian hearts. It was not, he said, for New Zealand to advise India what she should do, much as New Zealand would welcome continued partnership with India in the Commonwealth. But there was one consideration to be kept in mind. The people of the British dominions, he noted, 'do not regard dominion status as an imperfect kind of independence. On the contrary it is independence with something added and not independence with something taken away.'[4] This was precisely the point on which so many Indians had misgivings.

On 4 June Lord Mountbatten held a press conference on the British Government's plan attended by 300 representatives of the Indian and the world's press. Of the little less than 100 questions which he answered, with a mastery of substance and detail which made a remarkable impression upon his critical audience, those of greatest interest to the

[1] Canada, H. of C. Deb., 1947, vol. 4, pp. 3771–2 (Mansergh, *Documents*, ii. 702–3).
[2] Australia, H. of R. Deb., vol. 192, p. 3692 (ibid. p. 704).
[3] *The Times*, 5 June 1947 (ibid. p. 705).
[4] *New Zealand Herald*, 5 June 1947 (ibid. p. 704).

student of Commonwealth history concerned Indian fears of the implications of continued Commonwealth membership on the part of one only of the two successor states and continuing Indian doubts as to whether membership was tantamount to independence—let alone independence with something added to it. The following exchanges, in which Devadas Gandhi played a prominent part, are of some lasting importance:[1]

Question. It is said here [in the Statement] that the respective Constituent Assemblies have the right ultimately to elect to remain within the British Commonwealth or not. I want to point out that there is mischief in that provision?

The Viceroy. I absolutely disagree. The British Commonwealth of Nations is a completely free association of peoples. Each State is completely independent.... The whole essence of independence is that you must have complete freedom to do what you like....

Question. Nobody objects to interim Dominion Status. Suppose there are two Constituent Assemblies. It is open to one of them to declare itself absolutely independent and the other to declare itself a Dominion?...

The Viceroy. If you grant independence and at the same time try to impose restrictions, the independence becomes a mockery.

Question. . . . The point I want to put to Your Excellency is this. You know the history of the last few years. The two major parties have been asking for complete independence knowing full well all the implications of the Statute of Westminster. Since you are proceeding with the consent of the parties throughout, what will happen if one party is not a consenting party to what the other party is doing?

The Viceroy. I am simply amazed at these questions. If you are sincere in your demand for independence, it means that you have got perfect freedom to do what you like. There is no question of imposing any decision on you. There is no question of one party imposing its will on the other.

Question. I am afraid we are still at cross purposes on this particular point.... If you allow the Dominion Status to become a bone of contention to the rival parties, you are going to be charged with some kind of conspiracy behind it. Therefore, so far as the Dominion Status is concerned, we shall think of it when all sections of India want it. If to-morrow, we come and say that we must be admitted into the Commonwealth of Nations, nobody shall say 'no' to it. If you demand that India should have one voice and not two voices regarding the membership of the Commonwealth of Nations, you will surely be furthering your own aim.

The Viceroy. I do not think you have yourself understood what the Commonwealth of Nations is. It is not run by His Majesty's Government. His Majesty's Government represents only one Government and not the Commonwealth of Nations. Before this paragraph could go through, the Dominion Governments had to be consulted. I can assure you there is no sinister motive about. Living as neighbours alongside each other, the two Dominions will have a hundred and one problems that will arise in the course of the partition. If they will feel then that the time has come when one or both should leave the Commonwealth of Nations, they will presumably consult each other....

[1] Mountbatten, *Time Only to Look Forward*, pp. 44–47. See also Campbell-Johnson, *Mission with Mountbatten*, pp. 108–10.

Question. Will the Governor-General be appointed on the advice of the Dominion Governments? If so, is there any bar against there being separate Governors-General for the two States?

The Viceroy. The moment any State acquires Dominion Status, it chooses its own Governor-General. That Governor-General is chosen by the Prime Minister of the Government of the Dominion concerned. He submits his name to the King, who being a constitutional monarch, may discuss it but finally acts on the advice of the Government concerned. We have many examples on that. It is complete and absolute freedom to do exactly what you like. . . .

Question. May I ask whether each Dominion will have full responsibility for its own defences?

The Viceroy. Basically, each State, when it gets its independence, is wholly and solely responsible for its own defence. I must tell you that the process of partition of forces, if it is to be done in a way that will not cause the collapse of the morale and the disintegration of the army, must be done in an orderly and well-disciplined manner. When the partition has taken place, the States are absolutely at liberty to get together and have a combined plan for the defence of India or to make their own separate plans. From all the questions that have been asked, there is one thing which I sincerely believe is not yet clear to the people. Somehow people seem to have some doubts about this word 'Dominion Status'. It is absolute independence in every possible way, with the sole exception that the Member States of [the] Commonwealth are linked together voluntarily. In effect they look for support from each other and they are pulled together, by mutual trust and in due course affection.

The Indian Independence Act[1]

The Indian Independence Act, duly introduced into the House of Commons in accordance with the terms of the statement of 3 June, made provision for the setting up of two 'independent Dominions', the wording of the Preamble and of the text being in this respect an innovation in Commonwealth terminology. The first section of the Act stated that 'As from the fifteenth day of August, nineteen hundred and fortyseven, two independent Dominions shall be set up in India, to be known respectively as India and Pakistan'. The frontiers between them were to be delimited in accordance with the outcome of the procedures outlined on 3 June, and as from the appointed day the authority of the United Kingdom government in India lapsed, it being specifically stated that no Act of the United Kingdom passed on or after that day should extend, or be deemed to extend, to either of the two new dominions as part of the law of that dominion unless extended by a law of its own legislature. Likewise after 15 August His Majesty's government in the United Kingdom was to have no responsibility in respect of the government of any territories in British India; 'the suzerainty of His Majesty over the Indian States' was to lapse, and also all treaties or agreements with the tribal

---

[1] 10 and 11 Geo. 6, c. 30 (Mansergh, *Documents*, ii. 669–85).

areas. The words 'Indiae Imperator' and 'Emperor of India' were to be omitted henceforward from the Royal Style and Titles. The powers of the legislature of each dominion, for the purpose of drafting its constitution, were to be exercised by the Constituent Assembly of that dominion, and pending the enactments of their respective constitutions, each of the dominions and all the provinces were to be governed 'as nearly as may be in accordance with the Government of India Act, 1935', the powers of the Governor-General under the Act being specifically curtailed. In this there was something at once ironic for those who remembered the past and reassuring for those who attached importance to constitutional continuity. The Act which in India at the time of its passing was denounced, not unreasonably, for its extremely cautious approach to Indian self-government, was now to serve as the first foundation for independent self-government in India's two successor nation states.

The Indian Independence Act marked the ending of British rule in India. The Prime Minister,[1] in a speech which showed once again his insight into Indo-British relations, sought to place it in the perspective of history. The Act, he insisted, recorded not the abdication but the fulfilment of Britain's mission in India. It was the culminating point in a long course of events, foreshadowed in many reports and proposals, from those of Morley and Minto in 1909, down to those of Sir Stafford Cripps in 1942 and the Cabinet Mission of 1946. He recalled, not Macaulay, but Mountstuart Elphinstone writing in 1854 that

> we must not dream of perpetual possession, but must apply ourselves to bring the natives into a state that will admit of their governing themselves in a manner that may be beneficial to our interests as well as their own, and that of the rest of the world; and to take the glory of the achievement and the sense of having done our duty for the chief reward of our exertions.

And the Prime Minister remembered at the very opening of his speech Campbell-Bannerman's magnanimous gesture in restoring self-government to the defeated Boer republics, noting that 1947 marked not the first but the second time in little more than a generation in which Britain had voluntarily surrendered power enjoyed over another nation. It was well that these things should have been said, for there was in them much truth, if not the whole truth. They were inspired chiefly by one thing which might well prove transient—India's and Pakistan's continuing membership of the Commonwealth. Lord Halifax,[2] reminding the House of Lords that 'in the long run influence is a very much finer and more durable and more eternal thing than power', thought of the British Commonwealth founded and fostered in a soil of apparent contradictions as affording possibilities of fruitful partnership

---

[1] H. of C. Deb., vol. 439, coll. 2441–56 (Mansergh, *Documents*, ii. 685–96).
[2] H. of L. Deb., vol. 150, coll. 832–7 (ibid. pp. 696–700).

that took due account of the fact that 'nothing so much predisposes men to understand as the consciousness that they are understood'.[1] Yet if in Britain there was general acclaim, there was by no means general enthusiasm, and before a decade had passed many right-wing imperialists, psychologically unreconciled, were to talk not of the fulfilment of British rule in India but of policies of 'quit' and 'scuttle', just as some few in India and Pakistan spoke of abdication under duress. But the majority in all three countries preferred to think of a generous gesture, of a magnanimity of mind on the part of peoples and leaders alike, which held out for the future the prospect not of rancour and recrimination over the past but of fruitful co-operation. It was in that spirit that a Commonwealth in Asia came into existence, whose capacity to endure was conditional upon its survival.

The Princes; Pressure and Procrastination

On 15 March 1946 Mr. Attlee expressed the hope that the statesmen of British India and of princely India would be able to work out a solution of 'the problem of bringing together, in one great polity, these disparate constituent parts'. We must see, he said, that the Indian states find their due place, but there can be no positive veto on advance, and 'I do not believe for a moment that the Indian princes would desire to be a bar to the forward march of India'.[2] The hint of admonition in the Prime Minister's statement was underlined in the Cabinet Mission's Report. In their *Memorandum on States' Treaties and Paramountcy*[3] handed to the Chancellor of the Chamber of Princes on 12 May, but not published till 22 May 1946, it was affirmed that when a self-governing state, or states, were established in British India, His Majesty's government in the United Kingdom would not be able to carry out the obligations, and would accordingly cease to exercise the powers of paramountcy. The void would have to be filled either by the states entering into a federal relationship with British India or, failing this, entering into particular arrangements with the successor governments or government in British India when their form and constitution had been more clearly defined. The way was left open for representation of the Princely States in the Constituent Assembly after negotiation with their rulers. 'I regret', observed Pandit Nehru on 21 December 1946,[4] 'I say frankly that we have to meet the rulers' Negotiating Committee'. But it was not possible at that stage to reopen the question of representation of peoples as against princes. Resulting discussions proceeded leisurely, with the princes for the most part assuming that they stood to gain by a policy of 'wait and see'. It was a policy which, after the time-limit announced on 20 February setting a term to British rule in

---
[1] Lord Grey of Fallodon was here quoted by Lord Halifax.
[2] 15 March 1946, H. of C. Deb., vol. 420, coll. 1422–3.
[3] Cmd. 6835 (Mansergh, *Documents*, ii. 642–3).
[4] *Times of India*, 22 December 1946.

India, had great temptations and even greater dangers. It did not survive an assault from within. In April 1947 the Maharajah of Bikaner advised by his Dewan, Sardar K. M. Panikkar, agreed 'that the united front that is required to be put up by the States is ... not by adopting a policy of "wait and see" but by fully co-operating with the Constituent Assembly with all the benefits that will accrue on such a step'.[1] The Maharajah of Patiala assented and together they decided that their states should be represented in the Constituent Assembly despite the disapproval of princely colleagues. On 18 April waverers were further moved by Pandit Nehru's observation at the States People's Conference that any state which did not come into the Constituent Assembly would be treated as a hostile state. Liaqat Ali Khan advised rulers to 'disregard the idle threat' but the majority, not satisfied that it was idle, were unprepared to do so.[2] On the contrary, one by one they decided to participate in the work of the Constituent Assembly.

The decision announced early in June to foreshorten the period before a transfer of power threw into clearer relief the problem of the states in the final phase of their quasi-autonomous existence. If they did not accede to one or the other of the new successor dominions when paramountcy lapsed, then the subcontinent was faced at the least with administrative chaos. Yet the decision whether to do so or not rested in the hands of the rulers whose discretion in Jinnah's view was absolute, though in the view of the Congress this was not so, for, in Rajagopalachari's opinion, 'paramountcy came into being as a fact and not by agreement and on the British withdrawal the successor authority must inherit the fact along with the rest of the context'.[3] In practice, however, it was the larger states alone that were in a position to bargain. They received no encouragement to do so from Delhi. Early in July a States Department was set up in the capital with V. P. Menon, formerly Reforms Commissioner to the Government of India, as its administrative head and the formidable figure of Sardar Vallabhbhai Patel as its political chief. It was the policy of the new department to secure princely accession only on a basis that would not preclude the states from becoming subsequently an integral part of the new India.

On 25 July Lord Mountbatten for the first and last time addressed the Chamber of Princes.[4] He urged them, in language that must have seemed in disturbing contrast to what they had been accustomed to hear from his predecessors even when the coming into existence of an Indian federation lay in princely hands, to study sympathetically a draft instrument of accession

---

[1] Quoted in Menon, *Integration of the Indian States*, pp. 74–76.
[2] Ibid. p. 78.
[3] Quoted in Lumby, *Transfer of Power*, p. 233. See also Menon, *Integration of the Indian States*, pp. 79–87.
[4] For text of his speech see *Time Only to Look Forward*, pp. 51–56. See also Campbell-Johnson, *Mission with Mountbatten*, pp. 140–3 and Menon, *Integration of the Indian States*, pp. 108–9. A draft instrument of Accession is reprinted in Mansergh, *Documents*, ii. 705–7.

based on the relevant provisions of the Government of India Act, 1935[1] which he had had circulated to them as a basis for discussion. The instrument provided for accession on three subjects only, foreign affairs, defence, and communications. 'My scheme', said the Viceroy, 'leaves you with all the practical independence you can possibly use and makes you free of all those subjects which you cannot possibly manage on your own. You cannot run away from the Dominion Government which is your neighbour any more than you can run away from subjects for whose welfare you are responsible.' The Viceroy's royal blood, his prestige, and his gifts of persuasion provided a counterpart to the pressure which Patel applied more bluntly. The princes for the most part acted as they were prompted, and by 15 August 1947 fears of disintegration so widely entertained had been substantially dispelled. What had been achieved in so short time to resolve a problem that had vexed so many British statesmen in the past was impressive indeed. Yet history is likely to consider as much what was left undone as what was accomplished. Among the smaller states Junagadh, among the largest Hyderabad and Kashmir, had acceded to neither dominion when power was transferred. Kashmir lay on the frontiers of both successor states, it was neighbour to both, and while its ruler was Hindu, its people were predominantly Muslim. There was no state in the subcontinent the future of which, if left unsettled when the independent imperial authority withdrew, was more likely to occasion dissension between the two dominions. The failure to concentrate more closely upon the problem it presented was destined to prove an oversight fraught with grave consequence.

15 August 1947: 'A Tryst with Destiny'

Long years ago we made a tryst with destiny, and now the time comes when we shall redeem our pledge, not wholly or in full measure, but very substantially. At the stroke of the midnight hour, when the world sleeps, India will awake to life and freedom.... It is fitting that at this solemn moment we take the pledge of dedication to the service of India and her people and to the still larger cause of humanity.[2]

So Pandit Nehru addressed the Constituent Assembly, reminding it of India's 'unending quest' and the 'trackless centuries filled with the grandeur of her success and failures', and on the stroke of midnight members dedicated themselves 'in all humility' to the service of India and her people 'to the end that this ancient land attain her rightful place in the world and make her full and willing contribution to the promotion of world peace and the welfare of mankind'. In a new capital, hemmed in by the desert and the sea, a state not restored to independence but new to history came into being. The Muslims of India in 1940 had pledged themselves to fight and if necessary to die for Pakistan and had shown, in the words of Jinnah—Quaid-i-Azam, the Creator

---
[1] 26 Geo. V, c. 2, pt. 2, ss. 5 and 6 (Mansergh, *Documents*, i. 254–71).
[2] India, Constituent Assembly Deb., vol. 5, pp. 4–5 (ibid. pp. 700–1).

of Pakistan, many years later to be so named in the Preamble to the constitution of the republic—that they were 'a united nation'.[1] And in the capitals of the British Commonwealth of Nations, hitherto European in respect of its self-governing membership, men were pondering on the implications of its frontiers extended to include peoples of other culture and other colour. August 1947 was also a landmark in its history.

The note of rejoicing was quickly stilled by the blood bath that followed partition, especially in the Punjab. It is not known how many perished in this frenzy of fear and passion; but the number was very great. In the toll of human suffering there has to be added to the loss of life the plight of countless refugees whose wretched shelters were destined for years to line the streets of Calcutta, Karachi, and even of Delhi itself. The governments of the two dominions sought by every means in their power to limit the scale of the catastrophe, but there was not sufficient organized force at their disposal for the task. 'When the Ganges is in flood', wrote Gandhi, 'the water is turbid. The dirt comes to the surface.'[2] He did not wish to live to see 'Indian humanity becoming barbarian'. Yet often he had foreseen that for a period chaos would succed to British rule, and at last seemed to accept the prospect with fatalistic resignation. In the event death and destruction were confined to comparatively limited areas, but their scale prompted others to inquire whether it might not have been at the least reduced had power been transferred less hastily and had adequate measures to cope with foreseen calamity been taken. Here, however, there are many imponderables, and while it is possible that a more protracted transfer would have lessened or averted disaster, it is not certain. An imperial power abdicating its authority was not well placed to take measures to preserve law and order after its rule had ended.[3] Moreover the demand for Pakistan was a communal demand and by its very nature served to inflame communal passions. A longer period might not have stilled but further intensified them. It is against such risks that the gain of better administrative preparation must be weighed.[4]

[1] Mansergh, *Documents*, ii. 701–2.
[2] Tendulkar, *Mahatma*, vii. 475.
[3] Wilfrid Russell, *Indian Summer* (Bombay, Thacker, 1951), pp. 164–5 has well recorded some otherwise forgotten deeds of heroism by young British officers in the Punjab.
[4] It is to be noted that Pakistan would in all likelihood have been better equipped to deal with the problems of refugees. In April 1947 Liaqat Ali Khan, most concerned among Muslim leaders with the setting up of the new government in Pakistan, told the author that June 1948 was a date that did not give reasonable time for adequate preparations to be made. In June 1947 this period was, of course, greatly foreshortened and Pakistan began her independent existence heavily handicapped by the need for improvisation in the public services.

CHAPTER V

ASIAN MEMBERSHIP OF THE COMMONWEALTH

THE first inter-Asian Conference was held in Delhi in March 1947 by the deathbed of the British Empire in India, and to historians of another age it might, so Pandit Nehru supposed, well stand out 'as the landmark which divides the past of Asia from its future'. It was a meeting principally of the representatives of nations long subject either to foreign rule or to foreign tutelage, and the record of the discussions that took place at it is indispensable to an understanding of the temper and outlook of Asian peoples at that time. It was for them a time of high emotion. The day of Western imperialism was fast drawing to a close, and delegates entertained in the Viceroy's house felt that they were witnessing the last departing gleams of its sunset splendour, not only in New Delhi, but throughout a continent. For them the last page in the lamentable history of exploitation of the East by the West was being written and the Indian poetess, Mrs. Sarojini Naidu, voiced the sentiments of the hour when she cried from the rostrum: 'Fellow Asians... my comrades, my kinsmen arise; remember the night of darkness is over. Together, men and women, let us march forward to the Dawn.'[1]

Many delegates felt in their hearts that Asians should march alone when that dawn came and independence was theirs once more. The ending of Western imperialism would, and in the opinion of many should, bring to an end all formal relations with the West. There was a marked disposition to think in terms of an Asian bloc and of the neutralization at least of South and South-East Asia as a protection against future wars which were presumed to be Western alike in origin and interest. Asia for the Asians was thus deemed synonymous with an exclusive continentalism. Asian peoples should be united against war, against colonialism, against racial discrimination in all its forms, and in a resolve to promote the unity of Asia. These were ideas which did not lose their force and, despite the fears of smaller South-East Asian states when they contemplated their greater neighbours, India and China, and despite rivalries and bitter antagonism between India and Pakistan, the sense of an underlying unity of interest of Asian peoples long subject to Western rule was something that survived its passing. Yet the most remarkable feature of the Asian Conference of 1947 was the moderation, especially of the spokesmen of most South and South-East Asian countries in this hour

[1] The official report of the conference was published by the Asian Relations Organization under the title of *The Asian Relations Conference* in 1948. See also Russell, *Indian Summer*, ch. iv, and the impressions of the author in *Commonwealth and the Nations*, ch. iv.

of nationalist triumph.[1] They were resolved to assert their sovereign independence; they were not for the most part desirous of severing such ties with their former rulers as were deemed by them to be consistent with that independence. The distinction was of much moment for the future of the British Commonwealth. In 1947, apart from scattered island territories in the Indian Ocean, Burma, Malaya, Singapore, and Ceylon as well as the Indian subcontinent lay within its confines. What was to be their future relationship with it? Would their peoples wish to remain within or to go without? On the longer view, was it possible to reconcile nationalism, and more especially non-European nationalism, with Commonwealth membership? And if it were, did dominion status in its conventional form, worked out in relation to the needs and aspirations of colonies of European settlement overseas, offer a congenial or appropriate symbolism? The Irish Free State had not found that it did, and it alone of the dominions could claim with these Asian states to be a mother country. If it did not, was the Commonwealth sufficiently flexible to accommodate nation states of non-British and non-European origin? And even if proved to be so in constitutional terms, was it desirable that existing and well-tested cohesion of the Commonwealth should be risked in a venture into the politically unknown?

All these were questions of great potential importance for the future of the Commonwealth, but it lay less with Britian and the existing members than with Asian governments and peoples to decide whether or not they should be posed in concrete form. Among them the greater responsibility rested with the greater states, Pakistan and India, and ultimately it was the Indian decision on which the scale and significance of a Commonwealth experiment in Asia depended. Ceylon, Burma, and Malaya were likely to be much influenced by Indian action and Pakistan, the weaker successor state on the Indian subcontinent, was likely to determine her attitude largely in the light of Indian decisions. In 1947 recent history, the declared Congress aim of Purna Swaraj, and the resolve of the Constituent Assembly to draft a republican constitution all made it probable that once dominion status had served its immediate purpose, India would secede from the Commonwealth; and further that Burma and Malaya would follow her example, but that Ceylon and Pakistan, concerned to reinsure themselves against India's preponderant power, would remain within. Such expectations were, however, not fulfilled.

The Secession of Burma

'The British Government had never succeeded in capturing the imagination of the people; it rested on their acquiescence in overwhelming force but never on consent, and national sentiment had survived a hundred years of foreign

---

[1] Those from Malaya and from the areas of Indo-China under the control of Ho Chi Minh were an exception. They desired and failed to secure armed assistance against imperial governments.

rule.' Such is the bleak verdict of an English writer[1] on British rule in Burma. It is to be noted, however, that the overwhelming force was not in fact present in Burma but in reserve, and it is to be remembered that experience elsewhere in Asia and in Europe would suggest that, however beneficent and imaginative the alien rulers, national sentiment was likely to survive for more than a century. None the less, it remained true that there was a lack of imagination on the part of the British rulers. Burma, though formally separated from India in 1935 in conformity with a recommendation to that effect made in the Report of the Simon Commission, continued to be thought of in Whitehall less in terms of a country with a distinct identity and destiny of its own than as an appendage of the British Empire in India. Both before and after 1935 the goal of British rule in Burma was defined in relation to that marked out for India, and the most important statement of policy by the United Kingdom government, made in January 1931,[2] was a pledge that Burma would not be allowed to lag behind India on the road to self-government. 'The prospects of constitutional advance held out to Burma as part of British India', the statement read, 'will not be prejudiced by this decision [to effect separation] and . . . the constitutional objective after separation will remain the progressive realization of responsible Government in Burma as an integral part of the Empire.' At the time this explicit extension of the declaration on responsible government to a Burma whose administration was about to be separated from that of India was welcomed as an insurance against neglect. Burma's advance would not lag behind that of India. But what if India's lagged? That was a possibility whose baneful consequences for Anglo-Burmese relations were overlooked in Britain and in Burma alike. It was the outcome of the decision to relate Burma's constitutional advance, and thus in effect to subordinate her problems to those of India. The separate office of Secretary of State for Burma was created; but the Secretary of State for India continued to fill it.

There was no such apparent division of opinion in Burma as there was in India when war came. In October 1939, however, the Burmese political leaders formulated a request for a statement of British policy towards Burma. The Governor replied, but did not reassure them by reaffirming the intention of the British government to use its best endeavours to assist Burma to attain 'her due place in the British Commonwealth of Nations'.[3] On 23 February 1940 the Burmese House of Representatives adopted a resolution strongly reminiscent of the demands of the Indian National Congress, stating that Burma's willing participation in the war effort was dependent upon immediate acceptance of her claim to be 'recognized as an independent nation entitled to frame her own constitution'.[4] The British government responded

---

[1] J. S. Furnivall, 'Twilight in Burma; Reconquest and After', *Pacific Affairs*, March 1949, p. 16.   [2] Quoted in Cmd. 4004, p. 18.   [3] *The Times*, 8 November 1939.
[4] Burma, Proceedings of 1st H. of R., vol. 7, p. 416, and see generally pp. 363–416.

by stating that while dominion status was the ultimate goal, the decision of how and when it might be attained would have to be postponed until after the war. Such a prospect was highly unwelcome to Burmese nationalists, and their dissatisfaction was heightened by Japanese occupation of Indo-China in the autumn of 1940; for the Japanese, despite their long record of aggression in China, were popularly accepted in South-East Asia[1] as the champions of Asian nationalism. In the autumn of 1941, under threat of a Japanese assault upon the territories of the Western imperial powers in Asia, the Burmese Premier, U Saw, visited London to seek clarification of British intentions and sought assurances that Burma would be granted dominion status immediately after the war, subject to transitional arrangements allowing some continuing measure of imperial control over foreign affairs and defence. The Japanese struck before the Premier returned to his own country and because of reported communications with them since Pearl Harbour he was interned.[2] But that mattered little by comparison with the sudden transformation of the political scene.

A Burmese writer has testified to the impact of Japanese propaganda and the greater impact of Japanese victories on the Burmese peoples.

'Asia for Asians' [writes Dr. Maung Maung] was their cry, and their armies were marching with the torch of liberation in their hands, Tokyo radio said. More attractive than words were the victories. They might not carry the torch in their hands, but Japanese armies were triumphant, and the peoples of Burma were dazzled. Armies of an Asian nation, belonging to the great 'Asian brotherhood' that Japanese propaganda made much of, were putting the 'superior' and 'invincible' armies of the West to rout. It was an awe-inspiring scene for the peoples, terrible and terribly attractive.[3]

Thakin Nu, later to be one of the founders and Prime Minister of the Union of Burma, and then lodged with other nationalist leaders in jail by order of the government of Burma, resolved with them that if Britain which 'entered this great war to protect small countries and to defend their independence' proclaimed Burmese independence, or promised to do so after the war, they would help Britain against the 'fascist brigands who threaten the independence of small nations'; but if Britain would not do so then 'we will do all we can to hinder your war effort.'[4] No such declaration was, or indeed at that time could usefully have been issued by the British government whatever its views, but the resolution illustrates the dominance which the single aim of indepen-

[1] Cf. Thakin Nu, *Burma Under the Japanese* (London, Macmillan, 1954), pp. 1–2. It was a matter on which the Congress party in India were not so much better informed as better advised.

[2] See B. R. Pearn, *The Burman, 1939–44* (London, 1945), p. 11; see also Maurice Collis, *First and Last in Burma, 1941–8* (London, Faber, 1956), pp. 36–37.

[3] Maung Maung, *Burma and the Family of Nations* (Amsterdam, Djambatan, 1956), p. 91. Also see generally ch. viii entitled 'War and Occupation'.

[4] *Burma under the Japanese*, p. 7.

dence exercised over the minds even of those Burmese nationalists who, with Thakin Nu, had few illusions[1] about Japanese aims or methods.

The Burmese people soon experienced the cruelty and rapacity of the Japanese army of occupation. But they were none the less susceptible to the forms of independence which their new rulers conferred upon them and their desire to rid themselves of all alien government hardened into a fixed purpose. So it was that while nationalist movements formed under Japanese auspices turned against them and fought in co-operation with the returning British forces against a common foe, they were not fighting for a restoration of British rule. They were fighting to assert Burmese independence, for, as another Burmese writer has suggested, 'independence day dates back to August 1943, when, under Japanese occupation, Burma was declared independent. However bogus that declaration, it was no longer possible, from that moment, for Burmese nationalists to think in terms of anything less than complete political freedom.'[2] The movement of Burmese opinion was recognized by the Governor, Sir Reginald Dorman-Smith, and more fully by Lord Louis Mountbatten, then Supreme Commander, South-East Asia, but in London it was little understood and for the most part unsympathetically regarded. As a result its impact upon policy at each succeeding stage tended to be too little and too late to afford a reasonable opportunity of reconciling Burmese nationalism and Commonwealth membership.[3]

In May 1945 British policy towards Burma was defined in a White Paper which stated that the aim of the British government was 'to assist Burma's political development till she can sustain the responsibility of complete self-government within the British Commonwealth and consequently attain a status equal to that of the Dominions and of this country.' 'The ultimate objective'—again the unhappy phrase was used—of His Majesty's government was that representatives of the Burmese people, once a sufficient measure of agreement between the various parties and sections into which they were divided had been reached, 'should draw up a Constitution of a type which they themselves consider most suitable for Burma'.[4] In the meantime, however, the Constitution of 1935 was to remain in abeyance for three years, till December 1948, and during the interim period the Governor was to be responsible for the administration of affairs. The Burmese, however, little disposed in any event to consider dominion status as an 'ultimate objective', were sharply critical of the protracted procedure contemplated for its attainment. They

---

[1] It was his Communist friends who were chiefly responsible for impressing upon him the evil character of Japanese militarism and for further urging him to help the democratic side without reserve. Cf. ibid. pp. 2–3.

[2] Daw Saw Yin in *Empire*, January 1948. See also the highly personal account written by Nu, *Burma under the Japanese*, pp. 54–97 and Maung Maung, *Burma and the Family of Nations*, pp. 96–101.

[3] Collis, *First and Last in Burma*, provides evidence, supported by selected extracts from official communications, on these points. See especially chs. xxiii, xxvi, and xxxi.

[4] Cmd. 6635 (Mansergh, *Documents*, ii. 760–5).

wished to draft a constitution not after a return however limited in time to direct rule but forthwith. Nor were they mollified by a statement made on 20 October by Mr. Arthur Henderson, the Under-Secretary of State for Burma in the new Labour government, which declared that 'it is the policy and the wish of His Majesty's Government that Burma should attain full self-government within the British Commonwealth at the earliest moment that practical considerations make possible'.[1] While Mr. Henderson was at pains to emphasize that there would be no 'avoidable delay' in implementing this undertaking, there was criticism by almost all sections of opinion in Burma of the vagueness of British policy, and the absence of any time-limit for the achievement of self-government.[2]

The Anti-Fascist People's Freedom League (AFPFL), the most powerful political association in post-war Burma comprising, as it did, not a party but a grouping of all parties united in the demand for independence under the leadership of the youthful Aung San, rejected the White Paper proposals outright and refused to participate in the interim government. This rendered the position of the Governor seeking to implement the policy of the United Kingdom government in association with minority groups and discredited pre-war politicians intolerable—as it was intended to do. Meanwhile the League formulated its demands. At its first all-Burma Congress in January 1946 a resolution was adopted rejecting dominion status 'or any other status within the framework of British imperialism'.[3] 'Burma wants independence', said one of the leaders of the League, 'but Mr. Arthur Henderson has talked only of Dominion status'.[4] By September 1946 when the Governor's Executive Cabinet was reconstituted in order to include representatives of the AFPFL, the Labour government under pressure of circumstances and satisfied that the AFPFL represented, as they claimed, the great majority of the people, began to speak of other and more congenial things.

The desire of His Majesty's Government, said Mr. Attlee on 20 December 1946,

is that the Burmese people should attain their self-government by the quickest and most convenient path possible. . . . In particular, I would repeat, so far as Burma is concerned, what I have already said with regard to India. We do not desire to retain

---

[1] 29 October 1945, H. of C. Deb., vol. 415, col. 26. He was introducing the government's White Paper on Burma.

[2] See for example Burma, Legislative Council Proceedings, 1st session, vol. 1, no. 2, pp. 23, 25, and 37.

[3] *The Times*, 22 January 1946.

[4] Yet in this respect the views of the AFPFL were by no means so definite as some of their declarations might suggest. U Aung San, while maintaining that 'Britain's outlook would have to undergo a radical transformation if the Commonwealth was to be a living and ever developing system', did not exclude the possibility in his own words, that a synthesis might be brought about between the idea of the Commonwealth and the right of every nation to its independence. What he stressed was that the Burmese people must be 'masters of their own country'. Mr. Mackenzie King was, however, equally emphatic about Canadians of theirs.

within the Commonwealth and Empire any unwilling peoples. It is for the people of Burma to decide their own future, but we are certain that it will be to their interest, as it will be to ours, if they decide to remain within the Commonwealth and we sincerely hope that they will arrive at such a decision.

But they were under no compulsion to do so. In order 'to hasten forward the time when Burma shall realise her independence, either within or without the Commonwealth,'[1] Mr. Attlee announced the government's intention to invite representatives of the Executive Council to London for talks with the British government.

The outcome of the meeting between the Prime Minister and the Burmese delegation which took place in London in January 1947 was agreement that elections for a Constituent Assembly should be held in April and understanding at last between the British and Burmese leaders.[2] But while the Burmese were prepared to consider membership of the Commonwealth (renamed—they suggested—a 'United Commonwealth of Nations'), they wanted not traditional dominion status but something akin to external association about the nature of which they made inquiries in Dublin. They received no encouragement in this regard in London, principally for fear of prejudicing discussions about the nature of India's future relations with the Commonwealth, while they themselves misunderstood Indian intentions, believing that India was committed to secession.[3]

The elections for the Constituent Assembly resulted in the victory of the AFPFL, which won 173 seats out of 210. On 16 June 1947 its leader, Aung San, moved a resolution in the Constituent Assembly declaring that Burma should be an 'Independent Sovereign Republic to be known as the Union of Burma'. The resolution was unanimously adopted by the Assembly. The assassination of Aung San with four of his colleagues in the Executive Council a month later did not qualify the attitude of the Assembly towards Commonwealth membership, and when the draft constitution was approved in September all that remained to complete the process of separation was the enactment of the necessary legislation by the United Kingdom Parliament. For this purpose the Burma Independence Bill was introduced and duly passed.[4] It was declared that Burma was henceforward to be regarded neither as 'forming part of His Majesty's dominions nor entitled to His Majesty's protection'. Of the former association all that survived was a treaty which came into force on

---

[1] H. of C. Deb., vol. 431, col. 2342. Mr. Churchill concluded from this that Burma, too, was to be 'shorn away from the British Crown' and advised that 'that at least is a matter of which notice should be taken . . . even in this period, when we are getting so accustomed and indurated to the process of the decline and fall of the British Empire' (ibid. col. 2351).

[2] On this point see Hugh Tinker, *The Union of Burma* (London, Oxford University Press for RIIA, 1957), p. 22, and see generally ch. i.

[3] See Collis, *First and Last in Burma*, p. 288. He states that the Burmese leaders 'received a shock' when they learned of the Indian decision to remain.

[4] 11 Geo. 6, c. 3 (Mansergh, *Documents*, ii. 779–83).

4 January 1948: it provided for the settlement of outstanding financial questions, for the making of a commercial agreement, and for the reception by the Burmese government of a naval, military, and air force mission from the United Kingdom government.[1]

The impending secession of Burma called forth from the Prime Minister a reassertion of the principles of freedom which inspired the Commonwealth policy of the Labour government.

> The departure from the British family of nations of one of its members [said Mr. Attlee] must be an occasion for deep regret. It was the hope and desire of the Government that the people of Burma would recognise the great advantages which accrue from membership of the Commonwealth—a membership which, as one of the Dominion Prime Ministers said, is not a derogation from independence but an addition to it. But they have decided otherwise. In our view, nations have the right to decide on the nature of their own government. The British Commonwealth of Nations is a free association of peoples, not a collection of subject nations. When, therefore, after due consideration the elected representatives of the people of Burma chose independence, it was, I believe, the duty of His Majesty's Government to take the necessary steps to implement this decision.[2]

Ceylon

While Burma, a country within the British Commonwealth which was never a dominion, was resolving on secession, the island of Ceylon was pursuing its peaceful constitutional advance towards dominion status. At the Asian Conference ardent nationalists from other and less peaceful lands might allude in tones of some condescension to Ceylon's fight for freedom, but the gentlemanly pressure for independence exerted by its conservative nationalist leaders upon Whitehall made up in good sense what it lacked in political passion. As a result Ceylon acquired the status of a dominion of the British Commonwealth without bitterness, by orderly constitutional advance which made the manner of its attainment a source of unfailing satisfaction to British constitutional historians and its status in the academic world that of the model dominion.

Under the 1931 Donoughmore Constitution[3] Ceylon enjoyed representative, but not responsible, Cabinet government. The Constitution, while enabling the Ceylonese leaders to acquire experience in the art of government, did not bring into being a party system, and indeed the form of government it established in itself, quite apart from communal divisions, militated against such a possibility. In practice, moreover, the Constitution accentuated the predominance of the Sinhalese majority in the island, other minorities being

---

[1] Cmd. 7360 (Mansergh, *Documents*, ii. 775–9).
[2] 5 November 1947, H. of C. Deb., vol. 443, coll. 1836–7.
[3] It was based on the Report of the Special (Donoughmore) Commission on the Constitution, Cmd. 3131 of 1928 (extract in Mansergh, *Documents*, ii. 710–14).

largely excluded from office.[1] The offer of dominion status to India in 1942 stimulated Ceylonese politicians to demand an equal advance for Ceylon. They had worked the 'The London County Council' Constitution of 1931, while princely non-co-operation had rendered the central provisions of the Government of India Act, 1935 of no effect; they had co-operated in the war effort, the Indian politicians for the most part had not. Should not they be at least equally rewarded? The case was strong, it was skilfully presented by D. S. Senanayake, and it was in large measure conceded in 1943, though it is to be noted that it was events in India and British endeavours to secure a settlement there that opened the door to constitutional advance in Ceylon.

In 1943 the British government pledged itself to a post-war re-examination of the Ceylon Constitution with a view to the granting to Ceylon 'of full responsible Government under the Crown in all matters of internal civil administration', responsibility for defence and foreign affairs being specifically reserved to the imperial government. But while the framing of the constitution would require 'such examination of detail and such precision of definition as cannot be brought to bear so long as the whole of the energies of the Service and other Departments of His Majesty's Government remain focussed on the successful prosecution of the war', ministers were encouraged to formulate their own constitutional proposals for consideration when the war was over.[2] This concession was psychologically of much importance. Acceptance of any such proposals was made conditional upon their compliance with the conditions laid down in the White Paper and their subsequent approval by three-quarters of the members of the State Council of Ceylon, the second condition being waived later.

The ministers' proposals were submitted in February 1944. The British Government responded in July by appointing a Commission

to examine and discuss any proposals for constitutional reform in the Island which have the object of giving effect to the Declaration of His Majesty's Government on that subject dated the 26th May, 1943; and, after consultation with various interests in the Island, including minority communities, concerned with the subject of constitutional reform, to advise His Majesty's Government on all measures necessary to attain that object.[3]

The appointment of the Commission was viewed with suspicion inasmuch as it seemed likely to reopen the whole question of the constitution and to cause further delay in its enactment.[4] Yet in fact the Commission, under the

[1] For a full account see Jennings, *Commonwealth in Asia*, and also *The Dominion of Ceylon* (London, Stevens, 1952), ch. vi. Sir Ivor Jennings, Vice-Chancellor of the University of Colombo 1941–53, was constitutional adviser to the government of Ceylon at this time and writes with first-hand authority.
[2] Cmd. 6690 (Mansergh, *Documents*, ii. 716–21).
[3] Commission on Constitutional Reform (Soulbury Commission), Cmd. 6677. The terms of reference, recommendations, and the Epilogue are included in Mansergh, *Documents*, ii. 716–21.
[4] Jennings, *The Commonwealth in Asia*, p. 74.

chairmanship of Lord Soulbury, produced a report, written in the classic tradition of British state documents, illuminated with wit, well-grounded in good sense, which in substance approved the ministerial proposals submitted for their consideration.

The recommendations of the Soulbury Report accepted the principle of ministerial responsibility which, in the opinion of the members of the Commission, was essential to parliamentary government. They noted that many of Ceylon's political leaders had been educated in England, absorbed English political ideas, and resented any deviation from responsible government on the English parliamentary model; and while they recognized that the people of Ceylon had not reached the same stage of political development as the people of Britain, 'we think it better to devise a Constitution somewhat in advance of the stage already reached rather than behind it'. Members of the Commission did not doubt that there would be difficulties, but they preferred to place their trust in the power of education and the lessons of experience rather than procrastinate or embark upon constitutional experiments. 'It is easier', commented the Report on that second point with a wisdom greater than that of the Simon Commission some sixteen years earlier,

to propound new constitutional devices and fresh constructive solutions than to foresee the difficulties and disadvantages which they may develop. At all events, in recommending for Ceylon a Constitution on the British pattern, we are recommending a method of government we know something about, a method which is the result of very long experience, which has been tested by trial and error and which works, and, on the whole, works well.

Responsible parliamentary government was to be the prelude to dominion status because 'it is clearly not possible to reach that goal in a single step'.

The recommendations of the Soulbury Report were given effect in the Constitution of 1946.[1] It was not the Constitution of a dominion, but it was so drafted as to provide the basis for one, and in fact with the necessary amendments it became the Constitution of the dominion of Ceylon.[2] In June 1947 the Colonial Secretary, Mr. A. Creech-Jones, stated in the House of Commons that the United Kingdom government was preparing to negotiate with the government of Ceylon for the amendment of the Soulbury Constitution so as to give Ceylon full self-government in external as well as in internal affairs.[3] Accordingly, in November 1947, the Ceylon Independence Bill was introduced in Parliament, and it came into force on 4 February 1948. It was supplemented by agreements on defence and external affairs,[4] which were

---

[1] The Decisions of H.M.G. are to be found in Cmd. 6690 (Mansergh, *Documents*, ii. 721–3) and The Ceylon (Constitution) Order in Council, 1946 (ibid. pp. 723–8).
[2] Mansergh, *Documents*, ii. 723. For a full account of the drafting of the Constitution see Jennings, *Dominion of Ceylon*.
[3] H. of C. Deb., vol. 438, coll. 2015–17 (Mansergh, *Documents*, ii. 748–9).
[4] Cmd. 7257 (ibid. pp. 749–50).

signed on 11 November 1947. The agreement on defence between the two governments, terminated in 1956, made provision for 'such military assistance for the security of their territories, for defence against external aggression and for the protection of essential communications as it may be in their mutual interest to provide', and also permitted the United Kingdom to base naval and air forces and to maintain such land forces in Ceylon as might be mutually agreed as being necessary for the island's security. In the agreement on external affairs the government of Ceylon undertook to adopt and follow the resolutions of the past Imperial Conferences and to observe the accepted principles and practice of Commonwealth consultation. For its part the United Kingdom government undertook to support Ceylon's application for membership of the United Nations, which was not in fact secured till 1956 because of Soviet opposition.

The general significance of Ceylon's advance from colonial to dominion status was thought to be far-reaching. 'This is the first occasion in our history', said Lord Addison, the Lord Privy Seal and a former Dominions Secretary, in introducing the second reading of the Ceylon Independence Bill in the House of Lords on 4 December 1947, 'upon which a Colony, developing this system of self-government of its own accord, has deliberately sought to become a Dominion State in our Commonwealth . . . but we hope and expect it will not be the last.'[1] Encouraging, however, though the implication of Ceylonese membership might be to the government of the United Kingdom, it was on the decision of India and Pakistan that the significance of the Commonwealth in Asia ultimately depended. Would they follow the precedent set by Burma or the example of Ceylon?

India: A Republic Within the Commonwealth

The Meeting of Commonwealth Prime Ministers in London in October 1948 was a notable event in the history of the Commonwealth because, for the first time, the three new dominions of Asia sent representatives to such a gathering. But if this Meeting was the outward sign of the new phase in Commonwealth relations, a phase in which non-British and non-European peoples were to contribute as equals to discussions which went far to determine the character of the policies of individual Commonwealth governments, the form of their relationship was not discussed in full session at all. On the contrary, the conference concerned itself with questions of defence, security, and economic development,[2] and, though discussions about the Irish repeal of the External Relations Act irrupted on to the stage at the time that the Prime Ministers were meeting in London, the tacit agreement to leave constitutional questions affecting the Asian dominions on one side remained

---
[1] The Ceylon Independence Act (11 Geo. 6, ch. 7) together with an extract from Lord Addison's speech, H. of L. Deb., vol. 152, coll. 1204–6, are reprinted in Mansergh, *Documents*, ii. 756–8.   [2] The final communiqué is reprinted in ibid. pp. 1137–8.

unaltered. These Fabian tactics enabled the Prime Ministers of the Asian dominions to judge the value of Commonwealth consultation in the light of their personal experience before recommending any final decisions about their countries' membership, for it was felt that only by participation in the councils of the Commonwealth at the highest level might misapprehensions be dispelled and understanding of its working be acquired.[1]

There was evidence of a more favourable attitude to Commonwealth membership on the part of the political leaders of Pakistan and India at the end of the Prime Ministers' Meeting. Since India, Pakistan, and Ceylon 'have come into the Commonwealth', said Liaqat Ali Khan, the Prime Minister of Pakistan, 'its complexion has changed—now it is a Commonwealth of free nations who believe in the same way of life and in the same democracy. To my mind, these ideas are even stronger than racial ties.' In judicious phrases the Congress, meeting on 18 December 1948 at Jaipur, foreshadowed the coming rapprochement between India and the Commonwealth by resolving that

In view of the attainment of complete independence and the establishment of the Republic of India which will symbolise Independence and give to India the status among the nations of the world that is her rightful due, her present association with the United Kingdom and the Commonwealth of Nations will necessarily have to change. India, however, desires to maintain all such links with other countries as do not come in the way of her freedom of action and independence and the Congress would welcome her free association with independent nations of the Commonwealth for their common welfare and the promotion of world peace.[2]

The Jaipur Resolution, however, in reflecting the more sympathetic attitude of the Congress to Commonwealth membership, implicitly posed a problem which Commonwealth statesmen had now to resolve. It was a republican India that contemplated continued association with the Commonwealth. There was no presumption that India could or should renounce republicanism for membership. The question was, could the two be reconciled? The problem was, however, distinct in certain important respects from that which had been raised by Irish nationalists a quarter of a century earlier. India already had a dominion constitution, as Ireland had not; she was about to adopt a republican constitution from which the Irish Free State had been debarred by the threat of force, and she expressed a positive wish to co-operate as a full member with the other countries of the Commonwealth, whereas Ireland had sought only to be externally associated with them. The Indian request, however,

---

[1] The Prime Minister of India's conversation with Mr. Mackenzie King, the elder statesman of the overseas Commonwealth, on a sick bed on a last visit to London has been invested with dramatic significance by some commentators. They would seem to have allowed their imaginations to outrun the facts.

[2] Quoted by Pandit Nehru in speech to the Indian Constituent Assembly on 16 May 1949 (Mansergh, *Documents*, ii. 850).

contemplated the greater modification in the Commonwealth system inasmuch as its acceptance would involve the waiving of one of the hitherto essential conditions of membership, whereas the Irish envisaged no such change in the system but the addition to it of the distinct and external category of associated republic.

The Commonwealth Prime Ministers, including those of the three new dominions in Asia, met again in April 1949 to determine the issue after emissaries dispatched from London had held preliminary discussions in all Commonwealth capitals. Agreement was reached in the short period of six days. This was in itself a considerable achievement. The text of the communiqué issued at the conclusion of the Meeting tells best its own story:

During the past week the Prime Ministers of the United Kingdom, Australia, New Zealand, South Africa, India, Pakistan and Ceylon, and the Canadian Secretary of State for External Affairs have met in London to exchange views upon the important constitutional issues arising from India's decision to adopt a republican form of constitution and her desire to continue her membership of the Commonwealth.

The discussions have been concerned with the effects of such a development upon the existing structure of the Commonwealth and the constitutional relations between its members. They have been conducted in an atmosphere of goodwill and mutual understanding, and have had as their historical background the traditional capacity of the Commonwealth to strengthen its unity of purpose, while adapting its organization and procedures to changing circumstances.

After full discussion the representatives of the Governments of all the Commonwealth countries have agreed that the conclusions reached should be placed on record in the following declaration:

'The Governments of the United Kingdom, Canada, Australia, New Zealand, South Africa, India, Pakistan and Ceylon, whose countries are united as Members of the British Commonwealth of Nations and owe a common allegiance to the Crown, which is also the symbol of their free association, have considered the impending constitutional changes in India.

'The Government of India has informed the other Governments of the Commonwealth of the intention of the Indian people that under the new constitution which is about to be adopted India shall become a sovereign independent republic. The Government of India have however declared and affirmed India's desire to continue her full membership of the Commonwealth of Nations and her acceptance of The King as the symbol of the free association of its independent member nations and as such the Head of the Commonwealth.

'The Governments of the other countries of the Commonwealth, the basis of whose membership of the Commonwealth is not hereby changed, accept and recognize India's continuing membership in accordance with the terms of this declaration.

'Accordingly the United Kingdom, Canada, Australia, New Zealand, South Africa, India, Pakistan and Ceylon hereby declare that they remain united as free and equal members of the Commonwealth of Nations, freely co-operating in the pursuit of peace, liberty and progress.'

These constitutional questions have been the sole subject of discussion at the full meetings of Prime Ministers.[1]

The settlement reached, it will be noted, was specific, not general, in application. There was no decision that a republic, as such, could be a full member of the Commonwealth. The Meeting simply recorded that when India, under her new Constitution, became a sovereign independent republic, she would remain in accordance with her own wishes a full member of the Commonwealth and would acknowledge the King as a symbol of the free association of its independent member nations; and, as such, the Head of the Commonwealth. The Indian Republic, therefore, would owe no allegiance to the Crown and the monarch would have no place in its government.

There is a reference [Pandit Nehru explained to the Indian Constituent Assembly later] in connexion with the Commonwealth, to the King as the symbol of that association. Observe that the reference is to the King and not to the Crown. It is a small matter, but it has a certain significance. But the point is this, that in so far as the Republic of India is concerned, ... she has nothing to do with any external authority, with any king, and none of her subjects owe any allegiance to the King or any other external authority.[2]

It is in this respect, however, that the settlement involved a notable departure from the doctrine embodied in the Preamble to the Statute of Westminster in which the members of the Commonwealth were said to be 'united by a common allegiance to the Crown'. Republicanism, which in the past both in Ireland and in South Africa had been regarded as synonymous with secession, was thereby accepted as compatible with full membership. It was maintained that this compatibility extended only to the case of India, and that one exception did not constitute a category and did not modify the general conditions of Commonwealth membership. In 1955 and 1956 it was, however, agreed that Pakistan and Ceylon respectively should continue their membership on the same basis, and the root principle of equality governing intra-Commonwealth relations predicated that this should be so.

At first sight the Indian constitutional settlement seemed almost metaphysical in its refinement. It had, however, the merit of going a long way towards reconciling constitutional forms with political realities. In the older dominions, which were predominantly British in extraction, loyalty to the Crown had been a unifying force of transcendent value. For them the constitutional position remained unchanged. King George VI remained King of Canada, King of New Zealand, as he remained King of the United Kingdom. But in the case of India differences in race, in culture, and in recent experience suggested that other forms would be more appropriate, and the republican symbolism preferred by the Indian Constituent Assembly was

[1] Mansergh, *Documents*, ii. 846–7.
[2] India, Constituent Assembly Deb., vol. 8, pp. 2–10 (ibid. p. 847).

ASIAN MEMBERSHIP OF THE COMMONWEALTH

accepted by other members of the Commonwealth in April 1949 as compatible with membership.

There could be little question in London in April 1949 of the broad political advantages of the solution reached. The Commonwealth extended its frontiers beyond the circle of self-governing European peoples of European origin, and in so doing, it assumed an international[1] character—to which in the past it could pretend only with some qualification—for the successful outcome of the London Meeting implied that the association of Asian peoples with the older dominions, predominantly European in stock, might be not an episode but a continuing factor in its history. In this respect the use of the term 'Commonwealth of Nations' in the later paragraphs of the communiqué for 'British Commonwealth of Nations' which appeared in the first, though it marked no formal change in terminology, faithfully reflected a change in composition and outlook.

In India the Constituent Assembly endorsed the settlement reached in London with only one dissentient voice. This did not fairly reflect the balance of opinion within India, for the settlement was criticized by Socialists as well as by Communists both then and later. It was in fact Pandit Nehru's persuasive appeal[2] to the Indian Constituent Assembly, where the great majority continued to associate independence with secession, which proved decisive. In it he recalled the pledges, the thoughts, and the aspirations of the past and sought conscientiously to reconcile membership of the Commonwealth with them.

We join the Commonwealth [he said] obviously because we think it is beneficial to us and to certain causes in the world that we wish to advance. The other countries of the Commonwealth wish us to remain, because they think it is beneficial to them. ... In the world today where there are so many disruptive forces at work, where we are often on the verge of war, I think it is not a safe thing to encourage the breaking up of any association that one has ... it is better to keep a co-operative association going which may do good in this world rather than break it.

But membership, he argued, did not mean the abandonment of past ideals, any lessening of the desire for closer association with neighbouring Asian countries, any compromise in the struggle against racial discrimination and for the freedom of suppressed nationalities. He admitted that he was 'a bad bargainer', that he was not used 'to the ways of the market place', and that he had thought it, in London, 'far more precious to come to a decision in friendship and goodwill rather than to gain a word here and there at the cost of ill will', and he added 'the fact that we have begun this new type of association with a touch of healing will be good for us, good for them, and I think,

---

[1] At the Imperial War Conference in 1917, General Smuts, it is true, spoke of the British Empire as the only successful experiment in international government that had ever been tried, but the test, it must be conceded, was also less exacting at that time than in any other such experiment. [2] In the speech referred to on p. 252 above.

good for the world'. Here in the light of the recent past was magnanimity as well as statesmanship, and the Prime Ministers of the Commonwealth responded to it with imaginative understanding.

The Indian Prime Minister thought in terms of 'a new type of association'. Members of Commonwealth governments, while almost uniformly regretting India's decision to adopt a republican constitution, welcomed this new type of association as evidence of the flexibility of the Commonwealth and its capacity to meet changing circumstances.[1] The principal critics of the London Declaration were, therefore, to be found among those who had no desire to modify the old relationship. Mr. Winston Churchill was not to be numbered with them. To the surprise of many[2] the author of many challenging, even boisterous, criticisms of Indian independence in the past acclaimed the new settlement. He conceived that it did not lower but rather elevated the status of the Crown by investing the monarch with the new, symbolic but meaningful designation of 'Head of the Commonwealth', and always sensible of the magnanimous in politics, his heart was warmed by the thought that Indian leaders who had been imprisoned for many years, and recently at his direction, should have desired India's continuing membership of the Commonwealth.[3] Perhaps indeed he remembered the time, some forty-three years earlier, when as Under-Secretary of State for the Colonies he had defended the restoration of self-government to the defeated Boer republics against Mr. Balfour's sweeping criticism, and recalled that Campbell-Bannerman's magnanimous gesture had converted some of the outstanding Boer guerrilla leaders into staunch upholders of the British Commonwealth.[4] One of these survived to be the principal statesman within the Commonwealth to criticize the London Declaration.

General Smuts, defeated in the South African general election of 1948, was concerned first to underline that the London Declaration affected only the position of India and marked therefore 'no revolutionary departure', because 'for the rest the position remains as it was'.[5] In the London Declaration, as in the Statute of Westminster, there was a dual foundation to the Commonwealth: there was the 'free association of which the King ìs the symbol, and there is the common allegiance to the Crown'. An Indian republic would owe no allegiance, but with that exception 'there is no change whatever' and 'all that has happened . . . is to accommodate India into this system on an exceptional basis'. He recognized the weight of the strategic, economic, and political arguments in favour of giving India an exceptional position which

---

[1] Speeches of ministers in all Commonwealth countries commenting on the 1949 Declaration are included in Mansergh, *Documents*, ii. 847–75.
[2] Mr. Menzies, it is supposed, among them.
[3] See H. of C. Deb., vol. 464, coll. 371–4.
[4] Mr. Churchill was much moved on his first meeting with Pandit Nehru which took place after the 1949 Meeting.
[5] South Africa, H. of A. Deb., vol. 68, coll. 5565–9 (Mansergh, *Documents*, ii. 871–4).

would keep her within the Commonwealth. But they did not quiet his own anxieties: 'The King is something of a reality in our system, even if he does not exercise functions', and he was such a reality because of 'this common allegiance which the rest of us have retained'. With the breach in common allegiance there was a risk that the Commonwealth might become something merely symbolic, something which 'is merely a matter of language and has nothing behind it', with the result that the British Commonwealth might indeed live on but, like the Holy Roman Empire, merely as a name for hundreds of years after it had ceased to exist.

General Smuts's argument, addressed immediately to the republican Nationalist government which supplanted him in office, commands respect. His criticisms were seemingly more firmly grounded than Mr. Churchill's acclaim, for surely he was right in thinking that this political arrangement reflected a weakening, not a strengthening, of the position of the Crown in the Commonwealth. If the first concern had been to safeguard the position of the Crown and at the same time to maintain India's ties with the Commonwealth, the solution to be aimed at was external association on the Irish model. It is far from clear that either the Commonwealth governments or the many who acclaimed the London Declaration, in the belief that it preserved unimpaired, or even elevated, the position of the Crown, understood this. The root principle of the Commonwealth was equality. If one member, adopting a republican constitution, acquired membership on that basis, then, by virtue of that root principle of equality, all could do so. The way was, therefore, opened for a renunciation of allegiance on the part of other members of the Commonwealth and the enactment of republican constitutions without loss of membership. Unquestionably there were great advantages in this, chief among them being the removal of a barrier which had hitherto been interposed between republicanism and membership and which by its existence in the past had limited the appeal of the Commonwealth largely to peoples of British extraction.[1] It would have been an act not of statesmanship but of constitutional obscurantism with incalculable consequences for the future of the Commonwealth in Africa as well as in Asia to have rejected India's request for continuing membership in 1949 and thus to have sacrificed the unity of the Commonwealth to the symbol of that unity.[2] But while in principle the settlement would seem to have been well designed to meet a particular situation, it does not necessarily follow that it was well judged in every particular. India's relations with the Commonwealth inevitably would possess a character different from those of older European members, yet in defining the basis of the relationship in each instance as full membership there

---

[1] Cf. an article of much insight entitled 'Ireland and the British Commonwealth, 1931–7, by Professor James Hogan of University College, Cork, in *Ireland Today*, October 1937.

[2] The speech made by King George VI in welcoming the Commonwealth Prime Ministers in October 1948 suggested that he had no wish for such a sacrifice to be made (*The Times*, 15 October 1948).

was a tendency to underline similarities and to overlook differences. From this in turn there followed criticism, often founded in a deficient sense of political realities, when India as a full member did not conform to a pattern of behaviour associated with full membership. While obviously there was no difference in status, since all alike were independent, sovereign states, there was a difference in relationship which was expressed only in part in the 1949 formula. In this respect, therefore, it may be suggested that the formula, while statesmanlike in its main purposes, did not sufficiently relate constitutional forms to political realities.[1] Indian leaders, however, were more concerned to avoid any suggestion of inferiority in status, while those of older members were most anxious to minimize the apparent breach with the past.

Co-operation Without, Discord Within

The London Declaration of 1949 marked the climax to an important phase in British imperial policy in Asia. Its principal characteristic had been the granting to Asian peoples, formerly under British rule, of full freedom to determine their own destiny. India, Ceylon, Pakistan after a protracted period spent in the framing of its constitution, and Malaya decided to exercise that freedom to remain within the Commonwealth, Burma alone seceding. At root British policy was founded on the conviction that nationalism was the dominant force in Asia after the Second World War and that, contrary to past belief, this was not incompatible with the conception of a Commonwealth of free and equal nations but rather, on the contrary, that national states might find a congenial home within such a Commonwealth and might contribute much to its influence in promoting peace and goodwill among peoples of different racial origin. Commonwealth membership was acceptable on this interpretation to the majority of the newly independent peoples of South Asia because they were at last convinced that membership was a matter for them alone to decide and that it left their freedom of action wholly unimpaired. It was only because they were so convinced that the experiment of a Commonwealth in Asia could be undertaken.[2] It laboured at the outset under many

---

[1] The author's views were set out in a lecture entitled 'The Implications of Eire's Relations with the British Commonwealth of Nations' in October 1948 and reprinted in *The Commonwealth and the Nations*. The arguments against a treaty relationship were put by Dr. Malan in the South African House of Assembly (see p. 254 above) and carry conviction unless indeed the treaty was to be phrased in general terms imposing no specific obligations of a kind unwelcome alike to India and South Africa. K. M. Panikkar in *The Basis of an Indo-British Treaty* (New Delhi, Indian Council of World Affairs) had earlier discussed the possibility of a bilateral Anglo-Indian treaty.

[2] The secession of Burma afforded conclusive evidence that the Commonwealth at that time desired no unwilling members. It was so accepted, among other places, in the United States where the suggestion was made to the author after a meeting in New York that the secession was not the considered choice of the Burmese but the result of the deliberate policy of a British Labour government resolved to demonstrate to the world at large, and the United States in particular, that there was full freedom to secede.

liabilities and grievous problems, many of them inseparable from the transition from imperial to national rule, but with one outstanding asset. It was the governments and peoples of South Asia who decided that the experiment should be attempted. It was not, therefore, something imposed from above or without, but something inspired from within, and as a result, despite some misunderstandings, the relations between the older and the newer Asian members of the Commonwealth, South Africa always excepted, were conducted in an atmosphere of friendship and goodwill. The graver problems accordingly came not from without but from within.

Asian membership of the Commonwealth was related to tensions between India and Ceylon and India and Pakistan. In so far as Commonwealth membership was a reinsurance against more powerful neighbours, Ceylon placed high value upon it. Her strategic position in the Indian Ocean was at once an international asset and an international liability, for it prompted the sympathetic interest of those who wished to preserve the independence of South Asian states in the security and well-being of the island and at the same time attracted the attention of potential aggressors in the area. With the complete defeat of the Japanese in 1945 the principal anxiety of the Ceylon government was not aggression but the submersion of the Sinhalese by the multiplication of Indians within the island and the further immigration of Indians from South India. The preservation of power in Sinhalese hands by the restriction of voting rights and control of immigration were the means adopted to achieve this end and their equity was questioned in Delhi. In discussions which were at times acrimonious the government of Ceylon maintained its position, sensing that membership of the Commonwealth enabled it to treat with its formidable mainland neighbour on a basis of near equality. Since the Indian government in any event showed little disposition to force the issue, relations between the two governments were not seriously strained. It was far otherwise in respect of India and Pakistan.

Few anticipated that the partition of India could be brought about without suffering and turmoil. The slaughter in the Punjab that followed partition and the plight of refugees crowded by the thousand in improvised shelters along the streets of Calcutta or out into the desert that circled Karachi as far as the eye could see, was a continuing reminder of it, stirring the anger of those who had not themselves suffered. In such an atmosphere it was not easy for governments responsive to the popular will and to popular passion to exercise restraint, the more so since they too, and especially the government of Pakistan, were shadowed not only by memories of the past but by fears for the future.

The root cause of Indo-Pakistani tension in the years that followed partition, of which disputes about division of goods and services between the two governments, the vehement denunciation of Sir Cyril Radcliffe's boundary award in Pakistan,[1] and the destiny of Hyderabad, Junagadh, and above all Kashmir were no more than symptoms, was the acceptance on either side of irreconcilable interpretations of the causes of partition. To the Indian National Congress and to most Hindus this unnatural vivisection of Mother India was brought about, whether deliberately or otherwise was irrelevant, by imperial policies. British imperialists, said Mr. Nehru in the Indian general election campaign of 1957, 'sowed disunity among the Hindus and Moslems. . . . The result of this policy was the creation of Pakistan.'[2] But in Pakistan the British by implication were absolved from all such responsibility, for the state was deemed there to have come into being to protect and preserve the way of life of the Muslims of India, a people of a different culture, of a different faith, even of a different civilization from the Hindu majority in India. It was not easy in the light of the views they entertained for the Hindus to reconcile themselves to the existence of what they professed to regard as an artificially created communal state carved out of their historic homeland, or for the Muslims, despite the attainment of their goal of a separate state, not to feel that eternal vigilance was the condition of its survival. Moreover, the differences of view as to the root cause of partition had a continuing importance in respect of those Princely States whose future had not been finally determined by 15 August 1947. For the Indian government to concede that community should determine allegiance or frontiers would be to abandon the past pretensions of the Congress to speak for all India and to undermine the foundation of a secular state, which comprised many distinct communities, while the government of Pakistan, consistent with the past claims of the Muslim League, could not but maintain that community and frontier so far as possible should coincide, for to allow otherwise was to question the *raison d'être* of Pakistan itself. It was in no small degree because the future of Kashmir raised in acute form these fundamental differences in historical interpretation and outlook that it became the occasion of prolonged dispute between these two members of the Commonwealth.

There was agreement between the Congress, the League, and the British government that the final decision in respect of the accession or non-accession of the Princely States to either dominion should rest in the hands of their rulers.[3] This was an arrangement in which the Congress leaders had acquiesced with extreme reluctance, for it was their view that not the princes but the people of the states should determine their future, and it was only because it was deemed impracticable to arrange for a popular verdict in states where there had been no experience of the democratic process, and hence no machinery for ascertaining it, that their assent to this procedure was secured.

---

[1] It was stigmatized by Ministers as 'disgusting', 'abominable', and 'one-sided'; by *Dawn* as tantamount to the territorial murder of Pakistan which by its character absolved the government from its prior undertaking to accept it.

[2] *New York Times*, 22 February 1957.   [3] See above, pp. 236–7.

ASIAN MEMBERSHIP OF THE COMMONWEALTH

The leaders of the Muslim League, by contrast, underlined the authority of the princes, to whom they were traditionally more sympathetically disposed, and both Liaqat Ali Khan and Jinnah advised the princes in the strongest terms not to allow themselves to be hustled by the Congress or the Viceroy into making hasty or premature decisions.[1] The Muslim leaders, prompted, in part at least, by a desire to see India weakened by the continued quasi-autonomous existence of such states within her territory, in this would seem on the longer view to have misjudged their own interests. It was all-important for both successor states, in the light of the foreseeable, and foreseen, tensions that would follow partition, to remove uncertainties about the disposition of the states while the third party, the British, remained. It was particularly important in the case of Kashmir which, as has already been noted, had a common frontier with both dominions, a Hindu ruler and a Muslim majority population, and occupied a position of high strategic importance.

There was consistency neither in the Indian nor in the Pakistani arguments in respect of Kashmir, and, indeed, the complexities of the problems raised were such that this was hardly possible.[2] On 31 May 1947 Gandhi, consistent with the Congress view, said that in a free India they would have not princely raj but *panchayat* raj,[3] and that therefore in Kashmir it was not the Maharaja with his soldiery that would count but the Muslims who were the vast majority there. The same thing, he said, applied in Hyderabad and Bhopal.[4] Yet self-determination, in the atmosphere of the time, meant almost certainly decision on the basis of community. Was not this in practice, therefore, conceding the case for a state on communal lines? India's forceful action in Hyderabad, where a Hindu majority state was ruled by a Mohammedan Nizam with the aid of his Muslim *razakars*, and in Junagadh, a small predominantly Hindu state whose ruler acceded to Pakistan, was in principle, if not in method, reconcilable with Indian insistence on popular decision, for it was assuredly thus in each instance that the people would have decided. Indian policy remained outwardly at least consistent after tribal invasions of Kashmir, facilitated by Pakistan, finally persuaded a fickle and unworthy prince to accede to India; for while there was acceptance of the accession there was an assurance, albeit contingent on withdrawal of the invaders, that there would be a plebiscite. It was, however, the Indian leaders who were well placed to denounce the fickleness and irresponsibility of princes by which in this instance

[1] See Lumby, *Transfer of Power*, p. 233 and Menon, *Integration of Indian States*, p. 87.
[2] It would be out of place to give a detailed account of the course of this continuing dispute in this volume. For an authoritative account from an Indian standpoint see Menon, *Integration of Indian States*, ch. xx; from the British, Campbell-Johnson, *Mission with Mountbatten*, pp. 223–42; from the Pakistani the statement by the Hon. Mr. Liaqat Ali Khan on 'Kashmir and Inter-Dominion Disputes' on 19 January 1950 in the Pakistan Constituent Assembly and reprinted under this title by the Publications Department of the government of Pakistan. See also Mansergh, *Documents*, ii. 901–8 for speeches by Sir Muhammad Zafrulla Khan and Sir Benegal Rau at the Security Council in February 1950.
[3] Village council rule.
[4] Tendulkar, *Mahatma*, vii. 486.

they had so greatly profited, while Pakistani leaders who had sought to sustain princely authority, had now lost Kashmir by its arbitrary exercise.

The Kashmir situation, as seen by Sir Owen Dixon, the author of the most penetrating of the United Nations Reports upon it, in 1950

presented strange features. The parties had agreed that the fate of the State as a whole should be settled by a general plebiscite, but over a considerable period of time they had failed to agree on any of the preliminary measures which it was clearly necessary to take before it was possible to set up an organization to take a plebiscite.[1]

In the Indian view one necessary preliminary to the holding of a plebiscite was the withdrawal of all Pakistani forces, on the ground that in Kashmir Pakistan was an aggressor. Sir Owen Dixon was prepared to adopt the view that when the frontier of the state of Jammu and Kashmir was crossed on 20 October 1947 by hostile elements it was contrary to international law, and that the later movement of Pakistani forces into the state, in May 1948, was also inconsistent with international law. But while, and for this reason, he contemplated the earlier withdrawal of Pakistani troops, he considered that it was also necessary for Indian forces to be withdrawn on their side of the cease-fire line to secure the demilitarization of the whole of Kashmir and a free plebiscite.

Sir Owen Dixon's proposals for a phased withdrawal, like other and later proposals, foundered on Indian objections to all the particular suggestions that were made. With the passage of time other elements entered into an already complex dispute and Herr Jarring in 1957 was confronted, as Sir Owen Dixon had not been, with a situation which had not only dangerously crystallized but was merging increasingly with international and defence questions affecting the whole of South-East Asia. 'I could not', wrote this later United Nations Mediator,[2] 'fail to take note of the concern expressed in connexion with the changing political, economic and strategic factors surrounding the whole of the Kashmir question, together with the changing pattern of power relations in West and South Asia.' It was with foreboding that he concluded his report on a situation which 'has become progressively more difficult'.

The Kashmir dispute gravely weakened the Commonwealth in Asia, by making impossible intra-Commonwealth co-operation between the two principal members of it and by confronting existing members, reluctant to be drawn into the quarrel, with painful decisions at the United Nations and elsewhere. Despite Pakistani pressure for an award by a Commonwealth tribunal, the other governments of the Commonwealth, mindful of earlier

[1] Security Council, *Official Records*, 5th year, supplements, S/1791.
[2] Report on the Indian–Pakistan Question submitted in pursuance of the Resolution of the Security Council of 21 February 1957 (S/3821).

experience especially in respect of Anglo-Irish economic differences, were agreed that no such tribunal should be constituted save at the wish of both parties to the dispute. From India no such request was forthcoming. As in the past, the Congress had maintained that disputes between the principal communities in India were domestic disputes to be resolved by the Indian people themselves, so they maintained, despite partition, that the Kashmir dispute was a domestic dispute to be resolved within the subcontinent. This was not a doctrine, however remote its earliest enunciation, which made any strong appeal to the weaker party, which sought by contrast not to exclude other members of the Commonwealth but to draw them into the dispute. In this it was not altogether unsuccessful.

The Kashmir dispute emphasized what divided and obscured what united the two new dominions of the Indian subcontinent. In that respect it imperilled the security, weakened the economy, and diminished the external influence of both, India in particular damaging her international prestige by her clear resolve not to risk what had been gained by formal accession out of regard for assurances then given. Yet more significant even than a dispute of such far-reaching implications and unfortunate consequences was the fact that there had emerged in the Indian subcontinent two states of world importance, forming part of the Commonwealth of Nations. Independence to which they had aspired so long was theirs at last. The world awaited with interest the use that they would make of it.

> To Mecca hast thou turned in prayer
>   With aching heart and eyes that burn:
> Oh, Hajji, whither wilt thou turn
>   When thou art there, when thou art there?

CHAPTER VI

IRELAND: EXTERNAL ASSOCIATION, THE REPUBLIC AND SECESSION

External Association

IN the Constitution of 1937 no description was given to the independent sovereign state whose effective jurisdiction covered twenty-six of the thirty-two counties of Ireland. The omission was deliberate. Mr. de Valera explained in 1945 to the Annual Conference of the Fianna Fáil party that while the state was a 'sovereign, independent republic, unfortunately it did not cover the whole of Ireland', and for that reason he had not introduced into the Constitution 'the name of Poblacht na h'Éireann because that was a name which was sacred'. The words Poblacht na h'Éireann, or Republic of Ireland, he observed in the Dáil[1] the following year, were omitted from the Constitution 'simply because those words had a historical association with the country as a whole, when the Republic was declared here in 1919', and the name of the republic was sacred because the martyrs of 1916 had died for an all-Ireland republic. Fundamental to them and to their successors had been the conception of an inalienable national sovereignty over the whole island which, though in abeyance during centuries of alien rule, had remained in being independent of law, government, or administration. It represented a political reality which even by their own volition the Irish people could not destroy, for, in the language of Rousseau, even the people by the expression of its general will could not divest itself of the sovereignty which resided in it, and in the language of Mr. de Valera, even the people had no right to do wrong. It was thus a conception which was invested with an emotional and moral sanction so all-pervasive that any compromise or seeming subtraction from absolute sovereignty came to be regarded as a betrayal of the national cause.

Between the idea of a fundamental national sovereignty and the republican form of polity there was a close association which was the product of history and the lasting outcome of the 1916 rebellion. The dramatic appeal of the republic might have lessened with the passing of the years, but essentially the republic remained beyond all dispute or question the political ideal of nationalist Ireland. It was because Mr. de Valera was regarded as one of its principal architects and its most faithful champion that his political position remained for so long unassailable. When, therefore, he decided in 1937 that the republic should not be formally proclaimed while partition endured, he

[1] 19 June 1946, Dáil Deb., vol. 101, col. 2248.

was embarking on a course that nationalist opinion was prepared to follow, for the majority, too, had always conceived of the republic as an all-Irish republic. A republic for the twenty-six counties might prove politically desirable, but ideally it would be a shoddy make-believe which might, by its very existence, weaken the urge to unity.

When the Constitution of 1937 was introduced, Mr. de Valera claimed that not one comma of it would need to be altered if a republic were to be declared the next day,[1] thereby implying that it would not be necessary to introduce into the Constitution a formal description of the state. For such reticence the American Constitution afforded an honoured precedent. Moreover, in terms of political expediency, silence was golden. In 1937 the proclamation of the republic would have been regarded as a provocative act in Britain, though less certainly in the Commonwealth overseas, while everywhere it would have been interpreted as tantamount to secession. Therefore, over and above Mr. de Valera's own personal predilections, the dictates of political prudence counselled ambiguity.

The lack of a description of the state in the Constitution in itself in no way affected its character. The state, said Mr. de Valera in 1937, 'is a sovereign independent republic'. The form of government was in fact republican. It was only when the Constitution was interpreted with particular relation to the External Relations Act[2] which had been passed a year earlier that any question of allegiance to the Crown, however oblique, was introduced. Mr. de Valera insisted that, since the External Relations Act was not a constitutional law but an ordinary legislative enactment, permissive in character and open to repeal by the ordinary process of legislation, it was not to be regarded as part of the fundamental law of the state.[3] It was no more than an enabling act permitting the carrying out of the external policies of the state in a way provided for in Article 29[4] of the Constitution, and in so far as it conflicted with the Constitution or any provision of it it was null and void. As Mr. de Valera remarked with satisfaction, the Constitution made no change in respect of the conduct of foreign affairs except that it put 'the question of our international relations in their proper place—and that is outside the Constitution'.[5]

Mr. de Valera allowed that the arrangement made in the External Relations Act was unique. But then, he argued, the situation it was designed to fit was

[1] See Mansergh, *Survey, 1931–9*, p. 299.
[2] Executive Authority (External Relations) Act, 1936 (Mansergh, *Documents*, i. 321–2).
[3] See Mansergh, *Survey, 1931–9*, pp. 288–96.
[4] Section 4, sub-section 2 of Art. 29 provided: 'For the purpose of the exercise of any executive function of the State in or in connection with its external relations, the Government may, to such extent and subject to such conditions, if any, as may be determined by law, avail of or adopt any organ, instrument, or method of procedure used or adopted for the like purpose by the members of any group or league of nations with which the State is or becomes associated for the purpose of international co-operation in matters of common concern.'
[5] Dáil Deb., vol. 67, col. 60.

also unique.¹ On the one hand popular sovereignty and republican institutions combined to preclude membership of the British Commonwealth in its traditional form, on the other the existence of partition was then felt to preclude outright secession. Neither, however, constituted a barrier against association with the British Commonwealth from without. Such external association implied no retreat from national sovereignty, nor did it involve allegiance to the Crown, but equally it brought about no severance of Commonwealth ties such as might well have finally estranged majority opinion in Northern Ireland. It is true that Mr. de Valera did not conceive, as some of his critics from time to time suggested he did, that external association would in itself incline opinion in Northern Ireland towards unity. He laboured under no such illusion. On the contrary he recognized, as a political fact with which of necessity he had to reckon, the loyalty of the majority within the six counties to Crown and Commonwealth, and he felt that continued Irish association with the Northern Unionists in a form consistent with national sovereignty was a concession properly to be made by the majority to minority opinion.

In dealing with this question of Partition, . . . [said Mr. de Valera in 1947] the problem is how far ought the people in this part of Ireland [to] go to meet the views of the people in the other part so that there will be agreement both here and in the North? I believe that the Constitution as we have it, . . . as well as our association with the States of the British Commonwealth in the form in which it is at the moment, is the farthest that you can go to meet the views in the North and at the same time get agreement here.²

In a certain sense Mr. de Valera was a Commonwealth statesman. At first sight this seems a strangely paradoxical statement. Yet in moments of crisis such as occurred during the war, his first thought was to obtain the goodwill and the good offices of Commonwealth governments overseas. Moreover, despite his academic cast of mind, he shared the misgivings of Commonwealth statesmen about attempts to define too closely the difficult, imponderable questions of politics. Where, however, they customarily relied upon the authority of Edmund Burke, an Irishman, he, when challenged by his critics to be precise about Eire's external relations, defended his reluctance to do so by quoting the dictum of Joseph de Maistre to the effect that 'in all political systems there are relationships which it is wiser to leave undefined'.³ He regarded Ireland's association with the Commonwealth as peculiarly such a relationship. When the governments of the Commonwealth declared on 24 December 1937⁴ that they were prepared to treat the new Irish Constitution as not effecting a fundamental alteration in the position of the Irish Free State as a member of the British Commonwealth of Nations, he did not feel

[1] Dáil Deb., vol. 97, col. 2573 (Mansergh, *Documents*, ii. 765–6).
[2] Dáil Deb., vol. 107, col. 86 (ibid. p. 797). See also his remarks on the same lines in 1945 (Dáil Deb., vol. 97, col. 2740).   [3] Ibid. col. 2573.   [4] Mansergh, *Documents*, i. 366–7.

it incumbent upon him to clarify the position by expressing his own views, even though in fact he regarded his country as being no longer a member. 'The Government here', he recalled in 1945, 'did not feel called upon to make any comment. . . . We could only accept the British Government statement as the expression of a view taken by them in full knowledge of our position here at the time.'[1] Thus he placed the onus of determining whether Eire was associated with the Commonwealth and, if so, in what way, upon the governments of the Commonwealth. It was for them to prescribe the rules and to interpret them. Throughout the war years their attitude continued to be one of marked reserve. United Kingdom ministers avoided specific allusion to Eire as a dominion for reasons partly constitutional and partly political, arising from Eire's neutrality, and sought refuge in less specific allusion to membership of the Commonwealth. Thus in February 1944 Mr. Churchill declined to make a statement about the Irish relationship with the Commonwealth after the war, because of the 'many elements of gravity which it possesses'.[2] In March 1944 the Parliamentary Under-Secretary of State for Dominion Affairs said that 'broadly, Eire is treated by us as a member of the British Commonwealth of Nations, but she is, of course, excluded from the benefits of all special wartime arrangements'.[3]

But if the policy of governments was to let sleeping dogs lie, there were others whose delight it was to stir up scorpions. In the end it was not the Commonwealth without, but the opposition within that compelled Mr. de Valera to be more explicit. At home his position had both the traditional strength and the weaknesses of that of a man of the centre. In the late 1930's he was open to attack from the militant left; ten years later he was forced into a difficult and in the end impossible position by his opponents on the right, and ultimately driven from power by a coalition between them. It might have been supposed that the Fine Gael party, which had openly championed Commonwealth membership as late as the election of 1944, would have preferred the maintenance of some link, however imperfect, with the Commonwealth rather than none. Yet impelled by its implacable hostility to Mr. de Valera and to the External Relations Act, it came to adopt a position which it would hardly have deliberately chosen. By its sustained and bitter ridicule it compelled Mr. de Valera to expound and to define, and in so doing impaired that measure of popular acquiescence which alone could have enabled the ingenious and not unstatesmanlike experiment of external association to survive.

The Republic and the Commonwealth

It was not, however, the Fine Gael leaders, but the taunts of two independent members which first broke through the barriers of Mr. de Valera's

[1] Dáil Deb., vol. 97, col. 2574 (Mansergh, *Documents*, ii. 796).
[2] H. of C. Deb., vol. 396, coll. 1266–7.   [3] Ibid. vol. 398, col. 660.

reserve. One of them, Mr. Dillon, had been a member of the Fine Gael party, and, though closely associated with its leaders, was at that time in the political wilderness. The other, Mr. Oliver Flanagan, was at that time[1] an independent deputy in the traditional sense of being a deputy on whom politically nobody could depend. In 1944 Mr. Flanagan was anxious to discover whether Eire was a part of the British Commonwealth. He put the question to Mr. de Valera in the Dáil. Mr. de Valera referred him to Section 3 (1) of the External Relations Act[2] and Article 29 Section 4 (2) of the Constitution,[3] with the comment that he himself did not propose 'to try to paraphrase them or to give any definition to the relationship established by them save that contained in the words of the documents themselves'. Mr. Flanagan protested that his question had not been answered. Was Eire a part of the British Commonwealth or not? Yes or no? 'I think the Deputy will take some time to learn that you cannot always answer questions by "yes" or "no"', replied the Taoiseach. The relationship, he reiterated, was settled in 1936 and 1937 and, he added, 'we do not propose to change it at the moment'. 'Then we are a member of the British Commonwealth of Nations?' exclaimed Mr. Flanagan. 'Make up your own mind', responded the Taoiseach.[4]

But if in respect of membership of the Commonwealth Mr. de Valera remained unyielding, an inquiry about the nature of the state from Mr. Dillon in July 1945 elicited more positive results.

Mr. Dillon: Are we a republic or are we not, for nobody seems to know?
The Taoiseach: We are, if that is all the Deputy wants to know.
Mr. Dillon: This is a republic? That is the greatest news I heard for a long time. Now we know where we are.... When did it happen, can anyone tell us?...
The Taoiseach: You will hear all about it later.[5]

The following week Mr. de Valera was not perhaps quite so forthcoming as Opposition deputies had hoped. He talked about the republic with a fine impersonal detachment. Mr. Dillon, said the Taoiseach, pretended that he (Mr. de Valera) was the only person who knew the answer to the question whether Eire was a republic or not, but the answer did not rest with him at all. The state, constitutionally, was what it was and its character was to be tested by the definitions of the forms of state given in standard textbooks. Far be it from any particular person or government to settle so important a

[1] Subsequently he joined the Fine Gael party.
[2] Section 3 (1) reads: 'It is hereby declared and enacted that, so long as Saorstát Eireann is associated with the following nations, that is to say, Australia, Canada, Great Britain, New Zealand, and South Africa, and so long as the King recognized by those nations as the symbol of their co-operation continues to act on behalf of each of those nations (on the advice of the several Governments thereof) for the purposes of the appointment of diplomatic and consular representatives and the conclusion of international agreements, the King so recognized may, and is hereby authorised to, act on behalf of Saorstát Eireann for the like purposes as and when advised by the Executive Council so to do.'   [3] See above, p. 263 n. 4.
[4] 29 November 1944, Dáil Deb., vol. 95, coll. 1024–5.
[5] Ibid. vol. 97, coll. 2116–17.

question; the state was to be qualified politically only by observation of the state's institutions and by examination of its fundamental laws. To assist deputies in their diagnosis the Taoiseach then proceeded to quote from the definitions of a republic contained in the *Encyclopaedia Britannica*, the *Encyclopaedia Americana*, the *Shorter Oxford English Dictionary*, *Webster's International Dictionary*, the *New Standard Dictionary of the English Language*, and *Chambers's Dictionary*. Perhaps the last, with its succinct statement that a republic was 'a form of Government without a monarch in which the supreme power is vested in representatives elected by the people', alone gave him the precise phrasing he required. At any rate he quoted it last, concluding with the warning that if anyone still persisted in maintaining that Eire was not a republic he could no longer argue with him, for 'we have no common language'.[1]

The 'dictionary republic' invited ridicule.[2] Even with Mr. de Valera's backing it never looked like staying the Irish electoral course. It was too heavily handicapped. Irish nationalist opinion might have been persuaded that the declaration of the republic should be postponed till the country was united and might further, though with great reluctance, have conceded that, at least for years to come, republicanism and unity were incompatible aims. But the retrospective definition of a republic by reference to standard dictionaries satisfied neither their sense of politics nor their sense of drama. The one thing that had never been anticipated was the surreptitious advent of the republic.

Mr. de Valera, even if far-sighted in his aim, had been over subtle in his means. The republican whose overriding concern was unity felt, surely rightly, that much would be lost by the premature declaration of a republic for one part of Ireland, but, experienced in the drafting of constitutional laws, he failed to understand the reactions of less complex minds, inexperienced in such arts, to the notion that the state in which they lived was classified by the most respectable authors as a republic but was not so designated or formally described in its own Constitution or by its own government. Even the most devoted of his followers shared in the popular sense of unfulfilment, to which moreover were soon to be added doubts which proved ineradicable about the authenticity of the republic so surprisingly found to have been in existence for many years.

Mr. de Valera's admission that Eire was a republic served not to dampen but to revive interest in Ireland's relations with the Commonwealth. The

[1] Ibid. col. 2572 (Mansergh, *Documents*, ii. 794-6).
[2] Cf. Dr. O'Higgins's comment, Dáil Deb., vol. 97, col. 2607: 'That question' (about the republic) 'was not addressed to Webster. It was addressed to Taoiseach de Valera. Webster does not hold any function in this State, or in this Parliament'. Mr. McGilligan later commented: 'The Taoiseach said he did not want to interfere too much in the matter because of the difficulty of getting foreign Governments to recognise that we had a republic. Have we passed that stage? If not, the *Encyclopaedia Britannica* has not done well abroad, however it has gone down here amongst certain people' (ibid. vol. 106, col. 2322).

conventional characteristics of dominion status, as set out in the Balfour Report and the Preamble to the Statute of Westminster, were equality of status, free association, and common allegiance to the Crown. It was the third alone which confronted the governments of the United Kingdom and Eire with a problem. It was one not altogether easy to resolve. In essentials it amounted to this. If Eire was a republic it could not be a member of the British Commonwealth; if it were a member of the British Commonwealth it could not be a republic. The statement issued by the United Kingdom government, with dominion assent, in 1937 implied—common allegiance being one of the conventional characteristics of dominion status—that Commonwealth governments were satisfied that the text of the External Relations Act could be construed as evidence of Eire's continuing allegiance to the Crown. In the light of the wording of the Act and of the interpretation placed upon it by the Irish government this patient resolve to pretend that a state owed allegiance, even though its government stated categorically that it did not, had about it an element of absurdity. Implicitly such a contention committed the government of the United Kingdom to the view that after the enactment of the 1937 Constitution Eire was not a republic, for no one suggested that a republic, least of all an Irish republic, could owe allegiance to a king, even an 'external' king. Mr. de Valera's opponents, once the republic had acquired its dictionary *imprimatur*, were intent upon exposing the constitutional devices upon which the opinion of the United Kingdom government alone was based.

During the war years the provision of the External Relations Act authorizing the King's signature to letters of credence issued to Irish ministers and ambassadors on their appointment were allowed to fall into virtual abeyance, since to avoid embarrassment on either side, the Irish government appointed chargés d'affaires to fill new or vacated posts. But thereafter use was made once again of the procedure authorized by the External Relations Act. In Ireland, however, as elsewhere, nationalist sentiment had in the meantime hardened, and even those once disposed to admire Mr. de Valera's constitutional ingenuity as displayed in the External Relations Act were now embarrassed by the authority it gave for the open participation of the English King in the formal conduct of Eire's relations with foreign states. The opposition heightened such feelings of malaise on the part of some professed republicans by publicizing or insisting on the publication of the actual letters used in individual cases.

On 19 June 1946 Mr. Dillon read out in the Dáil the letter of credence presented by the Irish Minister to the King of Sweden. Its terms were as follows:[1]

My Brother,
   The Government of Ireland being desirous of maintaining the relations of friendship which exist between Ireland and Sweden, have advised me that they have

[1] Dáil Deb., vol. 101, coll. 2181–2.

judged it expedient that . . . be accredited to Your Majesty in the character of Envoy Extraordinary and Minister Plenipotentiary of Ireland.

The Irish Government feel assured that the choice of . . . would be perfectly agreeable to Your Majesty and that he will prove himself worthy of this mark of confidence.

I, therefore, request on behalf of the Government of Ireland that Your Majesty will give entire credence to all that . . . shall communicate to Your Majesty in their name, and I take this opportunity of renewing to Your Majesty the assurance of my sincere friendship, and of the unfeigned respect and esteem which I entertain for Your Majesty's person and character.

Given at my court at Buckingham Palace, 20th day of June, 1946.
I am, Sir, My Brother, Your Majesty's Good Brother George, Rex Imperator.
Countersigned—Eámon de Valera.

Mr. de Valera was at pains to underline the limited and particular significance of the royal signature. Such letters, he explained, were signed by the King in accordance with the provisions of the External Relations Act and as a matter of external policy. He emphasized the distinction that in consequence existed between the King's functions in Canada, South Africa, and Australia, where he acted as head of the state, and his functions in Eire where he 'is used by us as a mark of our association with these States'.[1] Yet Mr. Dillon was perhaps guilty of no exaggeration when he suggested a year later that deputies felt a sense of humiliation on learning that the Irish Ambassador to the Holy See presented 'to the Papal Secretary of State letters of credence addressed to the Holy Father by His Majesty King George VI', thereby imposing

on the Holy Father the diplomatic necessity of addressing a letter, in reply to credentials presented by the Ambassador of the Irish Republic, to the King of England, thanking him for the gracious terms of the letters of credence which have recently been presented by the Ambassador from the Irish Republic.[2]

Mr. McGilligan, another forceful critic, maintained that in all this the harm lay not in sending representatives abroad with letters of credence signed by the King, but in pretending that they were not so signed. He would rather see the arrangement ended than perpetuate a lie. In Eire they had no head of state, for the President was not the head of the state. He was more aptly described as an 'internal growth and a foreign body' for he had no relations internationally *vis-à-vis* other countries.

It was Mr. de Valera's belief that the republican Constitution balanced by

---

[1] Ibid. col. 2246.
[2] Ibid. vol. 106, col. 2326. It was in fact the Minister of External Affairs who received letters of credence addressed to the King and, in Mr. Dillon's mocking phrase, it was only after that had been done that the incoming diplomat might 'proceed to Arus an Uachtaran, there to drink a hospitable cup of tea'.

the republic's external association with the states of the British Commonwealth in the form sanctioned by the External Relations Act was the most that any Irish nationalist government could concede and at the same time preserve unity at home. After the war, with mounting criticism from the right and also from the extreme left, the risk that it might imperil national unity in the twenty-six counties without making any appreciable advance towards the reunion of the thirty-two was no longer to be ignored. Yet repeal of the Act would seemingly mean secession from the Commonwealth and that in turn would surely place a further barrier in the way of Irish unity. On this last point Mr. de Valera's fears were shared by his principal critic. In July 1945 Mr. Dillon declared that he was as certain

as that I am standing here that we can be members of the Commonwealth of Nations and retain the full sovereignty of the Irish people, not only in 26 counties but in 32, and I am equally certain that if we make the decision to break the link with the Commonwealth of Nations . . . we are surrendering for our time and for all foreseeable time, not only six counties of our national territory, but one-fifth of our population who, under existing conditions, do not want to come back to the Irish nation.[1]

General Mulcahy, the leader of the Fine Gael party after Mr. Cosgrave's retirement, with such considerations no doubt in mind, was judiciously reserved. He inclined to the view that Eire was still a member of the Commonwealth and argued simply that the External Relations Act created 'a certain amount of doubt' which would be better dispelled in the interest of the people.[2] But his colleagues were more disposed to vehement denunciations—Mr. McGilligan spoke of people 'going about shamefacedly' because the country was 'living a lie'[3]—and their dislike of qualified association was so great that failing full membership they came to adopt the position that no association at all with the Commonwealth, even at the risk of prejudicing future prospects of Irish unity, was to be preferred to external association. In this Mr. Dillon shared their views, or perhaps it would be more exact to say that they shared Mr. Dillon's. What they were Mr. Dillon made clear beyond doubt two years later. If he had to choose, so he told the Dáil in 1947, between the 'fraudulent make-believe' of the External Relations Act and 'cutting the painter altogether with the other nations of the Commonwealth', he would emphatically choose the latter.[4] In their acceptance of this view not all the Fine Gael leaders would seem to have calculated where their criticisms were likely to lead them in the end. Mr. de Valera, the Fabian revolutionary, deferred his decision, seemingly continuing to hope that if formal secession could be avoided republicanism and unity might ultimately be reconciled, while his more conservative, traditionally pro-Commonwealth critics, with

[1] Dáil Deb., vol. 97, col. 2598. 'Breaking the link' apparently covered external association as well as outright secession.
[2] Ibid. col. 2575.   [3] Ibid. vol. 106, col. 2322–3.   [4] Ibid. col. 2327.

long years in the political wilderness behind them, insisted on an end to all prevarication and procrastination. In one thing assuredly they succeeded. They impaired Mr. de Valera's confidence in the continuing usefulness of his own constitutional devices as he found it increasingly difficult to counter the attacks, and to tolerate the taunts, of his critics.

In all the debates on status—and they took place year by year on the Department of External Affairs Estimates—the twin questions of the form of government and membership of the Commonwealth were inextricably intertwined. Irish nationalist sentiment was insistent that full national sovereignty be recognized. Nothing that detracted from it, however useful or convenient in itself, should be permitted to remain. The Crown, the hated Oath of Allegiance, the Governor-General, all had been swept away, and yet there remained the suggestion that sovereignty was not complete. When Mr. de Valera explained the omission to designate the state a republic by reference to the hallowed precedent of the American Constitution, he carried conviction; but there was no such precedent for the use of the signature of an 'external' King for the accreditation of representatives to foreign countries.[1] Did it not in fact mean that through membership of, or association with, the Commonwealth the state was 'encumbered' by external forms and could never be 'a complete republic' so long as the King of another country was accepted by an Irish government as 'the one and only person entitled to accredit our representatives abroad or to sign international treaties for us'?[2] Thus the critics argued, and Mr. de Valera had no sufficient rejoinder. He had to rely on an appeal not to precedent or to emotion, but to reason. If, he argued in 1947, being in the Commonwealth implied in any way allegiance and acceptance of the King as King in Ireland, then Eire was not in the Commonwealth because she did not accept either of these things. And he went on:

Our position in relation to the Commonwealth is accepted and understood by the people who are immediately concerned in Britain, and it is understood by everybody who wants to understand it abroad. The only people who do not understand it are the people who do not want to understand it—the people who want to create political confusion. If there is any deception in the matter it is not deception on our part but deception on the part of those who, in the face of clear facts will still—because the situation is a bit delicate—try to create confusion about it.

Mr. Dillon: 'Delicate' is good.

The Taoiseach: This is a republican State. As a matter of our external policy, we are associated with the States of the British Commonwealth. We are not at the present time regarded as members of it, but we are regarded as associates.

Mr. Morrissey: Does that mean we are inside or outside?

The Taoiseach: It means that we are external to the British Commonwealth so long as the States in it regard the acceptance of allegiance to the King as the necessary

---
[1] See, for example, Mr. Norton's criticisms, ibid. vol. 97, coll. 2637–49.
[2] Ibid. col. 2649.

link. If that is the bond which they have, we have not that bond and we have made it quite clear that we have not that bond.[1]

Mr. de Valera was correct in saying that the position was understood by those immediately concerned in Britain and the Commonwealth overseas. By convention Commonwealth governments referred to Eire as a member, or even as a quasi-member of the Commonwealth, while in Britain successive Secretaries of State for Dominion Affairs continued to avoid the issue of whether the country was or was not a dominion. But continuing Irish association with the Commonwealth in some form was not open to doubt. As late as 22 April 1948 the Under-Secretary of State for Commonwealth Relations, Mr. Gordon-Walker, was asked in the House of Commons whether Irish assent to the alterations of the Royal Title consequential upon the change of status of India and Pakistan had been invited. His affirmative reply prompted the following exchange:

Sir R. Ross: Does that mean that Eire was consulted as a Dominion and had to give assent as a Dominion?
Mr. Gordon-Walker: It means that when the Eire Government were consulted... they said the change presented no difficulty to them. In other words, it assented in the change.
Sir R. Ross: Can the Minister say in what capacity Eire was consulted—as a foreign power or as a Dominion within the Commonwealth?
Mr. Gordon-Walker: Naturally, as a member of the Commonwealth—a Government within the Commonwealth.[2]

While there was thus general consent that Eire's association with the Commonwealth continued, there was tacit agreement between the governments principally concerned not to probe too closely into its precise character. For a short period such governmental restraint served its own very useful purpose. But it could not provide the foundation for a lasting relationship. For that the agreement of the governments of the Commonwealth to a re-interpretation and restatement of Irish relations with the Commonwealth in conformity with existing political realities was essential. So much Mr. de Valera realized. By 1947 he was prepared to contemplate the adoption of alternative means for the accrediting of the Irish representatives overseas, which might not necessarily involve a repeal of the External Relations Act but would allow of its falling into abeyance. 'If the method which we have so far used for indicating our association with the States of the British Commonwealth should not fulfill its purpose', he told the Dáil,[3] '... it is very easy, if we wish to do so, to transfer these powers to the President by an Act of this Legislature.' He had not himself deemed any such change desirable because he thought the existing arrangements a fitting 'external symbol' of

---

[1] Dáil Deb., vol. 107, col. 87 (Mansergh, *Documents*, ii. 797).
[2] H. of C. Deb., vol. 449, col. 1975.   [3] 24 June 1947, Dáil Deb., vol. 107, col. 93.

Eire's association with the Commonwealth, but once convinced that it was creating confusion in the minds of the Irish people he would, so he assured Opposition deputies, reconsider his opinion. In any event, he argued, the External Relations Act would have served a useful purpose simply by keeping in suspense the question of Ireland's relations with the Commonwealth long enough to enable her government to see whether the post-war changes arising from the transfer of power in India would bring into being a Commonwealth so modified in structure and character as to provide a natural and congenial resting place for an Irish republic. But this was not to be. Though Mr. de Valera held the door open for so long, at the critical moment responsibility passed to other hands. By-elections in October 1947 in Tipperary and Dublin, resulting in the victory of a new Republican party, foreshadowed the close of his long tenure of power and the ending of the experiment of external association.

The General Election, 1948

It was with the challenge of the new republican party, the Clann na Poblachta, that Mr. de Valera was principally preoccupied in the general election that followed. Like the Roman dictator at the battle of Lake Regillus, who from afar singled out among the Tuscan ranks the most dangerous of his foes:

> And far before the rest
> I see the dark grey charger
> I see the purple vest,

so Mr. de Valera marked out its leader, Mr. Seán MacBride—all the more clearly, be it said, because the horse he rode and the colours he wore had a distinct resemblance to those with which Mr. de Valera rode to battle against Mr. Cosgrave long ago. Sensitive, like Clemenceau and Nehru, to opposition from the Left, Mr. de Valera rightly detected in Mr. MacBride's new Republican party, which, though ill organized, nominated as many as ninety candidates, the force most likely to undermine his position. The appeal of the new party was to republican sentiment. Its leader, a barrister by profession, was the son of John MacBride, executed in 1916, and Mme Maud Gonne MacBride, the inspiration of Yeats's *Cathleen ni Houlihan*, and a militant champion of Irish nationalism.[1] To this impeccable national background Mr. MacBride added a forceful personality, and an insistence on the need for enthusiasm and integrity in Irish public life. Characteristic was the listing among his party's aims of the need to end 'political corruption, quibbling, jobbery and graft'. Like reforming and revolutionary parties before them, the new Republicans came forward as the 'sea-green incorruptibles'. In external policy it was their aim to carry the national revolution a stage further by the severance of the last formal tie with the Commonwealth.

[1] She founded in 1904 the 'Inginidhe na h'Éireann' which later developed into the better known Cumann na mBan.

There was no national issue in the strict sense of the word in the election campaign, but there was an all-pervasive national background heightened by Mr. MacBride's intervention. The parties were agreed in their desire to end partition, but it was Mr. MacBride who put forward the one positive suggestion, that members elected for Northern Ireland constituencies should take their seats in the Dáil. But if he obtained little support for this particular and impracticable proposal, he succeeded in creating an atmosphere in which all parties felt that something must be done to end partition. That had its importance later. So, too, and for the same reason, Mr. MacBride's advocacy of the repeal of the External Relations Act gave renewed prominence to an issue with which the parties rather than the people were much concerned. He had the open support of Labour, who had opposed the Act from the outset on the ground that it continued an association with the British Crown which should have been terminated when King Edward, in the words of Mr. William Norton, the Labour leader, 'voluntarily relinquished his objectionable rôle here'.[1] But on the other hand the principal opposition party, Fine Gael, however much they disliked the Act as such, remained to all outward appearance sympathetic to the Commonwealth connexion.

Under proportional representation Mr. de Valera's chances of a renewed overall majority were in any event remote, and they had been further diminished by a recent revision of electoral boundaries which increased the number of smaller three-member constituencies.[2] The only alternative was a coalition. This Fine Gael had advocated in 1944, and in 1948 they made it the principal plank in the party platform. Yet before a coalition could come into being formidable differences in outlook and policy had to be reconciled. How were Fine Gael, the party of the older industrialists and the larger farmers, with their faith in *laissez-faire* economics and their aversion to social reform, to find common ground in home affairs with the two sections into which the Labour party was split, or with Mr. MacBride and the new Republicans with their emphasis on the need for radical welfare policies? Wider still, to all appearance, was the gulf to be bridged in external affairs. Labour and the new Republicans were pledged to sever Ireland's relations with the Commonwealth by the repeal of the External Relations Act, while Fine Gael declared that if returned to power they would not alter the Constitution in relation to external affairs. 'The present position', General Mulcahy, the leader of the party, observed at Letterkenny in January 1948,[3] 'has been accepted by all members of the British Commonwealth as being in consonance with membership', and it was Commonwealth membership that the Fine Gael party had hitherto consistently championed.

[1] See Mansergh, *Survey, 1931–9*, p. 294, and Mr. Norton's speeches, in Dáil Deb., vol. 64, col. 1249, and vol. 97, coll. 2637–49.
[2] In the former five or seven-member constituencies, Fianna Fáil as the largest party had a better chance of securing the odd seat which would give it an overall majority.
[3] *Irish Times* and *Irish Press*, 28 January 1948.

The election took place early in February 1948, and the results showed that while Fianna Fáil with 68 seats remained by far the largest party in the new Dáil it had failed to secure an overall majority.[1] When the new Dáil assembled on 18 February Mr. de Valera's nomination as Taoiseach was defeated by 75 votes to 70.[2] Mr. J. A. Costello, a leading member, though not the leader, of the Fine Gael party, and one who, in his own words, was 'detached from the controversial bitternesses of the past',[3] was then proposed and, with the support of all the opposition groups, was elected by 75 votes to 68.[4] Left and Right had successfully combined to defeat the Centre. The composition of the new government faithfully reflected the relative strength of the parties thus strangely united. Fine Gael received five portfolios, the party leader, General Mulcahy, accepting the comparatively subordinate post of Minister of Education. Mr. Norton, the Labour leader, became deputy Prime Minister, Mr. MacBride Minister of External Affairs, and Mr. J. M. Dillon Minister of Agriculture. Mr. MacBride, in supporting Mr. Costello's nomination as Taoiseach, allowed that while 'the reintegration of this nation as a republic, free from any association with any other country' remained the ultimate political objective of his party, it could not claim to have received a mandate that 'would enable us to repeal, or seek to repeal the External Relations Act and such other measures as are inconsistent with our status as an independent republic'.[5] The repeal of the Act was also presumably among those matters to which Mr. Costello referred when he said that 'any points on which we have not agreed have been left in abeyance'. Yet it was difficult for a government composed of such diverse elements and which owed its accession to office very largely to the inroads which the new Republican party had made upon Mr. de Valera's traditional vote to let the question lie. Confronted by so formidable an opponent, its survival seemed conditional from the outset on two things; first on the maintenance of inter-party unity on essentials and secondly on not allowing itself to be outbid on a national issue by Mr. de Valera. That Mr. Costello should declare the ending of partition to be the principal objective of his government was therefore to be anticipated, but though in the first months of office relations with the Commonwealth would appear to have little preoccupied the administration, ministers were constantly on their guard lest on this question too they might be out-manœuvred.

The Repeal of the External Relations Act

The actions of the inter-party government could be rightly predicted only by an assessement of the balance of forces within it at any given time. On paper the advantage lay with the conservative elements. Fine Gael was the predominant partner and in internal affairs its controlling influence was assured by the placing of the key posts of Prime Minister and Minister for

---

[1] For full results see Appendix E, below, p. 442. [2] Dáil Deb., vol. 110, coll. 41–42.
[3] Ibid. col. 47.   [4] Ibid. coll. 45–46.   [5] Ibid. col. 25.

Finance in the hands of leading members of the party,[1] and by the backing of the Farmers' party[2] and most of the Independents for their conservative home policies. But in external affairs the position of Fine Gael was by no means so strong. Mr. MacBride held the External Affairs portfolio, and, poorly though his party had fared at the election, its contribution to the overthrow of Mr. de Valera had been decisive. The appeal of the party and of Labour was to republican-nationalist sentiment and it was more cogent than that of Fine Gael's now tepid declaration of faith in continuing Commonwealth membership. In any appeal to public opinion on an external issue the verdict would assuredly come down on the side of the 'root-and-branch' republicans. This was well understood by the members of Mr. MacBride's new and highly individualistic Republican party. Few of its members were prepared to concede with their leader that the electorate had given no mandate for change in Eire's relations with the British Commonwealth, and two of them, Mr. Con Lehane and Captain Peadar Cowan, who was expelled from the party in July 1948, embarrassed its leadership by actively skirmishing against what remained of the Commonwealth connexion.

In June 1948 Mr. Lehane obtained from Mr. Costello the long-delayed but none the less satisfying assurance that the 'national feelings of the majority of Irishmen . . . outraged by the failure to remove the statue of a foreign monarch from the Quadrangle at Leinster House', were to be assuaged by the government's approval of a scheme 'for the provision of parking accommodation for motor cars' which would involve the removal of Queen Victoria's statue.[3] While Captain Cowan disliked the oblique way in which this minor national objective was to be attained, it was a portent for the future. A government in which the conservative elements were strongly entrenched could sponsor radical nationalist measures with the assurance that these lay in political territory where the Opposition might skirmish but could enter into no general engagement. In the enactment of such measures, too, the Fine Gael party saw at long last an opportunity of seizing once again the national initiative from Mr. de Valera and, as it were incidentally, from some of their coalition partners. On the other hand, if they remained inactive there was the possibility that Captain Cowan would himself beg leave to introduce legislation to repeal the External Relations Act and proclaim the republic.[4]

---

[1] Mr. Norton, the Labour party leader, who was An Tanaiste (Deputy Prime Minister) and Minister for Social Security, was persuaded to restrict the scope of the social security legislation he sponsored after receiving public admonition from Mr. McGilligan, the Minister for Finance, on the paramount need for economy in social services.

[2] Clann na Talmhan.

[3] Dáil Deb., vol. 111, coll. 1785-6. The statue was objectionable not only on grounds of national sentiment. King Edward VII, who unveiled it, is said to have exclaimed when it was exposed to view, 'My God! Poor Mama'.

[4] Cf. Captain Cowan's speech, ibid. vol. 112, coll. 985-95. The concern of both Mr. MacBride and Mr. de Valera is reflected in the frequency and the astringency of their interruptions. Deputy Lehane, too, continued to act as a pace-maker (ibid. coll. 996 and 999).

Were that to happen the disruption of the inter-party government could scarcely be averted, for whatever action Fine Gael might take on their own, they could not, as a hitherto Commonwealth party, secede from the Commonwealth under the appearance of compulsion.

In June 1948 a strong Irish delegation under the leadership of Mr. Costello went to London to negotiate a new trade agreement with Britain. In the course of their visit Mr. Attlee alluded to the forthcoming meeting of Commonwealth Prime Ministers which was to be held in London in October. It was a meeting which had an importance all its own because it was to be the first at which the three new Asian dominions were to be represented. For that very reason it seemed to afford the most propitious of opportunities for the reappearance of Irish representatives in the innermost councils of the Commonwealth, if only because the enlargement of the Commonwealth by the addition of three strongly nationalist members of non-British extraction might be expected to bring into being a looser, and from the Irish point of view, more congenial, grouping than that of the former and predominantly British Commonwealth of pre-war years. If the available evidence suggests that Mr. de Valera alone of Irish leaders was wholly aware of some of the wider implications of the occasion,[1] the question of Irish representation was certainly considered by the Cabinet. They informed the United Kingdom government that if Eire were represented at the Conference her representatives would wish to have partition, and the basis of future Irish relations with the Commonwealth, considered.[2] But in thus stating the conditions of Irish participation the Irish government returned no explicit answer to the British invitation.

The most important consequence of discussion in the Cabinet about Irish representation at the Commonwealth Prime Ministers' Meeting was to make the inter-party government increasingly aware of the desirability of defining more precisely their attitude to the Commonwealth connexion. The case for so doing was further strengthened by the provisions of the British Nationality Act,[3] which provided that in United Kingdom law Irish citizens were no longer to be regarded as British subjects, though equally they were not to be regarded as foreigners. This was a compromise solution, worked out by a committee of Commonwealth nationality experts on which Eire was represented and which met in London in early 1947. It came close to realizing the Irish aim of reciprocal as distinct from common citizenship, and in so doing removed the more startling of the conflicts in the nationality law of the two countries and a long-standing source of Irish grievance. Mr. MacBride spoke

[1] He had visited Delhi on his way back from New Zealand and Australia.
[2] See Mr. Costello's speech, 10 May 1949, Dáil Deb., vol. 115, coll. 796–7.
[3] 11 and 12 Geo. 6, c. 56 (see Mansergh, *Documents*, ii. 949–68 and below, pp. 385–6). Its provisions were the subject of a not very illuminating discussion on the adjournment (Dáil Deb., vol. 111, coll. 1931–44). The Irish reaction was more satisfactorily indicated later (see ibid. vol. 112, coll. 908–22).

of the 'very serious effort to meet our viewpoint . . . made by Mr. Attlee's Government', and if the Act did not go the whole way towards satisfying Irish claims at least it represented 'a vast improvement on the position that has existed hitherto'.[1] Mr. MacBride interpreted the new measure of accord on citizenship legislation which the Act represented as an indication that henceforward those who desired to promote better Anglo-Irish relations would pay attention to the substance and not to the form. The difficulties in Anglo-Irish relations arose, he argued, not from any outworn prejudice but from concrete obstacles such as partition and short-sighted efforts to retain forms that could only serve as a reminder of an unhappy past, and as irritants endangering and frustrating the relationship they were meant to express. 'The Crown and outward forms that belong to British constitutional history', he concluded, 'are merely reminders of an unhappy past that we want to bury, that have no realities for us and only serve as irritants.'[2] By that test the External Relations Act could not survive.

The provisions of the British Nationality Act, in so far as they substituted reciprocal for common citizenship on the lines contemplated by the Sinn Féin leaders of 1921, in this one important particular tacitly endorsed the Irish view that Eire was not a member of the Commonwealth, but a state externally associated with it. Mr. MacBride indeed went so far as to say that the Labour government in Britain agreed that Eire was not a member of the Commonwealth,[3] but in a formal sense this would seem to have been an overstatement. On the other hand Mr. MacBride's own categoric assertion that Eire was not a member of the Commonwealth was in significant contrast to his predecessor's guarded circumlocution. It elicited in due course the inevitable inquiry from Captain Cowan: 'When and under what circumstances', he asked on 28 July, did Ireland cease 'to be a member of the British Commonwealth of Nations?' The process, explained Mr. Costello, was one of 'gradual development'. But, like the Minister of External Affairs, he too was satisfied that Ireland had ceased to be a member of the Commonwealth, though she still remained associated with it.[4]

In the definition and the redefinition of Irish relations with the Commonwealth the ending of partition remained a very important, but not always an overriding, consideration. When released from the cares of office Mr. de Valera embarked on a lengthy tour of the United States, Australia, New Zealand, and ultimately Great Britain in the hope of enlisting the sympathy of their peoples for the cause of Irish unity. If the government deemed it necessary to compete with so formidable a figure on an issue which he had made peculiarly his own it behoved it to move fast. On 23 July Mr. Costello seemingly snatched the initiative with the statement that for the first time since 1922 the country had a government which had some hope of ending

---

[1] 20 July 1948, Dáil Deb., vol. 112, col. 908.
[2] Ibid. col. 910.
[3] Ibid. col. 1019.
[4] Ibid. coll. 1555-6.

partition. 'I make that assertion', he said,[1] 'with all the confidence I have within me. To say any more would be to damage the advances that already have been made.' If the public, both in Britain and in Ireland, remained somewhat mystified by this cryptic pronouncement, summer visits to Ireland by a succession of British ministers, including the Prime Minister, Mr. Attlee, fostered a sanguine expectation of coming change in the twenty-six counties, for the more United Kingdom ministers repeated their assurances that they had come to Ireland merely for a holiday the more were their statements discounted.[2]

Irish preoccupation with partition, though intensified by considerations of party advantage, derived its strength from a deeply-rooted sense of injustice. Yet, powerful though the political and emotional urge to unity unquestionably was, the full realization of 'national' sovereignty, even for the twenty-six counties, remained the decisive motive force. In any conflict therefore between sovereignty and unity sovereignty came first, partly no doubt because the removal of any fetters or supposed fetters on Irish sovereignty lay within the competence of the Oireachtas while the removal of the border depended upon the opinions and actions of those over whom Eire exercised no control.

Both government and Opposition felt that the fulfilment of Ireland's national aspirations would be assisted by the positive goodwill of friendly countries overseas. But where Mr. de Valera continued to place his faith in co-operation with the oversea members of the Commonwealth, his successor in the Department of External Affairs directed his efforts less to the Commonwealth and more to Western Europe and the United States. This change in emphasis, never very clearly defined, was none the less perceptible. Mr. MacBride was much preoccupied in his period of office with the recovery of Western Europe, and, while in no way departing from the now traditional Irish policy of non-participation in any military pact or alliance,[3] encouraged the idea that Eire should play a full part in the recovery of Western Europe, and never hesitated to declare that her sympathies could not but be with the Christian West. The revival and extension of Irish association with Western Europe did not itself lessen the extent of Irish co-operation with the Commonwealth; it was simply a question of where the greater reliance should be placed and where the more active policy should be pursued.

While Mr. MacBride honourably kept by his admission that the electorate

---

[1] *Manchester Guardian*, 24 July 1948.
[2] The number of visits was remarkable. Mr. Attlee was in Ireland for three weeks from 30 July; he was followed by the Lord Chancellor, Lord Jowitt, who was there also for three weeks from 10 August, by Mr. Strauss, the Minister of Supply, and by Mr. P. J. Noel-Baker, Secretary of State for Commonwealth Relations. Mr. Attlee found on his visit that 'much of the old bitterness between English and Irish had passed away', but 'the division between North and South was still a rankling sore' (*As It Happened*, p. 190).
[3] The exchange of notes published in the Irish White Paper (P. no. 9934) on the Irish attitude to the North Atlantic Treaty summarizes the reasons for it. See below, p. 302.

had given no mandate for the repeal of the External Relations Act, he could not and did not disguise his own conviction that the Act provided no satisfactory basis for Irish association with the Commonwealth. He insisted, in particular, that Eire, though a sovereign independent state, had no head for external purposes, for the President could not be so described because he did not fulfil the functions normally associated with such an office.[1] Inevitably his observations served to accentuate prevailing doubts about the country's constitutional position, and on 5 August Captain Cowan once again expressed them. He asked the Taoiseach if Ireland's association with the Commonwealth might be terminated by unilateral action and whether Ireland was now an independent republic, and if not whether the government would indicate what steps were necessary to 'declare and establish Ireland as an independent republic'. To this inquiry Mr. Costello gave an answer which threw some light on the way in which his own mind was moving. He said that Ireland's association with the Commonwealth of Nations depended upon the factual position, and more particularly upon the reciprocal exchange of concrete benefits in such matters as trade and citizenship rights, and upon consultation and co-operation in matters of common concern. 'Our association with the nations of the Commonwealth', he said, 'is a free association, which, by virtue of its very freedom, could be determined by unilateral action.'[2] The question whether Eire was a republic or not he regarded as one purely of nomenclature, and he declined to go beyond the phrase of the Constitution which declared it to be a sovereign, independent, democratic state. More particularly he did not associate himself with Mr. de Valera's description of the state as a republic, thereby suggesting that if it were so to be described further legislation was required.

The conclusion to be drawn from Mr. MacBride's and Mr. Costello's constitutional commentaries was sharpened by the Deputy Prime Minister's denunciation of the External Relations Act in the debate on the adjournment on 6 August 1948. Mr. Norton said that he had been, as was indeed the case, at all times opposed to the Act, and he felt 'it would do our national self-respect good both at home and abroad if we were to proceed without delay to abolish the External Relations Act'.[3] Even though by deliberate intent very considerable latitude was allowed to the members of the inter-party government in the expression of their personal views, it was inconceivable that a Deputy Prime Minister could have used such language had not the question of repeal been considered and approved in principle in the Cabinet. The reaction of the Fianna Fáil party increased the probability of early legislative action. 'You will get no opposition from us', was Mr. de Valera's rejoinder to Mr. Norton's suggestion of immediate repeal, though he had earlier remarked that for his part he believed it was to the advantage of Ireland that

---

[1] See his heated exchange with Mr. de Valera on this point in Dáil Deb., vol. 112 coll., 1020–1. [2] Ibid. coll. 2105–6. [3] Ibid. coll. 2440–1.

she should continue to be associated with the states of the British Commonwealth.[1] But was such association conditional upon the continuance of the Act in the Statute book?

In the late summer of 1948 the inter-party government would seem to have agreed that the External Relations Act should be repealed but not to have decided upon the date of repeal and still less upon the relationship with the Commonwealth that should be established when this last constitutional tie was severed. Mr. Norton and possibly Mr. MacBride favoured repeal and secession. The emphasis which Mr. Costello placed upon the desirability of continuing Irish association with oversea dominions with large groups of population descended from Irish emigrants suggested strongly that while he contemplated repeal he did not have secession in mind. This interpretation would seem to be warranted not only by examination of the phrases which he used but by the whole history of the Fine Gael party, of which he was a member. To repeal the External Relations Act would be consistent with its record; to secede from the Commonwealth would render meaningless much of its history over two decades.

It was at this time of continuing indecision about the timing and the purpose of the repeal of the External Relations Act that Mr. Costello went to Canada to address the Canadian Bar Association. His speech, delivered in Montreal on 1 September 1948, consisted of a closely reasoned analysis of the development of Anglo-Irish relations.[2] Its principal theme was that the symbols appropriate to the older and predominantly British members of the Commonwealth were wholly unsuited to Irish circumstances. For British peoples overseas the Crown was a symbol, a rallying point for those who sprang from and recognized their common origin and their common motherland. If that sentiment of attachment had been somewhat diluted with the inclusion within the family circle of the Union of South Africa, the bond between the oversea dominions and the mother country remained. It was reflected in their constitutional and political structure, and constitutional forms were expressive of family loyalties and traditions. These forms, extended to the Irish Free State in 1921, aroused there very different emotions. 'Irish national instincts, deep-rooted in history', said Mr. Costello, 'recoiled from the forms which were to them, not the embodiment of their national pride . . . but the symbol of centuries of civil and religious persecution and confiscation.' The Crown in particular had become a symbol of political and religious ascendancy and was 'anathema to the vast majority of the Irish people'. By a narrow majority in the Dáil and by a rather larger majority in the country the Irish people accepted the Treaty in 1921-2, but even the party which supported it did so, as Michael Collins said, in the conviction

---
[1] Ibid. col. 2434.
[2] Published as *Ireland in International Affairs* (Dublin and Bray, Monument Press, 1948; Mansergh, *Documents*, ii. 797–801).

that the Treaty gave Ireland the freedom necessary to enable her people to achieve freedom. That freedom was achieved during the succeeding years by the removal of constitutional bonds or fetters, whether practical or theoretical, so that all restrictions on Irish sovereignty had been removed; the question confronting the Irish people was no longer whether their association with the Commonwealth represented a limitation upon their freedom or national sovereignty but whether the constitutional arrangements governing Ireland's association with the Commonwealth were in a form compatible with national sentiment and historical tradition. While Mr. Costello allowed that the successive steps taken by Mr. de Valera to remove the formal bonds linking the Irish Free State to the Commonwealth were to be explained as part of the process of bringing Irish political institutions into closer harmony with national sentiment, he was highly critical of the Act through which his predecessor had sought to symbolize the nature of Eire's new relationship with the Commonwealth. Not only, in his view, did the provisions of the External Relations Act contain 'inaccuracies and infirmities'[1] which of themselves caused confusion, but in principle the Act itself was misconceived.

Mr. Costello's address to the Canadian Bar Association clearly indicated the intention of his government to amend, or more probably repeal, the External Relations Act. It suggested, however, that this would be done in such a way as to leave unimpaired Ireland's relations with the Commonwealth. How it might be done was known to have been the subject of discussion with Mr. Mackenzie King, who, while affirming Canada's resolve to maintain full membership of the Commonwealth through a common allegiance to the Crown, conceded that in the Irish case a constitutional arrangement which acted only as an irritant could serve no useful purpose. But here again it was not contemplated that repeal would necessarily mean secession.

Thereafter the exact sequence of events is not without interest. On 4 September Mr. Costello dined with the Governor-General of Canada. The Governor-General was Field-Marshal Lord Alexander. He was an Ulsterman. Seeming discourtesies would appear to have inclined Mr. Costello towards the ending of what he was now more than ever disposed to consider an intolerable constitutional arrangement. On 5 September the *Sunday Independent* in Dublin published as its front-page news story an article by its political correspondent carrying the headline 'External Relations Act to Go'. The writer recalled that all the parties in the coalition government had denounced the External Relations Act as a dishonest deception in the past, and he instanced Mr. MacBride's comments in the Dáil[2] to the effect that outworn political forms could act only as irritants endangering and frustrating the

---

[1] In this criticism Mr. Costello was justified. The Act spoke of the King as the symbol of the *co-operation* of the members of the Commonwealth instead of their free *association*, and while it dealt with the appointment it made no provision for the reception of diplomatic representatives.   [2] Dáil Deb., vol. 112, col. 909.

relationship which they were intended to express and preserve, and Mr. Norton's forcibly expressed conviction[1] that Irish national honesty would rank all the higher if the External Relations Act were to go, as evidence that its early repeal was contemplated. The correctness of this conclusion, argued the correspondent, was confirmed by Mr. Costello's address to the Bar Association in Montreal and therefore an early announcement was to be expected. 'It is open to question', a student of Commonwealth affairs had remarked, '. . . whether the one remaining constitutional link embodied in the External Relations Act any longer possesses practical advantages outweighing its psychological disadvantages'.[2] 'Who today', commented the political correspondent, 'could say that it does. And that is why the Act may already be considered dead.'

The quotation of the important parts of this article by Canadian newspapers[3] prompted press inquiries which evidently impressed upon Mr. Costello the desirability of an early pronouncement.[4] In any event, at a press conference in Ottawa on 7 September, he announced the intention of his government to repeal the External Relations Act on the dual ground of its unsatisfactory character and of the impossibility of continuing Irish association with the Crown in any form. He did not say in his original statement whether repeal would or would not mean secession from the Commonwealth. It was only when a correspondent asked that question that Mr. Costello replied in the affirmative. Once he had done so, clearly there could be no going back.

It is no secret that Mr. Costello's colleagues in the Executive Council in Dublin, including Mr. Seán MacBride, his Minister for External Affairs, were taken unawares by his announcement. That the majority favoured the repeal of the Act in principle was not in question, but the timing of the announcement and the form in which it was made were matters in which the Taoiseach acted on his own initiative.[5] This had one important consequence. Had Mr. Costello not committed himself in Ottawa to the view that repeal meant secession, the nature of any future association between Eire and the Commonwealth might have been considered on its merits. As it was an irrevocable decision was taken on this point before the outstanding question of republican India's relations with the Commonwealth had been settled. By a delay of some six months, the Irish government would at the least have been able to consider to what extent the evolution of the Commonwealth, to which

[1] Ibid. col. 2440.
[2] Mansergh, 'The Implications of Eire's Relations with the British Commonwealth', *International Affairs*, January 1948.
[3] e.g. *Montreal Gazette, Ottawa Citizen,* 6 September 1948.
[4] The Irish High Commissioner had earlier stated that no further pronouncement was to be expected, which suggests that Mr. Costello changed his mind in view of the interest stimulated by the article in the *Sunday Independent* (see *Ottawa Citizen,* 6 September 1948).
[5] Mr. Attlee in his autobiography noted with his usual studied understatement, 'He [Mr. Costello] made a speech in Canada—which was, I believe, not premeditated' (*As It Happened,* p. 190).

Ireland in the past had contributed, allowed of informal Irish association with it on the basis not of constitutional law, but of consultation and free cooperation on matters of common interest. Some such continuing connexion might indeed have seemed the more logical outcome of Mr. Costello's policy, for, as he later observed on many occasions, the repeal of the External Relations Act was intended, by removing the last vestige of alien authority, to cement relations with Britain and with the oversea members of the Commonwealth. But internal political considerations confronted him with the hard choice of acting precipitately or risking the break-up of the inter-party government.

While Mr. Costello's announcement in Canada of the intention of his government to repeal the External Relations Act was unexpected, there was no occasion for surprise in the decision itself. The Minister for External Affairs, the Deputy Prime Minister, and finally the Taoiseach himself, had all made it abundantly clear in the course of the summer that such was the intention of the inter-party government. Yet the government of the United Kingdom, which was diplomatically represented in Dublin, appears to have been taken unawares, and it would seem from ministerial comments that it had given little or no consideration to the situation which would arise when the External Relations Act was repealed.[1] No doubt it might have anticipated that any Irish government contemplating such a step would have forewarned it as a matter of courtesy. Yet it was not something on which any confident expectation could or should have been founded, for, as the Lord Chancellor, Viscount Jowitt, observed later, there was no reason why Mr. Costello should have informed the United Kingdom government and the United Kingdom government had not the smallest complaint on the ground that he had not done so.[2] Mr. Costello's failure to do so in fact occasioned comment largely because of the fortuitous presence of United Kingdom ministers in Dublin during July and August.[3] Yet those visits in themselves make still more surprising an apparent failure in London to deduce that the only point about Irish policy that remained in doubt was the moment when the External Relations Act would be repealed and what, if anything, would replace it as the symbol of Irish association with the Commonwealth.

The situation which would be created by the repeal of the External Relations Act was not formally considered at the Meeting of Commonwealth Prime Ministers in October 1948, but advantage was taken of their presence in London to arrange separate discussions with Irish ministers on the consequences of secession. These discussions were held at Chequers, and the

---

[1] See the Lord Chancellor's comment, 15 December 1948, H. of L. Deb., vol. 159, col. 1089.
[2] Ibid. col. 1087.
[3] Mr. Costello may have feared that if informed of Irish intentions in advance the United Kingdom government would commit itself to a course of action from which, later, it might find it difficult to depart, even if it so desired.

Prime Ministers of the United Kingdom, Canada, and New Zealand, the Australian Minister for External Affairs, and the Irish Ministers for External Affairs and Finance took part.[1] The countries of the Commonwealth which were represented were those whose populations included a large number of people of Irish origin, and the meeting was understood to have been arranged on the initiative of the dominion representatives.[2] While it was agreed on all sides that the talks at Chequers were at once friendly and helpful, what emerged most clearly from them was that in respect of future Irish relations with the Commonwealth the Commonwealth was by no means united. While the United Kingdom ministers indulged in the gloomiest forecasts of the possible effect of secession on trade preferences and citizenship, dominion ministers were resolved that the severance of formal constitutional ties should not be the occasion for a wider breach.

Some attempts were made to dissuade the Irish government from the course of action on which it had embarked, but wholly without success. Had anyone spoken 'with the eloquence of Demosthenes and at greater length even than Mr. Gladstone', said the Lord Chancellor subsequently, 'I am convinced that he would have failed—as I failed.'[3] United Kingdom forebodings about the consequences of repeal were, however, a test of nerve and resolution and at least served the purpose of indicating beyond possibility of dispute that the Irish mind was made up. Even had the severance of the last formal tie with the Commonwealth involved the ending of trade preferences and of reciprocal citizenship arrangements, the Irish government would not have been deflected from its course. The somewhat artificial air of crisis in fact served not to weaken but to strengthen the cohesion of the inter-party government, while the Opposition, though making legitimate fun of the somersault of Fine Gael —whose sudden conversion to republicanism, in the words of Mr. MacEntee, was a 'skedaddle enough to make a skeleton merry'—could not oppose repeal and were politically out-manœuvred. Only Fine Gael deputies[4] in some Dublin constituencies where the Protestant minority was strongly represented were embarrassed. Some of them had made much at the general election of their party's pledge to effect no change in constitutional relations, and after Mr. Costello's Canadian pronouncements they were left explaining to a sceptical electorate that, strictly speaking, the repeal of the External Relations Act, inasmuch as it involved no amendment of the Constitution, was not within the meaning of the phrase 'constitutional change', and that in any event the assurance would have applied only if Fine Gael had been returned to power as a single party government. Elsewhere, however, Fine Gael gained rather

---

[1] On 17 October 1948. No official advisers were present at them.
[2] *The Times*, 18 October 1948. Neither the Asian dominions nor South Africa were represented at the Chequers meeting.
[3] 15 December 1948, H. of L. Deb., vol. 159, col. 1089 (Mansergh, *Documents*, ii. 818).
[4] Mr. Costello was among them.

than lost support by their change of front. In a deeper sense there was, indeed, less inconsistency in their purpose than the critics allowed. The course Fine Gael had adopted was intended to bring Eire closer, not to take her farther away from the Commonwealth. It was, said Dr. O'Higgins, the Minister of Defence, because they desired better relations with the Commonwealth that they had decided to repeal the Act. That was something Mr. Costello frequently emphasized.

On 24 November Mr. Costello introduced the Republic of Ireland Act.[1] The purpose of the Act was to repeal the External Relations Act, to declare that the description of the state should be the Republic of Ireland, and that the President, on the authority and the advice of the government, might exercise the executive power for any executive function of the state in connexion with its external relations. 'This Bill', said Mr. Costello,

will end forever, in a simple, clear and unequivocal way this country's long and tragic association with the institution of the British Crown and will make it manifest beyond equivocation or subtlety that the national and international status of this country is that of an independent republic.[2]

The Act was not to be regarded as the product of unthinking or negative nationalism, but was intended to clarify the position of the state and by so doing to increase national self-respect and to lead to closer friendship with the Commonwealth. The measure, Mr. Costello said, was not designed or conceived in any spirit of hostility to the British people or to the institution of the British Crown; on the contrary one result of its enactment would be that Eire's relationship with Britain would be 'far closer and far better, and will be put upon a better and firmer foundation than it ever has been before'. It would be 'unthinkable' for the Republic of Ireland to draw farther away from the nations of the Commonwealth with which 'we have had such long and, I think, such fruitful association in the past 25 or 26 years'.[3] Commonwealth countries would not be regarded as foreign by the Republic of Ireland, neither would the Republic be treated as a foreign country by Britain and the oversea members of the Commonwealth. Likewise arrangements would be made for a reciprocal citizenship, on the lines indicated in the Irish Nationality and Citizenship Act of 1935[4] and the British Nationality Act of 1948. Lastly, Mr. Costello discounted the widely entertained view that the Republic of Ireland bill would place a further, more formidable, barrier in the way of Irish unity as 'part of a foul press campaign'. This was debatable. It was, of course, true, as Mr. Costello observed, that no single approach had been made by the government of Northern Ireland towards either the dominion government of the Irish Free State or the externally associated government of

---

[1] Mansergh, *Documents*, ii. 802–8.
[2] Dáil Deb., vol. 113, col. 347 (Mansergh, *Documents*, ii. 802–8).
[3] Ibid. coll. 351 and 353.
[4] Mansergh, *Documents*, i. 314–19.

Eire, with the object of promoting the reunion of Ireland. But was it correct to deduce from this that the case for the perpetuation of what he described as 'the national indignity' of the External Relations Act rested on nothing more than 'the vain and vague hope that our ambiguous constitutional status . . . would prepare the way for co-operation from the Government of the six north-eastern counties of Ireland?'[1] While the majority in Northern Ireland were unlikely in any foreseeable future to take any initiative to end partition, the argument that no additional barrier should be placed in their way was not altogether insubstantial. The repeal of the External Relations Act, by taking the twenty-six counties outside the Commonwealth, ruled out the possibility of partition being resolved in a Commonwealth context. 'I hesitated about declarations of this sort', said Mr. de Valera, 'and I left a bridge for a long time, in the hope that by it it would be possible to bring about the unity of our country, that we were going to meet the sentiment of the minority... by means of association.'[2] Such from a nationalist standpoint was the essence of the case against the severance of formal ties with the Commonwealth by the proclamation of a twenty-six-county republic.

On 25 November[3] the United Kingdom government formally recorded that, while Eire would no longer be a member of the Commonwealth after the repeal of the External Relations Act, her government had stated that it recognized the existence of a specially close relationship between Eire and the Commonwealth countries and desired that it should be maintained. For its part, too, the United Kingdom government recognized the existence of these factual ties and was at one with the Irish government in desiring that close and friendly relations should continue and be strengthened. Accordingly the United Kingdom government declared that it would not regard the enactment of the Republic of Ireland Act as placing the Republic in the category of foreign countries or Irish citizens in the category of foreigners. On the contrary, the position of citizens of the Republic in the United Kingdom would be governed by the provisions of the British Nationality Act 1948, while the Irish government for its part stated its intention of bringing its legislation into line with that in Commonwealth countries so that in Eire citizens of Commonwealth countries would receive comparable treatment.

Some critics, notably Lord Simon,[4] doubted whether a mere statement of government intention sufficed to establish a situation by which the Republic of Ireland would remain neither a Commonwealth partner nor a foreign country. Was it possible, he asked, to add to the simple and long-established formula 'Are you a British subject, or are you a foreigner?' a 'third something which is neither one nor the other'? Moreover the meaning attributed to the

[1] Dáil Deb., vol. 113, col. 385.
[2] Ibid. col. 413 (Mansergh, *Documents*, ii. 808).
[3] H. of C. Deb., vol. 458, coll. 1413–15 (Mansergh, *Documents*, ii. 809).
[4] H. of L. Deb., vol. 159, coll. 1051–93 (Mansergh, *Documents*, ii. 811–16).

phrase 'a citizen of Eire' when the British Nationality Act was approved by Parliament was something quite different to that which it would acquire when Eire became a republic outside the Commonwealth. It was not really understood, argued Lord Simon,

> that the phrase 'a citizen of Eire', used in the Act when Eire was within the Commonwealth, could be given by the Government a connotation so wide as to cover a citizen of some future Republic called Eire which hereafter divorces itself from the Commonwealth altogether.

Again, what assurance had the government that other countries would regard a mere declaration of its own as sufficient to ensure that in international law Eire, not being a member of the Commonwealth, would none the less not be regarded as a foreign country?

To Lord Simon's questions there was in logic no very convincing answer. But statesmanship is something different from logic, and there was no doubt where the advantage of both Britain and Ireland lay. The long-established economic association and social ties between the two countries made impracticable, as the Lord Chancellor emphasized,[1] any complete severance of their relations. What should we gain, he inquired, by treating Eire's citizens as aliens, expelling them, as we should have to do, from our civil service, from our diplomatic service, from our army and our forces generally, and by a large-scale elaboration of the whole system of aliens' control which would in consequence be necessary? Yet he allowed, too, that it was not these practical considerations that were decisive in determining the reaction of the United Kingdom. It was the influence of the oversea dominions. It was the original intention of the United Kingdom government to insist that secession meant the ending of trade preferences and alien status for Irish citizens in the United Kingdom.[2] It was deflected from its course by pressure from the oversea dominions. 'If we had taken a different line from the one we decided to take', admitted the Lord Chancellor,[3] 'we should have acted in the teeth of the advice of the representatives of Canada, Australia, and New Zealand.' Here, therefore, was an outstanding illustration of the influence of oversea Commonwealth countries on United Kingdom policy, and as such it was an important landmark in Commonwealth history. It was also an ironic commentary on Irish policy which, while possibly promoting better relations with Britain, unquestionably weakened Irish ties with those friendly nations overseas.

---

[1] H. of L. Deb., vol. 159, coll. 1090–1.
[2] Cf. *Manchester Guardian*, 16 November 1948. The apparent concern of United Kingdom statesmen with the possible effect of secession upon trade preferences in this case was in marked contrast to their bland assumption a year earlier that there would be no difficulty in their continuance when Burma seceded (see Lord Listowel's comments, 25 November 1947, H. of L. Deb., vol. 152, col. 866; Mansergh, *Documents*, ii. 792).
[3] H. of L. Deb., vol. 159, col. 1090.

A Republic Proclaimed

The Irish government decreed that the Republic of Ireland Bill should not take effect, and the Republic not be proclaimed, until Easter Day 1949, the thirty-third anniversary of the Easter rising of 1916. Its choice of date was not welcomed by Mr. de Valera. This was not the republic for which Pearse and Connolly had died, and he declined to play any part in the formal inaugural ceremonies. Perhaps the reason for his critical aloofness helped to bring new life to the anti-partition campaign. In any event in the early months of 1949 the political pressure against Northern Ireland was intensified with consequences that diminished rather than increased the prospects of unity. Particularly unfortunate, from the point of view of the aims which its authors had in mind, was the decision of an all-party conference to raise funds to support anti-partition candidates within the six counties, for intervention served only to stiffen resistance.

At midnight on 17–18 April Eire formally left the British Commonwealth and the last constitutional tie with Britain was severed. From that moment the description of the state became the Republic of Ireland. The birth of the Republic was heralded by celebrations throughout the country which reached their climax in Dublin on Easter Monday. At the General Post Office, with memories of the 1916 Rebellion present in every mind, the tricolour was hoisted at noon and there followed a military parade watched by a subdued crowd. 'We believe', said the Taoiseach,[1] 'that what has been done today will ensure more cordial and closer co-operation between Ireland and Great Britain and the other members of the Commonwealth of Nations than could ever have existed under any conditions before.' King George VI, mindful 'of the neighbourly links which hold the people of the Republic of Ireland in close association with my subjects of the United Kingdom', expressed his goodwill to the President, and alluded to the 'most grateful memory' in which he held 'the services and sacrifices of the men and women of your country who rendered gallant assistance to our cause in the recent war'.[2] It seemed as if Mr. Costello's hopes of closer, friendlier relations were to be fulfilled. But in fact, though the republican goal had been achieved, the price in terms of unity had not yet been paid.

The Ireland Act, 1949[3]

In this atmosphere of goodwill and mutual congratulation the introduction of the Ireland Bill in the House of Commons provided a sharp reminder of tensions that were unresolved. The purpose of the Bill, in the words of its Preamble, was:

to recognize and declare the constitutional position as to the part of Ireland heretofore known as Eire, and to make provision as to the name by which it may be known

---

[1] *Irish Times*, 19 April 1949. [2] *The Times*, 18 April 1949.
[3] 12 & 13 Geo. 6, c. 41 (Mansergh, *Documents*, ii. 821–5).

and the manner in which the law is to apply in relation to it; to declare and affirm the constitutional position and territorial integrity of Northern Ireland and to amend, as respects the Parliament of the United Kingdom, the law relating to the qualifications of electors in constituencies in Northern Ireland.

The Act recognized that as from 18 April 1949 Eire ceased to be part of His Majesty's dominions and it confirmed that 'in no event will Northern Ireland or any part thereof cease to be part of His Majesty's dominions and of the United Kingdom without the consent of the Parliament of Northern Ireland'. It was this latter provision that provoked an angry outburst in Dublin. At a special session Mr. Costello, with the support of all the parties, moved that the Dáil should solemnly reassert the indefeasible right of the Irish nation to the unity and integrity of the national territory and reaffirm the sovereign right of the people of Ireland to choose its own form of government and through its democratic institutions to decide all questions of national policy free from outside interference. The claim of the United Kingdom Parliament to enact legislation affecting Ireland's territorial integrity was repudiated and the Dáil recorded its indignant protest against the introduction in the British Parliament of legislation 'purporting to endorse and continue the existing partition of Ireland'.[1]

The vehemence of the Irish reaction was sharpened by a sense of grievance on a matter of comparative detail. The Irish government felt that it had at the least been insufficiently forewarned by United Kingdom ministers of the nature of the renewed pledge they would feel it necessary to give to Northern Ireland when the Republic of Ireland seceded. On 28 October 1948 Mr. Attlee had stated that the United Kingdom government had always entertained, and continued to entertain, the view that no change should be made in the constitutional status of Northern Ireland without Northern Ireland's free agreement,[2] but it appears that at the meeting at Chequers on 17 October, and at the subsequent meeting in Paris on 17 November with the Irish ministers, the question of partition, though raised by the Irish representatives, was not discussed on the ground that it was outside the scope of the topics under review at these conferences. Neither, so Mr. Costello asserted, was there any suggestion of any kind made by British ministers that the Republic of Ireland Act would necessitate United Kingdom legislation in respect of partition. It might be that had the United Kingdom government been earlier forewarned of the intention of the Irish government to repeal the External Relations Act, it would itself have felt bound to indicate its own intentions about legislation affecting the position of Northern Ireland in advance. In any event lack of prior consultation did not affect the substance of the dispute. The protest of the Irish government against an Act of the United Kingdom

[1] 10 May 1949, Dáil Deb., vol. 115, col. 786 (Mansergh, *Documents*, ii. 826–30).
[2] H. of C. Deb., vol. 457, col. 239.

IRELAND

Parliament involving 'the further tightening of the ligature which was fastened round the body of Ireland by the Government of Ireland Act, 1920'[1] was addressed to that provision of the Ireland Act which specifically transferred the right of self-determination to the Parliament, not even to the people, of Northern Ireland. The Act of 1920 had paid lip service to the unity of Ireland, but the Act of 1949, by confirming that the United Kingdom Parliament itself could not, without the consent of the subordinate Parliament in Belfast, even adjust the boundary so as to transfer minorities to the Republic of Ireland, in fact meant that the boundary acquired an air of permanence and of rigidity in law which it had not hitherto possessed.[2] Since the area to be excluded from the Irish national Parliament in 1920 had in fact been determined by the Ulster Unionist party, who, on the admission of one of their own leaders, claimed an area in which Unionists would be assured indefinitely of a safe majority,[3] the reaction of republican Ireland was understandable, even though its leaders had themselves taken the initiative in bringing about the sequence of events which led to the enactment of the Ireland Act 1949.

Mr. Attlee maintained, in contradistinction to Mr. Costello, that it was not the United Kingdom government but the government of Eire which had tightened the ligature round the body of Ireland. In this the British Labour Prime Minister was not expressing a view entertained solely by British or foreign observers. In the past Irish leaders had taken the same view of the probable consequences of secession. Mr. Dillon's words spoken in 1945 and

[1] Dáil Deb., vol. 115, col. 788.
[2] The transfer of the responsibility from the United Kingdom to the Northern Ireland Parliament theoretically impaired the hitherto unitary character of the state, for if one part of a state through its local parliament is entitled to decide whether, in the words of Mr. Attlee, 'to stay in or leave the United Kingdom and Commonwealth' its subordination to the imperial Parliament in this very important respect apparently ceased so long as the Act was in force and was so interpreted. Even in federations such a right of secession is by no means uniformly admitted and theoretically at least the concession of such a right to a part of a unitary state detracts from and may even be held to destroy its unitary character. Professor J. L. Montrose, Dean of the Faculty of Law, Queen's University, Belfast, at a conference on Federalism, arranged by the Australian National University in 1951, took the view that 'the relation between the United Kingdom and the Province is one of devolution, but it could be substantially described as federation' in view particularly of the provisions of the Ireland Act 1949 (see G. Sawer, ed., *Federalism* (Melbourne, Cheshire for Australian National University, 1952), pp. 6–7 and 27).
[3] Captain Craig (afterwards Lord Craigavon and first Prime Minister of Northern Ireland) explained in the debate on the Government of Ireland Bill 1920 that if an Ulster Parliament, including, that is to say, all the nine counties of the Province of Ulster, were to be set up 'the Unionist majority would be about three or four, but in a six counties' Parliament, with 52 Members, the Unionist majority would be about 10.... We quite frankly admit that we cannot hold the nine counties.... Therefore, we have decided that, in the interests of the greater part of Ulster, it is better that we should give up those three counties [Cavan, Monaghan, and Donegal] rather than take on a bigger task than we are able to carry out' In fact, at the general election held on 10 February 1949 the Unionists' overall majority was 22, a result which added force to republican protests (29 March 1920, H. of C. Deb., vol. 127, coll. 990–1).

already quoted may here be recalled.[1] In the same debate, after denouncing Mr. de Valera's ambiguities and evasions, Dr. O'Higgins inquired:

> Does not the Taoiseach know, if he is a realist at all, that, whatever hope there is of securing the unity of this country, it will only be achieved with the aid of other members of the Commonwealth and within the Commonwealth of Nations? If any real Irishman had to choose between a united Ireland, a member of that Commonwealth, and a dismembered Ireland calling herself a republic and living her life as a dismembered, isolated little fragment, he would have no hesitation in arriving at his decision and making his choice.[2]

Mr. Dillon was Mr. Costello's Minister for Agriculture, Dr. O'Higgins his Minister for Defence.

The dispute about partition obscured the important provisions of the Ireland Act which gave legislative sanction[3] to the arrangement already made in respect of reciprocal citizenship by confirming that the Republic of Ireland was not to be regarded as a foreign country or its citizens as foreigners within the United Kingdom. Subsequently the overseas members of the Commonwealth (excepting Pakistan and Ceylon) enacted comparable legislation so that after the secession of the Republic of Ireland from the Commonwealth neither the Republic nor its citizens were regarded as 'foreigners' in the countries of the Commonwealth.[4]

Ireland's Relations with the Commonwealth, 1921–49: A Perspective View

Between 1921 and 1952 there were three distinct experiments in the ordering of Anglo-Irish relations. Two of them failed. The first was the experiment of Commonwealth membership embodied in the Anglo-Irish Treaty of 1921, in which the status of the Irish Free State was specifically associated with that of the senior dominion Canada, and generally with those of the oversea dominions. That experiment may be said to have come to an end in 1936–7 when the External Relations Act was passed and a new Constitution enacted with the sanction of popular approval. Then from 1936 to 1949 there was the experiment, not in a full but in an improvised form, of external association. During that period Eire owed no allegiance to the Crown and was not, in the Irish view, a member of the British Commonwealth of Nations, but a state whose association with it from without was symbolized by the King's signature to the letters of appointment of Irish representatives to foreign countries. With the decision to repeal the External Relations Act in the autumn of 1948 this experiment too was brought to a close and Eire, or the Republic of Ireland as she was now described, formally seceded from the British Commonwealth. She did not, however, become a foreign country, as did Burma which also seceded, and, while her citizens were no longer to be regarded as British

---

[1] 17 July 1945, Dáil Deb., vol. 97, col. 2598. See above, p. 270.   [2] Ibid. coll. 2609–10.
[3] Sections 2, 3, and 4.   [4] Mansergh, *Documents*, ii., section xix.

subjects or Commonwealth citizens, they retained a special non-foreign status.

The three successive experiments in the ordering of Anglo-Irish relations are recorded in the three different names which have been given or are commonly attributed to the sovereign state which comprises twenty-six of the thirty-two counties of Ireland. Between 1921 and 1937 she was known as the Irish Free State. In the Constitution of 1937 the name of the state was declared to be Eire, or in the English language, Ireland. Since the jurisdiction of her government extended only to twenty-six of the thirty-two counties this created confusion, and outside the twenty-six counties the name Eire was commonly, if incorrectly, used as though it were a synonymous successor title to the Irish Free State. In 1948, contrary to general belief, the name of the state was not changed by the Republic of Ireland Act.[1] Any such change would have necessitated an amendment of the Constitution. The Act merely declared that 'the description of the State shall be the Republic of Ireland'.[2] Evidently this refinement was too much for British draftsmen, for the Ireland Act 1949 speaks wrongly of 'The Republic of Ireland' as the name 'attributed thereto by the law thereof'.[3]

Yet the fate of these experiments in dominion status and external association, while final in the sense that neither could be repeated, determined the nature of what remained. Characteristic of Irish relations with the Commonwealth since 1921 had been an approach towards a finality that was never quite attained. Even the declaration of the Republic and secession did not effect the final break which in fear or in hope had been awaited for so many years. What was most remarkable after April 1949 was not how much but how little had been changed. It is because of that that it is not only relevant but important to consider, first, to what extent the secession of the Republic of Ireland from the Commonwealth transformed the relationship that had existed previously, and particularly in the preceding twelve years when Eire had been a state associated with the British Commonwealth, and, secondly, what were the more important practical consequences of secession. The two questions are indeed closely interrelated. With regard to the first, Mr. Churchill failed to detect any radical transformation in Anglo-Irish relations in 1949. Before then, he remarked, Eire so far as the Commonwealth was concerned was 'in and out'; thereafter it was 'out and in'. If generally Mr. Churchill's comments on Irish affairs were remarkable for pungency rather than precision, yet on this point legislation enacted in the United Kingdom and in the dominions went far towards endorsing his view. The Ireland Act of 1949 stated, as has been seen, that though Eire ceased from 18 April 1949 to be a part of His Majesty's dominions, yet 'notwithstanding that the Republic of Ireland is not part of His Majesty's dominions' she was not a foreign

[1] No. 22 of 1948.   [2] Section 2.
[3] Section 1, subsection 3.

country. Parallel legislation was enacted by other members of the Commonwealth. The New Zealand Republic of Ireland Act, 1950[1] went so far as to say that:

> All existing law ... shall, until provision to the contrary is made by the authority having power to alter that law, have the same operation in relation to the Republic of Ireland, and to persons and things in any way belonging or connected with the Republic of Ireland, as it would have had if the Republic of Ireland had remained part of His Majesty's dominions.

Was such language warranted? Did the formal act of secession make as little difference as that?

To answer this question it is necessary first to recall something of the history of external association, for Eire was not a full member of the Commonwealth when she seceded. She was in her own view an external associate, and in any view her membership was diluted. Even in United Kingdom law and practice external association had received qualified recognition after 1945; it was not, therefore, as though a full membership had ended in April 1949. The idea of an externally associated state had first been advanced in 1921 by the Sinn Féin leaders as an alternative to dominion status. Ireland, they had argued, being a mother country long subject to foreign rule, was not and never could be a dominion in spirit. That was a status appropriate to countries of settlement such as Canada and Australia, not to countries with long and cherished traditions of their own. Above all the Crown, which to British peoples, whether at home or settled overseas, symbolized their conception of law and constitutional government, remained for the Irish only the symbol of alien rule. On the other hand, the Sinn Féin leaders acknowledged the interdependence of Britain and Ireland and, in 1921, they went so far as to suggest that defence and foreign policy should be matters of common concern, while the very special relationship that existed between Ireland and the Commonwealth countries should be symbolized by Irish recognition of the King as head of the Commonwealth association. In his 'Document No. 2',[2] which constituted Mr. de Valera's republican alternative to dominion status and was drafted after the Treaty, Article 2 proposed that for 'purposes of common concern, Ireland shall be associated with the States of the British Commonwealth', and Article 6 'that, for purposes of the Association, Ireland shall recognize His Britannic Majesty as head of the Association'. But in Britain in 1921 such an idea was considered almost fantastic. Even eleven years later when Mr. de Valera returned to office and elaborated once again this conception of the appropriate relationship of an Ireland external to, but associated with, the Commonwealth, he found in Mr. J. H. Thomas, the Dominions

---

[1] No. 13 of 1950, Art. 3 (Mansergh, *Documents*, ii. 837).
[2] Reprinted in Dorothy Macardle, *The Irish Republic* (London, Gollancz, 1937), pp. 996–1000.

Secretary, a singularly unappreciative audience.[1] Yet, despite discouragement both within and without, Mr. de Valera was not to be deflected from his chosen course, and by the passage of the External Relations Act and of the Constitution the following year he partially achieved his purpose. It was not, however, arranged as neatly as might have been wished. For this the abdication was responsible, for it meant that the order of the legislation had to be reversed, the External Relations Act preceding the Constitution to which it was meant to be the sequel. More generally it demanded improvisation where deliberation was much needed. Yet whatever its defects, the External Relations Act fulfilled for a time the purpose its author had in mind. It made possible the continuing association of a country which, after 1937, was a republic in all but name with a Commonwealth of Nations owing common allegiance to the Crown. It may be that the solution was too subtle; certainly it had about it the air of a temporary expedient. But then time was needed not only for emotions to calm but also for the pattern of Commonwealth relations to evolve. And by this ingenious arrangement which, in the view of the United Kingdom government and the governments of the oversea dominions, effected no fundamental alteration in the position of the Irish Free State as a member of the Commonwealth, Mr. de Valera felt that he had attained the goal of an independent republic associated as a matter of external policy with the states of the British Commonwealth. When he was pressed to define exactly Eire's relationship with the Commonwealth he replied that was something which he alone could not do, thereby indicating that so long as the Commonwealth were satisfied that Eire fulfilled the conditions of associate membership, it was not for him to contest their opinion; likewise when urged by Mr. Dillon to declare whether Eire was a republic or not, he referred him to the Constitution and to the dictionary definition. The solution, however, absurd though the situations were to which it gave rise, had one quality of statesmanship. It closed no doors, or to use Mr. de Valera's own analogy, it 'burned no bridges'. But it was too subtle to last—and in fact it did not last quite long enough. That was one of the ironies of Commonwealth history.

In 1949 a republic—how inconceivable it had seemed a quarter of a century earlier—was accepted in accordance with its own expressed wishes as a full member of the Commonwealth. Irish experiments and direct inquiries in Dublin had encouraged Indians to think that after all a republic might be associated with the Commonwealth; and in the event the actual phrase by which the membership of India as a republic was reconciled with the Crown as the symbol of Commonwealth association had its Irish origin. The Irish, it is true, had never imagined that a republic could be a full member of the

[1] 'Mr. de Valera has told us... that his ultimate aim is the recognition of a United Ireland as a Republic with some form of association with the British Commonwealth in some circumstances and for some reasons and the recognition of the King as the head of the association. Any such proposals would be totally unacceptable to His Majesty's Government in the United Kingdom' (14 November 1933, H. of C. Deb., vol. 281, col. 727).

Commonwealth and the phrase they had contemplated in 1921 recognized the King as the head of the association, not as Head of the Commonwealth, which was the formula adopted in the London Declaration of 1949. Yet the intention of that earlier phrase, which embodied the essence of Mr. de Valera's thought, was to resolve the very problem which was resolved by the Commonwealth Prime Ministers in April 1949.[1] And at the very moment when it was so resolved Mr. de Valera was out of office for the first time since 1931. It is perhaps unprofitable but none the less interesting to speculate about what would have happened had things been otherwise. Is it conceivable that Mr. de Valera, had he been in office, could have done other than welcome the fulfilment in so large a measure of his own ideas and feel that thereby the door at last was opened for an agreed solution of Eire's relations with the Commonwealth? In August 1948, before Mr. Costello's fateful visit to Canada, he alluded to the changes that were taking place in the Commonwealth and contrasted the situation which had existed before 1939 with that which was now emerging. Ireland had never been in the position of Australia or Canada or New Zealand, where the great majority of the people could unquestionably accept allegiance to the Crown and inclusion in the British Empire. She was rather in the position South Africa had always been in, that India might adopt, and that Burma could have adopted, had not the test been 'allegiance . . . and inclusion in the British Empire'.[2] With the condition of allegiance waived, Mr. de Valera even contemplated 'internal' free association with republican status in the Commonwealth. Nor did he fail at the same time to express his own opinion that 'it is desirable, if we can, to be associated—I have no hesitation myself in saying this—with the States in the British Commonwealth', provided there was no ambiguity about the character of the association.[3] The 1949 Declaration, in accordance with which republican India remained a full member of the Commonwealth and not an associate, seemed therefore to reflect almost exactly the ideas Mr. de Valera entertained of the possible future form of Ireland's relationship with the Commonwealth. Republican India owed no allegiance to the Crown, however oblique, her ambassadors were accredited in the name of the Indian President, and not of the King as was the case in Eire before the repeal of the External Relations Act, and the recognition of the King (or Queen) as Head of the Commonwealth derived directly from Mr. de Valera's earlier phrase. Mr. Attlee, who as Prime Minister was chiefly responsible for Britain's response to the conflicting policies pursued by republican India and republican Ireland, believed that the Indian solution would have provided a more satisfactory basis for Anglo-Irish relations than 'the rather illogical relationship' which was brought into being as a result of the Irish decision to secede from the Commonwealth.[4]

[1] *The Times*, 28 April 1949; see above, pp. 250–2.
[2] Dáil Deb., vol. 112, coll. 2422–3.
[3] Ibid. col. 2434.
[4] *As It Happened*, p. 190.

Mr. Costello's inter-party government, in deciding that while India was to become a republic within, Ireland was to be a republic without, the Commonwealth, reached a different conclusion. It acted as it did for reasons not to be lightly discounted. Mr. Costello himself laid most emphasis upon two of them; upon the imperative needs for unity at home, or for taking the gun out of politics as it was more dramatically phrased, and for opening the way to frank friendship with Britain and the Commonwealth by removing the psychological barrier of the Crown and all ambiguity and source of friction in constitutional relationships. By a repeal of the External Relations Act friendship would henceforward, he urged, be easy and natural, not artificial and constricted, and it would be closer, for, to recall his own words, it would be unthinkable for the Republic of Ireland to draw farther away from the countries of the Commonwealth.

In 1949 external association was dead. There could, as Mr. de Valera admitted, be no going back. The boats were burned.[1] If attention has hitherto been focused on the interplay of party politics, it is not to be overlooked that there was a deeper reason for the failure of external association. It was an experiment which, like the experiment of dominion status that preceded it, failed to fulfil its principal purpose. In the 1920's Mr. Cosgrave's government believed that by being a loyal member of the Commonwealth it would bring closer the day when Ireland would be reunited; Mr. de Valera believed in 1936 and later that by refraining from the open declaration of a republic and by continuing Eire's association with the Commonwealth he too would at least leave the door open for reunion. But both felt that they had been mistaken. All parties had convinced themselves by 1949 that neither full dominion status nor still less external association would contribute toward the removal of the border. In the North the majority wished to remain part of the United Kingdom irrespective of whether the twenty-six counties became a dominion, an associated state, or an independent republic. In so far as British statesmen had conceived that partition and dominion status could form parts of one consistent whole they were altogether mistaken. Experience had shown that either there was a partitioned Ireland or there was an Irish dominion. There could not be both. There could not for the simple reason that within the twenty-six counties there was no solid basis of support, as the Fine Gael party learned to their cost, for Commonwealth policies. The Commonwealth votes were on the other side of the border.

The repeal of the External Relations Act was accepted both in London and in Dublin as tantamount to secession. In constitutional law this was not a necessary conclusion, since the London Declaration of April 1949 made it clear that allegiance to the Crown was no longer to be regarded as an essential condition of Commonwealth membership. Earlier British refusal to consider a relationship in which allegiance was not an integral part and later hardening

[1] 24 November 1948, Dáil Deb., vol. 113, col. 414.

of Irish opinion against any association with the Crown combined to produce this result. The real difference in the history of the relations of the Indian and Irish republics with the Commonwealth is to be found not in the field of constitutional theory but in the realm of political intention. India expressed an explicit desire to remain a full member after she had become a republic at a time when the United Kingdom and the other existing members of the Commonwealth were prepared to contemplate membership on that basis, Eire at the critical moment did not.

The Republic Outside the Commonwealth

The consequences of Irish secession are likely to unfold as the years go by. At this slight vantage point in time, it is only in relations between governments that they may be at all clearly discerned. When the Republic seceded the Lord Chancellor forecast that Ireland would not retain all the advantages of Commonwealth membership and, in particular, that she would be excluded from Commonwealth consultation and not be considered as a partner in Commonwealth defence matters.[1] This, in fact, happened. At the Commonwealth Finance Ministers' meeting held in London in January 1952, and at the discussions of the Commonwealth Prime Ministers on economic affairs in November and December 1952, the Republic was not represented. Yet Irish interest in these conferences, which were concerned with the strength and stability of the sterling area, could not be overlooked. Accordingly, after the January meeting had concluded, the Ministers for Finance and for Industry and Commerce[2] visited London for bilateral conversations with the Chancellor of the Exchequer. It is clear that however useful such bilateral conversations[3] were, they precluded contact between Irish ministers and ministers in the oversea Commonwealth countries. Likewise the Irish Ambassador in London might see the Secretary of State for Commonwealth Relations as occasion required, but he did not attend the meetings of the Secretary of State for Commonwealth Relations with dominion High Commissioners after April 1949. In Dublin also there was thereafter no occasion for the Taoiseach to have specially close contact with the representatives of Canada, Australia, or India. Indeed, were he to do so, representatives of other countries would have legitimate ground for complaint. In these ways, therefore, personal contact with the Commonwealth overseas declined. In the equally important field of written communications, the Republic of Ireland no longer came within the Commonwealth system. As a result the Irish government was deprived of Commonwealth sources of information, a deprivation no doubt especially noted in respect of events in the many countries in which the

[1] 15 December 1948, H. of L. Deb., vol. 159, coll. 1092–3.
[2] Mr. Seán MacEntee and Mr. Seán Lemass, who was also the Deputy Prime Minister.
[3] They would seem to have had a marked effect upon Irish financial policy, so much so that Mr. MacEntee was denounced by the Opposition as having 'out-Butlered Butler' in his Budget proposals.

Republic was not itself diplomatically represented. More generally the Commonwealth, as a result of secession, was precluded from exercising an influence on Irish policy, and the Irish deprived of opportunities of making their views heard in world affairs through one of the greater groupings of states. So much would seem to have been to the disadvantage of both parties and a clear loss.

The loss, however, was potential rather than actual. In fact Commonwealth consultation with Eire ceased in the early months of the war, at the request of the Irish government. It was not thereafter resumed. The Irish were represented at no Commonwealth ministerial conference after 1932, though their officials did attend conferences of experts, particularly that on nationality, between 1945 and 1949. In general, relations since the economic war (1932–8) were not normal, and if the force of the conclusion which has been drawn is not thereby much diminished, it is to be recorded that it was the prospect, not the actual existence, of intimate consultation between the Republic of Ireland and the Commonwealth countries overseas that virtually disappeared with secession. At a time when Western Europe was declining in influence and power and some of the Commonwealth countries overseas at least seemed to be treading the path to greatness, that is something not to be lightly disregarded. When Mr. Peter Fraser, who played an unostentatious but statesmanlike part in the resolution of Anglo-Irish difficulties, was asked what difference secession would make in New Zealand's attitude to Ireland he replied, 'What difference could there be? There has been friendliness always'.[1] But friendship, as Dr. Johnson once remarked, is something to be kept in constant repair, and after 1949 Irish opportunities for keeping their friendship with the oversea members of the Commonwealth in repair were sensibly diminished.

While the secession of the Republic of Ireland has lessened the intimacy of Irish relations with the oversea Commonwealth countries, no such easy verdict can be pronounced in respect of relations with Britain. Mr. Costello's hope that secession would remove misunderstanding was not wholly unfulfilled in the immediately succeeding years. Even in the realm of practical affairs it was probably, to go back to the example already given, an advantage to the Republic that her Ministers should have discussed the financial problems of the sterling area and trading relations with Britain on a reciprocal basis, for the problems were exceptional in character. In a wider field there would seem, too, to have been perceptible improvement in relations. At the time of the death of King George VI there could be no doubt that the general and sincere expression of sympathy in the Republic reflected a feeling which for the first time was uninhibited by political or constitutional reservations. Here the contrast with sentiment at the time of the death of George V was marked, and there seems little doubt that the disappearance of ambiguities in Anglo-Irish relations contributed to the changed atmosphere. Even among

[1] *Manchester Guardian*, 20 December 1948.

ex-Unionists who had been greatly shocked by the somersault of Fine Gael there were to be found some who then conceded, albeit sadly, that perhaps Mr. Costello had been right after all. Few perhaps, at this short distance in time, would be disposed to quarrel with Mr. Fraser's verdict. 'I regret', he said, 'that any country finds it necessary because of the sentiments of its people even to get away a little distance from us, but I believe there is more friendship in Southern Ireland for the British Commonwealth today than there has been in my lifetime.'[1] It is also to be noted that the Fine Gael party, which had hitherto stood, or had been regarded as standing, for the Commonwealth connexion, alone of the parties comprising the inter-party government greatly strengthened its position at the 1951 general election.

In the relationship that existed between Britain and Ireland after secession the reciprocal arrangements about citizenship (made possible, so far as the United Kingdom was concerned, by the continuing application of the provisions of the British Nationality Act under circumstances different in respect of Eire to those contemplated when the Act was drafted) were of first importance. Their effect, it will be recalled, was that in the United Kingdom citizens of Eire, though no longer British subjects, were not regarded as foreigners and in practice enjoyed the rights and obligations of citizenship, while in the republic citizens of the United Kingdom enjoyed reciprocal rights. In the relevant Irish citizenship order issued in 1949 it was stated that citizens of the United Kingdom and colonies 'shall, subject to law, enjoy in Ireland similar rights and privileges to those enjoyed by Irish citizens in the United Kingdom and Colonies by virtue of the British Nationality Act, 1948'.[2] Similar orders were made for Commonwealth members other than Pakistan and Ceylon, which included no special provision for citizens of the Republic in their Nationality Acts.

These citizenship arrangements, practical and sensible though they were, did not escape criticism. English people, many of whom were disposed to regard Irish insistence on a distinct and wholly separate nationality as an example of Irish contrariness, complained that by means of them the Irish were getting the advantages without assuming the responsibilities of Commonwealth membership. Nor indeed was it only Englishmen who questioned their appropriateness. In the *Oireachtas* one voice, that of Senator Margaret Pearse, sister of Patrick Pearse the leader of the 1916 Easter rising, protested that in Britain she felt herself to be an alien as much as she did in France, and would prefer to be so regarded.[3] Her father, as has been the case so often with extreme nationalists that it can hardly be coincidence, was English. Mr. George Bernard Shaw, too, after living in Britain for nearly half a century, though starting from a different premiss reached the same conclusion. 'I shall

[1] *Manchester Guardian*, 23 December 1948.
[2] Eire, Statutory Instrument, No. 1 of 1949.
[3] Senate Deb., vol. 36, col. 340.

always be a foreigner here,' he said, 'whether I have to register as an alien or not, because I am one of the few people here who think objectively. Englishmen are incapable of objectivity.'[1]

On balance, however, the arrangements would seem to have been to the advantage of both parties. It is true that the Irish were the more obvious beneficiaries in that the number of Irishmen coming to work in the United Kingdom exceeded the number of Englishmen engaging in business or seeking refuge from austerity or high taxation in the Republic. But then the principal reason why Irishmen came in such large numbers to the United Kingdom was because there was heavy and mostly unskilled work to be done there for which there was no sufficient alternative supply of labour. Nor must one think of men alone. In the years 1945–51 women emigrants exceeded men by nearly 40 per cent.[2] Most of them were employed in domestic work, or in factories and hospitals. Was it not in fact much to the advantage of Britain that there should be this labour reserve so conveniently to hand and that those drawn from it should not have to be registered as aliens? Indeed, the large administrative problems involved in any alternative would in any event almost certainly have precluded its adoption. Finally, in the event of a war in which Britain was involved and the Republic was neutral, alien status would place difficulties in the way of Irishmen volunteering to serve in the British forces. Would this be a wise or even a just arrangement in view of the number of Irishmen who served in the Second World War?

In the economic field the secession of Ireland made no formal difference in trading relations with Commonwealth countries. It was suggested in 1949 that the continuance of reciprocal preferential trading agreements with a country which had left the Commonwealth would be challenged by foreign governments as conflicting with the most-favoured-nation clause in commercial treaties and with the General Agreement on Tariffs and Trade at Geneva in 1947. On this point, however, the Irish government was always, and it seems rightly, confident. It argued that the very close and long-standing trading relationship between Britain and Ireland warranted exceptional treatment, and more particularly it pointed to the fact that the schedule to the Geneva Agreement listed the Commonwealth countries by name and individually, without any general heading implying that the preferences they exchanged were dependent upon Commonwealth membership.[3] In 1950 the Irish government concluded a formal agreement with the United States government in a Treaty of Friendship, Commerce, and Navigation in terms which ensured that the continuance of the existing trade preferences would not

---

[1] *News Chronicle*, 18 October 1948.

[2] In 1947, for example, 18,727 women received new travel permits, passports, and identity cards to go to employment, compared with 12,511 men (Ireland, Commission on Emigration and other Population Problems 1948–54, *Reports* (Dublin, Stationery Office, 1955), pp. 115–16, and Table 33, p. 324).

[3] Cmd. 7258, Art. 1 and Annex A.

be questioned by Washington.¹ The advantage to both Britain and the Republic of Ireland of a special trading relationship was not seriously questioned on either side, though its relative importance, like that of other Commonwealth agreements, had declined.

The Republic of Ireland, though not a member of the Commonwealth, remained after 1949 a member of the sterling area. No country, other than Britain herself, had then a greater interest in the maintenance of the strength of sterling as an international currency. That was mainly because of Ireland's large overseas investments, estimated in 1947 to amount to £150 per head of the population.² At the end of the war the Republic had in fact accumulated sterling balances amounting to some £400 million. Unlike the Egyptian or Indian sterling balances, the Irish represented payment not for services rendered but for food supplied at low prices during the war years when it was not possible to buy consumer or capital goods on any comparable scale from Britain. The existence of this balance temporarily at least had the effect of knitting the Irish economy yet more closely to that of the United Kingdom.

Secession brought about no significant change in Irish foreign policy. In an Exchange of Notes[3] with the United States government in 1949 Mr. Seán MacBride stated that while partition continued no Irish government, whatever its political views, could participate with Britain in a military alliance without running counter to the national sentiments of the people and thereby incurring the risk, in the event of a crisis, of civil war. In this view Irish membership of the North Atlantic Treaty Organization was precluded.

In the past, Whitaker's Almanack divided the world into the British Empire, the United States, and foreign countries. After 1949 the Republic of Ireland was added to the intermediate category. But if the Republic of Ireland was thus to be regarded as being neither a foreign country nor a member of the Commonwealth, the emphasis in describing her status might still be placed very differently. While it is true that in 1921 dominion status was imposed on the Irish Free State, that helps to explain, but does not alter the fact that she was an unsatisfactory dominion. From the first she worked for the dilution of dominion status, for the removal of the Crown from her Constitution, for the abolition of Privy Council appeals (though here Canada took the first step); she was the first dominion to replace the concept of common citizenship by that of reciprocal citizenship; she was the first, too, to set the example of neutrality in a major war, and finally the first to secede.[4] In English eyes this constituted a depressing and a discouraging record. On the other hand if the Republic of Ireland were regarded as a foreign country rather than as a former

---

[1] Ireland, Treaty Series, 1950, No. 7, Art. XX, No. 3, reads: 'The most favoured nation provisions of the present Treaty relating to the treatment of goods shall not apply to advantages accorded ... by Ireland to members of the British Commonwealth of Nations and their dependent territories.'

[2] R. C. Geary, 'Irish Economic Development since the Treaty', Studies, December 1951.

[3] No. 9934.

[4] Burma, which seceded a year earlier, had never been a dominion.

dominion how different might be the impression. Viewed in this light Britain might be thought of as having as her nearest neighbour a country remarkable amongst the countries of Western Europe for her effective working of the British parliamentary system, for the stability of her government, for her hitherto comparatively strong financial position; a country moreover which was a reservoir of labour, whose principal export was food of which some 90 per cent. came to the United Kingdom, and who despite neutrality sent, and might again send, material reinforcement in the form of volunteers to serve in the British forces in wartime. In short, was Britain not to be envied in her Atlantic neighbour? If here the contrast is deliberately heightened, does it not suggest that psychologically at least it was of importance that the United Kingdom should regard the Republic of Ireland more as a foreign country than as an ex-member of the Commonwealth with all that that implies? If in the opinion of most, though not all,[1] of the members of the Commonwealth Ireland took the wrong road in 1949, it is at least to be remembered that even the wrong road leads somewhere.

But if this was the more constructive approach from the British point of view it was by no means necessarily so from the Irish. The major objective of Irish policy remained the ending of partition. Here the possible contribution of the Commonwealth was consistently underestimated between 1921 and 1949, largely because Commonwealth relations are viewed in Ireland in the narrower context of Anglo-Irish history. The events of 1948-9 showed clearly that nowhere had the Republic better friends than in the oversea dominions. For that reason alone it might be thought important that the possibilities implicit in association in one form or another with the Commonwealth should be kept to the forefront in the Republic.

One fact of cardinal importance remains fundamental in all discussion of the consequences of Irish secession. It is the very special relationship which existed between Britain and Ireland, a relationship which remained even after 1949 more intimate, in every respect other than the political, than that of Britain with any of the oversea members of the Commonwealth. The census of 1951 showed that there were one and a half times as many citizens of Eire resident in the United Kingdom as there were citizens of all the other members of the Commonwealth put together.[2] The proportion of Irish exports that went to the United Kingdom, and the proportion of United Kingdom exports to the Republic were alike higher than those in the case of any dominion. The relationship between the two countries has existed since the beginning of time and presumably will continue until the end. It is a relationship parallel to the

[1] Mr. Fraser expressed the opinion that 'in the circumstances . . . the best thing was done' (*Manchester Guardian*, 23 December 1948).

[2] According to Great Britain, General Register Office, *Census 1951: Great Britain One per cent. Sample Tables* (London, HMSO, 1952), pt. 2, table ix. 1, there were some 530,000 persons born in Eire resident in Great Britain. The corresponding total from all oversea Commonwealth countries, colonies, protectorates, and mandated territories was 375,000.

relationships between Norway and Sweden, Portugal and Spain, Canada and the United States. For this reason the Republic of Ireland might secede from the Commonwealth without profoundly affecting her relations at least with Britain. All this deserves emphasis because it means that the secession of Ireland from the Commonwealth and its consequences is no guide to the consequences of secession by an oversea dominion. In their relations with Britain the Commonwealth is fundamental, for Ireland it was never more than a superstructure.

PART III
PROBLEMS OF INTERNATIONAL AND COMMONWEALTH RELATIONS

For as the nature of Foule weather, lyeth not in a showre or two of rain; but in an inclination thereto of many dayes together: so the nature of War, consisteth not in actuall fighting; but in the known disposition thereto, during all the time there is no assurance to the contrary. THOMAS HOBBES, *Leviathan*

... this greatest human experiment in political organization, this proudest political structure of our time, this precedent and anticipation of what one hopes may be in store for human society in years to come. J. C. SMUTS, 21 October 1942

CHAPTER VII

THE COMMONWEALTH, THE UNITED NATIONS, IMPERIAL DEFENCE, AND INTERNATIONAL SECURITY, 1945–52

Commonwealth Statesmen and the Post-War International Organization

EVEN in the early phases of the war the thoughts of Commonwealth statesmen were occupied with the problem of ensuring peace and upholding the rule of law in international society when victory was won. 'While the old order is destroying itself', said Mr. Mackenzie King on 4 September 1941,[1] a new relationship 'of men and nations has already begun its slow but sure evolution'. The spirit which inspired it found expression when Britain determined to put an end to aggression in Europe, when other nations of the Commonwealth took their place at Britain's side, when the United States 'resolved to lend its powerful aid to the nations which are fighting for freedom', and in the Atlantic Charter. Events themselves were combining to create 'one great brotherhood of freedom-loving peoples'. All this, in Mr. Mackenzie King's view, was to be welcomed, for 'a new world order to be worthy of the name is something that is born, not made'. It could not be reduced to writing at a conference table at some given moment; it was something that needed to grow in the hearts and minds of men. If, therefore, it 'is not already on its way before the war is over, we may look for it in vain'. But if it were, as he believed in 1941 it was, then it could assume shape and form 'only . . . through the leadership of the British Commonwealth of Nations and the United States of America working in whole-hearted cooperation toward this great end'. A condition of their doing so, Mr. Mackenzie King implied but did not say, was the abandonment of policies of isolation, and for this reason his Guildhall speech of September 1941 may be taken to mark the formal ending of Mr. Mackenzie King's reliance upon a policy of detachment in foreign policy which had been—partly from choice and partly from necessity—so marked a feature of Canadian and indeed of dominion policies in the inter-war years.

Mr. Mackenzie King's views at this time and later were more representative of Commonwealth opinion but less arresting in language and less provocative in content than those of General Smuts. Some three months before the Canadian Prime Minister spoke in London, General Smuts had expounded his ideas of the future world order from Pretoria.[2] To him it seemed clear that the day of the small independent sovereign state had passed and that 'we

---

[1] *The Times*, 5 September 1941.
[2] Broadcast, 'A Vision of the Future', 12 June 1941 (Holborn, i. 343–5).

are unmistakably in for larger groupings in that holistic process which fundamentally moulds all life and all history'. The pressure of the times was irresistibly forcing the free democracies 'representing the forward movement in our western civilization' into a great world organization. In it there would be various degrees of affinity. In the inner circle, and now foremost in resistance to Nazi tyranny, would be the nations of the Commonwealth, whose association 'is undoubtedly a precedent and a prototype for the large world association now in process of formation'. Closest to this inner circle was the United States of America, linked to it by the same ethic and the same political philosophy. The outer circle would be comprised of the democracies of Western Europe and other continents. But the new organization would not be universal in its membership. That was the mistake of the League of Nations, which attempted 'too wide a membership on too loose and nebulous a foundation'. Later such an association might expand into the wider international society of the future, but 'do not let us attempt more than is wisely possible for the immediate future after the war. Time is a real force, a great healer and a great builder.'

While General Smuts and Mr. Mackenzie King agreed about the importance of close association between the Commonwealth and the United States after the war, their conceptions of the membership and even of the nature of the new world organization were evidently very different. Yet for both, as for others, the determining factors were the lessons rightly or wrongly drawn from the past. Experience of the League of Nations, noted Sir Charles Webster, 'dominated all the discussions on the drafting of the Charter of the United Nations'[1] and, it may also be added, all discussion preliminary to the agreement to draft it as well.

The dominions collectively had as the first aim of their post-war policy the maintenance of great-power unity. This was not because they liked great-power leadership—on the contrary they wished for the most part even in wartime to make it more responsive to the opinion of the middle and smaller powers—but because they attributed the failure of the League to two things: to the absence of some of the great powers from the League and to the lack of great-power leadership, which was in large measure a consequence of it. 'Where are the great Powers leading us, who have not the faith to persevere?', complained South Africa's representative, Mr. te Water,[2] when he saw Franco-British resolution on sanctions against Italy petering out in attempts at faltering and undignified compromise with the aggressor. But when it was further asked why great-power leadership had failed so dismally on this and on other occasions the most important part of the answer seemed to be because the

---

[1] *The Making of the Charter of the United Nations History* (Creighton Lecture, University of London, 1946).

[2] In a speech to the Assembly of the League of Nations, 1 July 1936 (Mansergh, *Documents*, i. 158).

United States was never, and others of the great powers were only intermittently, members of the League. In the Australian and New Zealand view it was the absence of the United States that had rendered impracticable the imposition of sanctions against Japan when she embarked upon her career of aggression in 1931 or continued it in 1936–7.

In a non-universal League [Mr. S. M. Bruce told the Assembly of the League of Nations in September 1936] it is not possible to implement to the full the provisions of the Covenant, and to achieve what was the objective of the founders when they embodied certain sections in the Covenant; that is to say, by the universality of the League and its overwhelming power, they hoped to bring about the immediate cessation of aggression should it take place, or to prevent aggression from occurring. A non-universal League cannot do that.[1]

It was for this reason that General Smuts concluded that

the crux of this next great step in the organization of our world will be the attitude of the United States of America. . . . The failure of the League since 1932 is probably the main cause of the present world war. America's sporadic efforts to help from the outside proved unavailing. As a Member of the League her role would probably have been decisive. I must therefore conclude that just as world organization is essential, so America's membership in such an organization is no less essential.[2]

Limited membership, in fact, had resulted in a balance of power between the aggressor and peace-loving states and many therefore desired to replace it by universal membership which would ensure an overwhelming preponderance on the side of law and order. 'The new order', said Mr. Mackenzie King on 9 October 1942, 'must be a world order. It must be governed by a universal rule of law.'[3] When victory comes 'the peoples of the British Commonwealth and the people of the United States will be found at each other's side, united more closely than ever. But they will be part of a larger company. In that company all the nations now united in the defence of freedom will remain united in the service of mankind.'[4] But if universalism was to be the principle of membership, its chief attraction was that it predicated the membership of the great powers.

Whatever, therefore, the reservations entertained by dominion governments about the nature of the great-power leadership under which they fought in the Second World War, they were resolved that their demand for a more democratic peace-time association should not be pushed to the point at which great-power agreement and great-power participation in the new international organization would be imperilled. 'No peace', said Mr. Nash as early as

[1] League of Nations, *Official Journal*, special suppl. no. 255, pp. 75–77 (Mansergh, *Documents*, i. 150–2). [2] Broadcast, 12 June 1941 (Holborn, i. 343–5).
[3] Address to American Federation of Labour Convention (ibid. pp. 307–11).
[4] Address to the Pilgrims of the United States, New York, 2 December 1942 (ibid. pp. 311–15).

December 1942, 'will be practicable unless these four chief powers are in agreement.'[1] To the dominions the new order held out the promise of one telling advance upon the old—the great powers would be within, not without, the fold. It was not an advance to be lightly jeopardized.

While great-power membership of the new international organization came to be accepted by dominion governments as a condition of its effective survival, most of them were—but always subject to this paramount consideration—very much concerned to ensure that they should exert their due influence in its councils and indeed, if possible, rather more than was their due in terms of power and population. General Smuts, it is true, was prepared to contemplate a world ruled by Titans, but his dominion colleagues emphatically were not. Less preoccupied than he was with the problems of power, and less sensitive at this time to the dangers of post-war Soviet hegemony in Europe, they asserted, in the case of Dr. Evatt provocatively, the right of lesser powers to have their say and to exercise their restraining influence upon the great. In this they advocated a course which commended itself alike to the self-respect, to the self-interest, and to the idealism of the democratic peoples for whom they spoke. Implicit in the nature of their demands was a conflict of opinion, and perhaps of interest, with the government of the United Kingdom, one of the great powers whose authority it was hoped to confine within reasonable bounds.

On his visit to Washington in May 1943 Mr. Churchill was invited to sketch out his ideas of the post-war international order and his response to the invitation illustrates the differences in the approach of the United Kingdom and of the majority of dominion governments to this question. Mr. Churchill contemplated a supreme World Council in which the greatest powers, however reinforced, would exercise ultimate authority, and subordinate to it three Regional Councils, one for Europe, one for the American hemisphere, and one for the Pacific.[2] The central idea of the structure, said Mr. Churchill, was a three-legged stool—the World Council resting on three Regional Councils, and he attached much importance to the regional principle, since it was 'only the countries whose interests were directly affected by a dispute who would be expected to apply themselves with sufficient vigour to secure a settlement'. The conception was coupled with the idea of the closest association, including possibly reciprocal citizenship and the common use of strategic bases, between the United States and British Commonwealth. But despite dominion representation on regional councils, what was fundamental to Mr. Churchill's proposals was the hegemony of the greatest powers and it was precisely to this that dominion governments objected.

---

[1] Speech to the World Confederation of International Groupments, New York City, 4 December 1942 (Holborn, i. 337–40).
[2] None specifically for Asia or Africa, though China was a possible member of the World Council (see Churchill, iv. 717–19).

A draft statement of the intention to found a United Nations Organization, approved at the first Quebec Conference in September 1943 and issued in the name of the four sponsoring powers, the United States, the Soviet Union, the United Kingdom, and China, in the Moscow Declaration of 30 October the same year was more reassuring to the dominions and to other middle and smaller powers than some among them had come to expect. It stated that the four governments were agreed upon the necessity of establishing 'at the earliest practicable date a general international organization, based on the principle of the sovereign equality of all peace-loving states, and open to membership by all such states, large and small, for the maintenance of international peace and security'.[1] By asserting the sovereign equality of all peace-loving states the statement disposed of the notion much canvassed in the capitals of the great powers in the earlier years of the war and reappearing in a new guise in Mr. Churchill's proposals, that the three or four great powers should be vested with exclusive effective authority for the preservation of peace. Such recognition of the principle of equality was in accord with dominion sentiment and the concern of dominion governments henceforward was with its application in practice.

There were two ideas about the representation and the allocation of responsibility among members of the new international organization, which in one form or another enjoyed considerable support among some or all of the countries of the Commonwealth. One of these was regionalism, the other functionalism. Neither term had a single precise meaning but both had the attraction of suggesting ways in which great-power leadership might be diluted and some reality given to the principle of equality.

Regionalism within the Commonwealth was associated with the delegation of responsibility from the centre to a grouping of territories in a geographical area for particular or for more general purposes. The Eastern Group Supply Council established in Delhi,[2] the Middle East Supply Centre in Cairo, the appointment of a Resident Minister in West Africa,[3] the conference of East Africa Governors, the setting up of a Standing Joint Committee in the Caribbean, all came within the broad definition and in their several ways all afforded illustrations of the extent to which wartime needs had prompted at once decentralization of responsibility and some merging of local authority in a wider grouping. Some of these groupings proved ephemeral; some, notably in the West Indies, hastened the process of economic or political consolidation of the territories within them; while all served to popularize the notion that at a time when power tended to be concentrated in the hands of great states, regional groupings of this kind possessed

---

[1] Holborn, ii. 7–8.
[2] See above, pp. 84–85.
[3] For an account of his responsibilities see Viscount Swinton, *I Remember* (London, Hutchinson, 1948), chs. xvi–xix.

some inherent virtue. Few speeches on imperial policy of the later war period failed to allude to what was widely deemed to be a novel and encouraging development, whereas it was in fact in full accord with the nineteenth and twentieth-century pattern of consolidation of North American, New Zealand, Australian, and South African colonies into larger units. It was not the idea but the emphasis placed upon it and the faith reposed in it that were novel.[1]

The Anzac Agreement of 1944,[2] which constituted the most ambitious essay in regional planning among self-governing members of the Commonwealth in this period, represented, in the words of Dr. Evatt, the resolution of the two Pacific dominions to establish in their part of the world a regional system of defence because they had taken to heart 'the bitter experiences resulting from the failure to achieve collective security and the international order which must be based on security'. By taking the initiative and publishing the agreement Dr. Evatt believed that the two countries had 'given a lead on certain vital aspects of international relationships in the post-war world'.[3] This proved too large a claim.

The idea that regionalism might provide the foundation of the new world order was deemed unrealistic on closer examination chiefly because the power and resources necessary for security and welfare were not, in fact, evenly distributed among the regions but concentrated very largely in one. 'I should like to stress', observed Mr. Fraser in January 1944, 'that we entertain considerable doubts as to the practicability of regional bodies for the preservation of world peace, though we are entirely in accord with the idea of a system of regional defense'.[4] It was these doubts, increasingly shared, which focused greater attention on the Canadian Prime Minister's championship of the alternative and at root conflicting idea of functionalism.

In July 1943 Mr. Mackenzie King observed that while on the one hand authority in international affairs should not be concentrated exclusively in the largest powers, it could not on the other be divided equally among all the sovereign states of the United Nations, or all effective authority would disappear.[5] Representation on future international bodies should, therefore, 'neither be restricted to the largest states nor necessarily extended to all states'. It should be determined on a functional basis, so that states, whether large or small, which had the greatest contribution to make to the object in view should be admitted to membership. Functionalism was a principle that commended itself to Canadian altruism, good sense, and self-interest alike.

In the concluding years of the war and the early years of peace Canada, as was most strikingly demonstrated by her assistance to the United Nations Relief and Rehabilitation Administration, contributed impressively

---

[1] Cf. especially General Smuts's views, above, pp. 175–6.   [2] See above p. 181.
[3] 10 February 1944, Australia, H. of R. Deb., vol. 177, p. 73 (Mansergh, *Documents*, ii. 1166–8).
[4] He was speaking at the signing of the 1944 Anzac Agreement (Holborn, ii. 686–9).
[5] Canada, H. of C. Deb., 1943, vol. 5, p. 4558.

to reconstruction and welfare in the war-devastated areas of the world.[1] She played a leading part in a series of specialist conferences, notably on food and agriculture, civil aviation, and, at Bretton Woods, on international monetary and financial stabilization.[2] Her representation at such conferences, as Mr. Lester Pearson justly observed in 1944, 'has been functional and has been generally recognized as such'. But, as he also, and with equal justice, remarked, a series of functional bodies, however useful in promoting economic and social co-operation, would be a shaky foundation for a post-war international organization. 'There can be no full dinner-pail of nutritionally correct foods, financed by an international bank and carried swiftly to consumers over reduced tariff barriers by internationally supervised air lines, as long as there are wars and fears of war.'[3]

The Commonwealth Prime Ministers at their Meeting in May 1944 considered the implications of the Moscow Declaration of October 1943 and collectively affirmed that 'after the war a World Organization to maintain peace and security should be set up and endowed with the necessary power and authority to prevent aggression and violence'.[4] Mr. Mackenzie King observed later to the House of Commons in Ottawa, in part reference to these discussions in London, that 'in the organization of power it is for the most powerful states to take the lead', and the fact that that was being done was an instance of the 'correct application of the functional idea of international organization', which at least was satisfying to him. But while the Canadian Prime Minister was not therefore disposed to question the large powers to be vested in the Security Council, he was concerned about the representation of lesser countries on it. By what criteria should it be decided? Mr. Mackenzie King had little doubt about the answer. 'In determining what states should be represented on the council with the great powers it is, I believe, necessary to apply the functional idea. Those countries which have most to contribute to the maintenance of the peace of the world should be most frequently selected.'[5] This, however, was something about which the great powers had yet to be convinced.

Dominion governments were not represented at the Dumbarton Oaks Conference, membership of which was confined to the great powers. They had, however, already had an opportunity of discussing the major problems at issue with the government of the United Kingdom in May, and during the Conference itself, which sat from late August to early October 1944, United

[1] Canada was the third largest contributor in relief supplies to UNRRA.
[2] Later Canada's willingness and her capacity to contribute to the work of the specialized agencies of the United Nations likewise assured her of a particular place among the middle powers in relation to them. In 1947, when eight such agencies had been established, Canada was a member of all of them. For a more detailed account see *Canada in World Affairs, 1944–6*, chs. iv–vi.
[3] Speech at Winnipeg, 27 December 1944 (Holborn, ii. 622–5).
[4] Declaration of 16 May 1944 (Mansergh, *Documents*, i. 585–6).
[5] Canada, H. of C. Deb., 1944, vol. 6, pp. 5909–11 (Holborn, ii. 617–21).

Kingdom delegates met daily with the representatives of dominion diplomatic missions in Washington. At one remove, therefore, the dominions had an opportunity of influencing the course of the discussions denied to representatives of other lesser powers. On one point, however, they found that great-power opinion was immovable, and that was on the predominant and privileged position of the great powers in the new international organization. The veto was the most striking manifestation of this resolve but it extended far beyond the veto. 'No organization of peace', complained Mr. Pearson in comment on the Conference proposals in December 1944, 'should be based entirely on any small group—even of the mightiest powers'; and he urged the modification of great-power control and the abandonment of its corollary that outside the group of great powers all other states, Honduras and Canada for example, were equal. Above all, he complained, the position and importance of the middle powers were not sufficiently recognized—due, it need hardly be said, though Mr. Pearson said it, to great-power disregard of the functional principle.[1]

The reaction to the Dumbarton Oaks proposals in Australia and New Zealand was no more favourable than in Canada. Dr. Evatt, who had evinced no special interest in Canadian ideas about functional representation, reached the same broad conclusion as Mr. Pearson. Dr. Evatt at no time doubted that the Dumbarton Oaks proposals showed obvious signs of having been drawn up in the exclusive interest of major powers,[2] and at the San Francisco Conference he embarked on a bitter campaign against great-power pretensions. But there was a point beyond which dominion governments were not prepared to go, for, weighing on their minds, and in the last resort weighing decisively, was the sobering reflection that all prospect of peace depended upon great-power participation in the new international organization.

I know there was something like consternation after Dumbarton Oaks [observed General Smuts] when it became known that there was to be this special position and special functions for the Great Powers, but it was right, it is quite right. . . . Some very considerable sacrifices will have to be made by some of the lesser powers . . . in our own interests and those of world peace.[3]

London and San Francisco

There was a meeting of Commonwealth statesmen in London in April 1945 to consider the Dumbarton Oaks proposals for the charter for the United Nations, before the meeting of the Conference of the United Nations due to take place at San Francisco later that month. The aim of the London meeting was, to judge by the observations of dominion leaders, emphatically not to produce a common policy, or uniformity of view, but to exchange opinions

---

[1] Holborn, ii. 624–5.
[2] Australia, H. of Deb., vol. 184, pp. 5029–33.
[3] Speech at the Commonwealth Statesmen's Meeting, London, 1945 (Holborn, ii. 728–9).

and to frame individual policies in the light of discussions with Commonwealth colleagues. Our purpose, said Lord Cranborne at the opening session, 'is not to "gang up" against other nations or to obtain any sectional advantages for ourselves', but to contribute 'as best we may' to the creation of the new world organization. It was possible, he pointed out, doubtless chiefly for the enlightenment of transatlantic countries, to be a member of a family and a citizen of the world and it was as members of a family that they were deliberating together.[1]

The United Kingdom government did not expect that dominion governments would all subscribe to the agreements they had made with the other sponsoring powers at Yalta and Dumbarton Oaks. This expectation was well founded. The San Francisco Conference in 1945, like the Paris Peace Conference a year later, made plain to all the world that the dominions were little disposed to acquiesce in arrangements distasteful to them merely because they carried the imprimatur of United Kingdom sponsorship. If anyone believed that there was a Commonwealth bloc, the debates on the United Nations Charter must have proved a sharply disillusioning experience.

The division of opinion between the United Kingdom on the one hand and Canada, Australia, and New Zealand on the other at root concerned the place to be given to the great powers in the United Nations Charter. The United Kingdom, as a sponsoring power, defended the exceptional authority vested in the Security Council and expressed her conviction that such concentration was necessary in the interests of universal membership and the preservation of peace; she was not prepared to yield, even in respect of the veto, to demands strongly and at times vehemently expressed[2] by the middle powers, with the dominions chief among them, for a more democratic organization. Her attitude was understanding but in important matters uncompromising, and the dominions, lacking the support of a great power, emerged from the Conference with concessions to their respective viewpoints which were of secondary importance so far as the political provisions of the Charter were concerned.

There was little disposition on the part of dominion representatives at San Francisco to question the need for a strong Security Council. 'We felt', said Mr. Fraser,[3] 'that the Security Council ought to have great powers, and it has.' But at the same time Canada, Australia, and New Zealand wished to see the powers of the General Assembly, restricted in the Dumbarton Oaks proposals to the discussion of the general principles of international peace and

---

[1] *The Times*, 6 April 1945.

[2] So vehemently that Mr. Fraser, for example, found it necessary to reassure the New Zealand House of Representatives 'that no differences of opinion on the wording of the principles of the Charter between any of the dominions, or between any of the dominions and the Mother-country in any way has loosened our close ties' (24 July 1945, New Zealand, H. of R. Deb., vol. 268, p. 575; Mansergh, *Documents*, ii. 1091).

[3] New Zealand, H. of R. Deb., vol. 268, p. 578.

security, much enlarged. Dr. Evatt played a prominent part in pressing for such enlargement and in this he was warmly supported by the New Zealand delegation. The General Assembly, said Mr. Fraser, ought to be the Parliament of mankind, and should have virtually unrestricted powers of discussion. As a result of such pressure, from smaller European states as well as the dominions, its powers were widened so that it might discuss 'any questions or any matters within the scope of the present Charter or relating to the powers and functions of any organs provided in the present Charter', with the reservation that any dispute or situation under review by the Security Council was specifically excluded from recommendation by the General Assembly. Both Dr. Evatt[1] and Mr. Fraser seemingly underestimated the importance of that reservation.

The grand assault of the Australian and New Zealand governments was delivered against the veto, or to be more precise against the exercise of the veto by a single great power. They were prepared to recognize that the agreement of four of the five great powers should be necessary for condemnation of an aggressor but not that of all five. It appeared 'utterly ridiculous', said Mr. Fraser, that a great power could stop its own condemnation, and deplorable consequences, in his view, might follow were one great power to veto action against a small associate or satellite aggressor.[2] The Australian objection was similar. 'To us', said Dr. Evatt, 'it was a matter of principle that while the unanimity of the Great Powers could be justified as a prerequisite for enforcement action, no such justification existed for the right of veto on measures designed for the peaceful settlement of a dispute.'[3] The risk the Australian government had especially in mind was that one great power, not a party to a dispute, by exercising the right of veto could prevent its being dealt with by the Security Council even though the ten remaining members desired that this should be done. Australia accordingly pressed strongly for the acceptance of an amendment which would remove the individual veto on the Security Council's conciliation jurisdiction. The amendment was defeated after the sponsoring powers had intimated that they would not sign the Charter if it were accepted. By way of inadequate compensation the great powers affirmed that they would use the veto sparingly, only in an emergency, and never to block preliminary consideration and discussion by the Council of any dispute. Dr. Evatt deemed this undertaking 'important' in 1945. Twelve years later other epithets would seem more appropriate.

The Canadian government, while at one with the Australian and New Zealand governments in its dislike of the veto, was more ready to acquiesce in its insertion in the Charter in an absolute form on the ground that such was the price to be paid for great-power membership of the United Nations.

[1] 30 August 1945, Australia, H. of R. Deb., vol. 184, pp. 5016–39 (Mansergh, *Documents*, ii. 1101–7). Dr. Evatt's speech gives a general commentary on Australia's aims and achievements at the Conference.
[2] 24 July 1945, New Zealand, H. of R. Deb., vol. 268, pp. 579–80.
[3] Australia, H. of R. Deb., vol. 184, p. 5024.

The Canadian delegation, their Report reads,[1] 'took the view that while they could not accept the interpretation of the voting procedure as satisfactory, it was not too high a price to pay for a world organization which was good in other respects'. Canadian energies, accordingly, were spent less in much publicized but vain opposition to the great-power veto and more in seeking to secure due representation of the middle powers on the Security Council and to safeguard such states from the consequences of great-power predominance. Both ends were deemed to be in accord with the true application of the functional principle. They had also much to recommend them on grounds of prudence.

The Security Council was to be composed of eleven members. Five of the seats were allocated permanently to the five great powers, the remainder to be filled by election by the General Assembly. How, and in the light of what principles, was the General Assembly to exercise its electoral responsibilities? The Canadian government, in the amendment to Article 23 (1) which it sponsored, proposed that the General Assembly should make rules for the election of non-permanent members 'in order to ensure that due weight be given to the contribution of members to the maintenance of international peace and security and the performance of their obligations to the United Nations'.[2] In the Canadian view, thus summarized, eligibility for election to the Security Council should be related to the ability of nations to contribute to international peace and security and the extent to which they had already given evidence of their intention to do so.[3] There was deliberately no reference to geographical or regional considerations. The amendment was rejected chiefly because of Soviet opposition. The Canadian government was not, however, altogether dissatisfied with the wording of the article as finally agreed, for this stated that attention was to be paid *in the first instance* to the contribution of candidates to international peace and security and also to equitable geographical distribution. It was formally agreed by the sponsoring powers that geographical considerations were to be regarded as secondary.[4] Superficially, therefore, this appeared to be, if not a victory, at least a weighting of the scales in favour of the functional as against the regional principle of selection. This was important for Canada both in theory and seemingly also in practice, for recognition of a geographical or regional principle, in view of the permanent membership of the United States, would inevitably work to her disadvantage. But while it was thus intended that special consideration should be given to the claims of middle powers, the members of the General Assembly showed little disposition to do so when the time came for them to cast their votes, and there was no apparent remedy. So it was that at the first election of non-permanent members to the Security Council in 1946

[1] Quoted in *Canada in World Affairs, 1944–6*, p. 142.
[2] *Round Table*, September 1945, p. 363.
[3] Canada, H. of C. Deb., 1945, 2nd session, vol. 1, p. 1199.
[4] UNCIO, xi. 254, 298, and 414. See also *Canada in World Affairs, 1944–6*, pp. 138–9.

Canada, in dignified but undisguised disappointment, withdrew in favour of Australia after three ballots had failed to yield a sufficient margin of votes in her favour.[1] In subsequent elections geographical or regional considerations continued to prevail, and since the Commonwealth was apt to be regarded as a regional grouping by other members of the United Nations, one Commonwealth member was customarily elected to non-permanent membership of the Security Council. This again was an outcome unwelcome to the Canadian government, which had consistently declined to regard the Commonwealth as such a bloc or group to be represented by one of its members, and which noted also that it was likely to lead in practice to under-representation of the Commonwealth.

Apart from non-permanent membership of the Security Council, the Canadian and also the Australian governments were concerned to safeguard for themselves and for others of comparable status their own independence and reasonable freedom of action. In the last resort the great powers could exercise their veto, but the other states, having no such reinsurance, would have to rely upon the interpretation of the relevant provisions of the Charter to protect them from interference in their domestic affairs. Here, so it seemed to Dr. Evatt, was a striking justification of the need for vigilance on the part of the smaller powers, and, while an Australian amendment was rejected, later modifications, chiefly by the sponsoring powers in the light of the representations made to them, satisfied dominion critics. As a result, while the wide power of discussion given to the Assembly was not narrowly restricted, internal matters 'such as the migration policy of a State' did not fall within the scope of the organization.[2] This was a matter in which South African interest was as pronounced as Australian, and Article 2 (7) of the Charter afforded them in principle the safeguard they desired.[3]

A somewhat similar problem seemed likely to arise in the event of a challenge to the authority of the United Nations. The smaller powers had little to contribute, the great powers were entrenched behind their veto, whereas the so-called middle powers might well be called upon by the Security Council to furnish such assistance, including armed forces, as was deemed by the Security Council necessary to meet any given threat to peace or security. Under the Dumbarton Oaks proposals members undertook 'to accept the decisions of the Security Council and to carry them out', their only protection being that afforded by Article 3. The Canadian delegates, arguing by doubtful analogy that this was equivalent to taxation without representation, urged that in equity such orders should not be binding unless assented to by the power to whom they were given and after its representatives had had an opportunity of participating as a member in the Security Council's decisions.[4] Their

[1] See *Canada in World Affairs, 1944–6*, pp. 152–4 for a fuller account.
[2] Australia, H. of R. Deb., vol. 184, p. 5030.   [3] UNCIO, x. 434 and 439.
[4] Ibid. xii. 297, 303, 307, 327, and 417–19. See also *Canada in World Affairs, 1944–6*, pp. 138–40.

point was largely met, though not in respect of membership, in Article 44 of the Charter which provided that 'when the Security Council has decided to use force it shall, before calling upon a member not represented on it to provide armed forces... invite that member ... to participate in the decisions of the Security Council concerning the employment of contingents of that member's armed forces'. Canada, a permanent member of the Atomic Energy Commission, also sought with the same considerations in mind to make more explicit the arrangements for the representation of non-members of the Security Council at discussions by the Council of any questions which 'specially affected' their interests. In this they achieved some modest success.

Canada, Australia, and New Zealand were not supported by South Africa in their attempts to 'liberalize' the political provisions of the Charter of the United Nations. On the contrary, in essentials the weight of South Africa was thrown on the side of the sponsoring powers.[1] Peace, in General Smuts's view,[2] was the paramount concern, and only the great powers could ensure it. Therefore everything should in this respect be subordinated to fostering co-operation among them within the framework of the new international order. In the Security Council, he told the House of Assembly, 'there is no equality'. There was on the contrary a special position for all the great powers. That position was given because of the world's preoccupation with the idea of security against war. Under modern conditions each war became a great war. For that reason the war power concentrated in the hands of the few had become the dominating factor of the whole situation. The great powers could not be treated as though they were equal with smaller powers; they had in fact a quite special position and a special responsibility. Everything had moreover to be done to keep them together, and the aim of the other powers must be to create 'conditions of unanimity' among the great. The veto was necessary to bind them together; therefore the veto was 'absolutely right'. This was the great departure from the League of Nations and, in General Smuts's opinion, it was a departure soundly based on experience. To him the division between middle and great powers was not the division that mattered; what mattered was division among the great powers, and other ends, however desirable in themselves, must be sacrificed in an attempt, which he recognized might well prove vain, to avert it.

The creative contribution of the dominions at San Francisco was in respect of economic and social policy and the setting up of the Trusteeship Council. Their aim was to elevate the status and widen the scope of the Economic and Social Council. The Australian delegation secured an amendment to Article 55 stating that 'the United Nations shall promote ... high standards of living, full employment and conditions of economic and social progress

---

[1] UNCIO, xi. 352.
[2] 6 February 1946, South Africa, H. of A. Deb., vol. 55, coll. 1155–73 (Mansergh, *Documents*, ii. 1107–18).

and development', and a pledge that all members would take joint and separate action in co-operation with the organization for the achievement of these purposes.[1] They were purposes embodied in the 1944 Anzac Agreement, and their insertion in the Charter represented a notable success for Australian and New Zealand statesmanship. Further Canadian proposals, suggesting that the General Assembly should pay due regard to the 'adequate' representation on the Economic and Social Council of states of major economic importance—what might be described as a classic application of the functional principle—were rejected as being inconsistent with the older, more honoured, but possibly in the circumstances less useful, principle of equality.[2]

Mr. Fraser, New Zealand's Prime Minister, was Chairman of the Committee on Trusteeship, for him an honourable but inhibiting position, and dominion representatives, especially those of Australia[3] and New Zealand, worked hard and in varied company to make the Trusteeship Council at once a progressive and a practical instrument for ensuring by agreement a widening measure of effective international supervision of non-self-governing territories based upon the now internationally recognized paramountcy of native interests. This was a difficult task. At one extreme the colonial powers were concerned that the responsibilities of the Council should extend only to the territories of ex-enemy states, while at the other the anti-colonial majority in the United Nations desired to see them extended to all non-self-governing territories. This was a question on which United States opinion shifted during the course of the Conference itself and one on which New Zealand and Australia were not in agreement with the United Kingdom. There was a real risk that at a Conference where, as General Smuts noted, the temper of the majority of the delegates was markedly anti-colonial, the colonial powers might be altogether estranged and decline to co-operate in the working of the Trusteeship Council. It is largely to the credit of Australia and New Zealand[4] that such a break was averted and discussion turned to more constructive channels.

The Commonwealth contribution at San Francisco was considerable but the conference was for most Commonwealth delegations a disillusioning experience. There they were brought face to face with the growing rift between the Soviet Union and the Western world, which was to render otiose for years to come much of the detailed work that they had done. This rift was soon destined to widen into an open breach. The drafting of the peace treaties was the occasion though not the cause. Only in one respect were the dominion governments themselves directly concerned. They had conceived

---

[1] UNCIO, viii. 134–7 and Australia, H. of R. Deb., vol. 184, pp. 5028–33.

[2] UNCIO, x. 53.

[3] An example is the Australian addition of a new Part C (promotion of welfare and development) to the working paper of the Committee on the Trusteeship System (ibid. pp. 695–6).

[4] For an illuminating account of the importance New Zealand attached to the idea of Trusteeship, both at the preliminary Commonwealth Conference in London and at San Francisco, see Wood, ch. xxii.

that peace-making would be a matter for those who had played an active part in securing the defeat of the Axis powers.

> We consistently maintain [said Dr. Evatt], the right of all active belligerents to a full share in the framing of the peace. Those who have contributed substantially to victory are entitled to make a corresponding contribution to the peace. That is the only fair and democratic method of making the peace; and a just method of making a peace settlement is as important as the settlement itself.[1]

'We in Canada', said Mr. Mackenzie King[2] at the Paris Peace Conference in 1946, 'felt that the measure of our participation in the war against aggression would have warranted a similar measure of participation in the decisions of peace.' But the Soviet Union was inexorably resolved on a great-power peace, if indeed there was to be a peace at all, and not all the violent indignation of Dr. Evatt nor the pained remonstrances of Mr. Mackenzie King sufficed to qualify by one iota their resolve. 'We were fighting', said the Canadian Prime Minister, 'to prevent two countries from dominating the world, and we do not now wish to see one, two, three or four countries dominate the peace.'[3] When, however, he did see it—he himself remarked that the word 'commentator' sufficed to describe Canada's role in the making of the draft treaties[4]—he felt one gesture of protest remained open to him. He declined to leave Canadian troops, for whom there was to be no Canadian zone, to serve as part of the occupying forces in Germany and Austria. Unfortunately it was a gesture at the expense not of the Soviet Union but chiefly of the United Kingdom. But its target was great-power domination.[5]

The dominions signed the United Nations Charter not grouped together under the general heading British Empire, as they had signed the League of Nations Covenant and the peace treaties in 1919, but separately according to their alphabetic order among the nations. This has been regarded as symbolic of the advancement of their Commonwealth and international status in the intervening years. On a longer view, however, Yalta, Potsdam, Paris, Moscow marked a significant and depressing depreciation of their ability to influence international politics and a sorry reward for those who had fought so gallantly from first to last against what Mr. Mackenzie King had once called the 'forces

---

[1] Dr. Evatt's speech to the Australian House of Representatives, 13 March 1946 (H. of R. Deb., vol. 186, pp. 187–92) sets out Australian demands in respect of peace-making in Europe and in the Far East. He believed he had obtained several important concessions, but with the breakdown of the Foreign Ministers' Conference in Moscow their value disappeared.

[2] Canadian Information Service Weekly, 9 August 1946.

[3] Canada, H. of C. Deb., 1947, vol. 1, p. 57.

[4] Quoted in *Canada in World Affairs, 1944–6*, p. 214. Also see generally ch. vii.

[5] On this point and on others in preceding pages relating to Canada's policies in respect of the United Nations and the peace treaties I have had the benefit of reading a thesis submitted for the degree of Doctor of Philosophy at the University of Oxford by Dr. D. G. Anglin, Associate Professor of Political Science and International Relations at the University of Manitoba, entitled 'Canada and the Middle Powers: the Relations of Great and Small States in International Institutions'.

of evil'. In 1947 he was left fearing 'greatly the drying up of the springs of chivalry and generosity in many nations if the great powers in the world today are not prepared to recognize what has been done . . . by the other nations of the world in helping to save the freedom of the World'.[1]

The Anglo-Egyptian Treaty Negotiations

In the minds of Commonwealth statesmen almost without exception the United Nations and the British Commonwealth of Nations constituted not conflicting but complementary organizations. The Commonwealth association was deemed to be a principal buttress to the United Nations. In the Pacific dominions and in the United Kingdom especially it was also regarded as an insurance against the failure of the new experiment in international organization embodied in the United Nations Charter. On both counts the creation of a world organization was thought not to diminish the importance of the Commonwealth to its several members but to demand from it a contribution to peace which, by its world-wide composition and distinctive character, it alone could give.

During the war methods of Commonwealth co-operation through consultation had been much elaborated. After the war, as during and before it, much depended upon the good sense and discrimination with which these methods were worked. It may be suspected that had Mr. Churchill in his unique political career ever held the office of Secretary of State for Dominion Affairs some wartime misunderstandings might have been avoided. Be that as it may, it was not Mr. Churchill, but surprisingly Mr. Attlee, a wartime Dominions Secretary, whose good judgement on Commonwealth affairs was widely acknowledged even by political opponents, who in 1946 neglected to draw the proper distinction between consultation and information, and by so doing caused some passing annoyance to Mr. Mackenzie King and the composition of an important pronouncement on the working of the Commonwealth system.

The occasion was the revision of the Anglo-Egyptian Treaty of 1936.[2] Article 1 of the treaty had terminated the occupation of Egypt 'by the forces of His Majesty The King and Emperor', but the treaty had entitled the United Kingdom 'to station forces in Egyptian territory in the vicinity of the canal' in view of its importance as 'an essential means of communication between the different parts of the British Empire' for a period of not more than twenty years, at the expiry of which any disagreement between the two Governments was to be referred to the Council of the League of Nations.

Confronted with Egyptian demands, which had the evident backing of Egyptian nationalist sentiment, the Labour government in 1946 proposed the withdrawal by stages of all United Kingdom forces. This provoked vigorous inter-party controversy at Westminster, in the course of which attention was directed to the interests of the dominions, and inquiries made as to the attitudes

[1] Canada, H. of C. Deb., 1947, vol. 1, p. 58.   [2] Cmd. 5360.

of their governments. In reply Mr. Attlee committed himself to the statement that the revision of the Anglo-Egyptian Treaty, and the particular proposals made by the United Kingdom government involving the withdrawal of all British naval, military, and air forces from Egyptian territory by stages, had been 'agreed'[1] by the dominion Prime Ministers as the 'best method of approach'.[2] Mr. Mackenzie King at once explained in Ottawa that the Canadian government was not a party to any decision which had been taken, and had not offered any advice on any aspect of the negotiations leading to it.[3] Mr. Attlee on the same day confessed in London that he had been 'led away in the course of the Debate' into overstating the measure of dominion endorsement. In withdrawing, he took the opportunity of restating the principles on which consultation with the dominions was conducted, and this statement carried collective Commonwealth authority since its terms were agreed to in advance by dominion governments. Mr Attlee said:

It is our practice and our duty, as members of the British Commonwealth, to keep other members of the Commonwealth fully and continuously informed of all matters which we are called upon to decide, but which may affect Commonwealth interests. The object is to give them an opportunity of expressing their views in confidence, if they so desire. These views are taken fully into account, but the decision must be ours, and the other Governments are not asked, and would not wish, to share the responsibility for it. Dominion Governments follow the same practice.[4]

Mr. Bevin, the Secretary of State for Foreign Affairs, subsequently and carefully outlined the sequence of events. None of the dominions, he explained, had committed themselves to the 1936 treaty, though they had been fully consulted.[5] Responsibility had rested solely with the United Kingdom government. When the negotiations for the revision of the treaty were begun 'almost every document' which was relevant was sent to the dominion governments, and they were asked for their views. Discussion followed, but not decision. The Commonwealth governments reached no agreement and, as Mr. Bevin justly observed, it would not have been in accordance with accepted practice for a joint Commonwealth policy to have been evolved. Since 1923 responsibility had been vested in the member state primarily responsible for the negotiations, and its Commonwealth partners did not underwrite any agreement or treaty that resulted unless they specifically desired to do so. Mr. Bevin said that he could remember no specific case of a treaty, or the termination of a treaty, or a change in a treaty, in which a formal decision had been recorded by the dominions. Revision of the Anglo-Egyptian Treaty, in

[1] On this point there would seem to be some doubt. Clearly the Conservative Opposition had some reason to suppose that some difference of opinion existed. See Mr. Bevin's remark quoted below, p. 324, and *Canada in World Affairs, 1944–6*, pp. 227–30.
[2] 7 May 1946, H. of C. Deb., vol. 422, col. 858.
[3] 8 May 1946, Canada, H. of C. Deb., vol. 2, pp. 1324–5.
[4] H. of C. Deb., vol. 422, col. 1069 (Mansergh, *Documents*, i. 594–5).
[5] Ibid. vol. 423, col. 789; see also Mansergh, *Survey, 1931–9*, p. 434.

which at least three dominions—Australia, New Zealand, and South Africa—were specially interested, was therefore agreed to by the United Kingdom government on its own responsibility but in the light of preliminary discussions with those dominions.

If the negotiations on the Anglo-Egyptian Treaty underlined the looseness —to some critics the dangerous looseness—of the relationship between the Commonwealth countries even in major issues of foreign policy, it did at the same time emphasize the very great advantages of so flexible a system in affairs which were of importance to more than one of the Commonwealth countries but with which only one was sufficiently concerned to initiate negotiations that might lead to the abandonment of old or the undertaking of new and specific commitments. In the particular circumstances of 1946, the United Kingdom government had the advantage of learning the views of the Australian, New Zealand, and South African governments, the precise nature of which has not been made public, before finally deciding on its own policy. These views, it may be assumed, had been carefully considered, since each of these dominions had a traditional interest in this artery of Empire, and each had available, in Mr. Bevin's words, almost every relevant document, to enable them to form an independent judgement on the best course to be followed. Here was a case, therefore, in which consultation was active, and the United Kingdom government presumably benefited from the expression of other views than its own, though, as Mr. Bevin explained, while he and his colleagues took into account the opinions of the dominions, 'we are not tied by them and they are not tied by us'.

The 1946 Prime Ministers' Meeting

The second Meeting of Commonwealth Prime Ministers, held in April and May of 1946, was not so satisfactorily arranged as its predecessor. At no time during its sessions were the representatives of all the Commonwealth countries gathered together. At the outset the Prime Minister of Australia, Mr. Chifley, accompanied by his Minister for External Affairs, Dr. Evatt, was present, together with New Zealand's Deputy Prime Minister, Mr. Walter Nash, but it was not till the second week that they were joined by General Smuts, and Mr. Mackenzie King, arriving later still, did not reach London until Mr. Chifley had returned to Australia. Nor indeed did Mr. Mackenzie King evince any marked enthusiasm for the Meeting prior to its assembly. 'If I had consulted my own feelings at this time', he said in Ottawa, 'I would have remained here.' He also took the opportunity of assuring the House, though any such assurance might perhaps by then have been thought superfluous, that he would 'refrain from committing anyone in a manner that is likely to occasion embarrassment'.[1]

---

[1] Canada, H. of C. Deb., 1946, vol. 2, p. 1348. See also *Canada in World Affairs, 1944-6*, pp. 231-2.

The 1946 Meeting confirmed the character of its predecessor. What took place was officially described as an informal exchange of views, and throughout the proceedings any impression that the purpose of the Meeting was to make decisions or to reach agreement was discouraged. On their conclusion the talks were said to have contributed greatly to the elucidation of many problems and to a mutual understanding of the issues involved. Their range was wide, and it was recorded that among the subjects on which views were exchanged were the draft treaties with the satellite states in Europe; the treaty with Germany; co-operation in the South Pacific and in South-East Asia; and 'security responsibilities and arrangements for liaison between British Commonwealth Governments on military affairs'.[1] There followed an emphatic reassertion of faith in the system of intra-Commonwealth consultation. 'The existing methods of consultation', recorded the assembled dominion statesmen, 'have proved their worth. . . . They are peculiarly appropriate to the character of the British Commonwealth. . . . While all are willing to consider and adopt practical proposals for developing the existing system, it is agreed that the methods now practised are preferable to any rigid centralized machinery', which 'would not facilitate, and might even hamper, the combination of autonomy and unity which is characteristic of the British Commonwealth and is one of their great achievements'.[2]

The tributes paid to the working of the Commonwealth system were more outspoken in 1946 than they had been in 1944, no doubt partly because there was no inhibiting awareness of recent debate about methods of Commonwealth consultation to qualify them. But there would seem also to have been a greater conviction that in this respect the Commonwealth was travelling on the right road. Especially noteworthy was the language used by Dr. Evatt, who dismissed demands for 'a fixed and centralized co-ordination' as being based on a profound misunderstanding of the history and status of the dominions,[3] and described the discussions that had taken place in London as 'perhaps the most successful talks yet held within the Commonwealth'.[4] Such a tribute from a member of Australia's Labour government was not lightly to be discounted, and in this respect the 1946 Meeting may be said to mark the end, for some years at least, of official Australian efforts to secure some change in the system of Commonwealth consultation.

On his return to Ottawa Mr. Mackenzie King remained silent about the proceedings in London, and thus provoked a complaint that the Department

---

[1] See below, pp. 326-9.

[2] The final communiqué is printed in full in Mansergh, *Documents*, i. 595-6.

[3] These words are not necessarily to be regarded as a repudiation of the proposals which Mr. Curtin had outlined for a Commonwealth Council and Secretariat, for in the mind at least of the Australian government these proposals had never been conceived as detracting in any way from the full status of the dominions, however they might have been interpreted in imperialist circles outside Australia.

[4] In a statement issued on 23 May 1946 (*The Times*, 24 May 1946).

of External Affairs and its Minister 'should [not] carry all the information about external affairs in their vest pockets',[1] but members of the Australian government were more forthcoming. In London, they explained on their return, they had proposed that the function of developing the defence aspect of regional security in the Pacific should be assigned to Australia, and that it had been agreed that Australia should assume a greater responsibility and make a larger contribution, as her government wished, towards the defence of the British Commonwealth in the Pacific. Thus the outcome, as Mr. Chifley explained, was 'a further devolution of responsibility and planning for defence from a centralized to a regional basis'.[2] In that respect the Australian government had achieved some of the purposes Mr. Curtin had in mind when he suggested the creation of an Imperial Secretariat, though in ways other than those he had contemplated. The initiative taken in the signature of the Anzac Treaty of 1944 was followed by agreement upon devolution of defence responsibility in 1946, by a Commonwealth Conference in Canberra to discuss the terms of the Japanese peace settlement in 1947,[3] and by Australian command of Commonwealth occupation forces in Japan.[4]

The Reorganization of Commonwealth Defence

'Self-government begets self-defence.' So Liberal administrations maintained in the years that followed the great commercial revolution of the mid-nineteenth century, convinced on the one hand that free trade happily reconciled the higher interests of Britain and of humanity, and concerned on the other lest colonies that were no longer of economic advantage should continue to require financial assistance for defence.[5] The wish was father to the thought and the thought itself of limited validity. Joseph Chamberlain learned this in long and outspoken argument with colonial ministers, seeking, for the most part in vain, to persuade them to contribute more liberally in money or in ships to the forces of the Empire.[6] The dominions in fact were working towards co-ordinated, not unified, defence, partly because they were long accustomed to immunity from external danger, thanks to the supremacy of the Royal Navy, and still more because dominion patriotism early in the century led the dominions to favour not imperial forces under a unified imperial command but separate dominion forces to be merged in a larger whole only in the event of war. The central planning authority for the defence of the Empire

[1] Canada, H. of C. Deb., 1946, vol. 5, p. 5731.
[2] 19 June 1946, Australia, H. of R. Deb., vol. 187, pp. 1558–64.
[3] A part of its report is reprinted in Mansergh, *Documents*, ii. 1168–71.
[4] This experiment in unified Commonwealth command was not an unqualified success.
[5] For an account of earlier developments see N. H. Gibbs, *The Origins of Imperial Defence* (Oxford, Clarendon Press, 1955).
[6] Cf. his address at the opening of the Colonial Conference, 1897 (A. B. Keith, *Speeches and Documents on British Colonial Policy, 1763–1917* (London, Oxford University Press, 1948), pp. 216–21.

was therefore rightly named not the Imperial Committee of Defence but the Committee of Imperial Defence.[1] It was a United Kingdom body reinforced from time to time by dominion representation, and its function, in the words of Lord Haldane who conceived it, was not to command but to advise. It was this body that before the First World War and again between 1919 and 1939 planned the defence of the Empire, in accord with the principles of equality and on the foundation of that free co-operation which the Balfour Report had spoken of as the life-blood of the Empire. Yet in this field above all others there continued to be the most pronounced inequality between the dominions and the United Kingdom, an inequality greater in most instances than the resources of either would justify. The Liberal assertion that self-government begets self-defence, while sound in principle, was qualified until 1939 by the dominions' remoteness from dangers that would otherwise have moved their peoples to take sterner measures to protect their liberties.[2]

The Second World War had brought changes, psychological as well as material. Dominion peoples realized for the first time their own comparative defencelessness and their ultimate dependence upon their greater allies. This realization came home to them in full force at a time when it was also understood that the United Kingdom could not still be ranked with the greatest powers. Imperial defence was something that could no longer be assured by the Commonwealth alone, for in this respect the member nations were neither individually nor collectively self-sufficient. After 1945 the organization of Commonwealth defence, therefore, remained important but no longer of the highest importance.

The Commonwealth Prime Ministers addressed themselves to the problems of Commonwealth defence at their meeting in April 1946. Their discussions were followed by the publication of a White Paper on defence by the government of the United Kingdom.[3] For national defence it contemplated the establishment of a Defence Committee under the chairmanship of the United Kingdom Prime Minister, which would take over the functions of the Committee of Imperial Defence in respect of the United Kingdom. In respect of Commonwealth defence the White Paper noted that the conception of a central authority in London, representative of all the self-governing members of the Commonwealth, had never been recognized as practicable, even if it were desirable, and that in consequence co-operation in defence had always taken the form of promoting uniformity of organization, training, and equipment of forces, of maintaining the closest possible touch between Staffs, and of interchanging officers to promote a common doctrine and outlook on military affairs. 'Collaboration in war-time between the naval, land and air

---

[1] Amery, *Thoughts on the Constitution*, p. 146.
[2] On the relation between United Kingdom and dominion resources before 1939 see Mansergh, *Survey, 1931–9*, pp. 73–79.
[3] Cmd. 6923 (extract in Mansergh, *Documents*, ii. 1190–4).

forces from different parts of the Commonwealth', the White Paper concluded with some complacency, 'has thus been easy and effective.'[1] Accordingly the principles on which co-operation had rested in the past should continue to be applied, and reliance placed not upon any centralized machinery but upon methods of consultation which were in defence, as in politics 'peculiarly appropriate to the character of the British Commonwealth'. These same methods, it was thought, would prove fruitful in the development of ideas for regional defence which formed the natural starting-point for future progress in Commonwealth defence. Plans were accordingly submitted by the government of the United Kingdom, and favourable comments returned by dominion Prime Ministers, for the interchange of liaison officers to assist in the study of regional defence problems wherever the governments principally concerned so desired.

The 1946 White Paper proposals had two principal merits in the eyes of their sponsors. On the one hand it was thought that they would pave the way for machinery which, while giving full play to the independence of Commonwealth members, would be effective as a means of consultation and collaboration; on the other that their regional approach would fit well into any regional defence agreements made by members of the Commonwealth with neighbouring foreign countries under the aegis of the United Nations Charter. Both, it may be suggested, were in themselves considerable, but neither was likely to commend itself to the Conservative Opposition. The disappearance of the name 'Committee of Imperial Defence' seemed to them unnecessary and even unwise; the abandonment of all striving towards a more closely knit system of Commonwealth defence altogether deplorable. It is certainly the case that the White Paper, possibly with a view to appeasing Conservative critics, seemed to suggest that the Commonwealth defensive system based upon these arrangements would be altogether more substantial than a close examination of its foundations would seem to warrant. But, as Lord Chatfield[2] pointed out, the new Defence Committee's connexion with imperial defence as envisaged in the White Paper was 'weaker than it was, and it was never very strong'. The White Paper, he said, implied that before 1939 the various Staffs kept in 'the closest possible touch'. But when matters of 'a really secret nature' were discussed in the Committee of Imperial Defence there was not 'the closest possible touch', nor could there be in view of the uncertainty about the intentions of some of the dominions in the event of war. Nor were there common plans for military action. The risk now, so it seemed to him, was that dislike of central or rigid machinery would lead to no organization at all. Yet in the age of scientific warfare there must be organized Commonwealth defence, and the appointment of liaison officers would not provide that. Lord Hankey,[3]

---

[1] Cmd. 6923, p. 11.
[2] 16 October 1946, H. of L. Deb., vol. 143, coll. 283–90 (Mansergh, *Documents*, ii. 1194–9).
[3] Ibid. coll. 306–12 (Mansergh, *Documents*, ii. 1199–1203).

with the weight of long experience as Secretary to the Committee of Imperial Defence behind him, endorsed Lord Chatfield's principal criticisms. He thought the new proposals implied a drastic break with the past and the dropping of the name Committee of Imperial Defence, 'a black blot on the White Paper'. The imperial or Commonwealth element was minimized. The Secretary of State for Dominion Affairs was not to be included in the membership of the new Defence Committee nor was there provision for continuous high-level dominion representation. There was in fact no provision for the creation of appropriate machinery to enable Commonwealth governments to have an effective voice in policy and in higher control of planning.

The criticisms were substantial, even if the critics gave too little weight to the possibilities of co-ordination through consultation and paid insufficient regard to the diversity of dominion interests and their often specialized defence needs.[1] But it was of more importance that the Empire which the Committee of Imperial Defence was designed to serve had passed away. There had been a transformation in intra-Commonwealth political relations, but also, and this was more fundamental, there had been a change in the balance of world power. The concept of imperial defence in any absolute form was outdated. In its place there was the concept of regional defence agreements under the Charter of the United Nations. That was why, when the United Nations grievously disappointed the hopes of its sponsors and failed to achieve its primary purpose of maintaining international peace and security, it was not in imperial defence but in regional associations that the members of the Commonwealth, and not least the United Kingdom, sought refuge. In practice, therefore, the principal responsibility of the Defence Committee was not to plan the defence of the Commonwealth in isolation but rather to link together regional plans for defence in which Commonwealth members and foreign countries alike participated.[2] The Committee was well fitted to serve this more modest purpose, and in 1948 the Commonwealth Prime Ministers expressed satisfaction with its discharge of these important but limited responsibilities.[3]

The Commonwealth and Western European Union

By temperament British statesmen favour a pragmatic approach to foreign policy without always recognizing how powerfully inclination is reinforced by geography. Yet the fact that Britain is at once an island semi-detached from Europe and the heart of an overseas Empire has fundamentally determined the character of her foreign policy. The coming of the steelclad battleship, of the dreadnought and the submarine before the First World War, and more

---

[1] e.g., Canadian defence problems in the face of possible Arctic warfare.
[2] Much of this is implicit in Lord Addison's reply as Secretary of State for Dominion Affairs to the critics of the White Paper (H. of L. Deb., vol. 143, coll. 336–8; Mansergh, *Documents*, ii. 1203–4).   [3] Cmd. 7631, p. 4 (Mansergh, *Documents*, ii. 1204–5).

especially of the bomber and of the atomic bomb between 1919 and 1945, modified Britain's strategic position and lessened the strategic advantages she had hitherto enjoyed, but her essential interests remained little changed. The twin purposes of Britain's policy continued to be the safeguarding of her position in Europe by ensuring that neither the Low Countries nor France nor Western Germany after 1945 were controlled by an unfriendly Power; and the safety and well-being of her overseas Empire. In theory, and sometimes in practice, these twin purposes were not always easy to reconcile and after the Second World War, when the United Kingdom's margin in manpower and resources in relation to responsibilities was so tenuous, the task of reconciliation proved more exacting than at any time in the recent past. But its successful achievement was widely thought to be the condition of Britain's survival as a great power, and for that reason the relationship between the Commonwealth and the association of Western European States which was variously described as Western Union or Western European Union assumed much importance. The problem, however, though greater in urgency than at any earlier period in Britain's history, was the same in essentials and demanded the same pragmatic approach. Even with the coming of the atomic age geography allowed little scope for originality in foreign policy.

It was evident by 1943 that the Second World War would leave a vacuum in power, and therefore a lack of balance, in Central and Western Europe. General Smuts was the first Commonwealth statesman to suggest how it might best be filled. This he did in his speech to the Empire Parliamentary Association in November 1943. He was concerned, as has been seen, on the one hand to consolidate the Commonwealth by associating the self-governing dominions with the government of colonial territories falling within their geographical area, and on the other to extend its stabilizing influence to Europe by linking it with the free peoples on the Western European seaboard. What he said on this score is worth recalling.[1]

We have evolved a system in the Commonwealth which opens the door for developments of this kind. Today in the Commonwealth we have a group of sovereign States working together, living together in peace and in war, under a system that has stood the greatest strain to which any nations could be subjected. They are all sovereign States, they retain all the attributes and functions and symbols of sovereignty. Other neighbouring nations, therefore, living the same way of life, and with the same outlook, can with perfect safety say: 'That is our group; why are we not there? With full retention and maintenance of our sovereign status, we choose that grand company for our future in this dangerous world.'

The emphasis he placed on the retention and maintenance of full sovereign status is especially noteworthy. What General Smuts contemplated in 1943, and what the dominions naturally contemplated, was a union in Western Europe which would leave each member state within that union master in its

[1] Mansergh, *Documents*, i. 571; see also above, pp. 173–6.

own house. If there were to be co-ordinating authorities, dominion opinion welcomed them without misgiving so long as they did not infringe fundamentally upon national sovereignty. That was the sort of relationship which a decentralized Commonwealth understood, and the extension of it to Western Europe raised no particular problems, for it would leave the United Kingdom with a freedom of action sufficient to enable her to undertake and discharge obligations in other parts of the world.[1]

General Smuts's emphasis on national sovereignty was not to be found in the pronouncements on Western Union made by United Kingdom statesmen, and particularly by Mr. Bevin, who on 22 January 1948 launched the concept as the principal aim of Britain's foreign policy in Europe to a welcoming Western world.[2] On the contrary, so far as national sovereignty was concerned Mr. Bevin's words left an impression of judiciously considered imprecision. There was no doubting his deep conviction that 'the free nations of Western Europe must now draw closely together'. That had been rendered imperative by the scale of Russia's expansion and her ruthless communization of Eastern Europe, by the emergence once again of the police state, by the breakdown of the four-power discussions on Germany, and, finally, by the naked hostility of the Soviet Union to the European Recovery Programme. All this made the closing 'of the breach between East and West' the task for another day. What was imperative now, urged the Foreign Secretary, was the drawing together of 'the kindred souls' of the West to preserve at least in one part of Europe the liberties of men and nations. So much, it will be noted, rested firmly upon that foundation of traditional policy which Sir Eyre Crowe had expounded in his classic memorandum of January 1906,[3] for Western Union was also a 'league of defence'. But was it not something more as well? Defence was not its only goal even though it was the most clearly defined. What were the other purposes that had helped to bring Western Union into being? And once in being, was it likely to lead to the superseding of national sovereignties by the creation of an organic or a federal union, or even a loose confederation? Or was it best regarded as a military alliance refashioned to meet the demands of modern warfare? These were the questions which profoundly concerned the Commonwealth countries, for the answers would vitally affect their future relationship with the United Kingdom. But Mr. Bevin gave no precise answers. He spoke of federal union as a distant goal, but for

---

[1] The misuse of the word 'union' was a source of misunderstanding. By any definition union means something more than alliance or association; more than economic and political consolidation. In English history it applied to two formal acts of state—the Acts of Union with Scotland and Ireland—by which countries previously separate and distinct entered into a wider community, in which they merged their separate identities.

[2] H. of C. Deb., vol. 446, coll. 383–409.

[3] 'Memorandum on the Present State of British Relations with France and Germany', in G. P. Gooch and H. W. V. Temperley, *British Documents on the Origins of the War, 1898–1914*, vol. 3 (London, HMSO, 1928), p. 402.

the immediate future he wisely confined himself to emphasizing the need for taking one step at a time.

> If [he said on 22 January] we are to have an organism in the West it must be a spiritual union. While, no doubt, there must be treaties or, at least, understandings, the union must primarily be a fusion derived from the basic freedoms and ethical principles for which we all stand. . . . It is more of a brotherhood and less of a rigid system.[1]

The essence of Mr. Bevin's statesmanship, like that of Condorcet's philosophy, was 'a delicate liqueur wrapped up in cotton wool'.

But if the British approach to Western Union was empirical and its aim very largely undefined, that made the more important consultations with the partner-states in the Commonwealth preliminary to the Commonwealth Prime Ministers' Meeting in October 1948. On 5 May 1948 the Prime Minister asserted in the House of Commons that 'in all these matters we keep in the closest touch with the other Commonwealth countries. . . . We have kept in very very close touch, and we take very full account of their views.' In the same debate[2] the Prime Minister remarked that he

> was disturbed by the suggestion . . . that we might somehow get closer to Europe than to our Commonwealth. The Commonwealth nations are our closest friends. While I want to get as close as we can with the other nations, we have to bear in mind that we are not solely a European Power but a member of a great Commonwealth and Empire.

Through Britain, and at one remove, the dominions were thus in a position to influence developments in Western Europe.

Any crystallized or uniform Commonwealth reaction to Western Union was from the first ruled out both by the way in which the Commonwealth system worked and by the differences in approach to European problems created by the distinct regional interests and psychological characteristics of each self-governing nation within it. Nor was the elaborate system of intra-Commonwealth consultation, that 'continuing conference of Cabinets' of which Mr. Mackenzie King had earlier spoken, well calculated or even designed to produce prompt clear-cut reactions to new departures in long-term policy towards a continent in which the interests of the oversea dominions were not particular, but general. It was, with the possible exception of Canada, through the eyes of London that they looked out upon Europe. It was therefore in discussion, at times rather desultory or one-way discussion, initiated in correspondence and continued in conference in October, that the attitudes of Commonwealth members towards Western Union became more clearly defined. But their views continued to be an important consideration in the making of the United Kingdom's policy, as was evidenced by an exchange of

[1] H. of C. Deb., vol. 446, coll. 407–8. [2] Ibid. vol. 450, coll. 1316–19.

correspondence between Mr. Attlee and Mr. Churchill in August about the next steps to be taken in Western Europe. In the course of it the Prime Minister made it plain that, in the opinion of the government, Western Union 'has an important bearing on Commonwealth relations, and that in consequence the Government desire to exchange views with the Commonwealth Prime Ministers in October before expressing any definite view'.[1]

The early steps taken in Western Europe did not immediately concern oversea Commonwealth governments and to that extent they were at the outset more interested in the direction than in the details of policy. They observed that Western Union had two aspects, one economic, the other political, both of which involved the creation of consultative organizations on a considerable scale. On the economic side were the Benelux Customs Union, which came into existence formally in October 1947; the more general agreement for discussion on colonial problems of common interest between the United Kingdom, France, Belgium, and Portugal;[2] and last, and by far the most important, the Committee of European Economic Co-operation, set up after the sixteen-nation Paris Peace Conference of July-September 1947.[3] The political counterpart to the bodies created to further economic co-operation was on a more restricted scale. It was to be found in the Anglo-French Treaty of March 1947[4] and the five-power treaty signed at Brussels in March 1948.[5] The Brussels Treaty extended beyond the strictly political field, though its most important articles were those which provided for the setting up of joint consultative machinery for consultation on any situation constituting a threat to peace 'from whatever quarter' and the more specific commitment to joint defence in the event of aggression in Europe. But these were evidently steps towards a goal which was neither explicitly defined nor indeed clearly perceived.

Different opinions were expressed by Commonwealth statesmen about the developments that should be likely to flow from the Brussels Treaty. General Smuts spoke of the association of the Commonwealth and Western European countries as a means of bringing into being a third force. In a pre-election broadcast on 23 May 1948 he said that he thought of Western Union with United Kingdom membership as helping to create a third power group, the co-equal of the two colossi which dominated the world, whose emergence was highly to be desired.[6] Mr. Mackenzie King, once again by contrast, stated that Canada regarded the Brussels Treaty as a partial realization of the idea of collective security, and as such a step which might well be followed by other similar steps until an association was built up of all free states willing to

---

[1] Letter of 21 August, published on 25 August (*The Times*, 26 August 1948).
[2] See H. of C. Deb., vol. 446, coll. 17, 98, where Mr. Creech Jones answered a question on co-operation between West European colonial powers.
[3] Cmd. 7796. [4] Cmd. 7058. [5] Cmd. 7599.
[6] Mansergh, *Documents*, ii. 1133–5.

accept responsibilities of mutual assistance to prevent aggression and preserve peace.[1] The Canadian point of view was elaborated by Mr. St. Laurent on 29 April 1948, when he contemplated a collective security league, arising out of Western Union, in which Canada would play a full part.[2] 'The spread of aggressive communist despotism over western Europe', he said, 'would ultimately almost certainly mean for us war, and war on most unfavourable terms. It is in our national interest to see to it that the flood of communist expansion is held back.' Peace in Europe, said Dr. Evatt in an illuminating Australian comment, was the condition of peace in Asia. 'Peace and stability in the Pacific and in East Asia will be attainable only so far as there is peace and stability in Europe—Australia's concern in the European situation is therefore direct and vital.'[3] And since it was accepted in Australia and New Zealand that the Brussels Treaty improved the prospects of peace in Europe, Britain's signature of it was welcomed.

While the dominions thus approved Britain's participation in agreements designed to restore the shattered fabric of Western European economy, security, and civilization and acknowledged their own interest in the successful accomplishment of this purpose, their governments did not associate themselves formally with Britain in the signature of the Brussels Treaty. The precedents of 1939, when the guarantees extended to Greece, Rumania, and Poland carried the signature of the United Kingdom alone, were thus once more followed. This continued dominion reluctance to undertake a direct, formal commitment in Europe, and the reasons for it, were understood in the United Kingdom, and sufficiently understood in Western Europe to make it a matter of secondary importance. The dominions had assumed no obligations towards Poland, yet their reaction to the invasion of that country in 1939 had afforded evidence, too striking to be forgotten, that dominion dislike of specific commitments in Europe was not to be equated with indifference or isolationism. It was also clear that after 1945, by contrast with the years before the war, dominion reluctance to assume commitments in Western Europe was no longer founded in an objection to them in principle but an unwillingness to assume them in a region of which they themselves geographically did not form part. Some evidence of this was given in July 1948, when Canada joined in the Western Union defence talks as a member of the permanent military committee in London.[4]

Consideration of the possible implications of Western Union for the Commonwealth underlined certain factors of lasting importance in Commonwealth relations. One was that the United Kingdom was inescapably a European

[1] Canada, H. of C. Deb., 1948, vol. 3, p. 2303.
[2] Ibid. vol. 4, p. 3449 (Mansergh, *Documents*, ii. 1124–9).
[3] Broadcast from London, 27 July 1948.
[4] Ceylon had entered into certain loosely defined obligations with Britain in respect of mutual assistance against external aggression under the 1947 Defence Agreement (Cmd. 7257, p. 2; Mansergh, *Documents*, ii, 749–50). See also above, pp. 248–9.

power; with the often unwelcome consequence that the Commonwealth as a whole could not but be concerned with European affairs. Another was that, however absolute the independence and however real the equality of the dominions, the United Kingdom was the heart of the Commonwealth, and the Commonwealth was a centripetal system. The real efforts made by both old and new dominions to increase their representation in and co-operation with their fellow members of the Commonwealth could not alter the fact that the United Kingdom was the source to which they looked (with the exception of Canada, whose proximity to the United States once again placed her in a special position) for capital, for economic and technical assistance, and in some instances for immigrants as well. The way in which the Commonwealth had developed from a colonial system made this inevitable; it also made necessary a careful weighing by the United Kingdom of her responsibilities towards a Commonwealth of independent nations and of the means by which they might be reconciled with her responsibilities in Europe. It was because this was so that European and oversea Commonwealth countries remained suspicious each of the other's influence on United Kingdom policy, and so tended to represent their interests as conflicting whereas on balance they were more often complementary.

While responsibility for determining the extent of Britain's participation in Western Union clearly rested with the government of the United Kingdom, the United Kingdom saw it as a responsibility to be discharged in the light of older ties with the Commonwealth. 'The welfare of the Commonwealth and Empire must always be the first consideration', and it was therefore 'absolutely essential' that in a new development of British policy 'the Empire should be with us at every stage'. So Mr. Anthony Eden declared on behalf of the Conservative Opposition,[1] and Mr. Attlee, speaking for the Labour government, was no less insistent that it had always to be remembered that Britain had interests not in one but in all continents, and that she was not 'solely a European Power but a member of a great Commonwealth and Empire'.[2] These were facts which did not lessen Britain's responsibilities in respect of Western Union but went far to determine how they should be exercised. In particular, Britain's Commonwealth connexions precluded her participation in a Western European federal union, because such participation would necessarily mean the transfer of ultimate control over foreign policy and defence from the government of the United Kingdom to that of the federation, as well as a change in the status of the Crown, since the sovereign in Britain would be the head, no longer of an independent kingdom, but of a unit in a federal state. Western European suggestions for a constituent assembly to draft a federal or indeed any formal Constitution for Western European Union were viewed, therefore, with deep misgiving. That Britain 'should

[1] 5 May 1948, H. of C. Deb., vol. 450, coll. 1272–3 (Mansergh, *Documents*, ii. 1129–31).
[2] Ibid. coll. 1315–19 (Mansergh, *Documents*, ii. 1131–3).

join a federation on the continent of Europe', said Mr. Eden in 1952, 'is something which we know, in our bones, we cannot do.'[1]

While Britain's participation in any federal union was precluded by the nature of her Commonwealth connexions, it is also true that irrespective of any such considerations her people, mindful especially of their experience in 1940, were not at this time prepared to enter such a federation—so much was made clear in 1950 when the government of the United Kingdom was invited to participate in the Schuman Plan for the creation of a supranational High Authority to control Western European coal and steel industries but declined, while expressing a desire to be associated with it. A French commentator,[2] impressed by the nature of this response and the reasons which prompted it, concluded that external association might provide a formula which should guide Britain's relations with Western Europe. The phrase itself was apt, even if many of its Irish overtones were out of place, for Britain's attitude, largely though not exclusively determined by her Commonwealth ties, at this time was one favouring close association with, rather than membership of, Western European economic or political organizations. But British statesmen felt no need of a formula, nor did they feel it necessary to make a choice, for it was rather their aim to effect a reconciliation. The position was summed up by Mr. Menzies. 'The practical task of statesmanship', he said in 1950, was to see that whatever Britain did in Western Europe 'should be done not only in consultation with the other British countries but with their co-operation'; for provided there was full consultation there was 'no reason why British participation in Western European stability should not be in the widest and best sense of the term "British" and not merely that of the United Kingdom'.[3]

The North Atlantic Treaty

As late as May 1948 General Smuts still conceived Western Union with British membership as constituting a third or middle-power group at least equal to the other two, so that the security of the world 'will rest on a triangle of Power, and will not continue to be precariously poised between two great Powers facing each other across a broken Europe'.[4] But neither the United Kingdom, nor still less the Canadian, government envisaged such a possibility. Their endeavours were directed towards the expansion of the Western defensive grouping so as to include within its framework one of these great powers. For the idea of a balance of power they substituted that of a preponderance on the side of the peace-loving nations.

---

[1] Speech at Columbia University, 11 January 1952 (Mansergh, *Documents*, ii. 1156–7).

[2] Y. G. Brissonnière, '*Commonwealth d'abord*' (Paris, Domat Montchrestien, 1955), ch. xiii.

[3] R. G. Menzies, *The British Commonwealth of Nations in International Affairs*, Roy Milne Memorial Lecture (Sydney, Australian Institute of International Affairs, 1950).

[4] Broadcast 23 May 1948 (Mansergh, *Documents*, ii. 1133–5).

The policy of the Canadian government in this period is of particular interest to students of Commonwealth history. Before 1939 no dominion government had been more consistent in its opposition to specific commitments which would limit the freedom of the Canadian Parliament to decide on Canadian participation in war; and no dominion government had expressed greater devotion to the United Nations and to the principle of universalism on which it was founded after 1945. How then is one to account for the transformation in policy which is symbolized by Canada's sponsorship of the North Atlantic Treaty? There were many reasons, but chief among them were the lessons of recent experience. The world was once again threatened with aggression by a totalitarian military state. Even at San Francisco Mr. Mackenzie King was filled at times with the deepest forebodings of what the future might bring because of the inability of the new international organization then being shaped to provide security for peace-loving peoples.[1] Such fears, voiced intermittently by Mr. Mackenzie King, received outspoken expression from his Minister for External Affairs, Mr. St. Laurent, on 18 September 1947. Alarmed especially by Russia's exercise of the veto in the Security Council, he told the General Assembly that it 'would be folly' not to admit that the United Nations organization had been weakened, and that 'this veto privilege, . . . if it continues to be abused, may well destroy the United Nations'.

Nations, in their search for peace and co-operation [he warned delegates] will not, and cannot, accept indefinitely an unaltered Council which was set up to ensure their security and which . . . has become frozen in futility and divided by dissension. If forced, they may seek greater safety in an association of democratic and peace-loving states willing to accept more specific international obligations in return for a greater measure of national security.[2]

By their failure to offer united resistance to Nazi demands the democracies had earlier enabled Hitler to destroy his victims singly. That lesson at least was deeply graven on the mind of the Western world. 'We must', said Mr. St. Laurent in the Canadian House of Commons, 'at all costs avoid the fatal repetition of the history of the pre-war years when the nazi aggressor picked off its victims one by one. Such a process does not end at the Atlantic.'[3] But effective resistance was conditional in Canadian eyes upon United States participation in an organized defensive system. That had been withheld before 1939; it was forthcoming after 1945. In the earlier period the Western world without United States support could hope at best to establish a balance of power; in the later, with United States participation, the peace-loving states might reasonably expect to possess a decisive preponderance.

[1] Bruce Hutchison, *The Incredible Canadian* (Toronto, Longmans, 1953), p. 410.
[2] Canada, Dept. of External Affairs, *Canada at the United Nations, 1947* (Ottawa, King's Printer, 1948), pp. 178-80.
[3] In the speech referred to on p. 334 above.

United States association with the United Kingdom in a Western Alliance would further fulfil one of the principal aims of Canadian policy by bringing together her greater North American neighbour and her principal Commonwealth partner in a common association for a common aim. That aim was to deter, if necessary by force, further Soviet expansion in Europe.

The formation of such a defensive group of free states [said Mr. St. Laurent] would not be a counsel of despair but a measure of hope. It would not mean that we regarded a third world war as inevitable; but that the free democracies had decided that to prevent such a war they would organize so as to confront the forces of communist expansionism with an overwhelming preponderance of moral, economic and military force and with sufficient degree of unity to ensure that this preponderance of force is so used that the free nations cannot be defeated one by one.[1]

The aim was one that commended itself particularly to Catholic and traditionally isolationist Quebec. The Nazi-Soviet alliance of August 1939 had contributed notably to French-Canadian support for Canada's entry into the Second World War, while the revelations of Soviet espionage in 1945[2] confirmed a rooted conviction that despite the wartime alliance Russian Communism was at all times the most deadly menace to the Catholic Church and to the way of life it enjoined.

Je sais que dans ma province [said the Prime Minister in an appeal to his French Canadian fellow countrymen], parmi les gens de ma race et de ma religion, on ne veut pas que se reproduisent ici les désastres qui sont survenus dans tant de pays européens, ni que se développe la situation qui a donné lieu à cette persécution religieuse dans des autres démocraties d'Europe dont tout le monde civilisé se scandalise.[3]

Finally, the retreat from universalism which regional alliances of necessity involved was thought of as a temporary refuge provided for in the Charter of the United Nations, not in itself prejudicing the ultimate prospects for realization of the larger aim. The provisions of the Charter, explained Mr. St. Laurent, were a floor under rather than a ceiling over the responsibilities of member states. If some preferred to go even below that floor, others need not be prevented from moving upwards.[4]

The signing of the North Atlantic Treaty in April 1949 was an oblique recognition on the part of the United States that Britain and Canada had been right, in September 1939, in deciding that resistance must be offered to Nazi aggression, and that there was no lasting safety to be found in detachment

---

[1] In the speech referred to on p. 334 above.
[2] Canada, Royal Commission to Investigate the Facts Relating to and the Circumstances Surrounding the Communication, by Public Officials and other Persons in Positions of Trust, of Secret and Confidential Information to Agents of a Foreign Power, *Report* (Ottawa, King's Printer, 1946).
[3] Quoted in *Canada in World Affairs, 1949 to 1950*, p. 23. (Canada, H. of C. Deb., 1949, vol. 3, p. 2065). Also see generally ch. 1.
[4] Speech of 18 September 1947, in *Canada at the United Nations, 1947*, p. 180.

and isolation even for the greatest, or geographically most-favoured, powers. But more than this it embodied the conviction, born of common experience in the Second World War, that those who thought alike should work together to preserve the things they cherished in peace as in war. The North Atlantic Treaty, to Canadian statesmen especially, was not a reversion to the past but a step forward into the future. Mr. Mackenzie King had welcomed the Brussels Treaty 'as far more than an alliance of the old kind'.[1] The North Atlantic Treaty even more emphatically was not to be thought of as a grouping of powers, as an 'old fashioned military alliance' to quote the phrase used by Mr. St. Laurent, but as an association of democratic and like-minded peoples resolved to strengthen and preserve their way of life and ultimately to bring into existence a true community of North Atlantic peoples. It had an economic, social, and above all a moral purpose. It was, said Mr. St. Laurent, 'based on the common belief of the North Atlantic nations in the values and virtues of our Christian civilization'.[2] If, therefore, the non-military clauses of the Alliance were Canadian in inspiration and even in drafting, that was because the Canadian government attached from the outset so much importance to them. It hoped that the need for the military provisions of the treaty might in time disappear with a strengthening of the United Nations organization, but that the conception of a North Atlantic community would remain.

The North Atlantic Treaty,[3] like the 1944 Anzac Agreement and the 1947 provision for continuing United States–Canadian defence co-operation, was expressly related to the provisions of the United Nations Charter. It was deemed to be not a 'regional arrangement' determined primarily by geographical considerations as was contemplated under Article 53 of the Charter, but an association of nations linked by a community of interests provided for by Article 51. The distinction was important not for purposes of identification, but in terms of procedure. The prior authorization of the Security Council was required for enforcement actions by regional associations under Article 53, but not for individual or collective measures of self-defence under Article 51. In this way the exercise of a Russian veto against the treaty was circumvented.

The signatories of the North Atlantic Treaty expressed themselves as being concerned not to weaken but to strengthen the United Nations. Article 7

---

[1] Canada, H. of C. Deb., 1948, vol. 3, p. 2303.
[2] Canada, H. of C. Deb., 1949, vol. 3, p. 2063. Cf. also the comment by the author of *Canada in World Affairs, 1949 to 1950* (p. 23): 'Mr. St. Laurent's emphasis in explaining the nature and purposes of the treaty was characteristic as well of the man as of his fellow countrymen in general: it was liberal and it was Christian.'
[3] Cmd. 7789 (Mansergh, *Documents*, ii. 1142–4). There is an extensive literature on the North Atlantic Treaty Organization, but for the purposes of this study the reader will find especially helpful the official review of the first five years of its operation: *NATO; the First Five Years*, by Lord Ismay (Paris, NATO, 1954).

of the treaty specifically stated that its terms did not affect and should not be interpreted as affecting in any way 'the primary responsibility of the Security Council for the maintenance of international peace and security'. But while the preamble to the treaty reaffirmed their faith in the purposes and principles of the Charter, it also expressed their determination to safeguard 'the freedom, common heritage and civilization of their peoples'. Article 4 provided accordingly that the parties to the treaty should consult together whenever 'in the opinion of any of them, the territorial integrity, political independence or security of any of the Parties is threatened', and Article 5, the hard core of the treaty, provided that, in the event of armed attack against one or more of them in Europe or North America, it should be considered an attack against them all and consequently each would assist the victim of such aggression 'by taking forthwith . . . such action as it deems necessary, including the use of armed force, to restore and maintain the security of the North Atlantic area'. The deterrent force of the obligations thus assumed was materially reinforced by Article 3, which provided that the 'Parties, separately and jointly, by means of continuous and effective self-help and mutual aid, will maintain and develop their individual and collective capacity to resist armed attack'.

The terms of a treaty are less important than the purpose which inspired them and the spirit in which they are applied. While, therefore, under Article 5 the action to be taken by signatories of the treaty in the event of an attack upon one of them is a matter to be decided by their respective governments, collective resistance to such aggression was, at least in the early years of the alliance, never in doubt, nor was the resolve of the signatories to build up in the West, by mutual co-operation extending from the military to the social and economic fields, a sufficient strength to discourage thoughts of aggression on the part of the rulers of Soviet Russia. For this purpose a North Atlantic Council, with a defence committee[1] and secretariat, was created, and if the signatories of the treaty accepted no formal diminution of their separate sovereignties they were prepared to limit their own freedom of action by committing themselves collectively in peace, and if necessary in war, to the achievement of common purposes. Canada's subscription to the aims of the treaty, and more particularly to the means adopted for their fulfilment, marked a revolution in Canadian thinking on foreign policy, even though there was no commitment under Article 5 to go to war without the prior sanction of the Canadian Parliament.

The Canadian contribution to the North Atlantic Treaty was important partly because Canada was at once a North American and a Commonwealth country, and partly because Canadian thinking on the problems of international security had a depth and a coherence which made the influence of her government greater than the stature of the country alone would have

[1] Under Art. 9.

justified. In particular, the Canadian government emphasized the importance of co-operation within the framework of the United Nations Charter. It had from the outset conceived of a treaty in conformity with the provisions of the Charter, and, as has been noted, the Preamble reaffirmed the faith of the signatories in the purpose and principles of the Charter, Article 7 emphasized the primary responsibility of the Security Council for the preservation of peace, and the concluding section of Article 5 provided that measures of collective defence against aggression by the treaty powers should be reported immediately to the Security Council and 'be terminated when the Security Council has taken the measures to restore and maintain international peace and security'. So much indeed was a condition of Canadian participation in the treaty. But the Canadian government was at least equally concerned to ensure that the treaty, once it had served the immediate purposes which had called it into being, should help to establish a North Atlantic Community of free peoples. It was this concept indeed which gave to the treaty much of its appeal to the Canadian people, and not least to formerly isolationist sentiment in Quebec. The menace to the Western world, as Mr. St. Laurent never ceased to emphasize, was not only military, it was at least equally spiritual and ideological. Therefore, defence against it was to be thought of not only in military terms. Article 2 of the North Atlantic Treaty reflected these ideas, but it did not express them in terms as explicit as the Canadian government would have liked.[1] None the less its members attached and continued to attach much importance to the non-military aspects of the treaty. Canada, and especially French-Canada, had long feared lest her people should be drawn into what Sir Wilfrid Laurier as early as 1902 had spoken of as 'the vortex of European militarism',[2] and on grounds of principle and policy alike Mr. St. Laurent's government required reassuring evidence that the North Atlantic Treaty was something 'far more than an old fashioned military alliance'.[3] 'Convincing proof of the peaceful intention of our alliance', said Mr. Lester Pearson, Canadian Secretary of State for External Affairs, in a broadcast at the conclusion of the seventh session of the North Atlantic Council in 1951,

is found in the fact that during these past few days in Ottawa we have devoted many hours to a serious and heartening discussion of the non-military aspects of the

---

[1] Art. 2 read: 'The Parties will contribute toward the further development of peaceful and friendly international relations by strengthening their free institutions, by bringing about a better understanding of the principles upon which these institutions are founded, and by promoting conditions of stability and well-being. They will seek to eliminate conflict in their international economic policies and will encourage economic collaboration between any or all of them.'

[2] Domestic opposition to the treaty was evidently overestimated by the Canadian government, for during the debate Mr. Lester Pearson replied forcefully to criticisms that were in fact never made (Canada, H. of C. Deb., 1949, vol. 3, pp. 2093–101).

[3] Ibid. p. 2063 (Mansergh, *Documents* ii. 1151).

treaty. This marks, I think, an historic turning point in its development. . . . To build the North Atlantic community, as we are now pledged to do, will not be a short or easy task[1]

but, as he told the Canadian House of Commons, it was one 'worthy of our finest efforts and our greatest zeal'.

The Canadian government sought to maintain a balance between the short-term and the long-term objectives of NATO while not doubting that the pressing problem of the early years was the building up of sufficient strength to ensure survival; others in their preoccupation with the short-term paid but scant regard to the long-term aim. If in this respect the Canadian voice was not a voice crying in the wilderness, it was a voice heard for the most part with respectful indifference. To many, and to most in Western Europe, the satisfying thing about the North Atlantic Treaty was that it was an old-fashioned military alliance reinforced by more efficient administrative machinery for peace-time preparation. So it was that when Canada at last embarked on 'a crusade' she found, as other crusaders before her, that the company in which she marched was often moved by less exalted aims than those which she professed.

The Commonwealth and the Devaluation of Sterling, September 1949

In 1949 the sterling area and the Commonwealth did not coincide. The sterling area included Iceland, Iraq, a former British mandated territory, and Burma and the Republic of Ireland, both of whom had until recently been within the Commonwealth; it did not include Canada, the senior dominion. None the less the sterling area was essentially a grouping of British countries, all lying within the British trading system and brought together by common interests and by pressures to which all in greater or lesser degree had been subjected. Like the Commonwealth, it was not artificially constructed but developed gradually, and the pre-war sterling area has been described 'as simply a group of countries which banked in London'.[2] This group was not even formally designated 'the sterling area' till 1939, nor was its extent defined until 1941.[3] During and after the Second World War its importance increased and its character changed with the acceptance by its members of a restriction which in practice precluded the free conversion of their sterling balances into dollars. This restriction was the result of an agreement prompted by external pressure upon sterling, for there was no central authority

---

[1] *Canadian Weekly Bulletin* (Dept. of External Affairs, Ottawa), 28 September 1951 (Mansergh, *Documents*, ii. 1154–6). The speech as a whole throws much light on Canadian foreign policy at this time.

[2] Hugh Gaitskell, 'The Sterling Area', *International Affairs*, April 1952, p. 171. Mr. Gaitskell wrote on the steling area with the authority of a former lecturer in economics who was also former Chancellor of the Exchequer.

[3] *Defence (Finance) Regulation 1939 (No. 10)*, and *The Defence (Finance) (Definition of Sterling Area) (No. 5) Order, 1941*. The second is reprinted in Mansergh, *Documents*, ii. 1013–14.

or machinery by which it was, or could be, imposed.[1] The first meeting of the Finance Ministers of the Commonwealth did not in fact take place until the summer of 1949, and like the meetings of Commonwealth Prime Ministers, possessed no executive authority. The Finance Ministers, however, advised both their respective governments, with whom responsibility for individual action rested, and also the Chancellor of the Exchequer, who possessed a special status among them. This arose from particular circumstances at that time. The sterling area was, to quote Mr. Gaitskell, 'a very loosely knit affair without any constitution', in which the banker-customer relationship of earlier years, when Britain as the banker promised to honour every cheque that was presented and convert into whatever currency was required, had given way to 'something like a consumers' co-operative bank in which the customers had agreed to do certain things, namely to restrict dollar purchases.'[2] But Britain remained the banker, predisposed as bankers are, to doing what she deemed best for her customers without attaching too much importance to the customers' opinions.

Problems of currency exchange dominated sterling-area policies after 1945. Britain's own position was peculiarly vulnerable to any recession, especially to any drop in demand for exports to the dollar area, partly because of her exceptional need at the time for imports from the dollar area, and partly because the sale of the greater part of her dollar investments in 1940 had deprived her of much of the invisible dollar balances with which she had been accustomed to cushion herself against an unfavourable turn in the terms of trade.[3] With the ending of Lend-Lease Britain, as the outcome of her war efforts, was left, in the words of the official historian of her wartime financial policy, 'the greatest debtor in the history of the world'.[4] Some of the consequences were seen in 1948–9 when there was a rapid decline in the gold reserves of the sterling area, caused in part by dominion over-expenditure of dollars in relation to earnings. Faced with this, the second, and the more serious post-war exchange crisis, the Commonwealth Finance Ministers meeting in London in July 1949 asserted that the long-term remedy must be the achievement of a pattern of world trade in which the dollar and non-dollar countries could operate together, within one single multilateral system.[5] Its achievement, as they recognized, would require on the one hand a very large expansion of the earnings of the sterling area; on the other national trading policies, especially on the part of the United States, the largest creditor nation, which would make

[1] For a detailed account of the sterling area, its interests and its policies see U.S.A., Economic Cooperation Administration, *The Sterling Area: an American Analysis* (London, 1951).
[2] Gaitskell, *The Sterling Area*, p. 171.
[3] Cf. speech by Sir Stafford Cripps, 14 July 1949, H. of C. Deb., vol. 467, coll. 673–94 (Mansergh, *Documents*, ii. 1015–19).
[4] R. S. Sayers, *Financial Policy, 1939–45* (London, HMSO and Longmans, 1956), p. 486. (*History of the Second World War*, U.K. Civil series.)
[5] Final communiqué, 18 July 1949 (Mansergh, *Documents*, ii. 1020–1).

such a multilateral system of world trade and payments practicable. It was in any event a distant goal, but it was one which in later and more favourable circumstances determined the direction of long-term Commonwealth economic policies. In the meantime to meet the crisis of 1949 the United Kingdom government decided upon restrictive measures and the Commonwealth Finance Ministers agreed to recommend comparable measures to their governments in order to protect the remaining reserves of the sterling area. Two months later, however, the United Kingdom government concluded that a drastic short-term remedy was imperative, and on 18 September announced the devaluation of the pound sterling in relation to the United States dollar.[1] Similar steps were taken by other Commonwealth countries within the sterling area, with the one exception of Pakistan, whose government decided against any devaluation of the Pakistani rupee. The Canadian government made the necessary adjustments in respect of the exchange value of the Canadian dollar.[2]

The devaluation of the pound sterling served to illuminate the nature of the financial relations within the sterling area and the Commonwealth. Devaluation was decided upon by the United Kingdom government as a last and in some respects desperate remedy to check the drain upon the gold reserves of the sterling area. Advance information of the intentions of the United Kingdom government to devalue the pound sterling would have largely defeated its purpose, for it would have increased the drain on the sterling reserves. According to the subsequent statement of the Indian Finance Minister, Dr. John Matthai,[3] the possibility of devaluation was not discussed at the meeting of the Commonwealth Finance Ministers in July. There was, he said, 'not even so much as a reference to the subject at the Conference'. Resolutions were framed representing the views of the Finance Ministers on the measures that should be taken by the sterling-area countries to increase their dollar resources and relieve their dollar expenditure, and these were, again in the words of India's Finance Minister, 'to provide the basis on which the British Chancellor of the Exchequer, so to speak the Managing Agent of the Sterling Area, was to hold talks . . . with the U.S.A. Treasury and with the Canadian Government'. The United Kingdom government's decision to devalue the pound, reached before the Washington talks, was not the outcome of further consultation with Commonwealth governments. On the contrary they were informed only very shortly before

---

[1] For a discussion on the immediate background to devaluation see Commonwealth Relations Conference, 4th, Bigwin Inn, Ontario, September 1949, *The Changing Commonwealth, Proceedings*, ed. by F. H. Soward (Toronto, Oxford University Press for CIIA, 1950).

[2] The speeches of the Finance Ministers of Canada, Australia, New Zealand, South Africa, India, Pakistan, and Ceylon on the devaluation are reprinted in Mansergh, *Documents*, ii. 1022–45.

[3] Constituent Assembly of India (Legislative) Deb., vol. 5, no. 1, pp. 9–21 (ibid. pp. 1029–38).

devaluation. They had not, however, supposed that the categorical denials given by the Chancellor of the Exchequer to any suggestion that the pound might be devalued necessarily excluded the possibility that it would be devalued. On 16 and 17 September the implications of devaluation were discussed at a meeting of the International Monetary Fund in New York, while in London the Commonwealth Relations Office called a meeting of the High Commissioners, at which the High Commissioner for Pakistan was unable to be present, to inform them of the action the United Kingdom government proposed to take. There were also telegraphic communications between Delhi and Karachi and Delhi and Colombo, but they did not suffice to remove causes of misunderstanding in the very short time left to oversea Commonwealth governments to determine their respective courses of action.[1] Dr. Matthai, making due allowance for the extreme difficulties of the situation, felt that Sir Stafford Cripps had exceeded the brief given him by the Commonwealth Finance Ministers in July, whereas Sir Stafford evidently felt free to make his decision in the light of the discussions of the Finance Ministers but in no way limited by them. This was an interpretation consistent with the convention that prevailed at meetings of Commonwealth Prime Ministers; but extended to a financial question of the greatest moment to all the members of the Commonwealth it appeared to some, and more especially to the Asian, members of the Commonwealth, too loose to safeguard their interests. It was very largely as a result of experience in September 1949,[2] and of the failure, partly through lack of time, to ensure reasonable opportunities for the co-ordination of Indian, Pakistani, and Ceylonese financial policies, that these Asian members, so insistent on the need for the greatest flexibility in intra-Commonwealth discussions, were later well disposed towards proposals for the strengthening of the machinery of consultation on economic and financial policy.

The Colombo Conference, January 1950

The creation of a stable relationship between the sterling and the dollar areas was not to be resolved by any one act, however drastic, and it continued in the years after 1949 as the major problem in the financial relations of the Commonwealth with the United States. Its effects extended beyond the financial and the economic into the political field, for exchange stability and the policies of economic expansion that were in no small measure conditional upon its attainment were thought of as part of the struggle of the non-Communist world to preserve itself from the penetration of Communist doctrine. Because contracting living standards and economic and social

[1] See the speech of the Finance Minister for Ceylon, Mr. Jayawardene, who stated that he was not consulted by the Indian government (Mansergh, *Documents*, ii. 1042).

[2] Cf. the statement by Dr. Matthai: 'I feel we have been placed in a position which led not merely to inconvenience to ourselves but also inconvenience to our neighbours, Ceylon and Pakistan, and I think every effort should have been made to avoid the inconvenience that was caused in that way' (ibid. p. 1034).

instability were generally deemed most favourable to the spread of Communist ideas, so financial stability and rising living standards were thought to provide the best protection against them. In this there was at once much truth and some dangerous over-simplification. It was, however, a belief that influenced the governments of Canada and more particularly of the United States in their decisions to assist the economic recovery of Western Europe as an indispensable counterpart to the military defences of the North Atlantic area and one also which directed greater attention to the far graver problems of raising living standards in the Colonial Empire and in Southern Asia.

The government of the United Kingdom acted with generosity and foresight when it came to the conclusion that social services and state enterprises were also appropriate for export to economically backward areas. The Colonial Development Act of 1929[1] was a first tentative step; the Development and Welfare Act of 1940,[2] prompted by the deplorable evidences of neglect enshrined in the Report of the West India Royal Commission,[3] was a splendidly defiant affirmation of a new faith at an hour when Britain and the Empire were threatened as never before in their history.[4] Under the postwar Labour administration state-sponsored enterprises[5] were widely and by no means always judiciously extended to colonial territories, as egg-farming ventures in the Gambia and a groundnuts extravaganza in Tanganyika testified to a public that was warmly appreciative of the ironic flavour of failures attributable to the miscalculations of civil service planning.[6] But while such experience counselled prudence, the resolve to continue with the extension of development and welfare policies to economically backward areas remained. It was strengthened by awareness of the attractions of Communism in its new expansionist phase for the poorer—now illuminatingly described as the underprivileged—peoples of the world, but it did not derive from it. In respect of Commonwealth territories the origins of such policies may be clearly traced back through the Colonial Development and Welfare Acts to the struggle for social services and nationalization of basic industries in the United Kingdom.

The discussions at the meeting of the Foreign Ministers of the Commonwealth in Colombo in January 1950 served more immediately to illustrate the interrelationship of economic and social with political considerations; for,

[1] 20 Geo. V, c. 5 (extract in Mansergh, *Documents*, ii. 1073-4).
[2] 3 & 4 Geo. 6, c. 40 (ibid. pp. 1075-6).
[3] Cmd. 6174 (relevant extract in ibid. pp. 1074-5).
[4] See especially speech by the Rt. Hon. Malcolm MacDonald, 21 May 1940, H. of C. Deb., vol. 361, coll. 41-51 (ibid. pp. 1077-9). A further Colonial Development and Welfare Act was passed in 1945 (8 & 9 Geo. 6, c. 20; ibid. pp. 1079-80).
[5] Colonial Development and Overseas Food Corporations were created under the Overseas Resources Development Act 1948, 11 & 12 Geo. 6, c. 15 (ibid. pp. 1082-7).
[6] The wholesale damage and destruction to agricultural machinery unsuited to the East African terrain prompted the comment (playing on Mr. Churchill's historic appeal to the United States), 'Give us the job and we will finish the tools'.

paradoxically enough, the most important contribution of the Foreign Ministers was not in the realm of foreign policy as traditionally understood but in the inauguration of the Colombo Plan for the promotion of the economic development of the countries of South and South-East Asia. Their meeting was notable also for other reasons. It was the first conference of Commonwealth Foreign Ministers to be held, and it was also the first ministerial conference to take place in Asia. Both were of political and psychological importance. Mr. Senanayake, the Prime Minister of Ceylon, who presided, observed that the holding of the conference in the island was practical proof that all members of the Commonwealth were of equal standing, irrespective of size, race, or creed, and he thought it especially appropriate that Ceylon should be chosen for the first meeting of Commonwealth Foreign Ministers because with the addition of its Asian members the Commonwealth had acquired a new influence in Asia at a time when the continent was confronted with some of the gravest international problems of the day.

The official statement issued at the end of the Colombo Conference was couched in characteristically general terms.[1] It said the discussions had 'once again demonstrated that among all members of the Commonwealth there is a continuing and substantial community of outlook' in their approach to world problems; that most of the time of the Conference had been spent in a comprehensive review of South-East Asia where progress was recognized to depend mainly upon the improvement of economic conditions, and that recommendations to this end, including the establishment of an economic consultative committee, were to be made to Commonwealth governments. Since the Australian delegation led by Mr. P. C. Spender, the Minister for External Affairs, had taken the initiative in advancing proposals for a concerted Commonwealth approach to the problem of raising living standards in Southern Asia,[2] it was agreed that this committee should hold its first meeting in Australia. The Foreign Ministers considered that, while world problems were indivisible, Asia was 'at the moment the main focus of interest and an area of special urgency'; but they were divided in their views on outstanding Asian problems, notably that of Indo-China. They disposed temporarily of a much-debated subject by recording their agreement that there need be no inconsistency between Britain's closer association with Western Europe and the maintenance of her traditional links with the Commonwealth. The success of the conference was widely acclaimed; but Pandit Nehru, in describing it as a 'remarkable and significant' event, placed its contribution in perspective by adding that at least it 'helps us to prevent things from going completely astray'.[3]

In May 1950 the Commonwealth Economic Consultative Committee on

[1] Final communiqué, 14 January 1950 (Mansergh, *Documents*, ii. 1186–8).
[2] Cf. speech by Mr. P. C. Spender, Australia, H. of R. Deb., vol. 211, pp. 3186–8 (ibid. ii. 1071–3).
[3] *Annual Register*, 1950, p. 84.

economic aid for South-East Asia, set up by the Colombo Conference, met at Sydney.[1] It recommended that the development of South-East Asia should proceed by progressive stages under six-year plans, which were to be fomulated in the light of full statements of the economic situation and development programme of each participating country. In addition there was to be a Commonwealth Technical Assistance Committee with headquarters at Colombo.

In September 1950 the Consultative Committee met again in London to consider the six-year development plans prepared by the governments of India, Pakistan, Ceylon, Malaya, Singapore, and North Borneo.[2] In sum these plans contemplated a total expenditure of £1,868 million over the six years, of which £1,084 million would require external finance. Under the agreement the participating countries of Asia were to provide a proportion of the capital and the remainder was to be contributed from outside sources. The United Kingdom and other Commonwealth governments (excepting that of South Africa which felt that development in Africa must be its principal preoccupation) gave prompt assurances of their intention to assist in the working out of these national programmes for development through self-help and mutual aid. Those assurances were fulfilled. But while the plan was Commonwealth inspired, it was not intended that it should remain an exclusively Commonwealth undertaking either in its financing or in its application.

We countries of the Commonwealth [said Mr. Gaitskell] have taken the initiative in this enterprise but we desire no monopoly. Our work supplements and does not duplicate the efforts of the United Nations and other interested agencies. We shall welcome the co-operation of all governments concerned to maintain the independence and assist the progress of South East Asia.[3]

Nor was the aid to be given under the plan to be confined to Commonwealth countries. On the contrary, all in the area were invited to participate in its implementation.

The national programmes[4] submitted by the states of South-East Asia were on a modest scale and it was temptingly easy for those outside Asia to overestimate the possible Colombo Plan contribution to the raising of living standards in South and South-East Asia. Visitors from the older dominions seeing machinery for irrigation works or tractors on experimental farms inscribed 'supplied by Canada under the Colombo Plan' or 'supplied by Australia under the Colombo Plan' often fell into this temptation—one incidentally to which visitors from the United Kingdom were not exposed, since the greater part of the United Kingdom's substantial contribution was made

[1] Final communiqué, 19 May 1950 (Mansergh, *Documents*, ii. pp. 1053-5).
[2] Cmd. 8080 (ibid. pp. 1055-69).
[3] cf. Mr. P. C. Gordon Walker's speech to the Royal Empire Society, 12 October 1950 (Mansergh, *Documents*, ii. 1216-17).
[4] The development programmes are given in some detail in Cmd. 8080.

through the release of accumulated war-time sterling balances. Among Asians, however, while there was an appreciation of such external assistance, it was customarily related to the assumption that it was the harbinger of more substantial aid. The plan, in the words of the Indian Finance Minister, Mr. Chintaman Deshmukh, contained 'the seeds of international economic cooperation'.[1] In contrast with the implied premiss of the older members of the Commonwealth, that assistance on their part was generous or politic or more usually both, was the prevailing Asian presumption that it was a first and overdue recognition of the claims of social justice. In 1951 some 7 per cent. of the world's population enjoyed some 42 per cent. of its income, while 55 per cent. of its people enjoyed only 10 per cent. of its income. The older members of the Commonwealth were to be numbered with the wealthy minority, the newer with the under-privileged majority. This uneven distribution of the world's wealth, thus reflected within the Commonwealth, was described by the *Eastern Economist* as 'absolutely wicked' and something which it was the moral responsibility of more privileged nations to help to redress.

The Colombo Plan was essentially an essay in economic co-operation. Whatever may prove to be the final assessment of its contribution to development and welfare in South and South-East Asia in relation to capacity and needs, by its conception and execution it influenced significantly the shaping of post-war Commonwealth relations. Apart from the Technical Assistance Committee in Ceylon, the Plan was not directed or administered by any common authority. National governments were responsible for the assessment of needs and capacities for development, the role of the Consultative Committee being confined to co-ordination, criticism, and advice. Ultimate authority rested at all times with individual governments. Yet the association of the governments of the older and wealthier members of the Commonwealth with their newer and economically more backward partners was well calculated to promote at the least greater understanding. Nor were such opportunities confined to ministers and government officials. As a result of the Colombo Plan there was, for example, an increased flow of Asian students to Australian universities, where hitherto, except at Perth, the Commonwealth's Indian Ocean university, they had been almost unknown; there was a corresponding increase in the number of technicians from older Commonwealth countries working for a period of years in Southern Asia. If, once again, the scale of such interchanges was easily exaggerated, it was equally not to be overlooked. Economically and socially the Colombo Plan helped to give some cohesion to a Commonwealth recently enlarged by the addition of its three Asian members. It was enabled to do so because the Plan was not directly associated, even if it was also not unrelated, to Western endeavours to contain Communism in Asia. There was in any event no conviction that it could do so. The belief

---

[1] India, Parliamentary Deb., vol. 6, no. 11, pt. 2, col. 841 (Mansergh, *Documents*, ii. 1069–70).

'that we can buy off communism and purchase peace for ourselves merely by stepping up our economic assistance' was described by Mr. Lester Pearson at the 1955 meeting of the Consultative Committee as 'nothing but a comforting illusion'. That required something more than money or aid; it required mutual understanding, respect, and support for 'the genuine leaders of the Asian people'.[1]

The Commonwealth and the Korean War

The identity of the 'genuine leaders of the Asian peoples' was a matter upon which agreement could not be presumed. Few in Asia believed that the Emperor Bao Dai in Indo-China was entitled to that description, but at the Colombo Conference the Foreign Ministers of the older members of the Commonwealth were prepared so to regard him. Could a Communist be a 'genuine leader', or a Communist government an acceptable government in Asia? After the overthrow of Chiang Kai-shek and the Kuomintang in China, these were matters that caused no little heart-searching among Commonwealth governments. While the Communist victory there caused little surprise in Southern Asia, its impact elsewhere was heightened by its unexpectedness, and partly for that reason caused much emotional disturbance in the United States, with which Commonwealth governments of necessity had to reckon in the shaping of their policies.

The Indian and Pakistani governments recognized the People's government in Peking as the *de facto* government of China, Mr. Nehru explaining that India's action in this respect implied not moral approval but a recognition of political realities. It was not, he told the Indian Parliament on 17 March 1950, a question of approving or disapproving the change, but of recognizing a major event in history and dealing with it.[2] He had no doubt the Communist régime was firmly established and that 'there was no force likely to supplant it'. The government of the United Kingdom, much influenced by Indian assessments of the position in China, adopted the same course. The leader of the Opposition, Mr. Churchill, implicitly accepted Mr. Nehru's premiss in remarking that 'the reason for having diplomatic relations is not to confer a compliment, but to secure a convenience'.[3] Canada, Australia, New Zealand, and South Africa, however, withheld recognition, after consultation which the Lord Chancellor, Lord Jowitt, described[4] as closer, more continuous, and more direct than any which had hitherto taken place between oversea members of the Commonwealth and the United Kingdom. The result was that in respect of a major question of Asian policy the United Kingdom found herself in accord with the newer Asian members of

---

[1] *Annual Register, 1955*, p. 76.
[2] India, House of the People Deb., vol. 3, p. 1699.
[3] 17 November 1949, H. of C. Deb., vol. 469, col. 2225.
[4] 17 March 1950, H. of L. Deb., vol. 166, col. 88.

the Commonwealth; the older members, in agreement with the government of the United States,[1] and thereby committed to the recognition of Chiang Kai-shek, exiled on the island of Formosa, as 'the genuine leader' of the Chinese people, and his government as the government of one of the great powers entitled to a permanent seat on the Security Council. Rarely have folly and presumption been more closely allied.

On 27 June 1950 the forces of the North Korean Communist-controlled government crossed the 38th parallel. On 28 June the Security Council, the representative of the Soviet Union being absent at that time because of the Soviet boycott, condemned the aggression of North Korea. The governments of the members of the Commonwealth who were not members of the Security Council subsequently expressed their approval of the resolution,[2] and on 5 July Mr. Attlee, the Prime Minister of the United Kingdom, spoke of the 'striking unity of view' displayed by its member nations. The older members of the Commonwealth contributed to the United Nations forces in Korea, their ground troops later being formed into a Commonwealth Division. But they fought under United Nations command in a United Nations war. The great bulk of the United Nations forces in Korea were, however, United States forces. Their commander was General MacArthur. As the war progressed it became increasingly uncertain whether General MacArthur considered himself a United Nations commander or a United States commander, or indeed whether in practice he was prepared to acknowledge any such external authority. Partly because of this uncertainty, partly because of misgivings in Asia about the aims of the United States, the Commonwealth countries were drawn together neither for the first nor for the last time in order to exercise a restraining influence upon United States policies. Pandit Nehru, especially after the crossing of the 38th parallel on 8 October 1950 against strong Indian advice to the contrary,[3] was outspoken in his complaints that the Western powers were too much disposed to make decisions affecting vast areas of Asia without understanding the real needs or the minds of the people there. A statement made by President Truman on 30 November 1950 suggesting that the United States was contemplating the use of the atomic bomb in Korea[4] startled Commonwealth capitals and increased the disquiet of the Asian members. In December 1950 the Prime Minister of the United Kingdom, urged by other Commonwealth governments and especially by that of India, went to Washington as the emissary of the greater part of the

[1] It is not to be assumed that they simply followed the United States lead; on the contrary, there is evidence to suggest that their decisions were reached independently. But this is a matter on which there is not sufficient published evidence in each instance on which to base a firm conclusion.
[2] The United Kingdom was the only Commonwealth member of the Security Council at this date; Ceylon was not at the time a member of the United Nations, her application for membership having been rejected by the exercise of the veto by the Soviet Union.
[3] See below, pp. 357-60 for some more detailed considerations of Indian foreign policy.
[4] Council on Foreign Relations, *The United States in World Affairs, 1950*, p. 418.

Commonwealth to impress upon the government of the United States their common desire to avoid all risk of extending the war in Korea. Shortly after Mr. Attlee's return in January 1951 the Commonwealth Prime Ministers met in London. At the conclusion of their Meeting they issued an uninformative communiqué and a separate Declaration affirming the principles which were guiding their policies.[1] This restated at once their resolve to strengthen their defences 'with all speed and diligence' so long as the fear of aggression remained, and their desire themselves to seek peace. In a passage unusual in an official statement of this character the Declaration went on:

> The great antidote to war is hope; its greatest promoter is despair. When we say that war is not inevitable, we do not just mean that we shall prepare and be strong, and that our strength may deter aggression. We also mean that, in a world worn out and distorted by war, there must be an overwhelming majority of the people of all lands who want peace. We must not despair of reaching them. In all our discussions we have made it clear to each other, as we now do to the world, that as Commonwealth Prime Ministers we would welcome any feasible arrangement for a frank exchange of views with Stalin or with Mao Tse Tung. We should, in the name of common humanity, make a supreme effort to see clearly into each other's hearts and minds.

The Declaration of early 1951, which was devoid neither of eloquence nor of emotion, marked a measure of agreement among all members of the Commonwealth not destined to be reached again in the immediately succeeding years. Asian endorsement of the resolution of the Security Council condemning the aggression of North Korea, coupled with a shared anxiety to limit the area of conflict and to bring about an early peace, had made it possible. Thereafter the course of events in Korea and deep differences of opinion about the possibility of a settlement with Communist China and about the nature of the war in Indo-China drove them apart. Korea more and more came to be interpreted in Asia not, as in the West, as a war to vindicate the authority of the United Nations, but as a war between great imperialist groupings fought out on Asian soil with little regard to Asian suffering, and likely to leave behind 'the peace of the grave'. Where the Western powers drew from it encouraging conclusions on the value of collective resistance to aggression, peoples in Southern Asia came to regard it as an object lesson on the importance of remaining uncommitted to the great-power blocs.

The Pacific Security Agreement, 1951

Mr. Menzies returned from the Prime Ministers' Meeting seemingly convinced that a world war provoked by Communist aggression was not so much a possibility as a probability. Three years, he warned the Australian people in March 1951, 'not a minute more', was the time in which they had to prepare.[2]

---

[1] Both in Mansergh, *Documents*, ii. 1206–9.
[2] 7 March 1951, Australia, H. of R. Deb., vol. 212, p. 78.

Australians, temperamentally little disposed to heed even the most sombre prognostications of Prime Ministers, were as much interested and some of them equally disturbed at that time by the concluding phase of the negotiations for a peace treaty with Japan. The terms of such a treaty had been discussed at the Commonwealth Conference in Canberra in 1947. At that conference 'security against future aggression by Japan was a major concern . . . throughout all its discussions on all subjects', and delegates 'directed particular attention to ensuring that Japan would not be in a position to rearm or to recreate dangerous war potential'.[1] In succeeding years the Australian and New Zealand governments continued to press for the imposition of terms which would exclude the possibility of a resurgence of Japanese military and naval power in the foreseeable future. This view was not in accord with the predominant United States opinion, which increasingly favoured the rearming of Japan as a bulwark against future Communist expansion in the Far East. Where the Australians continued to think of an enemy from whose brutalities their fellow countrymen had suffered so recently and so cruelly, the United States had come to think of a future ally in a war against Sino-Russian Communist imperialism. It was the United States view that prevailed. The price exacted by New Zealand and Australia was the Pacific Security Agreement.

Experience in 1941–2 had impressed upon all parties in Australia and New Zealand the need for solid guarantees for the future security of their countries. While it was true that both Britain and the United States had good reasons on grounds of self-interest alone to come to their assistance in the event of danger, it was also true that these two dominions lay on the perimeter both of the British Commonwealth and of the United States defensive systems. The latter was a matter of major importance. Might they not in certain circumstances be regarded as expendable in Washington? The existence of that doubt was the principal argument for a reinsurance agreement between New Zealand and Australia on the one hand and the United States on the other. It was reinforced by other considerations.

Experience of co-operation with the American forces in the Second World War had convinced many Australians that the American forces worked best to prepared plans, and that plans for the defence of the Pacific were more likely to be prepared, and in good time, if a formal agreement existed. Closely allied to this was the feeling that the increasing scale of American commitments in other parts of the world might lead to a neglect of the South Pacific in the absence of any such formal undertaking. In 1951 there was moreover much evidence to suggest that most important decisions, in respect, for example, of the allocation of raw materials and of manpower, were being taken by the North Atlantic Treaty powers, and that there was in consequence a serious risk that the views of the Australian and New Zealand governments

[1] Final Conference Communiqué (Mansergh, *Documents*, ii. 1170–1).

might not be heard before decisions were reached. Mr. Spender on more than one occasion expressed his anxiety on this score, and while he did not suggest that there was any lack of goodwill or of full Commonwealth consultation, he felt that inevitably Australian views were being heard in the North Atlantic Treaty Organization always at second-hand, and not always in time. To remedy this the Australian government was anxious itself to have a direct line to Washington, and felt that the negotiation of a formal agreement with the United States would best provide it.[1]

The negotiation of the North Atlantic Treaty inevitably suggested that to balance the Atlantic Treaty in the West there should be a Pacific Treaty in the East. Yet the needs and the circumstances of the two areas were very different. The Atlantic Treaty was a superstructure. It followed upon various defensive agreements in Western Europe—the Dunkirk Treaty, the Brussels Treaty, and the working out of plans for future economic and political co-operation. It did not precede them. No such developments, however, had taken place on the continent of Asia. There was indeed no suggestion that any state other than its original signatories, and perhaps Japan, would participate in the Pacific Security Agreement. It stood by itself; it was a possible foundation.[2]

The provisions of the Pacific Security Agreement were modelled on those of the North Atlantic Treaty and the wording of certain provisions in each was identical.[3] There was the same insistence that the agreement was intended not to detract from, but to buttress, the authority of the United Nations, and the Preamble reaffirmed the faith of the signatories 'in the purposes and principles of the Charter'. But in respect of obligation the wording of the Pacific Security Agreement was weaker than that of its Atlantic counterpart. Article 4, described by Mr. Casey as 'the heart of the treaty',[4] recorded the recognition of each signatory that 'an armed attack in the Pacific area on any of the parties would be dangerous to its own peace and safety' and declared that it would 'act to meet the common danger in accordance with its constitutional processes'. Article 5 of the North Atlantic Treaty, it will be recalled, by contrast spoke of an armed attack against one or more of the signatories as being considered 'an armed attack against all', and coupled this with specific references to the action to be taken by each party 'forthwith in concert with other signatories to restore and maintain the security of the North Atlantic area'.

[1] Mr. Spender, by resigning from ministerial office in 1951 and proceeding to Washington as Australian Ambassador, gave further indication of the importance he attached to 'the line to Washington'.
[2] But since United States policy aimed at ensuring United States' interests and stability in the area by a chain of agreements rather than by a single comprehensive alliance, it was not a foundation on which the principal partner in the Pacific Security Agreement was likely to build.
[3] Art. 1 of both treaties and Arts. 3 and 4 of the North Atlantic Treaty are identical with Arts. 2 and 3 of the Pacific Security Agreement except for the addition of 'in the Pacific' in the later treaty. For text see Mansergh, *Documents*, ii. 1171–3.
[4] Australia, H. of R. Deb., 1st session 1951, no. 11, pp. 1708–9 (ibid. pp. 1173–5).

While the North Atlantic Treaty left the nature of the action to be taken and the aid to be given to the discretion of each party, it implied at least a greater obligation, and indeed at the time of its ratification alarm was expressed in the United States at the insertion of a statement that an attack upon one should be considered an attack upon all parties to the treaty. This accounts for the substitution in later regional agreements, including the Pacific Security Agreement, of the phrase 'would endanger its own peace and safety' long since associated with the enunciation of the Monroe Doctrine. In turn, however, this phrase, designed to reassure the United States, disturbed some Australian Members of Parliament.[1] Officially, however, it was maintained that too much emphasis should not be placed upon such verbal distinctions. Mr. Dulles, for the United States, observed on the signature of the Pacific Security Agreement that 'our fates have been joined', and the Australian and New Zealand governments were satisfied that this was so. Some critics, notably in New Zealand, questioned whether anything of substance had been gained. The United States, they argued, would help to defend Australia and New Zealand, treaty or no treaty, if it suited her interest, and conversely no such assistance would be forthcoming irrespective of any treaty if it were not deemed to be in the interest of the United States to afford it. On this argument, therefore, the Pacific dominions had undertaken an obligation without securing any very real return. It was an argument of doubtful validity. Indeed the question that would seem to have disturbed larger sections of New Zealand and Australian opinion was not whether United States assistance would be forthcoming in the circumstances contemplated in the agreement but rather whether Australia and New Zealand would be drawn against their will in the wake of United States policies in the Far East and in Asia as a whole.[2] So it was that from the date of the signing of the agreement Australia and New Zealand joined the ranks of those who deemed the exercise of a restraining influence upon the United States to be an important aspect of their foreign policy.

The Pacific Security Agreement was the first treaty signed by Australia and New Zealand with a foreign country. Mr. Casey assured the Australian, and Mr. Doidge the New Zealand, House of Representatives that there had been the closest consultations with the government of the United Kingdom throughout the negotiation of the agreement and that the same consultation and close association would be continued in the working of a treaty which recognized in its Preamble that the two dominions had defence obligations outside as well as inside the Pacific area because of their membership of the

[1] See Australia, H. of R. Deb., vol. 216, p. 7.

[2] The wording of Art. 5 of the treaty was partly responsible for such misgivings. It read: 'For the purposes of Article 4, an armed attack on any of the Parties is deemed to include an armed attack on the metropolitan territory of any of the Parties, or on the island territories under its jurisdiction in the Pacific or on its armed forces, public vessels or aircraft in the Pacific'. Might not aircraft, for example, whether by chance or design provoke an attack?

British Commonwealth of Nations.[1] But while Mr. Attlee's Labour government was prepared to acquiesce in the negotiation of a Pacific treaty to which Britain was not a party, Mr. Churchill was not. On his return to office he felt his freedom of action to be impaired but his sense of dissatisfaction undiminished. 'It is one thing', he told Mr. Morrison in October 1952, 'to do harm and another thing to get it undone.'[2] Mr. Menzies offered courteous but incomplete explanations later in the same month.

There are good reasons [he said] which I shall not recount in detail, why the three Governments concerned consider that the treaty should be confined, for the present at any rate, to the original signatories. If anybody should be under the misapprehension that this entails any drawing away from the Mother Country I repeat the assurance which I have given previously in public, that no such movement is intended or, in fact, has taken place. Our adherence to our Mother Country ... to the general British connexion, and to the Commonwealth generally is precisely what it always has been. It is generally acknowledged that the hard core of democracy for the future must be the closest possible relationship between the British peoples and the American people. The treaty is only a local manifestation of closer British-American relations. To my mind, it is not by any means necessary that every self-governing member of the Commonwealth should be a party to every treaty or arrangement entered into with the United States of America.[3]

Mr. Casey spoke[4] in general terms of possible future expansion of the treaty organization. But the United Kingdom remained outside. In a treaty negotiated by three states, one of which was among the greatest of world powers, in this as in other matters it was the will of the one that prevailed.[5]

The Pacific Security Agreement was more important for the Commonwealth than the North Atlantic Treaty in that it marked the formal association and dependence of members of the Commonwealth outside North America upon the United States. Canada on any reckoning lay within the American defensive system; Australia and New Zealand did not. They came within it because of the acknowledged inability of the United Kingdom to underwrite their security. In that respect it was a change of direction the significance of which was heightened by the fact that, contrary to the belief widely entertained in the United Kingdom, it was not the United States that wished by means of the treaty to seduce Australia and New Zealand from their allegiance to the Commonwealth, but rather two conservative and traditionally imperialist

[1] Australia, H. of R. Deb., 1st session 1951, no. 11, pp. 1708–9; New Zealand, H. of R. Deb., 2nd session 1951, no. 3, pp. 318–19 (Mansergh, *Documents*, ii. 1173–7).
[2] H. of C. Deb., vol. 505, col. 28.
[3] Australia, Senate Deb., vol. 220, p. 2951 (Written Answers).
[4] At the first Anzus Council Meeting, 10 August 1952 (*Current Notes*, vol. 23, no. 8, August 1952).
[5] Whether the governments of Australia and New Zealand debated the issue and were convinced by or acquiesced in United States arguments, or whether they themselves had independently concluded that Britain should not be a signatory has not been revealed. One of the first two hypotheses is the more probable.

governments in Australia and New Zealand that persuaded the United States to underwrite their security in return for their acquiescence in the United States notions of an appropriate peace treaty with Japan. It was indeed the hope of the two dominions that their traditional association with Britain could at all times be reconciled with their new treaty relationship with the United States and thus remain unimpaired. 'Where Britain stands we stand: where she goes we go.' So Mr. Holland declared in London early in 1951. Within a few weeks he was reported to have asserted in Washington that New Zealand would 'stand by the United States through thick and thin, right or wrong'. Opposition speakers at home found in these two statements much scope for diverting criticism.[1] But in effect what Mr. Holland was saying was that New Zealand, like Canada, could no longer contemplate with equanimity any serious divergence between United States and United Kingdom policies.

India, South Asia, and the Policy of Non-Alignment

While the older members of the Commonwealth, other than South Africa, sought refuge in regional defence agreements, the newer Asian members placed their faith in a policy of non-alignment. Principle, preconception, and calculation, all alike prompted them to do so. Consequently in the early years of self-government the Asian members, divided by domestic differences, were united in their refusal to be drawn into the cold war. Pandit Nehru was the principal exponent of the policy of non-alignment and partly because of his many expositions of the principles that inspired it and the purposes it was intended to serve, it is a policy most fruitfully examined in an Indian context. But the measure of support Pandit Nehru's utterances on this theme commanded, even among those in South Asia most critical of his other aims and actions, suggests that this was a policy, largely predetermined by history and economic circumstances, which was well grounded in popular emotion. It was indeed judged by its principal sponsor to be a policy not of negation but of construction, the product not of isolationism but of the re-entry of Asia into world history, the symbol not of impotence but of Asian enlightenment.

Tradition and experience both prompted Indian statesmen, like United States historians after the First World War, to attribute responsibility for the calamity of world war not to countries or to individuals but to a declining sense of moral values in politics throughout the whole of the Western world. The awful irruption of Japan in Eastern and South-East Asia little modified such indiscriminate condemnation, for had not Japan in blindly following Western ways cut herself off from the heart of Asia? Even when claims to moral

---

[1] Cf. *The Standard* (New Zealand), 31 January 1951. There was some dispute as to whether Mr. Holland had said that New Zealand would follow the United States 'through right and wrong' or 'through right or wrong'. Some of the criticism was skilfully deflected from the substance of Mr. Holland's remarks to this rather fine textual distinction.

superiority, which were peculiarly irritating to Englishmen who had entertained such notions at other times, were disavowed, the argument was sustained by reasoning from experience.

> I do not mean to say [commented Pandit Nehru] that we in Asia are in any way superior, ethically or morally, to the people of Europe. In some ways I imagine we are worse. There is, however, a legacy of conflict in Europe. In Asia at the present moment at least, there is no such legacy. . . . That is a very great advantage for Asia and it would be folly in the extreme for Asia, for India, to be dragged in the wake of the conflicts in Europe.[1]

Asia or India—the two were not always clearly distinguished by the Indian Prime Minister—at all costs, therefore, must not become entangled in alliances with the Western powers. The Western powers generally neither welcomed this conclusion nor greatly relished the reasons advanced for it.

In the early years of independence India, Pakistan, and Ceylon, while preserving full freedom of action, inclined perceptibly towards the West. Ceylon, barred from membership of the United Nations, was closely associated with Britain not only through her membership of the Commonwealth but also by the terms of the 1947 defence agreement.[2] Pakistan, struggling for survival, had one dominant external preoccupation—Kashmir—to which all else was subordinated, and despite early disappointment continued, with occasional and deliberately provocative glances towards Moscow, to place her hopes of a favourable outcome upon the support of the Western powers. The Indian government, threatened by Communist subversion which in 1950 'bordered on open revolt',[3] sought strength and stability in association with Asian neighbours and Commonwealth partners. If India was estranged from Pakistan over Kashmir, and bitterly critical of South Africa's racial policies at the United Nations, she found understanding with Labour governments in the United Kingdom, Australia, and New Zealand and the Liberal government in Canada. Australia and New Zealand were represented at the Delhi Conferences on Indonesia,[4] and their governments showed themselves, as did that of the United Kingdom, to be sympathetic to Asian nationalist aspirations. Nationalism and Commonwealth membership, it appeared, were not contradictory but compatible, and even complementary, concepts. But after 1950, when India exercised her greatest influence on United Kingdom policy, and the Commonwealth perhaps its greatest influence in Washington, Indian policy, while remaining unchanged in principle, was no longer coloured by a pro-Western

---

[1] India, Constituent Assembly (Legislative) Deb., vol. 2, pt. 2, pp. 1225–36.
[2] See above, pp. 248–9.
[3] The phrase was used by the Indian Prime Minister who was outspoken at that time in his denunciations of the Indian Communist party and its members, chiefly on the ground that they were not a national party but one which accepted orders from without.
[4] See Report of the Conference on Indonesia held in Delhi in January 1949 (Mansergh, *Documents*, ii. 1177–80).

bias, no longer vigorously condemned by Moscow for that very reason, and became by 1955–6 one of independence so regarded by East and West alike.[1]

The reasons for adjustment in India's attitude to the Western powers were not general but particular. In Asia the Western powers decided to pursue policies against the advice and in conflict with the known views of the Indian government. In Korea India advised most strongly against the crossing of the 38th parallel. On 30 September 1950 Pandit Nehru said that the Indian government believed that every effort should be made to bring the Korean War to a conclusion and 'that it would be wrong to carry on military operations.... Therefore we think that the U.N. forces should not go beyond the 38th parallel till all other means of settlement have been explored.'[2] India's advice was disregarded. With Pakistan she urged recognition of the People's government in Peking. The United Kingdom, much influenced by Asian views, did recognize it; neither the United States nor any of the older members of the Commonwealth followed her example. There were sharp differences with the United States over the peace treaty with Japan in 1951. In Indo-China the Indian government advised against recognition of the French puppet Emperor Bao Dai. Such recognition, however, was accorded by the United Kingdom, the United States, Australia, and New Zealand. It was followed by Soviet and Asian recognition of Ho Chi Minh. India, in the words of her Prime Minister, was not ready to jump into the fray 'though unquestionably her government believed that continuing attempts to maintain a French sponsored regime involved greater risks to peace than possible extension of communist influence'.[3] The Western powers disagreed. This disagreement was sharpened when the Indian government later, and no longer with the support of Pakistan, protested against the extension of defence agreements to the Middle East and South-East Asia and against Western aid to Pakistan,

---

[1] J. C. Kundra, *Indian Foreign Policy, 1947–54* (Groningen, Wolters, 1955), has much useful and detailed material on this point and broadly speaking reaches this conclusion. Modifications in the Soviet attitudes to the principal Indian leaders are recorded in the comments upon them in successive editions of the Soviet Encyclopaedias. Thus in the *Small Soviet Encyclopaedia* (1930) Gandhi's 'moderate views' were said to reflect 'the mood of the petty bourgeoisie and in particular that of craftsmen' and he had 'lost his former influence as he is needed neither by the bourgeoisie ... nor by the masses'. In the *Large Soviet Encyclopaedia* (1952) Gandhi appeared as 'the author of the reactionary political doctrine of Gandhiism' who had resolutely rejected the united action of Indians with other oppressed nations and with European workers, and forced on the Indian nationalist movement a religious ideology instead of a revolutionary programme. His role in the development of the national liberation movement reflected the traitorous position of the large Indian bourgeoisie and landowners. Marshal Bulganin, addressing the Indian Parliament on 21 November 1955 and sympathizing with the brave struggle of the Indian people against colonial oppression, spoke of the great significance in this struggle 'of the ideas and leadership of the outstanding Indian national leader Mahatma Gandhi'. Nehru, 'the head of the petty bourgeois wing of the Congress' in 1939 was likewise rehabilitated in Soviet eyes by 1955.

[2] Quoted in Kundra, *Indian Foreign Policy*, p. 133.

[3] 9 September 1954 to Delhi Press Association (see *Times of India*, 10 September 1954).

which in her view would serve only to bring the cold war to the Indian subcontinent and to alter the balance of power there to India's disadvantage.

'You may like it or dislike it but like an earthquake it has happened just the same.' So Pandit Nehru said of the death of Western imperialism in Asia. However, it took an unconscionable time in dying. The conflict in Indo-China, Pandit Nehru told the Lok Sabha, despite its complexity was in its origin and essential character a movement of resistance to colonialism, and attempts were being made to deal with such resistance 'by the traditional methods of suppression and divide and rule'.[1] The risk, as he conceived it, was that Western alliances would be used to maintain surviving Western colonial outposts in Asia beyond the natural, historic term of their existence. In 1949, when asked about India's reaction to the North Atlantic Treaty, Pandit Nehru said that India had been kept informed but not consulted 'because we are not in it at all', and he added that India's membership of the Commonwealth did not in any way connect India with the North Atlantic Treaty. But on 13 June 1952 there appeared for the first time a new note of criticism. The North Atlantic Treaty, said Pandit Nehru, began as a defence organization but later extended its role to the defence of the colonial possessions of its members.[2] India took 'a very serious view' of this because she was unalterably opposed to colonial rule wherever it existed. Subsequent Portuguese appeals to her partners in the North Atlantic Treaty to ensure regard for Portuguese sovereignty in Goa and the response they elicited hardened this antipathy in India to the principal Western alliance, while in Pakistan the association of NATO with repressive French policies in North Africa provoked a correspondingly unfavourable reaction.

While opposed after 1952 to the whole system of Western alliances in which the United Kingdom was a principal partner, and to colonial empires, of which the British was still the largest, the Indian government under Pandit Nehru's leadership remained a convinced supporter of the Commonwealth and a believer in 'its healing touch'.[3] In the same speech in which the Indian Prime Minister first denounced the North Atlantic Treaty he reaffirmed in categorical terms all he had said in the past about the importance to India of her ties with the Commonwealth. 'We propose to continue these bonds', he told his critics,[4] 'and I see no reason why we should break these bonds which are of advantage to us.' Despite the differences on major issues of foreign policy which divided India from the older members of the Commonwealth, the importance of membership remained for both.

[1] 24 April 1954 (*The Hindu*, 25 April 1954).
[2] Dr. Kundra (*Indian Foreign Policy*, p. 121) notes that by the end of 1950 India had received only $4·5 million from the United States as compared with $35·5 million to Formosa and $6·2 sanctioned for Indo-China. Indian dislike of aid 'with strings' partly explains this relative disparity.
[3] See Indian Constituent Assembly Deb., vol. 8, pp. 2–10 (Mansergh, *Documents*, ii. 847–57). [4] 12 June 1952, India, House of the People Deb., vol. 2, no. 1, coll. 1665–9.

South Africa, the Western Alliances, and the United Nations

The Union of South Africa was a member of none of the Western alliances. This was rather because of its geographical situation than by deliberate choice. Anti-Communist feeling among the majority of the European ruling class in the Union was pronounced. In his pre-election statement of the Nationalist party programme on 20 April 1948 Dr. Malan declared that one of the tasks of a Nationalist government would be to rescue the South African nation from the 'foreign complexes' which inhibited the Smuts government, and still more 'from the ever-encroaching and all-destroying Communist cancer'.[1] This aim was closely associated with the principal plank in the party's election programme, the saving of white civilization 'from vanishing in the black sea of South Africa's non-European population'. Nothing indeed was to be permitted which impaired absolute European sovereignty, and to that end the policy of *apartheid* was enunciated. Native and Coloured rights to 'self-respecting development in their own sphere' were to be maintained, but their separateness from each other and still more from their European rulers was to be enforced by law and political discrimination against them. Urban Natives were to be domiciled in separate townships 'with proper attention to health and housing conditions' and only Natives assured of work were to be admitted to the urban areas. There was to be no equality in political, social, or economic rights[2] and the admission of Natives to European institutions of higher education was to cease absolutely. As for the Indians, they were deemed unassimilable. Their immigration was to cease and as many as possible were to be repatriated 'with the co-operation of India and other countries'. Here, in outline, was a programme for the perpetual domination of the majority by a privileged minority and it was a programme founded on difference of colour and race. It was enunciated at a time when the Commonwealth, of which South Africa was a member, had for the first time embraced non-European states in equal partnership, and within a few years of the inclusion of a statement on human rights within the United Nations Charter. It was a programme which brought to the Nationalists a majority of seats, though not of votes, in the 1948 election,[3] and five years later brought them a more decisive electoral victory. Its consequences for South Africa, for the Commonwealth, and for the world are still unfolding.

Communism is a creed that appeals to the under-privileged and the oppressed. The proclaimed intention of the Nationalist party was to depress the status of non-Europeans in the Union and, what was more important in the particular circumstances, to deprive them of all prospect of attaining, whatever their qualifications, the rights and responsibilities of full citizenship. It

---

[1] *Cape Times*, 21 April 1948.
[2] The Transvaal Constitution of 1856 had a clause to this effect.
[3] See Appendix E, p. 442 below. Weightage had been given by agreement to the platteland constituencies at the time of Union.

was this ultimate goal more than any intermediate measures which dismayed South Africa's Commonwealth partners and non-Commonwealth members of the Western alliances. In 1949 Dr. Malan alluded tentatively to the possibility of South Africa's association with the North Atlantic Treaty powers even though the Union lay outside the geographical area of the treaty. But the reaction was discouraging, for South Africa's association with 'the free world' was thought likely to prove a liability rather than an asset in the ideological warfare with Communism. Moreover, by necessity as much as by choice, South Africa was bound in any event to resist Communist military expansion in her own area of strategic interest, which extended to North Africa and the Middle East. The question that remained was whether South Africa under Nationalist leadership and imposing a policy of racial inequality at home was not in fact encouraging the spread of Communism among non-Europeans within and without her borders.

South African policies were the occasion of much debate and denunciation at the United Nations. Three distinct questions were at issue; the future of South-West Africa, the treatment of South African citizens of Indian descent, and the application of a policy of racial discrimination.

The United Nations Charter had made provision for territories held under mandate to be placed under the control of a Trusteeship Council.[1] South Africa alone of the mandatory powers declined to do so, maintaining that in this final discretion rested with the administering power. In 1946 South Africa proposed the incorporation of South-West Africa in the Union in the interest both of its inhabitants, who were said to favour it, and of the Union. India, questioning whether the wishes of the inhabitants had been truly ascertained, opposed any such action. The General Assembly of the United Nations formally resolved that it was unable to accede to the incorporation of the territory in the Union, and recommended that it be placed under the international Trusteeship Council, the South African government being invited to draft a trusteeship agreement for consideration by the General Assembly. This was rejected by the Union government on 23 July 1947 in view of 'the wish, clearly expressed by the overwhelming majority of all the native races . . . and by unanimous vote on the part of the European representatives', in favour of incorporation.[2] Neither side subsequently departed in essentials from their respective and irreconcilable viewpoints. In 1948 South-West Africa was in effect incorporated in the Union.

Indian championship of the rights of South African citizens of Indian descent and her indictment of the policy of racial discrimination commanded a varying but on the whole substantial measure of support in the United Nations.[3] It was the contention of the Indian government that South Africa's

[1] Arts. 75–85.
[2] U.N. doc. A/134.
[3] For a fuller account see K. P. Karunakaran, *India in World Affairs, August 1947*–

discriminatory racial policies were 'a serious violation of the purposes and principles of the Charter on which the United Nations is founded'.[1] In reply the Union government sought not to justify or debate these policies but to exclude them from discussion by the United Nations. In its view they were matters of domestic policy and the South African government protested against the assumption of a jurisdiction which was explicitly excluded by Article 2(7) of the Charter. This, in its view, was 'one of the most fundamental provisions of the Charter' and was plainly intended to have an overriding effect.

> Not only [said Mr. Louw] is it listed among the basic principles which are set forth in Article 2 of the First Chapter, and which govern the whole Charter, but it opens with the very significant words '*Nothing contained in the present Charter shall authorize...*'. Without this paragraph (7), I make bold to say, there could have been, and there would have been no Charter. Without it, South Africa would most certainly not have been a member of the United Nations.[2]

It was a conflict, old in history, between those who appealed to the spirit and those who relied upon the letter. The South African argument was unquestionably well grounded, but in a world which thought and spoke, though more rarely acted, in terms of human rights and racial equality, this little inhibited denunciation of her racial policies. 'Apart from its being wrong, it is an attempt to reverse certain inevitable historical processes at work.' So Pandit Nehru spoke[3] of continuing colonialism in Asia, but he might equally well have used the words of South Africa's racial policies, for they would in that context have commanded even more widespread assent. The Western powers, notably Britain herself, stood for a tradition of equality, irrespective of race or colour or religion, and the open repudiation of that tradition by a member nation of the Commonwealth could not but weaken the Commonwealth as a whole. Communism was to be resisted not only, nor even chiefly, by the organization of military strength but by ideas, by policies of economic development and social welfare. So Western statesmen claimed, but South African policies offered a disturbing commentary on what they were saying.

The Elaboration of Commonwealth Alliances: A Perspective View

In September 1939 the dominions had no particular commitments binding them to go to war in Europe or in Asia. They had not subscribed to the obligations assumed by the United Kingdom in the Locarno Treaties of 1925, in the

---

January 1950 (Calcutta, Oxford University Press for Indian Council of World Affairs, 1952), ch. vii.

[1] Letter from the Representative of India to the Secretary-General of the United Nations, 12 July 1948 (Mansergh, *Documents*, ii. 908–10).

[2] South Africa, *The Treatment of Indians in the Union of South Africa: Discussion and Proceedings in the United Nations (September 1948–May 1949)*. (Pretoria, Government Printer; Mansergh, *Documents*, ii. 910–13.)

[3] In Delhi, 9 September 1954.

Anglo-Egyptian Treaty and in the renewed guarantee of Belgian neutrality both of 1936; in the guarantees given to Poland, Rumania, and Greece in March–April 1939, or in the Anglo-Turkish alliance of the same year. Their policies of detachment were enshrined in the phrase 'no commitments'. They were founded not so much upon a cool assessment of what might best serve the cause of peace and the interests of the Commonwealth as upon an emotional revulsion against the alliances and power politics of the Old World and a desire to disentangle dominion policies from those of the United Kingdom. Considerations of status and of foreign policy at that time were thus inextricably intertwined. Once status had become something that no longer needed to be asserted, a reconsideration of dominion policies was in any circumstances likely. The particular circumstances in which that reconsideration took place prompted a course of action in marked contrast to that generally pursued by the dominions between 1919 and 1939, with the result that by 1952 and still more by 1957 (for this is an occasion when it is illuminating to extend by a few years the period under consideration in this book) the member nations of the Commonwealth had entered either severally or individually into a great variety of alliances, treaties, or agreements committing them to particular courses of action in particular circumstances.[1] The freedom of action the dominions had acquired by disentangling their policies from those of the United Kingdom was thus at their own will limited by international obligations which they had decided to assume.

The extent and variety of the alliances, treaties, and other agreements entered into by members of the Commonwealth may be placed in perspective by summarizing briefly the more important of them. In Europe the United Kingdom alone of Commonwealth members was a party to the Dunkirk Treaty with France, 1946 and the Brussels Treaty, 1947 and associated with Western European Union, 1955, all of which committed her to armed assistance in the event of an attack upon one or more of the signatories to these treaties. Britain and Canada among Commonwealth members were signatories to the North Atlantic Treaty in 1949, Britain and Pakistan to the Baghdad Pact, 1954, Britain, Pakistan, Australia, and New Zealand to the South-East Asian Treaty, 1954. Canada, apart from her membership of the North Atlantic Treaty, was associated with the United States in the defence of North America under the 1940 Ogdensburg Agreement as extended for peacetime purposes in 1947 and 1949. Australia and New Zealand, pledged to mutual aid and assistance under the intra-Commonwealth Anzac Agreement of 1944, both subscribed to the Pacific Security (Anzus) Agreement in 1951 with the United States and to the South-East Asia (Manila) Treaty in 1954. South Africa was a member of no regional pact, but under an agreement signed in June 1955 guaranteed the maintenance of the Simonstown naval base by the Union and its use by the United Kingdom and her allies in time

[1] See Mansergh, *Survey, 1931–9*, pp. 365–6.

of war whether the Union herself were neutral or not.[1] The South African government had also indicated its intention to assist in the defence of the Middle East and its government had asserted that in the event of a major war against Communist aggression South Africa would not be neutral. Pakistan, a member of the Baghdad Pact, was linked by bilateral treaties with Turkey, Iraq, and Persia in the Middle East and associated with the United States not only through common membership of the South-East Asia Treaty Organization but also by acceptance of United States military aid under an agreement reached in 1954. Ceylon was associated with the United Kingdom through the 1947 defence agreement until its abrogation in 1956 at the wish of the Ceylonese government. India, like South Africa, but for altogether different reasons, was a member of no military agreements. She entered, however, into a number of treaties of mutual friendship, first with neighbouring countries, later with others geographically more remote. Over and above treaties that were military or political in their principal purposes, members of the Commonwealth participated in a large number of treaties for economic and social purposes. Among them may be mentioned Britain's membership of OEEC and of the Council of Europe, the participation of all members of the Commonwealth other than South Africa in the Colombo Plan, United Kingdom, Australian, and New Zealand membership of the South Seas Commission, Asian membership of ECAFE, South African association with various organizations for economic planning and research in Africa.

The number of Commonwealth commitments entered into by Commonwealth members during and after the Second World War indicates the independent action taken and the responsibility assumed by them in these years.[2] It was at once the product of maturity and of experience. The Nazi technique of picking off prospective victims one by one disillusioned those who believed that aggressors might be appeased or their own safety secured by a policy of detachment. Accordingly faith was placed, as some few distinguished but lonely voices had advocated in the years before the Second World War, in collective security and collective measures for defence. But the distaste for military alliances remained. The new agreements were rarely so described. Canadian statesmen, once the foremost champions of a policy of no commitments, were insistent that their new regional security agreements were something different from, and morally superior to, old-fashioned military pacts; and in respect of their greater awareness of the economic and social conditions of peace perhaps the claim was warranted. But the hard core of the regional defensive treaties was none the less military. The members of the Commonwealth who subscribed to them were brought directly and not indirectly, as

---

[1] Cmd. 9520. For earlier arrangements see Mansergh, *Survey, 1931–9*, pp. 76, 235.
[2] The fact that the United States had military alliances with forty-two nations in 1957 helps to put this in perspective. The United States alliances were listed in the *New York Times*, 23 March 1957.

before 1939, into the area where military decisions were made. This marked the principal change in the character of the post-war Commonwealth and accounted for the fact that foreign policy had become the principal preoccupation of its members. That in turn posed new questions as to the scope and purpose of their partnership, the ends it best might serve, and the means by which its members might most usefully co-operate.

CHAPTER VIII

THE COMMONWEALTH AT THE ACCESSION OF QUEEN ELIZABETH II

I am His Majesty's Australian Prime Minister.... We are royal, not republican; British, wherever we may be.

R. G. MENZIES, 1950

I am something more than Prime Minister. We are the children of the Indian revolution and its fire still burns in our veins.

JAWAHARLAL NEHRU, 1956

THE nature of the Commonwealth, it goes almost without saying, is not easy to understand. Englishmen would be much disappointed if it were, for the incapacity of foreigners to comprehend the working of British institutions is for them a source of unfailing satisfaction. The sort of tribute English people most cherish is that of the German commentator who observed in 1938[1] that the British Empire 'gives an impression of unsystematic genius in the Englishman, who has no sense of structural beauty or orderly creation. To him nothing is wrong, however illogical, so long as the machine works'.

I believe [said the Lord Chancellor in introducing the British Nationality Bill in the House of Lords ten years later] that of all the remarkable contributions which our race has made to the art of government, the conception of our Empire and Commonwealth is the greatest. Of course it may be said, and said with truth, that it lacks a logical foundation and that it is difficult to expound or explain it. Indeed, even St. Athanasius himself would have found this subject one which called for all his skill.[2]

'La solution du problème', observed the Quebec newspaper *Le Soleil* on the 1949 Declaration on India's republican membership, 'est dans la bonne tradition britannique; elle est à la fois efficace et dépourvue de logique.'[3] At root such satisfaction derived from a belief that indifference to logic implied concentration on practical results. The essence of the German compliment lay in its concluding words—'so long as the machine works'. Since 1938 the Commonwealth had become less shapely and almost wholly devoid of structural beauty, but the satisfaction of knowing that, as a result, it had become still more difficult for foreigners to understand was tempered in some quarters by doubts about its continuing capacity to work.

[1] *Berliner Tageblatt*, 20 August 1938.
[2] H. of L. Deb., vol. 155, col. 754 (Mansergh, *Documents*, ii. 968).
[3] *Le Soleil*, 29 April 1949, quoted in *Canada in World Affairs, 1949 to 1950*, p. 45.

'The old structural unity of the Empire has gone', observed Mr. Menzies with unconcealed anxiety in Adelaide on 26 June 1950; 'it has been succeeded by structural variety.' If the process goes on, he continued, this unity may give place

> to a purely functional association based upon friendship and common interest but necessarily lacking the old high instincts and instantaneous cohesion which sprang from the fact that we were, all over the British world, as indeed we remain in the old Dominions, the King's subjects and the King's men.[1]

There was implicit in Mr. Menzies's words a doubt that has long afflicted men of conservative temper and orderly mind as they watched the apparent loosening of the fabric of imperial unity. It was not a doubt peculiar to the bleak years of the mid-twentieth century; on the contrary it dated back at least to the earliest days of separate dominion foreign policies. It received forcible expression from Mr. R. B. Bennett in the Canadian House of Commons in 1927 when he sensed that with the setting up of a separate Canadian legation in Washington Canada was 'entering on a great adventure, the last great adventure in our relation to the British Empire', for did not this diplomatic departure indicate the acceptance of 'the doctrine of separation'?[2] In a more exalted quarter the intention of the Canadian government later in the year to accredit diplomatic missions to France and Japan had, so the King's Private Secretary Lord Stamfordham remarked, 'rather taken H.M.'s breath away'.[3] Such doubts and misgivings were more widespread, particularly in the Pacific dominions, as has been seen, after the enactment of the Statute of Westminster and all that that implied. So much may be recalled to dispose of the notion that misgivings about the increasing structural variety of the Commonwealth were novel: they were as old as the Commonwealth itself. The fact that they had hitherto been discounted by history prompted contemporaries to look at them critically in their later manifestations though it did not warrant the presumption that they would prove as unfounded in the future as in the past. Jeremiah, after all, is numbered with the major prophets.

In the 'Statute-of-Westminster British Commonwealth',[4] if an inelegant but reasonably exact phrase may be used to describe this community of nations in the form in which it existed between 1931 and 1949, the status of the self-governing member nations was reasonably clearly defined. Its three distinguishing characteristics, as set out in the Balfour Report of 1926 and in the Preamble to the Statute of Westminster, were equality of status, freedom of association, and common allegiance to the Crown. Equality of status and

---

[1] His speech was later published as *The British Commonwealth of Nations in International Affairs* and in part reprinted in Mansergh, *Documents*, ii. 1211–13.
[2] 13 April 1927, Canada, H. of C. Deb., 1927, vol. 2, p. 2472.
[3] Nicolson, p. 471 n.
[4] On the laws and conventions of the Statute-of-Westminster Commonwealth see K. C. Wheare, *The Statute of Westminster and Dominion Status*, 5th ed.

freedom of association combined to ensure the effective independence of the dominions, common allegiance the unity of the Commonwealth. But by 1952 no such equilibrium existed in theory or in practice. Equality of status and freedom of association remained characteristics of full membership in a Commonwealth that was more than British, but the condition of common allegiance had lost its overall validity. Moreover, while equality of status and freedom of association were meaningful phrases in the Statute-of-Westminster Commonwealth they were subsequently, save for those non-self-governing territories which aspired to the inner circle of the self-governing elect, little more than interesting period pieces. Once a challenge, they had become a relic. Was it not otiose in 1952 to describe great nations such as Canada or India as being equal in status, in no way subordinate one to another, and freely associated in the Commonwealth? Of course they were equal in status one with another and with the United Kingdom, not subordinate one to another, and not merely freely associated but free to dissociate should they so desire. What was of interest, therefore, was no longer the status of the dominions but the ways in which the independent member nations of the Commonwealth regarded their membership, and the part it played in the shaping of their outlook and the determination of their policies. Had the weighing down of the scales on the side of autonomy impaired unity? Did the nations now mean more than the Commonwealth which collectively they comprised?

The Place of the Crown in the Commonwealth

These questions may be approached first by considering the position of the Crown in the Commonwealth, the Crown which, to recall Mr. Baldwin's words to King Edward VIII in the abdication crisis, is 'the last link of Empire that is left'. The task is made somewhat easier by the contemporary preference for exact and descriptive, in place of traditional and often pretentious Royal Titles. The ministers of King George I light-heartedly acclaimed him King of France while the *Grand Monarque* was still alive, but the ministers of Queen Elizabeth II scrutinized with care the appropriateness of the titles with which she was to be invested. Was it right to acclaim her Queen of 'the British Dominions beyond the Seas' when some of them were not British and none of them considered the ambiguous designation 'Dominion' wholly felicitous? And in a Commonwealth of many faiths could the Queen everywhere be fittingly described as 'Defender of the Faith'? Even the question of whether it would be proper to have in the title the traditional words, 'by the Grace of God' was weighed, so Mr. St. Laurent told the Canadian House of Commons, with due Prime Ministerial deliberation[1] and different conclusions reached about it. What mattered was not tradition but exactitude. 'It makes', said Mr. Solon Low, the Social Credit leader, in the same debate, 'little or no

---

[1] 3 February 1953, Canada, H. of C. Deb., 1952–3, vol. 2, p. 1566.

difference ... what elements are used to constitute the title of Her Majesty the Queen so long as those elements do indeed portray accurately the present relationship between the sovereign and the different parts of the Commonwealth.'[1] For this the constitutional historian at least is grateful since it meant that the Queen's titles in themselves constituted a precise, if brief, description of the place of the Crown in the Commonwealth at the time of her accession.

Throughout the reign of King George VI it had been recognized that the King was as much King of Canada or King of Australia as he was King of Great Britain. But his title did not make this clear. He was at the close of his reign 'George the Sixth, by the Grace of God, of Great Britain, Ireland and the British Dominions beyond the Seas, King, Defender of the Faith'.[2] In the accession Proclamations of the new Queen the several and particular relationships of the Monarch to the countries over which she reigned were more clearly indicated. In the United Kingdom she was proclaimed 'Queen of this Realm and all Her other Realms and Territories, Head of the Commonwealth', and to this extent identical language was employed in the accession Proclamations in Australia, New Zealand, Pakistan, and Ceylon; though, curiously enough, Canada and South Africa, for once not in the vanguard, used the older comprehensive formula of 'the British Dominions beyond the Seas'. The Commonwealth Prime Ministers' Meeting in London in December 1952 conceded the need both for re-definition and for variety in the Queen's titles which the accession Proclamations in their newer form had suggested. In the existing stage of Commonwealth relations they considered that it would be more in accord with the established constitutional position were each member of the Commonwealth to devise for its own use a form of title expressing its relationship with the Crown in terms most appropriate to its circumstances while retaining a substantial element common to all. They agreed, said Mr. St. Laurent, to disagree, and there were therefore to be, for the first time, several—to be exact seven—Royal Titles describing in formal language the relationship to the Crown of the seven member nations of the Commonwealth which were monarchies at that time. The then solitary republic, India, owing no allegiance, acknowledged the Queen as Head of the Commonwealth. The once heretical doctrine of the divisibility of the Crown was thus embedded in the new orthodoxy. The Commonwealth expressed its unity in 'a new Athanasianism of many crowns in one monarchy'.[3]

In the oversea territories which formed the hard core of the older British Commonwealth—Canada, Australia, and New Zealand—the Queen was uniformly styled 'Elizabeth the Second, by the Grace of God of the United Kingdom, Canada [or Australia or New Zealand] and her other Realms and

---

[1] H. of C. Deb., 1952–3, vol. 2, p. 1571.
[2] The title Emperor of India was deleted by the Indian Independence Act, 1947 (10 & 11 Geo. 6, c. 30, s. 7, ss. 2).
[3] The phrase is that of Dr. Percival Spear.

Territories Queen, Head of the Commonwealth, Defender of the Faith'. This was in conformity with the form adopted in the United Kingdom and followed the language used in the United Kingdom accession Proclamation with the word 'all' omitted.[1] It is also to be noted that the United Kingdom title alone defined the United Kingdom as being of 'Great Britain and Northern Ireland'. This was a nettle which other members of the Commonwealth did not see fit to grasp. More important was the retention of 'United Kingdom'—even though undefined—in the titles adopted by the three older dominions. In them the Queen, while Queen of Canada, Australia, or New Zealand, was also specifically named Queen of the United Kingdom. To their respective governments this seemed both appropriate to present circumstances and expressive of their historical evolution.

Her Majesty [said the Canadian Prime Minister] is now the Queen of Canada but she is the Queen of Canada because she is Queen of the United Kingdom and because the people of Canada are happy to recognize as their Sovereign the person who is the Sovereign of the United Kingdom. It is not a separate office. It is the recognition of the traditional development of our institutions.[2]

South Africa and Ceylon adopted a different course. Both countries named the Queen as their Queen, as Queen of her other Realms and Territories and as Head of the Commonwealth, but not as Queen by the Grace of God or as Queen of the United Kingdom. Though the form of title was identical in these two countries the reasons for its adoption would seem to have been different. Mr. Dudley Senanayake, the Prime Minister, spoke of Ceylon's choice of title as being an affirmation of Ceylon's continuing membership of the Commonwealth and it was not until the change of government in 1956 that Ceylon decided upon the adoption of a republican Constitution. In South Africa the use of the same formula was specifically intended to implant nationalist doctrine on the divisibility of the Crown in the Royal Title itself. The allegation made by leaders of the United party that the choice of title was designed to facilitate the declaration of a republic, while no doubt not without foundation, lacked substance because no form of title recommended by the South African government, approved by the South African Parliament,[3] embodied in South African law could constitute a barrier to the declaration of a republic should the people and Parliament of South Africa desire to establish it. This in itself, however, underlined the compromise implicit in the South African title. It was intended to divide opinion least and, like all such middle-of-the-road

---

[1] Did the Commonwealth Prime Ministers perhaps consider the phrase 'all her other Realms and Territories' a trifle pretentious, a little too reminiscent of far-flung dominion over palm and pine?

[2] 3 Febuary 1953, Canada, H. of C. Deb., 1952–3, vol. 2, p. 1566.

[3] It was approved on 20 February 1953. See South Africa, Senate Deb., 1953, coll. 1086–1108.

expedients, it was attacked from both sides. While English-speaking South Africans saw in it further evidence of a loosening of ties with the United Kingdom, Nationalist republicans, according to *Die Burger*, would not be moved by any change of title to accept the hereditary monarchy of Britain as a living symbol of South African nationhood, but would be made still more conscious of the anachronistic character of the monarchy by the title 'Queen of South Africa'.[1] In the light of such comment the absence of the words 'by the Grace of God' may be assumed to have had a political rather than a theological significance.

The government of Pakistan, in contrast with those of Ceylon and South Africa, recommended that in Pakistan Her Majesty should be styled 'Queen of the United Kingdom and of her other Realms and Territories' without reference to her as Queen of Pakistan. The reason was not far to seek. In January 1953 the Prime Minister presented to the Constituent Assembly the report of the special committee appointed to consider the form of government to be adopted in Pakistan, and the committee recommended the 'establishment of a truly Islamic democracy' in which the Head of the State should be, like the great majority of the people, a Muslim. He was to be an elected President with power to make treaties, to declare peace and war, and to receive and accredit ambassadors, and allegiance, as in India, would be due no longer to the Queen, but to the state and its elected head. It was not until 1956 after many vicissitudes that Pakistan enacted a Constitution, but in this respect there was no important modification. It was as a republic that Pakistan remained a member of the Commonwealth after that date.

The strength of republican opinion in South Africa and the proposed republican form of the Constitution of Pakistan and later Ceylon enhanced the already great importance of the agreement of April 1949 enabling India to remain at her own request a full member of the Commonwealth on the coming into force of her republican Constitution in January 1950. As a republic India recognized the Queen, as later Pakistan and Ceylon were to do, as the symbol of the Commonwealth association and, as such, the Head of the Commonwealth.[2] But Indians owed no allegiance to the Crown, and the Crown played no such part, however tenuous, in the conduct of India's external relations as it did, for example, in Eire between 1936 and 1949 when the External Relations Act was in force. To put the difference in its extreme form, under the Irish dispensation the King, at least in the United Kingdom view, would have been at war when Eire was at war (though not necessarily at peace when Eire was at peace), but should India be at war, the Queen is not in law thereby also at war. This might have some important consequences.

[1] Quoted in *Observer*, 21 December 1952.
[2] For this reason India participated in the discussions on the Royal Style and Titles, though no individual action on the part of her government was required to implement the agreements reached.

More generally the wording of the 1949 agreement, with its assertion that republican India would remain a full member of the Commonwealth and not, for example, constitutionally an associate member, underlined that allegiance to the Crown was no longer a condition of full membership. Subsequently there emerged a Commonwealth more evenly divided as between monarchical and republican states, the symbol of whose unity lay in their common recognition of the Queen as Head of the Commonwealth, not in their common allegiance to the Crown.

The designation 'Head of the Commonwealth' was common to all the Queen's titles.[1] When this title was first given to King George VI in 1949 Mr. Churchill observed that it seemed to him not to depreciate but rather to elevate the status of the Crown.[2] Certainly the new title recognized for the first time the symbolic position of the monarch in relation to the Commonwealth as something distinct from the position of the Crown as an integral part of the constitutions of the member nations of the Commonwealth other than India. In this respect, therefore, it can be said that the accommodation of a republic within the Commonwealth prompted the formal recognition of a long-existing duality to which General Smuts alluded when he spoke of the free association of which the King was the symbol, and the common allegiance to the Crown.[3] Yet if in this there was truth it was not the whole truth, and it is well to remember the origin of the title Head of the Commonwealth in placing an interpretation on it. When Pandit Nehru recommended the acceptance of the London Declaration to the Indian Constituent Assembly he was insistent that, while the Republic of India might associate with other countries which were monarchies, under her Constitution and in her government 'she has nothing to do with any external authority', and in respect of India the King had a status but no functions at all. There could be no compromise on the question of allegiance to any external authority or on the sovereignty and the independence of the Indian Republic.[4] The recognition of the King as the symbol of the Commonwealth association and as such the Head of the Commonwealth was acceptable, therefore, on the assumption that it in no way detracted from India's position as a sovereign republic. The title, 'Head of the Commonwealth' had, thus, an explicit meaning in a particular context; to extend, to amplify that meaning in a broader context was to place upon it a political interpretation not well founded in history. We have it on authority that new wine should not be poured into old bottles. It was perhaps almost equally unwise to pour old wine into new bottles, or in other words to read old meanings into a new title.

---

[1] The phrase 'her other Realms and Territories' was also common to all.
[2] See above, pp. 254–5.
[3] 11 May 1949, South Africa, H. of A. Deb., vol. 68, coll. 5565–9.
[4] 16 May 1949, Indian Constituent Assembly Deb., vol. 8, pp. 2–10 (Mansergh, *Documents*, ii. 847–8). See above, pp. 253–4.

Monarchical and Republican Membership

Within the post-Statute-of-Westminster Commonwealth there was constitutional dualism. In the majority of the member nations Her Majesty was Queen, in a minority she was not. 'With us the King is not merely the symbol and head of an external association but is himself a real presence in our local self-government', said Mr. Menzies in 1950 of Australia's position in the Commonwealth.

> I am His Majesty's Australian Prime Minister. Mr. Chifley is His Majesty's Leader of the Opposition. The courts are the King's courts and it is the King's writ which issues from them . . . Every Member of Parliament takes the Oath of Allegiance. We are royal, not republican; British, wherever we may be.[1]

So much could be said in 1957 of the United Kingdom, of New Zealand, of Canada with some, and of South Africa with very considerable, reservations. It could not be said at all of India, Pakistan, or Ceylon. The more sharply the distinction is drawn between a monarchical and a republican form of government the greater the importance that is to be attached to this difference. Mr. Peter Fraser spoke in 1949[2] of the dominions as 'crowned republics', suggesting that constitutional monarchy had come to embrace so many of the virtues associated in the past with a republic that in such form of government republicanism was transcended. Just as he once aptly suggested that dominion status amounted to 'independence plus',[3] so he would seem to have thought of constitutional monarchy on the British model as 'republicanism plus', that is to say republicanism buttressed by those elements of tradition and stability which are the unique contribution of a long-established monarchy. But such a pragmatic view is sharply contested, for example, by Professor Wheare who commented, without particular reference to Mr. Fraser's views, that it would be an error to suppose that a modern constitutional monarchy is no more than a 'crowned republic'.[4] In his view the virtues which monarchy exhibits, no less than the dangers to which it is prone, mark it off as a distinct form not of constitution and government only but also of society and community.

> We assert something significant [he adds later] . . . when we say that while the Constitutions of Eire and New Zealand resemble each other in that both are written and unitary and both establish a parliamentary executive, they differ in that the Irish Constitution is rigid and supreme, while the Constitution of New Zealand is flexible and subordinate to the legislature, and in that the Irish Constitution is republican and that of New Zealand is monarchical.

---

[1] *The British Commonwealth of Nations in International Affairs*, pp. 3-4.
[2] In Belfast with characteristic intrepidity.
[3] To be precise it seems that it was not Mr. Fraser but a journalist who coined this phrase in foreshortening for cabling the New Zealand Prime Minister's less epigrammatic statement that dominion status 'was independence with something added to it'.
[4] K. C. Wheare, *Modern Constitutions* (London, Oxford University Press, 1951), pp. 43-45.

If there is substituted throughout this passage India for Eire, the contrast between the constitutional position of countries which are alike full members of the Commonwealth is described in essentials. If we agree with Mr. Fraser, the existing constitutional dualism within the Commonwealth will not seem of major importance; if we agree with Professor Wheare, we will necessarily be driven towards Mr. Menzies's conclusion that while there was a structural or organic relationship between the monarchical states of the Commonwealth, the relationship of its republican members was largely functional.

The historian, in recognizing that there is insufficient evidence on which to reach any final conclusion, may feel disposed to doubt whether the question can properly be posed in so absolute a form. Was not the distinction between Commonwealth members which were monarchies and those which were republics often blurred in practice? Ceylon was a constitutional monarchy at the date of the Queen's accession; the Queen was enthusiastically welcomed on her visit to Colombo in 1954; so distinguished an authority as Sir Ivor Jennings believed in 1956 that a monarchical symbolism was securely founded in the historical tradition of the Ceylonese people.[1] In the same year, however, Mr. Bandanaraike won a decisive electoral victory on a republican platform. Was Ceylon in 'organic relationship' with the Commonwealth while her Constitution was monarchical and did that relationship become purely functional when she decided to adopt a republican Constitution? Is the character of membership really so simple and so easily definable as Mr. Menzies supposed? Would the declaration of a republic in South Africa, transform the character of the Union's membership?

The Representatives of the Crown

The existence of a fundamental distinction between constitutional monarchies and republics within the Commonwealth also seems less easy to maintain in the light on the one hand of the symbolic status of the Crown in relation to its republican members and on the other of the representation of the Crown in its oversea monarchical members by a Governor-General nominated by the governments of those members. India and Pakistan, it has been noted, are no less sovereign republics because they acknowledge the Queen as the symbol of the Commonwealth association and as such the Head of the Commonwealth, but this symbolic recognition at the least implies that in the minds of the Indians and Pakistanis there is no deep gulf fixed between the republican and monarchical forms of government. It presupposes, too, a readiness to acknowledge the reality and the strength of a monarchical tie elsewhere in the Commonwealth, for what state would accord even symbolic recognition to an institution or person whose traditional status was felt to be devoid of meaning or reality? While, therefore, there is no detraction from the republicanism of India or Pakistan there is on their part recognition of the

[1] 'Crown and Commonwealth in Asia', *International Affairs*, April 1956.

unifying force of the Crown in a Commonwealth in which they are full members. Such recognition may reasonably be held to blunt the edge of the theoretical distinction between republicanism and constitutional monarchy from the republican side. It is also blunted from the monarchical side by reason of the monarch's inability to play a personal role in the several realms which comprise the fundamental monarchical membership of the Commonwealth.

In 1926 it was declared that the Governor-General of a dominion held in all essential respects the same position in relation to the administration of public affairs in a dominion as was held by the King in Great Britain. For this reason a Governor-General's relations with his ministers should be in accord with the same rules and constitutional conventions as the sovereign observes in relations with United Kingdom ministers. But how were these rules to be defined or these constitutional conventions to be interpreted in practice? Could definition and interpretation be entrusted solely to a Governor-General who must inevitably lack the mystique of a monarch and might well be politically inexperienced?

It was taken for granted [wrote Sir Harold Nicolson in his life of King George V] that the relations between the King and his Ministers in the Dominions would be governed by the same general principles and conventions as had for so long regulated the relations between the King and successive Prime Ministers and Cabinets in the United Kingdom. It was soon realised that the circumstances were not identical, or even analagous. When transplanted in a different soil and climate, the seedling did not produce the same sort of tree.[1]

So much was evidently true, but psychologically yet more important was the fact that transplantation was not and never could be more than theoretical. The person of the monarch was not transplanted. Royal tours might bring the monarchy to distant dominions but they were no sufficient substitute for royal residence. New Zealand, Australia, and Canada were monarchies but they were monarchies without a resident monarch. In itself that necessarily modified the role and diminished the distinctively monarchical character of these states even though, as in Australia and New Zealand, remoteness might enhance the emotional attachment to the Crown.

Between 1926 and 1952 the role of the monarch in the government of the oversea member nations of the Commonwealth perceptibly declined. For this there were two principal reasons. The first derived somewhat paradoxically from the right of direct access of dominion Prime Ministers to the sovereign, the second from the right of dominion governments to advise the sovereign on the appointment of a Governor-General. The right of direct access brought in its train certain psychological problems. Ordinarily it was unlikely that the monarch would be able to establish the intimate personal

[1] Nicolson, pp. 474-5.

relations with dominion ministers that he could maintain with successive governments in London. Nor could he make his influence so readily or so surely felt in issues some of which must inevitably fall outside the range not necessarily of knowledge but of familiarity. For their part dominion ministers, too, lacked that instinctive feeling which plays so decisive a part in maintaining a proper balance between the remaining prerogatives of the sovereign and the rights of ministers, and would seem on occasions to have pressed their advice beyond conventional limits. Direct relationship, therefore, tended to limit the discretionary authority of the sovereign by making him dependent upon the advice of dominion governments to an extent identical in theory but greater in practice than he was upon the advice of the United Kingdom government, because it was more difficult for him to exert his influence in states where he did not normally reside.

In ordinary circumstances it was not the monarch but his representative who was called upon to exercise the Royal Prerogatives in dominion affairs. No matter how highly respected or well regarded the King's representative might be, he could aspire to be no more than a representative. The exercise of his discretionary authority was scrutinized with little of that reverential awe naturally accorded to the monarch, and in the event of dispute between a Governor-General and a Prime Minister, acrimony was likely to be little tempered by regard for high office alone. In 1953 Sir John Kotelawala replied to inquiries from the Governor-General, Lord Soulbury, about a decision taken by the government not to fly the Union Jack nor play 'God Save the Queen' at official functions with a terseness conventionally avoided in dealing with the head of a state.

Although Ceylon is an independent country [noted Sir John] there are three points which the people of Ceylon are unable to understand. First why in this free country should there be a foreign Governor-General? Second and third: Why should there be an English flag and an English national anthem in free Ceylon?

'The second and third have been suitably dealt with', he concluded a trifle ominously, 'which may kindly be taken note of.'[1] If Sir John's language, which seemed from time to time somewhat too vehement to Afro-Asian conferences and London tea merchants as well as to English Governors-General, may be supposed exceptional, the same cannot be thought of that of Mr. Mackenzie King. Mr. Mackenzie King, wrote Lord Byng on 29 June 1925 to King George V, 'will probably take a very vitriolic line against myself, in spite of his protestations of friendship—this seems only natural'.[2] But had the King refused a dissolution on questionable grounds to a United Kingdom Prime Minister, such a line would not have seemed natural at all. On the contrary the natural course would have been to protect the Crown from all

---

[1] *The Times*, 11 November 1953; see also his autobiography, *An Asian Prime Minister's Story* (London, Harrap, 1956).
[2] Nicolson, pp. 476–7.

criticism or, to put the contrast in other terms, in the dominions the Governor-General is regarded, should occasion arise, as a legitimate target for criticism, in Britain the King or Queen is not. The Imperial Conference of 1926 might resolve that a Governor-General's functions in a dominion were 'similar in all essentials' to those of the Sovereign in the United Kingdom and the Governor-General might scrupulously abide by the constitutional precedents in the light of which relations between King and Cabinet had evolved, but the attitudes and spirit in which such constitutional conventions were applied were not the same. The Queen's representative is not the Queen.

In the United Kingdom and in imperialist strongholds overseas the view was widely entertained that the growing practice of appointing dominion nationals as Governors-General had in effect weakened the link with the Crown. It was not a view wholly substantiated or wholly discredited by experience. The appointment of a Royal Duke or close relative of the reigning monarch certainly strengthened the personal association with the Crown; the appointment of a distinguished English peer unquestionably reminded dominion citizens of the close association of their country with the United Kingdom; while all such overseas appointments could enrich the political experience especially of a smaller dominion and ensure that the Crown was kept wholly dissociated from party politics. But such theoretical advantages carried with them corresponding risks. The actions of a British Governor-General tended to be suspect among more extreme nationalists until there was good evidence that the holder of the office did not regard the politics of the dominion at the apex of whose government he was placed through the window of Britain's self-interest. That suspicion, however ill-founded, told heavily in favour of Mr. Mackenzie King in his controversy with Lord Byng, and had a United Kingdom Governor-General refused a dissolution to General Hertzog in the heated atmosphere of September 1939, as did Sir Patrick Duncan, the controversy might have reached the intensity that provokes a civil war.[1] If, therefore, the appointment of Governors-General from the United Kingdom was satisfying to imperialist sentiment, it was for the same reason suspect to nationalist opinion, and as it strengthened the links of the Commonwealth on the one hand, it might subject them to exceptional strains on the other. This second consideration was one that weighed the more heavily with dominion governments in an age of triumphant nationalism, and it is not to be doubted that they were in the best position to judge what was best calculated to preserve the internal unity of their countries. They were also, however, concerned with power and, other things being equal, the weaker the Governor-General the stronger the Prime Minister. Professor Crisp faithfully reflected the opinion at least of Australian Labour governments when he wrote that 'in becoming ever more innocuous and unobtrusive' the office of Governor-General 'has provided an ever more

[1] Cf. Mansergh, *Survey, 1931–9*, p. 397.

satisfactory keystone to the constitutional arch'.[1] This happens not when the post is filled by a Royal Duke but when it is occupied by a loyal veteran nominated by the party in power.

From the outset of its career as a dominion the Irish Free State desired the appointment of Irish nationals as Governors-General. In itself this did not necessarily involve any departure from the procedure then customarily followed. While it remained the responsibility of the Prime Minister of the United Kingdom to submit the names of candidates for appointment, the list itself was prepared in consultation with the dominion government concerned. After 1926, however, and as a result of the conclusions then reached, dominion Prime Ministers contended, not unreasonably, that henceforward such appointments should be made on the advice of dominion Cabinets alone. In 1929 Mr. Scullin proposed the appointment of Sir Isaac Isaacs as first Australian-born Governor-General of the Commonwealth of Australia. King George V demurred, not on the ground that Mr. Scullin's nominee was an Australian, but

upon the principle that any local man, whether in politics or not, must have local political predilections, political friends and political opponents—whereas a nominee from England had no local politics and would therefore, as the King's representative, stand aloof from all politics as much as the Sovereign does at home.

Mr. Scullin was adamant. The King told him that he had departed 'from the time-honoured custom of informally suggesting names to the Sovereign in order to ascertain whether such persons were likely to be acceptable' and that there was no record of the King's wishes in such cases being ignored. The King added that Sir Isaac Isaacs was personally unknown to him, that he was 75 years of age,[2] and that no Australian could be selected without having some party bias. Mr. Scullin remained unmoved and the King, sensing 'the supreme importance' of his decision in imperial relations, yielded; and Mr. Scullin's nominee once installed in office sent to the King 'private letters of immense length, describing his own benevolent activities and', as the King's biographer remarks with gentle irony, 'the party dissensions which rendered federal politics of such interest to the outside observer'.[3] None the less the manner of the appointment, as the King foresaw, created a precedent which dominion governments customarily and courteously disregarded in succeeding years but to which none the less appeal could be made at any time.

Neither in India, nor in Pakistan, nor in Ceylon during their brief period as monarchical members of the Commonwealth, was the sovereign disposed to question the advice tendered by their respective governments. In these

---

[1] L. F. Crisp, *The Parliamentary Government of the Commonwealth of Australia* (London, Longmans, in association with the Wakefield Press, Adelaide, 1949), p. 236.

[2] Sir Isaac Isaacs in fact lived till he was 95.

[3] Nicolson, pp. 477–82. Chapter xxviii of this biography, of which these pages form a part, is an important and sometimes overlooked contribution to Commonwealth history.

countries, and in South Africa after the accession of the Nationalist party to office in 1948, the recommendation of the government concerned, while made with due regard to traditional forms and courtesies, was final in the sense that these governments did not in fact desire their recommendations to be subject to royal review. They nominated for the office of Governor-General persons who under later republican constitutions might reasonably have been expected to fill the office of President, and indeed Major-General Iskander Mirza, the last Governor-General of Pakistan, was the first provisional President of the new Islamic Republic of Pakistan. Once again this suggests that the distinction between monarchical and republican members of the Commonwealth at a given time and in particular instances may have been of secondary importance.

The political symbolism of a nation embodies at once much of its traditions and its aspirations and, in so doing, may serve as the most powerful of unifying forces. Within the Commonwealth the monarchy has served and continues to serve such a purpose in the United Kingdom itself and wherever people of British stock are settled. Likewise, though recent in their adoption, it may be that in India and in Pakistan, as earlier in the United States and France, republican institutions will be accorded that emotional loyalty which can mean so much in terms of national cohesion and unity. But where there are settled communities of differing cultural or racial origins within a single state a political symbolism equally cherished by all communities is something often sought but rarely found. In Canada the proximity of so very great a republican neighbour has contributed to the success of the monarchy in providing a symbolism which, while emotionally less compelling among the French-speaking and more recent European immigrant groups—which together now comprise more than half the population—than among the descendants of English-speaking settlers, none the less serves to unite a country whose greatest need is unity. While republican sentiment exists it is not challenging. As *Le Devoir* commented on the republican resolution of the Pakistani Constituent Assembly in 1953,

> La proclamation de la république n'a rien d'urgent pour les Canadiens. Il n'y a pas lieu de négliger des réclamations essentielles sur le terrain religieux ou sur le terrain culturel pour hâter l'avènement d'un régime qui sera l'aboutissement inévitable de notre évolution constitutionnelle. Il n'y a pas lieu de provoquer des querelles violentes pour imposer plus vite un régime qui finira par s'imposer de lui-même.[1]

This in itself was an implied tribute to the reconciling character of the monarchy in Canada.

In South Africa republicanism by contrast was not the Laodicean faith of a minority but the conviction of a majority. 'The soul of the Afrikaner' was republican and despite many temptations had not been denationalized by the

[1] *Le Devoir*, 13 January 1953.

policies of Botha, Hertzog, and Smuts, for the Afrikaner had remained 'true to his soul'. So Mr. Strijdom claimed in September 1953,[1] adding, 'the independence which we visualize must eventually end in a republic'. If, therefore, the monarchy survived in South Africa, its survival was to be attributed not to the support of a majority of the European population but to the fact that in a country deeply divided in its devotion to differing political symbolisms, that which existed could not be replaced without further prejudicing the cohesion and perhaps even the existence of the Union. Both Canada and more strikingly South Africa made plain that within a monarchical member state there may exist republican sentiment, just as within a republican member state there may exist monarchical sentiment. Political realities once again may be lost to view behind some neat constitutional classification.

While the distinction between monarchical and republican members may have been more apparent than real, whether considered in terms of political practices or political sentiment, it is not suggested that this was universally the case. Monarchism in Australia and New Zealand, republicanism among Irishmen or Afrikaners meant something more than a preference for a particular form of government. It was over and above this at once a challenge and an assertion of political faith. Monarchism in Australia and New Zealand was the expression of the attachment of British peoples settled in the far Pacific to the homeland of their faith and their fathers; republicanism in Ireland after 1916 and among Afrikaners symbolized the way of life to which they aspired. Emotion in each case powerfully reinforced reason, but the political importance of such emotion is at no time to be underestimated simply because it cannot be measured by social scientists or documented by historians. Not for nothing did Mr. Strijdom speak of the 'soul of the Afrikaner'.

Monarchical sentiment has been, and continues to be, a principal buttress of Commonwealth unity, but of republicanism the most that can be said is that while after 1949 it was no longer necessarily incompatible with Commonwealth membership, history had largely determined in each case the extent to which it interposed a continuing psychological barrier to full acceptance of the Commonwealth. In Asia republicanism was a by-product of independence; in Ireland and in South Africa republicanism was inextricably associated with a struggle for independence, with the result that the former was more easily associated with continued Commonwealth membership than the latter. When in April 1949 General Smuts affirmed[2] that 'my personal view, in substance, is that there is no middle course between the Crown and the Republic, between in and out of the Commonwealth', he was speaking in terms of the history and aspirations of South African republicanism which were by no means identical with those of republicanism in Asia. India and Pakistan found just such a middle course congenial to them.

[1] *The Times*, 23 September 1953.
[2] *Johannesburg Star*, 9 April 1949.

The element of constitutional variety introduced in 1949 represented the most important change that had taken place in the constitution of the Commonwealth since 1931, and its acceptance marks off the post-1949 Commonwealth from the Statute-of-Westminster Commonwealth of 1931–49. With it there was introduced on the one hand a new, and therefore incalculable, element in Commonwealth relations, and on the other a greater element of flexibility which enabled the relationship of all members of the Commonwealth to be defined in terms that more nearly represented and reflected political and psychological realities. Of the first more remains to be said in a broader political setting, but the importance of the second may be appropriately noted here. Irish membership of the Commonwealth had about it from the outset an element of compulsion, and Ireland seceded. But Asian membership was founded in freedom, and it was by their own choice that India, Pakistan, and Ceylon decided to remain within the Commonwealth. 'We want no unwilling members', said Mr. Attlee, and the action of his government in respect of Burma showed that these were no empty words. Those who believe that partnership in common enterprises freely undertaken counts for more than formal unity, traditionally expressed and uniformly imposed, saw in this not a weakening but a strengthening of the Commonwealth. For with the modification of traditional forms to meet new circumstances there was little change in the relationship of the older members of the Commonwealth to the Crown. For them the monarchy remained, in the words of Sir Harold Nicolson, 'the magnet of loyalty, the emblem of union, the symbol of continuity and the embodiment of national, as distinct from class or party feeling.'[1] Its position in them had been in no way impaired; in some respects it had been strengthened. Elsewhere in countries where republican sentiments prevailed its elimination from domestic affairs virtually excluded the possibility of its being a source of friction in external relations.

Nationality and Citizenship

If the Crown was to be regarded as the keystone of the constitutional arch, citizenship and nationality constituted its foundation. The existence of a common nationality was traditionally regarded as fundamental to the conception of Empire or Commonwealth. In the past the common law rule had been that all persons born within the King's dominions (together with some further special categories) were British subjects, and that common law rule was given statutory effect in the general provisions of the British Nationality and Status of Aliens Act of 1914.[2] But if this status was common to all who owed allegiance to the Crown, the privileges it gave were conditioned in practice by the policies of the individual member states of the Commonwealth. The concept

---

[1] Nicolson, p. 120. [2] 4 & 5 Geo. V, c. 17.

of common status derived indeed from a more spacious past. It had long ceased to confer, for example, a universal right to enter, still less to settle, in any of the King's dominions at will, a cause of complaint in non-European areas of the Commonwealth notably against Australian and South African immigration policies. The common status of British subject none the less retained practical as well as symbolic significance. Wherever a British subject went within the Commonwealth, his status was that of a citizen, not of a foreigner. The children of British subjects could marry citizens of any part of the Commonwealth without losing or changing their nationality. In the United Kingdom itself, any British subject from wherever he might come found the door open to him for employment in the public services and the professions, as though he had been born there. From that both the United Kingdom and the overseas empire had gained in the past, and in the United Kingdom there was a general consensus of opinion that this open door, so rightly prized, should not be even partly closed by the provisions of nationality legislation designed to bring the law of the United Kingdom and of the dominions into conformity with a changing outlook and practice.

The acquisition by the dominions of more distinct political identities especially during and after the First World War produced at once a need and a desire to determine more precisely the members of their own several communities. Various steps were taken to this end in Canada, South Africa, and especially the Irish Free State and the Imperial Conference of 1937 considered claims for the fuller recognition of dominion nationalities.[1] It was, however, in the words of the Report, 'in no way suggested that any change should be made in the existing position regarding the common status based on the British Nationality and Status of Aliens Act of the United Kingdom and the corresponding enactments in other parts of the British Commonwealth'. But attention was drawn to the fact that over and above the common status, British subjects generally speaking had a connexion with one or other member of the Commonwealth and that in the absence of rules determining that connexion practical difficulties arose. There was, however, in 1937 no general agreement that all members of the Commonwealth should follow the practice of some and introduce legislation defining their own citizens and nationals, and no major change was introduced until after the Second World War. In the meantime some difficulties had arisen.

It was, for example, felt necessary by the Australian delegation at San Francisco to raise the question whether nationals of different states of the Commonwealth could, under the statute of the International Court of Justice, which provides for one judge only of any nationality, be judges at the same time. This point had been raised but not resolved in 1929,[2] and in fact no

---

[1] Cmd. 5482, section XIV (relevant extract in Mansergh, *Documents*, ii. 930–5).
[2] Manley O. Hudson, *The Permanent Court of International Justice, 1920–1942* (New York, Macmillan, 1943), p. 367.

judge from a dominion had ever been elected to the Permanent Court of International Justice. An amendment to the draft statute was agreed so that Article 3 (2) of the International Court of Justice should read: 'A person who for the purposes of membership in the Court could be regarded as a national of more than one state shall be deemed to be a national of the one in which he ordinarily exercises civil and political rights'.[1] Whether the Australian delegation were anxious that nothing should stand in the way of the dominions' playing their full part in the work of the United Nations or whether questions of Commonwealth nationality were at that time much in their minds is not clear, but at least the incident suggested the insufficiency for some purposes of existing nationality legislation in the British Commonwealth.

The Canadian Citizenship Act of 1946,[2] by creating a new code of Canadian citizenship, in the words of the Lord Chancellor,[3] 'completely shattered' the common code of citizenship which had hitherto prevailed in principle though it had shown many signs of breaking down in practice. The purpose of the Canadian Act was succinctly summarized by the Secretary of State who introduced it. 'We are seeking', said Mr. Paul Martin in the Canadian House of Commons, 'to establish clearly a basic and definite Canadian citizenship which will be the fundamental status upon which the rights and privileges of Canadians will depend.' And the spirit which inspired it was equally well stated later in the same speech when Mr. Martin declared that 'for a young nation, Canada has done great things . . . and it is time we know what a Canadian is. . . . There has been too little, not too much, national pride in this country.'[4]

The Canadian Citizenship Act defined citizenship in Canada and did not dissolve the common bond of British subject. Under it, all Canadian citizens were declared to be British subjects. But they were British subjects because they were Canadian citizens, not, as had formerly for the most part been the case, Canadian citizens because they were British subjects. In other words, the dominion citizenship from which common nationality was derived was henceforward to be fundamental in Canada and not as hitherto British subjecthood. Citizenship, as Lord Jowitt observed, was now to be the gateway through which nationality was achieved.[5]

The breach made in the common status code by the Canadian Act was fatal to it and the United Kingdom and subsequently other members of the Commonwealth concluded that the only alternative consistent with the nature of the Commonwealth was a system based on individual determination of citizenship by each member state with the common status deriving from it.

[1] Leland M. Goodrich and Edvard Hambro, *Charter of the United Nations*, 2nd ed. (London, Stevens, 1949), p. 611. See also UNCIO, xiii. 143, 209, and 471.
[2] 10 Geo. VI, c. 15, as amended in 1950 by 14 Geo. VI, c. 29 (Mansergh, *Documents*, ii. 934–5). [3] H. of L. Deb., vol. 155, col. 756 (Mansergh, *Documents*, ii. 969).
[4] Canada, H. of C. Deb., 1946, vol. 1, pp. 503–10 (ibid. pp. 944–9).
[5] On this point see his speech referred to below, p. 385 n.

The British Nationality Act, 1948, drafted after consultation with representatives of the other dominions and with their concurrence, was intended to bring United Kingdom practice into conformity with the Canadian precedent. Its main intention therefore was to establish a local citizenship, that of the United Kingdom and the Colonies, which would be distinguishable from that of the British subject status common to the whole of the Empire. This required the introduction of the new designation of 'citizen of the United Kingdom and Colonies'. It was a designation that lacked elegance, and it was criticized on that score in the debate in the House of Lords. Lord Altrincham further maintained that it was a description of something that was politically unreal and that the term 'citizen', reputedly uncongenial to colonial peoples, was anyway a word tainted with undesirable republican associations.[1] The former objection was substantial. There was not that degree of homogeneity between the widely scattered colonial peoples and the inhabitants of Britain to justify a collective designation. The Lord Chancellor, indeed, did not defend it on its merits, but rather on the ground that there appeared to be no more appropriate alternative in view of dominion insistence that the generic term 'British subject' should not be used to describe the local citizenship of a part or parts of the Commonwealth. It might, however, have been wiser and more in accord with social and political realities to have contemplated a separate local citizenship for the United Kingdom and a series of colonial or regional citizenships for the non-self-governing peoples overseas, many of whom were advancing rapidly towards self-government or independence.

Some of the most complex and controversial provisions of the British Nationality Act related to Ireland and their political implications have been considered in an earlier chapter. In this context, however, it is also useful to summarize their intention in the broader context of Commonwealth nationality and citizenship legislation. Under the Irish Nationality Act of 1935 an Irish citizen might not acquire dual nationality. He could not, therefore, in Irish law, be an Irish citizen and a British subject. Until 1948 this was not recognized by the British government, who continued to regard Irish citizens as British subjects. 'An impertinence' is how Mr. de Valera was wont to describe their attitude. The provisions of the Nationality Bill, worked out in collaboration with Irish experts at the 1947 Conference on Nationality, contemplated a reasonable compromise. Broadly speaking, they recognized the principle of reciprocal as against common citizenship, by giving Irish citizens in the United Kingdom the privileges, but not the status, of British subjects and to United Kingdom citizens corresponding privileges in Eire. There was further

---

[1] The debate on the Bill in the House of Lords was of high quality. The speeches of the Lord Chancellor, Lord Jowitt, and the principal critic of the Bill, Lord Simon, are included in Mansergh, *Documents*, ii. 968–79. For an incisive criticism of the ideas underlying the British Nationality Act see 'The British Subject', *Round Table*, June 1948.

allowance made for any Irish citizen who wished, for reasons of sentiment or occupation, to remain a British subject. Accordingly after the enactment of the Act Irish citizens were regarded neither as aliens in Britain or elsewhere in the Commonwealth (except in Pakistan and Ceylon whose Nationality Acts failed to make special provision for them), nor as British subjects; and likewise citizens of Commonwealth countries were given a corresponding non-foreign status in the Republic of Ireland.[1]

The British Nationality Act made the terms 'British subject' and 'Commonwealth citizen' interchangeable. The purpose of this provision, introduced in an amendment by the government, was to provide alternative phraseology for peoples for whom the words 'British subject' evoked no happy memories. To some colonial peoples, to Indians and to Irishmen, to some Afrikaners and French-speaking Canadians, the words 'British subject' implied subjection to Britain or to the British Crown. For them the term 'Commonwealth citizen' was intended to provide a more congenial alternative duly taking account of the fact that the Commonwealth was composed of many peoples of varied cultures, traditions, and susceptibilities to whom names and symbols had a significance often little understood by those whose destiny it had been not to be ruled but to rule.[2]

Legislation on the lines laid down in the Canadian Citizenship Act, 1946 and the British Nationality Act, 1948, was enacted by members of the Commonwealth, with the exception of India, between 1948 and 1951.[3] The character of this legislation varied, but in respect of the Commonwealth the pattern may be most briefly and clearly stated by quoting two provisions of the Australian Act.

In this Act, unless the contrary intention appears—'alien' means a person who is not a British subject, an Irish citizen or a protected person (Section 5 (1)).

A person who, under this Act, is an Australian citizen or, by an enactment for the time being in force in a country to which this section applies, is a citizen of that country shall, by virtue of that citizenship, be a British subject.

The countries to which this section applies are the following countries, namely, the United Kingdom and Colonies, Canada, New Zealand, the Union of South Africa, Newfoundland, India, Pakistan, Southern Rhodesia and Ceylon. (Section 7, subsections (1) and (2).)

Most but not all of the members of the Commonwealth conformed in letter or in spirit to the intention of these provisions. There were significant variations, especially in the South African Citizenship Act,[4] in which no mention was made of a common status either under the older British subject or the

---

[1] For a lawyer's analysis of the issues see R. F. V. Heuston, 'British Nationality and Irish Citizenship', *International Affairs*, January 1950, pp. 77–96.

[2] The susceptibilities of Channel Islanders and Manxmen were also catered for; section 33 authorizing their designation as 'citizens of the United Kingdom, Islands and Colonies'.

[3] The relevant portions of these Acts are reprinted Mansergh, *Documents*, ii. 930–1009.

[4] No. 44 of 1949.

newer Commonwealth citizen description. The omission was deliberate. It was no longer possible, Dr. Dönges maintained on behalf of the government, to talk of common status after the London Conference of 1949, since there was no longer a common allegiance. 'Since a common allegiance is no longer an essential condition of Commonwealth membership', he argued,[1] there could not be a common subjecthood, circumscribing common status and since there was no question of a super-state, 'there cannot be a common citizenship'. Accordingly the South African Act was framed in terms of reciprocal citizenship arrangements with other Commonwealth countries and with Eire; and these, it may be added, were conceived in no generous spirit, in respect either of registration for Union citizenship or of voting rights.

The Making of Commonwealth Constitutions

Excellence in the art of government has been regarded by a long line of imperial statesmen as Britain's greatest contribution to the peoples over whom she has ruled. It is the one imperial claim which has not been strongly challenged by her former subject peoples. Irish nationalists and Indian Congressmen, Afrikaners, in spite of many backward glances to a patriarchal Boer state, Gold Coast pioneers of African independence alike have tacitly accepted its validity. Inspired for the most part by English political thinkers—not for nothing was Mahatma Gandhi described as the last of the Great Victorians[2]— what they demanded during their struggle for independence was the more radical and more rapid extension of British parliamentary institutions to their own territories. It was the British rulers, indeed, who customarily urged the need for caution, who underlined, as in the telling imagery of the Simon Report, that 'the British parliamentary system . . . has been fitted like a well-worn garment to the figure of the wearer, but it does not follow that it will suit everybody'.[3] But despite such implied or stated misgivings, in the end they were apt to yield, however reluctantly, to nationalist pressures.

We are well aware [wrote the authors of the Soulbury Report] that self-government of the British Parliamentary type, carried on by means of a technique which it has taken centuries to develop, may not be suitable or practicable for another country, and that where the history, traditions and culture of that country are foreign to those of Great Britain, the prospects of transplanting British institutions with success may appear remote. But it does not follow that the invention of modifications or variations of the British form of government to meet different conditions elsewhere will be any more successful. . . . At all events, in recommending for Ceylon a Constitution on the British pattern we are recommending a method of government we know something about, a method which is the result of very long

---
[1] South Africa, Senate Deb., 1949, col. 5532; see generally coll. 5524–56.
[2] By a reviewer in *The Economist*.
[3] *Report of the Indian Statutory Commission*, vol. ii: *Recommendations*, Cmd 569, 1930, pp. 6–7.

experience, which has been tested by trial and error and which works, and, on the whole, works well.[1]

So the demand of the politically-conscious majority in Ceylon, in India, in Malaya, in West Africa, and elsewhere, though not everywhere, for parliamentary institutions on the British model was in time conceded. Whether or not it was 'the best form of government' it was the form of government to which hitherto dependent peoples in the British Empire aspired and about which their British rulers knew most.

After 1945 Commonwealth constitution-making was on a large scale[2] both in the newly independent countries of Asia and in non-self-governing territories elsewhere. In the former it was for the most part indigenous; in the latter it was undertaken more usually from without. In the history of Europe many constitutions have been drafted by well-intentioned academics for dissembling Empires; in this particular phase of Commonwealth history the academics, no doubt, were well intentioned but the Empire was not dissembling. Its rulers had embarked on a policy of self-government for hitherto dependent peoples as soon as political conditions allowed and so long as their own interests or security did not thereby appear to be unduly affected. The enactment of constitutions on the British parliamentary model for non-European, as earlier for European, peoples provided one of the more important aspects of Commonwealth history at this time.

There was one important difference between the British constitution and those of all Commonwealth members overseas. The former was unwritten and flexible, the latter were written and rigid. British statesmen and English academics indeed customarily attributed the excellence of the British constitution to the fact that it did not exist in written form, and the achievements of the Commonwealth to the fact that almost everything of importance in Commonwealth relations had been so wisely left undefined. This, however, induced in the minds neither of statesmen, nor lawyers, nor academics any reluctance to provide written constitutions for other parts of the Commonwealth, which so far as possible defined the rules and conventions of the English government. But while the constitutions of oversea Commonwealth members were all alike in as much as they were written and rigid, there was a distinction between those of the older members of the Commonwealth which were embodied in Acts of the United Kingdom Parliament, and those, first of Eire, then of India and Pakistan, which were embodied in Acts of their own

---

[1] *Ceylon: Report of the Commission on Constitutional Reform*, September 1945, Cmd. 6677 (Mansergh, *Documents*, ii. 718–21).

[2] See Martin Wight, *Colonial Constitutions 1947* (Oxford University Press, 1952), Mansergh, *Documents*, ii. section xxii, and W. I. Jennings and C. M. Young, *Constitutional Laws of the Commonwealth*, 2nd ed. (Oxford University Press, 1952), where the British are described as 'the largest manufacturers of written Constitutions the world has ever seen' (p. 43). Sir Ivor Jennings himself was by no means the least among them.

THE ACCESSION OF QUEEN ELIZABETH II

several Parliaments. It was because this was so that the location and nature of the powers of constitutional amendment and of judicial review were regarded historically as of crucial importance in determining the degree of constitutional autonomy enjoyed by the older members of the Commonwealth, whereas in Eire after 1937 and in India and Pakistan, the source of authority from the outset being indigenous and their constitutions being embodied not in Acts of the United Kingdom Parliament but of their own Parliaments, such questions did not arise. Paradoxically, therefore, it was members of the Commonwealth that had long enjoyed effective autonomy which still wore some of 'the badges of colonialism' while those recently emancipated from colonial rule were clothed in the full vesture of the sovereign statehood.

The Removal of Surviving Inequalities in Status in New Zealand and Canada

With the enactment of the Statute of Westminster the dominions listed in section 1 of the Act became in effect independent states if and when they so desired. Neither Australia nor New Zealand adopted the Statute until 1943 and 1947 respectively,[1] and in the same year the latter formally acquired authority to amend her own Constitution. How and why this came about is of interest.

Section 8 of the Statute of Westminster, inserted at the request and with the consent of the government of New Zealand, provided that nothing in the Act should be deemed to confer any power to repeal or alter the Constitution Act of New Zealand otherwise than in accordance with the law existing before the Statute was passed. Any amendment of the New Zealand Constitution after 1931 had accordingly to be enacted by the Parliament of the United Kingdom, at the request and with the consent of the government of New Zealand. The adoption of the Statute of Westminster by New Zealand in 1947 would seem to have transferred effectively such overriding authority from the Parliament of the United Kingdom to the Parliament of New Zealand, but in order, as the New Zealand Prime Minister, Mr. Fraser, remarked, 'to make assurance doubly sure' the New Zealand government, with the approval of the New Zealand Parliament, submitted for enactment by the Imperial Parliament an amendment to the New Zealand Constitution Act explicitly conferring the power of constitutional amendment upon the New Zealand Parliament. This draft amendment, duly enacted at Westminster, brought legal forms into correspondence with actual fact, for by convention the Parliament at Westminster enacted any amendment desired by the New Zealand government and Parliament.[2] The authority given by the 1947 amendment was used by a conservative government in 1950 to abolish the Legislative Council, or Upper House, on

[1] See Mansergh, *Survey, 1931–9*, pp. 17–18. For texts of the Australian and New Zealand Statute of Westminster Adoption Acts see Mansergh, *Documents*, i. 6–7, and for comment pp. 20–35.

[2] Constitution Amendment (Request and Consent) Act (No. 44 of 1947) (Mansergh, *Documents*, i. 8). Mr. Fraser's speech in the New Zealand House of Representatives, 7 November 1947, is reprinted ibid. pp. 29–33.

the ground not that it was a reactionary influence but more simply that it was inefficient and superfluous. New Zealand thereby acquired the first unicameral legislature in the self-governing Commonwealth.[1]

New Zealand sought full power of constitutional amendment not because of any desire to assert her independence from the mother country—such a notion was expressly repudiated by her Prime Minister—but in order to remove an anomaly and to end an anachronism. Nor was there in New Zealand or in Australia, where amendment of the Constitution was vested by the Commonwealth of Australia Act in Parliament and people, any expressed desire to terminate appeals to the Judicial Committee of the Privy Council, even at a time when elsewhere in the self-governing Commonwealth such a process had almost reached its possible limit.[2] In Canada, a land of mixed cultural settlement, such questions were, however, otherwise regarded.

'In its progress towards full self-government, Canada until the present time has retained two badges of colonialism.' So Mr. Garson, the Minister of Justice, observed in the Canadian House of Commons in 1949.[3] One of the 'badges of colonialism' was the inability of the Canadian Parliament to amend the British North America Act, the other the continuance of a right of appeal from Canadian courts to the Judicial Committee of the Privy Council. It was the desire of the Canadian government to remove both and Mr. Garson's comments were made in the course of a speech introducing a bill to end all appeals to the Judicial Committee of the Privy Council. The competence of the Canadian Parliament to do so had been affirmed in 1947 in a judgment of the Judicial Committee in *Attorney-General for Ontario* v. *the Attorney-General for Canada and Others, 1947*,[4] and the phrasing of the Amending Act left no doubt of its intention. 'The Supreme Court', it was stated, 'shall have, hold and exercise exclusive ultimate appellate civil and criminal jurisdiction within and for Canada; and the judgment of the Court shall, in all cases, be final and conclusive.'[5] Mr. Garson considered the enactment of the Bill to be 'an historic occasion' and believed that if 'in smallness of mind and meannesss of spirit' Canadians needlessly perpetuated a situation in which the authority to amend their Constitution was vested in the Parliament of another country, even though its people 'be of our own blood', they would be 'unworthy of the efforts and sacrifices of our fellow Canadians, and undeserving of the bounty which Providence has bestowed upon our country.'

The removal of the second 'badge of colonialism' proved a more complex matter. Section 7 of the Statute of Westminster, inserted at the request and with the consent of the Canadian government, expressly excluded the repeal,

---

[1] If one excepts the brief period before the enactment of the 1937 Constitution when the Irish Free State was without a Senate.
[2] See Mansergh, *Survey, 1931–9*, pp. 31–35. Ceylon abolished Privy Council appeals in 1956.
[3] Canada, H. of C. Deb., 1949, 2nd session, vol. 1, pp. 69–75 (Mansergh, *Documents*, i. 53–62).   [4] Law Reports, Appeal Cases, 1947, 127 (ibid. pp. 39–53).
[5] 13 Geo. VI, c. 37, s. 3 (ibid. p. 53).

amendment, or alteration of the British North America Acts, 1867 to 1930 from the application of the Statute. The British North America (No. 2) Act, 1949,[1] transferred to the Canadian Parliament the authority to amend certain parts of the Constitution without resort to the Parliament of the United Kingdom. The intention of this Act was clear. It was to invest the Canadian Parliament with authority to amend 'the Canadian Constitution'—a term broader in its meaning than the phrase 'British North America Acts, 1867 to 1930' used in Section 7 of the Statute of Westminster—to the extent that agreement existed within Canada that such power should be conferred upon it. This meant in practice that the federal Parliament then acquired power to amend those sections of the Constitution which did not bear upon exclusive powers of the provinces or upon educational and language rights, but that amendment of provisions which treated of such matters continued to be reserved to the United Kingdom Parliament. Constitutional conferences called in 1950 with a view to securing agreement between dominion and provincial governments on a procedure which would make possible a wholly Canadian amending power failed of their purpose and while the intention remains, the means have not as yet been found.[2]

South African Interpretations of Inequality

In the Union of South Africa appeals to the Judicial Committee of the Privy Council were abolished in 1949,[3] but the bearing of the Statute of Westminster upon the amendment of the Constitution, or more precisely upon the amendment of the entrenched clauses of the Constitution and the future of the High Commission Territories, posed perplexing and controversial questions of more than domestic interest or importance on the nature and application of the root principle of equality in Commonwealth relations.

It was a condition of Union in 1909 that equal-language rights for the two European settler-communities in South Africa and existing franchise rights in Cape Province should be safeguarded. This was done by placing them outside the ordinary process of constitutional amendment and providing, in section 152 of the South Africa Act, that at the third reading a two-thirds majority of the total number of the members of both Houses of the South African Parliament sitting together should be required for their amendment. Section 152, which thus *inter alia* entrenched sections 35 and 137 on voting and language rights respectively, was itself entrenched and could be amended only by the same process. The protection thus provided was thought to be substantial at the time, Lord Crewe observing in the House of Lords on

[1] 12, 13, & 14 Geo. VI, c. 81 (ibid. pp. 90–91).

[2] See W. L. Livingston, *Federalism and Constitutional Change* (Oxford, Clarendon Press, 1956), pp. 82–104 for a concise historical analysis of the problem. For a detailed study see P. Gérin-Lajoie, *Constitutional Amendment in Canada* (Toronto, 1950).

[3] Act to Amend the South Africa Act, 1909, so as to abolish appeals to the Privy Council (No. 16 of 1950) (Mansergh, *Documents*, i. 63).

behalf of the government, and with special reference to the Cape franchise for non-Europeans, that 'there does not seem to be much risk' of its being abolished.[1] In this his opinion was justified by subsequent events. Between 1950 and 1955, under extreme pressure from a Nationalist government, the two Houses of Parliament in joint session at Cape Town failed to yield the necessary two-thirds majority for the abolition of the Cape franchise entrenched in Article 35. But was such a majority legally required for its amendment after the enactment of the Statute of Westminister?

The Statute of Westminster, in repealing the Colonial Laws Validity Act, enabled the dominions to enact legislation repugnant to British statutes. The South Africa Act was a British statute, and if a dominion government were no longer restricted by the provisions of British statutes, could it not remove the restrictive power embodied in section 152—the entrenching provision of the South Africa Act—and amend the entrenched articles of the Act themselves by ordinary process of legislation or otherwise as it might itself determine? It is true, and it was generally accepted, that there were moral as well as legal considerations at issue. The entrenched clauses provided safeguards the insertion of which in the South Africa Act had been a condition of Union. Generals Hertzog and Smuts accordingly in requesting the enactment of the Statute of Westminster stated that the request was made 'on the understanding that the proposed legislation will in no way derogate from the entrenched provisions of the South Africa Act'. By making such a reservation, however, the leaders of the two principal parties at the least suggested a doubt in their own minds as to the continued validity in law of the special provisions for the amendment of these clauses after the enactment of the Statute of Westminster. Their doubts were seemingly confirmed in 1937 when the Appellate Division of the Supreme Court of South Africa, in *Ndlwana* v. *Hofmeyr*, accepted such an interpretation without, however, explaining their grounds for so doing. When Dr. Malan, in accordance with the professed Nationalist policy of *apartheid*, resolved to abolish the Cape franchise, he sought the opinion of the government's law advisers[2] and of Professor E. C. S. Wade, the Downing Professor of the Laws of England at Cambridge. Both accepted the view, seemingly endorsed by the Appellate Court in 1937, that in law the entrenched clauses were 'no longer entrenched'. The law advisers' argument was that, while up to the date of the Statute of Westminster the validity of the procedure laid down in sections 35 and 152 of the South Africa Act could 'not have been open to doubt', a material alteration was brought about by its enactment. In their view these and other entrenched sections derived their effective force

[1] 27 July 1909, H. of L. Deb., 1909, vol. 2, col. 761.
[2] Opinion of the Government's Law Advisers on the amendment of the Entrenched Clauses in the South Africa Act (Mansergh, *Documents*, i. 91–97). The Speaker's ruling on the franchise legislation subsequently introduced and making provision, *inter alia*, for the separate representation in Parliament and in the Provincial Council of Cape Province of Europeans and non-Europeans was given in the House of Assembly, 11 April 1951.

from the Colonial Laws Validity Act, which rendered any Act of the Union Parliament adopted otherwise than in accord with the terms of the entrenched sections void and inoperative. But these limitations upon the legislative competence of the Union Parliament prior to 1931 were removed by section 2 (1) of the Statute of Westminister, which repealed the Colonial Laws Validity Act and so deprived sections 35 and 152 of the South Africa Act of their effectiveness. As Mr. Justice van Zyl observed in the Cape Supreme Court:

> The effect of the passing of the Statute of Westminster was to withdraw from the Union the sovereignty of the Parliament of the United Kingdom and to make the Union Parliament the sovereign legislature in the Union with power to repeal or amend any British act, order, rule or regulation in so far as the same is part of the law of the Union.

On these grounds, therefore, the law advisers concluded that

> it follows that Sections 35 and 152 (and the other entrenched sections) of the South Africa Act no longer involve any limitation whatsoever upon the legislative competence of Parliament; that they can be repealed or amended by Parliament in the ordinary way without compliance with the requirements of Section 152....

This conclusion, they argued, was in conformity with the fact that after 1931, and as re-stated in South African law, in the Status of the Union Act, 1934, the Parliament of the Union was the supreme and sovereign legislative authority in the Union and could itself determine the procedure it would adopt for the making of laws. Professor Wade's opinion was no different in substance. The Union Parliament, in his view, could not ignore the relevant provisions for its procedure as a legislature, but it could repeal them at its will, and so far as the entrenched clauses were concerned, 'they ceased to be entrenched so soon as the Union Parliament acquired in 1931 equal powers with the United Kingdom Parliament'.[1]

Dr. Malan's government thereupon introduced the Separate Representation of Voters' Bill, which proposed to remove the Cape Coloured voters from the common roll. It was passed by ordinary legislative procedure. Its validity was challenged in the Courts. In *Harris* v. *Dönges* the Appellate Court, deliberately rejecting the interpretation accepted in 1937, declared the Act invalid because it had not been passed in accord with procedure prescribed in the relevant provisions of the South Africa Act. In a long and closely reasoned judgment[2] delivered by Chief Justice Centlivres they argued that the Statute of Westminster had in fact not affected the validity of the procedures laid down in the entrenched clauses of the South Africa Act. It was the case that the Statute of Westminster conferred upon the Union Parliament a power

---

[1] Published as Appendix II in Geoffrey Marshall's *Parliamentary Sovereignty and the Commonwealth* (Oxford, Clarendon Press, 1957).

[2] South Africa Law Reports, 1952 (2), May, pp. 428–72 (ibid. pp. 97–113). See also Professor D. V. Cowen's *Parliamentary Sovereignty and the Entrenched Sections of the South Africa Act* (Cape Town, Juta, 1951).

which it did not possess prior to the enactment of the Statute, namely to pass a law repugnant to existing or future laws of the United Kingdom. But prior to the Statute of Westminster the Union Parliament had full power to amend the South Africa Act. It was not possible to justify the inference that there was any intention to repeal or modify the provisions of Section 152 of the South Africa Act in Section 2 (2) of the Statute of Westminster. The existence of these provisions constituted no impairment of South African sovereignty. 'A state can be unquestionably sovereign although it has no legislature which is completely sovereign.' To say that the Union was not a sovereign state simply because its Parliament, functioning bicamerally, had not the power to amend certain sections of the South Africa Act was to state 'a manifest absurdity'. Those sections could be amended by Parliament sitting unicamerally. The entrenched clauses were specially protected not by the Colonial Laws Validity Act but by the South Africa Act itself, which was the Constitution of the Union. An Act of Parliament could not be questioned by the Courts but a measure affecting the entrenched clauses passed in disregard of the prescribed procedure was no Act of Parliament and was therefore void. The earlier decision of the Appellate Court was wrong and therefore it was right for the Court to depart from it.[1]

The Nationalist government, like Henry VIII anxious to carry through a revolution by constitutional means, reacted sharply to a judgment which frustrated its purpose. The Court, claimed Dr. Malan,[2] had no right to challenge the validity of an Act of Parliament.

> The situation which has now arisen [he continued] is an intolerable one, and the Government would be grossly neglecting its duty towards the people ... if steps are not taken to put an end to this confusing and dangerous situation. It is imperative that the legislative sovereignty of Parliament should be placed beyond any doubt.

The government accordingly introduced legislation which was passed by both Houses creating a new High Court of Parliament composed of all members of Parliament and invested with the power to review any decision of the Appellate Court that challenged an Act of Parliament. The new High Court of Parliament reversed the Supreme Court's decision in *Harris* v. *Dönges*, but was itself declared invalid by the Supreme Court on the ground that it was a device to accomplish something already declared illegal. Dr. Malan, once more rebuffed in the courts but fortified by an impressive victory at the polls in 1953, pursued his aim but changed his method. In 1955 the Nationalist government enlarged the membership of the Senate from 48 to 84 and altered the method

---

[1] It is noteworthy that the majority of the assenting Judges, Mr. Justice Greenberg, Mr. Justice Schreiner, Mr. Justice van den Heever, and Mr. Justice Hoexter, were Afrikaners. It is also to be noted that the judgment not only conflicted with the advice Dr. Malan had received from the experts he had consulted but also challenged the assumptions of most constitutional historians, including the present author (see *Survey*, *1931–9*, p. 22).

[2] South Africa, H. of A. Deb., vol. 78, coll. 3124–5.

of election so as to secure the required two-thirds majority. In 1956 the goal was reached and the Separate Representation of Voters' Bill became law. To most Nationalists this seemed a notable vindication of the sovereignty of Parliament; to the Opposition party the attainment by unconstitutional means of an end which destroyed the essential basis of the compact of 1909. The Union of South Africa had achieved full equality of status, but was not its government using that external equality to underline or create domestic inequalities? It was because this was widely felt to be the case that citizens in the Commonwealth felt strongly that action inconsistent with the spirit of the Commonwealth and with the conventions of parliamentary government was a matter of more than domestic South African significance.

Inequalities in status are not susceptible of uniform definition. In the view of South Africa's Nationalist government the entrenched clauses of the South Africa Act detracted from the sovereignty of the Union Parliament and thereby deprived it of full equality of status with the Parliament of the United Kingdom, which could amend all United Kingdom law by ordinary process of legislation. The Appellate Court did not agree, but Dr. Malan by circumventing their judgment attained his end. The entrenched clauses were not, however, in his view the only inequality under which the Union laboured. In 1951 he complained bitterly to the visiting Secretary of State for Commonwealth Relations, Mr. P. C. Gordon Walker, that the failure to transfer the High Commission Territories of Basutoland, Bechuanaland, and Swaziland to the Union as contemplated in the South Africa Act was something that 'affects our equal status and place among the other members of the Commonwealth as well as our self-respect as a nation'.

South Africa [he continued] is an independent country and recognized as such. Constitutionally she stands on a footing of equality with the other members of the Commonwealth and with other independent nations. But in one vital respect she differs from them all, and that is, that within her embrace, and even actually within her borders, she is compelled to harbour territories, entirely dependent upon her economically and largely also for their defence, but belonging to and governed by another country. Such a condition, I venture to say, will not for a single moment be tolerated in their case, either by Canada or Australia or New Zealand, not to speak of India or Pakistan or Ceylon or Britain herself.[1]

The desire of South Africans to see the High Commission Territories transferred to the Union was not confined to any one party and indeed was in itself altogether understandable. In the particular circumstances, however, the notion that the continued government of these Territories by the United Kingdom constituted inequality of status was questionable. An implication of inequality in a certain context is not inequality.

Section 151 of the South Africa Act provided that the King, with the advice of the Privy Council, might on addresses from the Houses of Parliament of the

[1] Mansergh, *Documents*, ii. 928–9.

Union transfer the Territories to the Union upon terms and conditions set out in a schedule to the Act and embodying certain principles and safeguards of native rights drafted and agreed by the South African National Convention and accepted by the Parliament of the United Kingdom. The schedule was designed therefore as a guarantee that the existing rights of the Natives should not be prejudiced in the event of any transfer of responsibility, but its effectiveness for this purpose was impaired by the enactment of the Statute of Westminster because the powers of reservation and disallowance by which the guarantee was underwritten were thereby deprived of their validity. But the United Kingdom remained in a position to protect Native interests because of two pledges given in the House of Commons when the South Africa Act was before it. The first pledge was that the House would have the fullest opportunity of considering any such transfer before a decision was reached and the second that 'the wishes of the Natives of these territories will be most carefully considered before any transfer takes place'. In all subsequent discussion on this question the viewpoint of the United Kingdom government on these two pledges remained constant[1]—the Native inhabitants must be consulted and the United Kingdom Parliament must have an opportunity of expressing its views. Pressure at Westminster to declare that pledges of consultation should be reinterpreted to mean consent, and pressure from successive South African governments to reinterpret it as a formality in the light of the Natives' inability to decide what was in their own best interest, were alike firmly rejected, though on the second point the United Kingdom government weakened its moral position by the establishment in 1953 of a Federation of the Rhodesias and Nyasaland despite evidence of Native opposition to it. But this did not offer a precedent for the transfer of Native peoples from the jurisdiction of one government to that of another in the face of their strong opposition. Nor could it reasonably be maintained that refusal to do so was in conflict with the root principle of equality which determined Commonwealth relations. In so far as the terms of the South Africa Act presumed that the High Commission Territories would ultimately be incorporated in the Union, it was a presumption based on the conviction that South African Native policy would be of such a character as would cause the Native inhabitants of the Territories to view such a transfer with equanimity. That presumption was not fulfilled. In the history of the Commonwealth colonial territories in Canada, in Australia, and in South Africa itself had come together to form self-governing dominions. But their association had been of their own free will, and to compel the High Commission Territories to enter the Union against the wishes of their inhabitants would have been a departure from Commonwealth

---

[1] There is extensive documentation of this dispute, of which a selection is reprinted in Mansergh, *Documents*, ii. pp. 913–30. See also Union of South Africa, *Negotiations regarding the transfer to the Union of South Africa of the Government of Basutoland, the Bechuanaland Protectorate, and Swaziland* (Pretoria, Govt. Printer, 1952–3).

tradition which would have introduced a new element of inequality. This is underlined by the manner of Newfoundland's ultimate union with Canada.

The Incorporation of Newfoundland in the Canadian Confederation

In November 1947 Canadian proposals for confederation were submitted to a Constitutional Convention set up to determine the future of the island, whose affairs had been administered by a Commission of Government since 1934. These proposals were studied by the delegates who, however, decided early in 1948 that only the two following forms of government should be placed before the people at the proposed referendum: (1) Responsible Government as it existed prior to 1934; (2) Commission of Government. A resolution recommending that confederation with Canada should also be placed on the ballot was defeated in February that year by 29 votes to 16. Many electors protested strongly against the decision to deprive them of this third choice. The United Kingdom government, with whom ultimate responsibility rested, accepting the view that the issues arising from confederation were sufficiently clear to enable the people of Newfoundland to express an opinion on them, and taking into account the considerable minority of the Convention in favour of such a course, ruled that confederation should be included as a third choice at the first referendum.

The voting in the referendum, which was held on 3 June, resulted as follows:

	Votes
For Responsible Government	69,230
For confederation with Canada	63,110
For Commission of Government for a further period of five years	21,944

The total number of voters eligible to vote at the referendum was 176,297, and the proportion who voted was therefore remarkably high.

It had been provided in the Referendum Act that there should be a second referendum if there were not an absolute majority for any of the three choices at the first vote and that the form of government for which the smallest number of votes was cast in the first referendum should be omitted from the ballot paper at the second poll. Accordingly a second referendum omitting the alternative of continued government by Commission took place on 22 July. The result of this second ballot showed a small but clear majority in favour of confederation with Canada. The voting was as follows:

For confederation	78,451
For Responsible Government	71,217[1]

[1] In Labrador the vote was 2,802 in favour of confederation and 645 for Responsible Government.

The comparatively small majority in favour of confederation invited the question whether it was sufficient to decide the constitutional future of Newfoundland. Some of the protagonists of Responsible Government maintained that it was not, and a petition for the restoration of Responsible Government was organized and subsequently presented at the Bar of the House of Commons for submission to the United Kingdom government. It was argued, on the other hand, that the great bulk of the people were satisfied both with the way in which the decision had been reached and with its finality.

The Canadian government, after considering the result of the second referendum, announced that in its view it could be accepted as decisive. Mr. Mackenzie King stated that a definite majority of the electorate of Newfoundland had expressed its wishes in favour of confederation and that the result was 'clear and beyond possibility of misunderstanding'. Because of this the Canadian government and the people of Canada welcomed the result of the plebiscite and felt that the union would seal in constitutional terms 'a close and fraternal association that has existed in war and in peace between the two countries over many years'. The United Kingdom for her part concurred in this conclusion. Accordingly the Canadian government proceeded to make arrangements for the entry of Newfoundland into the Confederation on the basis outlined in 1947. After detailed discussions between representatives of the Canadian government and of Newfoundland agreement was reached, Newfoundland entered the Canadian Confederation,[1] and her members were welcomed in the House of Commons in Ottawa in September 1949, when, moved by the occasion, some among them made speeches of exceptional length extolling the wealth and attractions of the province.

Throughout the negotiations the Canadian government made it abundantly clear that while it hoped to be able to welcome Newfoundland as the tenth province in the Canadian Confederation she was to become so, if indeed she did, only of her own free will. If the procedure adopted, ensuring, as it did, to the people of Newfoundland every opportunity of expressing their wishes, had any general validity in Commonwealth relations, it suggested that it was the South African government which was departing from Commonwealth convention in demanding the transfer of the High Commission Territories to the Union irrespective of the wishes of their inhabitants and that it was the United Kingdom government which, by making consultation a prior condition of such transfer, was acting in accordance with it. Inequality, a word much used, is also a word that has been sometimes abused in Commonwealth history.

Commonwealth Consultation: A Perspective View

The London Declaration of April 1949 was regarded, and rightly regarded, as signal evidence of the adaptability of the Commonwealth to changing cir-

[1] The relevant documents are reprinted in Mansergh, *Documents*, ii. 896–902.

THE ACCESSION OF QUEEN ELIZABETH II

cumstances. There is, however, some risk lest its dramatic qualities should obscure the underlying pattern of Commonwealth development. If equality were the root principle, its chief manifestation was progressive decentralization of power and responsibility. 'In the Commonwealth', said General Smuts,[1] 'we follow to the limit the principle of decentralization.' In no respect was this more true or more important than of the system of consultation that had first evolved in accordance with the needs and desires of the older dominions.

When the Dominions Office was established as a separate department with its own Secretary of State in July 1925, the relationships between the United Kingdom and the dominions on the one hand and the United Kingdom and the colonies on the other were departmentally distinguished, but it was not until 1930 that the offices of the Secretaries of State for the Colonies and for Dominion Affairs were separated and Dominion Affairs became the entire responsibility of a principal Secretary of State.[2] Even thereafter responsibility for the two departments remained for a period of four years in the hands of one Secretary of State, Mr. J. H. Thomas, and again for a short period in 1938–9 in the hands of Mr. Malcolm MacDonald.[3] Until 1939, too, interchange between the staffs of the two departments was frequent and until 1946 the Dominions and Colonial Offices shared a joint establishment. The continuing association of the Dominions with the Colonial Office rather than with the Foreign Office, as would have been more logical in view of the duties of this 'foreign office with family feeling', had administrative consequences of some importance. It meant that at the outset senior officials of the new department were almost wholly drawn from the former Colonial Office. It meant, too, that the method of recruitment to the Dominions Office was through the normal machinery of the Home Civil Service Examination and, more particularly, that until 1946 candidates who might have expressed a preference for the Colonial Office were liable to transfer at any time to the Dominions Office, where their responsibilities would be different in kind. In Whitehall this was a matter of little moment, but it had, at least in theory, its disadvantages in the staffing of the offices of the United Kingdom High Commissioners overseas. The officials from whom selection was normally made had been chosen on their qualifications as administrators without any particular regard to their aptitude for diplomacy, even though while serving overseas their duties were predominantly diplomatic in character. It was for that reason that greater interchange with Foreign Office personnel was frequently recommended but perhaps wisely not adopted on any considerable scale.[4]

---

[1] In a speech to the Empire Parliamentary Association, 25 November 1943 (ibid. i. 568–75).
[2] The history of the office is conveniently summarized in the *Commonwealth Relations Office Handbook, 1952* (London, HMSO, 1951), p. 7.
[3] See Appendix B, p. 425 below.
[4] Individuals from the Foreign Service were seconded to serve in the offices of High Commissioners with increasing frequency after 1939, but it is a matter for curious reflection that

The tradition of the junior was not easily assimilated by members of the senior department. It was a problem best left to time to resolve.

The Dominions Office, renamed the Commonwealth Relations Office in 1947, provided the central machinery for intra-Commonwealth consultation. Its principal duty was to give as much background information as possible about developments in foreign affairs to the dominion governments. In the ordinary course its contact in the dominion capitals was with the dominion Departments of External Affairs, though there were varieties of ways in which communications could be sent in accordance with their importance. Thus a matter of the highest importance would usually be the subject of a communication from Prime Minister to Prime Minister, though it is to be noted that such communications did not necessarily dispose of a problem more quickly than was possible by other means. A Prime Minister in a dominion was a member of a Cabinet collectively responsible to his Parliament, and he was rarely in a position to take an important decision without consulting with his colleagues. For that reason, in theory though not always in practice, individual decisions on major questions by heads of governments were precluded. Mr. Mackenzie King, in his address to both Houses of Parliament at Westminster in May 1944, rightly laid emphasis upon the fact that Commonwealth consultation was part of a continuing conference of *Cabinets*. The machinery for consultation worked in relation to the British conception of parliamentary government; and many proposals for its reform, admirable in themselves, by overlooking this elementary but fundamental consideration, showed themselves remote from political realities.

It was at no time deemed sufficient that dominion governments should be informed. They had also to be informed at the earliest possible moment. The prospect of working out a policy in agreement was directly related to the promptitude with which discussions were initiated. It was, as we have seen, on this question of speed in communications that the most serious difficulties arose, and it was a problem to which attention was devoted at the Commonwealth Prime Ministers' Meetings of 1944 and 1946. Though responsibility for failures to consult in time, or, at all in the case of the Polish guarantee, 1939 or of the Cairo Conference, 1943[1] mostly rested with the United Kingdom simply because the initiative continued to lie with it as one of the great powers, there were occasions when responsibility for the breakdown of the system lay with the dominion departments of External Affairs, understaffing of the Australian Department, for example, being thought responsible for unfortunate delays in the circulation of plans for the conduct of the Pacific War

the officials of the Dominions Office overseas as a general rule were deemed more diplomatic than the professional diplomats who were serving temporarily with them.

[1] The Australian and New Zealand governments were disturbed not by the content of the Cairo Conference declaration of December 1943 on the nature of the peace to be imposed upon Japan but by the exclusive great power responsibility for its drafting (cf. Wood, ch. xxiii and H. V. Evatt, *Australia in World Affairs* (Sydney, 1946), p. 99).

to the Australian Prime Minister in March–April 1942. It was no chance that the Canadian Prime Minister Mr. Mackenzie King, who had been the most satisfied with the war-time machinery of Commonwealth consultation, should have taken the greatest pains to build up a Department of External Affairs outstanding in the quality of its personnel.[1]

Towards the end of the war Lord Cranborne, who was Secretary of State for Dominion Affairs for the second time from 1943 to 1945, alluded to the elaboration of the system of consultation that had taken place during the war without radical change in method.

> Every day [he remarked] sheaves of telegrams go out from the Dominions Office on all and every subject of mutual interest—foreign affairs, economic developments, military co-operation, even domestic issues here which are likely to interest our partners. We tell them everything we can, and we consult them on every point that arises of any importance in the international field.[2]

Foreign Office telegrams received from, and sent to, diplomatic posts abroad constituted the raw material of the information on international affairs sent out to dominion governments. The department of the Foreign Office known as the Commonwealth Liaison Department[3] sorted these telegrams, on an average 133 per day, for the express purpose of ensuring that the Commonwealth countries were kept fully informed on all questions likely to be of interest to them. The volume of outgoing communications was consequently considerable, and in 1946 the number of telegrams alone handled by the Dominions Office was over 23,000. Nor did this figure represent a purely temporary phenomenon due to post-war conditions. The total of circular telegrams in 1947 was more than 15,000 where in 1937 it had been less than 4,000, and the exchange of written dispatches had increased correspondingly. It was not surprising that General Smuts should have remarked after the 1946 Prime Ministers' Meeting that the problem was no longer one of too little but of too much information reaching dominion capitals. Their digestive capacity was stretched to, or even beyond, its natural limit.

Important though the increased scale of written communications unquestionably was, it could have achieved little had not personal contact between Commonwealth governments been correspondingly strengthened. The dominion governments had long been represented by High Commissioners in London, but not till the war years was the pattern filled out, so

---

[1] It so happens that many of its higher officials had been university dons before they became civil servants.

[2] From a speech of 19 February 1945, reprinted in R. Frost, ed. *The British Commonwealth and World Society* (London, Oxford University Press for RIIA, 1947), p. 166.

[3] This Department worked in association with the department of the Dominions Office responsible for the dispatch of information derived from Foreign Office telegrams to the Commonwealth governments concerned. This information was arranged by the Commonwealth Liaison Department in consultation with the appropriate political departments of the Foreign Office and with the Dominions Office.

that inter-dominion representation by High Commissioners was virtually complete only by 1945.[1] Thereafter London was not the only capital where comprehensive personal discussions between representatives of Commonwealth governments could take place, even if in fact, as was perhaps inevitable, they occurred rarely elsewhere. During the war, and indeed so long as London remained the principal capital within the Commonwealth, discussions there had the greatest importance.

To some, as has been seen, it was a source of complaint, to others a source of satisfaction, that responsibility for the higher direction of the war was concentrated first in London and then, so far as the dominions were concerned, in London and in Washington. But it was so, and it gave exceptional importance to the daily meetings[2] held between the Secretary of State for Dominion Affairs and the dominion High Commissioners in London. These meetings, continued at less frequent intervals after the war, were informal and the exchange of views that took place at them might cover any topic which any member saw fit to raise. Their immediate practical purpose was the conveying of up-to-date and accurate information about wartime developments to the dominion representatives for transmission when they deemed it desirable to their governments, but they served equally as a channel by which the views or the representations of dominion governments could be conveyed by their High Commissioners to the Secretary of State or to the Foreign Secretary.[3]

The post of Colonial Secretary has been traditionally regarded as one of secondary political importance. It is true that Joseph Chamberlain, declining the proffered Chancellorship, raised it to a new eminence, but it was not long before it slipped back in political standing. The office of Secretary of State for Dominion Affairs shared something of the same fate and for much the same reasons. The Dominions Secretary was concerned with overseas affairs, usually of little dramatic interest, in a field in which controversial issues did not ordinarily arise, and where therefore he had few opportunities of impressing his personality upon his own electorate. It was only rarely that a politician of the highest calibre and of equal ambition accepted such a post with enthusiasm. A glance at the list of Secretaries of State for Dominion Affairs, or Commonwealth Relations[4] suggests that, with the two notable exceptions of Mr. Eden and Mr. Attlee during the war, they were men of eminence and standing who were not likely to reach the highest political office. No doubt because the post lay outside the main stream of domestic party politics, it attracted men who are not anxious to engage whole-heartedly in the rough and tumble of political life.[5] In the case of Mr. Eden and Mr. Attlee the circum-

---

[1] See Appendix C, pp. 431–6 below.
[2] For an account of their origin see Mansergh, *Survey, 1931–9*, p. 433.
[3] It was usual for the Minister of State or some high official in the Foreign Office to be present so that the issues of foreign policy could be authoritatively expounded when need arose.
[4] Appendix B, p. 425 below.
[5] It is not suggested that this is necessarily to their discredit.

stances were exceptional. Mr. Eden, while Dominions Secretary, had general, if undefined, responsibilities in respect of foreign affairs, and Mr. Attlee combined the office with that of Deputy Prime Minister. The position reverted to normal with the appointments successively of Lord Cranborne and Viscount Addison, who held the office between them from 1943 to 1947 and who both combined the post of Dominions Secretary with that of Leader of the House of Lords. This had some advantages, since many of the more important debates on Commonwealth affairs took place in the Upper House, but they were outweighed by the disadvantages of untimely distractions from departmental affairs.

More important than the burden of responsibility falling upon the Secretary of State for Dominion Affairs or Commonwealth Relations was his personal influence with his Cabinet colleagues. The post carried Cabinet rank in peace-time but during the war Lord Cranborne was not a member of the War Cabinet during either of his two periods of office though, as he explained in 1941,[1] he attended meetings of the War Cabinet regularly so as to be able to inform the dominion High Commissioners of all matters which concerned them. Important, however, though such inside knowledge unquestionably was, attendance at the War Cabinet on such terms was a negative rather than a positive asset from the point of view of dominion governments. What concerned them was that their opinions should be put forcibly, if need be, to the War Cabinet by a spokesman whom the members of the Cabinet respected and who took part in their discussions. At that time dominion critics maintained that while the system allowed the most liberal interchange of information, it did not always permit of dominion points of view carrying their appropriate weight in the making of policy. It was that criticism which led from time to time to the suggestion either that the Dominions Secretary should be a full member of the Cabinet, or alternatively that dominion governments should deal direct with the Foreign Office. The argument on which this was founded was that the Dominions Secretary, and indeed the Dominions Office, was a buffer between dominion governments and the department where policy was shaped, and that in the process of transmission from one Whitehall department to another the dominions' representations lost weight. The argument was not altogether convincing.[2] It is doubtful if in practice the Foreign Secretary, heavily preoccupied with his traditional responsibilities, would normally have been able to devote sufficient time to Commonwealth affairs, whilst on major issues access to him by dominion High Commissioners

---

[1] 2 April 1941, H. of L. Deb., vol. 118, col. 968 (Mansergh, *Documents*, i. 534–7).

[2] On the other hand it had the support of Sir William Clark, former United Kingdom High Commissioner to Canada and to the Union of South Africa who suggested in 1944 that 'we and the Dominion Governments would be on a more comfortable parity if our Foreign Office and Dominions Office were merged into a Department of External Affairs' (*United Empire*, Nov.–Dec. 1944, p. 197). His address on 'The British Commonwealth and International Relations' has many points of interest.

was always open. On balance, therefore, it would seem to have been much to the advantage of Commonwealth governments that there was a minister constantly concerned with their interests and prepared to give his full attention to their affairs. But even when so much was allowed, clearly it remained important that he should be a man of standing among his colleagues.

From all this it would seem that the essential qualifications of a Dominions Secretary were that he should be an influential member of the Cabinet and that he should have a capacity for understanding the dominion point of view. But these qualifications alone were not sufficient to ensure that the machinery of intra-Commonwealth consultation would work well on the personal side. Almost equally important were the personalities and the influence of the dominion High Commissioners in London. This was particularly the case during the war, when the value of consultation depended in no small measure upon the attention paid to the views of a dominion High Commissioner in London by his home government.

What manner of men were chosen by dominion governments to represent them in London?[1] To that no concise answer is possible, for inevitably the qualities demanded differed in each case. It is noteworthy that the Australian government, which aimed consistently at influencing United Kingdom policy from within, should have appointed to the post of High Commissioner in London a succession of men rich in political experience. From 1933 to 1945 the post was held by the Rt. Hon. S. M. Bruce (afterwards Viscount Bruce of Melbourne), who was also Australian representative in the War Cabinet in the later war years and who had been Prime Minister of Australia from 1923 to 1929. He was a man whose experience and standing in Australia alone ensured that the highest regard would be paid to the views he expressed in London. Lord Bruce was succeeded in 1946 by Mr. Beasley, Minister of Defence in Mr. Chifley's Labour government, and he was followed in turn by Mr. Eric Harrison, who retained the Defence portfolio while in London, and then by Sir Thomas White, a former Minister of Commerce. Australia's preoccupation with defence and trade in these years clearly influenced her choice of representatives[2] in London, though it was more important that in every case they had previously held high political office. The practice followed by New Zealand was rather similar, Mr. W. J. Jordan, who was New Zealand High Commissioner from 1936 to 1951, having previously been a Labour Member of Parliament and his successor, Mr. F. W. Doidge, Minister of External Affairs at the time of his appointment.

For rather different reasons the Union of South Africa, too, relied upon the appointment of political High Commissioners. From 1929 to 1939 the post of High Commissioner in London was held by Mr. C. T. te Water, who had been a member of the House of Assembly from 1924 to 1929 and who was an outstanding and courageous spokesman for collective security at Geneva at

[1] See Appendix C, pp. 431–2 below. [2] Or Ministers Resident.

the time when the League was faltering before Mussolini's loud-mouthed menaces. His successor, Mr. S. F. Waterson, had also been in politics before entering government service, and he returned to South Africa in 1942 to assume ministerial office in General Smuts's administration. In London he was succeeded by Colonel Deneys Reitz, whose distinguished political career, culminating in his elevation to the post of Deputy Prime Minister, never reconciled him to 'Pretorian servitude'.[1] Famed in his youth for the guerrilla exploits which are recorded in the pages of *Commando* and *Trekking On*, he brought with him to London in the eve of his days a directness of approach and shrewdness of judgement acquired in a lifetime of adventure, and an outdoor personality that seemed strangely out of place in the drab corridors of the Dominions Office. He in turn was succeeded in 1944 by Mr. Heaton Nicholls, also a member of the United party, whose independence of view did not always make him the ideal back-bencher at Cape Town. The Republic of India, whose High Commissioner was accredited to the Crown, not to the United Kingdom government, was served in London by two political personalities of first importance, Mr. V. K. Krishna Menon, and Mrs. Pandit, a sister of Pandit Nehru, the Indian Prime Minister.

Canada and Eire preferred to appoint either civil servants or men with a non-political background and a tradition of public service to the office of High Commissioner in London. Canada, the senior dominion, whose High Commissioner took precedence until the 1948 Commonwealth Prime Ministers' Meeting decided that precedence should be in order of seniority of appointment, nominated four distinguished men to fill the post between 1931 and 1952. All of them—Mr. Howard Ferguson, Mr. Vincent Massey, Mr. Norman Robertson, and Mr. Dana Wilgress—remained outside the political arena. Mr. Vincent Massey, of whose service in London during the war Mr. Mackenzie King spoke on several occasions with warm appreciation,[2] became in 1952 the first Canadian-born Governor-General of Canada. Mr. Norman Robertson, who succeeded him as High Commissioner in 1946, had been Under-Secretary of State for External Affairs from 1941 and his period as High Commissioner in London was interrupted from 1949 to 1951 to allow of his return to Ottawa to serve as Clerk to the Privy Council and Secretary to the Cabinet. Mr. Wilgress, who had been Canadian Minister and then Canadian Ambassador to the Soviet Union from 1942 to 1947, served in London in the intervening years. Mr. J. W. Dulanty, who was appointed High Commissioner for the Irish Free State in 1930, survived long enough in that office to become first Ambassador for the Republic of Ireland in July 1950.[3] Pakistan and Ceylon also relied upon non-political representation in London.

---

[1] The phrase was his own.   [2] e.g. Canada, H. of C. Deb., 1943, vol. 1, p. 44.
[3] Although the Irish Free State became a Republic in April 1949, the office of High Commissioner was not brought into conformity for over a year.

Since dominion High Commissioners normally addressed their communications to their respective Departments of External Affairs, it was a matter of importance that for a long period Prime Ministers in most dominions retained the External Affairs portfolios in their own hands. In Canada the offices of Prime Minister and Secretary for External Affairs were not formally separated till 1947, when Mr. St. Laurent was appointed Secretary for External Affairs. In South Africa General Smuts, like General Hertzog before him, retained the External Affairs portfolio in his own hands until his fall from office in 1948, when Dr. Malan appointed a separate minister, as did his successor Mr. Strijdom. In Dublin, Mr. de Valera also was his own Minister of External Affairs throughout his long period of office from 1932 to 1948, but with the accession of Mr. Costello's inter-party government the two offices were once again separated, and External Affairs entrusted to Mr. Seán MacBride.[1] In New Zealand the practice was more variable but the offices were more often than not combined in these years, and Mr. Peter Fraser was his own External Affairs Minister from 1943 to 1949. Only in Australia, of the older members, had the offices consistently been separated since 1931. In the Asian member states there is by comparison little experience. In India Mr. Nehru retained the External Affairs portfolio in his own hands; in Pakistan the two offices were separate from 1947 till 1956 while in the same period in Ceylon they were united.

The association of the offices of Prime Minister and Minister for External Affairs in the dominions had some bearing on the conduct of intra-Commonwealth relations, particularly during the war years. The practice had both advantages and disadvantages. Inasmuch as it meant that communications of importance from London were submitted directly to the highest political authority in the dominions, that was a gain. On the other hand the many and inevitable preoccupations of the dominion Prime Ministers during the war left them with insufficient time to devote to departmental matters, with the result that decisions were often delayed because there was no minister who could deal with them in the ordinary way of business. One consequence was that permanent officials often felt compelled to take decisions themselves on matters of ministerial but not prime ministerial importance, and in Ottawa, in Pretoria, in Dublin, and in Wellington permanent Under-Secretaries in the External Affairs Departments thus acquired a status not often accorded, even informally, to civil servants, and with it a considerable influence on the working of the Commonwealth system.

It is not to be supposed that the retention of the External Affairs portfolio in prime ministerial hands was fortuitous. On the contrary, it is to be attributed primarily to a sense of its importance coupled with an appreciation of the political delicacy of some of the questions for which the departments were

---

[1] When Mr. de Valera returned to office once more in 1951 he, too, appointed a separate Minister.

responsible. The second consideration applied with particular force at particular times in Pretoria, Delhi, and Dublin, where it was maintained that only the head of the government could deal with questions which might at any moment arise and which might have sharp political repercussions at home. In Ottawa, too, it had some relevance, if only because of Mr. Mackenzie King's constant preoccupation with matters that might have some bearing on Canadian status and Canadian unity.

The External Affairs departments in the dominions were able to consult the United Kingdom High Commissioners accredited to their respective governments, as well as their own representatives in London, on any point on which they required information or elucidation. Until 1941 such appointments had been made from the ranks of the civil service, though not always from the Colonial or Dominions Offices. Thus Sir Edward Harding, who was Permanent Under-Secretary of State at the Dominions Office from 1930 to 1940, served as United Kingdom High Commissioner to the Union of South Africa from 1940 to 1941; Sir Harry Batterbee, who was an Assistant Under-Secretary of State at the Dominions Office from 1930 to 1938, served as first United Kingdom High Commissioner in New Zealand from 1939 to 1944; and Sir Geoffrey Whiskard, also an Assistant Under-Secretary of State at the Dominions Office, served as first High Commissioner in Australia from 1936 to 1941. On the other hand Sir William Clark, who served successively in Ottawa and in Pretoria between 1928 and 1938, had previously been Comptroller-General of the Department of Overseas Trade, and Sir Gerald Campbell, who served in Ottawa from 1938 to 1941, was a member of the consular service. With the enhanced importance of United Kingdom-dominion relations during the war, a policy of appointing United Kingdom High Commissioners with political experience was initiated. In 1941 three such 'political' High Commissioners were appointed. All had at some period held Cabinet office. Sir Ronald Cross, a Conservative Member of Parliament, resigned from his post as Minister of Economic Warfare to go to Canberra as High Commissioner; Mr. Malcolm MacDonald, who had held ministerial office continuously since 1936, was appointed High Commissioner to Canada; and Lord Harlech, who as Mr. Ormsby-Gore had been a member of Mr. Baldwin's second administration, was appointed to Pretoria. Only in Wellington, and in Dublin, where Sir John Maffey filled the post of United Kingdom representative with rare distinction from 1939 to 1949, was the civil service tradition continued.

The advantage of 'political' High Commissioners in wartime was evident. As Lord Cranborne stated in 1941, the United Kingdom High Commissioners in the dominions were 'in the closest possible contact both with the Dominion Prime Ministers and with the Dominion Governments',[1] and they were fully informed by telegram of wartime political developments from London, so as

[1] H. of L. Deb., vol. 118, coll. 966–71 (Mansergh, *Documents*, i. 93–94).

to be in a position to represent the views of the United Kingdom government with authority. The political High Commissioners were accustomed to dealing with Cabinet Ministers on familiar and equal terms, and they were well placed to understand political factors which in wartime might at any moment become of critical importance. They were accustomed, too, to the taking of quick decisions and to assuming responsibility for them. If in the nature of things their appointment was a temporary device, for in peace-time politicians with a future do not welcome overseas appointments and those only with a past rarely have much to contribute, unquestionably it served a most useful purpose. Mr. MacDonald's understanding of the Canadian Prime Minister and Lord Harlech's association with General Smuts were by no means least among the personal factors which contributed to the success of Commonwealth co-operation in wartime.

These political appointments served to raise the standing of the United Kingdom High Commissioners in the dominions and, equally important, with their home government. During the war the staffs of the High Commissioners' offices were reinforced to deal with additional work and to undertake new duties. By 1945 information sections had been added to assist in the dissemination of information about developments in the United Kingdom, and at about the same time the old-established Trade Commissioner organization was more closely associated with the High Commissioner's Office, the senior Trade Commissioner becoming the High Commissioner's principal economic adviser. Expansion of staff was intended to free the High Commissioners themselves from excessive office work and there was greater appreciation of the need for travel by the High Commissioner and by members of his staff if their representational duties were to be adequately discharged. All this once more underlined the importance of personalities, for, though the duties of the High Commissioners might be predominantly diplomatic, they themselves were, in a sense in which Foreign Service colleagues in foreign countries were not, the spokesmen of one partner community to another.

After the war non-political appointments were once more the order of the day. Again they were not made exclusively from the Dominions Office, the principal reason being that that office, whose total administrative staff at that time did not exceed thirty-five, had an inadequate pool upon which to draw. The emergence of the three new dominions in Asia in 1947–8 underlined in this respect its limited resources. Of the first High Commissioners appointed to these dominions only one was chosen from the Dominions Office, that is to say from among those whose principal experience had been in the field of Commonwealth relations. For the rest reliance was placed upon the Foreign Service, and at a time when first Burma, and later India and Pakistan, were deciding whether to remain members of the British Commonwealth of Nations or to secede from it the United Kingdom representatives in their capitals

THE ACCESSION OF QUEEN ELIZABETH II

were men whose experience and training had lain outside the Commonwealth. This was a liability which served, even if only negatively, to demonstrate the political importance of the office of the High Commissioner and the measure of the possible personal contribution of a High Commissioner to the fruitful working of the Commonwealth system. In the Commonwealth the men have always mattered more than the machine.

The elevation of the office of High Commissioner led to some change in emphasis in the practice of Commonwealth consultation. Direct government-to-government communication was once the general practice, and continued to be extensively used, but at the same time the United Kingdom, Canada, and India increasingly adopted the practice of cabling not direct to the government with which they wished to communicate but to their High Commissioner in the member state concerned. The High Commissioner might then discuss the matter personally with its government and cable his reply. This procedure helped to make consultation less formal than when reliance was placed on inter-governmental communications alone. In 1952 10,470 telegrams came into the Commonwealth Relations Office from its overseas posts, and 17,840 were sent out to them. Over and above these there was correspondence on a comparable scale. But there was no uniformity in practice, some Commonwealth governments using their High Commissioners as intermediaries less than others. It is important, however, not to overlook the increased importance of this channel of communication.

Parallel with the growing importance of the High Commissioners within the Commonwealth was the expansion of the dominion diplomatic representation without. In 1939 Canada had four[1] and Australia had only two representatives in foreign capitals. In 1956 Canada was represented diplomatically in 42 foreign countries; Australia in 22; New Zealand in 4; South Africa in 17; India in 48; Pakistan in 27; and Ceylon in 5. Far from depending upon the Foreign Office for information about developments in Europe, in Asia, and in other parts of the world, some oversea members of the Commonwealth were in a position to provide information to London on a considerable and a growing scale. They were, however, slow to do so. In 1948 Lord Bruce estimated that 90 per cent. of the information circulated originated in the United Kingdom, and even if due allowance was not made in this calculation for the extent to which some governments, notably the Canadian, used their High Commissioners' Offices in London for the transmission of information, the implication of the figure is not open to serious doubt.[2] Increased representation overseas, somewhat paradoxically, enhanced the potential value of consultation within the Commonwealth perhaps particularly in respect of regional policies or interests. In 1951 there was, for example, a greater volume of communication from Canberra to Delhi than from Canberra to any other

---

[1] One of them was accredited both to the Belgian and to the Netherlands governments.
[2] H. of L. Deb., vol. 153, coll. 1102–8 (Mansergh, *Documents*, i. 597–602).

Commonwealth capital except London, and not excepting Wellington. More generally there was a growth of intra-Commonwealth consultation among oversea members as well as between each of them individually and the United Kingdom. The close understanding between India and Canada in the later stages of the Korean War and their continued co-operation on many issues at the United Nations was a significant factor in international as well as in Commonwealth history at this time.

A more active role in foreign policy increased the potential benefits to be derived from prior consultation within the Commonwealth of Nations. In this way there developed the practice of preliminary Commonwealth conferences, which met informally before the more important wartime and postwar international conferences. One notable instance already recorded was the Meeting of Commonwealth statesmen in London in April 1945 to discuss their attitudes towards the Dumbarton Oaks proposals. These informal gatherings were usually described with some reserve in view of United States and other susceptibilities about the existence of 'blocs' other than their own.[1] It was, however, the custom for Commonwealth Foreign Ministers and leaders of Commonwealth delegations to discuss questions of policy and of tactics before and during international conferences. Even where there was no possibility of agreement, as on colonial questions between the Asian and the older members of the Commonwealth, these consultations took place in the hope, and usually with the result, of an amicable public expression of differences. Such consultation among Commonwealth representatives in foreign capitals was also frequent.

> In Washington [wrote Sir Oliver Franks on the conclusion of his term as British Ambassador] I saw how that unity [of the Commonwealth] worked. Every fortnight except in the summer the eight Ambassadors of the Commonwealth met in our Embassy to exchange views and consult informally together. We discussed everything: the movement of affairs in the world, the latest phase of American policy—and the opinions of our different countries about them. We did not mince words. Even difficulties between individual members, like Kashmir, were regularly talked over by all of us, including India and Pakistan, with conviction but without heat.[2]

Prime Ministers and their Meetings

The 'continuing conference of Cabinets' of which Mr. Mackenzie King spoke so highly was made technically possible by improved methods of communication; it derived from, and well expressed, a growing sense of equality in partnership. Where the Imperial Conference by its name and character presumed concentration of power, the Meetings of Commonwealth Prime

---

[1] Cf. both on the scale of such discussions and on allusions to blocs Lord Addison's speech in the House of Lords 17 February 1948 (H. of L. Deb., vol. 153, coll. 1154–8; ibid. pp. 602–7).

[2] Sir Oliver Franks, *Britain and the Tide of World Affairs* (London, Oxford University Press, 1955), p. 17.

Ministers recognized its dispersal. Such meetings, therefore, were in conformity with the political realities in the post-Statute-of-Westminster Commonwealth. At the outset of the war some, as has been seen, lamented the failure to re-create an Imperial War Cabinet; towards its close others expressed their anxiety lest the apparent lapse of the Imperial Conference would mean less effective and less frequent consultation.[1] Those who attended such meetings, and some among them had experience of earlier Imperial Conferences, seemingly did not share these doubts about their effectiveness, while in respect of frequency of meetings at least there was no comparison between the two. Imperial Conferences were normally held every five years; there were Meetings of Commonwealth Prime Ministers in 1944, 1946, 1948, 1949, 1951, within our period, and in 1953, 1954, 1955, and 1957 beyond it, and during these years they were supplemented by meetings of Commonwealth Foreign, Finance, and Defence Ministers. Thus, while there was an apparent loosening of the formal fabric, there was an increase in ministerial as in official consultation due principally to the more active concern of oversea members of the Commonwealth with problems of foreign policy, but also to a new and significant preoccupation with economic and welfare policies.

The usefulness of the Meetings of Prime Ministers at the apex of the system of Commonwealth consultation was related to the personalities of the Prime Ministers themselves and their willingness and ability to discuss common problems fruitfully together. The fact that they all alike presided over Cabinets responsible to Parliaments created a presumption, but no more than a presumption, that they would have a common approach to the problems which confronted them when they met together. Yet in itself this was not enough. The success or failure of meetings so informal in character, so flexible in their working arrangements, depended exceptionally upon the spirit in which they were held and upon the men who attended them.

From the close of the First World War to the ending of the Statute-of-Westminster Commonwealth in 1949 there were many outstanding personalities among Commonwealth leaders, but over this extended period the influence of two of them, General Smuts and Mr. Mackenzie King, in the highest councils of the Commonwealth was especially pronounced. They were men of different temperament and contrasted achievement, the one chiefly preoccupied with ends, the other principally with means.

Something of General Smuts's influence in the Commonwealth certainly was due to his past. In the eyes of Britain and indeed of the world the Boer commando leader, become a staunch upholder of what in different guise he once had challenged, was a man to compel attention.[2] But at root it was not romantic

[1] See, for example, 'Half a Conference', *Round Table*, September 1948, pp. 731–5.
[2] On one convivial wartime evening Mr. John Dulanty, Ireland's High Commissioner in London by whose conversation, it was later written, no man was ever bored, said to Colonel

appeal or dramatic conversion but hard thought that made General Smuts a chief architect of the Commonwealth. He gave to an idea and a name substance and form; he enriched it with the magnanimity of his personality. About its character and contribution to the world he had thought not only long and deeply but creatively. At home his ideal was openly challenged, and as a result the Commonwealth never became for him something that could be accepted; on the contrary it was always something to work for and to justify in deed as well as in word. That was one reason why he contributed so much to its development. The South African background helps also to explain something that might otherwise appear somewhat paradoxical in General Smuts's contribution to Commonwealth affairs. In his own country he was thought of (except by imperialists in Natal) as a great imperialist; in the councils of the Commonwealth he was known equally as the unswerving champion of dominion autonomy long before the Balfour Report or the Statute of Westminster had established it in convention and in law. In fact he believed the Commonwealth should be a brotherhood of independent states and he was therefore at all times insistent that equality should be realized in practice as well as in theory. As early as 1917 he had described the Commonwealth as the only successful experiment in international government that had ever been made and it was his conviction, as that of Botha before him, that the foundation of that success was equality and free cooperation. Decentralization was his watchword and to the last he was resolutely opposed to all attempts to recreate a centralized empire. At the end of his days in 1948 he dismissed proposals put forward by Lord Bruce in the House of Lords[1] for an Imperial Council or Secretariat with the terse comment 'the more machinery we have the more friction there will be' Co-operation between the countries of the Commonwealth should be allowed, in his view, to develop freely along its own natural lines unrestricted by forms and institutions. Yet while General Smuts believed in decentralization he also believed in a strong Commonwealth. He believed that the Commonwealth had a great part to play in world affairs and that it could play it only if it were strong and united. No man contributed more than he to that unity and that strength which in two world wars evoked the admiration of mankind, and which indeed but for his leadership in September 1939 might have been gravely impaired in the second by South African neutrality. Yet by an ironic destiny this soldier-statesman who was ever reaching outwards from the land of his birth and his boyhood and seeking to promote the wider community of the Commonwealth and of the whole world failed at the last to achieve that unity at home which would indirectly have so greatly strengthened the Commonwealth. Perhaps no man could have done this; but perhaps also the

Deneys Reitz, 'You know, when I read General Smuts' speeches and heard your broadcasts I said to myself "those fellows there have been nobbled by the British" ' (Reitz, *No Outspan*, p. 257).   [1] In the speech referred to on p. 409 above.

gaze of the world statesman strayed too often from distasteful and tedious problems nearer home. At the last he paid, as General Hertzog had paid before him, for one grave political miscalculation. Had not the two Generals formed a coalition and then a Fusion government in 1933–4, the Purified Nationalists would not have had occasion to secede from the Nationalist party, and would therefore not have been left amid the wartime wreckage of the Fusion experiment as the virtually unchallenged heirs of the Nationalist tradition and the only serious contenders for power. The election of 1948 was a logical sequel to the formation of the Fusion government fifteen years earlier. General Smuts did not apparently foresee this consequence, but his Canadian contemporary, Mr. Mackenzie King, a man of lesser talent but of greater political penetration, might well have done so.

Mr. Mackenzie King was essentially a Canadian, not a Commonwealth or a world statesman. That was at once his weakness and his strength. He was chosen leader of the Liberal party in 1919, and twenty-nine years later, in 1948, the year of Smuts's electoral defeat, he gave a final accounting of his stewardship to the National Liberal Convention in Ottawa. The record was impressive. The party had fought 7 elections under his leadership and had won 6 of them. It had been in power for 21 of those 29 years and its greatest electoral triumph lay before it. In Canada Mr. Mackenzie King surpassed both Sir John Macdonald's and Sir Wilfrid Laurier's long tenure of the office of Prime Minister, and in a wider field, in April 1948, to his own undisguised satisfaction, he surpassed Sir Robert Walpole's hitherto unchallenged record. They had other things in common and part of what Lecky wrote of Walpole might also be written of Mr. Mackenzie King.

As a statesman the chief object of his policy was to avoid all violent concussions of opinion. He belonged to that class of legislators who recognize fully that government is an organic thing, that all transitions to be safe should be the gradual product of public opinion, that the great end of statesmanship is to secure a nation's practical well-being, and allow its social and industrial forces to develop unimpeded, and that a wise minister will carefully avoid exciting violent passions, provoking reactions, offending large classes and generating enduring discontents.[1]

Like Walpole, too, Mr. Mackenzie King had many critics within Canada and without, and it is no occasion for surprise that the biographers of his earlier years[2] should have conceived as great a distaste for the subject of their biography as Macaulay for James II. Some have sought for the secret of his political success in the personality of a man who in the eyes of Canadian commentators[3] has bade fair to rival Talleyrand 'as the most impenetrable

[1] *History of England in the Eighteenth Century* (1879), i. 329.
[2] H. S. Ferns and B. Ostry, *The Age of Mackenzie King* (London, Heinemann, 1955). The author noted in 1953 that students at the University of Toronto chose as a topic for debate 'Mackenzie King: Patriot or Rogue?', but few of his colleagues thought the matter one for surprise or even for comment. Toronto, of course, is not Canada.
[3] e.g. Hutchison, *The Incredible Canadian*.

and incomprehensible of men', but more probably if more prosaically is it to be looked for in his understanding of men and a knowledge, acquired in his early years as a professional industrial conciliator, of the anatomy of a twentieth-century industrial society and of the tensions to which it is a prey. Unity at home was his constant concern and his lasting achievement. It was an achievement of outstanding importance to the Commonwealth as well as to Canada.

Mr. Mackenzie King did not contribute significantly to the ideas which moved the Commonwealth or the ideals which stirred the emotions of its peoples. He laboured on a more pedestrian plane. He was interested chiefly in the working out of a pattern of a Commonwealth co-operation which in no way impaired national responsibility for policy. If General Smuts was one of the seminal minds of the Commonwealth Mr. Mackenzie King was its great parliamentarian. More than any other he reconciled the practice of responsible parliamentary government in the dominions with the machinery of intra-Commonwealth consultation. Negation was the weapon he chiefly employed, and abroad as at home he applied it with deadly effect. Yet in his later years he, who at Imperial Conferences had so often been the spokesman of 'Canada's everlasting no', became an elder statesman of the Commonwealth, the intimate adviser of the Crown, visited by the monarch on his London sickbed, and a man whose idiosyncracies became known beyond the confines of the Canadian capital where for long they had brought pain and pleasure to those in his exacting service.[1] In the history of the Commonwealth his reputation will depend largely upon the success or failure of the new principles and methods applied in the conduct of Commonwealth relations, for which he, more than any other single man, was responsible.

Some Problems of Multi-Racial Membership

In the United Kingdom, and in Australia especially, the pattern of Commonwealth development prompted some misgiving. Two reasons for this may be suggested. The first was procedural. By their very character the informal meetings of Commonwealth Prime Ministers precluded much in the way of subsequent publicity. Exchanges of view, however useful, did not provide interesting material for communiqués. As a result the best that could be said about most communiqués issued after Commonwealth meetings was that

---

[1] Mr. Mackenzie King's collection of ruins, assembled in a field near his country home at Kingsmere, was especially notable. They were composed of masonry, woodwork, and even stained glass brought together from historic sites. A story was told in 1941 of a Canadian messenger carrying a small suitcase to a waiting aircraft on which the Canadian Prime Minister was travelling back to Canada. The messenger was breathing so heavily that a secretary asked him if anything was the matter. He replied 'Yes, and you'd feel there was something the matter too if you were carrying a large piece of Buckingham Palace in your bag'. German bombs and royal favour had given Mr. Mackenzie King a notable addition to his collection of ruins.

they never shrank from a restatement of the obvious. The worst that could be said of them was said by Mr. Lester Pearson, who, in ironic allusion to the communiqué issued after the Colombo Meeting of Foreign Ministers in 1950, remarked that 'if, at the time of Magna Carta, a communiqué had been issued from Runnymede, it would probably have said: "There has been a full and friendly discussion of feudal rights, and the conference decided to make some recommendations to King John." '[1] But while the uninformative nature of the published record had something to do with contemporary doubts about the working of the Commonwealth, such official reticence was almost certainly in the interest of Commonwealth co-operation.

The second and more fundamental reason for misgiving went to the very roots of the multi-racial Commonwealth itself. It was widely agreed that self-government was the foundation, the fundamental principle, of the Commonwealth. But it was not by chance that most Englishmen spoke of responsible rather than national self-government. Mr. Gathorne-Hardy has written that English opinion as a whole never accepted the principle of self-determination as logically defined by President Wilson in 1918, and indeed 'under the terser synonym of "home rule" it had been vigorously repudiated by a large section of the population'.[2] If this assertion is somewhat too categorical there was among Englishmen widespread mistrust of other peoples' nationalism. Yet in the Commonwealth as enlarged in 1947 both the self-government and the national character of its member nations were of the greatest importance, especially in Asia. Thus in 1948 Mr. Liaqat Ali Khan, commenting on the changed complexion of the Commonwealth said: 'It is a Commonwealth of free nations who believe in the same way of life and in the same democracy', and in whose common forms of government is to be found 'a bond of unity stronger than either kinship or kingship'. And a year later Mr. Nehru, in an address to the Canadian Parliament, spoke of the way in which a reconciliation between Indian nationalism and British imperialism was brought about as 'an outstanding example of the peaceful solution of difficult problems', to which 'the rest of the world might well pay heed'. That reconciliation rested upon the assumption that there was no fundamental conflict between nationalism and Commonwealth membership. First and foremost India and Pakistan were national states and for them their Commonwealth membership had meaning and vitality because and in so far as it derived from a national source. Our co-operation, said Mr. Nehru, 'will have the greater strength that common endeavour derives from a sense that it is inspired and sustained by the free will of free peoples'.[3] Implicit in such assertions were the overtones of an age-old debate to which history alone in

---

[1] This is quoted and the point is also considered in Mansergh, *Documents*, i. xxxix.

[2] G. M. Gathorne-Hardy, *A Short History of International Affairs, 1920–1939*, 4th ed. (London, Oxford University Press for RIIA, 1950), p. 23.

[3] 24 October 1949, Canada, H. of C. Deb., 2nd sess., vol. 2, p. 1103 (Mansergh, *Documents*, ii. 1211).

each instance can furnish the materials for an answer. Coleridge believed that 'the key to the declension of the Roman Empire' was to be found not, as Gibbon suggested, in the decay of its central imperial institutions but in the imperial character overlaying and finally destroying the national character, so that Rome under Trajan was an Empire without a nation.[1] If he was right this at least was a danger the British Commonwealth had avoided, for there it was the nations that overlaid the Empire. But that in turn brought its problems and other dangers.

The association of Britain and dominions of European settlement overseas in one Commonwealth with Eastern peoples whose frontiers, as Macaulay reminded the House of Commons in 1833, the legions of Trajan never crossed, and which lay beyond the point where the phalanx of Alexander refused to proceed, was indeed little less remarkable than the government of India for a century and a half by the people of a small island in the Atlantic. It is, therefore, a matter of no surprise that the reconciliation of non-European nationalisms with the unity of a hitherto European-dominated Commonwealth should have constituted one of the major problems of its new multiracial membership. The limitation of the area even of recent common experience between the Asian and European member states accentuated it. For before the Second World War the peoples of South Asia were beset by different cares, oppressed by the thought of different dangers, and seeking different ends. One result was that the lessons they learned from recent history were not the same. For the older members of the Commonwealth the experiences which conditioned their outlook were of the dismal and wellnigh disastrous consequences of appeasement in the 1930's, of the struggle for a year, alone and ill prepared, against the might of Hitler's Germany, and of victory followed by the re-emergence in Eastern Europe of a new and seemingly equally formidable totalitarian threat to peace and security. The lesson most deeply graven on their minds was of the need to unite in time in resolute resistance to aggression, wherever it might occur. But in Asian minds what remained uppermost was the struggle to overthrow imperialism in the 1930's, its largely successful outcome in the 1940's, and disturbing reminders from South-East Asia that remnants of imperial rule still survived there. Where the former remembered how the Nazi tyrant picked off his victims one by one, the latter recalled the years of subjection to imperial rule. All the opprobrious significance of the term 'appeasement' in the West was invested in the term 'colonialism' in the East. They were two words that epitomized respectively the experiences of the older and of the Asian members. Their implications were very different.[2]

[1] *Table Talk*.
[2] These reflections were prompted by the discussion on foreign policy and defence at the fifth unofficial Commonwealth Relations Conference held at Lahore in 1954, and this paragraph is largely reproduced from the concluding chapter of Mansergh, *The Multi-Racial Commonwealth* (RIIA, 1955).

Differences in recent experience had two important consequences. The first, outlined earlier,[1] was Asian emphasis on non-alignment by contrast with Western insistence that security was to be found only by association in defensive agreements; the second, of which something remains to be said, was Asian dislike of colonialism in all its forms and British support for it in some of them.

In theory the Asian attitude to colonialism, and the racial discrimination psychologically so closely associated with it, was one of uncompromising hostility. In practice, Indian, Pakistani, and Ceylonese opinion, however, tended to make some qualified exception in favour of British colonial rule. While this in no way detracted from their condemnation of colonialism as a method of government even for backward peoples, it implied acknowledgement of the quality of much of Britain's colonial administration and also of the fact that self-government was the aim of Britain's colonial policy. While the Asian members desired greater authority in colonial matters to be vested in the United Nations, especially through a more liberal or even a strained interpretation of Article 73 of the Charter, they were prepared to recognize that the declared goal of British colonial policy was something of which they could unreservedly approve, and in respect of Britain their criticisms were, therefore, principally directed to two things. In the first place, they doubted whether any imperial government, including that of Great Britain, was likely to transfer power to a colonial people at the first possible moment that that people was ready to assume responsibility for its own affairs; and secondly, they feared lest Britain's association with 'reactionary' imperial powers in the North Atlantic Treaty and other defence agreements should deflect her from her declared policy of self-government for colonial territories. The 'discreditable company' which Britain kept at the United Nations was condemned vigorously by Asian delegates at the Lahore Commonwealth Relations Conference in 1954, and they complained that Britain, having discovered, as she had shown by her actions in Asia, the sovereign remedy of self-government for colonial discontent, seemed concerned to preserve the secret for herself and to discourage her Western European allies from applying it in their subject territories.

Differences of attitude and opinion on colonial and racial policies made the Commonwealth sensitive and perhaps vulnerable to inter-racial tensions. Certainly South African racial policies, long matters of dispute with the government of India, imposed a strain upon Commonwealth relations, while for its part the government of South Africa, committed as it was to policies of racial inequality at home, found difficulty in keeping in step with a community of states the membership of which included European and non-European peoples on a basis of equality. It was indeed for this reason that the admission of

---

[1] See above, ch. vii.

African states was thought likely to bring into question South Africa's continued membership of the Commonwealth.

In 1952 at Cape Town Dr. Malan expressed strong objection to the admission of a West African negro state to full membership.

Here [he said] we encounter a preposterous absurdity in existing Commonwealth relations. The Commonwealth is a closed group, all free and equal, and consequently one would expect that with the admission of new members all would have an equal say, because such a development might affect the whole being and character of the group. But what do we find? Acting of her own accord and without consultation with or approval of other group members, England recently added India, Pakistan and Ceylon to the Commonwealth; and now she intends to continue the process without limitation.[1]

Dr. Malan was mistaken in some of his facts, for the dominions had been consulted about the admission of the Asian members[2] and there was no question of their not being consulted about the possible admission of African states. But the South African objection was essentially not to the procedure adopted but to the end in view. It gave widespread credence to the assumption that the South African government would attempt to veto any such proposal for admission and inspired misgiving in West Africa lest the South African government might be able to block African membership by the exercise of a supposed veto power. Such fears were based on misunderstanding of Commonwealth procedure and practice. On the one hand it was a well-established convention that the strongly expressed views of a majority of members of the Commonwealth should be accepted and on the other there was no possibility of the exercise of a veto since there was no voting at Commonwealth conferences. Indeed a more careful scrutiny of what Dr. Malan said suggested that he himself was not unmindful of this, but wished in the first place to ensure that South Africa was fully consulted, and in the second place to register a protest, even though ineffective, against the admission of African states to Commonwealth membership, partly on grounds of conviction and partly for reasons of domestic politics. Open conflict of opinion was avoided and Ghana was admitted to full membership in 1957. But the underlying cause of dispute remained.

Influence and Power

Misgivings about the continuing cohesion of the Commonwealth were associated with doubts about the capacity of the Commonwealth, in terms of

---

[1] 23 February 1951 (Mansergh, *Documents*, ii. 1287–8).

[2] For the Asian precedents see ibid. pp. 702–5, and for Mr. Gordon Walker's statement on the procedure to be followed on future occasions see H. of C. Deb., vol. 488, col. 1199 (ibid. pp. 1288–9). The distinction between the grant of responsible self-government, a matter for the United Kingdom government alone, and full membership of the Commonwealth, a matter for all existing members, is to be noted.

power, to influence events decisively. National power is difficult to weigh[1] and to think in terms of Commonwealth power was to enter into the realm of imponderables; for in such terms there was no Commonwealth but only the states which composed it. Yet British peoples were inclined, perhaps on that account, to ponder too little on the realities of power. When King George VI died, United States commentators did not think first, as did their colleagues in Britain, of the extension of the self-governing Commonwealth to Asia but of the contraction of the Empire during his reign. Burma had gone, Ireland had gone; while India and Pakistan remained within the Commonwealth, Britain was no longer a land power controlling what had been hitherto if not the greatest, then the most efficient, military force on the mainland of Asia, and no longer possessed a Pacific fleet sufficient to enable her to rank as a great power in the Far East. In an able and penetrating work widely used at that time in North American universities Professor Hans J. Morgenthau[2] wrote, regretfully be it said, of Britain's role as the 'holder' of the balance of power as having come to an end, and of her friendship as being in consequence 'no longer of decisive importance'.

In the metaphorical language of the balance of power [he observed] one might say, rather crudely but not without truth, that, while in the Russian scale there is a weight of seventy, the weight of the American scale amounts to a hundred of which seventy is the United States' own strength, ten that of Great Britain, and the remainder that of the other actual or prospective allies. Thus, even if the British weight were removed from the American scale and placed into the Russian, the heavier weights would still be in the American scale.

No people, and one long accustomed to greatness least of all, likes being told, however tactfully, that it no longer counts in the scales of power, but sometimes it gives cause for wholesome reflection. In international politics few things are likely to lead more quickly to humiliation or disaster, as the French learned in Morocco in 1905–6 and the Poles in the years before the outbreak of the Second World War, than a policy based upon an overestimate of national power. Might not the emphasis so often placed after the Second World War on British influence on world affairs by way of compensation for the relative decline in British power be used as an easy but dangerous refuge from a difficult or even painful recognition of facts? On the other hand might not the American accent on organized power be too pronounced? Was it right, was it wise to overlook, as many American writers did, the ill-organized, but latent power of the Commonwealth? After all, there was a time not so distant when the Commonwealth had withstood alone the weight of Nazi power. Had its cohesion, its relative strength declined so much since then? At the turn of the century Lord Salisbury observed with penetration

[1] Mr. H. C. Hillmann made an interesting attempt to do so in RIIA, *The World in March 1939*.
[2] *Politics Among Nations* (New York, Knopf, 1948), p. 274.

that the most remarkable thing in the modern world was that the great powers were becoming greater, the small powers counting for less and less. How right he was! By 1952, Professor Morgenthau asserted, only two giants remained. And yet very great though the two greatest powers had become, was it possible that they overestimated their own greatness, and unduly discounted the possibility that the distance between them and their nearest competitors in power would not increase but lessen, and so reproduce in due course a multiple balance of power on a world scale? Might not that law of balance, which Canning likened to a law of nature, exercise its influence again in the pattern not of continental but of world politics?

No such speculation about a future balance of power modified the sense of the importance of the newly forged ties between members of the Commonwealth and the United States. In the Atlantic, in the Pacific, and later in South Asia, through Pakistan, they were linked in formal alliances. 'Let it roll', said Mr. Churchill of United States-Commonwealth wartime co-operation, and after 1945 it rolled, albeit uncertainly, forward. Its extension in the future was often lightly assumed, especially in those member nations, Canada, the United Kingdom, Australia, and New Zealand, who formed the hard core of the older British Commonwealth, and who were also most strongly drawn, by reason of history, language, and racial origin, to the United States, as though the healing of the breach in the English-speaking world was necessarily a part of a pre-ordained historical process and therefore independent of statesmanship. Yet, weighed against such facile assumptions, there was on the one hand the sensitiveness that arose from a relationship of dependence. 'We are all suppliants now', commented a Canadian official, and in itself that did not make for easy Commonwealth-United States relations. And on the other, and by way of counterpart, there were the difficulties that arose from unaccustomed responsibilities of leadership. The presumption of friendship made tensions arising from both not easier but more difficult to resolve. 'Cosmus Duke of Florence', so Bacon tells us, had 'a Desperate Saying against Perfidious or Neglecting Friends, as if those wrongs were unpardonable; "You shall reade" (saith he) "that we are commanded to forgive our Enemies; But you never reade that we are commanded, to forgive our Friends".' It was something not seldom required of the English-speaking peoples at this time.

The Coronation of Queen Elizabeth II was an occasion for the expression of unbounded faith in the future of the Commonwealth and Empire by writers who had hitherto shown little interest in either and who were apparently inspired by a steady resolve to press, beyond the limits of sense and endurance, analogies with sixteenth-century Tudor England. Like King Philip III of Spain, who was supposed to possess a gift of second sight which caused him to see a corpse on the ground whenever a murder was committed in any part of his dominions, and to which courtiers attributed his habit of looking upwards, many of them seemed fearful of what they might see were they to look down. Yet 'know thyself' is a wise maxim for nations as for individuals, and those who prefer indulgence in fanciful parallels with other ages are usually those with least confidence in their own. But for others, though there was light and shade in the picture of the Commonwealth as it moved into the second half of the twentieth century, there was lacking neither faith nor hope. Some cause for such tempered optimism was to be found in the wide extent and the closeness of Commonwealth co-operation at this time. 'These gentlemen', wrote Mr. Ramsay MacDonald of the dominion Prime Ministers in 1930, for the information of King George V, 'are very kittle cattle and have to be handled very carefully'.[1] They were 'kittle cattle' because of their sensitiveness on matters of status. But with all vestige of inequality removed, co-operation was no longer thus inhibited. Further cause derived from a sense of opportunity inspired by the extension of the Commonwealth to Asia. The Commonwealth, so it seemed to contemporaries, constituted an experiment in international co-operation that was supremely worth undertaking. If the Commonwealth was able to bring about understanding between the East and the West, the day might come, said Mr. St. Laurent in 1951, 'when we will look back on the achievement of the freedom and independence of India, Pakistan and Ceylon as the greatest event in Commonwealth history'.[2] At a time when the liberal democratic world appeared so often on the defensive the Commonwealth, it seemed, had embarked on an experiment which had about it a quality of greatness. If it succeeded then some among the peoples of the Western world, of Asia and Africa might be saved from the isolation, the suspicions and some of the bitter rivalries which had caused wars and destroyed earlier civilizations; if it failed it might none the less help, as Bryce conceived the Holy Roman Empire in its day had done, to pass on to other ages the feeling of 'a brotherhood of mankind, of a commonwealth of the whole world'.[3]

[1] Quoted in Nicolson, p. 483.
[2] In a broadcast given in London on 10 January 1951 (Mansergh, *Documents*, ii. 1214–15).
[3] *The Holy Roman Empire* (London, Macmillan, 1925), ch. xxii.

APPENDIX A

GOVERNORS-GENERAL OF THE DOMINIONS, 1931–52

CANADA

The Earl of Bessborough	1931
Lord Tweedsmuir of Elsfield	1935
Major-General the Earl of Athlone	1940
Field-Marshal the Rt. Hon. Viscount Alexander of Tunis	1946
Rt. Hon. Vincent Massey	1952

AUSTRALIA

Rt. Hon. Sir Isaac Isaacs	1931
Brig.-General the Rt. Hon. Lord Gowrie	1936
Major-General Sir Winston J. Dugan (Acting)	1944
H.R.H. the Duke of Gloucester	1945
Rt. Hon. W. J. McKell	1947
Field-Marshal Sir William Slim	1952

NEW ZEALAND

Rt. Hon. Lord Bledisloe	1930
Rt. Hon. Viscount Galway	1935
Marshal of the R.A.F. the Lord Newall	1941
Lieut. General Sir Bernard Freyberg (Lord Freyberg 1951)	1946
Lieut. General Sir Willoughby Norrie	1952

SOUTH AFRICA

The Rt. Hon. the Earl of Clarendon	1931
Rt. Hon. Sir Patrick Duncan	1937
Rt. Hon. N. J. de Wet (Officer Administering the Government)	1943
Major the Rt. Hon. G. Brank van Zyl	1946
Hon. E. G. Jansen	1951

IRISH FREE STATE

Mr. James McNeill	1927
Mr. Donal Buckley	1932

INDIA

The Earl Mountbatten of Burma	1947
Sri Chakravarty Rajagopalachari	1948

APPENDIX A

PAKISTAN

Mr. M. A. Jinnah	1947
Hon. Khwaja Nazimuddin	1947
Hon. Ghulam Mohammad	1951

CEYLON

Sir Henry Monck-Mason Moore	1948
Rt. Hon. Lord Soulbury	1949

APPENDIX B

COMMONWEALTH PRIME MINISTERS, MINISTERS OF FINANCE, DEFENCE, AND EXTERNAL AFFAIRS, 1931–52[1]

UNITED KINGDOM

Prime Minister

Rt. Hon. J. Ramsay MacDonald	5 June 1929
Rt. Hon. Stanley Baldwin	7 June 1935
Rt. Hon. Neville Chamberlain	28 May 1937
Rt. Hon. W. S. Churchill	10 May 1940
Rt. Hon. C. R. Attlee	26 July 1945
Rt. Hon. W. S. Churchill	26 October 1951

Chancellor of the Exchequer

Rt. Hon. Philip Snowden	7 June 1929
Rt. Hon. Neville Chamberlain	6 November 1931
Rt. Hon. Sir John Simon	28 May 1937
Rt. Hon. Sir H. Kingsley Wood	12 May 1940
Rt. Hon. Sir John Anderson	24 September 1943
Rt. Hon. Hugh Dalton	27 July 1945
Rt. Hon. Sir Stafford Cripps	13 November 1947
Rt. Hon. H. T. Gaitskell	19 October 1950
Rt. Hon. R. A. Butler	27 October 1951

Minister for the Co-ordination of Defence

Rt. Hon. Sir Thomas Inskip	13 March 1936
Admiral of the Fleet the Rt. Hon. Lord Chatfield	28 January 1939

Minister of Defence

The Prime Minister, Rt. Hon. W. S. Churchill	11 May 1940
The Prime Minister, Rt. Hon. C. R. Attlee	27 July 1945
Rt. Hon. A. V. Alexander	4 October 1946
Rt. Hon. E. Shinwell	28 February 1950
The Prime Minister, Rt. Hon. W. S. Churchill	26 October 1951
Field-Marshal the Rt. Hon. Viscount Alexander of Tunis	28 January 1952

[1] Date when appointment was announced, unless otherwise stated.

APPENDIX B

Secretary of State for Foreign Affairs

Rt. Hon. Arthur Henderson	7 June 1929
The Most Hon. the Marquess of Reading	25 August 1931
Rt. Hon. Sir John Simon	9 November 1931
Rt. Hon. Sir Samuel Hoare	7 June 1935
Rt. Hon. R. A. Eden	22 December 1935
Rt. Hon. Viscount Halifax	25 February 1938
Rt. Hon. R. A. Eden	23 December 1940
Rt. Hon. Ernest Bevin	27 July 1945
Rt. Hon. H. S. Morrison	9 March 1951
Rt. Hon. R. A. Eden	27 October 1951

Secretary of State for Dominion Affairs

Rt. Hon. J. H. Thomas	6 June 1930
Rt. Hon. Malcolm MacDonald	22 November 1935
Rt. Hon. Lord Stanley	16 May 1938
Rt. Hon. Malcolm MacDonald	30 October 1938
Rt. Hon. Sir Thomas Inskip (later Viscount Caldecote)	28 January 1939
Rt. Hon. R. A. Eden	3 September 1939
Rt. Hon. Viscount Caldecote	14 May 1940
Rt. Hon. Viscount Cranborne (later Lord Salisbury)	3 October 1940
Rt. Hon. C. R. Attlee (Deputy Prime Minister)	19 February 1942
Rt. Hon. Viscount Cranborne	25 September 1943
Rt. Hon. Viscount Addison	3 August 1945

Secretary of State for Commonwealth Relations

Rt. Hon. Viscount Addison	3 July 1947
Rt. Hon. P. J. Noel-Baker	14 October 1947
Rt. Hon. P. C. Gordon Walker	28 February 1950
General the Rt. Hon. Lord Ismay	27 October 1951
The Most Hon. the Marquess of Salisbury	12 March 1952
Rt. Hon. Viscount Swinton	24 November 1952

Secretary of State for India

Rt. Hon. W. Wedgwood Benn	7 June 1929
Rt. Hon. Sir Samuel Hoare	25 August 1931
The Most Hon. the Marquess of Zetland	7 June 1935
Rt. Hon. L. S. Amery	13 May 1940
Rt. Hon. Lord Pethick-Lawrence	3 August 1945
Rt. Hon. the Earl of Listowel	17 April 1947

Secretary of State for Burma

The Most Hon. the Marquess of Zetland	1 April 1937
Rt. Hon. L. S. Amery	13 May 1940

APPENDIX B

Rt. Hon. Lord Pethick-Lawrence   3 August 1945
Rt. Hon. the Earl of Listowel   17 April 1947

Secretary of State for the Colonies

Rt. Hon. Lord Passfield	7 June 1929
Rt. Hon. J. H. Thomas	25 August 1931
Rt. Hon. Sir Philip Cunliffe-Lister	9 November 1931
Rt. Hon. Malcolm MacDonald	7 June 1935
Rt. Hon. J. H. Thomas	22 November 1935
Rt. Hon. W. G. A. Ormsby-Gore	29 May 1936
Rt. Hon. Malcolm MacDonald	16 May 1938
Rt. Hon. Lord Lloyd	12 May 1940
Rt. Hon. Lord Moyne	8 February 1941
Rt. Hon. Viscount Cranborne	22 February 1942
Rt. Hon. O. F. G. Stanley	22 November 1942
Rt. Hon. G. H. Hall	3 August 1945
Rt. Hon. A. Creech Jones	4 October 1946
Rt. Hon. James Griffiths	28 February 1950
Rt. Hon. Oliver Lyttelton	27 October 1951

CANADA

Prime Minister

Rt. Hon. R. B. Bennett	7 August 1930
Rt. Hon. W. L. Mackenzie King	23 October 1935
Rt. Hon. L. S. St. Laurent	15 November 1948

Minister of Finance

The Prime Minister, Rt. Hon. R. B. Bennett	7 August 1930
Hon. E. N. Rhodes	3 February 1932
Hon. C. A. Dunning	23 October 1935
Hon. James Ralston	6 September 1939
Hon. J. L. Ilsley	8 July 1940
Hon. D. C. Abbott	10 December 1946

Minister of National Defence

Lieut.-Col. the Hon. D. M. Sutherland	7 August 1930
Hon. Ian Mackenzie	23 October 1935
Hon. Norman Rogers	19 September 1939
Hon. James Ralston	5 July 1940
Gen. the Hon. A. G. L. McNaughton	2 November 1944
Hon. D. C. Abbott	18 April 1945
Hon. Brooke Claxton	12 December 1946

Secretary of State for External Affairs

The Prime Minister, Rt. Hon. R. B. Bennett   7 August 1930

APPENDIX B

The Prime Minister, Rt. Hon. W. L.
   Mackenzie King   23 October 1935
Rt. Hon. L. S. St. Laurent   4 September 1946
Hon. Lester Pearson   10 September 1948

AUSTRALIA[1]

Prime Minister

Rt. Hon. J. H. Scullin	22 October 1929
Rt. Hon. J. A. Lyons	6 January 1932
Rt. Hon. Sir Earle Page	7 April 1939
Rt. Hon. R. G. Menzies	20 April 1939
Hon. A. W. Fadden	29 August 1941
Rt. Hon. J. Curtin	7 October 1941
Rt. Hon. F. M. Forde (Acting)	6 July 1945
Rt. Hon. J. B. Chifley	13 July 1945
Rt. Hon. R. G. Menzies	19 December 1949

The Treasurer

Hon. E. G. Theodore	29 January 1931
The Prime Minister, Rt. Hon. J. A. Lyons	6 January 1932
Hon. R. G. Casey	3 October 1935
The Prime Minister, Rt. Hon. R. G. Menzies	26 April 1939
Hon. P. C. Spender	14 March 1940
Hon. A. W. Fadden	28 October 1940
The Prime Minister, Hon. A. W. Fadden	29 August 1941
Hon. J. B. Chifley	7 October 1941
The Prime Minister, Rt. Hon. J. B. Chifley	13 July 1945
Rt. Hon. A. W. Fadden (Sir Arthur Fadden 1951)	19 December 1949

Minister of Defence

Hon. A. E. Green	October 1941
Hon. J. B. Chifley	3 March 1931
Senator the Rt. Hon. Sir George Pearce	6 January 1932
Hon. R. A. Parkhill	12 October 1934
Hon. H. V. C. Thorby	29 November 1937
Brigadier the Hon. G. A. Street	7 November 1938
The Prime Minister, Rt. Hon. R. G. Menzies	13 November 1939
Rt. Hon. R. G. Menzies	29 August 1941
The Prime Minister, Rt. Hon. J. Curtin	7 October 1941

[1] Date when sworn in.

APPENDIX B

Rt. Hon. J. A. Beasley — 6 July 1945
Hon. J. Dedman — 1 November 1946
Hon. E. J. Harrison — 19 December 1949
Senator the Hon. P. A. M. MacBride — 11 May 1951

Minister of External Affairs

The Prime Minister, Rt. Hon. J. H. Scullin — 22 October 1929
Hon. J. G. Latham — 6 January 1932
Senator the Rt. Hon. Sir George Pearce — 12 October 1934
Rt. Hon. W. M. Hughes — 29 November 1937
Hon. Sir Henry Gullett — 26 April 1939
Hon. J. McEwen — 14 March 1940
Hon. Sir Frederick Stewart — 28 October 1940
Rt. Hon. H. V. Evatt — 7 October 1941
Hon. P. C. Spender — 19 December 1949
Rt. Hon. R. G. Casey — 26 April 1951

NEW ZEALAND[1]

Prime Minister

Rt. Hon. G. W. Forbes — 28 May 1930
Rt. Hon. M. J. Savage — 6 December 1935
Rt. Hon. P. Fraser — 1 April 1940
Rt. Hon. S. G. Holland — 13 December 1949

Minister of Finance

The Prime Minister, Rt. Hon. G. W. Forbes — 28 May 1930
Hon. W. D. Stewart — 22 September 1931
Rt. Hon. J. G. Coates — 28 January 1933
Hon. W. Nash (P.C. 1946) — 6 December 1935
The Prime Minister, Rt. Hon. S. G. Holland — 13 December 1949

Minister of Defence

Hon. J. G. Cobbe — 28 May 1930
Hon. Frederick Jones — 6 December 1935
Hon. T. L. MacDonald — 13 December 1949

Minister of External Affairs

The Prime Minister, Rt. Hon. G. W. Forbes — 28 May 1930
The Prime Minister, Rt. Hon. M. J. Savage — 6 December 1935
Hon. F. Langstone — 1 April 1940

[1] Date when sworn in.

APPENDIX B

The Prime Minister, Rt. Hon. P. Fraser   7 July 1943
Hon. F. W. Doidge   13 December 1949
Hon. T. C. Webb   19 September 1951

SOUTH AFRICA

Prime Minister and Minister of External Affairs
  General the Hon. J. B. M. Hertzog   30 June 1924
  Rt. Hon. J. C. Smuts   6 September 1939
  Hon. D. F. Malan   4 June 1948

Minister of Finance
  Hon. N. C. Havenga   30 June 1924
  Hon. J. H. Hofmeyr   6 September 1939
  Hon. F. C. Sturrock   15 January 1948
  Hon. N. C. Havenga   4 June 1948

Minister of Defence
  Hon. F. H. Creswell   30 June 1924
  Hon. O. Pirow   30 March 1933
  The Prime Minister, Rt. Hon. J. C. Smuts   6 September 1939
  Hon. F. C. Erasmus   4 June 1948

IRELAND: EIRE

President of the Executive Council: Taoiseach
  Mr. William T. Cosgrave   9 September 1922
  Mr. Éamon de Valera   9 March 1932
  Mr. John A. Costello   18 February 1948

Minister for Finance
  Mr. Ernest Blythe   20 September 1923
  Mr. Seán MacEntee   9 March 1932
  Mr. Seán T. O'Kelly   14 September 1939
  Mr. Frank Aiken   25 June 1945
  Mr. Patrick McGilligan   18 February 1948

Minister for Defence
  Mr. Desmond Fitzgerald   23 June 1927
  Mr. Frank Aiken   9 March 1932
  Mr. Oscar Traynor   24 September 1939
  Dr. T. F. O'Higgins   18 February 1948

Minister for External Affairs
  Mr. Patrick McGilligan   12 October 1927
    The President, Éamon de Valera   9 March 1932
  Mr. Seán MacBride   18 February 1948

INDIA

The Prime Minister, Minister of External Affairs and Commonwealth Relations
    The Hon. Pandit Jawaharlal Nehru   15 August 1947

Minister of Finance
    Hon. Shanmukham Chetty   15 August 1947
    Hon. Dr. John Matthai   30 September 1948
    Hon. C. D. Deshmukh   25 May 1950

Minister of Defence
    Hon. Sardar Baldev Singh   15 August 1947
    Hon. N. Gopalaswami Ayyangar   13 May 1952

PAKISTAN

Prime Minister and Minister of Defence
    Hon. Liaqat Ali Khan   15 August 1947
    Hon. Khwaja Nazimuddin   24 October 1951

Minister of Finance and Economic Affairs
    Hon. Ghulam Mohammad   15 August 1947
    Hon. Mohammed Ali   24 October 1951

Minister of Foreign Affairs and Commonwealth Relations
    Hon. Sir Muhammad Zafrulla Khan   15 August 1947

CEYLON

Prime Minister, Minister of Defence and External Affairs
    Rt. Hon. D. S. Senanayake   4 February 1948
    Hon. Dudley Senanayake   25 March 1952

Minister of Finance
    Hon. J. R. Jayawardene   4 February 1948

APPENDIX C

COMMONWEALTH REPRESENTATION WITHIN THE COMMONWEALTH, 1931–52

HIGH COMMISSIONERS FOR THE DOMINIONS IN THE UNITED KINGDOM

Canada

The Hon. G. H. Ferguson	1930
The Hon. Vincent Massey	1935
Mr. N. A. Robertson	1946
Mr. L. D. Wilgress	1949
Mr. N. A. Robertson	1952

Australia

Major-General the Hon. Sir G. de L. Ryrie	1927
Rt. Hon. S. M. Bruce	1933
Rt. Hon. J. A. Beasley[1]	1945
Mr. N. R. Mighell (Acting High Commissioner)	1949
Hon. E. J. Harrison[2] (Resident Minister)	1950
Mr. T. W. (later Sir Thomas) White	1951

New Zealand

Sir Thomas Wilford	1930
Sir James Parr	1934
The Hon. W. J. Jordan (P.C. 1946)	1936
Mr. F. W. Doidge	1951

South Africa

Mr. C. T. te Water	1929
Mr. S. F. Waterson	1939
Colonel the Hon. Deneys Reitz	1942
Mr. G. Heaton Nicholls	1944
Mr. L. Egeland	1948
Dr. A. L. Geyer	1950

Ireland High Commissioner, Ambassador for the Republic of Ireland, July 1950[3]

Mr. J. W. Dulanty	1930
Mr. F. H. Boland	1950

[1] Mr. Beasley was appointed as Resident Minister and retained his portfolio as Minister for Defence, holding full Cabinet rank until November 1946. He assumed the title of High Commissioner in August 1946.

[2] Mr. Harrison retained his appointment as Minister for Defence and membership of the Cabinet while holding office.

[3] The Commonwealth Relations Office remains the Department responsible for relations with the Irish Republic.

APPENDIX C

India
    Mr. V. K. Krishna Menon   1947
    Mr. B. G. Kher   1952

Pakistan
    Habib I. Rahimtoola   1947
    Mr. M. A. H. Ispahani   1952

Ceylon
    Sir Oliver Goonetilleke   1948
    Mr. E. A. P. Wijeyeratne   1951

REPRESENTATIVES OF THE COMMONWEALTH IN CANADA

High Commissioner for the United Kingdom in Canada
    Sir William Clark   1928
    Sir Francis L. C. Floud   1935
    Sir Gerald Campbell   1938
    Rt. Hon. Malcolm MacDonald   1941
    Sir Alexander Clutterbuck   1946
    Sir Archibald Nye   1952

High Commissioner for the Commonwealth of Australia in Canada
    Major-General Sir William Glasgow   1939
    Hon. Alfred Stirling   1945
    Rt. Hon. F. M. Forde   1946
    Professor Sir Douglas Copland   1953

High Commissioner for New Zealand in Canada
    Hon. David Wilson   1944
    Hon. James Thorn   1947
    Mr. T. C. A. Hislop   1950

Accredited Representative, later High Commissioner (1945), for the Union of South Africa in Canada
    Mr. D. de Waal Meyer   1938
    Dr. P. R. Viljoen   1945
    Mr. H. H. Woodward (Acting H. C.)   1949
    Mr. A. A. Roberts   1949

High Commissioner for Eire in Canada, Ambassador for the Republic of Ireland, April 1950
    Hon. J. J. Hearne   1939
    Mr. Seán Murphy   1950

APPENDIX C

High Commissioner for India in Canada

Hon. Sardar Hardit Singh Malik	1947
Hon. S. K. Kirpalani	1949
Mr. R. R. Saksena	1951

High Commissioner for Pakistan in Canada

Hon. Mohammed Ali	1949

REPRESENTATIVES OF THE COMMONWEALTH IN AUSTRALIA

Representative, later High Commissioner (1936) in the Commonwealth of H.M.'s Government in the United Kingdom

Mr. E. T. Crutchley (Acting Representative)	1931
Sir Geoffrey Whiskard	1936
Rt. Hon. Sir Ronald Cross	1941
Rt. Hon. E. J. Williams	1946
Sir Stephen Holmes	1952

High Commissioner for Canada in the Commonwealth of Australia

Mr. Charles J. Burchell	1939
Major-General Victor Odlum	1941
The Hon. Mr. Justice T. C. Davis	1942
Mr. Kenneth Greene	1947
Major-General the Hon. L. R. La Flèche	1949
Mr. C. M. Croft (Acting H.C.)	1950
Mr. C. Fraser Elliot	1951

High Commissioner for New Zealand in the Commonwealth of Australia

Mr. C. A. Berendsen	1943
The Hon. J. G. Barclay	1944
Mr. G. E. Alderton	1950

High Commissioner for the Union of South Africa in the Commonwealth of Australia

Dr. P. R. Viljoen	1949
Mr. G. C. Nel (Acting H.C.)	1951

High Commissioner for Eire in the Commonwealth of Australia, Ambassador of the Irish Republic, September 1950

Dr. the Hon. T. J. Kiernan	1946

High Commissioner for India in the Commonwealth of Australia

Sir Raghunath P. Paranjpye	1944
Lieut.-Colonel Daya Singh Bedi	1948
Rajkumar K. S. Duleepsinhji	1950

High Commissioner for Pakistan in the Commonwealth of Australia
 Yusuf Abdoola Haroon   1950

High Commissioner for Ceylon in the Commonwealth of Australia
 Mr. J. Aubrey Martenz   1949

REPRESENTATIVES OF THE COMMONWEALTH IN NEW ZEALAND

High Commissioner for the United Kingdom in New Zealand
 Sir Harry Batterbee   1939
 Sir Patrick Duff   1945
 Sir Roy Price   1949

High Commissioner for Canada in New Zealand
 Dr. W. A. Riddell   1940
 Mr. A. Rive   1946

High Commissioner for the Commonwealth of Australia in New Zealand
 Mr. Thomas D'Alton   1943
 Mr. A. R. Cutler   1946

High Commissioner for Pakistan in New Zealand, Resident in Australia
 Yusuf Abdoola Haroon   1950

REPRESENTATIVES OF THE COMMONWEALTH IN SOUTH AFRICA

High Commissioner for Basutoland, the Bechuanaland Protectorate, and Swaziland, and High Commissioner for the United Kingdom in the Union of South Africa
 Sir Herbert Stanley   1930
 Sir William Clark   1935
 Sir Edward Harding   1940
 The Rt. Hon. Lord Harlech   1941
 Sir Evelyn Baring   1944
 Sir John Le Rougetel   1951

High Commissioner for Canada in the Union of South Africa
 Dr. Henry Laureys   1940
 Mr. Charles J. Burchell   1944
 Mr. J. C. MacGillivray (Acting)   1945
 Mr. E. D'Arcy McGreer   1946
 Mr. T. W. L. MacDermot   1950

High Commissioner for the Commonwealth of Australia in the Union of South Africa
 Sir G. Knowles   1946
 Mr. Alfred Stirling   1948
 Mr. J. P. Quinn (Acting H.C.)   1951
 Lieut.-Colonel W. R. Hodgson   1952

APPENDIX C 435

High Commissioner for India in the Union of South Africa

    Sir Shafa'at Ahmad Khan   1941
    R. M. Deshmukh   1944
    High Commissioner withdrawn   1946

REPRESENTATIVES OF THE COMMONWEALTH IN EIRE

British Representative in Eire, Ambassador to the Republic of Ireland, July 1950

    Sir John Maffey (later Lord Rugby)   1939
    Sir Gilbert Laithwaite   1949
    Sir Walter Hankinson   1951

High Commissioner for Canada in Eire, Ambassador to the Republic of Ireland, April 1950

    Mr. J. H. Kelly   1940
    Mr. J. D. Kearney   1941
    Mr. Merchant M. Mahoney   1945
    Mr. E. J. Garland (Acting H.C.)   1946
    Hon. W. F. A. Turgeon   1946

High Commissioner for the Commonwealth of Australia in Eire, Chargé d'Affaires to the Republic of Ireland, September 1950

    Mr. W. J. Dignam   1946
    Dr. W. A. Wynes   1950
    N. St. C. Deschamps   1952

REPRESENTATIVES OF THE COMMONWEALTH IN INDIA

High Commissioner for the United Kingdom in India

    Mr. T. H. (later Sir Terence) Shone   1946
    Sir Archibald Nye   1949
    Sir Alexander Clutterbuck   1952

High Commissioner for Canada in India

    Mr. J. D. Kearney   1947
    Mr. W. F. Chipman   1949

High Commissioner for the Commonwealth of Australia in India

    Lieut.-General Sir Iven Mackay   1943
    Mr. H. R. Gollan   1949
    Professor W. R. Crocker   1952

High Commissioner for Pakistan in India

    Zahid Hussain   1947
    Muhammad Ismail   1948

APPENDIX C

Representative, High Commissioner (1949) for Ceylon in India

    Mr. M. W. H. de Silva   1946
    Mr. C. Coomaraswamy   1949

REPRESENTATIVES OF THE COMMONWEALTH IN PAKISTAN

High Commissioner for the United Kingdom in Pakistan

    Sir Laurence Grafftey-Smith   1947
    Sir Gilbert Laithwaite   1951

High Commissioner for Canada in Pakistan

    Mr. D. M. Johnson   1949
    Mr. K. P. Kirkwood   1952

High Commissioner for the Commonwealth of Australia in Pakistan

    Mr. J. E. Oldham   1949
    Major-General L. E. Beavis   1952

High Commissioner for India in Pakistan

    Sri Prakasa   1947
    Dr. Sita Ram   1949
    Major-General Khub Chand (Acting)   1950
    Dr. Mohan Sinha Mehta   1951

High Commissioner for Ceylon in Pakistan

    Mr. T. B. Jayah   1950

REPRESENTATIVES OF THE COMMONWEALTH IN CEYLON

High Commissioner for the United Kingdom in Ceylon

    Sir Walter Hankinson   1948
    Sir Cecil Syers   1951

High Commissioner for Australia in Ceylon

    Hon. C. W. Frost   1948
    Dr. J. W. Burton   1951
    Mr. A. R. Cutler   1952

High Commissioner for India in Ceylon

    Mr. V. V. Giri   1947
    Mr. Raghavachary   1950
    Mr. K. P. Kesava Menon   1951

High Commissioner for Pakistan in Ceylon

    Haji Abdus Sattar Saith   1952

APPENDIX D

COMMONWEALTH REPRESENTATION IN FOREIGN COUNTRIES, 1931–52

CANADA

1931	*December 1939*	*1945*	*1952*	
France*	Belgium and	Argentina	Argentina	Iceland*
Japan*	the Nether-	Belgium	Belgium	Italy
U.S.A.*	lands*	Brazil	Brazil	Japan
Advisory	France*	Chile*	Chile	Luxemburg*
Officer	Japan*	China	Cuba	Mexico
to the	U.S.A.*	Czechoslovakia*	Czechoslovakia†	Netherlands
League of	Permanent	Cuba*	Denmark*	Norway*
Nations,	Delegate,	France	Finland*	Peru
Geneva	League of	Greece	France	Poland†
	Nations	Luxemburg*	Germany	Portugal*
		Netherlands*	Greece	Sweden
		Norway*		Switzerland
		Peru		Turkey
		U.S.A.		United Nations
		U.S.S.R.		(Permanent
		Yugoslavia*		Representative)
				U.S.A.
				U.S.S.R.
				Yugoslavia

AUSTRALIA

1931	*December 1939*	*1945*	*1952*	
	U.S.A.*	Brazil*	Brazil*	Japan
		Chile*	Burma*	Netherlands
		China*	Egypt*	Philippines*
		France*	France	Thailand*
		Netherlands*	Germany	United Nations
		U.S.A.*	Indo-China*	(Permanent
		U.S.S.R.*	Indonesia	Representative)
			Israel*	U.S.A.
			Italy*	U.S.S.R.

* denotes the rank of Envoy Extraordinary and Minister Plenipotentiary or of Minister and † that of Chargé d'Affaires; otherwise, representatives have the rank of Ambassador.

APPENDIX D

NEW ZEALAND

1931	1939	1945	1952
		U.S.A.*	France†
		U.S.S.R.*	United Nations (Permanent Delegate)
			U.S.A.

SOUTH AFRICA

1931	December 1939	1945	1952	
Italy*	Belgium*	Belgium*	Argentina*	United Nations
Netherlands*	France*	France	Belgium*	(Permanent
U.S.A.*	Italy*	Greece*	Brazil*	Representa-
	Netherlands*	Netherlands*	Chile*	tive)
	Portugal*	Portugal*	Egypt*	U.S.A.
	Sweden*	Sweden*	France	
	U.S.A.*	U.S.A.*	Germany*	
	Accredited Representative to the League of Nations		Greece*	
			Italy*	
			Netherlands	
			Portugal*	
			Spain*	
			Sweden*	

EIRE

1931	December 1939	1945
France*	France and Belgium*	France and Belgium*
Germany*	Germany†	Germany†
Holy See*	Holy See*	Holy See*
U.S.A.*	Italy*	Italy*
League of Nations (Permanent Delegate)	Spain*	Portugal†
	U.S.A.*	Spain*
		Switzerland†
		U.S.A.*

INDIA
1952

Afghanistan	Czechoslovakia	Japan (Head of Mission)	Switzerland*
Argentina	Denmark*	Jordon*	Syria*
Austria*	Egypt	Lebanon*	Thailand
Belgium	Ethiopia*	Luxemburg*	Turkey
Brazil	Finland*	Mexico	United Nations (Permanent Representative)
Burma	France	Nepal	U.S.A.
Chile*	Germany	Netherlands	U.S.S.R.
China	Indonesia	Norway*	Vatican*
	Iran	Philippines*	Yugoslavia†
	Iraq*	Portugal†	
	Italy†	Sweden*	

APPENDIX D

PAKISTAN
1952

Afghanistan	Iran
Belgium	Iraq*
Brazil	Italy*
Burma	Japan
China	Jordon, Lebanon and Syria*
Denmark, Finland, Norway, Sweden*¹	Netherlands†
Egypt, Saudi Arabia*	Spain
France	Turkey
Germany	United Nations (Permanent Representative)
Indonesia	U.S.A.
	U.S.S.R.

CEYLON

Burma
Italy*
U.S.A.

[1] Minister Resident in Stockholm.

APPENDIX E

RESULTS OF PARLIAMENTARY ELECTIONS IN THE COMMONWEALTH, 1931-52

UNITED KINGDOM

Parties	October 1931 Seats	October 1931 Votes[1]	November 1935 Seats	November 1935 Votes	July 1945 Seats	July 1945 Votes	February 1950 Seats	February 1950 Votes	October 1951 Seats	October 1951 Votes
Conservative (formerly Unionist) and Associates	521	13,134,301	431	11,791,461	212	9,960,809	298	12,501,983	321	13,724,418
Liberal	33	1,405,102	17	1,377,962	12	2,245,319	9	2,621,489	6	730,551
Labour and Associates	56	6,865,330	163	8,614,748	389	12,149,605	315	13,295,736	295	13,948,385
Independents and others	5	254,671	4	217,666	18	623,216	2	350,269	3	198,969
Total	615	..	615	..	640	..	624	..	625	..

CANADA

Parties	June 1930 Seats	June 1930 Votes	October 1935 Seats	October 1935 Votes	March 1940 Seats	March 1940 Votes	June 1945 Seats	June 1945 Votes	June 1949 Seats	June 1949 Votes
Liberal (together with Liberal Progressives and Independent Liberals)	91	1,774,333	178	2,060,890	184	2,411,197	127	2,170,625	193	2,926,029
Conservative (later Progressive-Conservative)	139	1,930,470	40	1,312,537	40	1,396,749	68	1,455,453	41	..
Social Credit	..	..	17	182,767	10	119,038	13	214,998	10	..
Co-operative Commonwealth Federation	..	..	7	392,715	8	370,710	29	822,661	13	..
Labour	3	55,047	..	..	..	..	..	..	..	..
Independents and others	12	132,906	3	457,945	3	161,167	8	582,393	5	..
Total	245	..	245	..	245	..	245	..	262	..

[1] These figures do not take into account 61 constituencies returning Conservative supporters unopposed and 6 constituencies returning unopposed Labour supporters.

COMMONWEALTH OF AUSTRALIA

Parties	December 1931		September 1934		October 1937		September 1940		August 1943		September 1946		December 1949		April 1951	
	Seats	Votes	Seats	Votes	Seats	Votes	Seats	Votes	Seats	Votes	Seats	Votes	Seats	Votes	Seats	Votes
United Australia Party, later Liberal Party	38	1,409,490	32	1,287,581	28	1,158,835	25	} 1,743,282	14	1,085,324	17	1,398,932	54	1,813,782	} 69	2,298,512
Country Party	13	431,305	15	480,279	17	350,082	14		9	366,978	12	515,374	20	500,349		
Labour (including Federal, State and Lang Labour)	18	1,194,536	27	1,495,679	29	1,325,614	34	1,866,853	49	2,117,167	43	2,159,956	47	2,149,958	52	2,174,840
Independents and others	2	136,703	..	287,846	..	218,306	1	93,655	2	552,996	..	116,906	..	140,300	..	92,547
Total	71	..	74	..	74	..	74	..	74	..	72	..	121	..	121	..

NEW ZEALAND

Parties	December 1931		November 1935		October 1938		September 1943		November 1946		November 1949		August 1951	
	Seats	Votes	Seats	Votes	Seats	Votes	Seats	Votes	Seats	Votes	Seats	Votes	Seats	Votes
Labour	25	244,881	55	292,965	53	528,296	44	410,594	42	536,798	34	469,766	30	446,545
National and Reform Party	29 22	396,004 73,626	19	280,222	25	381,080	34	368,119	38	507,043	46	515,649	50	518,721
Independents and others	4	714,511	6	179,450	2	37,022	2	83,221	..	3,070	..	9,717	..	1,837
Total	80	..	80	..	80	..	80	..	80	..	80	..	80	..

APPENDIX E

UNION OF SOUTH AFRICA

Parties	June 1929		May 1933		May 1938		July 1943		May 1948	
	Seats	Votes	Seats	Votes	Seats	Votes	Seats	Votes	Seats	Votes
Nationalist	78	144,907	75	..	27	259,450	43	347,057	70	442,338
Afrikaner Party	..	..	..	..	..	..	..	..	9	
Labour Party	8	31,883	4	..	3	43,193	9	..	6	
United Party	..	..	..	..	111	445,871	89	610,143 (includes Ind. and others)	65	559,331
South African Party (Dominion Party 1938-43)	61	156,398[1]	61	..	8	57,759	7	..	..	..
Independents and others	1	13,544	10	..	1	30,848	2	..	..	64,385
Total	148	..	150	..	150	..	150	..	150	..

[1] This figure does not include nine seats returned unopposed.

IRISH FREE STATE: EIRE

Parties	February 1932		June 1933		July 1937		June 1938		June 1943		May 1944		February 1948	
	Seats	Votes	Seats	Votes	Seats	Votes	Seats	Votes	Seats	Votes	Seats	Votes	Seats	Votes
Fianna Fáil	72	566,475	77	689,458	68	599,524	77	668,000	66	557,574	76	595,433	68	553,917
Fine Gael (formerly Cumann na nGaedheal)	57	449,810	48	417,467	48	461,258	45	428,000	32	307,651	30	249,231	31	262,202
Labour (including National Labour)	7	98,285	8	79,222	13	132,657	9	129,000	17	208,813	12	139,499	19	146,831
Independents	12	117,333	9	68,892	8	131,488	7	61,000	8	108,975	7	95,177	14	112,816
Farmers	5	41,302	11	126,795	..	..	..	..	14	149,328	13	137,984	5	71,686
Clann na Poblachta	..	..	..	..	..	..	..	..	..	..	..	..	10	173,166
Total	153	..	153	..	138	..	138	..	137	..	138	..	147	..

APPENDIX E

REPUBLIC OF INDIA
General Election 1952

Party	Seats*	Votes
Congress	362	47,588,000
Socialist	12	11,129,000
K.M.P. Party	10	6,147,000
Communist and Allies	27	5,723,000
Scheduled Caste Federation	2	2,438,000
Independents	36	15,792,000
Others	40	17,171,000
Total	489	..

* The total number of seats is 497 which includes seats filled other than by direct election.

CEYLON
Election June 1952

	Seats
Government	
United National Party	54
Pamial Congress	4
Labour	1
Independent	10
Opposition	
Sri Lanka Freedom Party	9
Lanka Sama Samaj	9
Communist	3
Joint Sama-Samaj-Communist	1
Federalist	2
People's Republican Party	1
Total*	94

* This does not include the six members to be nominated by the Governor-General to represent interests not already represented by elected members.

INDEX

A.B.D.A. Command, 136, 141.
Addison, Lord, 249, 403.
Africa: defence of 'white civilization' modifies South African Nationalist opposition to war, 35–36; Smuts emphasizes danger of hostile control of French and Belgian colonies, 44–45.
Africa, East: conference of East African Governors, 311.
Africa, North: Pakistan's disapproval of NATO's association with French repressive policy, 360.
Africa, South:
  Communism: opposition of the European ruling classes, 361–2 and cf. 365.
  Equal language rights: safeguarded at Union (1909), 391–2.
  High Commission territories: Union claims to, 395–7.
  Political parties: the reunion of Hertzogite and Gesuiwerde Nationalists, 33 n.3, 76; the Ossewa Brandwag, 78; Pirow's New Order group, 78; fundamental divisions within the reunited Nationalists, 78–79; Hertzog's resignation from party, 79; the general election of 1943, 159, 442; Smuts and the division of the Nationalist party, 413.
  Racial policy: denounced by India, 358; *apartheid*, 361–2; discrimination against citizens of Indian descent, 362–3; abolition of the Cape franchise, 391, 392–5; criticisms of the admission to the Commonwealth of Asian and African States, 417–18.
  Republicanism: associated with the demand for separate peace, 155–7; the precedent of Ireland, 155; Nationalist motion for establishment of republic defeated (1942), 155–7; the draft constitution in *Die Burger*, 157–8; republican gains in election of 1943, 159.
  Second World War: declaration of war, 3–4; rejection of compulsory service outside Africa, 29, 35–36; the Nationalist parties and opposition to war with Germany, 33–36; deficiencies in preparation, 36; effect of Italy's entry into the war, 76; Nationalist motion for separate peace, rejected (August 1940), 76–77; Nationalist belief in inevitability of German victory, 76–77, 77–78; represented at Eastern Group Conference (1940), 84; reaction to Japanese successes, 158; increased support for the war effort (1942–3), 158–60.
  South-West Africa, incorporated in Union, 362.
  See also BRITISH COMMONWEALTH; CROWN; DOMINIONS; HERTZOG; LOUW; MALAN; PIROW; SMUTS; SOUTH AFRICA ACT; STRIJDOM; UNITED NATIONS.
Africa, South-West: desire to retain modifies South African Nationalist opposition to war, 35; incorporated in Union of S. Africa, 362.
Africa, West: Gt. Britain appoints Resident Minister, 311 and n.3.
Age, The (Melbourne), 170.
Alexander, F.-M. Lord, 143, 282.
Alexander, Mr. A. V., 214.
Altrincham, Lord, 385.
Amery, L. S.: on the drafting of the Balfour Report, 9 n.4; proposes creation of Imperial War Cabinet, 25; on nationalist opposition in the dominions to centralized institutions, 26; on Indian representation on the Pacific War Council, 137 n.2; member of Cabinet sub-committee for Indian affairs, 145.
Anderson, Sir John, 145.
Anglo-American Combined Boards, 128–30.
Anglo-Egyptian Treaty (1936), *see under* TREATIES AND AGREEMENTS.
Anglo-Irish Agreement (1938), *see under* TREATIES AND AGREEMENTS.
Anglo-Irish Treaty (1921), *see under* TREATIES AND AGREEMENTS.
Anglo-Japanese Agreement, *see under* TREATIES AND AGREEMENTS.
Anglo-Russian Agreement (1941), *see under* TREATIES AND AGREEMENTS.
Anti-Fascist People's Freedom League (Burma), 244.
Antigua, 49.

Arabia, and the Balkans campaign (1941), 97 n.3.
Asian Conference (1947), 239–40.
Assam, in partition between India and Pakistan, 213, 216, 230.
Atlantic Charter, 120, 144, 193–4.
Atomic Energy Commission, 319.
Attlee, Mr. C. R.: as Secretary for Dominions, 93, 402–3; chairman of Cabinet sub-committee for Indian affairs, 145; and the Cripps Mission to India, 146; and the Labour party's Indian policy, 211 f.; and the Cabinet Mission to India (1946), 214–15; on Lord Halifax's support of Labour party's Indian policy, 227 n.1; plans for transfer of power to India, 229; on the Indian Independence Act (1947), 234; on the relation of the Princely States to an independent India, 235; on secession of Burma, 246; his visit to Ireland raises hopes of the abolition of partition, 279 and n.2; on Mr. Costello's announcement of his decision to repeal the External Relations Act, 283 n.5; discusses secession problems with Irish Ministers, 284–5; counters Irish protests against the Ireland Act (1949), 291; on the relation to the Commonwealth of republican India and Ireland, 296; and the Anglo-Egyptian treaty, 322 f.; on Western Union and Commonwealth relations, 332 f.; urges on the U.S.A. the danger of extending the Korean War, 351–2; rejects the use of force to preserve Commonwealth membership, 382.
Auchinleck, General Sir C. J. E., 116 f.
Aung San, U, 244–5.
Australia:
Labour party: increased appreciation of Commonwealth unity, 167 and n.2; sympathy with Asian nationalism, 358.
Second World War: declaration of war, 3; defence organization in 1939, 28; plans for employment of forces, 30–33; co-operation with New Zealand in defence matters, 31–32; requests for appreciations of military situation, 41 n.1; Parliament and the declaration of war on German allies, 43 and n.3, 135; Lend-Lease agreement with U.S.A., 56 n.4; represented at Eastern Group Conference (1940), 84 f.; fears of Japanese invasion, 86, 139–42; appointment of first Australian Minister at Washington, 86 f.; efforts to improve relations with Japan, 86–87; co-ordination of British and Australian policy in the Far East (1940), 87–88; concern for defence deficiencies at Singapore and conference (1940), 88–89; demand for closer collaboration between Australian and Imperial Governments, 89–90; and the campaign in Greece, 95–102, 105–6; the Syrian campaign (1941), 102–3, 104 n.2; control and disposition of forces, 104; concern at withdrawal of U.S. fleet to Atlantic, 109; proposals for Imperial War Cabinet, 110–15; appointment of Sir Earle Page as special envoy in London, 113–14; Canadian and Australian views on imperial co-operation contrasted, 115; the Tobruk dispute, 116–17; and the relative importance of the Middle and Far East, 117–18, 120; urges necessity of British Commonwealth warning to Japan (1941), 118, 119–20; Australian reliance on U.S. naval strength in the Pacific, 120–1; divergent views on Japan of Australia and U.K. in December 1941, 122–3; reactions to Japan's entry into war, 130–5; complains of U.K.'s neglect of Far Eastern defence, 131–2; seeks American assistance in Malaya, 132; requests for representation in War Cabinet (1942), 134–5; protests against proposed agreement for unified command in south-west Pacific (1941–2), 136; the Pacific War Councils, 136–9; conflict with British view of Japanese intentions (1942), 139–42; loss of division at Singapore, 141; refusal of British request for diversion of troops to Rangoon, 141–2; the 'Casey incident', 142–3; popular reaction to Japanese successes (1942), 144; revulsion from colonial system of government after Japanese successes, 144; discussion of Japanese peace settlement and command of occupation forces, 326 and n.4.
See also BRITISH COMMONWEALTH; BRUCE; CASEY; CROWN; CURTIN; DOMINIONS; EVATT; FADDEN; HASLUCK; IMPERIAL WAR CABINET; JAPAN; MENZIES; TREATIES AND

INDEX

Australia (*cont.*):
    AGREEMENTS; UNITED NATIONS; WAR CABINET.
Australia-New Zealand Agreement (1944), *see under* TREATIES AND AGREEMENTS.
Azad, Dr. Maulana: rejects the 'August offer', 83, 207; as Muslim President of Congress Party, 206; at the Simla Conference, 208; welcomes the Labour victory in general election (1945), 210.

Badoglio, Marshal, 169.
Baghdad Pact, *see under* TREATIES AND AGREEMENTS.
Bahamas, 49.
Baldwin, Mr. Stanley: on Mackenzie King's 'cold feet', 16 n.1; on the Crown as 'last link of Empire', 369.
Balfour, Earl of: on common interests as bond of Empire, 10; criticizes the restoration of self-government to Boer republics, 254.
Balfour Report: its statement of imperial relationships criticized, 6–7, 8; effect on formulation of imperial foreign policy, 10–17; and dominion status of Irish Free State, 59, 268; allegiance to the Crown an indispensable condition of dominion status, 225, 368–9; *cf. also* STATUTE OF WESTMINSTER.
Baluchistan, in partition between India and Pakistan, 213 f., 216, 230.
Bandanaraike, S. W. R. D., 375.
Bao Dai, 350, 359.
Basutoland, 395–6.
Batterbee, Sir Harry, 407.
Beasley, Mr. J. A., 404.
Bechuanaland, 395–6.
Belgium, guarantee of neutrality (1936), 364.
Benelux Customs Union (1947), 333.
Bengal: in partition between India and Pakistan, 213 f., 216, 230; riots (1946), 221 f.
Bengal, Bay of, 143.
Bennett, Maj.-Gen. Gordon, 141.
Bennett, Mr. R. B., on separation of Canadian from British foreign representation, 368.
Berehaven, 63 f.
Bermuda, 49.
Bevin, Ernest: on revision of the Anglo-Egyptian Treaty, 323–4; on Western European Union, 331–2.
Bihar, 154; riots (1946), 221 f.
Bikaner, Maharajah of, 236.
Birkenhead, 1st Earl of, 203.

Blackwell, Mr. L., 156–7.
Blamey, General: criticizes plan for Balkans campaign (1941), 99 n.2, 105–6; informs Australian Government of use of Australian troops in Syria, 102; on the control of dominion forces in the field, 107; and the Australian forces in Tobruk, 116.
Blomberg, F.-M. von, 23.
Blumentritt, Gen., 73 n.1.
Bombay, riots of 1946, 222.
Borden, Sir Robert: on the place of the dominions in imperial defence, 14; on the Imperial War Cabinet (1917–18), 25.
Borneo, North, 348.
Bose, Subhas Chandra, 154, 212 and n.3.
Botha, Gen., on benefits of decentralization in the Empire, 9, 176.
Bracken, Mr. John, 179.
Brissonnière, Y. G., 336.
British Commonwealth:
  Alliances: summary of commitments, 363–5.
  Asian members, and non-alignment policy: the first Asian Conference (1947), 240–1; the desire to avoid entanglement in Western conflict, 357–9, 360; India and non-alignment, 358–9; Indian disagreements with Western policy in Asia, 359–60; continued regard for Commonwealth ties, 360.
  China: the granting or withholding of *de facto* recognition of the People's Government, 350–1.
  Constitutions: making of, 387–9; amendment in New Zealand and Canada, 389–91; unicameral legislature, 390 and n.1.; amendment of the South Africa Act, 391–5.
  Consultation and intra-Commonwealth representation, 400–9; common discussion on foreign policy, 410; *and see below* Prime Ministers' Meetings.
  Defence: Australia and security of the Pacific, 326; devolution of responsibility on a regional basis, 326; postwar reorganization, 326–9; proposals of the 1946 White Paper, 327–9; the Pacific Security Agreement, 352–7; agreement for use of Simonstown naval base (1955), 364–5; post-war security agreements, 365–6.
  Economic co-operation: the Colombo Conference and Plan, 345–50.
  Education: the Colombo Plan and Asian students in Australia, 349.

British Commonwealth (*cont.*):
Finance Ministers' meetings, 343–4, 345, 411.
Financial relations, international: Bretton Woods (1944), 313; devaluation of sterling (1949), 342–5; Colombo Conference and Plan (1950), 345–50.
Foreign Ministers' meetings, 346–7, 411, 415.
International organization, post-war: Commonwealth statesmen's views, 307–10; conflict with British opinion and interests, 310, 314 f., 410; the wartime development of regionalism, 310–11; regionalism and functionalism in the new world order, 311–12; reaction to the Moscow Declaration (1943, United Nations), 311, 313; criticism and consideration of the Dumbarton Oaks proposals, 313–15, 410.
Korean War, 350–2.
Monarchical and republican membership, 374–6, 380–2.
Multi-racial membership, 414–18; S. African criticism of admission of Asian and African states, 417–18.
Nationality and citizenship, 382–7; the British Nationality Act (1948) and reciprocal arrangements with Ireland, 287–8, 300–1, 385–6; the traditional common status of British subjects, 382–3; dominions' legislation before the Second World War, 383; Australia raises the question of dominion nationality at San Francisco Conference, 383–4; the Canadian Citizenship Act (1946), 384; post-war dominions' legislation, 386–7.
Power and influence in the modern world, 418–21; as a unique form of political society, 187–8; gains in vitality with decline of colonialism, 194.
Prime Ministers' Meetings, 410–11, 414–15; (1944), 181–7, 400; (1946), 324–6, 400; (1948), 249–50, 329; (1949), 251–2, 296.
Privy Council, abolition of appeals to Judicial Committee of, 390 f.
Second World War: entry into war, 3–4; superficial explanations of the Nazi régime, 21–22; suggested reconstitution of the Imperial War Cabinet, 25–27; mobilization and employment of dominion forces, 28–36; dominions' rejection of conscription for overseas service, 29; provisions for wartime co-operation, 36–38; the munitions industry, 37; supply of information to, and consultation with, the dominions: the first ministerial conference, 38–41; dominions' criticism of British defence positions on the Western Front, 39; machinery for consultation, 40–41; assessments of the military and political position (May 1940), 41; the fall of France and crisis of 1940, 41–42; declaration of war on Italy, 43; action before consultation (offer of union to France, Oran), 43–44; the attempt on Dakar, 44–45, 46, 85; the need for discretion in disseminating information, 45–46; the Eastern Group Conference and Supply Council (1940), 84–85; methods of communication and co-operation with U.K., 90–95; and the campaign in Greece (1941), 95–102; control and disposition of forces, 103–7; dominions commanders' influence on strategic planning, 106–7; dominion representation in War Cabinet (1941), 107–10; and the Anglo-Russian Agreement, 108; Australian proposals for Imperial War Cabinet, 110–15; the problem of priority between the Middle and Far East, 117–18; dominions consulted on possible warning to Japan (August 1941), 118; effect on Commonwealth co-operation of U.S. entry into the war, 127–30; and the Combined Boards, 128–30; declaration of war on Finland, Hungary, and Rumania, 135; manpower and casualties, 189; stimulus to Commonwealth unity, 189–90.
Structural reform, post-war: discussions (1943–4), 164–87; Curtin's suggestions for an Imperial Secretariat, 165–73, 176 f., and cf. 325 n.3, 326; anticipation of post-war decline of U.K., 173, 178; Smuts on the future role of the Commonwealth, 173–6, 177 f.; Lord Halifax's views, 176–80; the Prime Ministers' Meeting (May 1944), 181–7.
See also individual states, and BALFOUR REPORT; COLOMBO CONFERENCE; COMMITTEE OF IMPERIAL DEFENCE; COMMONWEALTH RELATIONS OFFICE;

INDEX

British Commonwealth (*cont.*):
CROWN; DOMINIONS; IMPERIAL COMMITTEE OF DEFENCE; MUNICH CRISIS; STATUTE OF WESTMINSTER; TREATIES AND AGREEMENTS; UNITED NATIONS.

British Empire: prospect of independence for colonial peoples as incentive in Second World War, 4–5; Hitler's attitude to, 19–21; American recognition of the importance to the U.S.A. of its integrity, 119–20; the significance of Japanese successes, 143–4; the war and the attack on colonialism, 191–4; Churchill rejects U.S. trusteeship proposals, 192; British colonialism distinguished from Nazi tyranny, 193; restricted application of the Atlantic Charter, 193–4; colonial development and welfare, 346; American view of its post-war decline in power, 419–20. *See also* BRITISH COMMONWEALTH; BURMA; CEYLON; COLONIALISM; COMMITTEE OF IMPERIAL DEFENCE; DOMINIONS; IMPERIAL CONFERENCES; IMPERIAL WAR CABINET; INDIA.

British Guiana, 49.

British Nationality Act (1948): reciprocal citizenship arrangements between U.K. and Ireland, 277–8, 287–8, 300–1, 385–6; Commonwealth citizenship, 386.

British Nationality and Status of Aliens Act (1914), 382 f.

British North American Act (1867), 390–1.

Bruce, Lord: on German threat to Syria, 102; and the Japanese threat (1941), 118; conflict with British views on defence of the Far East (December 1941), 122; on the failure of the League of Nations to check aggression, 309; as Australian High Commissioner in London, 404; on exchange of information within the Commonwealth, 409.

Bulganin, Marshal, 359 n.1.

Burke, Edmund, 264.

Burma:
British rule, last phase of, 240–6, 256 and n.2; excluded from the Atlantic Charter, 193; the war and demand for independence, 240–2; discontent with U.K. offer of ultimate dominion status, 243–4; the AFPFL demands independence (1946), 244 f.

Independence and secession, 245–6; effect on trade preferences, 288 n.2.

India, separation from (1935), 241.

Second World War: entry (1939), 3, 4; plans for Australian reinforcements (1939), 30; represented at Eastern Group Conference (1940), 84; Japanese advance in, 138, 191; Australia refuses to divert troops to, 141–2; fall of Rangoon, 143; effect of Japanese successes and propaganda, 242; resistance to the Japanese a fight for independence, 243.

See also AUNG SAN, U; SAW, U.

Burma Independence Act (1947), 245.

Burma Road, 87 f.

Butler, J. R. M., 99.

Butler, Mr. R. A., 145.

Byng, Lord, 6, 377 f.

Cairo Conference (1943), 166, 400 and n.1.

Calcutta, the 1946 riots, 221 f.

Campbell, Sir Gerald, 407.

Campbell-Bannerman, Sir Henry, 234, 254.

Canada:
Commonwealth development, post-war: Canadian views, 171, 176, 178–9, 180; opposition to centralized dominion organization, 183, 185.

Newfoundland incorporated in the Confederation, 175, 397–8.

Reconstruction and welfare, post-war, 312–13.

Second World War: declaration of war, 3; plan for industrial and military assistance, 29–30; first division dispatched to France (June 1940), 42; interest in British attack on Dakar, 44; misgivings at bombardment of Oran, 44; reaction of French Canadians to fall of France, 44 n.3; and negotiations for U.S. lease of bases in Newfoundland, 50, 53–54; Ogdensburg Agreement and Canada–U.S. Joint Board on Defence, 51–53, 77; Roosevelt's pledge of assistance in case of attack (August 1938), 52; the Hyde Park Agreement with U.S.A. (1941), 56, 57–58; supply of war material to Britain and assistance in currency difficulties, 56–57; and termination of Anglo-Japanese Agreement (1940), 87–88; views on co-operation with U.K. and rejection of Imperial War Cabinet, 90–95; control and disposition of forces, 103–4; Dieppe raid, 104; contrast between Canadian and Australian views on imperial

Canada (*cont.*):
co-operation, 115; included in Combined Anglo–American Boards, 128–9; rejects proposed agreement for unified command in south-west Pacific (1941–2), 136; and Pacific War Council, 137; Canadian troops in fall of Hong Kong, 141; French Canadian feeling roused by Nazi–Soviet pact (1939), 338.
See also BRITISH COMMONWEALTH; CROWN; DOMINIONS; IMPERIAL WAR CABINET; KING, W. L. MACKENZIE; PEARSON; ST. LAURENT; TREATIES AND AGREEMENTS; UNITED NATIONS.

Canadian Citizenship Act (1946), 384, 386.

Casey, Mr. R. G., 38; criticizes British defence positions on Western Front (1939), 39; urges concessions in the Far East (1940), 86–87; and proposed Commonwealth warning to Japan (December 1941), 123; his appointment as Minister of State in Cairo, 142–3; on Gandhi, 222; on the Pacific Security Agreement, 354 ff.

'Cash and carry' replaced by Lend-Lease, 55.

Centlivres, Chief Justice, 393.

Ceylon:
Development plan, 348.
Dominion status, 240, 246–9; the Donoughmore Constitution (1931), 246–7; the Soulbury Report and 1946 Constitution, 247–8, 387–8; the Ceylon Independence Bill (1947), 248–9; agreements on defence and external affairs, 248–9, 358, 365.
India, tension with, 257.
Second World War: entry (1939), 4; represented at Eastern Group Conference (1940), 84.
See also SENANAYAKE, D. S., and DUDLEY.

Chamberlain, Sir Austen, 17 n.2.
Chamberlain, Joseph, 13–14, 326, 402.
Chamberlain, Mr. Neville: 38 ff., 63 f.; see also MUNICH CRISIS.
Chanak crisis (1922), 11, 15.
Channel Islands, in British Nationality Act, 386 n.2.
Chatfield, Lord, 63 f., 93–94, 328–9.
Chiang Kai-shek, Gen., 145, 350.
Chifley, Mr. J. B., 324, 326.
China: Britain agrees to close the Burma Road (1940), 87 f.; represented on Pacific War Council, 137 n.2; *de facto* recognition by India, Pakistan, U.K., of People's Government, 350, 359; older dominions and U.S.A. recognize Formosa Government, 350–1; Korean War, 350–2.

Church, Catholic: Hitler's attitude to, 19; French Canadian feeling roused by the Russian threat to, 338 and cf. 341.

Churchill, Mr. W. S.:
China: on recognition *de facto* of the People's Government, 350.
Commonwealth and Empire: on the Statute of Westminster, 8; on restricted application of the Atlantic Charter, 144, 193; views on the future of the Commonwealth (1944), 182; resistance to American anti-colonialism, 192; distinguishes between British colonialism and Nazi tyranny, 193; on the granting of self-government to Burma, 245 n.1; views on post-war international organization, 310 f.; and Western Union, 333; criticizes the Pacific Security Agreement, 356; on the title 'Head of the Commonwealth', 373; *see also below* India; Ireland.
India: lack of sympathy with Indian nationalism, 82; opposes the Government of India Bill (1935), 82, 199; on exclusion of India from the Atlantic Charter, 144; advocates strong government, 145; and the Cripps Mission, 146–7, 153; Indian suspicion of his concern for the depressed classes, 203; his contempt for the Constituent Assembly, 226; welcomes the London Declaration of India's position in the Commonwealth, 254 f.; his meeting with Nehru, 254 n.4.
Ireland, and neutrality, 58; denounces return of Irish ports to Irish sovereignty (1938), 64; his comments on Irish neutrality, 64–65; suggests visit of U.S. naval squadron, 68; on the effect of Irish refusal to allow use of ports, 73–74, 75; urges U.S. interest in securing Irish bases, 74; appeal to de Valera after Japanese attack on U.S.A., 160; and U.S. request for expulsion of Axis representatives in Dublin, 162, 163 n.; on republican Ireland's relation to the Commonwealth, 265, 293.

Japan: appreciation of Japanese intentions (1940), 86; doubts of appease-

INDEX

451

Churchill, Mr. W. S. (*cont.*):
ment policy in the Far East (1940), 87; the Atlantic meeting and consultation, 118–20; expects Japanese attack to be delayed until Russian collapse (October 1941), 122; unwilling to anticipate American reaction to Japanese aggression, 122–3; reassures New Zealand after Pearl Harbour, 131; and Curtin's complaints after Japanese entry into war, 131–2; and Pacific War Councils, 136 ff.; differs from Australian view of Japanese intentions (1942), 139–43; seeks to divert Australian division to Rangoon, 140–2; on the fall of Singapore, 143; and declaration of war on Japan, 160.

Second World War: reaction to the Munich crisis, 12 n.1; contact with dominions during crisis of 1940, 41–42; anticipates Hitler's drive to the east (1940), 42; retains fighter squadrons in Britain (1940), 42; his decision to attack Dakar, 44; on Britain's isolation in summer 1940, 46; and the destroyer–bases agreement with U.S.A., 46, 48–49, 49–50, 53; efforts to influence American opinion after fall of France, 47–48; doubts about declared aims of the Ogdensburg Agreement, 53; and Lend-Lease, 54 f.; and the campaign in Greece, 97 ff.; consults General Freyberg on general defence strategy, 107; his eve of invasion broadcast (June 1941), 107–8; and the Anglo-Russian Agreement (1941), 108; his personal control of war policy, 109, 127; Menzies criticizes his neglect of dominion war interests, 109–10; and proposal for Imperial War Cabinet, 110; opposes dominion representation in War Cabinet, 112–13; regrets Menzies's fall from office, 115–16; and the Tobruk dispute, 116–17; on the paramount importance of the Middle Eastern theatre, 117; and the Munitions Assignments Board, 128; and Canada's membership of the Combined Food Board, 129; and Curtin's request for Australian representative on War Cabinet, 134–5; and appointment of Casey to Cairo, 142–3; and stationing of U.S. troops in Northern Ireland, 160–1.

Ciano, Count Galeazzo, 43, 126.

Clark, Sir William, 407.
Claxton, Mr. Brooke, 50.
Coldwell, Mr. M. J., 179.
Collins, Michael, 281–2.
Colombo Conference and Plan (1950), 345–50, 365.
Colonial Conference (1902), 13.
Colonial Development Act (1929), 346.
Colonial Development and Welfare Acts (1940 and 1945), 346.
Colonial Laws Validity Act (1865), 7 n.4, 392 ff.
Colonial Office, 14, 399.
Colonialism: revulsion from, in U.K. and Australia, after Japanese successes, 143–4; opposition to, common to Russia and U.S.A., 191–2; the United Nations Trusteeship Council, 320; Nehru on the conflict in Indo-China, 360; Asian attitude to British colonial policy, 417; *see also* BRITISH EMPIRE; COLOMBO CONFERENCE.
Combined Boards (Anglo-American), 128–30.
Committee of European Economic Co-operation, 333.
Committee of Imperial Defence, 36–37, 131 f., 182, 326–7.
Commonwealth Consultative Economic Committee, 347–8, 349.
Commonwealth Liaison Department (Foreign Office), 401.
Commonwealth Relations Conference (Lahore, 1954), 416 n.1, 417.
Commonwealth Relations Office (Dominions Office), 169, 399–400, 401.
Commonwealth Supply Council, 128.
Commonwealth Technical Assistance Committee, 348 f.
Communism: ideological aspects of the North Atlantic Treaty, 339, 341; welfare and development of backward peoples as defence against, 346 and cf. 349–50; Commonwealth concern with progress in Asia, 350; Commonwealth Prime Ministers (1951) seek exchange of views with Communist leaders, 352; danger to Indian stability (1950), 358; opposition to, of European ruling class in S. Africa, 361–2 and cf. 365. *See also* CHINA; U.S.S.R.
Conscription for overseas service rejected by dominions, 29.
Cooper, Mr. Duff, 73 n.4, 118, 121–2, 144 n.1.
Coral Sea, U.S. naval success, 127.
Corregidor, 141.

INDEX

Cosgrave, Mr. W. T., 297.
Costello, Mr. J. A., member of the Fine Gael party, 275; succeeds de Valera as Taoiseach, 275; leads trade mission to London (1948), 277; is confident of the ending of partition (1948), 278–9; his views on Ireland's connexion with the Commonwealth, 278, 280, 281–2; his criticism of the External Relations Act, 282; decides to repeal the External Relations Act, 282–4; on the Republic of Ireland Act, 286–7; on the proclamation of the Republic, 289; protests against the Ireland Act (1949), 290; on republican Ireland's relation to the Commonwealth, 297.
Council of Europe, 365.
Coupland, Sir Reginald, 144, 146.
Cowan, Captain Peadar, 276, 278, 280.
Craigavon, Lord, 67–68, 291 n.3.
Cranborne, Lord, 93 f., 211, 314–15, 401, 403.
Crerar, Mr. T. A., 38 f.
Crete, the campaign of 1941, 95–102.
Crewe, Lord, 391–2.
Cripps, Sir Stafford: proposes constitutional changes for India (1942), 145; his mission to India (1942), 146–55, 191, 207, 210, 224, 234; and the Cabinet mission to India (1946), 214, 220; and the devaluation of sterling (1949), 344–5.
Crisp, Prof. L. F., 378–9.
Cross, Sir Ronald, 407.
Crown:
    Commonwealth, place in, 368–74; allegiance to, an indispensable condition of dominion status, 225, 268, 368–9; no longer an indispensable condition of full membership after 1949, 369, 372; monarchical and republican membership of the Commonwealth, 374–5, 380–2; dominion Prime Ministers' right of direct access to the sovereign, 376–7.
    India's relation to, as a republic, 251–3, 372–3; the London Declaration, 251–2, 296 ff., 373.
    Ireland's relation to, 294–8, 372; repudiation of allegiance, 59; de Valera's views on Irish allegiance, 264; the royal signature on Irish Ministers' letters of credence, 268–9, 271, 272–3; Costello on Irish attitude to, 281; criticism of treatment of, in the External Relations Act, 282 and n.; effect on Ireland's relation to, of the abdication of Edward VIII, 295.
    Representatives of, in the dominions, 376–80; the position of the Governor-General, 376–8; the appointment of dominion or U.K. nationals, 378–9; procedure of appointment, 379–80.
    Royal style and titles: legislation affecting, discussed at conference of 1929, 7 and n.4.; omission of 'Indiae Imperator', 234, 272; 'Head of the Commonwealth', 251, 254, 296, 373, 375; of Queen Elizabeth II, 369–70, 370–2; of King George VI, 370; relation to Commonwealth indicated by, 369–73.
    See also EXTERNAL RELATIONS ACT; IRELAND: Republicanism.
Curtin, Mr. John: on Commonwealth co-operation, 89; and the campaign in Greece, 101; urges Australian representation in War Cabinet, 112, 114, 134; succeeds Fadden as Prime Minister, 117; on Australia's military position at fall of Singapore, 130 n.3; complains of U.K. neglect of Far Eastern defence, 131; seeks U.S. assistance in Malaya, 132; urges reinforcement of Singapore, 132; his *Herald* article and emphasis on U.S. aid in the Pacific, 132–3, 166–7; refuses request for diversion of Australian division to Rangoon, 140–2; and appointment of Casey to Cairo, 142–3; and Axis representatives in Dublin, 162; his proposal for an Imperial Secretariat, 166–73, 171, 176 ff., and cf. 325 n.3, 326; on the Anzac Agreement, 181; on development of Commonwealth consultative machinery, 183, 184–5.
Curzon, Lord, 198.
Cyprus, 116.
Czechoslovakia, 34; see also MUNICH CRISIS.

Dakar, British attempt on (1940), 44–45, 46, 85, 166.
Daladier, M. Édouard, 39.
Davis, H. W. C., on von Treitschke's political thought, 22 n.3.
Daw Saw Yin, 243 and n.2.
Dawson, Mr. Geoffrey, 7, 12.
Deakin, Mr. Alfred, 14.
Denk, Hans, 34 n.5.
Denmark, places Greenland under temporary protection of U.S.A., 58.

INDEX

Deshmukh, Chintaman, 349.
de Valera, Mr. Eamon:
  Combines offices of Prime Minister and External Affairs, 406.
  External association and the republic: his rejection of dominion status, 59; reasons for delay in proclaiming republic, 262–3, 271; his interpretation of the External Relations Act, 263–4; pressure on, to define Ireland's position, 265–73; and the 'dictionary republic', 267, 295; and the Prime Ministers' Meeting (1948), 277; will not oppose repeal of External Relations Act, 280–1 and cf. 276 n.4; fears that secession may delay the ending of partition, 287, 297; dissociates himself from proclamation of the Republic, 289; the experiment of external association, 294–8; on the Irish Nationality Act (1935), 385.
  Overseas tour (1948), 278.
  Second World War and neutrality, 60–61; refuses to provide Irish bases for Britain, 58; his efforts for internal unity, 60–61, 66–67; fears British seizure of Irish ports, 62–63; protests against German invasion of Holland and Belgium, 65; formation of National Defence Council (1940), 66–67; refuses political concessions in return for admission of British forces, 68; determination to resist German invasion, 68, 73; complains of both German and British blockades, 74; rejects Churchill's appeal after attack on Pearl Harbour, 160; protests at stationing of U.S. troops in Northern Ireland, 161; rejects request for expulsion of Axis representatives, 162–3.
  Succeeded as Taoiseach by Costello, 275.
Dieppe raid, 104.
Dill, General Sir John, 96, 98, 117.
Dillon, Mr. J. M.: urges precise definition of Ireland's status, 266, 268–9, and n.2, 271, 295; on repeal of the External Relations Act, 270; in Coalition Government (1948), 275.
Dixon, Sir Owen, 260.
Doidge, Mr. F. W., 355–6, 404.
Dominions:
  Constitutions: written constitutions contrasted with flexibility of English, 388; of older dominions, contrasted with those of newer, 388–9; amendment of, 389–97.
  Diplomatic representation, 409; the Royal signature on Irish Ministers' letters of credence, 268–9, 271, 272–3; Canada accredits representatives abroad (1927), 368; of Pakistan and India, 372.
  Foreign policy: imperial, recognition of right to share in determination, 5–6; the effect of equality of status with inequality of function, 10–17, 177; reactions to the Munich crisis, 11–12, 13, 15–16; share in determination of policy in First World War, 12; delays and difficulties involved in consultation, 17–18; relations between dominions illustrated by Anglo-Egyptian Treaty negotiations (1946), 323–4; initiation of separate dominion policies, 368; the Departments for External Affairs, 400–1, 406; association of offices of Prime Minister and Secretary for External Affairs, 406–7.
  High Commissioners in London, 401–2, 404–5; of Britain in the dominions, 407–9.
  Status: Balfour Report, Statute of Westminster, and precise definition, 5–10, 368–9; draft formula defining (1926), 224; reactions to Indian Constituent Assembly's resolution on Indian status, 224–5; allegiance to the Crown an indispensable condition, 225; reaction to India's acceptance of dominion status, 231; Lord Mountbatten on the position of India and Pakistan, 231–3; the problem of a republican India as a member of the Commonwealth, 250–6; the London Declaration (1949) on India's status, 251–6, 296 f., 373, 398–9.
  United Kingdom, departmental responsibility for, 399–400; the office of Secretary of State for Dominion Affairs, 399, 402–4.
  See also individual states and statesmen and BALFOUR REPORT; BRITISH COMMONWEALTH; CROWN; IMPERIAL WAR CABINET; MUNICH CRISIS; STATUTE OF WESTMINSTER; TREATIES AND AGREEMENTS; UNITED NATIONS; WAR CABINET.
Dominions Office, *see* Commonwealth Relations Office.
Dönges, Dr. T. E., 387.

454 INDEX

Donoughmore Constitution (1931, Ceylon), 246–7.
Donovan, Colonel W. J., 58.
Dorman-Smith, Sir Reginald, 243.
Dulanty, Mr. J. W., 405, 411 n.3.
Dulles, Mr. J. F., on the Pacific Security Agreement, 355.
Dumbarton Oaks Conference (1944), 313–14, 318, 410.
Dunkirk Treaty (1947), *see under* TREATIES AND AGREEMENTS.

East Indies, occupied by Japan, 137.
Eastern Group Conference and Supply Council (1940–1), 84–85, 311.
Economic Council for Asia and the Far East (ECAFE), 365.
Economist, The, criticizes Irish policy of neutrality, 73.
Eden, Mr. Anthony: and the first wartime ministerial conference, 38; discussions with Smuts in Middle East, 94; and the campaign in Greece (1941), 96 ff.; on Western Union in the light of Commonwealth relations, 335–6; as Secretary of State for Dominion Affairs, 402–3.
Egypt: dispatch of First New Zealand Echelon, 39; *see also* TREATIES AND AGREEMENTS.
Eire, *see* IRELAND: Name, changes of.
Elibank, Lord, 93.
Elizabeth II, Queen, her titles, 369–70, 370–2.
Elphinstone, Mountstuart, 234.
Empire Air Training Scheme, 37.
Empire Clearing House, 128.
European Recovery Programme, 331.
Evatt, Mr. H. V.: criticizes composition of the Munitions Assignments Board, 129–30; as Australian Minister for External Affairs, 135; and declaration of war on Hungary, Finland, and Rumania, 135; and the Pacific War Council, 136 f.; at the Washington Pacific Council, 138 f.; differs from Churchill's appreciation of Far Eastern position (1942), 143; on Curtin's proposal for an Imperial Secretariat, 169; on the Anzac Agreement, 181, 312; on granting of dominion status to India, 231; at 1946 Prime Ministers' Meeting, 324; satisfied with machinery for Commonwealth consultation (1946), 325; on Australia's concern with Western Union, 334.

United Nations: urges the rights of the middle powers in post-war international organization, 310; criticizes the Dumbarton Oaks proposals, 314; hostility to great-power pretensions, 314; urges larger powers for the General Assembly, 315–16; attacks the exercise of the veto by a single great power, 316; on the need to safeguard smaller powers against international interference in domestic matters, 318; on the right of all active belligerents to share in framing peace treaties, 321 and n.1.
External Relations Act (1936), 58, 249, 263–87 *passim*, 295, 297–8; *see also* COSTELLO; DE VALERA; IRELAND: Republicanism.

Fadden, Mr. A. W.: on use of Australian troops in Greece, 98, 100–1, 106; on control and disposition of Australian forces, 104; succeeds Menzies as Prime Minister, 112; and the Tobruk dispute, 116–17; succeeded as Prime Minister by Curtin, 117.
Fascism, antagonism to, in India and the colonies, 5.
Ferguson, Mr. Howard, 405.
Fiji islands, 30.
Finland, 43 n.3, 135.
First World War: contrast between declaration of war in 1914 and 1939, 3; dominions' share in determination of policy, 12; the Imperial War Cabinet, 12, 25; function of the Committee of Imperial Defence, 327.
Flanagan, Mr. Oliver, 266.
Formosa, 351: *see also* CHIANG KAI-SHEK.
France: the collapse of 1940, 41–42; — effect in the dominions, 190; — effect in the Far East, 190–1; Churchill's offer of union, 43; Free French press for intervention in Syria, 102; Vichy Government's responsibility for Japan's advance in S.E. Asia, 191; *see also* DAKAR; INDO-CHINA; ORAN; SYRIA.
Franks, Sir Oliver, 410.
Fraser, Mr. Peter: on the Nazi régime, 22; at the first wartime ministerial conference, 38; urges declaration of war aims, 39 n.1; attends War Cabinet meetings (1941), 95, 107 f.; and the campaign in Greece, 99–100; on proposed Imperial War Cabinet, 110, 115; on Curtin's proposed Imperial Secretariat, 171 n.1; on the

Fraser, Mr. Peter (*cont.*):
  Anzac Agreement, 181; unconvinced of need for structural reform of the Commonwealth, 185–6; on granting of dominion status to India, 231; discusses secession problems with Irish Ministers, 285; on republican Ireland's relation to New Zealand, 299; on improved relations between republican Ireland and U.K., 300; doubts practicability of regionalism in the post-war world order, 312; on monarchical and republican membership of the Commonwealth, 374 f.; and amendment to the New Zealand Constitution Act, 389.
  United Nations: attacks the position of the great powers in the Security Council, 315 n.2; on the need for a strong Security Council, 315; attacks the exercise of the veto by a single great power, 316; urges larger powers for the General Assembly, 316; and the Trusteeship Council, 320.
Freyberg, General B.: appointed to command of 2nd New Zealand Expeditionary Force, 31; and the campaign in Greece (1941), 97, 105 f.; his instructions as commander, 104–5; views on defence strategy (1940), 106–7.
Furnivall, J. S., 240–1.

Gaitskell, Mr. Hugh, 342 and n.2, 343, 348.
Gambia, 346.
Gamelin, Gen., 39.
Gandhi, Devadas, 232.
Gandhi, Mahatma M. K.: unwilling to take advantage of British reverses in 1940, 81; opposes any assistance to the war effort, 82; and non-violent non-resistance, 154; and civil disobedience, 144; — civil disobedience as protest against the 'August offer,' 207; and rejection of the proposals of the Cripps Mission, 150, 191, 207, 210; imprisoned (1943), 154; on Hindu–Muslim antagonism as obstacle to self-government, 201; accuses Britain of creating internal divisions in India, 201–2, 203 f.; his insistence on a constitution drafted and implemented by Indians, 204–5; and the Muslim claim to separate nationhood, 207; failure of talks with Jinnah (1944), 207; hopes of early independence in 1946, 212; and the Cabinet mission (1946), 215; — his qualified welcome of their proposals, 218–19; his pilgrimage during the riots of 1947, 221–2; Casey's assessment, 222; suggests appointment of League Government (1947), 229; acquiescence in partition, 229, 230–1; on the riots after partition, 238; on the Princely States after partition, 259; Soviet view of, 359 n.1; his debt to Victorian English political thought, 387.
Garson, Mr. S. S., 390.
Gathorne-Hardy, G. M., 415.
General Agreement on Tariffs and Trade (1947), 301.
George V, King, 3; misgivings about definition of dominion status, 7 and cf. 368; and appointment of Sir Isaac Isaacs as Governor-General of Australia, 379.
George VI, King, 3, 255 n.2, 289; his style and titles, 370, 373.
Germany:
  Hitler and the Nazi challenge, 18–25; Munich and the end of appeasement, 18–19; Hitler's attitude to the British Empire, 19–21.
  Second World War: reaction of U.S.A. to submarine warfare in the Atlantic (1941), 58, 74–75; seeks to benefit from Irish neutrality, 60 ff.; plans for invasion of Britain, 70–71; plans for invasion of Ireland, 71–73; declares war on U.S.A., 126.
  See also HITLER; IRELAND: Second World War; IRISH REPUBLICAN ARMY; NATIONAL SOCIALISM; RAEDER.
Ghana, 418.
Glazebrook, G. P. de T., 13.
Goa, 360.
Government of India Act:
  (1919): 79, 199.
  (1935): 9, 199; nullification of, a condition of Congress participation in war effort, 81; modified application pending framing of new constitution, 234; non-co-operation of the Princes, 247.
Government of Ireland Bill (1920), 291 n.3.
Gray, Mr. David, 67–68, 69, 73.
Great Britain:
  Defence: White Paper proposals (1946), 327–9.
  Foreign policy: continued interest in

Great Britain (cont.):
  security of Low Countries and Germany, 329–30.
  Indian independence: attitude to granting of self-government (1919–39), 198–200; the charge of fomenting communal antagonisms, 201–2, 203; failure to appreciate the representative character of Congress, 203; delay in appreciating Muslim demand for Pakistan, 206; the Labour victory in general election (1945), 210–11; Conservative and Labour parties' sympathies, 211; attitudes to the Indian Independence Act, 235.
  See also ATTLEE; BRITISH COMMONWEALTH; CHURCHILL; CROWN; DOMINIONS; GERMANY; HITLER; INDIA; IRELAND; MUNICH CRISIS; TREATIES AND AGREEMENTS; UNITED NATIONS; WAR CABINET.
Greece: the campaign of 1941, 95–102, 105–6, 117; guarantee of 1939, 364.
Greenberg, Mr. Justice, 394 n.1.
Greenland, 58.
Grigg, Sir James, 145.
Gullett, Sir Henry, 29.

Haig, Sir Harry, 200.
Hailey, Lord, 5.
Haldane, Lord, 36 n.2, 327.
Halifax, Viscount, 18, 25; and the destroyer–bases agreement, 53; and termination of Anglo-Japanese Agreement, 87–88; his views on the post-war development of the Commonwealth, 176–80, 182; views on Indian self-government, 199; does not condemn Labour party policy in India, 226–7; on the Indian Independence Act (1947), 234–5.
Hall, H. Duncan, 37.
Hankey, Lord, 328–9.
Harding, Sir Edward, 407.
Harlech, Lord, 407.
Harriman, Mr. Averell, 122.
Harris v. *Dönges*, 393 f.
Harrison, Mr. Eric, 404.
Hasluck, Paul, 33, 89, 96, 103.
Haushofer, Prof., 20 f.
Havenga, Mr. N. C., 79.
Hegel, G. W. F., 22 f.
Held, German agent captured in Ireland, 66 n.2.
Hempel, Herr Eduard, 61–62.
Henderson, Mr. Arthur, 244.
Herald (Melbourne), 132, 167.

Herenigde (reunited) Nationalist party in South Africa, 33 n.3; *see also* AFRICA, SOUTH: Political parties.
Hertzog, Gen. J. B. M.: insists on complete equality of status for dominions, 6; on world appeasement as the mission of the Commonwealth, 15; reaction to German invasion of Czechoslovakia, 19; his motion (January 1940) that 'the war with Germany should be ended', 33–35, 78–79; urges separate peace with Germany and Italy (1940), 76–77, 78; fundamental difference with Malan on question of the republic, 78–79; resigns from Nationalist party, 79; draft formula defining dominion status (1926), 224; conflict with Governor-General over dissolution of Parliament (1939), 378; and the legality, under the Statute of Westminster, of amending the entrenched clauses (S. Africa Act), 392; combines offices of Prime Minister and External Affairs, 406.
Hinsley, F. H., 127.
Hitler, Adolf, 18; his attitude to the British Empire, 19–21; attitude to the Catholic Church, 19; his estimate of western democracies' reaction to invasion of Czechoslovakia, 20; and plans for invasion of Britain, 70–71; — and of Ireland, 72; and the Soviet–Japanese non-aggression pact, 121; urges Japanese attack on Britain in Far East, 124–5; conceals from Japan his plan to invade Russia, 125; urges Japan to attack Vladivostok, 125–6; reaction to Japanese attack on Pearl Harbour, 126; his colonial ambitions, 193; *see also* MUNICH CRISIS.
Hoare–Laval Pact, *see under* TREATIES AND AGREEMENTS.
Ho Chi Minh, 240 n., 359.
Hoexter, Mr. Justice, 394 n.1.
Holland: invaded by Germany, 65; freezing of Japanese assets (1941), 118; represented in Pacific War Council, 136, 137 n.2; naval losses in the Java Sea (1941), 141.
Holland, Mr. S. G., 357 and n.
Hong Kong, represented at Eastern Group Conference (1940), 84; falls to Japanese (1941), 140–1.
Hopkins, Mr. Harry, 109 n.4, 122, 138, 153.
Hossbach Memorandum (1937), 19 and n.4.

INDEX

Hughes, Mr. W. M., 6 and n., 89–90.
Hull, Mr. Cordell, 68–69, 75, 129.
Hungary, 43 n.3, 135.
Hyde Park Agreement, *see under* TREATIES AND AGREEMENTS.
Hyderabad, 237, 258 f.

Iceland, included in the sterling area, 342.
Imperial Conferences, 183–4; (1921), 6 and n.1, 14; (1926), 6, 224; — resolution on functions of a Governor-General, 376; (1929), 7 and n.4; (1930), 6; (1937), 15, 28; — and dominion nationality and status, 383.
Imperial War Cabinet: in First World War, 12, 25, 91; suggested reconstitution, 25–27; — Australian opinion, 89–90; — discussed and rejected in Canada and Britain, 90–95; — Australian proposals, 110–15; *see also* WAR CABINET.
India:
Asian Relations Conference (1947), Indian influence at, 239–40.
Ceylon, relations with, 257.
Commonwealth membership: the Jaipur resolution (1948), 250; the London Declaration (1949) on her Commonwealth membership, 251–6, 296 f., 373, 398–9.
Communist party, 358 n.3.
Congress: demands independence as condition of support for the war effort, 4, 81; angered by declaration of war by external authority, 79; concessions to Muslim and British views, 82–83; rejection of the 'August offer', 83–84; the 'Quit India' movement, 153–5, 207; accuses Britain of creating communal antagonisms, 201–2, 203 f., 258; demands constituent assembly to draft United India constitution, 205; slowness in appreciating Muslim demand for Pakistan, 206; and the Simla conference (1945), 208–9; and the elections of 1946, 209, 213–14; condemns departure from non-violence (1946), 212; defends the Indian National Army prisoners, 212; conditional acceptance of the Cabinet Mission's proposals, 219–20; and the Interim Government, 219–21; welcomes imposition of time-limit, 227; accepts partition in principle, 229; attitude to the Princely States in independent India, 236; *see also below* Cripps Mission; Independence.
Constitution (1950), 224, 372.
Cripps Mission, 146–55, 207; rights of the proposed Indian Union and position in the Commonwealth, 147–8, 152–3; Congress's criticisms and responsibility for its failure, 148, 149–50, 151–2, 207; reaction of the princes, 148–9; dissatisfaction of the Muslim League, 149, 207; Gandhi's attitude, 150, 207; the problem of control of the defence of India, 150–1, 152.
Foreign policy, consultation before independence, 17 n.1.
Independence: rejection of the 'August offer', 83–84, 144, 146, 154, 206–7; sub-committee of the Cabinet considers constitutional change (1942), 145–6; non-violent non-resistance and the Congress 'Quit India' resolution, 153–5; Muslim League condemns Congress 'open rebellion', 154; British attitude to self-government (1919–39), 198–200; self-government delayed by Hindu–Muslim antagonism, 200–1, 203; emergence of the Muslim demand for Pakistan and the Congress 'Quit India' resolution, 201–8; the Simla conference (1945), 208–9; the elections of 1946, 209, 213–14; disappointment after the Labour victory in British general election (1945), 210, 211–12; Labour sympathy with Congress, 211; the Cabinet Mission (1946) and election of constituent assembly, 214–19, 234; — its constitutional proposals, 217–19; — statement on the future position of the Princely States, 235; the Interim Government, 219–21; the Constituent Assembly, 222–5; the Objectives Resolution and implications of 'sovereign independent republic', 223–5; time-limit imposed, 225–7; Lord Mountbatten as Viceroy and shortening of time-limit, 227–33; acceptance in principle of partition and plans for transfer of power, 229–33; Lord Mountbatten on India's dominion status, 231–3; the Indian Independence Act (1947), 233–5; *see also above* Cripps Mission.
Indian Civil Service, Indianization of, 227.

India (cont.):
Indian National Army, 154, 212.
Kashmir, conflict with Pakistan, 258–61 and cf. 358.
Mahasabha party, eliminated in 1946 elections, 213.
Muslim League: fears British agreement with Congress's conditions for participating in war effort, 80; the demand for Pakistan (1940), 80, 205–6; condemns Congress's 'open rebellion', 154; Jinnah's position in, 201; belief in fundamental nature of Hindu–Muslim division, 201 f., 204; rejects the Cripps proposals, 207; and the 'August offer', 207; the Simla conference (1945), 208–9; and the elections of 1946, 209, 213–14; rejects Cabinet Mission's proposal for a 'truncated' Pakistan (1946), 216; — accepts their proposals for constituent assembly and interim government, 219; — withdrawal of acceptance, and 'direct action' for Pakistan, 221 f., 225–6; and the Interim Government, 219–21; welcomes imposition of time-limit, 227.
Nationalist party, eliminated in 1946 elections, 213.
North Atlantic Treaty, attitude to, 360.
Partition: the Muslim demand for Pakistan (1940), 80, 205–6; Hindu–Muslim antagonism and the theory of the two nations, 202–3, 258; British Labour party's lack of sympathy with Muslim League, 211; mounting tension in 1946, 212; Sikh fears of, 212, 215, and cf. 216, 230; the elections of 1946 and complexity of the problem in the provinces, 213–14; provinces claimed by Congress and the Muslim League, 213–14; the Cabinet mission (1946) favours a Union of India, 215–17; — its report on Muslim and non-Muslim population in areas claimed for Pakistan, 216; Muslim League calls for 'direct action' for Pakistan, 221; riots, and the 'Great Calcutta Killing', 221–2; Congress accepts partition in principle, 229; the division of the provinces, 230, 233; the Indian Independence Act (1947), 233–5; the Princely States, 235–7, 258–9; independence for India and Pakistan (August 1947), 237–8; riots after partition, 238, 257; Pakistan's hopes of Western powers' support in Kashmir, 358.
Second World War: declaration of war, 3, 79; not consulted on decision, 3 ff.; possible Australian reinforcements (1939), 30; represented at first war-time ministerial conference (1939), 38; general condemnation of Nazi aggression, 79–80; reaction of Congress party and Muslim League, 79–80, 80–81; general support from the princes for the war effort, 80; effect of the German victories in 1940, 81; Congress's proposals for co-operation with the Government (July 1940), 82–83; represented at the Eastern Group Conference and Supply Council, 84–85; represented on Pacific War Council, 137; effect of her exclusion from the Atlantic Charter, 144, 193; Japanese successes accentuate Hindu–Muslim rivalry, 144–5.
See also ATTLEE; BRITISH COMMONWEALTH; CHURCHILL: India; COLOMBO CONFERENCE; CROWN; GANDHI; GOVERNMENT OF INDIA ACT; GREAT BRITAIN: India; JINNAH; KHAN, LIAQAT ALI; LINLITHGOW; MOUNTBATTEN; NEHRU; WAVELL.
Indian Independence Act (1947), 233–5.
Indian Statutory Commission (Simon Commission), 241.
Indo-China, 118, 191, 347, 350, 359 f.
Indonesia, 358.
International Court of Justice, 383–4.
Iraq, 97 n.3, 342, 365.
Ireland, Republic of:
Constitution (1937): as precedent for India, 225; the omission of a formal definition of the State, 225, 262 f., 266; and the Anglo-Irish Treaty (1921), 292; the name Eire, 293.
Farmers' party, supports Fine Gael, 276.
Fianna Fáil, loses overall majority in 1948 election, 275; will not oppose repeal of External Relations Act, 280.
Fine Gael party, 265–6, 270; and external association, 274, 276, 300; its position in the 1948 Coalition Government, 275–6; change of attitude with announcement of decision to repeal the External Relations

INDEX

Ireland (*cont.*):
  Act, 285–6; its position strengthened in 1951 election, 300.
Labour party: advocates repeal of External Relations Act, 274; represented in 1948 Coalition Government, 275.
Name, changes of, 293.
Nationality and citizenship, provisions of U.K. Nationality Act (1948), 277–8, 286–8, 300–1.
Partition: ending of the war as an opportunity for extreme nationalists, 60, 61–62; suggested for abandonment of neutrality, 67–68; as cause for delay in proclaiming the republic, 262–3, 291–2, 297; MacBride suggests representation in the Dáil of Northern constituencies, 274; abolition of, the aim of the Coalition Government (1948), 275; Irish request consideration at Prime Ministers' Meeting (1948), 277; Costello's confidence about abolition (1948), 278–9; Irish desire for overseas countries' sympathy, 278 f.; hopes raised by British Ministers' visits, 279 and n.2; the desire for sovereignty stronger than that for unity, 279; the effect of the Republic of Ireland Act, 286–7; safeguards for Northern Ireland in the Ireland Act, 290–1; incompatibility of dominion status and, 297; with partition, military alliance with Britain impossible, 302.
Republican party (Clann na Poblachta), 273–4; and the general election (1948), 275.
Republicanism and the Commonwealth connexion: consequences of dominion status, 58–59, 224–5, 240, 250–1; taken as precedent by South African nationalists, 155; — and in India, 225, 295; — and in Burma, 245; external association with Commonwealth nations, 264–5; pressure on de Valera to define Ireland's position, 265–73; 'the dictionary republic', 267, 295; the royal signature on Irish Ministers' letters of credence, 268–9, 271, 272–3; the question of the repeal of the External Relations Act, 269–72, 274; U.K. and dominion views on her status, 272; the general election (1948) and Coalition Government, 273–5; repeal of the External Relations Act, 275–88; Republicanism strengthened by the 1948 election, 275–6; question of Irish participation in Prime Ministers' Meeting (1948), 277; the decision to repeal the External Relations Act, 281–6; discussion of secession problems with Commonwealth Prime Ministers (October 1948), 284–5; the Republic of Ireland Act, 286–8, 293; United Kingdom attitude to republic in Ireland, 287–8; — influence of dominion opinion, 288; the Republic proclaimed, 289; the Ireland Act (1949), 289–92, 293–4; review of relations with Commonwealth (1921–49), 292–8; the effect of secession on relationship to the Commonwealth, 293–8; comparison between the relations of Ireland and India, 296, 298; the Coalition Government's view of relation to the Commonwealth, 297; the Republic outside the Commonwealth, 298–304; excluded from Commonwealth consultation and information, 298–9; improved relations with Gt. Britain, 299–300; economic effects of secession, 301–2, 303; — effect on foreign policy, 302; Britain's neighbour as a foreign country, 302–3; the durability of Ireland's relation with Britain, 303–4.
Second World War and neutrality, 3 f., 58–75; press censorship, 60, 164; de Valera's efforts for internal unity, 60–61, 66–67; German caution in attitude to pro-German element, 61–62; de Valera fears British seizure of ports, 62–63; termination by 1938 Agreement of harbour facilities accorded in 1921 Treaty, 63–64; effect of denial of ports on protection of Atlantic convoys, 65, and cf. 73–74, 75; reaction to German invasion of Holland and Belgium, 65; landing and dropping of German agents, 65–66; formation of National Defence Council (1940), 66–67; unity suggested as return for abandonment of neutrality, 67–68; refusal of political concessions in return for admission of British forces, 68; determination to resist German invasion, 68, 73; U.S.A. rejects suggestion of visit of naval squadron to Irish ports, 68–69; British fears

INDEX

Ireland (*cont.*):
of German assault on Ireland, 69; appeal to U.S.A. for war material refused, 69–70, 74–75; German war strategy favours exclusion of Ireland from blockade, 70; German plans for invasion, 71–73; U.K. economic restrictions, 74; food supplies from Ireland to Britain, 74 n.3, 302; American pressure on behalf of Britain, 74–75; the moral, political, and constitutional basis of neutrality, 75; rejection of request for expulsion of Axis representatives, 161–3; U.K. Government overestimates influence of U.S.A., 163; Irish volunteers in British forces, 164, 303.

Sinn Féin, recognizes interdependence of Britain and Ireland (1921), 294.

Sterling area, included in, 342.

See also CHURCHILL: Ireland; CROWN; COSTELLO; DE VALERA; DILLON; IRISH FREE STATE; IRISH REPUBLICAN ARMY; MACBRIDE; MCGILLIGAN; NORTON.

Ireland Act (1949), 289–92, 293–4.

Ireland, Northern: union rejected as return for abandonment of Irish neutrality, 67–68; arrival of U.S. troops, 161; de Valera on external association as a concession to Northern views on partition, 264; provisions of the Ireland Act (1949), 290–1.

Irish Free State, 293; *see also* IRELAND.

Irish Nationality and Citizenship Act (1935), 286.

Irish Republican Army: the Phoenix Park raid (December, 1939), 60; German caution in attitude to, 61–62; offer to defend German Legation in case of violation of neutrality, 62; association with German agents, 66 n.1; rejects de Valera's plea for unity (1940), 67.

Ironside, Gen., 39.

Irwin, Lord, *see* HALIFAX, Viscount.

Isaacs, Sir Isaac, 379.

Italy: British Chief of Staff's assessment of attitude in May 1940, 41; declares war on Britain and France, 43; the dominions declare war, 43; effect in S. Africa of Italy's entry into war, 76; Australia informed of surrender negotiations, 169; *see also* MUSSOLINI; TREATIES AND AGREEMENTS: Hoare-Laval Pact.

Jamaica, 49.

Jammu, 260.

Japan: Australian fears of hostility (1939), 31; U.K. assessment of attitude in May 1940, 41; fears of aggression in the Pacific (1940), 85; Australian efforts to improve relations (1940), 86–87; Australia declares war, 43 n.3; U.K. agrees to close the Burma road, 87 f.; termination of Anglo-Japanese Agreement, 87–88; the approach to war, 115–23; Anglo-American consultation and U.S. warning (1941), 118–20; the threat to Thailand, 118; freezing of Japanese assets in U.S., U.K., and Holland (1941), 118; occupation of Indo-China, 118; non-aggression pact with Russia, 121; optimistic estimates in Singapore and Washington of the position in September 1941, 121–2; divergence of U.K. and Australian views in late 1941, 122–3; proposed U.K. warning (December 1941), 123; attack on Pearl Harbour, 124, 126;—reactions to, 130–5; entry into war determined independently of German advice, 124–6; immediate and lasting effects of Japanese intervention, 126–7; the attack in S.E. Asia, 139–42; advance in Burma, 143–4; the Indian National Army, 154; U.K. declares war, 160; anti-Western rather than anti-colonial outlook, 191; as champion of Asian nationalism, 242; effect of success and propaganda in Burma, 242; the League of Nations' failure to stop her aggression, 309; discussion of peace settlement (1947) and Australian command of occupation forces, 326 and n.4; Australian and New Zealand views on peace terms conflict with U.S.A., 353; *see also* HITLER; HONG KONG; INDO-CHINA; MALAYA; RANGOON; SINGAPORE; TREATIES: Pacific Security Agreement.

Jarring, Herr, 260.

Jennings, Sir Ivor, 247 n.1, 375.

Jinnah, M. A., on Hindu–Muslim antagonism as obstacle to self-government, 201; his position in the Muslim League, 201; belief in fundamental nature of Hindu–Muslim division, 201 f., 205; and the 'August offer', 207; failure of talks with Gandhi (1944), 207; and the Simla conference (1945), 208 f.; critical of Labour party's proposals (1945), 212; provinces claimed for

INDEX 461

Jinnah, M. A. (*cont.*):
Pakistan, 213; and the Cabinet mission (1946), 215; rejects Cabinet mission's proposal for 'truncated' Pakistan, 216; agrees with their proposals, 219; agreement withdrawn, 220–1; and the interim government, 220–1; conversations in London (1946), 226; discussions with Lord Mountbatten, 228; on the princes' right to decide their relations with independent Indian dominions, 236; as the creator of Pakistan, 237; and the Princely States after partition, 259; *see also* INDIA: Independence *and* Muslim League.

Joint Chiefs of Staff Committees, 127 f., 130.

Jordan, Mr. W. J., 404.

Jowitt, Lord, 279 n.2; on dominions' influence on the British Nationality Act (1948), 288 and cf. 385 n.; on republican Ireland's position in the Commonwealth, 298; on Commonwealth attitude to the People's Government in China, 350; on the British concept of Empire and Commonwealth, 367; on the Canadian Citizenship Act, 384.

Junagadh, 237, 258 f.

Kashmir dispute, 258–61; Pakistan's hopes of Western powers' support, 358.

Kenya: Smuts on S. Africa's responsibility for defence, 35.

Kesselring, F.-M. von, 73 n.1.

Khan, Abdul Ghaffar, 213–14.

Khan, Liaqat Ali: member of the Interim Government, 221; and the 1946 riots, 222; and representation of the Princely States in the Constituent Assembly, 236; on the time-limit imposed for Indian settlement, 238 n.4; on the Commonwealth after Indian independence, 250, 415; and the Princely States after partition, 259 and n.2.

Khan, Sir Muhammad Zafrullah, 38.

King, Mr. W. L. Mackenzie:
Commonwealth and international relations: supports appeasement in imperial foreign policy, 15, 16 and n.1; views on the preservation of peace in the post-war world, 179–80; on post-war relations within the Commonwealth, 186 f.; and draft formula of dominion status (1926), 224; on granting of dominion status to India, 231; discusses repeal of the External Relations Act, 282; discusses secession problems with Irish Ministers, 285; on the place of the Commonwealth in the post-war world, 307; urges universal membership of future organization, 309; advocates the principle of functionalism, 312, 313; on representation in the Security Council, 313; protests against framing of peace treaties by great powers, 321; and the revision of the Anglo-Egyptian Treaty, 322 f.; on the 1946 Prime Ministers' Meeting, 324 f.; on post-war Commonwealth consultation, 332, 400; on the Brussels Treaty, 333–4, 339; alarm at failure of United Nations to preserve security, 337; his controversy with the Governor-General, 377–8; on the incorporation of Newfoundland, 398; his character and achievement as a statesman, 413–14; personal idiosyncracies, 414 and n.

Second World War: on Canada's entry into war, 4; rejects (1939) conscription for overseas expeditionary force, 29; on the first wartime ministerial conference, 38; on Italy's declaration of war, 43; justifies the bombardment of Oran, 44; on American conviction of Nazi invincibility (1940), 47; and lease to U.S.A. of British bases, 50–51; and the Joint Board on Defence, 51–53; and the Hyde Park Agreement (1941), 57; urged by Churchill to press for visit of U.S. squadron to Irish ports, 68; on termination of Anglo-Japanese Agreement (1940), 88; on methods of co-operation between Canada and U.K., 90–93; rejects suggestion of Imperial War Cabinet, 90–93, 110 f., 114–15; views on the Anglo-American Combined Boards, 129; and Pacific War Councils, 137, 139; and Axis representatives in Dublin, 162; and the Canadian reinforcement crisis (1944–5), 189; declines to leave Canadian troops in occupying forces in Europe, 321.

Korean War, 350–2; Indian conflict with Western policy, 351, 359.

Kotelawala, Sir John, 377.

Labrador, 397 n.

Langer, W. L., and S. E. Gleason, 48.

Latham, Sir John, 87.
Laurier, Sir Wilfrid, 14, 341, 413.
League of Nations, 10; and the Italo-Abyssinian war, 15; Commonwealth statesmen's criticisms, 308–9; experience of, influences drafting of United Nations Charter, 308, 319; failure to check Japanese aggression, 309.
Lebanon, 102.
Lehane, Mr. Con, 276 and n.4.
Lemass, Mr. Seán, 298 n.2.
'Lend-Lease', 54–57, 343.
Lingard, C. C., and R. G. Trotter, *Canada in World Affairs*, 173.
Linlithgow, Lord: opposes hasty constitutional changes in India (1939), 80; Nehru's criticism of, 82; on the Eastern Group Conference (1940), 84; and Cripps's proposals (1939) for Indian settlement, 147 n.2; and the Cripps Mission to India, 150, 153; views on Indian self-government, 199 f.; on Gandhi's attitude to the Government of India Act (1935), 204.
Lloyd George, Mr. David, 6 n., 14 ff.
Locarno Treaties, 10, 363.
Long, Gavin, 28, 132.
Lothian, Lord, 47 ff.
Louw, Mr. Eric, 34, 363.
Low, Mr. Solon, 369–70.
Lyons, Mr. J. A., 31–32.
Lyttelton, Mr. Oliver, 85, 116–17.

MacArthur, Gen., 121–2, 130 n.1, 141, 351.
Macaulay, Lord, 197 f., 228, 234, 416.
MacBride, John, 273.
MacBride, Maud Gonne, 273 and n.
MacBride, Mr. Seán: leader of the new Republican party in Ireland, 273; views on partition, 274; and repeal of the External Relations Act, 274, 276 n.4, 279–80, 281, 282–3, 284; in Coalition Government (1948), 275 f.; on the British Nationality Act, 278; seeks sympathy for abolition of partition, 279; on impossibility, under partition, of military alliance with Britain, 302; as Secretary for External Affairs, 406; *see also* IRELAND: Republican party.
Macdonald, Sir John, 413.
MacDonald, Mr. Malcolm, 399, 407.
MacDonald, Mr. Ramsay, 421.
MacEntee, Mr. Seán, 298 nn.2, 3.
McEwen, Mr. J., 87 f.
McGilligan, Mr. Patrick: insists on complete equality of status for dominions, 6; on the 'dictionary republic', 267 n.2; on the falsity of Ireland's position, 269 f.; as Minister of Finance in the Coalition Government (1948), 275–6, 276 n.1.
McKell, Mr. W. J., 89.
McNaughton, Gen., 103, 107.
Maffey, Sir John, 73, 407.
Maistre, Joseph de, 264.
Malan, Dr. D. F.: opposition to S. African participation in the war, 33, 35; disclaims sympathy with Nazism, 34; urges separate peace with Germany and Italy (1940), 76 f.; opposes the Ossewa Brandwag and New Order group, 78; fundamental difference with Hertzog on question of the republic, 78–79; on Ireland as a precedent for breaking connexion with Britain, 155; motion for the establishment of republic (1942), 155–7; and the draft republican constitution in *Die Burger*, 157; on republican victory in election of 1943, 159; his arguments against a treaty relationship between members of the Commonwealth, 256 n.1; on the danger of Communism, 361; urges dissociation from 'foreign complexes', 361; and *apartheid*, 361; and amendment of the entrenched clauses (S. Africa Act), 392–3, 394–5; appoints separate minister for foreign affairs, 406; criticizes admission to the Commonwealth of Asian and African states, 417–18.
Malaya: represented at Eastern Group Conference (1940), 84; and defence in the Far East, 88; the Japanese threat in 1941, 118; Australia seeks American assistance, 132; Japanese occupation, 191; at Asian Relations Conference (1947), 240; decides on Commonwealth membership, 256; development plan, 348; *see also* SINGAPORE.
Man, Isle of, in British Nationality Act, 386 n.2.
Mansergh, N., 283, 394 n.1.
Manstein, F.-M. von, 73 n.1.
Marshall, Gen. G. C., 120.
Martin, Mr. Paul, 384.
Marwick, Mr. W. J., 156.
Massey, Mr. Vincent, 92, 405.
Matsuoka, Yosuké, 124 f.
Matthai, Dr. John, 344, 345 n.2.
Maung Maung, Dr., 242.
Menon, V. K. Krishna, 405.

INDEX

Menon, V. P., 83 f., 236.
Menzies, Mr. R. G.:
  Commonwealth and international relations: criticizes the Balfour Report, 7; on Curtin's proposals for an Imperial Secretariat, 167; on dominions' allegiance to the Crown, 225; on Britain's participation in Western Union, 336; warns Australia of the approach of a third world war (1951), 352; defends the Pacific Security Agreement, 356; on post-war structural changes in the Empire, 368; on Australia's relation to the Crown, 374.
  Second World War: on Australia's entry into war, 3; urges retention of democratic institutions in wartime, 24; rejects (1939) conscription for service overseas, 29; and New Zealand's decision (September 1939) to send troops overseas, 32; expresses concern at Dakar incident, 45, 85; discusses defence problems of Singapore (1940), 88–89; attends War Cabinet meetings (1941), 90, 94 f.; and the campaign in Greece, 95–102, 106; on Churchill's broadcast (June 1941), 107–8; concern at withdrawal of U.S. fleet from Pacific, 109; on concentration of power in Churchill's hands, 109, 127; criticizes Churchill's attitude to dominion war interests, 109–10; proposes Imperial War Cabinet, 110–15; Australian opposition to his return to London (August 1941), 111–12; succeeded as Prime Minister by Fadden, 112, 115–16; favours warning to Japan (August 1941), 118; on Australian representation in the War Cabinet, 134.
Middle East Supply Centre (1941), 85, 311.
Midway Island, U.S. naval victory, 127.
Mirza, Maj.-Gen. Iskander, 380.
Montagu, Edwin, 152.
Montrose, Prof. J. L., 291 n.2.
Morgenthau, Prof. Hans J., 419 f.
Morgenthau, Henry, 56.
Mountbatten, Lord: as Viceroy in India, 227–33; his statements on the dominion status of India and Pakistan, 231–3; on the position of the Princely States after Indian independence, 236–7; appreciates Burmese aims in resisting Japan, 243.
Mulcahy, Gen.: on Ireland's relation to the Commonwealth, 270; on the External Relations Act, 274; in Coalition Government (1948), 275; *see also* IRELAND: Fine Gael.
Munich Agreement (1938), 166.
Munich crisis: reaction in the dominions, 11–12, 13, 15–16; destruction of Czechoslovakia ends policy of appeasement, 18–19; Hitler's estimate of the reaction of Western democracies, 20; Australia consulted, 170.
Munitions Assignments Board, 128.
Munro, Sir Thomas, 197, 199.
Mussolini, Benito, 24, 126.

Naidu, Mrs. Sarojini, 222, 239.
Nash, Mr. Walter, 138 f., 309–10, 324.
National Defence Council (Ireland), 66–67.
National Socialism, 21, 22–25, 78.
Nazi–Soviet Pact, *see under* TREATIES AND AGREEMENTS.
Nazimuddin, K., 372.
Ndlwana v. *Hofmeyr*, 392.
Nehru, Pandit Jawaharlal: on failure to consult India on declaration of war (1939), 4; reaction to British reverses in 1940, 81; proposals for co-operation with Government in war effort (July 1940), 82–83; his criticism of Lord Linlithgow, 82; his comment on Churchill, 82–83; rejects the 'August offer', 83, 207; minimizes danger of Japanese attack on India (1939), 143; and civil disobedience, 144; and the Cripps Mission to India, 146; on Gandhi and the Cripps Mission, 150; imprisoned (1943), 154; urges resistance to Japanese, 154; associated with defence of Indian National Army prisoners, 212 n.4; and the Cabinet Mission (1946), 215; and the interim government, 221; and the 1946 riots, 222; and the Constituent Assembly, 222–3, 224; quotes Ireland as precedent, 225; accepts partition in principle (February 1947), 229; and discussion with the Princes' Negotiating Committee, 235; on India's entry into independence, 237; on the Asian Relations Conference (1947), 239; and India's decision to retain Commonwealth membership, 253–4; his meeting with Churchill, 254 n.4; accuses U.K. of causing communal divisions, 258; on Colombo Conference, 347; on recognition, *de facto*, of People's Government in China, 350; on the

Western powers' neglect of Asian opinion in the Korean War, 351; denounces Indian Communist party, 358 n.3; advocates policy of nonalignment, 357 f.; on India's policy towards Indo-China, 359; Soviet view of, 359 n.1; on importance to India of Commonwealth ties, 360; on the death of Western imperialism in Asia, 360; on the conflict in Indo-China, 360; on the North Atlantic Treaty, 360; on the London Declaration (1949), 373; combines offices of Prime Minister and External Affairs, 406; on the reconciliation of Indian nationalism and British imperialism, 415; *see also* INDIA: Congress *and* Independence.

New Guinea, 127, 140.

New Zealand:
Asian nationalism, sympathy with, 358.
External Affairs Department, established (1943), 91 n.
Hoare–Laval pact, dissociated from, 13 n.1.
Ireland: the New Zealand Republic of Ireland Act (1950), 294.
Second World War: declaration of war, 3 and n.1; dissatisfaction with Munich Agreement, 13 and n.1, and cf. 29; insufficiency of defence preparations, 29; plans for employment of forces, 30–32; co-operation with Australia in defence matters, 31–32; dispatch of First New Zealand Echelon to Egypt, 32, 39; Lend-Lease agreement with U.S.A., 56 n.4; represented at Eastern Group Conference (1940), 84; fears of Japanese aggression (1940), 86; concern for defence deficiencies at Singapore and conference (1940), 88–89; and the campaign in Greece, 96 n., 97–102, 105–6; control and disposition of forces, 104–5; reaction to Pearl Harbour, 131; and the Pacific War Councils, 136 f.; the possibility of a Japanese invasion, 185 and n.1.
Structural reform of post-war Commonwealth, views on, 185–6; critical of Curtin's proposed Imperial Secretariat, 171.
See also BRITISH COMMONWEALTH; CROWN; DOMINIONS; FRASER; JAPAN; NASH; TREATIES AND AGREEMENTS; UNITED NATIONS.

New Zealand Constitution Act (1852, amended 1947), 389–90.

Newall, Air Marshal Sir C., 42.
Newfoundland: lease of bases by U.S.A., 49 f., 53–54; incorporated in Canadian Confederation, 175, 397–8.
Nicholls, Mr. Heaton, 405.
Nicolson, Sir Harold, 9, 379; on the Sovereign's relation to his Ministers in the dominions, 376.
Nishtar, Abdur Rab, 222.
Noel-Baker, Mr. P. J., 279 n.2.
North Atlantic Council, 341.
North Atlantic Treaty, *see under* TREATIES AND AGREEMENTS.
North Atlantic Treaty Organization, 302, 337–8, 353–4.
North Borneo, *see* BORNEO, North.
North-West Frontier Province, in partition between India and Pakistan, 213–14, 230.
Norton, Mr. William, 274 f., 276 n., 280 f., 283 f.
Nu, Thakin, 242.
Nyasaland, 35, 396.

Ogdensburg Agreement, *see under* TREATIES AND AGREEMENTS.
O'Higgins, Dr. T. F., 267 n.2, 286, 292.
Oran, British ultimatum to French naval forces and bombardment, 43–44.
Orange Free State, 79.
Ormsby-Gore, Mr. W. G. A., *see* HARLECH, Lord.
Ossewa Brandwag, 78.

Pacific Security Agreement, *see under* TREATIES AND AGREEMENTS.
Pacific War Councils, 136–9.
Page, Sir Earle: Australian Envoy Extraordinary in London, 114, 135; urges retention of British fleet at Singapore, 121; disagrees with British view on defence of the Far East, 122; views on closer liaison between Australia and Britain, 133–4; and diversion of Australian division to Rangoon, 141.
Pakistan: formally recognized as dominion by Indian Independence Act (1947), 233; at Asian Relations Conference (1947), 240; assertion of separate nationhood and culture, 258; and Kashmir dispute, 258–61, 358; development plan (Colombo), 348; India protests at Western aid to, 359–60; attitude to the North Atlantic Treaty, 360; *see also* INDIA: Partition; JINNAH.

Palestine, 84, 97 n.3.
Pandit, Mrs., 405.
Panikkar, K. M., 236.
Patel, Sardar Vallabhbhai, 221 f., 236 f.
Patiala, Maharajah of, 236.
Pearl Harbour, 124, 126, 130 and n.2.
Pearse, Senator Margaret, 300.
Pearson, Mr. Lester: on the place of functional bodies in post-war organization, 313; criticizes the Dumbarton Oaks proposals, 314; on the North Atlantic Treaty, 341 n.2, 341–2; on resistance to communism in Asia, 350; on the Colombo Foreign Ministers' Meeting (1950), 415.
Permanent Court of International Justice, 383–4.
Persia, treaty with Pakistan, 365.
Pethick-Lawrence, Lord: on Indian self-government, 210; and the Cabinet Mission to India (1946), 214, 217, 220; on Gandhi, 215, 219.
Pirow, Mr. Oswald, 34–35, 36, 78, 156; participation in the war, 34–35.
Poland: the British guarantee, 18 n.2, 177, 364; dominions' reaction to invasion, 334.
Port Darwin, 140.
Portugal, seeks NATO support for sovereignty in Goa, 360.
Prime Ministers' Meetings, *see under* BRITISH COMMONWEALTH.
Privy Council, abolition of dominions' appeal to Judicial Committee of, 390 f.
Punjab, in partition between India and Pakistan, 214, 216, 230.
Purvis, Mr. Arthur, 54.

Rabaul, 140.
Radcliffe, Sir Cyril, 257.
Raeder, Admiral, 45 n.1, 50, 53, 70–71, 117 n.6.
Rajagopalachari, C., 145; angered by the 'August offer', 207; and the Cabinet Mission (1946), 215; member of the interim government, 221; on the position of the Princely States in independent Indian dominions, 236.
Ralston, Col. J., 103–4.
Rangoon, 140 ff.
Rauschning, Hermann, 20.
Red Sea, removed from list of areas forbidden to U.S. shipping (1941), 58.
Reitz, Col. D., 38 f., 405.
Rhodesia, 157; the Federation of 1953, 396.
Rhodesia, Southern, 84.

Ribbentrop, J. von., 124 f.
Robertson, Mr. Norman, 405.
Roosevelt, President Franklin D.: on Italy's declaration of war, 43; and Churchill's request for loan of American destroyers, 46, 48–49, 49–50; on necessity of assisting Britain (1940), 48; and the Joint Board on Defence, 51–53; his pledge to assist Canada in case of attack (August 1938), 52; and Lend-Lease, 55; extends U.S.A. patrol area in Atlantic (April 1941), 58; fails to persuade de Valera to provide Britain with bases, 58; and Irish neutrality, 58, 67 f., 69–70; urges Ireland to allow use of ports by Britain, 74; on the Atlantic as the decisive battlefield, 108; the Atlantic meeting (1941) and consultation on Japan, 118–20; and proposed U.S. and British warnings to Japan (December 1941), 123; and dominion membership of Combined Boards, 129; and Australian appeal for reinforcements in Malaya, 132; forms the Washington Pacific Council, 138; supports British request for diversion of Australian troops to Rangoon, 140; orders abandonment of Corregidor, 141; on the appointment of Casey to Cairo, 143; on the Atlantic Charter, 144; fails to influence Churchill's Indian policy, 145 f., 153; sends U.S. troops to Northern Ireland, 160–1; and Axis representatives in Dublin, 162.
Round Table, 59–60, 111.
Royal Air Force: Empire Air Training Scheme, 37; fighter squadrons retained in Britain (1940), 42.
Rugby, Lord, *see* MAFFEY, Sir John.
Rumania, 43 n.3, 135, 364.
Russell, Seán, 62 and n.2.

St. Laurent, Mr. L. S., 190; on Western Union, 334; fears of abuse of the veto in the U.N., 337; urges defensive grouping of free states against Russian expansion, 337 f.; on the North Atlantic Treaty, 337 ff.; on Russian threat to the Catholic Church, 338, and cf. 341; on the Royal titles, 369, 371; as Secretary for External Affairs, 406; on the independence of India and Ceylon, 421.
St. Lucia, 49.
Salisbury, Lord, 9, 419–20.
San Francisco Conference, 314–22, 383; *see also* UNITED NATIONS.

INDEX

Savage, Mr. M. J., 29, 31–32.
Saw, U, 242.
Schreiner, Mr. Justice, 394 n.1.
Schuman Plan, 336.
Scullin, Mr. J. H., 379.
Second World War: declaration of war by U.K. and the dominions, 3–4; discussion on declaration of war aims, 39 and n.1; results in the end of Western colonialism in Asia, 190–1, 194; *see also under combatant nations, and* BRITISH COMMONWEALTH; CHURCHILL; HITLER; IRELAND; IMPERIAL WAR CABINET; KING, W. L. MACKENZIE; MENZIES; RAEDER; ROOSEVELT; SMUTS; WAR CABINET.
Seeley, J. R., 198.
Senanayake, D. S., 247, 347.
Senanayake, Dudley, 371.
Separate Representation of Voters' Act (S. Africa, 1956), 393, 395.
Shaw, G. B., 300.
Shedden, Sir Frederick, 167 n.1.
Sherwood, R. E., 119, 142 n.1.
Shinwell, Mr. E., 182.
Simla Conference (1945), 208–9.
Simon, Lord, 38, 145, 287–8, 385 n.
Simon Commission, *see* INDIAN STATUTORY COMMISSION.
Sind, in partition between India and Pakistan, 213, 216, 230.
Singapore: plan for reinforcement from New Zealand and Australia (1939), 30 f.; its importance as naval base, 86 and cf. 117; Defence conference (1940), 88–89; U.S.A. insist on U.K. responsibility for defence, 109; the Japanese threat in 1941, 118; Australia urges necessity of strengthening defences, 121 f., 131–2; Hitler urges Japanese attack (March 1941), 124 f.; fall of, 138, 141, 143, 191; development plan, 348.
Singh, Master Tara, 212.
Smith, Mr. Ellis, 38 n.1.
Smuts, Gen. J. C.:
Commonwealth and international relations: insists on complete equality in status of dominions, 6; on benefits of decentralization, 9, 169, 175 f., 399; his part in drafting the League of Nations Covenant, 12; supports appeasement in imperial policy, 16; his views on the post-war role of the Commonwealth, 173–6, 177 f., 182–3, 412; on the Prime Ministers' Meeting (1944), 184; his tribute to the Commonwealth (1942), 194; urges India to remain in the Commonwealth, 231; on the London Declaration (1949), 254–5, 373; his criticism of the League of Nations, 308 f., 319; on post-war international organization, 308–9, 310; on the importance of great-power unity in the United Nations, 319; on the Brussels Treaty, 333; views on Western Union, 330–1, 333, 336; on republican membership of the Commonwealth, 381; and the legality of amending the entrenched clauses (S. Africa Act), 392; as a chief architect of the Commonwealth, 411–13.
External Affairs Ministry combined with Premiership, 406.
Nationalist party: his responsibility for the breach, 413.
Political theorist, 24 n.2, 173–6 f.
Second World War: on South Africa's entry into war, 3–4; compulsory service outside the Union, 29, 35–36; —and use of troops outside Africa, 36; his position in South African Parliament at outbreak of war, 33; and the Nationalist opposition to war, 33–36; on South Africa's responsibility for defence of 'white civilization' in Africa, 35–36; on deficiencies in South Africa's preparations for war, 36; advises against decision to retain fighter squadrons in Britain (1940), 42; justifies bombardment of Oran, 44; fully informed of attack on Dakar, 44–45; emphasizes danger of hostile control of French and Belgian colonies, 44–45; his political position strengthened (May–November 1940), 76, 78 f.; and discussion on reconstitution of Imperial War Cabinet, 94; consulted on campaigns in Africa and Greece, 98 f., 102, and cf. 94; his influence on general war policy, 107; opposes proposed Imperial War Cabinet, 110 f., 115; his leadership essential to South Africa's war effort, 111; parliamentary motion reaffirms declaration of war and membership of Commonwealth (1942), 157; his position in S. Africa strengthened (1942–3), 158–9; on the collapse of France, 190–1.
Soulbury, Lord, 248, 377.
Soulbury Report, and Ceylon's 1946 Constitution, 248, 387–8.

INDEX

South Africa, *see* AFRICA, South.
South Africa Act, amendment of, 391–7.
South African Citizenship Act, 386–7.
South African War, 13.
South Pacific Commission, 175.
South Seas Commission, 365.
Spain, British assessment of attitude in May 1940, 41.
Spender, Mr. P. C., 106, 347, 354 and n.1.
Stark, Admiral H. R., 120.
Status of the Union Act (1934), 393.
Statute of Westminster (1931): and definition of dominion status, 6–10; and dominion status of Ireland, 59, 268; allegiance to the Crown an indispensable condition of dominion status, 225, 368–9; the relation of dominions to the Crown modified by India's republican membership, 251–3; adopted by Australia and New Zealand, 389; provisions governing amendment of constitutions, 389–90, 391–2; and the legality of amending the entrenched clauses (S. Africa Act), 392–4; *see also* BALFOUR REPORT; CROWN; DOMINIONS: Status.
Sterling, devaluation of (1949), 342–5.
Stewart, Sir Frederick, 87 f.
Stimson, Mr. H. L., 52.
Strauss, Mr. J. G. N., 279 n.2.
Strijdom, Mr. J. G., 381; urges renunciation of Commonwealth membership, 77; associates republicanism with demand for separate peace, 155; appoints separate Secretary for Foreign Affairs, 406.
Suez Canal, 117, 322.
Sunday Independent (Dublin), forecasts repeal of the External Relations Act, 282–3, 283 n.4.
Sun Yat Sen, 202.
Swart, Mr. C. R., 159.
Swaziland, 395–6.
Syria, the campaign of 1941, 102–3, 104 n.2.

Tanganyika, 35, 346 and n.6.
te Water, Mr. C. T., 308, 404–5.
Thailand, 118, 123, 191.
Thomas, Mr. J. H., 294–5, 399.
Times, The: repudiates necessity to define imperial relationships, 7 f.; *History of,* 11; reaction to Munich crisis, 11; *see also* DAWSON.
Tobruk, Australian forces in, 116–17.
Toynbee, Dr. A. J., 19.

Treaties and Agreements:
Anglo-Egyptian Treaty (1936), 166, 322–4; dominions' attitude to withdrawal of British troops, 323; dominions dissociated from responsibility for, 323–4, 364.
Anglo-French Treaty (Dunkirk, 1947), 333 and n., 354, 364.
Anglo-Irish Agreement (1938), 63–64.
Anglo-Irish Treaty (1921), 63, 281–2, 292.
Anglo-Japanese Agreement (1940), 87–88.
Anglo-Russian Agreement (1941), 108.
Anglo-Turkish Treaty (1939), 364.
Australia–New Zealand (Anzac) Agreement (1944), 175, 181, 312, 326, 339, 364.
Baghdad Pact, 364 f.
Brussels Treaty (1948), 333–4, 339, 354, 364.
Hoare–Laval pact (1935), 13 and n.1, 18 n.2, and cf. 308.
Hyde Park Agreement (Canada–U.S.A., 1941), 56 f.
Irish–U.S.A. Treaty of Friendship, Commerce, and Navigation (1950), 301–2.
Lend-Lease, 54–56.
Locarno Treaty (1925), 10, 363.
Munich Agreement (1938), 166.
Nazi–Soviet Pact (1939), 338.
North Atlantic Treaty (1949), 336–42; the Irish attitude, 279 n.3; reasons for Canadian sponsorship, 337–8; Canadian policy aims at the inclusion of the U.S.A., 337–8; U.S.A. recognizes the impossibility of isolation, 338–9; ideological aspects, 339, 341; provisions for collective resistance to aggression, 340; importance of the Canadian contribution, 340–2; the Pacific Security Agreement inspired by Australian and New Zealand reactions to, 353–4; provisions of, compared with Pacific Security Agreement, 354–5, 354 n.3; attitude to, in India and Pakistan, 360; Irish participation in NATO precluded, 302.
Ogdensburg Agreement (Canada–U.S.A., 1940), 51–53, 57, 77, 364.
Pacific Security Agreement (Anzus, 1951), 352–7, 364; inspired by Australian and New Zealand reactions to NATO, 353–4; as the price of acquiescence in U.S. views on

Treaties and Agreements (*cont.*):
    Japanese peace treaty, 353, 356–7; possibility of Japanese participation, 354; provisions of, compared with North Atlantic Treaty, 354–5, 354 n.3; in relation to the U.S.A., 354 and n.2, 355, 356–7; consultation with U.K., 355–6; Conservative and Labour attitude to in U.K., 356.
    Simonstown Naval Base Agreement (1955), 364–5.
    South-East Asia (Manila) Treaty (1954), 364 f.
    Tripartite Agreement (Germany, Italy, Japan, 1940), 124–5.
    Western European Union, 329–36, 364.
Treitschke, H. von, 22–23.
Trinidad, air base, 49.
Truman, President Harry S., 351.
Turkey: Chanak crisis (1922), 11, 15; and the Balkans campaign (1941), 97 n.3; treaty with Pakistan, 365.

Uganda, 35.
Union of Soviet Socialist Republics: British assessment of attitude in 1940, 41; the Anglo-Russian Agreement (1941), 108; non-aggression pact with Japan, 121; German intention to attack concealed from Japan, 125; Hitler urges Japan to attack Vladivostok, 125–6; ideological basis of anti-imperialism, 191–2; opposes Canadian proposals for election of non-permanent members of the Security Council, 317; rift with West opens with framing of peace treaties, 320–1; hostility to European Recovery Programme, 331; use of the veto at U.N. prompts Canadian sponsorship of NATO, 337–8; Nazi-Soviet pact and Canada's entry into the war, 338; attitude to principal Indian leaders, 359 n.1; *see also* COMMUNISM.
United Nations: drafting of the Charter influenced by experience of the League of Nations, 308, 319; the draft statement and Moscow Declaration (1943), 311, 313; Dumbarton Oaks (1944), 313–14, 410; effect on Commonwealth defence organization of its failure to preserve peace, 329; NATO and the Canadian retreat from universalism, 337–8; relation of the North Atlantic Treaty to the Charter, 338, 339–40, 341.
    General Assembly, 315–16; Australia safeguards smaller powers from interference in domestic matters, 318.
    Kashmir dispute, 260.
    Korean War, 351–2, 359.
    San Francisco Conference (1945), 314–22; dominions' opposition to great-power pretensions, 315, 316–19, 321–2; disagreement between Great Britain and the dominions, 315, 320; dominions' contribution in economic and social policy, 319–20; dominions' disappointment at the outcome, 320; the dominions and the signing of the Charter, 321; Australia raises the question of dominions' nationality, 383–4.
    Security Council, 315 f.; Mackenzie King on representation in, 313; Commonwealth agreement on need for strength, 315; dominions' dislike of great-power predominance, 315–17; Canada and, 317–19; U.S.A. and U.K. recognize Nationalist China's right to permanent seat, 350–1; *see also below* Veto.
    South African problems, 362–3.
    Trusteeship Council: Australian and New Zealand disagreement with U.K. 320; South Africa refuses control to, of mandated territories, 362.
    Veto: dominions attack its exercise by single great power, 314, 315, 316–17; U.K. defends, 315; Smuts on necessity of, 319; Canadian alarm at Russia's use of, 337; avoidance of Russian veto against North Atlantic Treaty, 339.
    See also BRITISH COMMONWEALTH: International organization.
United Nations Relief and Rehabilitation Administration, 312.
United Provinces (India), 154.
United States of America: influences British attitude to constitutional reform in India, 145–6; anti-colonialism, 191–2; Commonwealth statesmen's views on post-war relation to the Commonwealth, 308 ff.; its responsibility for failure of the League of Nations, 308–9; recognizes Nationalist China, 350–1; Korean War, 351; recognizes Bao Dai, 359; military alliances (1957), 365 n.2.

United States of America (*cont.*):
  Second World War: views on U.K.'s position at the fall of France, 46–48; destroyers–bases agreement, 46–47, 48–50, 53–54; the Joint Board on Defence, 51–53; Lend-Lease, 54–57; extension of Atlantic patrol area (April 1941), 58; temporary protection of Greenland, 58; Red Sea removed from list of areas prohibited to U.S. shipping, 58; urges Ireland to allow Britain use of ports, 74–75; Anglo-American staff talks on war priorities, 108–9; U.S. warning to Japan (1941), 118–20; Germany declares war on, 126; effect of entry into war on Commonwealth co-operation, 127–30; Anglo-American Combined Boards, 128–30; and the Pacific War Councils, 137–8; the Washington Pacific Council, 138–9; U.S. troops land in Australia, 140; arrival of troops in Northern Ireland, 161.
  See also COLOMBO CONFERENCE; HOPKINS; HULL; IRELAND: Second World War; MACARTHUR; ROOSEVELT; STERLING; TREATIES AND AGREEMENTS; UNITED NATIONS.

van den Heever, Mr. Justice, 394 n.1.
van der Merwe, Dr. M. J., 34.
van Zyl, Mr. Justice, 393.
Versailles Treaty, Hertzog and, 33–34.
Victoria, Queen, statue of, 276 and n.3.
Vladivostok, 125–6.

Wade, Prof. E. C. S., 392 f., and cf. 394 n.1.
Walker, Mr. P. C. Gordon, 395.
War Cabinet: Chamberlain rejects suggestion of Empire Council with representative in, 38; — proposal again rejected (1940), 90; Australian demand for representation, 89–90, 112; — Curtin's request for Australian representative, 134–5; dominion representation (1941), 95, 107–10; attended by Australian Envoy Extraordinary, 134.
Warlimont, Gen., 73 n.1.
Waterson, Mr. S. F., 405.
Wavell, F.-M.: and the campaign in Greece, 96, 98; instructed to occupy Syria, 102; and unified command in south-west Pacific, 136; on collapse of the ABDA Command, 141; and Simla Conference (1945), 208 f.; and the Cabinet Mission to India (1946), 215; and formation of an Interim Government, 220–1; succeeded as Viceroy by Lord Mountbatten, 227.
Webster, Sir Charles, 308.
Welles, Mr. Sumner, 119.
West Indies: lease of U.K. bases, 48–50; the Standing Joint Committee, 311; the Colonial Development and Welfare Act (1940), 346.
Western European Union, *see under* TREATIES AND AGREEMENTS.
Wheare, K. C., 374 f.
Wheeler-Bennett, J. W., 12 n.1.
Whiskard, Sir Geoffrey, 407.
White, Sir Thomas, 404.
Wilgress, Mr. L. D., 405.
Willkie, Mr. Wendell, 58, 192, 193–4.
Winant, Mr. J. G., 58.
Wood, Prof. F. L. W., 3 n.1, 7 n.1.

Yalta, 192, 315.
Yugoslavia, 97 n.3.

Zetland, Marquess of, 80, 199, 200, 202 n.
Zimmern, Sir Alfred, 9 and n.1.